W9-BNL-636

Programming C# 4.0

SIXTH EDITION

Programming C# 4.0

Ian Griffiths, Matthew Adams, and Jesse Liberty

O'REILLY®

Beijing · Cambridge · Farnham · Köln · Sebastopol · Taipei · Tokyo

Programming C# 4.0, Sixth Edition

by Ian Griffiths, Matthew Adams, and Jesse Liberty

Copyright © 2010 Ian Griffiths and Matthew Adams. All rights reserved.
Printed in the United States of America.

Published by O'Reilly Media, Inc., 1005 Gravenstein Highway North, Sebastopol, CA 95472.

O'Reilly books may be purchased for educational, business, or sales promotional use. Online editions are also available for most titles (*http://my.safaribooksonline.com*). For more information, contact our corporate/institutional sales department: 800-998-9938 or *corporate@oreilly.com*.

Editors: Mike Hendrickson and Laurel Ruma
Production Editor: Adam Zaremba
Copyeditor: Audrey Doyle
Proofreader: Stacie Arellano

Indexer: Jay Marchand
Cover Designer: Karen Montgomery
Interior Designer: David Futato
Illustrator: Robert Romano

Printing History:

July 2001:	First Edition.
February 2002:	Second Edition.
May 2003:	Third Edition.
February 2005:	Fourth Edition.
December 2007:	Fifth Edition.
August 2010:	Sixth Edition.

Nutshell Handbook, the Nutshell Handbook logo, and the O'Reilly logo are registered trademarks of O'Reilly Media, Inc. *Programming C# 4.0*, the image of an African crowned crane, and related trade dress are trademarks of O'Reilly Media, Inc.

Many of the designations used by manufacturers and sellers to distinguish their products are claimed as trademarks. Where those designations appear in this book, and O'Reilly Media, Inc. was aware of a trademark claim, the designations have been printed in caps or initial caps.

While every precaution has been taken in the preparation of this book, the publisher and authors assume no responsibility for errors or omissions, or for damages resulting from the use of the information contained herein.

ISBN: 978-0-596-15983-2

[M]

1280336486

Table of Contents

Preface xv

1. Introducing C# 1
Why C#? Why .NET?   1
The .NET Framework Class Library   2
Language Style   3
    Composability   4
    Managed Code   5
    Continuity and the Windows Ecosystem   6
C# 4.0, .NET 4, and Visual Studio 2010   7
Summary   9

2. Basic Programming Techniques 11
Getting Started   11
Namespaces and Types   14
Projects and Solutions   19
Comments, Regions, and Readability   24
    Bad Comments   26
    XML Documentation Comments   26
Variables   28
    Variable Types   28
Expressions and Statements   35
    Assignment Statements   38
    Increment and Decrement Operators   38
Flow Control with Selection Statements   39
    if Statements   40
    switch and case Statements   45
Iteration Statements   47
    foreach Statements   48
    for Statements   50
    while and do Statements   52

    Breaking Out of a Loop   53
  Methods   55
  Summary   58

3. Abstracting Ideas with Classes and Structs **59**
  Divide and Conquer   59
    Abstracting Ideas with Methods   59
    Abstracting Ideas with Objects and Classes   62
  Defining Classes   64
    Representing State with Properties   64
    Protection Levels   66
    Initializing with a Constructor   68
    Fields: A Place to Put Data   72
    Fields Can Be Fickle, but const Is Forever   75
    Read-only Fields and Properties   76
  Related Constants with enum   79
  Value Types and Reference Types   82
  Too Many Constructors, Mr. Mozart   88
  Overloading   88
    Overloaded Methods and Default Named Parameters   89
  Object Initializers   92
  Defining Methods   95
    Declaring Static Methods   98
  Static Fields and Properties   99
    Static Constructors   101
  Summary   102

4. Extensibility and Polymorphism **103**
  Association Through Composition and Aggregation   104
  Inheritance and Polymorphism   106
  Replacing Methods in Derived Classes   109
    Hiding Base Members with new   109
    Replacing Methods with virtual and override   112
  Inheritance and Protection   114
  Calling Base Class Methods   116
  Thus Far and No Farther: sealed   118
  Requiring Overrides with abstract   121
  All Types Are Derived from Object   127
    Boxing and Unboxing Value Types   127
  C# Does Not Support Multiple Inheritance of Implementation   132
  C# Supports Multiple Inheritance of Interface   132
  Deriving Interfaces from Other Interfaces   135
    Explicit Interface Implementation   136

The Last Resort: Checking Types at Runtime   141
Summary   142

5. Composability and Extensibility with Delegates **143**
Functional Composition with delegate   150
Generic Actions with Action<T>   156
Generic Predicates with Predicate<T>   160
Using Anonymous Methods   162
Creating Delegates with Lambda Expressions   163
Delegates in Properties   165
Generic Delegates for Functions   167
Notifying Clients with Events   171
     Exposing Large Numbers of Events   180
Summary   183

6. Dealing with Errors **185**
When and How to Fail   191
Returning Error Values   194
     Debugging with Return Values   200
Exceptions   201
     Handling Exceptions   207
     When Do finally Blocks Run?   214
     Deciding What to Catch   215
     Custom Exceptions   218
Summary   220

7. Arrays and Lists **221**
Arrays   221
     Construction and Initialization   222
     Custom Types in Arrays   225
     Array Members   230
     Array Size   236
List<T>   243
     Custom Indexers   247
     Finding and Sorting   253
Collections and Polymorphism   254
     Creating Your Own IEnumerable<T>   258
Summary   264

8. LINQ **265**
Query Expressions   265
     Query Expressions Versus Method Calls   267
     Extension Methods and LINQ   268

let Clauses 271
LINQ Concepts and Techniques 271
    Delegates and Lambdas 271
    Functional Style and Composition 273
    Deferred Execution 274
LINQ Operators 275
    Filtering 275
    Ordering 276
    Concatenation 279
    Grouping 280
    Projections 282
    Zipping 288
    Getting Selective 289
    Testing the Whole Collection 291
    Aggregation 292
    Set Operations 294
    Joining 295
    Conversions 296
Summary 297

9. Collection Classes **299**
Dictionaries 299
    Common Dictionary Uses 301
    IDictionary<TKey, TValue> 308
    Dictionaries and LINQ 309
HashSet and SortedSet 310
Queues 311
Linked Lists 312
Stacks 313
Summary 314

10. Strings **315**
What Is a String? 316
The String and Char Types 317
Literal Strings and Chars 318
    Escaping Special Characters 319
Formatting Data for Output 322
    Standard Numeric Format Strings 323
    Custom Numeric Format Strings 329
    Dates and Times 332
    Going the Other Way: Converting Strings to Other Types 336
    Composite Formatting with String.Format 337
Culture Sensitivity 338

Exploring Formatting Rules 340
Accessing Characters by Index 341
Strings Are Immutable 341
Getting a Range of Characters 343
Composing Strings 344
Splitting It Up Again 346
Upper- and Lowercase 347
Manipulating Text 348
Mutable Strings with StringBuilder 349
Finding and Replacing Content 353
All Sorts of "Empty" Strings 355
Trimming Whitespace 357
Checking Character Types 360
Encoding Characters 360
Why Encodings Matter 362
Encoding and Decoding 363
Why Represent Strings As Byte Sequences? 370
Summary 370

11. Files and Streams **371**
Inspecting Directories and Files 371
Examining Directories 374
Manipulating File Paths 375
Path and the Current Working Directory 376
Examining File Information 377
Creating Temporary Files 381
Deleting Files 381
Well-Known Folders 383
Concatenating Path Elements Safely 387
Creating and Securing Directory Hierarchies 388
Deleting a Directory 394
Writing Text Files 396
Writing a Whole Text File at Once 396
Writing Text with a StreamWriter 397
When Files Go Bad: Dealing with Exceptions 400
Finding and Modifying Permissions 404
Reading Files into Memory 409
Streams 413
Moving Around in a Stream 419
Writing Data with Streams 421
Reading, Writing, and Locking Files 422
FileStream Constructors 423
Stream Buffers 423

Setting Permissions During Construction	424
Setting Advanced Options	425
Asynchronous File Operations	425
Isolated Storage	428
Stores	429
Reading and Writing Text	430
Defining "Isolated"	431
Managing User Storage with Quotas	436
Managing Isolated Storage	436
Streams That Aren't Files	439
An Adapting Stream: CryptoStream	443
In Memory Alone: The MemoryStream	444
Representing Binary As Text with Base64 Encoding	444
Summary	447

12. XML **449**

XML Basics (A Quick Review)	449
Elements	450
XHTML	451
X Stands for eXtensible	452
Creating XML Documents	452
XML Elements	455
XML Attributes	456
Putting the LINQ in LINQ to XML	459
Searching in XML with LINQ	461
Searching for a Single Node	465
Search Axes	466
Where Clauses	466
XML Serialization	467
Customizing XML Serialization Using Attributes	469
Summary	471

13. Networking **473**

Choosing a Networking Technology	473
Web Application with Client-Side Code	474
.NET Client and .NET Server	477
.NET Client and External Party Web Service	479
External Client and .NET Web Service	480
WCF	481
Creating a WCF Project	481
WCF Contracts	482
WCF Test Client and Host	483
Hosting a WCF Service	486

	Writing a WCF Client	493
	Bidirectional Communication with Duplex Contracts	501
	HTTP	511
	WebClient	512
	WebRequest and WebResponse	516
	Sockets	522
	IP, IPv6, and TCP	523
	Connecting to Services with the Socket Class	528
	Implementing Services with the Socket Class	531
	Other Networking Features	536
	Summary	537
14.	**Databases**	**539**
	The .NET Data Access Landscape	539
	Classic ADO.NET	540
	LINQ and Databases	544
	Non-Microsoft Data Access Technologies	545
	WCF Data Services	546
	Silverlight and Data Access	546
	Databases	547
	The Entity Data Model	548
	Generated Code	551
	Changing the Mapping	554
	Relationships	555
	Inheritance	562
	Queries	563
	LINQ to Entities	563
	Entity SQL	568
	Mixing ESQL and LINQ	570
	The EntityClient ADO.NET Provider	571
	Object Context	571
	Connection Handling	571
	Creating, Updating, and Deleting	574
	Transactions	576
	Optimistic Concurrency	581
	Context and Entity Lifetime	583
	WCF Data Services	584
	Summary	588
15.	**Assemblies**	**589**
	.NET Components: Assemblies	589
	References	590
	Writing Libraries	593

Protection	595
Naming	598
Signing and Strong Names	599
Loading	601
Loading from the Application Folder	602
Loading from the GAC	603
Loading from a Silverlight .xap File	603
Explicit Loading	604
Summary	605

16. Threads and Asynchronous Code **607**
Threads	609
Threads and the OS Scheduler	611
The Stack	613
The Thread Pool	620
Thread Affinity and Context	622
Common Thread Misconceptions	623
Multithreaded Coding Is Hard	629
Multithreading Survival Strategies	632
Synchronization Primitives	634
Monitor	634
Other Lock Types	645
Other Coordination Mechanisms	649
Events	649
Countdown	650
BlockingCollection	650
Asynchronous Programming	651
The Asynchronous Programming Model	652
The Event-Based Asynchronous Pattern	655
Ad Hoc Asynchrony	656
The Task Parallel Library	656
Tasks	657
Cancellation	663
Error Handling	665
Data Parallelism	666
Parallel For and ForEach	667
PLINQ: Parallel LINQ	669
Summary	670

17. Attributes and Reflection **671**
Attributes	671
Types of Attributes	672
Custom Attributes	673

Reflection 677
 Inspecting Metadata 678
 Type Discovery 679
 Reflecting on a Specific Type 681
 Late Binding 683
Summary 686

18. Dynamic **687**
Static Versus Dynamic 687
 The Dynamic Style and COM Automation 689
The dynamic Type 690
 Object Types and dynamic 693
dynamic in Noninterop Scenarios? 703
Summary 706

19. Interop with COM and Win32 . . . . **707**
Importing ActiveX Controls 707
 Importing a Control in .NET 708
Interop Assemblies 711
 No PIA 712
64-bit Versus 32-bit 713
P/Invoke 716
Pointers 720
C# 4.0 Interop Syntax Enhancements 725
 Indexed Properties 725
 Optional ref 726
Summary 727

20. WPF and Silverlight **729**
Xaml and Code Behind 731
 Xaml and Objects 735
Elements and Controls 738
 Layout Panels 739
 Graphical Elements 748
 Controls 755
 User Controls 760
Control Templates 761
 Styles 764
 The Visual State Manager 766
Data Binding 767
 Data Templates 769
Summary 773

21. Programming ASP.NET Applications 775
    Web Forms Fundamentals   775
        Web Forms Events   776
        Web Forms Life Cycle   778
    Creating a Web Application   779
        Code-Behind Files   780
        Adding Controls   781
        Server Controls   783
    Data Binding   784
        Examining the Code   789
        Adding Controls and Events   790
    Summary   794

22. Windows Forms 795
    Creating the Application   796
        Adding a Binding Source   797
    Controls   800
        Docking and Anchoring   805
    Data Binding   806
    Event Handling   811
    Summary   813

Index 815

Preface

Microsoft unveiled the .NET Framework in 2000, and in the decade that followed, it became an extremely popular choice for developing software for Windows. While .NET supports many programming languages, it is most strongly associated with the language designed specifically for the platform: C#.

C# has grown considerably since its launch. Each new version enabled new programming techniques—C# 2.0 added generics and enhanced functional programming capabilities, then integrated query features and yet more powerful functional capabilities arrived in C# 3.0, and now C# 4.0 adds new dynamic language capabilities.

The .NET Framework has grown with the language. Back in .NET 1.0, the class libraries offered relatively patchy coverage of the underlying Windows capabilities. Moreover, the library features that were unique to .NET, rather than being wrappers for something else, were relatively modest. Now, as well as more comprehensive platform coverage we have a GUI framework (WPF), much stronger database capabilities, powerful support for concurrent execution, and an extensive set of communication services (WCF), to name just a few of the available features. And the features that have been there since version 1.0, such as web support (ASP.NET), have been fleshed out substantially.

.NET is no longer limited to running just on Windows. Some people recognized its potential for platform independence early on, but for years, Microsoft supported C# just on Windows, leaving open source projects to offer the only way to run C# on other systems. But in 2008, the release of Silverlight 2 saw C# code running with Microsoft's full support on non-Windows platforms such as the Mac for the first time.

The C# language has come a long way since 2000, in both reach and size. Our goal with *Programming C# 4.0* is to show how to use C#.

How This Book Is Organized

The book begins by looking at the details of the C# language that you will use in everyday programming. We then look at the most common parts of the .NET Framework class library that you will also use very regularly. Next, we move into some more specialized areas of the framework. Finally, we look at some of the application frameworks for building Windows and web applications in .NET.

Chapter 1, *Introducing C#*
This chapter talks about the nature of C# and its relationship with the .NET Framework.

Chapter 2, *Basic Programming Techniques*
In this chapter, we show the core elements of C# code—the steps required to get up and running, and fundamental features such as variables, flow control, loops, and methods.

Chapter 3, *Abstracting Ideas with Classes and Structs*
C# supports object-oriented programming, and this chapter describes the language features dedicated to these techniques.

Chapter 4, *Extensibility and Polymorphism*
This chapter continues the discussion from the preceding chapter, illustrating how C# supports inheritance, interfaces, and related concepts.

Chapter 5, *Composability and Extensibility with Delegates*
C# isn't limited to object-oriented programming—it also supports some very powerful functional programming idioms. This chapter shows how these can sometimes be more flexible and also simpler than OO techniques.

Chapter 6, *Dealing with Errors*
All programs encounter failures, whether due to programming errors, unexpected input, network failures, or a host of other eventualities. This chapter shows the options for detecting and responding robustly to errors.

Chapter 7, *Arrays and Lists*
This chapter shows the tools C# offers for representing simple collections of information.

Chapter 8, *LINQ*
It's not enough merely to be able to represent collections, so this chapter shows how you can use the integrated query features in C# to process your collections of data.

Chapter 9, *Collection Classes*
This chapter shows some of the more specialized classes for working with collections in particular ways.

Chapter 10, *Strings*
Text is a particularly important data type for most applications, so this chapter shows how text is represented, and how you can format data into textual form.

Chapter 11, *Files and Streams*
This chapter shows how to store information on disk and read it back in, and how to perform other filesystem operations. It also shows how some of the abstractions used when working with files can be applied in other scenarios.

Chapter 12, *XML*

This chapter shows the classes offered by the .NET Framework for processing XML, and how these can work in conjunction with the LINQ features in C#.

Chapter 13, *Networking*

In this chapter, we look at the various techniques for communicating over a network.

Chapter 14, *Databases*

This chapter shows how to access a database from C#.

Chapter 15, *Assemblies*

In this chapter, we show how to compile code into libraries for reuse, and how programs made up from multiple components work.

Chapter 16, *Threads and Asynchronous Code*

Many programs need to deal with concurrency, and this chapter shows the tools and techniques available.

Chapter 17, *Attributes and Reflection*

C# has the ability to inspect the structure of code, which makes it easier to automate certain kinds of tasks. This chapter shows the API for doing this, and how you can extend the structural information through attributes.

Chapter 18, *Dynamic*

One of the new features in C# 4.0 is support for dynamic binding. This is particularly useful in certain interop scenarios, as we discuss in this chapter.

Chapter 19, *Interop with COM and Win32*

Sometimes it's necessary for C# code to communicate with components not designed to be used from .NET. This chapter shows how to do this with both COM components and Win32-style DLLs.

Chapter 20, *WPF and Silverlight*

WPF and Silverlight offer very similar programming models for building user interfaces. This chapter shows how to use that model from C#.

Chapter 21, *Programming ASP.NET Applications*

This chapter shows how to use ASP.NET, the part of the .NET Framework designed for building web applications.

Chapter 22, *Windows Forms*

This chapter shows how to use Windows Forms, which is a wrapper around the classic Windows user interface mechanisms. While it is less flexible than WPF, it can offer an easier way to integrate with old components such as ActiveX controls.

Where to Find Features New in C# 4.0 and .NET 4

Although this book is written to be read as a whole, we expect that some readers will want to look for the features new to C# 4.0, and also to .NET 4. Since our goal is to show how the C# language is used today, we have avoided structuring the book around the history of the language, because you will use language features of varying ages in combination. As it happens, one of the new features in C# 4.0 serves a very specific purpose, so it gets its own chapter, but for the most part, new language features are spread throughout the book, because we aim to mention them where you need to know about them. We cannot point you at a particular set of chapters, so instead, here's a quick guide to where we discuss these features.

Chapter 1 talks about the broad goals behind the new features in C# 4.0. Chapter 3 shows the use of default values and named arguments (and these come up again very briefly in Chapters 11 and 17). Chapter 7 describes variance, a rather technical feature of the type system that has some useful implications for collection types. Chapter 16 talks about the extensive new multithreading support added in .NET 4. Chapter 18 is dedicated entirely to a new language feature: support for dynamic programming. Chapter 19 describes the new no-PIA feature, and some features that allow more elegant code in some interop scenarios.

Who This Book Is For

If you have some basic knowledge of C# but want to brush up your skills, or if you are proficient in another programming language such as C++ or Java, or even if C# is your first programming language, this book is for you.

What You Need to Use This Book

To make the best use of this book, please obtain the latest release of Visual Studio 2010. Any edition will do, including the free Express edition for C#, which can be downloaded from *http://www.microsoft.com/express/*.

For Chapter 14 you will need a copy of SQL Server or SQL Server Express. Some editions of Visual Studio will install SQL Server Express for you by default, so you may already have this.

The example source code for this book is available through the O'Reilly site at *http://oreilly.com/catalog/9780596159832/*.

Conventions Used in This Book

The following font conventions are used in this book:

Italic is used for:

- Pathnames, filenames, and program names
- Internet addresses, such as domain names and URLs
- New terms where they are defined

`Constant Width` is used for:

- Command lines and options that should be typed verbatim
- Names and keywords in program examples, including method names, variable names, and class names

`Constant Width Italic` is used for:

- Replaceable items, such as variables or optional elements, within syntax lines or code

`Constant Width Bold` is used for:

- Emphasis within program code

Pay special attention to notes set apart from the text with the following icons:

 This is a tip. It contains useful supplementary information about the topic at hand.

 This is a warning. It helps you solve and avoid annoying problems.

Using Code Examples

This book is here to help you get your job done. In general, you may use the code in this book in your programs and documentation. You do not need to contact us for permission unless you're reproducing a significant portion of the code. For example, writing a program that uses several chunks of code from this book does not require permission. Selling or distributing a CD-ROM of examples from O'Reilly books *does* require permission. Answering a question by citing this book and quoting example code does not require permission. Incorporating a significant amount of example code from this book into your product's documentation *does* require permission.

We appreciate, but do not require, attribution. An attribution usually includes the title, author, publisher, and ISBN. For example: "*Programming C# 4.0*, Sixth Edition, by Ian Griffiths, Matthew Adams, and Jesse Liberty. Copyright 2010 Ian Griffiths and Matthew Adams, 978-0-596-15983-2."

Safari® Books Online

Safari Books Online is an on-demand digital library that lets you easily search over 7,500 technology and creative reference books and videos to find the answers you need quickly.

With a subscription, you can read any page and watch any video from our library online. Read books on your cell phone and mobile devices. Access new titles before they are available for print, and get exclusive access to manuscripts in development and post feedback for the authors. Copy and paste code samples, organize your favorites, download chapters, bookmark key sections, create notes, print out pages, and benefit from tons of other time-saving features.

O'Reilly Media has uploaded this book to the Safari Books Online service. To have full digital access to this book and others on similar topics from O'Reilly and other publishers, sign up for free at *http://my.safaribooksonline.com/?portal=oreilly*.

Acknowledgments

From Ian Griffiths

I want to thank the technical reviewers, whose feedback helped to improve this book: Nicholas Paldino, Chris Smith, Chris Williams, Michael Eaton, Brian Peek, and Stephen Toub.

Everyone at O'Reilly has provided a great deal of support and patience throughout the project, so many thanks to Mike Hendrickson, Laurel Ruma, Audrey Doyle, and Sumita Mukherji. Thanks also to John Osborn for getting things started in the early days of this project, and for getting Matthew and me on board as O'Reilly authors in the first place, all those years ago.

Thank you to my coauthor for not learning his lesson from the last book and agreeing to write another with me. And finally, thank you to Jesse Liberty for asking us to take over his book.

From Matthew Adams

I'd like to add my thanks to those of my coauthor to all those at O'Reilly whose patience, help, and support have made this book possible, and to all our reviewers whose feedback has been invaluable.

In addition, I'd like to add a nod to Karolina Lemiesz, coffee wizard at the Starbucks where most of my text was written, for the constant supply of ristretto, and an education in coffee tasting when work got too much.

As always, my partner Una provided the necessary foundation of love and support (despite her own book deadlines). And finally, anyone who tells you that squeezing a book out of an author is a breeze is clearly deluded, but my coauthor makes it look easy. My thanks go to him especially for his forbearance, wit, and friendship. And good dinners.

CHAPTER 1

Introducing C#

C#—pronounced "See Sharp"—is a programming language designed for Microsoft's .NET platform. Since its first release in 2002, C# has found many roles. It is widely used on the server side of websites, and also on both the client and server in line-of-business Windows desktop applications. You can write smartphone user interfaces and Xbox 360 games in C#. More recently, Microsoft's Silverlight platform has made C# an option for writing Rich Internet Applications that run in a web browser.

But what kind of language is C#? To understand a language well enough to use it effectively, it's not enough to focus purely on the details and mechanisms, although we'll be spending plenty of time on those in this book. It is equally important to understand the thinking behind the details. So in this chapter, we'll look at what problems C# was built to solve. Then we'll explore the style of the language, through aspects that distinguish it from other languages. And we'll finish the chapter with a look at the latest step in the evolution of C#, its fourth version.

Why C#? Why .NET?

Programming languages exist to help developers be more productive. Many successful languages simplify or automate tedious tasks that previously had to be done by hand. Some offer new techniques that allow old problems to be tackled more effectively, or on a larger scale than before. How much difference C# can make to you will depend on your programming background, of course, so it's worth considering what sorts of people the language designers had in mind when they created C#.

C# is aimed at developers working on the Windows platform, and its syntax is instantly familiar to users of C or C++, or other languages that draw from the same tradition, such as JavaScript and Java. Fundamental language elements such as statements, expressions, function declarations, and flow control are modeled as closely as possible on their equivalents in C family languages.

A familiar syntax is not enough of a reason to pick a language, of course, so C# offers productivity-enhancing features not found in some of its predecessors. Garbage collection frees developers from the tyranny of common memory management problems such as memory leaks and circular references. Verifiable type safety of compiled code rules out a wide range of bugs and potential security flaws. While C or C++ Windows developers may not be accustomed to those features, they will seem old hat to Java veterans, but Java has nothing to compete with the "LINQ" features C# offers for working with collections of information, whether in object models, XML documents, or databases. Integrating code from external components is remarkably painless, even those written in other languages. C# also incorporates support for functional programming, a powerful feature previously most commonly seen in academic languages.

Many of the most useful features available to C# developers come from the .NET Framework, which provides the runtime environment and libraries for C#, and all other .NET languages, such as VB.NET. C# was designed for .NET, and one of the main benefits of its close relationship with the .NET Framework is that working with framework features such as the class library feels very natural.

The .NET Framework Class Library

Working in C# means more than using just the language—the classes offered by the .NET Framework are an extremely important part of the C# developer's everyday experience (and they account for a lot of this book's content). Most of the library functionality falls into one of three categories: utility features written in .NET, wrappers around Windows functionality, and frameworks.

The first group comprises utility types such as dictionaries, lists, and other collection classes, as well as string manipulation facilities such as a regular expression engine. There are also features that operate on a slightly larger scale, such as the object models for representing XML documents.

Some library features are wrappers around underlying OS functionality. For example, there are classes for accessing the filesystem, and for using network features such as sockets. And there are classes for writing output to the console, which we can illustrate with the obligatory first example of any programming language book, shown in Example 1-1.

Example 1-1. The inevitable "Hello, world" example

```
class Program
{
    static void Main()
    {
        System.Console.WriteLine("Hello, world");
    }
}
```

We'll examine all the pieces shown here in due course, but for now, note that even this simplest of examples depends on a class from the library—the `System.Console` class in this case—to do its job.

Finally, the class library offers whole frameworks to support building certain kinds of applications. For example, Windows Presentation Foundation (WPF) is a framework for building Windows desktop software; ASP.NET (which is not an acronym, despite appearances) is a framework for building web applications. Not all frameworks are about user interfaces—Windows Communication Foundation (WCF) is designed for building services accessed over the network by other computer systems, for instance.

These three categories are not strict, as quite a few classes fit into two. For example, the parts of the class library that provide access to the filesystem are not just thin wrappers around existing Win32 APIs. They add new object-oriented abstractions, providing significant functionality beyond the basic file I/O services, so these types fit into both the first and second categories. Likewise, frameworks usually need to integrate with underlying services to some extent—for example, although the Windows Forms UI framework has a distinctive API of its own, a lot of the underlying functionality is provided by Win32 components. So the three categories here are not strict. They just offer a useful idea of what sorts of things you can find in the class libraries.

Language Style

C# is not the only language that runs on the .NET Framework. Indeed, support for multiple languages has always been a key feature of .NET, reflected in the name of its runtime engine, the *CLR* or *Common Language Runtime*. As this name implies, .NET is not just for one language—numerous languages have access to the services of the .NET Framework class library. Why might you choose C# over the others?

We already mentioned one important reason: C# was designed specifically for .NET. If you are working with .NET technologies such as WPF or ASP.NET, you'll be speaking their language if you work in C#. Compare this with C++, which supports .NET through extensions to the original language. The extensions are carefully thought out and work well, but code that uses .NET libraries just looks different from normal C++, so programs that bridge the worlds of .NET and standard C++ never feel completely coherent. And the dual personality often presents dilemmas—should you use standard C++ collection classes or the ones in the .NET class library, for example? In native .NET languages such as C#, such questions do not emerge.

But C# is not unique in this respect. Visual Studio 2010 ships with three languages designed for .NET: C#, VB.NET, and F#. (Although VB.NET follows on from its non-.NET Visual Basic predecessors, it was radically different in some important ways. It is a native .NET language with a VB-like syntax rather than VB 6 with .NET capabilities bolted on.) The choice between these languages comes down to what style of language you prefer.

F# is the odd one out here. It's a functional programming language, heavily influenced by a language called ML. Back in 1991, when your authors were first-year students, our university's computer science course chose ML for the first programming language lectures in part because it was so academic that none of the students would previously have come across anything like it. F# is still at the academic end of the spectrum despite having climbed far enough down the ivory tower to be a standard part of a mainstream development environment. It excels at complicated calculations and algorithms, and has some characteristics that can help with parallel execution. However, as with many functional languages, the cost of making some hard problems easier is that a lot of things that are easy in more traditional languages are remarkably hard in F#— functional languages are adept at complex problems, but can be clumsy with simple ones. It seems likely that F# will mostly be used in scientific or financial applications where the complexity of the computation to be performed dwarfs the complexity of the code that needs to act on the results of those calculations.

While F# feels distinctly *other*, VB.NET and C# have a lot of similarities. The most obvious factor in choosing between these is that VB.NET is easier to learn for someone familiar with Visual Basic syntax, while C# will be easier for someone familiar with a C-like language. However, there is a subtler difference in language philosophy that goes beyond the syntax.

Composability

A consistent theme in the design of the C# programming language is that its creators tend to prefer general-purpose features over specialized ones. The most obvious example of this is LINQ, the Language *IN*tegrated Query feature added in C# 3.0. Superficially, this appears to add SQL-like query features to the language, providing a natural way to integrate database access into your code. Example 1-2 shows a simple query.

Example 1-2. Data access with LINQ

```
var californianAuthors = from author in pubs.authors
                         where author.state == "CA"
                         select new
                         {
                             author.au_fname,
                             author.au_lname
                         };
foreach (var author in californianAuthors)
{
    Console.WriteLine(author);
}
```

Despite appearances, C# doesn't know anything about SQL or databases. To enable this syntax, C# 3.0 added a raft of language features which, in combination, allow code of this sort to be used not just for database access, but also for XML parsing, or working with object models. Moreover, many of the individual features can be used in other contexts, as we'll see in later chapters. C# prefers small, composable, general-purpose features over monolithic, specialized ones.

A striking example of this philosophy is a feature that was demonstrated in prototype form in C#, but which eventually got left out: XML literals. This experimental syntax allowed inline XML, which compiled into code that built an object model representing that XML. The C# team's decision to omit this feature illustrates a stylistic preference for generality over highly specialized features—while the LINQ syntax has many applications, XML literal syntax cannot be used for anything other than XML, and this degree of specialization would feel out of place in C#.[*]

Managed Code

The .NET Framework provides more than just a class library. It also provides services in subtler ways that are not accessed explicitly through library calls. For example, earlier we mentioned that C# can automate some aspects of memory management, a notorious source of bugs in C++ code. Abandoning heap-allocated objects once you're done with them is a coding error in C++, but it's the normal way to free them in .NET. This service is provided by the CLR—the .NET Framework's runtime environment. Although the C# compiler works closely with the runtime to make this possible, providing the necessary information about how your code uses objects and data, it's ultimately the runtime that does the work of garbage collection.

Depending on what sorts of languages you may have worked with before, the idea that the language depends heavily on the runtime might seem either completely natural or somewhat disconcerting. It's certainly different from how C and C++ work—with those languages, the compiler's output can be executed directly by the computer, and although those languages have some runtime services, it's possible to write code that can run without them. But C# code cannot even execute without the help of the runtime. Code that depends entirely on the runtime is called *managed code*.

Managed compilers do not produce raw executable code. Instead, they produce an intermediate form of code called IL, the Intermediate Language.[†] The runtime decides exactly how to convert it into something executable. One practical upshot of managed code is that a compiled C# program can run on both 32-bit and 64-bit systems without modification, and can even run on different processor architectures—it's often possible

---

[*] VB.NET supports XML literals. Since C# 2.0 shipped, the C# and VB.NET teams have operated a policy of keeping the feature sets of the two languages similar, so the fact that VB.NET picked up a feature that C# abandoned shows a clear difference in language philosophy.

[†] Depending on whether you read Microsoft's documentation, or the ECMA CLI (Common Language Infrastructure) specifications that define the standardized parts of .NET and C#, IL's proper name is either MSIL (Microsoft IL) or CIL (Common IL), respectively. The unofficial name, IL, seems more popular in practice.

for code that runs on an ARM-based handheld device to run unmodified on Intel-based PCs, or on the PowerPC architecture found in the Xbox 360 game console.

As interesting as CPU independence may be, in practice the most useful aspect of managed code and IL is that the .NET runtime can provide useful services that are very hard for traditional compilation systems to implement well. In other words, the point is to make developers more productive. The memory management mentioned earlier is just one example. Others include a security model that takes the origin of code into account rather than merely the identity of the user who happens to be running the code; flexible mechanisms for loading shared components with robust support for servicing and versioning; runtime code optimization based on how the code is being used in practice rather than how the compiler guesses it might be used; and as already mentioned, the CLR's ability to verify that code conforms to type safety rules before executing it, ruling out whole classes of security and stability bugs.

If you're a Java developer, all of this will sound rather familiar—just substitute *bytecode* for *IL* and the story is very similar. Indeed, a popular but somewhat ignorant "joke" among the less thoughtful members of the Java community is to describe C# as a poor imitation of Java. When the first version of C# appeared, the differences were subtle, but the fact that Java went on to copy several features from C# illustrates that C# was always more than a mere clone. The languages have grown more obviously different with each new version, but one difference, present from the start, is particularly important for Windows developers: C# has always made it easy to get at the features of the underlying Windows platform.

Continuity and the Windows Ecosystem

Software development platforms do not succeed purely on their own merits—context matters. For example, widespread availability of third-party components and tools can make a platform significantly more compelling. Windows is perhaps the most striking example of this phenomenon. Any new programming system attempting to gain acceptance has a considerable advantage if it can plug into some existing ecosystem, and one of the biggest differences between C# and Java is that C# and the .NET Framework positively embrace the Windows platform, while Java goes out of its way to insulate developers from the underlying OS.

If you're writing code to run on a specific operating system, it's not especially helpful for a language to cut you off from the tools and components unique to your chosen platform. Rather than requiring developers to break with the past, .NET offers continuity by making it possible to work directly with components and services either built into or built for Windows. Most of the time, you won't need to use this—the class library provides wrappers for a lot of the underlying platform's functionality. However, if you need to use a third-party component or a feature of the operating system that doesn't yet have a .NET wrapper, the ability to work with such unmanaged features directly from managed code is invaluable.

 While .NET offers features to ease integration with the underlying platform, there is still support for non-Windows systems. Microsoft's Silverlight can run C# and VB.NET code on Mac OS X as well as Windows. There's an open source project called Mono which enables .NET code to run on Linux, and the related Moonlight project is an open source version of Silverlight. So the presence of local platform integration features doesn't stop C# from being useful on multiple platforms—if you want to target multiple operating systems, you would just choose not to use any platform-specific features.

So the biggest philosophical difference between C# and Java is that C# provides equal support for direct use of operating-system-specific features and for platform independence. Java makes the former disproportionately harder than the latter.

The latest version of C# contains features that enhance this capability further. Several of the new C# 4.0 features make it easier to interact with Office and other Windows applications that use COM automation—this was a weak spot in C# 3.0. The relative ease with which developers can reach outside the boundaries of managed code makes C# an attractive choice—it offers all the benefits of managed execution, but retains the ability to work with any code in the Windows environment, managed or not.

C# 4.0, .NET 4, and Visual Studio 2010

Since C# favors general-purpose language features designed to be composed with one another, it often doesn't make sense to describe individual new features on their own. So rather than devoting sections or whole chapters to new features, we cover them in context, integrated appropriately with other, older language features. The section you're reading right now is an exception, of course, and the main reason is that we expect people already familiar with C# 3.0 to browse through this book in bookstores looking for our coverage of the new features. If that's you, welcome to the book! If you look in the Preface you'll find a guide to what's where in the book, including a section just for you, describing where to find material about C# 4.0 features.

That being said, a theme unites the new language features in version 4: they support dynamic programming, with a particular focus on making certain interoperability scenarios simpler. For example, consider the C# 3.0 code in Example 1-3 that uses part of the Office object model to read the Author property from a Word document.

Example 1-3. The horrors of Office interop before C# 4.0

```
static void Main(string[] args)
{
    var wordApp = new Microsoft.Office.Interop.Word.Application();

    object fileName = @"WordFile.docx";
    object missing = System.Reflection.Missing.Value;
```

```
object readOnly = true;
Microsoft.Office.Interop.Word._Document doc =
    wordApp.Documents.Open(ref fileName, ref missing, ref readOnly,
        ref missing, ref missing, ref missing, ref missing, ref missing,
        ref missing, ref missing, ref missing, ref missing, ref missing,
        ref missing, ref missing, ref missing);

object docProperties = doc.BuiltInDocumentProperties;
Type docPropType = docProperties.GetType();
object authorProp = docPropType.InvokeMember("Item",
    BindingFlags.Default | BindingFlags.GetProperty,
    null, docProperties,
    new object[] { "Author" });
Type propType = authorProp.GetType();
string authorName = propType.InvokeMember("Value",
    BindingFlags.Default |BindingFlags.GetProperty,
    null, authorProp,
    new object[] { }).ToString();

object saveChanges = false;
doc.Close(ref saveChanges, ref missing, ref missing);


Console.WriteLine(authorName);
}
```

That's some pretty horrible code—it's hard to see what the example does because the goal is lost in the details. The reason it is so unpleasant is that Office's programming model is designed for dynamic languages that can fill in a lot of the details at runtime. C# 3.0 wasn't able to do this, so developers were forced to do all the work by hand.

Example 1-4 shows how to do exactly the same job in C# 4.0. This is a lot easier to follow, because the code contains only the relevant details. It's easy to see the sequence of operations—open the document, get its properties, retrieve the Author property's value, and close the document. C# 4.0 is now able to fill in all the details for us, thanks to its new dynamic language features.

Example 1-4. Office interop with C# 4.0

```
static void Main(string[] args)
{
    var wordApp = new Microsoft.Office.Interop.Word.Application();

    Microsoft.Office.Interop.Word._Document doc =
        wordApp.Documents.Open("WordFile.docx", ReadOnly: true);
    dynamic docProperties = doc.BuiltInDocumentProperties;
    string authorName = docProperties["Author"].Value;
    doc.Close(SaveChanges: false);

    Console.WriteLine(authorName);
}
```

This example uses a couple of C# 4.0 features: it uses the new `dynamic` keyword for runtime binding to members. It also uses the support for optional arguments. The `Open` and `Close` methods take 16 and 3 arguments, respectively, and as you can see from Example 1-3, you need to provide all of them in C# 3.0. But Example 1-4 has only provided values for the arguments it wants to set to something other than the default.

Besides using these two new features, a project containing this code would usually be built using a third new interop feature called *no-PIA*. There's nothing to see in the preceding example, because when you enable no-PIA in a C# project, you do not need to modify your code—no-PIA is essentially a deployment feature. In C# 3.0, you had to install special support libraries called *primary interop assemblies* (PIAs) on the target machine to be able to use COM APIs such as Office automation, but in C# 4.0 you no longer have to do this. You still need these PIAs on your *development* machine, but the C# compiler can extract the information your code requires, and copy it into your application. This saves you from deploying PIAs to the target machine, hence the name, "no-PIA".

While these new language features are particularly well suited to COM automation interop scenarios, they can be used anywhere. (The "no-PIA" feature is narrower, but it's really part of the .NET runtime rather than a C# language feature.)

Summary

In this chapter we provided a quick overview of the nature of the C# language, and we showed some of its strengths and how the latest version has evolved. There's one last benefit you should be aware of before we get into the details in the next chapter, and that's the sheer quantity of C# resources available on the Internet. When the .NET Framework first appeared, C# adoption took off much faster than the other .NET languages. Consequently, if you're searching for examples of how to get things done, or solutions to problems, C# is an excellent choice because it's so well represented in blogs, examples, tools, open source projects, and webcasts—Microsoft's own documentation is pretty evenhanded between C# and VB.NET, but on the Web as a whole, you're far better served if you're a C# developer. So with that in mind, we'll now look at the fundamental elements of C# programs.

CHAPTER 2

Basic Programming Techniques

To use a programming language, you must master the fundamentals. You need to understand the elements required to construct a working program, and learn how to use the development tools to build and run code. You also need to become familiar with the everyday features for representing information, performing calculations, and making decisions. This chapter will introduce these core features of the C# language.

Getting Started

We'll be working in Visual Studio, the Microsoft development environment. There are other ways to build C# programs, but Visual Studio is the most widely used and it's freely available, so we'll stick with that.

 If you don't have Visual Studio, you can download the free Express edition from *http://www.microsoft.com/express/*.

In the first part of this chapter, we'll create a very simple program so that you can see the bare minimum of steps required to get up and running. We'll also examine all of the pieces Visual Studio creates for you so that you know exactly what the development environment is doing for you. And then we'll build some slightly more interesting examples to explore the C# language.

To create a new C# program, select the File→New Project menu option, or just use the Ctrl-Shift-N shortcut. This will open Visual Studio's New Project dialog, shown in Figure 2-1, where you can pick the kind of program you want to build. In the Installed Templates list on the lefthand side, ensure that the Visual C# item is expanded, and inside that, select the Windows item—applications that run locally on Windows are the easiest to create. We'll get into other kinds of programs such as web applications later in the book.

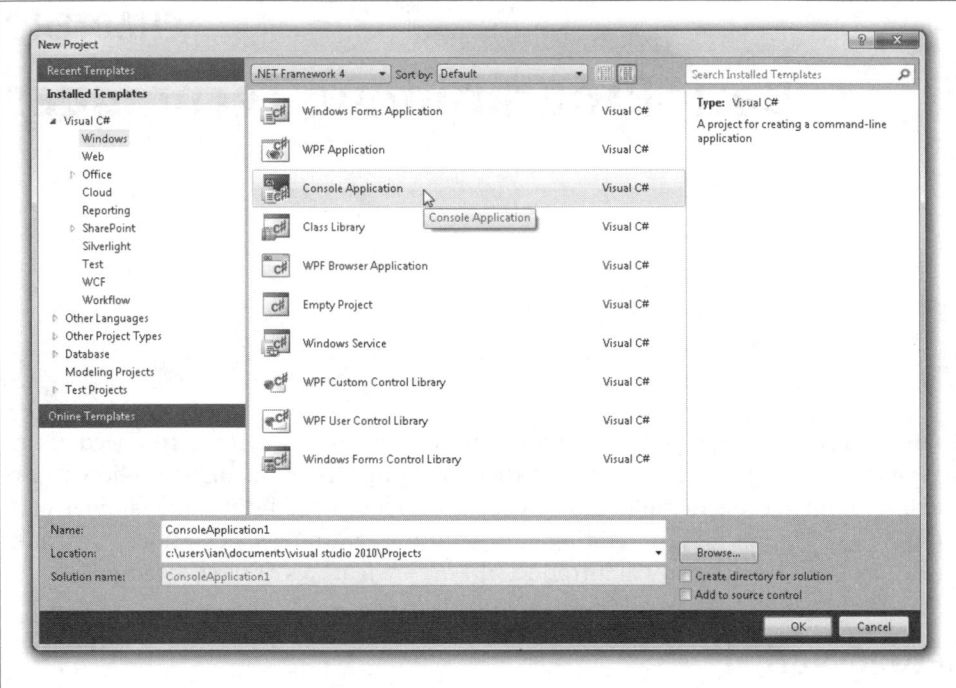

Figure 2-1. Visual Studio's New Project dialog

In the dialog's center, select the Console Application template. This creates an old-fashioned command-line application that runs in a console window. It might not be the most exciting kind of program, but it's the easiest to create and understand, so that's where we'll start.

You need to pick a name for your program—by default, Visual Studio will suggest something unimaginative such as `ConsoleApplication1`. In the Name field near the bottom of the dialog, type `HelloWorld`. (OK, so that's equally unimaginative, but at least it's descriptive.) Visual Studio also wants to know where you'd like to put the project on your hard disk—put it wherever you like. It can also create a separate "solution" directory. That's something you'd do in a larger program made up of multiple components, but for this simple example, you want the "Create directory for solution" checkbox to be unchecked.

When you click the OK button, Visual Studio will create a new *project*, a collection of files that are used to build a program. C# projects always contain source code files, but they often include other types of files, such as bitmaps. This newly created project will contain a C# source file called *Program.cs*, which should be visible in Visual Studio's text editor. In case you're not following along in Visual Studio as you read this, the code is reproduced in Example 2-1. By the way, there's no particular significance to the filename *Program.cs*. Visual Studio doesn't care what you call your source files; by convention, they have a *.cs* extension, short for C#, although even that's optional.

Example 2-1. The code in a freshly created console application

```
using System;
using System.Collections.Generic;
using System.Linq;
using System.Text;

namespace HelloWorld
{
    class Program
    {
        static void Main(string[] args)
        {
        }
    }
}
```

This program doesn't do anything yet. To turn it into the traditional first example, you'll need to add one line of code. This will go in between the two lines that contain the most-indented pair of braces ({ and }). The modified version is shown in Example 2-2, with the new line in bold.

Example 2-2. The traditional first example, "Hello, world"

```
using System;
using System.Collections.Generic;
using System.Linq;
using System.Text;

namespace HelloWorld
{
    class Program
    {
        static void Main(string[] args)
        {
            Console.WriteLine("Hello, world");
        }
    }
}
```

This example is now ready to run. From the Debug menu select the Start Without Debugging item, or just press Ctrl-F5. The program will run, and because you've written a console application, a console window will open. The first line of this window will contain the text "Hello, world" and this will be followed by a prompt saying "Press any key to continue..." Once you've finished admiring the fruits of your creation, press a key to dismiss the window.

 Don't use Debug→Start Debugging or F5—this will run the application in Visual Studio's debugging mode, which doesn't keep the window open once the application has finished. That's not helpful for this example, which will most likely run to completion and then close the window before you've had a chance to see the output.

Now that we have a complete program, let's look at the code to see what each part is for—all of the pieces are things you'll deal with every time you write in C#. Starting from the top, *Program.cs* has several lines beginning with `using`:

```
using System;
using System.Collections.Generic;
using System.Linq;
using System.Text;
```

These *using directives* help the C# compiler work out what external code this particular source file will be using. No code is an island—to get any useful work done, your programs will rely on other code. All C# programs depend on the .NET Framework class library, for example: the one line of code we added to our program uses the class library to display a message. Using directives can declare an intent to use classes from any library—yours, Microsoft's, or anyone's. All the directives in our example start with `System`, which indicates that we want to use something from the .NET Framework. This text that follows the `using` keyword denotes a *namespace*.

Namespaces and Types

The .NET Framework class library is big. To make it easier to find your way around the many services it offers, the library is split into namespaces. For example, the `System.IO` namespace offers I/O (Input/Output) services such as working with files on disk, while `System.Data.SqlClient` is for connecting to a SQL Server database.

A namespace contains *types*. A type typically represents either a kind of information or a kind of object. For example, there are types that provide the core forms of information used in all programs, such as `System.String` which represents text, or the various numeric types such as `System.Double` or `System.Int32`. Some types are more complex—for example, the `System.Net.HttpWebRequest` class represents an HTTP request to be sent to a web server. A few types do not represent any particular thing, but simply offer a set of services, such as the `System.Math` class, which provides mathematical functions such as `Sin` and `Log`, and constants such as π or the base of natural logarithms, *e*. (We will explore the nature of types, objects, and values in much more detail in the next chapter.)

All types in the .NET Framework class library belong to a namespace. The purpose of a using directive is to save you from typing the namespace every single time you need to use a class. For example, in a file that has a `using System;` directive you can just write `Math.PI` to get the value of π, instead of using the full name, `System.Math.PI`. You're not required to write using directives, by the way—if you happen to enjoy typing, you're free to use the fully qualified name. But since some namespaces get quite long—for example, `System.Windows.Media.Imaging`—you can see how the shorthand enabled by a using directive can reduce clutter considerably.

You might be wondering why namespaces are needed at all if the first thing we usually do is add a bunch of using directives to avoid having to mention the namespace anywhere else. One reason is disambiguation—some type names crop up in multiple places. For example, the ASP.NET web framework has a type called `Control`, and so do both WPF and Windows Forms. They represent similar concepts, but they are used in completely different contexts (web applications versus Windows applications). Although all of these types are called `Control`, they are distinct thanks to being in different namespaces.

This disambiguation also leaves you free to use whatever names you want in your own code even if some names happen to be used already in parts of the .NET class library you never knew existed. Since there are more than 10,000 types in the framework, it's entirely possible that you might pick a name that's already being used, but namespaces make this less of a problem. For example, there's a `Bold` class in .NET, but if you happen not to be using part of the library it belongs to (WPF's text services) you might well want to use the name `Bold` to mean something else in your own code. And since .NET's own `Bold` type is hidden away in the `System.Windows.Documents` namespace, as long as you don't add a using directive for that namespace you're free to use the name `Bold` yourself to mean whatever you like.

Even when there's no ambiguity, namespaces help you find your way around the class library—related types tend to be grouped into one namespace, or a group of related namespaces. (For example, there are various namespaces starting with `System.Web` containing types used in ASP.NET web applications.) So rather than searching through thousands of types for what you need, you can browse through the namespaces—there are only a few hundred of those.

 You can see a complete list of .NET Framework class library namespaces, along with a short description of what each one is for, at *http://msdn .microsoft.com/library/ms229335*.

Visual Studio adds four namespace directives to the *Program.cs* file in a new console project. The `System` namespace contains general-purpose services, including basic data types such as `String`, and various numeric types. It also contains the `Console` type our program uses to display its greeting and which provides other console-related services, such as reading keyboard input and choosing the color of your output text.

The remaining three using directives aren't used in our example. Visual Studio adds them to newly created projects because they are likely to be useful in many applications. The `System.Collections.Generic` namespace contains types for working with collections of things, such as a list of numbers. The `System.Linq` namespace contains types used for LINQ, which provides convenient ways of processing collections of information in C#. And the `System.Text` namespace contains types useful for working with text.

The using directives Visual Studio adds to a new C# file are there just to save you some typing. You are free to remove them if you happen not to be using those namespaces. And you can add more, of course.

Removing Unwanted Using Directives

There's a quick way to remove unwanted using directives. If you right-click anywhere on your C# code, the context menu offers an Organize Usings item. This opens a submenu that includes a Remove Unused Usings item—this works out which using directives are surplus to requirements, and removes them. The submenu offers another option designed to appeal to those who like to keep their source code tidy—its Remove and Sort entry can remove unused using statements and then sort the rest into alphabetical order. This menu is shown in Figure 2-2.

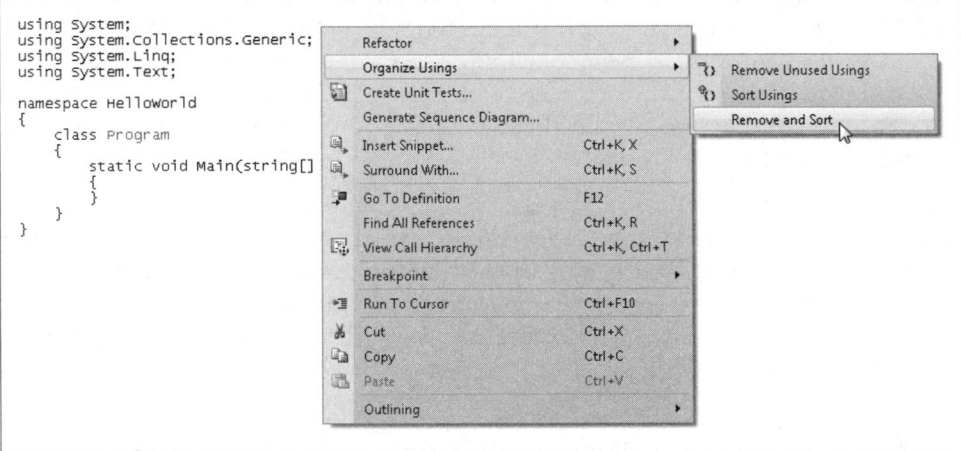

Figure 2-2. Tidying up using directives

The using directives are not the end of our simple program's encounter with namespaces. In fact, the very next line of code after these directives is also concerned with namespaces:

```
namespace HelloWorld
{
    ...
}
```

While using directives declare which namespaces our code consumes, this `namespace` keyword tells the compiler what namespace we plan to provide—the types we write in our programs belong to namespaces just like the types in the class library.* Here, Visual Studio has presumed that we'd like to put our code into a namespace named after the project we created. This is a common practice, although you're free to use whatever

---

* Strictly speaking, you can leave out the namespace, in which case your types will end up in the so-called *global namespace*. But this is considered a poor practice—you'll normally want your own code to reap the same benefits that class libraries get from namespaces.

---

names you like for your namespaces—there's no requirement that the namespace name match the program name.

 The C# compiler will even let you put your own code into namespaces whose names begin with System, but you should not do this (at least, not unless you work for Microsoft and are adding types to some future version of .NET's class library). You're likely to cause confusion if you break the convention that System namespaces contain .NET Framework types.

Notice that the namespace is followed by an open brace ({). C# uses braces to denote containment—here, everything inside these braces will be in our HelloWorld namespace. Since namespaces contain types, it should come as no great surprise that the next line in the file defines a type. Specifically, it defines a *class*.

The .NET Framework class library isn't the only thing that gets to define classes—in fact, if you want to write any code at all in C# you must provide a type to contain that code. Some languages (such as C++) do not impose this constraint, but C# is an object-oriented (OO) programming language. We'll explore OO concepts in the next chapter, but the main impact on our "Hello, world" example is that every bit of C# code must have a type that it calls home.

There are a few different ways to define types in C#, which we'll get to in the next few chapters, but for the present simple example, the distinctions are not yet relevant. So we use the most common, a class:

```
class Program
{
    ...
}
```

Again, note the braces—as with the namespace contents, the class's contents are delineated by a pair of braces.

We're still not quite at the code yet—code lives inside a class, but more specifically, it must live inside a particular *method* inside a class. A method is a named block of code, which may optionally return some data. The class in our example defines a method called Main, and once again we use a pair of braces to show where it starts and ends:

```
static void Main(string[] args)
{
    ...
}
```

The first keyword here, static, tells C# that it's not necessary to create a Program object (Program being the class that contains this method, remember) in order to use this method. As you'll see in the next chapter, a lot of methods require an object, but our simple example doesn't need one.

The next keyword is **void**. This tells the compiler that our method doesn't return any data—it just does some work. Many methods return information. For example, the **System.Math** class's **Cos** method calculates the cosine of its input, and since it doesn't know what you want to do with that result, it provides it as a return value—the output of the method. But the code in this example is rather more proactive than that—it decides to show a message on the screen, so there's nothing for it to return.[†] On methods that return data, you'd write the type of data being returned here, but since there's nothing to return in this case, the nothingness is denoted by the **void** keyword.

The next part, **Main**, is the name of the method. This happens to be a special name—the C# compiler will expect your program to provide one static method called **Main**, and it'll run that method when the program is launched.

The method name is followed by a *parameter list*, which declares the input the method requires. This particular example's parameter list is (**string[] args**), which says that it expects just a single input and that the code will refer to it using the name **args**. It expects this input to be a sequence of text strings (the square brackets indicating that multiple strings may be passed instead of just one). As it happens, this particular program doesn't use this input, but it's a standard feature of the specially named **Main** method—command-line arguments are passed in here. We'll return to this later in the chapter when we write a program that makes use of command-line arguments, but for now, our example doesn't use it. So we'll move on to the final part of the example—the code inside the **Main** method that was the one part we added to Visual Studio's contributions and which represents the only work this program does:

```
Console.WriteLine("Hello, world");
```

This shows the C# syntax for invoking a method. Here we're using a method provided by the **Console** class, which is part of the .NET Framework class library, and it is defined in the **System** namespace. We could have written the fully qualified name, in which case the code would look like this:

```
System.Console.WriteLine("Hello, world");
```

But because of the **using System;** directive earlier, we can use the shorter version—it means the same thing, it's just more concise. The **Console** class provides the ability to display text in a console window and to read input typed by the user in an old-fashioned command-line application. In this case, we're invoking the class's **WriteLine** method, passing it the text **"Hello, world"**. The **WriteLine** method will write whatever text we provide out to the console window.

---

† This is the essential difference between the so-called *functional* and *procedural* approaches to coding, by the way. Code that just performs a computation or calculation and returns the result is called "functional" because it's similar in nature to mathematical functions such as cosine, and square root. Procedural code tends to perform a sequence of actions. In some languages, such as F#, the functional style dominates, but C# programs typically use a mixture of both styles.

You'll have noticed that the dot (.) is being used to mean different things here. We can use it to delineate the namespace name and the type name; for example, System.Console means the Console type in the System namespace. It can also be used to break up a namespace name, as in System.IO. Our example also uses it to indicate that we want to use a particular method provided by a class, as in Console.WriteLine. And as you'll see, the dot turns up in a few other places in C#.

Broadly speaking, the dot signifies that we want to use something that's inside something else. The C# compiler works out from context exactly what that means.

Although we picked over every line of code in this simple example, we haven't quite finished exploring what Visual Studio did for us when we asked it to create a new application. To fully appreciate its work, we need to step out of the *Program.cs* source file and look at the whole project.

Projects and Solutions

It's rare for a useful program to be so simple that you would want all of its source code in one file. You may occasionally stumble across horrors such as a single file containing tens of thousands of lines of code, but in the interest of quality (and sanity) it's best to try to keep your source code in smaller, more manageable chunks—the larger and more complex anything gets the more likely it is to contain flaws. So Visual Studio is built to work with multiple source files, and it provides a couple of concepts for structuring your programs across those files: *projects* and *solutions*.

A project is a collection of source files that the C# compiler combines to produce a single output—typically either an executable program or a library. (See the sidebar on the next page for more details on the compilation process.) The usual convention in Windows is that executable files have an *.exe* extension while libraries have a *.dll* extension. (These extensions are short for *executable* and *dynamic link library*, respectively.) There isn't a big difference between the two kinds of file; the main distinction is that an executable program is required to have an entry point—the Main function. A library is not something you'd run independently; it's designed to be used by other programs, so a DLL doesn't have its own entry point. Other than that, they're pretty much the same thing—they're just files that contain code and data. (The two types of file are so similar that you can use an executable as though it were a library.) So Visual Studio projects work in much the same way for programs and libraries.

Source Code, Binary, and Compilation

The *.exe* and *.dll* files produced by Visual Studio do not contain your source code. If you were to look at the *HelloWorld.exe* file produced by our example, it would not contain a copy of the text in the *Program.cs* file. C# is a *compiled language*, meaning that during the development process, the source is converted into a binary format that is easier for the computer to execute. Visual Studio compiled your code automatically when you ran the program earlier.

Not all languages work this way. For example, JavaScript, a language used to add dynamic behavior to web pages, does not need to be compiled—your web browser downloads the source for any JavaScript required and runs it directly. But there are a few disadvantages with this.

First, source code tends to be rather verbose—it's important that source code be meaningful to humans as well as computers, because when we come to modify a program, we need to understand the code before changing it. But a computer can work with very dense binary representations of information, which makes it possible for compiled code to be much smaller than the source, thus taking up less space on disk and taking less time to download.

Second, human-readable representations are relatively hard work for computers to process—computers are more at home with binary than with text. Compilation provides the opportunity to convert all the human-readable text into a form more convenient for the computer in advance. So compiled code tends to run faster than a system that works directly with the source. (In fact, although JavaScript was not designed to be compiled, modern JavaScript engines have taken to compiling script after downloading it to speed things up. This still leaves it at a disadvantage to a language such as C# where compilation happens during development—when a script runs for the first time with such a system, the user of the web page has to wait while the script is downloaded and compiled.)

Some languages compile code into native *machine language*—the binary code that can be executed directly by a computer's CPU. This offers a performance benefit: code compiled in this way doesn't require any further processing to run. However, .NET languages don't do this, because it limits where a compiled program can execute. As we mentioned in the first chapter, .NET languages compile into a so-called Intermediate Language (IL for short). This is a binary representation, so it's compact and efficient for computers to process, but it's not specific to any particular CPU type, enabling .NET programs to run on either 32-bit or 64-bit machines, or on different CPU architectures. The .NET Framework converts this IL into native machine language just before running it, a technique referred to as JIT (Just In Time) compilation. JIT compilation offers the best of both worlds: it's much faster than compiling from the source, but it still retains the flexibility to target different machine types.

 Some project types produce neither libraries nor executables. For example, there's a project type for building *.msi* (Windows Installer) files from the outputs of other projects. So strictly speaking, a project is a fairly abstract idea: it takes some files and builds them into some kind of output. But projects containing C# code will produce either an EXE or a DLL.

A solution is just a collection of related projects. If you are writing a library, you'll probably want to write an application that uses it—even if the library is ultimately destined to be used by other people, you'll still want to be able to try it out for testing and debugging purposes, so it's useful to be able to have one or more applications that exercise the library's functionality. By putting all of these projects into one solution, you can work with the DLL and its test applications all at once. By the way, Visual Studio always requires a solution—even if you're building just one project, it is always contained in a solution. That's why the project's contents are shown in a panel called the *Solution Explorer*, shown in Figure 2-3.

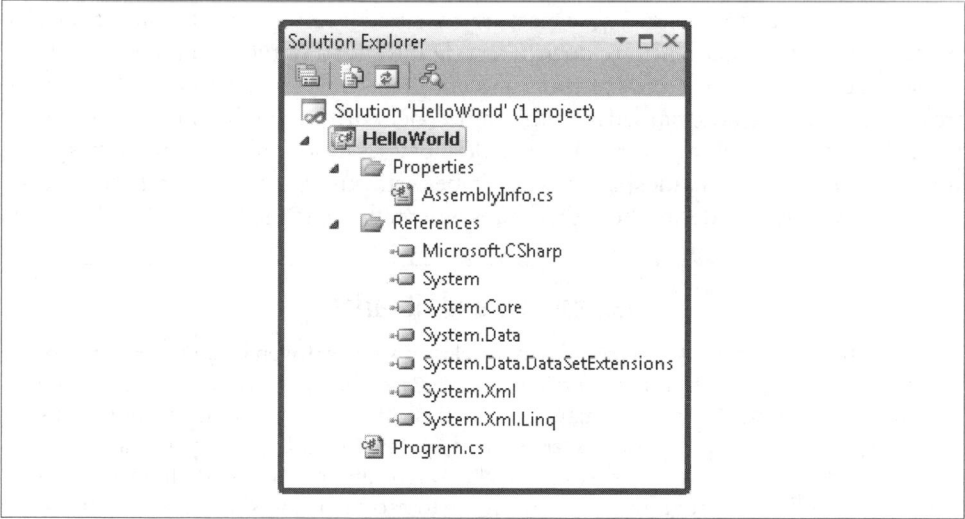

Figure 2-3. HelloWorld project in the Solution Explorer

The Solution Explorer is usually visible on the righthand side of Visual Studio, but if you don't see it you can open it with the View→Solution Explorer menu item. It shows all the projects in the solution—just the HelloWorld project in this example. And it shows all the files in the solution—you can see the *Program.cs* file we've been examining near the bottom of Figure 2-3. Farther up is an extra file we haven't looked at, called *AssemblyInfo.cs*. If you open this you'll see that Visual Studio puts version number and copyright information in that file—users will see this information if they view the compiled output's properties in Windows Explorer.

 You might find that on your system, the Solution Explorer doesn't show the Solution node that's visible at the top of Figure 2-3, and just shows the HelloWorld project. Visual Studio can be configured to hide the solution when it contains just a single project. If you don't see the solution and would like to, select the Tools→Options menu item, and in the Options dialog that opens select the Projects and Solutions item. One of the options will be the "Always show solution" checkbox—check this if you want to see the solution in the Solution Explorer even when you've got only one project.

Besides the C# source files, the Solution Explorer as shown in Figure 2-3 also has a References section. This contains a list of all the libraries your project uses. By default, Visual Studio populates this with a list of DLLs from the .NET Framework class library that it thinks you might find useful.

You might be experiencing déjà vu right now—didn't we already tell the compiler which bits of the library we want with using directives? This is a common cause of confusion among developers learning C#. Namespaces are not libraries, and neither one is contained by the other. These facts are obscured by an apparent connection. For example, the System.Data library does in fact define a load of types in the System.Data namespace. But this is just a convention, and one that is only loosely followed. Libraries are often, but not always, named after the namespace with which they are most strongly associated, but it's common for a library to define types in several different namespaces and it's common for a namespace's types to be distributed across several different libraries. (If you're wondering how this chaos emerged, see the sidebar below.)

Namespaces and Libraries

The distribution of types across DLLs in the class library is driven by a combination of efficiency requirements and history. The System.Core library is a good example of the latter. There is no System.Core namespace—this library defines types in numerous namespaces including System, System.IO, and System.Threading. But you'll also find types in these same three namespaces in the System library and also a library called mscorlib. (All .NET programs have a reference to mscorlib, and since it's mandatory, Visual Studio doesn't show it in the Solution Explorer. It's where critical types such as System.String and System.Int32 are defined.) One of the reasons System.Core exists as a separate DLL is that it first appeared in version 3.5 of .NET. With versions 3.0 and 3.5 of .NET, Microsoft chose to put completely new functionality into new DLLs rather than altering the DLLs that were provided in version 2.0. This packaging decision—choosing which types go in which DLLs—was independent from the conceptual decision of which types belong in which namespaces.

History doesn't explain the whole story, though. Even the very first version of .NET split its namespaces across multiple libraries. One common reason for this was to avoid loading code that is never used. You wouldn't want a desktop application to waste time and memory by loading the libraries for building web applications. In some cases, namespaces are actually a pretty good guide to partitioning—chances are good that if you use one type from one of the System.Web namespaces, you're going to be using lots of them. But there are a few cases in which namespaces are not the best way to determine packaging. For example, the System.Printing namespace is split across two libraries: the System.Printing library contains general print-related classes, but the ReachFrame work library adds extra types to the namespace that you may need if you're working with a particular kind of printable document called an XPS file. If you're not using that feature, you don't need a reference to that specialized DLL.

This raises a question: how do you know where to find things? It's frustrating when adding a reference to the System.Printing library fails to give you access to the types in the System.Printing namespace that you were looking for. Fortunately, the help pages for each type tell you both the namespace and the library file (assembly) containing the type.

The upshot is that the C# compiler cannot work out which libraries you want from your using directives, because in general it's not possible to deduce which libraries are required from the namespaces alone. So a project needs to list which libraries it uses, and then individual source files in that project can declare which namespaces they are using. Visual Studio provides you with a set of references that it hopes will be useful, and for this very simple example, we're not actually using most of them.

 Visual Studio notices when your code doesn't use all of the libraries your project references, and automatically omits references to any unused libraries. This makes your binary slightly smaller than it would be if unnecessary references were left in.

You can add or remove references to suit whatever program you're building. To remove a reference, you can just select the library in the Solution Explorer and press the Delete key. (As it happens, our program is so simple that it depends only on the mandatory mscorlib library, so you could remove every DLL shown, and as long as you also remove any unused using directives from the source code, the program will still work.) To add a reference to a library, you can right-click on the References item and choose the Add Reference menu item. We'll explore all of this in more detail in Chapter 15.

It's almost time to move on from "Hello, world" and start to explore more of the core language features, but first let's recap what we've seen. The one line of executable code in our program invokes the WriteLine method of the System.Console class to print a message. This code lives inside a method whose special name, Main, marks it out as the method to run when the program starts. That method is contained by a class called Program, because C# requires all methods to belong to a type. This class is a member of the HelloWorld namespace, because we chose to follow the convention of having our namespace match the name of the compiled binary. Our program uses the using directives supplied by Visual Studio to be able to refer to the Console class without needing to specify its namespace explicitly. So if you take one more look at the program, you now know what every single line is for. (It is reproduced in Example 2-3, with the unused using directives removed.)

Example 2-3. "Hello, world" again (with fewer using directives)

```
using System;

namespace HelloWorld
{
    class Program
    {
        static void Main(string[] args)
        {
            Console.WriteLine("Hello, world");
        }
    }
}
```

With the whole example in one place, you can see clearly that the code is indented to reflect the structure. This is a common practice, but it's not strictly necessary. As far as the C# compiler is concerned, when it comes to the space between elements of the language, there's no difference between a single space, multiple spaces or tabs, or even blank lines—the syntax treats any contiguous quantity of whitespace as it would a single space.‡ So you are free to use space in your source code to improve legibility. This is why C# requires the use of braces to indicate containment, and it's also why there's a semicolon at the end of the line that prints out the message. Since C# doesn't care whether we have one statement of code per line, split the code across multiple lines, or cram multiple statements onto one line, we need to be explicit about the end of each instruction, marking it with a ; so that the compiler knows where each new step of the program begins.

Comments, Regions, and Readability

While we're looking at the structure and layout of source code, we need to examine a language feature that is extremely important, despite having precisely no effect on the behavior of your code. C# lets you add text to your source file that it will completely ignore. This might not sound important, or even useful, but it turns out to be vital if you want to have any hope of understanding code you wrote six months ago.

There's an unfortunate phenomenon known as "write-only code." This is code that made some kind of sense to whoever wrote it at the time, but is incomprehensible to anyone trying to read it at a later date, even if the person reading it is its author. The best defense against this problem is to think carefully about the names you give the

---

‡ With the odd exception: in a string constant such as the "Hello, world" text in this example, whitespace is treated literally—C# presumes that if you put, say, three spaces in some text enclosed in double quotes, you really want three spaces.

features of your code and the way you structure your programs. You should strive to write your code so that it does what it looks like it does.

Unfortunately, it's sometimes necessary to do things in a nonobvious way, so even if your code is sufficiently clear that it's easy to see *what* it does, it may not be at all clear *why* it does certain things. This tends to happen where your code meets other code—you might be interacting with a component or a service that's idiosyncratic, or just plain buggy, and which works only if you do things in a particular way. For example, you might find that a component ignores the first attempt to do something and you need to add a redundant-looking line of code to get it to work:

```
Frobnicator.SetTarget("");
Frobnicator.SetTarget("Norfolk");
```

The problem with this sort of thing is that it's very hard for someone who comes across this code later on to know what to make of it. Is that apparently redundant line deliberate? Is it safe to remove? Intrigue and ambiguity might make for engaging fiction, but these characteristics are rarely desirable in code. We need something to explain the mystery, and that's the purpose of a comment. So you might write this:

```
// Frobnicator v2.41 has a bug where it crashes occasionally if
// we try to set the target to "Norfolk". Setting it to an empty
// string first seems to work around the problem.
Frobnicator.SetTarget("");
Frobnicator.SetTarget("Norfolk");
```

This is now less mysterious. Someone coming across this code knows why the apparently redundant line was added. It's clear what problem it solves and the conditions under which that problem occurs, which makes it possible to find out whether the problem has been fixed in the most recent version of the offending component, making it possible to remove the fix. This makes it much easier to maintain code in the long run.

As far as C# is concerned, this example is identical to the one without comments. The // character sequence tells it to ignore any further text up to the end of the line. So you can either put comments on their own line as shown earlier, or tack them onto the end of an existing line:

```
Frobnicator.SetTarget("");  // Workaround for bug in v2.41
```

Like most of the C-family languages, C# supports two forms of comment syntax. As well as the single-line // form, you can write a comment that spans multiple lines, denoting the start with /* and the end with */, for example:

```
/* This is part of a comment.
   This continues to be part of the same comment.
   Here endeth the comment. */
```

Bad Comments

While comments can be very useful, many, sadly, are not. There are a couple of particularly common mistakes people make when writing comments, and it's worth drawing attention to them so that you know what to avoid. Here's the most common example:

```
// Setting target to empty string
Frobnicator.SetTarget("");
// Setting target to Norfolk
Frobnicator.SetTarget("Norfolk");
```

These comments just repeat what the code already said. This is clearly a waste of space, but it's surprisingly common, particularly from inexperienced developers. This may be because they've been told that comments are good, but they have no idea what makes a good comment. A comment should say something that's not obvious from the code and which is likely to be useful to anyone trying to understand the code.

The other common form of bad comment looks like this:

```
// Setting target to Norfolk
Frobnicator.SetTarget("Wiltshire");
```

Here, the comment contradicts the code. It seems like it shouldn't be necessary to say that you shouldn't do that, but it's surprising how often you see this sort of thing in real code. It usually happens because someone modified the code without bothering to update the comment. A quick review of the comments after a code change is always worth doing. (Not least because if you've not paid enough attention to detail to notice that the comments are no longer accurate, chances are there are other problems you've not noticed.)

XML Documentation Comments

If you structure your comments in a certain way, Visual Studio is able to present the information in those comments in tool tips whenever developers use your code. As Example 2-4 shows, documentation comments are denoted with three slashes, and they contain XML elements describing the target of the comment—in this case, there's a description of a method, its parameters, and the information it returns.

Example 2-4. XML documentation comments

```
/// <summary>
/// Returns the square of the specified number.
/// </summary>
/// <param name="x">The number to square.</param>
/// <returns>The squared value.</returns>
static double Square(double x)
{
    return x * x;
}
```

If a developer starts writing code to invoke this method, Visual Studio will show a pop up listing all available members matching what she's typed so far, and also adds a tool tip showing the information from the <summary> element of the selected method in the list, as Figure 2-4 shows. You'll see similar information when using classes from the .NET Framework—documentation from its class libraries is provided as part of the .NET Framework SDK included with Visual Studio. (The C# compiler can extract this information from your source files and put it in a separate XML file, enabling you to provide the documentation for a library without necessarily having to ship the source code.)

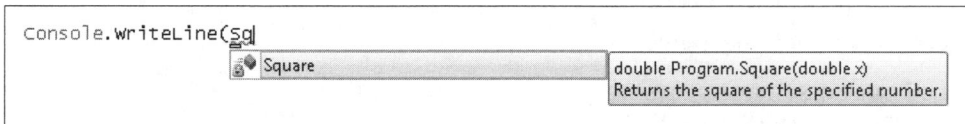

Figure 2-4. Summary information from XML documentation

The <param> information shows up as you start to type arguments, as Figure 2-5 shows. The <returns> information doesn't appear here, but there are tools that can build documentation from this information into HTML files or help files. For example, Microsoft provides a tool called Sandcastle, available from *http://www.codeplex.com/Sandcastle*, which can generate documentation with a similar structure to the documentation for Microsoft's own class libraries.

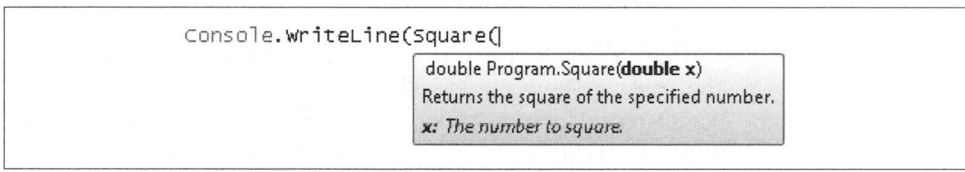

Figure 2-5. Parameter information from XML documentation

We're moving on from "Hello, world" now, so this is a good time to create a new project if you're following along in Visual Studio as you read. (Select File→New Project or press Ctrl-Shift-N. Note that, by default, this will create a new solution for your new project. There's an option in the New Project dialog to add the new project to the existing solution, but in this case, let it create a new one.) Create another console application and call it RaceInfo—the code is going to perform various jobs to analyze the performance of a race car. Let Visual Studio create the project for you, and you'll end up with much the same code as we had in Example 2-1, but with the Program class in a namespace called RaceInfo instead of HelloWorld. The first task will be to calculate the average speed and fuel consumption of the car, so we need to introduce the C# mechanism for holding and working with data.

Variables

C# methods can have named places to hold information. These are called *variables*, because the information they contain may be different each time the program runs, or your code may change a variable while the program runs. Example 2-5 defines three variables in our program's `Main` method, to represent the distance traveled by the car, how long it has been moving, and how much fuel it has consumed so far. These variables don't vary at all in this example—a variable's value *can* change, but it's OK to create variables whose value is fixed.

Example 2-5. Variables

```
static void Main(string[] args)
{
    double kmTravelled = 5.14;
    double elapsedSeconds = 78.74;
    double fuelKilosConsumed = 2.7;
}
```

Notice that the variable names (`kmTravelled`, `elapsedSeconds`, and `fuelKilosConsumed`) are reasonably descriptive. In algebra it's common to use single letters as variable names, but in code it is a good practice to use names that make it clear what the variable holds.

 If you can't think of a good descriptive name for a variable, that's often a symptom of trouble. It's hard to write code that works if it's not clear what information the code is working with.

These names indicate not just what the variables represent, but also their units. This is of no significance to the compiler—we could call the three variables `tom`, `dick`, and `harry` for all it cares—but it's useful for humans looking at the code. Misunderstandings about whether a particular value is in metric or imperial units have been known to cause some extremely expensive problems, such as the accidental destruction of spacecraft. This particular race team seems to use the metric system. (If you're wondering why the fuel is in kilograms rather than, say, liters, it's because in high-performance motor racing, fuel is typically measured by weight rather than volume, just like it is in aviation. Fuel tends to expand or contract as the temperature changes—you get better value for your money if you refill your car in the morning on a cold day than in the middle of a hot day—so mass is more useful because it's a more stable measure.)

Variable Types

All three of the variable declarations in Example 2-5 start with the keyword `double`. This tells the compiler what kind of information the variable holds. For this example, we're clearly working with numbers, but .NET offers several different numeric types. Table 2-1 shows the complete set, and it may look like a bewildering assortment of options, but in practice the choice usually goes one of three ways: int, double, or decimal, which represent integers, floating-point, or decimal floating-point numbers, respectively.

Table 2-1. Numeric types

C# name	.NET name	Purpose
float	System.Single	Whole numbers and a limited range of fractions, with a wide range of values thanks to "floating point." Occupies 32 bits of space.
double	System.Double	Double-precision version of float—same idea, but using 64 bits.
byte	System.Byte	Non-negative integer. Occupies 8 bits. Represents values from 0 to 255.
sbyte	System.SByte	Signed integer. Occupies 8 bits. Represents values from −128 to 127.
short	System.Int16	Signed integer. Occupies 16 bits. Represents values from −32,768 to 32,767.
ushort	System.UInt16	Non-negative integer. Occupies 16 bits. Represents values from 0 to 65,535.
int	System.Int32	Signed integer. Occupies 32 bits. Represents values from −2,147,483,648 to 2,147,483,647.
uint	System.UInt32	Nonnegative integer. Occupies 32 bits. Represents values from 0 to 4,294,967,295.
long	System.Int64	Signed integer. Occupies 64 bits. Represents values from −9,223,372,036,854,775,808 to 9,223,372,036,854,775,807.
ulong	System.UInt64	Nonnegative integer. Occupies 64 bits. Represents values from 0 to 18,446,744,073,709,551,615.
(none)	System.Numerics.BigInteger	Signed integer. Grows in size as required. Value range limited only by available memory.
decimal	System.Decimal	Supports whole numbers and fractions. Slightly less efficient than double, but provides more predictable behavior when using decimal fractions.

Integers

The int type (short for *integer*) represents whole numbers. That's clearly no use for our example, because we're dealing with numbers such as 5.14, and the closest that an int can get to that value is 5. But programs often deal with discrete quantities, such as the number of rows returned by a database query or the number of employees reporting to a particular manager. The principal advantage of an integer type is that it's exact: there's no scope for wondering if the number is really 5, or maybe just a number quite close to 5, such as 5.000001.

Table 2-1 lists nine types capable of representing integers. The ninth, BigInteger, is a special case that we'll get to later. The other eight support four different sizes, with a choice between the ability and inability to represent negative numbers.

Unsigned numbers may seem less flexible, but they are potentially useful if you need to represent values that should never be negative. However, the unsigned integer types are not widely used—some programming languages don't support them at all, and so you'll find that the .NET Framework class library tends to use the signed types even when the unsigned ones might make more sense. For example, the `Count` property available on most collection types is of type `int`—a signed 32-bit integer—even though it does not make sense for a collection to contain a negative number of items.

 Unsigned integers can also represent larger numbers than their signed equivalents. They don't need to use up a bit to represent the sign, so they can use that to extend the range instead. However, this is something you should be wary of depending on. If you're so close to the limits of a type's range that one more bit makes a difference, you're probably in danger of overflowing the type's range in any case, and so you should consider a larger type.

Besides the signed/unsigned distinction, the various types offer different sizes, and a correspondingly different range of values. 32 bits is a popular choice because it offers a usefully wide range of values and is efficient for a 32-bit processor to work with. 64-bit types are used for the (fairly rare) occasions when you're dealing with large enough quantities that a 32-bit representation's range of a couple of billion is insufficient. 16-bit values are rarely used, although they occasionally crop up when having to deal with old programming interfaces, file formats, or network protocols.

The 8-bit `byte` type is important because binary I/O (e.g., working with files or network connections) is mostly byte-oriented. And for reasons of historical convention, bytes buck the trend in that the unsigned type is used more widely than the signed `sbyte` type. But outside of I/O, a byte is usually too small to be useful.

So in practice, `int` is the most widely used integer type. The fact that C# even offers you all these other choices can seem a little archaic—it harks back to the time when computers had so little memory that 32-bit numbers looked like an expensive choice. It gets this from its C-family connections, but it does turn out to be useful to have this control when you need to work directly with Windows APIs, as you'll see in Chapter 19.

Notice that most of the types in Table 2-1 have two names. C# uses names such as `int` and `long`, but the .NET Framework calls these types by longer names such as `System.Int32` and `System.Int64`. The shorter C# names are *aliases*, and C# is happy to let you use either. You can write this:

```
int answer = 42;
```

or this:

```
System.Int32 answer = 42;
```

or, if your C# source file has a `using System;` directive at the top, you can write this:

```
Int32 answer = 42;
```

All of these are equivalent—they produce exactly the same compiled output. The last two are equivalent simply because of how namespaces work, but why does C# support a completely different set of aliases? The answer is historical: C# was designed to be easy to learn for people who are familiar with the so-called C family of languages, which includes C, C++, Java, and JavaScript. Most of the languages in this family use the same names for certain kinds of data types—most use the name `int` to denote a conveniently sized integer, for example. So C# is merely following suit—it allows you to write code that looks like it would in other C-family languages.

By contrast, the .NET Framework supports many different languages, so it takes the prosaic approach of giving these numeric data types descriptive names—it calls a 32-bit integer `System.Int32`. Since C# lets you use either naming style, opinion is divided on the matter of which you should use.§ The C-family style (`int`, `double`, etc.) seems to be the more popular.

Version 4 of the .NET Framework introduces an extra integer type that works slightly differently from the rest: `BigInteger`. It does not have a C-style name, so it's known only by its class library name. Unlike all the other integer types, which occupy a fixed amount of memory that determines their range, a `BigInteger` can grow. As the number it represents gets larger, it simply consumes more space. The only theoretical limit on range is the amount of memory available, but in practice, the computational cost of working with vast numbers is likely to be the limiting factor. Even simple arithmetic operations such as multiplication can become rather expensive with sufficiently vast numbers. For example, if you have two numbers each with 1 million decimal digits— each number occupies more than 400 kilobytes of memory—multiplying these together takes more than a minute on a reasonably well-specified computer. `BigInteger` is useful for mathematical scenarios when you need to be able to work with very large numbers, but in more ordinary situations, `int` is the most popular integer type.

Integers are all very well for countable quantities, but what if you need the ability to represent something other than a whole number? This is where floating-point types come in.

Floating point

The `double` and `float` types both offer the ability to support numbers with a fractional component. For example, you can represent the value 1.5 with either of these types, which you can't do with any of the integer types. The only difference between `double` and `float` is the level of precision available: since floating-point numbers have a fixed size, they can offer only a limited amount of precision. This means that they cannot represent *any* fraction—the limited precision means floating-point numbers can only represent most numbers approximately.

---

§ Whenever more than one way of doing something exists in a programming system, a schism inevitably forms, offering the opportunity for long and pointless arguments over which is "better."

Floating Point

If you're wondering why these are called *floating-point* types, the name is a technical description of how they work internally. These numbers contain a fixed number of binary digits to hold the value, and then another number that says where the . should go. So the *point* is a binary point, the binary equivalent of a decimal point. It's *floating* because it can move around.

A `float` offers about seven decimal places of precision, whereas a `double` offers about 17. (Strictly speaking, they offer 23 and 52 binary places of precision, respectively. These are binary formats, so their precision does not correspond to an exact number of decimal places of precision.) So the following code:

```
double x = 1234.5678;
double y = x + 0.0001;
Console.WriteLine(x);
Console.WriteLine(y);
```

prints out what you'd expect:

```
1234.5678
1234.5679
```

If instead we use the float type:

```
float x = 1234.5678f;
float y = x + 0.0001f;
Console.WriteLine(x);
Console.WriteLine(y);
```

we get this:

```
1234.568
1234.568
```

This often surprises new developers, but it's normal, and is by no means unique to C#. If only a limited amount of space is available, you simply cannot represent all possible numbers with complete accuracy. Floating point, approximate as it is, is the standard way to represent noninteger numbers in most programming languages, and you'll see this sort of inaccuracy anywhere.

Notice that when modifying the code to use float instead of double, we added the letter *f* to the end of the constants—0.0001f instead of just 0.0001, for example. This is because C# treats a number with a decimal point as a value of type double, and if we try to store this in a variable of type float, we risk losing data due to the lower precision. Such code is treated as an error, hence the need to explicitly tell C# that we know we're working with single-precision floating-point values, with the *f* suffix. If you have a double you really would like to turn into a float, and you are prepared to tolerate the loss of precision, you can tell C# this with a *cast* operator. For example:

```
double x = 1234.5678;
double y = x + 0.0001;
float impreciseSum = (float) (x + y);
```

The (float) syntax here is a cast, an explicit instruction to the compiler that we want to convert the type. Since we are being explicit, the compiler does not treat this as an error.

For a lot of applications, limited precision is not too big a problem as long as you're aware of it, but there's a slightly subtler problem that afflicts double and float. They are both binary representations, because that's the most efficient way of packing precision into the space available. However, it means that you can get some surprising-looking results when working in decimal. For example, the number 0.1 cannot be represented accurately as a finite-length binary fraction. (For much the same reason that 1/9 cannot accurately be represented as a finite-length decimal fraction. In either case, you end up with a recurring [i.e., infinitely long] number: 1/9 in decimal is 0.1111 recurring; 1/10 in decimal is 0.1, but in binary it's 0.00011001100110011 recurring.) Take the following example:

```
float f1 = 0.1f;
float f2 = f1 + 0.1f;
float f3 = f2 + 0.1f;
float f4 = f3 + 0.1f;
float f5 = f4 + 0.1f;
float f6 = f5 + 0.1f;
float f7 = f6 + 0.1f;
float f8 = f7 + 0.1f;
float f9 = f8 + 0.1f;
Console.WriteLine(f1);
Console.WriteLine(f2);
Console.WriteLine(f3);
Console.WriteLine(f4);
Console.WriteLine(f5);
Console.WriteLine(f6);
Console.WriteLine(f7);
Console.WriteLine(f8);
Console.WriteLine(f9);
```

(We'll see how to avoid such highly repetitive code when we get to loops later in the chapter, by the way.) This shows the following rather suspect output:

```
0.1
0.2
0.3
0.4
0.5
0.6
0.7
0.8000001
0.9000001
```

The inability to represent 0.1 accurately is not initially obvious, because .NET rounds the numbers when displaying them, masking the problem. However, as we keep adding numbers together, the inaccuracies add up and eventually start to become visible. As you can imagine, accountants don't like this sort of thing—if those numbers happened to represent fund transfers measured in billions of dollars, having $0.0000001 billion ($100) suddenly appear out of nowhere every eight transactions would be considered a bad practice. This is why there's a special numeric type just for working in decimal.

Decimal floating point

The decimal type (or System.Decimal, as .NET calls it) is superficially very similar to double and float, except its internal representation is adapted to decimal representations. It can represent up to 28 decimal digits of precision, and unlike the two binary floating-point types, any number that can be written as a 28-digit (or fewer) decimal can be represented completely accurately as a decimal variable. The value 0.1 fits comfortably into 28 digits with room to spare, so this would fix the problem in the previous example. The decimal type still has limited precision; it just has less surprising behavior if you're looking at all your numbers in decimal.

So if you are performing calculations involving money, decimal is likely to be a better choice than double or float. The trade-off is that it's slightly less efficient—computers are more at home in binary than decimal. For our race information application, we don't have any particular need for decimal fidelity, which is why we're using the double type in Example 2-5.

Getting back to that example, recall that we defined three variables that hold the distance our car has traveled, how long it took, and how much fuel it burned in the process. Here it is again so that you don't have to flip back to it:

```
static void Main(string[] args)
{
    double kmTravelled = 5.141;
    double elapsedSeconds = 78.738;
    double fuelKilosConsumed = 2.7;
}
```

Now that we've looked at the numeric types, the structure of these lines is pretty clear. We start with the type of data we'd like to work with, followed by the name we'd like to use, and then we use the = symbol to assign a value to the variable. But assigning constant values isn't very exciting. You can get the computer to do more useful work, because you can assign an *expression* into a variable.

Expressions and Statements

An expression is a piece of code that produces a value of some kind. We've actually seen several examples already, the most basic being the numbers we're assigning into the variables. So in our example, a number such as:

```
5.141
```

is an expression. Expressions where we just tell C# what value we want are called *literal* expressions. More interestingly, expressions can perform calculations. For example, we could calculate the distance traveled per kilogram of fuel consumed with the expression in Example 2-6.

Example 2-6. Dividing one variable by another

```
kmTravelled / fuelKilosConsumed
```

The / symbol denotes division. Multiplication, addition, and subtraction are done with *, +, and -, respectively.

You can combine expressions together too. The / operator requires two inputs—the dividend and the divisor—and each input is itself an expression. We were able to use variable names such as kmTravelled because a variable name is valid as an expression—the resultant value is just whatever that variable's value is. But we could use literals, as Example 2-7 shows. (A trap awaits the unwary here; see the sidebar on the next page.)

Example 2-7. Dividing one literal by another

```
60 / 10
```

Or we could use a mixture of literals and variable names to calculate the elapsed time in minutes:

```
elapsedSeconds / 60
```

or a multiplication expression as one of the inputs to a division expression to calculate the elapsed time in hours:

```
elapsedSeconds / (60 * 60)
```

Integer Versus Floating-Point Division

There's a subtle difference between how division works in Examples 2-6 and 2-7. Since the two literals in Example 2-7 do not contain decimal points, the compiler treats them as integers, and so it will perform an integer division. But since the `kmTravelled` and `fuelKilosConsumed` variables are both floating-point, it will use a floating-point division operation. In this particular case it doesn't matter, because dividing 60 by 10 produces another integer, 6. But what if the result had not been a whole number? If we had written this, for example:

```
3/4
```

the result would be 0, as this is an integer division—4 does not go into 3. However, given the following:

```
double x = 3;
double y = 4;
```

the value of `x/y` would be `0.75`, because C# would use floating-point division, which can deal with nonwhole results. If you wanted to use floating-point calculations with literals, you could write:

```
3.0/4.0
```

The decimal point indicates that we want floating-point numbers, and therefore floating-point division, so the result is 0.75.

(The parentheses ensure that we divide by 60 * 60. Without the parentheses, this expression would divide by 60, and then multiply by 60, which would be less useful. See the sidebar on the next page.) And then we could use this to work out the speed in kilometers per hour:

```
kmTravelled / (elapsedSeconds / (60 * 60))
```

Expressions don't actually do anything on their own. We have described a calculation, but the C# compiler needs to know what we want to do with the result. We can do various things with an expression. We could use it to initialize another variable:

```
double kmPerHour = kmTravelled / (elapsedSeconds / (60 * 60));
```

or we could display the value of the expression in the console window:

```
Console.WriteLine(kmTravelled / (elapsedSeconds / (60 * 60)));
```

Both of these are examples of *statements*.

Whereas an expression describes a calculation, a statement describes an action. In the last two examples, we used the same expression—a calculation of the race car's speed—but the two statements did different things: one evaluated the expression and assigned it into a new variable, while the other evaluated the expression and then passed it to the `Console` class's `WriteLine` method.

Order of Evaluation

C# has a set of rules for working out the order in which to evaluate the components of an expression. It does not necessarily work from left to right, because some operators have a higher *precedence* than others. For example, imagine evaluating this:

1.0 + 3.0 / 4.0

from left to right. Start with 1.0, add 3.0 which gets you to 4.0, and then divide by 4.0—the result would be 1.0. But the conventional rules of arithmetic mean the result should be one and three quarters. And that's just what C# produces—the result is 1.75. The division is performed before the addition, because division has higher precedence than division.

Some groups of operators have equal precedence. For example, multiplication and division have equal precedence. When expressions contain multiple operations with the same precedence, mathematical operations are evaluated from left to right. So 10.0 / 2.0 * 5.0 evaluates to 25.0. But parentheses trump precedence, so 10.0 / (2.0 * 5.0) evaluates to 1.0.

Some programming books go into great depths about all the details of precedence, but it makes for exceptionally tedious reading—C# has 15 different levels of precedence. The details are important for compiler writers, but of limited value for developers—code that relies heavily on precedence can be hard to read. Using parentheses to make evaluation order explicit can often improve clarity. But if you would like the gory details, you can find them at *http://msdn.microsoft.com/en-us/library/aa691323*.

An expression's type matters. The examples we just looked at involve numbers or numeric variables, and are of type double or int. Expressions can be of any type, though. For example, ("Hello, " + "world") is an expression of type string. If you wrote an assignment statement that tried to assign that expression into a variable of type double, the compiler would complain—it insists that expressions are either of the same type as the variable, or of a type that is implicitly convertible to the variable's type.

Implicit conversions exist for numeric types when the conversion won't lose information—for example, a double can represent any value that an int can, so you're allowed to assign an integer expression into a double variable. But attempting the opposite would cause a compiler error, because doubles can be larger than the highest int, and they can also contain fractional parts that would be lost. If you don't mind the loss of information, you can put a *cast* in front of the expression:

```
int approxKmPerHour = (int) kmPerHour;
```

This casts the kmPerHour (which we declared earlier as a double) to an int, meaning it'll force the value to fit in an integer, possibly losing information in the process.

A variable doesn't have to be stuck with its initial value for its whole life. We can assign new values at any time.

Assignment Statements

The previous section showed how to assign an expression's value into a newly declared variable:

```
double kmPerHour = kmTravelled / (elapsedSeconds / (60 * 60));
```

If at some later stage in the program's execution new information becomes available, we could assign a new value into the kmPerHour variable—assignment statements aren't required to declare new variables, and can assign into existing ones:

```
kmPerHour = updateKmTravelled / (updatedElapsedSeconds / (60 * 60));
```

This overwrites the existing value in the kmPerHour variable.

C# offers some specialized assignment statements that can make for slightly more succinct code. For example, suppose you wanted to add the car's latest lap time to the variable holding the total elapsed time. You could write this:

```
elapsedSeconds = elapsedSeconds + latestLapTime;
```

This evaluates the expression on the righthand side, and assigns the result to the variable specified on the lefthand side. However, this process of adding a value to a variable is so common that there's a special syntax for it:

```
elapsedSeconds += latestLapTime;
```

This has exactly the same effect as the previous expression. There are equivalents for the other mathematical operators, so -= means to subtract the expression on the right from the variable on the left, *= does the same for multiplication, and so on.

Increment and Decrement Operators

While we're looking at how to update values, we should also look at the increment and decrement operators. If we want to maintain a lap count, we could add one each time the car completes a lap:

```
lapCount += 1;
```

The C programming language's designers considered adding one to be a sufficiently important case to devise an even more special syntax for it, called the increment operator, which C# duly offers:

```
lapCount++;
```

There's also a decrement operator, --, which subtracts one. This example is a statement, but you can also use the increment and decrement operators in the middle of an expression:

```
int currentLap = lapCount++;
```

But be careful. The expression on the right of this assignment statement means "evaluate the *current* value of lapCount and then increment lapCount *after* getting its current value." So if lapCount was 3 before executing this statement, currentLap would be 3 and lapCount would be 4 after executing it. If you want to use the updated value, you put the increment (or decrement) operator before its target:

```
int currentLap = ++lapCount;
```

You could write a program that consisted entirely of variable declaration, assignment, increment, and method invocation statements. However, such a program wouldn't be very interesting—it would always execute the same sequence of statements just once in the same order. Fortunately, C# provides some more interesting statements that allow a program to make decisions that dynamically change the flow of execution through the code. This is sometimes referred to as *flow control*.

Flow Control with Selection Statements

A selection statement selects which code path to execute next, based on the value of an expression. We could use a selection statement to work out whether the race car is likely to run out of fuel in the next few laps, and display a warning if it is. C# offers two selection statements: if *statements* and switch *statements*.

To illustrate selection in action, we need to make a slight change to the program. Right now, our example hardcodes all of its data—the distance traveled, fuel consumed, and time elapsed are compiled into the code as literals. This makes selection statements uninteresting—the program would make the same decision every time because the data would always be the same. For the decision to be meaningful, we need to modify the program to accept input. Since we're writing a console application, we can supply the necessary information as command-line arguments. We could run the program passing in the total distance, elapsed time, and fuel consumed, for example:

```
RaceInfo 20.6 312.8 10.8
```

We can write a modified version of the program that picks up these command-line values instead of hardcoding them, as shown in Example 2-8.

Example 2-8. Reading command-line inputs

```
static void Main(string[] args)
{
    double kmTravelled = double.Parse(args[0]);
    double elapsedSeconds = double.Parse(args[1]);
    double fuelKilosConsumed = double.Parse(args[2]);
}
```

There are a few interesting features to point out here before we add a selection statement. First, recall from earlier that the Main method, our program's entry point, is passed a sequence of strings representing the command-line arguments in a variable called args. This sequence is an *array*, a .NET construct for holding multiple items of a particular type. (You can make arrays of anything—numbers, text, or any type. The `string[]` syntax indicates that this method expects an array of strings.) In an expression, we can retrieve a particular item from an array by specifying a number in square brackets after the array variable's name. So the first three lines in our method here use `args[0]`, `args[1]`, and `args[2]` to get the first, second, and third items in the array—the three command-line arguments in this case.

C-family languages tend to number things from zero, and C# follows suit. This may seem a little idiosyncratic, but it makes sense to the computer. You can think of it as saying how far into the array you want to look. If you want to look at the thing right at the start of the array, you don't need to go any distance at all, so an offset of zero gets you the first item. If you're British, you'll recognize this logic from floor numbering—the first floor in a building in Great Britain is not the one at street level; you have to go up one flight of stairs to get to the first floor.

Also notice the use of `double.Parse`. Command-line arguments are passed as text, because the user can type anything:

```
RaceInfo Jenson Button Rocks
```

But our program expects numbers. We need to do something to convert the strings into numbers, and that's what `double.Parse` does: it expects the text to contain a decimal number, and converts it into a double-precision floating-point representation of that number. (If you're wondering what it would do if the text wasn't in fact a number, it'll throw an exception. Chapter 6 explains what that means and how to deal with it gracefully, but for now it means our program would crash with an error.)

This example illustrates that method invocations can also be expressions—the `double` type's `Parse` method returns a value of type `double`, meaning we can use it to initialize a variable of type `double`.

But that's all by the by—the point here is that our program now gets data that could be different each time the program runs. For example, a race engineer in the pit lane could run the program with new distance, timing, and fuel information each time the car completes a lap. So our program can now usefully make decisions based on its input using selection statements. One such statement is the `if` statement.

if Statements

An `if` *statement* is a selection statement that decides whether to execute a particular piece of code based on the value of an expression. We can use this to show a low-fuel warning by adding the code in Example 2-9 at the end of our example's `Main` method. Most of the code performs calculations in preparation for making the decision. The `if` statement toward the end of the example makes the decision—it decides whether to execute the block of code enclosed in braces.

Example 2-9. if statement

```
double fuelTankCapacityKilos = 80;
double lapLength = 5.141;

double fuelKilosPerKm = fuelKilosConsumed / kmTravelled;
double fuelKilosRemaining = fuelTankCapacityKilos - fuelKilosConsumed;
double predictedDistanceUntilOutOfFuel = fuelKilosRemaining / fuelKilosPerKm;
double predictedLapsUntilOutOfFuel =
        predictedDistanceUntilOutOfFuel / lapLength;

if (predictedLapsUntilOutOfFuel < 4)
{
    Console.WriteLine("Low on fuel. Laps remaining: " +
        predictedLapsUntilOutOfFuel);
}
```

To test this, we need to run the program with command-line arguments. You could open a command prompt, move to the directory containing the built output of your project, and run it with the arguments you want. (It'll be in the *bin\Debug* folder that Visual Studio creates inside your project's folder.) Or you can get Visual Studio to pass arguments for you. To do that, go to the Solution Explorer panel and double-click on the Properties icon. This will open the project's properties view, which has a series of tabs on the lefthand side. Select the Debug tab, and in the middle you'll see a "Command line arguments" text box as shown in Figure 2-6.

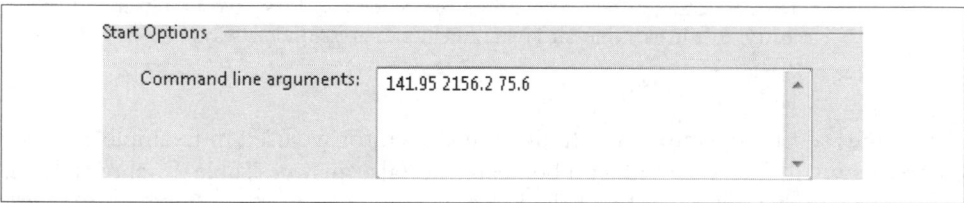

Figure 2-6. Passing command-line arguments in Visual Studio

If you run the program with arguments corresponding to just a few laps (e.g., 15 238 8) it won't print anything. But try running it with the following arguments: 141.95 2156.2 75.6. It'll predict that the car has about 1.6 laps of fuel remaining. The if statement in Example 2-9 tests the following expression:

```
predictedLapsUntilOutOfFuel < 4
```

The < symbol means "less than." So the code in braces following the if statement runs only if the number of predicted laps of fuel is less than 4. Clearly, 1.6 is less than 4, so in this case it'll run that code, printing out the following:

```
Low on fuel. Laps remaining: 1.60701035044548
```

You need to use the right kind of expression in an `if` statement. In this case, we've performed a comparison—we're testing to see if a variable is less than 4. There are only two possible outcomes: either it's less than 4 or it isn't. So this expression is clearly different in nature to the expressions performing mathematical calculations. If you were to modify the program so that it prints the value of that expression:

```
Console.WriteLine(predictedLapsUntilOutOfFuel < 4);
```

it would display either `True` or `False`. The .NET Framework has a special type to represent such an either/or choice, called `System.Boolean`, and as with the numeric types, C# defines its own alias for this type: `bool`.‖ An `if` statement requires a Boolean expression. So if you try to use an expression with a numeric result, such as this:

```
if (fuelTankCapacityKilos - fuelKilosConsumed)
```

the compiler will complain with the error "Cannot implicitly convert type 'double' to 'bool'." This is its way of saying that it expects a `bool`—either true or false—and you've given it a number. In effect, that code says something like "If fourteen and a half then do this." What would that even mean?

 The C language decided to answer that question by saying that `0` is equivalent to false, and anything else is equivalent to true. But that was only because it didn't have a built-in Boolean type, so its `if` statement had to be able to work with numeric expressions. This turned out to be a frequent cause of bugs in C programs. Since C# does have a built-in `bool` type, it insists that an `if` statement's expression is always of type `bool`.

C# defines several operators which, like the `<` operator we used in Example 2-9, can compare two numbers to produce a Boolean true/false answer. Table 2-2 shows these. Some of these operators can be applied to non-numeric types too. For example, you can use the `==` and `!=` operators to compare strings. (You might expect the other comparison operators to work too, telling you whether one string would come before or after another when sorted alphabetically. However, there's more than one way to sort strings—it turns out that the method used varies based on language and culture. And rather than have an expression such as `text1 < text2` mean different things in different contexts, C# simply doesn't allow it. If you want to compare strings, you have to call one of the methods provided by the `String` class that lets you say how you'd like the comparison to work.)

‖ The Boolean type is named after George Boole, who invented a branch of mathematical logic that uses just two values: true and false. His system is fundamental to the operation of all digital electronics, so it's a shame that C# doesn't see fit to spell his name properly.

Table 2-2. Comparison operators

C# operator	Meaning
<	Less than
>	Greater than
<=	Less than or equal to
>=	Greater than or equal to
==	Equal to
!=	Not equal to

Just as you can combine numeric expressions into more complex and powerful expressions, C# provides operators that let you combine Boolean expressions to test multiple conditions. The && operator combines two Boolean expressions into a single expression that's true only if both conditions are true. In our race example, we might use this to hide the low-fuel warning if we're near the end of the race and the car has enough fuel to make it to the finish line. Imagine that we added an extra argument to pass in the number of remaining laps in the race, and an additional variable to hold that value; we could write:

```
if ((predictedLapsUntilOutOfFuel < 4) &&
    (predictedLapsUntilOutOfFuel < remainingLapsInRace))
{
    Console.WriteLine("Low on fuel. Laps remaining: " +
        predictedLapsUntilOutOfFuel);
}
```

This has the same effect as the following slightly more verbose code:

```
if (predictedLapsUntilOutOfFuel < 4)
{
    if (predictedLapsUntilOutOfFuel < remainingLapsInRace)
    {
        Console.WriteLine("Low on fuel. Laps remaining: " +
            predictedLapsUntilOutOfFuel);
    }
}
```

Only if both conditions are true will the message be displayed. There's also a || operator. Like &&, the || operator combines two Boolean expressions, but will be **true** if *either* of them is true.

if...else

The `if` statement examples we've looked at so far just decide whether to execute some optional code, but what if we want to choose between two actions? An `if` statement can optionally include an `else` section that runs if the condition was false, as in this hypothetical post-race example:

```
if (weWonTheRace)
{
    Sponsors.DemandMoreMoney();
}
else
{
    Driver.ReducePay();
}
```

One type of if/else test comes up often enough that C-family languages have a special syntax for it: sometimes you want to pick between one of two values, based on some test. You could write this:

```
string messageForDriver;
if (weWonTheRace)
{
    messageForDriver = "Congratulations";
}
else
{
    messageForDriver = "You're fired";
}
```

Sometimes it's more convenient to be able to put this inside an expression. This can be done with the *ternary* operator, so called because it contains three expressions: a Boolean test expression, the expression to use if the test is true, and the expression to use if the test is false. The syntax uses ? and : characters to separate the expressions, so the basic pattern is *test* ? *resultIfTrue* : *resultIfFalse*. We can collapse the previous `if...else` example to a single assignment statement by using the ternary operator in the expression on the righthand side of the assignment:

```
string messageForDriver = weWonTheRace ?
                    "Congratulations" :
                    "You're fired";
```

You don't have to space it out like this, by the way—we put the two options on separate lines to make them easy to see. But some people like to use the ternary operator to condense as much logic as possible into as little space as possible; this is either admirable conciseness or impenetrable terseness, depending on your personal tastes.

You can string multiple `if...else` tests together. To see how that might be useful in our example, consider how in motor racing, incidents or weather conditions may cause the race stewards to initiate certain safety procedures, such as temporarily disallowing overtaking maneuvers while wreckage is cleared from the track, releasing the safety car for the drivers to follow slowly if the wreckage is particularly spectacular, or in extreme cases "red-flagging" the race—a temporary complete halt followed by a restart. Each of these has its own appropriate response, which can be dealt with by a chain of if...else if...else statements, as shown in Example 2-10.

Example 2-10. Testing multiple conditions with if and else

```
string raceStatus = args[3];
if (raceStatus == "YellowFlag")
{
    Driver.TellNotToOvertake();
}
else if (raceStatus == "SafetyCar")
{
    Driver.WarnAboutSafetyCar();
}
else if (raceStatus == "RedFlag")
{
    if (ourDriverCausedIncident)
    {
        Factory.OrderNewCar();
        Driver.ReducePay();
        if (feelingGenerous)
        {
            Driver.Resuscitate();
        }
    }
    else
    {
        Driver.CallBackToPit();
    }
}
else
{
    Driver.TellToDriveFaster();
}
```

While this works, there's an alternative. This pattern of choosing one option out of many is sufficiently common that C# has a special selection statement to handle it.

switch and case Statements

A switch statement lets you specify a list of expected values, and what to do for each value. The values can be either strings or integral types. (Integral types include int, short, etc.—you cannot switch on floating-point numbers. Enumeration types, which are discussed in Chapter 3, are considered to be integral types for the purposes of a switch statement.) We can use this to rewrite Example 2-10 as shown in Example 2-11.

Example 2-11. Testing multiple conditions with switch and case

```
string raceStatus = args[3];
switch (raceStatus)
{
case "YellowFlag":
    Driver.TellNotToOvertake();
    break;

case "SafetyCar":
    Driver.WarnAboutSafetyCar();
    break;

case "RedFlag":
    if (ourDriverCausedIncident)
    {
        Factory.OrderNewCar();
        Driver.ReducePay();
        if (feelingGenerous)
        {
            Driver.Resuscitate();
        }
    }
    else
    {
        Driver.CallBackToPit();
    }
    break;


default:
    Driver.TellToDriveFaster();
    break;

}
```

 The break keyword you can see at the end of each case is present mainly for consistency with other C-like languages. In C and C++, if you leave off the break, the code will "fall" out of one case through to the next. So if we left off the break in the YellowFlag case, we'd end up telling drivers not to overtake and then warning them about the safety car. This would be a bug—and in general, you almost always don't want fall-through. It's unfortunate that in C and C++ fall-through was the default. C# changes this: if you want fall-through you must ask for it explicitly by writing goto case "SafetyCar". But despite fall-through no longer being the implicit default, you still need to write the same break statement as you would in other C-family languages when you don't want fall-through—if you leave it out you'll get an error.

You might be wondering what is the point—this does exactly the same as Example 2-10, so why do we need a different syntax? As it happens, we don't—there's nothing you can do with switch and case that you can't do with if and else. But switch and case offer one useful advantage: they make it clear what we're doing—we're looking at a single expression (`raceStatus`) and we're choosing one of a number of options based on the value of that expression. A developer familiar with C# can look at this code and understand the structure of the decision-making process at a glance. With the previous example, you would need to look at each `else if` statement in turn to make sure it wasn't doing something more complex—chained `else if` statements are more flexible than `switch` statements, because each new link in the chain is allowed to test a completely different expression, but that flexibility comes at the cost of making it harder to understand the code. Sometimes a self-imposed constraint can make code easier to read and maintain, and a `switch` statement is a good example of that.

Selection statements make programs considerably more useful than they would otherwise be—they enable programs to make decisions. But our examples are still rather straightforward—they run just once, from start to finish, with the odd variation in the execution flow. The amount of work that is done is pretty trivial. So there's another kind of statement that plays to a computer's greatest strength: the ability to perform simple repetitive tasks many times over.

Iteration Statements

An *iteration statement* allows a sequence of other statements to be executed several times. (Repeated execution is also often known as a *loop* because, like the race car, the code goes round and round again.) This seems like it could be useful in our race data analysis—race cars usually complete many laps, so we will probably have multiple sets of data to process. It would be annoying to have to write the same code 60 times just to process all the data for a 60-lap race. Fortunately, we don't have to—we can use one of C#'s iteration statements.

Imagine that instead of passing in timing or fuel information as command-line arguments, the data was in files. We might have a text file containing one line per lap, with the elapsed time at the end of each lap. Another text file could contain the remaining fuel at the end of each lap. To illustrate how to work with such data, we'll start with a simple example: finding the lap on which our driver went quickest.

Since this code is a little different from the previous example, start a new project if you want to follow along. Make another console application called `LapAnalysis`.

To be able to test our code we'll need a file containing the timing information. You can add this to your Visual Studio project. Right-click on the `LapAnalysis` project in the Solution Explorer and select Add→New Item from the context menu. (Or just press Ctrl-Shift-A.) In the Installed Templates section on the left, select the General category under Visual C# Items, and then in the central area select Text File. Call the file *LapTimes.txt* and click Add. You'll need this file to be somewhere the program can get to. Go to the Properties panel for the file—this is usually below the Solution Explorer panel, but if you don't see it, right-click on *LapTimes.txt* in the Solution Explorer and select Properties. In the Properties panel, you should see a Copy to Output Directory property. By default, this is set to "Do not copy". Change it to "Copy if newer"—Visual Studio will ensure that an up-to-date copy of the file is available in the *bin\Debug* folder in which it builds your program. You'll need some data in this file. We'll be using the following—these numbers represent the elapsed time in seconds since the start of the race at the end of each lap:

```
78.73
157.2
237.1
313.8
390.7
470.2
```

The program is going to read in the contents of the file. To do this, it'll need to use types from the `System.IO` namespace, so you'll need to add the following near the top of your *Program.cs* file:

```
using System.IO;
```

Then inside the `Main` method, use the following code to read the contents of the file:

```
string[] lines = File.ReadAllLines("LapTimes.txt");
```

The `File` type is in the `System.IO` namespace, and its `ReadAllLines` method reads in all the lines of a text file and returns an array of strings (`string[]`) with one entry per line. The easiest way to work through all these entries is with a `foreach` *statement*.

foreach Statements

A `foreach` statement executes a block of statements once for every item in a collection such as an array. For example, this:

```
foreach (string line in lines)
{
    Console.WriteLine(line);
}
```

will display every line of text from the `lines` array we just built. The block to execute each time around is, as ever, delimited by a { } pair.

We have to provide the C# compiler with two things at the start of a `foreach` loop: the variable we'd like to use to access each item from the collection, and the collection itself. The `string line` part declares the first bit—the so-called *iteration variable*. And then the `in lines` part says that we want to iterate over the items in the `lines` array. So each time around the loop, `line` will contain the next string in `lines`.

We can use this to discover the fastest lap time, as shown in Example 2-12.

Example 2-12. Finding the fastest lap with foreach

```
string[] lines = File.ReadAllLines("LapTimes.txt");
double currentLapStartTime = 0;
double fastestLapTime = 0;
foreach (string line in lines)
{
    double lapEndTime = double.Parse(line);
    double lapTime = lapEndTime - currentLapStartTime;
    if (fastestLapTime == 0 || lapTime < fastestLapTime)
    {
        fastestLapTime = lapTime;
    }
    currentLapStartTime = lapEndTime;
}
Console.WriteLine("Fastest lap time: " + fastestLapTime);
```

The `currentLapStartTime` begins at zero, but is updated to the end time of the previous lap each time around the loop—we need this to work out how long each lap took, because each line of the file contains the total elapsed race time at each lap. And the `fastestLapTime` variable contains the time of the fastest lap yet found—it'll be updated each time a faster lap is found. (We also update it when it's zero, which it will be the first time we go around.)

This finds the fastest lap time—76.7 seconds in the example data we're using. But it doesn't tell us which lap that was. Looking at the numbers, we can see that it happens to be the fourth, but it would be nice if the program could tell us. One way to do this is to declare a new variable called `lapNumber`, initializing it to 1 outside the loop, and adding one each time around, to keep track of the current lap. Then we can record the lap number on which we found the fastest time. Example 2-13 shows a modified version, with the additional code in bold.

Example 2-13. Fastest lap including lap number

```
string[] lines = File.ReadAllLines("LapTimes.txt");
double currentLapStartTime = 0;
double fastestLapTime = 0;
int lapNumber = 1;
int fastestLapNumber = 0;
foreach (string line in lines)
{
    double lapEndTime = double.Parse(line);
    double lapTime = lapEndTime - currentLapStartTime;
    if (fastestLapTime == 0 || lapTime < fastestLapTime)
    {
        fastestLapTime = lapTime;
        fastestLapNumber = lapNumber;
    }
    currentLapStartTime = lapEndTime;
    lapNumber += 1;
}
Console.WriteLine("Fastest lap: " + fastestLapNumber);
Console.WriteLine("Fastest lap time: " + fastestLapTime);
```

If you're trying this out, this might be a good opportunity to acquaint yourself with Visual Studio's debugging features—see the sidebar below.

The Debugger

When your code includes flow control statements that can vary the sequence of operations, or how many times code runs, it can be useful to inspect the execution. If your code doesn't work quite how you expect, you can watch what it does one line at a time by using Visual Studio's built-in debugger.

If instead of running the program normally you run it with the Debug→Step Into menu item (or the F11 keyboard shortcut if you're using the C# profile for Visual Studio), it will run the code one line at a time—each time you choose Step Into, it will run one more line of code. And if you hover your mouse pointer over a variable, it will show you the current value, allowing you to see the current state of your program, as well as its current position.

You can also arrange for the program to stop in the debugger when it reaches a particular point by setting a *breakpoint*, either by clicking in the left margin of the code editor or by putting the cursor on the line in question and selecting Debug→Toggle Breakpoint. A red dot appears in the margin to indicate that the code will stop when it reaches this point. Breakpoints are active only if you run the program from within the debugger, so you need to make sure you start with Debug→Start Debugging (or press F5) if you want breakpoints to work.

Visual Studio's debugger is a powerful and flexible system—these simple techniques barely scratch its surface, but they are very useful when trying to diagnose troublesome behavior in a program.

Example 2-13 works well enough, but there's an alternative iteration statement you can use for this sort of scenario: a for *statement*.

for Statements

A for statement is a loop in which some variable is initialized to a start value, and is modified each time around the loop. The loop will run for as long as some condition remains true—this means a for loop does not necessarily have to involve a collection, unlike a foreach loop. Example 2-14 is a simple loop that counts to 10.

Example 2-14. Counting with a for loop

```
for (int i = 1; i <= 10; i++)
{
    Console.WriteLine(i);
}
Console.WriteLine("Coming, ready or not!");
```

The for keyword is followed by parentheses containing three pieces. First, a variable is declared and initialized. Then the condition is specified—this particular loop will iterate for as long as the variable i is less than or equal to 10. You can use any Boolean expression here, just like in an if statement. And finally, there is a statement to be executed each time around the loop—adding one to i in this case. (As you saw earlier, i++ adds one to i. We could also have written i += 1, but the usual if arbitrary convention in C-style languages is to use the ++ operator here.)

Earlier we recommended using variable names that are long enough to be descriptive, so you might be raising an eyebrow over the use of i as a variable name. There's a convention with **for** loops where the iteration variable just counts up from zero—short variable names such as i, j, k, x, and y are often used. It's not a universal convention, but you'll see it widely used, particularly with short loops.

We're using this convention in Example 2-14 only because you will come across it sooner or later, and so we felt it was important to show it. But it's arguably not an especially good way to write clear code, so feel free to choose more meaningful names in your own code.

We could use this construct as an alternative way to find the fastest lap time, as shown in Example 2-15.

Example 2-15. Finding the fastest lap with for

```
string[] lines = File.ReadAllLines("LapTimes.txt");
double currentLapStartTime = 0;
double fastestLapTime = 0;
int fastestLapNumber = 0;
for (int lapNumber = 1; lapNumber <= lines.Length; lapNumber++)
{
    double lapEndTime = double.Parse(lines[lapNumber - 1]);
    double lapTime = lapEndTime - currentLapStartTime;
    if (fastestLapTime == 0 || lapTime < fastestLapTime)
    {
        fastestLapTime = lapTime;
        fastestLapNumber = lapNumber;
    }
    currentLapStartTime = lapEndTime;
}
Console.WriteLine("Fastest lap: " + fastestLapNumber);
Console.WriteLine("Fastest lap time: " + fastestLapTime);
```

This is pretty similar to the **foreach** example. It's marginally shorter, but it's also a little more awkward—our program is counting the laps starting from 1, but arrays in .NET start from zero, so the line that parses the value from the file has the slightly ungainly expression lines[lapNumber - 1] in it. (Incidentally, this example avoids using a short iteration variable name such as i because we're numbering the laps from 1, not 0— short iteration variable names tend to be associated with zero-based counting.) Arguably, the **foreach** version was clearer, even if it was ever so slightly longer. The main advantage of `for` is that it doesn't require a collection, so it's better suited to Example 2-14 than Example 2-15.

while and do Statements

C# offers a third kind of iteration statement: the `while` *loop*. This is like a simplified `for` loop—it has only the Boolean expression that decides whether to carry on looping, and does not have the variable initialization part, or the statement to execute each time around. (Or if you prefer, a `for` loop is a fancy version of a `while` loop—neither `for` nor `foreach` does anything you couldn't achieve with a `while` loop and a little extra code.) Example 2-16 shows an alternative approach to working through the lines of a text file based on a `while` loop.

Example 2-16. Iterating through a file with a while loop

```
static void Main(string[] args)
{
    using (StreamReader times = File.OpenText("LapTimes.txt"))
    {
        while (!times.EndOfStream)
        {
            string line = times.ReadLine();
            double lapEndTime = double.Parse(line);
            Console.WriteLine(lapEndTime);
        }
    }
}
```

The `while` statement is well suited to the one-line-at-a-time approach. It doesn't require a collection; it just loops until the condition becomes false. In this example, that means we loop until the `StreamReader` tells us we've reached the end of the file.# (Chapter 11 describes the use of types such as `StreamReader` in detail.) The exclamation mark (!) in front of the expression means *not*—you can put this in front of any Boolean expression to invert the result. So the loop runs for as long as we are *not* at the end of the stream.

> We could have used a `for` loop to implement this one-line-at-a-time loop—it also iterates until its condition becomes false. The `while` loop happens to be a better choice here simply because in this example, we have no use for the variable initialization or loop statement offered by `for`.

#You'll have noticed the `using` keyword on the line where we get hold of the `StreamReader`. We use this construct when it's necessary to indicate exactly when we've finished with an object—in this case we need to say when we're done with the file to avoid keeping operating system file handles open.

The approach in Example 2-16 would be better than the previous examples for a particularly large file. The code can start working straight away without having to wait for the entire file to load, and it will use less memory because it doesn't build the array containing every single line—it can hold just one line at a time in memory. For our example lap time file with just six lines of data, this won't make any difference, but if you were processing a file with hundreds of thousands of entries, this while-based example could provide noticeably better performance than the array-based examples.

 This does *not* mean that while is faster than for or foreach. The performance difference here is a result of the code working with the file in a different way, and has nothing to do with the loop construct. In general, it's a bad idea to focus on which language features are "fastest." Performance usually depends on the way in which your code solves a problem, rather than which particular language feature you use.

Note that for and while loops might never execute their contents at all. If the condition is false the first time around, they'll skip the loop entirely. This is often desirable—if there's no data, you probably want to do no work. But just occasionally it can be useful to write a loop that is guaranteed to execute at least once. We can do this with a variation on the while loop, called the do while loop:

```
do
{
    Console.WriteLine("Waiting...");
}
while (DateTime.Now.Hour < 8);
```

The while keyword and condition come at the end, and we mark the start of the loop with the do keyword. This loop always executes at least once, testing the condition at the end of each iteration instead of the start. So this code will repeatedly show the message "Waiting..." until the current time is 8:00 a.m. or later. If it's already past 8:00 a.m., it'll still write out "Waiting..." once.

Breaking Out of a Loop

It can sometimes be useful to abandon a loop earlier than its natural end. In the case of a foreach loop, this might mean stopping before you've processed every item in the collection. With for or while loops, you get to write the loop condition so that you can stop under whatever conditions you like, but it can sometimes be more convenient to put the code that makes a decision to abandon a loop somewhere inside the loop body rather than in the condition. For these eventualities, C# provides the break keyword.

We saw `break` already in a `switch` statement in Example 2-11—we used it to say that we're done with the `switch` and want to `break` out of that statement. The `break` keyword does the same thing in a loop:

```
using (StreamReader times = File.OpenText("LapTimes.txt"))
{
    while (!times.EndOfStream)
    {
        string line = times.ReadLine();
        if (line == "STOP!")
        {
            break;
        }
        double lapEndTime = double.Parse(line);
        Console.WriteLine(lapEndTime);
    }
}
```

This is the loop from Example 2-16, modified to stop if it comes across a line in the input file that contains the text "STOP!" This breaks out immediately, abandoning the rest of the loop and leaping straight to the first line of code after the enclosing loop's closing brace. (In that case, this happens to be the enclosing `using` statement's closing brace, which will close the file handle.)

 Some people regard this use of `break` as bad practice. It makes it harder to understand the loop. When a loop contains no `break` statements, you can understand its lifetime by looking at the `while` (or `for`, or `foreach`) part. But if there are `break` statements, you need to look at more of the code to get a complete understanding of when the loop will finish.

More generally, flow control that jumps suddenly out of the middle of a construct is frowned upon, because it makes it much harder for someone to understand how execution flows through a program, and programs that are hard to understand tend to be buggy. The computer scientist Edsger Dijkstra submitted a short letter on this topic in 1968 to an academic journal, which was printed under a now infamous heading, "Go-to statement considered harmful". If you're interested in iconic pieces of computing history, or if you'd like a detailed explanation of exactly why this sort of jumpy flow control is problematic, you can find the original letter at *http://www.cs.utexas.edu/users/EWD/ewd02xx/ EWD215.PDF*.

To recap what we've explored so far, we've seen how to work with variables to hold information, how to write expressions that perform calculations, how to use selection statements that decide what to do, and how to build iteration statements that can do things repeatedly. There's one more basic C# programming feature we need to look at to cover the most important everyday coding features: methods.

Methods

As we saw earlier, a *method* is a named block of code. We wrote a method already—the `Main` method that runs when our program starts. And we used methods provided by the .NET Framework class library, such as `Console.WriteLine` and `File.ReadAll Lines`. But we haven't looked at how and why you would introduce new methods other than `Main` into your own code.

Methods are an essential mechanism for reducing your code's complexity and enhancing its readability. By putting a section of code into its own method with a carefully chosen name that describes what the method does, you can make it much easier for someone looking at the code to work out what your program is meant to do. Also, methods can help avoid repetition—if you need to do similar work in multiple places, a method can help you reuse code.

In our race car example, there's a job we may need to do multiple times: reading in numeric values from a file. We did this for timing information, but we're going to need to do the same with fuel consumption and distance. Rather than writing three almost identical bits of code, we can put the majority of the code into a single method.

The first thing we need to do is declare the method—we need to pick a name, define the information that comes into the method, and optionally define the information that comes back out. Let's call the method `ReadNumbersFromFile`, since that's what it's going to do. Its input will be a text string containing the filename, and it will return an array of double-precision floating-point numbers. The method declaration, which will go inside our `Program` class, will look like this:

```
static double[] ReadNumbersFromFile(string fileName)
```

As you may recall from the discussion of `Main` earlier, the `static` keyword indicates that we do not need an instance of the containing `Program` type to be created for this method to run. (We'll be looking at nonstatic methods in the next chapter when we start dealing with objects.) C# follows the C-family convention that the kind of data coming out of the method is specified before the name and the inputs, so next we have `double[]`, indicating that this method returns an array of numbers. Then we have the name, and then in parentheses, the inputs required by this method. In this example there's just one, the filename, but this would be a comma-separated list if more inputs were required.

After the method declaration comes the method body—the statements that make up the method, enclosed in braces. The code isn't going to be quite the same as what we've seen so far—up until now, we've converted the text to numbers one at a time immediately before processing them. But this code is going to return an array of numbers, just like `File.ReadAllLines` returns an array of strings. So our code needs to build up that array. Example 2-17 shows one way of doing this.

Example 2-17. A method for reading numbers from a file

```csharp
static double[] ReadNumbersFromFile(string fileName)
{
    List<double> numbers = new List<double>();
    using (StreamReader file = File.OpenText(fileName))
    {
        while (!file.EndOfStream)
        {
            string line = file.ReadLine();
            // Skip blank lines
            if (!string.IsNullOrEmpty(line))
            {
                numbers.Add(double.Parse(line));
            }
        }
    }
    return numbers.ToArray();
}
```

This looks pretty similar to the example `while` loop we saw earlier, with one addition: we're creating an object that lets us build up a collection of numbers one at a time—a `List<double>`. It's similar to an array (a `double[]`), but an array needs you to know how many items you want up front—you can't add more items onto an existing array. The advantage of a `List<double>` is that you can just keep adding new numbers at will. That matters here because if you look closely you'll see we've modified the code to skip over blank lines, which means that we actually don't know how many numbers we're going to get until we've read the whole file.

Once you're done adding numbers to a list, you can call its `ToArray()` method to get an array of the correct size. This list class is an example of a *collection class*. .NET offers several of these, and they are so extremely useful that Chapters 7, 8, and 9 are related to working with collections.

Notice the `return` keyword near the end of Example 2-17. This is how we return the information calculated by our method to whatever code calls the method. As well as specifying the value to return, the `return` keyword causes the current method to exit immediately, and for execution to continue back in the calling method. (In methods with a **void** return type, which do not return any value, you can use the `return` keyword without an argument to exit the method. Or you can just let execution run to the end of the method, and it will return implicitly.) If you're wondering how the method remembers where it's supposed to go back to, see the sidebar on the next page.

With the `ReadNumbersFromFile` method in place, we can now write this sort of code:

```csharp
double[] lapTimes = ReadNumbersFromFile("LapTimes.txt");
double[] fuelLevels = ReadNumbersFromFile("FuelRemainingByLap.txt");
```

The Call Stack

When you invoke a method, the CLR allocates some memory to keep track of that method's state. This state includes incoming arguments and local variables. When a method calls out to another method, the method state also remembers where we were in the calling method's code to be able to carry on later.

If you have nested method calls—if a first method calls a second method which calls a third method, for example—you end up with a sequence of method states, and this sequence is often referred to as the *call stack*. In general, a *stack* is a sequence of items where you can add or remove items only at the end of the sequence; by convention, we use the terms *push* and *pop* to describe adding and removing stack items. So when C# code invokes a new method, it pushes a new method state record onto the call stack. When the method returns, either because execution reaches the end or because we've hit a `return` statement, the current method state is popped from the call stack, and then execution resumes from where the previous method state record says the calling method had reached.

You can look at the call stack in the Visual Studio debugger. The Debug→Windows→Call Stack menu item displays a window showing a list of all the current methods in the call stack. You can double-click on any of these items to see the current location, and if you've opened any of the debug windows that show local variable state from the Debug→Windows menu, these will show local variables for the method you select.

It doesn't take a lot of effort to understand that this code is reading in numbers for lap times and fuel levels from a couple of text files—the code makes this aspect of its behavior much clearer than, say, Example 2-12. When code does what it says it does, you make life much easier for anyone who has to look at the code after you've written it. And since that probably includes you, you'll make your life easier in the long run by moving functionality into carefully named methods.

 This idea of moving code out of the middle of one method and into a separate method is very common, and is an example of *refactoring*. Generally speaking, refactoring means restructuring code without changing its behavior, to either simplify it, make it easier to understand and maintain, or avoid duplication. There are so many ways to refactor code that whole books have been written on the topic, but this particular refactoring operation is so useful that Visual Studio can automate it. If you select some code and then right-click on the C# editor window, it offers a Refactor→Extract Method menu item that does this for you. In practice, it's not always that straightforward—you might need to restructure the code a little first, before you're in a position to factor out the pieces you'd like to move into a method. Example 2-17 had to work slightly differently from any of the previous examples to package the code into a reusable method. But while it may require some work, it's a useful technique to apply.

Summary

In this chapter, we looked at some of the most important concepts involved in the everyday writing of C#. We saw how to create and run projects in Visual Studio. We saw how namespaces help us work with the .NET Framework class library and other external code, without getting lost in the thousands of classes on offer. We used variables and expressions to store and perform calculations with data. We used selection statements to make decisions based on input, and iteration statements to perform repetitive work on collections of data. And we saw how splitting your code into well-named methods can enhance the reusability and readability of your code. In the next chapter, we'll step outside the world of methods and look at C#'s support for object-oriented programming.

CHAPTER 3

Abstracting Ideas with Classes and Structs

In the previous couple of chapters, we looked at some basic programming techniques such as loops and conditions, and used some of the data types built into the language and platform, such as `int` and `string`.

Unfortunately, real programs—even fairly simple ones—are much, much more complicated than the examples we've built so far. They need to model the behavior of real-world objects like cars and planes, or ideas like mathematical expressions, or behaviors, like the transaction between you and your favorite coffee shop when you buy a double espresso and a brownie with your bank card.

Divide and Conquer

The best way to manage this complexity is to break a system down into manageable pieces, where each piece is small enough for us to understand completely. We should aim to craft each piece so that it fits neatly into the system as a whole with a small enough number of connections to the other pieces that we can comprehend all of those too.

Abstracting Ideas with Methods

We've already seen one tool for dividing our code into manageable pieces: methods. A method is a piece of a program that encapsulates a particular behavior completely. It's worth understanding the benefits of methods, because the same principles apply to the classes and structs that are this chapter's main subject.

 You will often see the term *function* used instead of *method*; they're related, but not identical. A function is a method that returns something. Some methods just do some work, and do not return any value. So in C#, all functions are methods, but not all methods are functions.

Methods offer a contract: if we meet particular conditions, a method will do certain things for us. Conditions come in various forms: we might need to pass arguments of suitable types, perhaps with limits on the range (e.g., negative numbers may not be allowed). We may need to ensure certain things about the program's environment—maybe we need to check that certain directories exist on disk, or that there's sufficient free memory and disk space. There may be constraints on *when* we are allowed to call the method—perhaps we're not allowed to call it if some related work we started earlier hasn't completed yet.

Likewise, there are several ways in which a method can hold up its side of the bargain. Perhaps it will just return a string or a number that is the result of a calculation involving the method's inputs. It might change the state of some entity in our system in some way, such as modifying an employee's salary. It may change something about the system environment—the method might install a new device driver, or change the current user's color scheme, for example. Some methods interact with the outside world by sending messages over the network.

Some aspects of the contract are formalized—a method's parameter list defines the number and type of arguments we need to pass, for example, and its return type tells us what, if anything, to expect as a return value. But most of the contract is informally specified—we rely on documentation (or sometimes, conversations with the developer who wrote the method) to understand the full contract. But understand it we must, because the contract is at the heart of how methods make our lives easier.

Methods simplify things for us in two ways. If we are the *user* of a method, then, as long as its internal implementation conforms to the contract, we can treat it as a "black box." We call it, we expect it to work as described, and we don't need to worry about *how* it worked. All its internal complexity is hidden from us, freeing us to think about ideas like "increase this employee's salary," without getting bogged down by details such as "open a connection to the database and execute some SQL."

If, on the other hand, we are the *developer* of a method, we don't need to worry about who might call us, and why. As long as our implementation works as promised, we can choose any means of implementation we like—perhaps optimizing for speed, or size, or (more often than not) simplicity and maintainability. We can concentrate on details like whether we're using the right connection string, and whether the SQL query modifies the database as intended, without needing to ask ourselves questions like "should we even be adjusting this particular employee's salary at all?"

So, one objective of good design is to *hide distracting details* and *expose a simple model* to your client. This practice is called *encapsulation*, and it's harder than it looks.

As is so often the case in life, making something look easy takes years of practice and hard work. It can also be a thankless task: if you devise a contract that is a model of clarity, people will probably think it was easy to design. Conversely, unnecessary complexity is often mistaken for cleverness.

While methods are essential for achieving encapsulation, they do not guarantee it. It's all too easy to write methods whose contract is unclear. This often happens when developers do something as an afterthought— it can be oh so tempting to add a bit of extra code to an existing method as a quick solution to a problem, but this risks making that's method's responsibilities less clear.

A method's name is often a good indicator of the clarity of the contract— if the name is vague, or worse, if it's an inaccurate description of what the method does, you're probably looking at a method that does a bad job of encapsulation.

One of the great things about methods is that we can use them to keep breaking things into smaller and smaller pieces. Suppose we have some method called `PlaceOrder`, which has a well-defined responsibility, but which is getting a bit complicated. We can just split its implementation into smaller methods—say, `CheckCustomerCredit`, `AllocateStock`, and `IssueRequestToWarehouse`. These smaller methods do different bits of the work for us.

This general technique, sometimes called *functional decomposition*, has a long history in mathematics. It was explored academically in computing applications as early as the 1930s. Bearing in mind that the first working programmable computers didn't appear until the 1940s, that's quite a pedigree. In fact, it has been around for so long that it now seems "obvious" to most people who have had anything to do with computer programming.

That's not the end of the story, though. Methods are great for describing the *dynamics* of a system—how things change in response to particular input data (the method arguments), and the results of those changes (a function's return value, or a method's side effects). What they're not so good at is describing the current *state* of the system. If we examine a set of functions and a load of variables, how can we work out which pieces of information are supposed to be operated on by which functions? If methods were the only tool available for abstraction, we'd have a hard time telling the difference between the `double` that describes my blood pressure, and can be operated on by this method:

```
void LowerMyBloodPressure(double pressureDelta)
```

and the `double` that describes my weight and can be affected by this method:

```
void EatSomeDonuts(int quantityOfDonuts)
```

As programs get ever larger, the number of system state variables floating around increases, and the number of methods can explode exponentially. But the problems aren't just about the sheer number of functions and variables you end up with. As you try to model a more complex system, it becomes harder to work out which functions and variables you actually need—what is a good "decomposition" of the system? Which methods relate to one another, and to which variables?

Abstracting Ideas with Objects and Classes

In the 1960s, two guys called Dahl and Nygaard (they're Norwegian) were working on big simulation systems and were struggling with this problem. Because they worked on simulating real things, they realized that their code would be easier to understand if they had some clear way to group together all of the data and functions related to a particular type of real thing (or a particular *object*, we might say).

They designed a programming language that could do this, called Simula 67 (after the year of its birth), and it is generally recognized as the grandmother of all the languages we'd call *object-oriented*, which (of course) includes C#.

They had hit upon two important concepts:

- The *class*: a **description** of a collection of data and the functions that operate on them
- The *object*: an **instance** of a collection of data and the functions that operate on them (i.e., an instance of a class)

With these simple ideas, we can remove all doubt over which functions operate on which data—the *class* describes for us *exactly* what goes with what, and we can handle multiple entities of the same kind by creating several *objects* of a particular class.

Object-oriented analysis

As an example, let's think about a very simple computer system that maintains the information for an air traffic control (ATC) operation. (Safety notice: if you happen to be building an ATC system, I strongly recommend that you *don't* base it on this one.)

How does (this particular, slightly peculiar) ATC system work? It turns out that we've got a bunch of people in a big room in Washington, tracking a large number of planes that buzz around the airport in Seattle. Each plane has an identifier (BA0049, which flies in from London Heathrow, for instance). We need to know the plane's position, which we'll represent using three numbers: an altitude (in feet); the distance from the airport control tower (in miles); and a compass heading (measured in degrees from North), which will also be relative to the tower. Just to be clear, that's not the direction the aircraft itself is facing—it's the direction we'd have to face in order to be looking at the plane if we're standing in the tower. We also need to know whether the aircraft is coming in to us, or away from us, and how fast. This, apparently, is quite important. (A more comprehensive model might include a second compass heading, representing the exact direction the plane is facing. But to keep this example simple, we'll just track whether planes are approaching or departing.)

As the planes come in, the controllers give them permission to take off or land, and instruct them to change their heading, height, or speed. The aim is to avoid them hitting each other at any point. This, apparently, is also quite important.

At present they have a system where each controller is responsible for a particular piece of airspace. They have a rack which contains little slips of plastic with the aircraft's ID on it, ordered by the height at which they are flying. If they are coming in to the airport, they use a piece of blue plastic. If they are going away, they use white plastic. To keep track of the heading, distance, and speed, they just write on the slip with a china graph pencil.* If the plane moves out of their airspace, they hand the plane over to another controller, who slips it into his own rack.

So that's our specification.

In reality, a safety-critical system such as ATC would have a more robust spec. However, when lives are not at stake, software specifications are often pretty nebulous, so this example is, sadly, a fair representation of what to expect on your average software project.

Armed with this brilliant description we need to come up with a design for a program which can model the system. We're going to do that using object-oriented techniques.

When we do an object-oriented analysis we're looking for the different *classes* of object that we are going to describe. Very often, they will correspond to real things in the system. For a class to represent these real objects properly, we need to work out what information it is going to hold, and what functions it will define to manipulate that information. In general, any one piece of information will belong to exactly one object, of exactly one class.

Not all of your classes will represent real-world objects. Some will relate to more abstract concepts like collections, or commands. However, designs that wander too far into the realms of the wholly abstract are often "clever" but not necessarily "good".

In our ATC example, it's clear that we have a whole lot of different planes buzzing round the airport. It would therefore seem logical that we would model each one as an object, for which we would define a class called `Plane`.

Because C# is a language with object-oriented features, we have a simple and expressive way of doing that.

---

* A special kind of crayon, designed for writing on glossy surfaces such as plastic.

Defining Classes

We can start out with the simplest possible class. It will have no methods, and no data, so as a model of a plane in our system, it leaves something to be desired, but it gets us started.

If you want to build your own version as you read, create a new Console Application project just as we did in Chapter 2. To add a new class, use the Project→Add Class menu item (or right-click on the project in the Solution Explorer and select Add→Class). It'll add a new file for the class, and if we call it *Plane.cs*, Visual Studio will create a new source file with the usual using directives and namespace declaration. And most importantly, the file will contain a new, empty class definition, as shown in Example 3-1.

Example 3-1. The empty Plane class

```
class Plane
{
}
```

Right; if we look back at the specification, there's clearly a whole bunch of information we've got about the plane that we need to store somewhere. C# gives us a handy mechanism for this called a *property*.

Representing State with Properties

Each plane has an identifier which is just a string of letters and numbers. We've already seen a built-in type ideal for representing this kind of data: string. So, we can add a property called Identifier, of type string, as Example 3-2 shows.

Example 3-2. Adding a property

```
class Plane
{
    string Identifier
    {
        get;
        set;
    }
}
```

A property definition always states the type of data the property holds (string in this case), followed by its name. By convention, we use *PascalCasing* for this name—see the sidebar on the next page. As with most nontrivial elements of a C# program, this is followed by a pair of braces, and inside these we say that we want to provide a getter and a set-ter for the property. You might be wondering why we need to declare these—wouldn't any property need to be gettable and settable? But as we'll see, these explicit declarations turn out to be useful.

PascalCasing and camelCasing

Most programming languages, including C#, use whitespace to separate elements of the code—it must be clear where one statement (or keyword, variable, or whatever) ends and the next begins, and we often rely on spaces to mark the boundaries. But this gives us a problem when it comes to naming. Lots of features of a program have names—classes, methods, properties, and variables, for example—and we might want to use multiple words in a name. But we can't put a space in the middle of a name like this:

```
class Jumbo Jet
{
}
```

The C# compiler would complain—the space after `Jumbo` marks the end of the name, and the compiler doesn't understand why we've put a second name, `Jet`, after that. If we want to use multiple words in a name, we have to do it without using spaces. C# programmers conventionally use two styles of capitalization to put multiple words in a name:

- *PascalCasing*, where each word starts with a capital letter. This is used for types, properties, and methods.
- *camelCasing*, where the first word starts with a lowercase letter and all subsequent words get a capital. This is used for parameters and fields.

Pascal casing takes its name from the fact that it was a popular style among Pascal programmers. It's not a widely used language today, but lots of developers cut their teeth on it a decade or three ago when drainpipe trousers, trilby hats, and black-and-white print T-shirts were the latest in fashion (or at least, they were in parts of Europe). And, by no coincidence whatsoever, Anders Hejlsberg (a key figure in the C# design team) also designed Borland's Turbo Pascal.

As for camel casing, that name comes from the fact that uppercase letters only ever appear in the middle of the name, meaning you get one or more humps in the middle, like a camel.

There's a wrinkle in these conventions. Acronyms generally get treated as though they are words, so if you had a class for an RGB color you might call it `ColorRgb`, and a color with an alpha channel might be `ColorArgb`. (The .NET Framework class libraries include types that refer to `Argb`, and people often mistakenly think that the "Arg" is short for "argument" rather than Alpha, Red, Green, and Blue.)

There's an exception to this exception: two-letter acronyms are usually capitalized. So a person's intelligence quotient might be recorded as `PersonIQ`.

These naming conventions are optional, but strongly recommended to help people understand your code. MSDN offers an extensive set of guidelines for these sorts of conventions at *http://msdn.microsoft.com/library/ms229042*.

If we create an instance of this class, we could use this `Identifier` property to get and set its identifier. Example 3-3 shows this in a modified version of the `Main` function in our *Program.cs* file.

Example 3-3. Using the Plane class's property

```
static void Main(string[] args)
{
    Plane someBoeing777 = new Plane();

    someBoeing777.Identifier = "BA0049";

    Console.WriteLine(
        "Your plane has identifier {0}",
        someBoeing777.Identifier);

    // Wait for the user to press a key, so
    // that we can see what happened
    Console.ReadKey();
}
```

But wait! If you try to compile this, you end up with an error message:

```
'Plane.Identifier' is inaccessible due to its protection level
```

What's that all about?

Protection Levels

Earlier, we mentioned that one of the objectives of good design is encapsulation: hiding the implementation details so that other developers can use our objects without relying on (or knowing about) how they work. As the error we just saw in Example 3-3 shows, a class's members are hidden by default. If we want them to be visible to users of our class, we must change their *protection level*.

Every entity that we declare has its own protection level, whether we specify it or not. A class, for example, has a default protection level called `internal`. This means that it can only be seen by other classes in its own assembly. We'll talk a lot more about assemblies in Chapter 15. For now, though, we're only using one assembly (our example application itself), so we can leave the class at its default protection level.

While classes default to being `internal`, the default protection level for a class member (such as a property) is `private`. This means that it is only accessible to other members of the class. To make it accessible from *outside* the class, we need to change its protection level to `public`, as Example 3-4 shows.

Example 3-4. Making a property public

```
class Plane
{
    public string Identifier
    {
```

```
        get;
        set;
    }
}
```

Now when we compile and run the application, we see the correct output:

```
Your plane has identifier BA0049
```

Notice how this is an opt-in scheme. If you don't do anything to the contrary, you get the lowest sensible visibility. Your classes are visible to any code inside your assembly, but aren't accessible to anyone else; a class's properties and methods are only visible inside the class, unless you explicitly choose to make them more widely accessible.

When different layers specify different protection, the effective accessibility is the lowest specified. For example, although our property has `public` accessibility, the class of which it is a member has `internal` accessibility. The lower of the two wins, so the `Identifier` property is, in practice, only accessible to code in the same assembly.

It is a good practice to design your classes with the smallest possible public interface (part of something we sometimes call "minimizing the surface area"). This makes it easier for clients to understand how they're supposed to be used and often cuts down on the amount of testing you need to do. Having a clean, simple public API can also improve the security characteristics of your class framework, because the larger and more complex the API gets, the harder it generally gets to spot all the possible lines of attack.

That being said, there's a common misconception that accessibility modifiers "secure" your class, by preventing people from accessing private members. Hence this warning:

 It is important to recognize that these protection levels are a convenient design constraint, to help us structure our applications properly. They are not a security feature. It's possible to use the reflection features described in Chapter 17 to circumvent these constraints and to access these supposedly hidden details.

To finish this discussion, you should know that there are two other protection levels available to us—`protected` and `protected internal`—which we can use to expose (or hide) members to developers who derive new classes from our class without making the members visible to all. But since we won't be talking about derived classes until Chapter 4, we'll defer the discussion of these protection levels until then.

We can take advantage of protection in our `Plane` class. A plane's identifier shouldn't change mid-flight, and it's a good practice for code to prevent things from happening that we know shouldn't happen. We should therefore add that constraint to our class. Fortunately, we have the ability to change the accessibility of the getter and the setter individually, as Example 3-5 shows. (This is one reason the property syntax makes use declare the `get` and `set` explicitly—it gives us a place to put the protection level.)

Example 3-5. Making a property setter private

```
class Plane
{
    public string Identifier
    {
        get;
        private set;
    }
}
```

Compiling again, we get a new error message:

```
The property or indexer 'Plane.Identifier' cannot be used in this context because
the set accessor is inaccessible
```

The problem is with this bit of code from Example 3-3:

```
someBoeing777.Identifier = "BA0049";
```

We're no longer able to set the property, because we've made the setter `private` (which means that we can only set it from other members of our class). We wanted to prevent the property from changing, but we've gone too far: we don't even have a way of giving it a value in the first place. Fortunately, there's a language feature that's perfect for this situation: a *constructor*.

Initializing with a Constructor

A constructor is a special method which allows you to perform some "setup" when you create an instance of a class. Just like any other method, you can provide it with parameters, but it doesn't have an explicit return value. Constructors always have the same name as their containing class.

Example 3-6 adds a constructor that takes the plane's identifier. Because the constructor is a member of the class, it's allowed to use the `Identifier` property's `private` setter.

Example 3-6. Defining a constructor

```
class Plane
{
    public Plane(string newIdentifier)
    {
        Identifier = newIdentifier;
    }

    public string Identifier
    {
        get;
        private set;
    }
}
```

Notice how the constructor looks like a standard method declaration, except that since there's no need for a return type specifier, we leave that out. We don't even write void, like we would for a normal method that returns nothing. And it would be weird if we did; in a sense this does return something—the newly created Plane—it just does so implicitly.

What sort of work should you do in a constructor? Opinion is divided on the subject—should you do *everything* required to make the object ready to use, or the minimum necessary to make it safe? The truth is that it is a judgment call—there are no hard and fast rules. Developers tend to think of a constructor as being a relatively low-cost operation, so enormous amounts of heavy lifting (opening files, reading data) might be a bad idea. Getting the object into a fit state for use is a good objective, though, because requiring other functions to be called before the object is fully operational tends to lead to bugs.

We need to update our Main function to use this new constructor and to get rid of the line of code that was setting the property, as Example 3-7 shows.

Example 3-7. Using a constructor

```
static void Main(string[] args)
{
    Plane someBoeing777 = new Plane("BA0049");

    Console.WriteLine(
        "Your plane has identifier {0}",
        someBoeing777.Identifier);

    Console.ReadKey();
}
```

Notice how we pass the argument to the constructor inside the parentheses, in much the same way that we pass arguments in a normal method call.

If you compile and run that, you'll see the same output as before—but now we have an identifier that can't be changed by users of the object.

 Be very careful when you talk about properties that "can't be changed" because they have a private setter. Even if you can't set a property, you may still be able to modify the state of the object referred to by that property. The built-in string type happens to be immune to that because it is immutable (i.e., it can't be changed once it has been created), so making the setter on a string property private does actually prevent clients from changing the property, but most types aren't like that.

Speaking of properties that might need to change, our specification requires us to know the speed at which each plane is traveling. Sadly, our specification didn't mention the units in which we were expected to express that speed. Let's assume it is miles per hour, and add a suitable property. We'll use the floating-point `double` data type for this. Example 3-8 shows the code to add to `Plane`.

Example 3-8. A modifiable speed property

```
public double SpeedInMilesPerHour
{
    get;
    set;
}
```

If we were to review this design with the customer, they might point out that while they have some systems that do indeed want the speed in miles per hour the people they liaise with in European air traffic control want the speed in kilometers per hour. To avoid confusion, we will add another property so that they can get or set the speed in the units with which they are familiar. Example 3-9 shows a suitable property.

Example 3-9. Property with code in its get and set

```
public double SpeedInKilometersPerHour
{
    get
    {
        return SpeedInMilesPerHour * 1.609344;
    }
    set
    {
        SpeedInMilesPerHour = value / 1.609344;
    }
}
```

We've done something different here—rather than just writing `get;` and `set;` we've provided code for these accessors. This is another reason we have to declare the accessors explicitly—the C# compiler needs to know whether we want to write a custom property implementation.

We don't want to use an ordinary property in Example 3-9, because our `SpeedInKilometersPerHour` is not really a property in its own right—it's an alternative representation for the information stored in the `SpeedInMilesPerHour` property. If we used the normal property syntax for both, it would be possible to set the speed as being both 100 mph and 400 km/h, which would clearly be inconsistent. So instead we've chosen to implement `SpeedInKilometersPerHour` as a wrapper around the `SpeedInMilesPerHour` property.

If you look at the getter, you'll see that it returns a value of type `double`. It is equivalent to a function with this signature:

```
public double get_SpeedInKilometersPerHour()
```

The setter seems to provide an invisible parameter called `value`, which is also of type `double`. So it is equivalent to a method with this signature:

```
public void set_SpeedInKilometersPerHour(double value)
```

 This `value` parameter is a *contextual keyword*—C# only considers it to be a keyword in property or event accessors. (Events are described in Chapter 5.) This means you're allowed to use `value` as an identifier in other contexts—for example, you can write a method that takes a parameter called `value`. You can't do that with other keywords—you can't have a parameter called `class`, for example.

This is a very flexible system indeed. You can provide properties that provide real storage in the class to store their data, or *calculated properties* that use any mechanism you like to get and/or set the values concerned. This choice is an implementation detail hidden from users of our class—we can switch between one and the other without changing our class's public face. For example, we could switch the implementation of these speed properties around so that we stored the value in kilometers per hour, and calculated the miles per hour—Example 3-10 shows how these two properties would look if the "real" value was in km/h.

Example 3-10. Swapping over the real and calculated properties

```
public double SpeedInMilesPerHour
{
    get
    {
        return SpeedInKilometersPerHour / 1.609344;
    }
    set
    {
        SpeedInKilometersPerHour = value * 1.609344;
    }
}

public double SpeedInKilometersPerHour
{
    get;
    set;
}
```

As far as users of the `Plane` class are concerned, there's no discernible difference between the two approaches—the way in which properties work is an encapsulated implementation detail. Example 3-11 shows an updated `Main` function that uses the new properties. It neither knows nor cares which one is the "real" one.

Example 3-11. Using the speed properties

```
static void Main(string[] args)
{
    Plane someBoeing777 = new Plane("BA0049");

    someBoeing777.SpeedInMilesPerHour = 150.0;

    Console.WriteLine(
        "Your plane has identifier {0}, " +
        "and is traveling at {1:0.00}mph [{2:0.00}kph]",
        someBoeing777.Identifier,
        someBoeing777.SpeedInMilesPerHour,
        someBoeing777.SpeedInKilometersPerHour);

    someBoeing777.SpeedInKilometersPerHour = 140.0;

    Console.WriteLine(
        "Your plane has identifier {0}, " +
        "and is traveling at {1:0.00}mph [{2:0.00}kph]",
        someBoeing777.Identifier,
        someBoeing777.SpeedInMilesPerHour,
        someBoeing777.SpeedInKilometersPerHour);

    Console.ReadKey();
}
```

Although our public API supports two different units for speed while successfully keeping the implementation for that private, there's something unsatisfactory about that implementation. Our conversion relies on a magic number (1.609344) that appears repeatedly. Repetition impedes readability, and is prone to typos (I know that for a fact. I've typed it incorrectly once already this morning while preparing the example!) There's an important principle in programming: *don't repeat yourself* (or *dry*, as it's sometimes abbreviated). Your code should aim to express any single fact or concept no more than once, because that way, you only need to get it right once.

It would be much better to put this conversion factor in one place, give it a name, and refer to it by that instead. We can do that by declaring a *field*.

Fields: A Place to Put Data

A field is a place to put some data of a particular type. There's no option to add code like you can in a property—a field is nothing more than data. Back before C# 3.0 the compiler didn't let us write just get; and set;—we always had to write properties with code as in Example 3-9, and if we wanted a simple property that stored a value, we had to provide a field, with code such as Example 3-12.

Example 3-12. Writing your own simple property

```
// Field to hold the SpeedInMilesPerHour property's value
double speedInMilesPerHourValue;

public double SpeedInMilesPerHour
{
    get
    {
        return speedInMilesPerHourValue;
    }
    set
    {
        speedInMilesPerHourValue = value;
    }
}
```

When you write just `get;` and `set;` as we did in Example 3-8, the C# compiler generates code that's more or less identical to Example 3-12, except it gives the field a peculiar name to prevent us from accessing it directly. (These compiler-generated properties are called *auto properties*.) So, if we want to store a value in an object, there's always a field involved, even if it's a hidden one provided automatically by the compiler. Fields are the only class members that can hold information—properties are really just methods in disguise.

As you can see, a field declaration looks similar to the start of a property declaration. There's the type (`double`), and a name. By convention, this name is camelCased, to make fields visibly different from properties. (Some developers like to distinguish fields further by giving them a name that starts with an underscore.)

We can modify a field's protection level if we want, but, conventionally, we leave all fields with the default `private` accessibility. That's because a field is just a place for some data, and if we make it `public`, we lose control over the internal state of our object. Properties always involve some code, even if it's generated automatically by the compiler. We can use private backing fields as we wish, or calculate property values any way we like, and we're free to modify the implementation without ever changing the public face of the class. But with a field, we have nowhere to put code, so if we decide to change our implementation by switching from a field to a calculated value, we would need to remove the field entirely. If the field was part of the public contract of the class, that could break our clients. In short, fields have no innate capacity for encapsulation, so it's a bad idea to make them `public`.

Example 3-13 shows a modified version of the `Plane` class. Instead of repeating the magic number for our speed conversion factor, we declare a single field initialized to the required value. Not only does this mean that we get to state the conversion value just once, but we've also been able to give it a descriptive name—in the conversions, it's now obvious that we're multiplying and dividing by the number of kilometers in a mile, even if you happen not to have committed the conversion factor to memory.

Example 3-13. Storing the conversion factor in a field

```
class Plane
{
    // Constructor with a parameter
    public Plane(string newIdentifier)
    {
        Identifier = newIdentifier;
    }

    public string Identifier
    {
        get;
        private set;
    }

    double kilometersPerMile = 1.609344;

    public double SpeedInMilesPerHour
    {
        get
        {
            return SpeedInKilometersPerHour / kilometersPerMile;
        }
        set
        {
            SpeedInKilometersPerHour = value * kilometersPerMile;
        }
    }

    public double SpeedInKilometersPerHour
    {
        get;
        set;
    }
}
```

Notice how we're able to initialize the field to a default value right where we declare it, by using the = operator. (This sort of code is called, predictably enough, a *field initializer*.) Alternatively, we could have initialized it inside a constructor, but if the default is a constant value, it is conventional to set it at the point of declaration.

What about the first example of a field that we saw—the one we used as the backing data for a property in Example 3-12? We didn't explicitly initialize it. In some other languages that would be a ghastly mistake. (Failure to initialize fields correctly is a major source of bugs in C++, for example.) Fortunately, the designers of .NET decided that the trade-off between performance and robustness wasn't worth the pain, and kindly initialize all fields to a default value for us—numeric fields are set to zero and fields of other types get whatever the nearest equivalent of zero is. (Boolean fields are initialized to false, for example.)

There's also a security reason for this initialization. Because a new object's memory is always zeroed out before we get to see it, we can't just allocate a whole load of objects and then peer at the "uninitialized" values to see if anything interesting was left behind by the last object that used the same memory.

Defining a field for our scale factor is an improvement, but we could do better. Our 1.609344 isn't ever going to change. There are always that many kilometers per mile, not just for this instance of a `Plane`, but for any `Plane` there ever will be. Why allocate the storage for the field in every single instance? Wouldn't it be better if we could define this value just once, and not store it in every `Plane` instance?

Fields Can Be Fickle, but const Is Forever

C# provides a mechanism for declaring that a field holds a constant value, and will never, ever change. You use the `const` modifier, as Example 3-14 shows.

Example 3-14. Defining a constant value

```
const double kilometersPerMile = 1.609344;
```

The platform now takes advantage of the fact that this can never change, and allocates storage for it only once, no matter how many instances of `Plane` you `new` up. Handy.

This isn't just a storage optimization, though. By making the field `const`, there's no danger that someone might accidentally change it for some reason inside another function he's building in the class—the C# compiler prevents you from assigning a value to a `const` field anywhere other than at the point of declaration.

In general, when we are developing software, we're trying to make it as easy as possible for other developers (including our "future selves") to do the right thing, almost by accident. You'll often hear this approach called "designing for the pit of success." The idea is that people will fall into doing the right things because of the choices you've made.

Some aspects of an object don't fit well as either a normal modifiable field or a constant value. Take the plane's identifier, for example—that's fixed, in the sense that it never changes after construction, but it's not a constant value like `kilometersPerMile`. Different planes have different identifiers. .NET supports this sort of information through read-only properties and fields, which aren't quite the same as `const`.

Read-only Fields and Properties

In Example 3-5, we made our `Plane` class's `Identifier` property **private**. This prevented users of our class from setting the property, but our class is still free to shoot itself in the foot. Suppose a careless developer added some code like that in Example 3-15, which prints out messages in the `SpeedInMilesPerHour` property perhaps in order to debug some problem he was investigating.

Example 3-15. Badly written debugging code

```
public double SpeedInMilesPerHour
{
    get
    {
        return SpeedInKilometersPerHour / kilometersPerMile;
    }
    set
    {
        Identifier += ": speed modified to " + value;
        Console.WriteLine(Identifier);
        SpeedInKilometersPerHour = value * kilometersPerMile;
    }
}
```

The first time someone tries to modify a plane's `SpeedInMilesPerHour` this will print out a message that includes the identifier, for example:

```
BA0048: speed modified to 400
```

Unfortunately, the developer who wrote this clearly wasn't the sharpest tool in the box—he used the += operator to build that debug string, which will end up modifying the `Identifier` property. So, the plane now thinks its identifier is that whole text, including the part about the speed. And if we modified the speed again, we'd see:

```
BA0048: speed modified to 400: speed modified to 380
```

While it might be interesting to see the entire modification history, the fact that we've messed up the `Identifier` is bad. Example 3-15 was able to do this because the `SpeedInMilesPerHour` property is part of the `Plane` class, so it can still use the **private** setter. We can fix this (up to a point) by making the property read-only—rather than merely making the setter **private**, we can leave it out entirely. However, we can't just write the code in Example 3-16.

Example 3-16. The wrong way to define a read-only property

```
class Plane
{
    // Wrong!
    public string Identifier
    {
        get;
    }
```

```
    ...
}
```

That won't work because there's no way we could *ever* set `Identifier`—not even in the constructor. Auto properties cannot be read-only, so we must write a getter with code. Example 3-17 will compile, although as we're about to see, the job's not done yet.

Example 3-17. A better, but incomplete, read-only property

```
class Plane
{
    public Plane(string newIdentifier)
    {
        _identifier = newIdentifier;
    }

    public string Identifier
    {
        get { return _identifier; }
    }
    private string _identifier;
    ...
}
```

This turns out to give us two problems. First, the original constructor from Example 3-6 would no longer compile—it set `Identifier`, but that's now read-only. That was easy to fix, though—Example 3-17 just sets the explicit backing field we've added. More worryingly, this hasn't solved the original problem—the developer who wrote the code in Example 3-15 has "cleverly" realized that he can "fix" his code by doing exactly the same thing as the constructor. As Example 3-18 shows he has just used the `_identifier` field directly.

Example 3-18. "Clever" badly written debugging code

```
public double SpeedInMilesPerHour
{
    get
    {
        return SpeedInKilometersPerHour / kilometersPerMile;
    }
    set
    {
        _identifier += ": speed modified to " + value;
        Console.WriteLine(Identifier);
        SpeedInKilometersPerHour = value * kilometersPerMile;
    }
}
```

That seemed like a long journey for no purpose. However, we can fix this problem— we can modify the backing field itself to be read-only, as shown in Example 3-19.

Example 3-19. A read-only field

```
private readonly string _identifier;
```

That will foil the developer who wrote Example 3-15 and Example 3-18. But doesn't it also break our constructor again? In fact, it doesn't: read-only fields behave differently from read-only properties. A read-only property can *never* be modified. A read-only field can be modified, but only by a constructor.

Since read-only fields only become truly read-only after construction completes, it makes them perfect for properties that need to be able to be different from one instance to another, but which need to be fixed for the lifetime of an instance.

Before we move on from `const` and `readonly` fields, there's another property our `Plane` needs for which `const` seems like it could be relevant, albeit in a slightly different way. In addition to monitoring the speed of an aircraft, we also need to know whether it is approaching or heading away from the airport.

We could represent that with a `bool` property called something like `IsApproaching` (where `true` would mean that it was approaching, and `false` would, by implication, indicate that it was heading away). That's a bit clumsy, though. You can often end up having to negate Boolean properties—you might need to write this sort of thing:

```
if (!plane.IsApproaching) { ... }
```

That reads as "if not plane is approaching" which sounds a bit awkward. We could go with:

```
if (somePlane.IsApproaching == false) { ... }
```

That's "if is approaching is false" which isn't much better. We could offer a second, calculated property called `IsNotApproaching`, but our code is likely to be simpler and easier to read (and therefore likely to contain fewer bugs) if, instead of using `bool`, we have a `Direction` property whose value could somehow be either `Approaching` or `Leaving`.

We've just seen a technique we could use for that. We could create two constant fields of any type we like (`int`, for example), and a property of type `int` called `Direction` (see Example 3-20).

Example 3-20. Named options with const int

```
class Plane
{
    public const int Approaching = 0;
    public const int Leaving = 1;

    // ...

    public int Direction { get; set; }
}
```

This lets us write code that reads a bit more naturally than it would if we had used just `true` and `false`:

```
someBoeing777.Direction = Plane.Approaching;
if (someAirbusA380.Direction == Plane.Leaving) { /* Do something */ }
```

But there's one problem: if our `Direction` property's type is `int`, there's nothing to stop us from saying something like:

```
someBoeing777.Direction = 72;
```

This makes no sense, but the C# compiler doesn't know that—after all, we told it the property's type was `int`, so how's it supposed to know that's wrong? Fortunately, the designers of C# have thought of this, and have given us a kind of type for precisely this situation, called an `enum`, and it turns out to be a much better solution for this than `const int`.

Related Constants with enum

The `enum`[†] keyword lets us define a type whose values can be one of a fixed set of possibilities. Example 3-21 declares an `enum` for our `Direction` property. You can add this to an existing source file, above or below the `Plane` class, for example. Alternatively, you could add a whole new source file to the project, although Visual Studio doesn't offer a file template for `enum` types, so either you'd have to add a new class and then change the `class` keyword to `enum`, or you could use the Code File template to add a new, empty source file.

Example 3-21. Direction enum

```
enum DirectionOfApproach
{
    Approaching,
    Leaving
}
```

This is similar in some respects to a class declaration. We can optionally begin with a protection level but if, like Example 3-21, we omit that, we get `internal` protection by default. Then there's the `enum` specifier itself, followed by the name of the type, which by convention we PascalCase. Inside the braces, we declare the members, again using PascalCasing. Notice that we use commas to separate the list of constants—this is where the syntax starts to part company with `class`. Unusually, the members are publicly accessible by default. That's because an `enum` has no behavior, and so there are no implementation details—it's just a list of named values, and those need to be `public` for the type to serve any useful purpose.

[†] It's short for "enumeration," by the way. So it's often pronounced "e-noom" or, depending on where you're from, "e-nyoom." However, some developers (and one of the authors) ignore the etymology and pronounce it "ee numb" because that's how it looks like it should sound.

 Notice that we've chosen to call this `DirectionOfApproach`, and not the plural `DirectionsOfApproach`. By convention, we give `enum` types a singular name even though they usually contain a list. This makes sense because when you use named entries from an enumeration, you use them one at a time, and so it would look odd if the type name were plural. Obviously, there won't be any technical consequences for breaking this convention, but following it helps make your code consistent with the .NET Framework class libraries.

We can now declare our `Direction` property, using the enumeration instead of an integer. Example 3-22 shows the property to add to the `Plane` class.

Example 3-22. Property with enum type

```
public DirectionOfApproach Direction
{
    get;
    set;
}
```

There are some optional features we can use in an `enum` declaration. Example 3-23 uses these, and they provide some insight into how `enum` types work.

Example 3-23. Explicit type and values for enum

```
enum DirectionOfApproach : int
{
    Approaching = 0,
    Leaving = 1
}
```

In this declaration, we have explicitly specified the *governing type* for the enumeration. This is the type that stores the individual values for an enumeration, and we specify it with a colon and the type name. By default, it uses an `int` (exactly as we did in our original const-based implementation of this property), so we've not actually changed anything here; we're just being more explicit. The governing type must be one of the built-in integer types: `byte`, `sbyte`, `short`, `ushort`, `uint`, `long`, or `ulong`.

Example 3-23 also specifies the numbers to use for each named value. As it happens, if you don't provide these numbers, the first member is assigned the value 0, and we count off sequentially after that, so again, this example hasn't changed anything, it's just showing the values explicitly.

We could, if we wanted, specify any value for any particular member. Maybe we start from 10 and go up in powers of 2. And we're also free to define duplicates, giving the same value several different names. (That might not be useful, but C# won't stop you.)

We normally leave all these explicit specifiers off, and accept the defaults. However, the sidebar on the next page describes a scenario in which you would need to control the numbers.

Bit Fields with [Flags]

You can create a special kind of enum called a [Flags] enum, also known as a *bit field*. A bit field is just an ordinary numeric value used in a particular way. When you view a bit field value in binary, each bit represents a particular setting. For example, we could define a bit field to represent the toppings on a bowl of ice cream. We might use the least significant bit to indicate whether a chocolate sauce topping is required. And we could use a different bit to indicate whether chocolate sprinkles are required.

The thing that makes bit field enum types different from normal ones is that you can use any *combination* of values. Because each value gets a whole bit of the number to itself, you can choose for that bit to be either 0 or 1 independently of the value of any other bits.

You indicate that your enum works this way by annotating it with a [Flags] attribute, and specifying the values of the members to correspond to the relevant bit patterns. (Actually, the [Flags] attribute turns out to be optional—the compiler ignores it, and lets you use any enum as though it were a bit field. The .NET Framework only uses the attribute to work out how to convert enumeration values to text. However, it's a useful signpost to tell other developers how your enum is meant to be used.) Typically, you define a name for each bit, and you can also name some common combinations:

```
[Flags]
enum Toppings
{
    None = 0x00,                // Special zero value
    ChocolateSauce = 0x01,
    ToffeeSauce = 0x02,
    ChocolateSprinkles = 0x04,
    Chocoholic = 0x05,          // Combined value, sets 2 bits
    Greedy = 0x07               // Everything!
}
```

We're using hexadecimal representations because it's easier to relate them to the binary values—each hex digit corresponds exactly to four binary digits.

We can combine the values together using the | operator (binary OR), for example:

```
// (011)
Toppings saucy =
    Toppings.ChocolateSauce | Toppings.ToffeeSauce;
```

We can use the binary AND operator (&) to see whether a particular flag has been set:

```
static bool DoYouWantChocolateSauceWithThat(Toppings t)
{
    return (t & Toppings.ChocolateSauce) != 0;
}
```

When defining bit fields, you might not want to allow certain combinations. For example, you might reject the **saucy** combination, requiring customers to pick, at most, one kind of sauce. Unfortunately, there are no language or platform mechanisms for enforcing that kind of constraint, so you'd need to write code to check for illegal combinations in any method that accepted arguments of this type. (Or you could consider an alternative design that does not use an enum at all.)

 If you don't specify explicit values, the first item in your list is effectively the default value for the enum (because it corresponds to the zero value). If you provide explicit values, be sure to define a value that corresponds to zero—if you don't, fields using your type will default to a value that's not a valid member of the enum, which is not desirable.

We can now access the enumeration property like this:

```
someBoeing777.Direction = DirectionOfApproach.Approaching;
```

We've clearly made some progress with our Plane class, but we're not done yet. We have a read-only property for its Identifier. We can store the speed, which we can get and set using two different properties representing different units, using a const field for the conversion factor. And we know the direction, which will be either the Approaching or the Leaving member of an enum.

We still need to store the aircraft's position. According to the specification, we've got two polar coordinates (an angle and a distance) for its position on the ground, and another value for its height above sea level.

We're likely to need to do a lot of calculations based on this position information. Every time we want to create a function to do that, we'd need three parameters per point, which seems overly complex. (And error-prone—it'd be all too easy to inadvertently pass two numbers from one position, and a third number from a different position.) It would be nicer if we could wrap the numbers up into a single, lightweight, "3D point" type that we can think of in the same kind of way we do int or double—a basic building block for other classes to use with minimum overhead.

This is a good candidate for a *value type*.

Value Types and Reference Types

So far, we've been building a class. When creating an instance of the class, we stored it in a named variable, as Example 3-24 shows.

Example 3-24. Storing a reference in a variable

```
Plane someBoeing777 = new Plane("BA0049");
someBoeing777.Direction = DirectionOfApproach.Approaching;
```

We can define another variable with a different name, and store a reference to the same plane in that new variable, as shown in Example 3-25.

Example 3-25. Copying a reference from one variable to another

```
Plane theSameBoeing777ByAnotherName = someBoeing777;
```

If we change a property through one variable, that change will be visible through the other. Example 3-26 modifies our plane's `Direction` property through the second variable, but then reads it through the first variable, verifying that they really are referring to the same object.

Example 3-26. Using one object through two variables

```
theSameBoeing777ByAnotherName.Direction = DirectionOfApproach.Leaving;
if (someBoeing777.Direction == DirectionOfApproach.Leaving)
{
    Console.WriteLine("Oh, they are the same!");
}
```

As Shakespeare might have said, if only he'd found his true vocation as a C# developer:

> That which we call `someBoeing777`
> By any other name would smell as sweet.

Assuming you like the smell of jet fuel.

When we define a type using `class`, we always get this behavior—our variables behave as references to an underlying object. We therefore call a type defined as a `class` a *reference type*.

 It's possible for a reference type variable to be in a state where it isn't referring to any object at all. C# has a special keyword, `null`, to represent this. You can set a variable to `null`, or you can pass `null` as an argument to a method. And you can also test to see if a field, variable, or argument is equal to `null` in an `if` statement. Any field whose type is a reference type will automatically be initialized to `null` before the constructor runs, in much the same way as numeric fields are initialized to zero.

The `enum` we declared earlier and the built-in numeric types (`int`, `double`) behave differently, though, as Example 3-27 illustrates.

Example 3-27. Copying values, not references

```
int firstInt = 3;
int secondInt = firstInt;

secondInt = 4;

if (firstInt != 4)
{
    Console.WriteLine("Well. They're not the same at all.");
}
```

When we assign `firstInt` to `secondInt`, we are *copying the value*. In this case, the variables hold the actual value, not a reference to a value. We call types that behave this way *value types*.

People often refer to reference types as being allocated "on the heap" and value types "on the stack." C++ programmers will be familiar with these concepts, and C++ provided one syntax in the language to explicitly create items on the stack (a cheap form of storage local to a particular scope), and a different syntax for working on the heap (a slightly more expensive but sophisticated form of storage that could persist beyond the current scope). C# doesn't make that distinction in its syntax, because the .NET Framework itself makes no such distinction. These aspects of memory management are completely opaque to the developer, and it is actively wrong to think of value types as being always allocated on a stack.

For people familiar with C++ this can take a while to get used to, especially as the myth is perpetuated on the Web, in the MSDN documentation and elsewhere. (For example, at the time of this writing, *http://msdn.microsoft.com/library/aa288471* states that structs are created on the stack, and while that happens to be true of the ones in that example when running against the current version of .NET, it would have been helpful if the page had mentioned that it's not always true. For example, if a class has a field of value type, that field doesn't live on the stack—it lives inside the object, and in all the versions of .NET released so far, objects live on the heap.)

 The important difference for the C# developer between these two kinds of types is the one of reference versus copy semantics.

As well as understanding the difference in behavior, you also need to be aware of some constraints. To be useful, a value type should be:

- Immutable
- Lightweight

Something is immutable if it doesn't change over time. So, the integer 3 is immutable. It doesn't have any internal workings that can change its "three-ness". You can replace the *value* of an int variable that currently contains a 3, by copying a 4 into it, but you can't change a 3 itself. (Unlike, say, a particular Plane object, which has a Direction property that you can change anytime you like without needing to replace the whole Plane.)

 There's nothing in C# that stops you from creating a mutable value type. It is just a bad idea (in general). If your type is mutable, it is probably safer to make it a reference type, by declaring it as a class. Mutable value types cause problems because of the copy semantics—if you modify a value, it's all too easy to end up modifying the wrong one, because there may be many copies.

It should be fairly apparent that a value type also needs to be pretty lightweight, because of all that copying going on. Every time you pass it into a function, or assign it to a variable, a copy is made. And copies are generally the enemy of good performance. If your value type consists of more than two or three of the built-in types, it may be getting too big.

These constraints mean it is very rare that you will actually want to declare a value type yourself. A lot of the obviously useful ones you might want are already defined in the .NET Framework class libraries (things like 2D points, times, and dates). Custom value types are so rare that it was hard to come up with a useful example for this book that wasn't already provided in the class libraries. (If you were wondering why our example application represents aircraft positions in such an idiosyncratic fashion, this is the reason.)

But that doesn't mean you should never, ever declare a value type. Value types can have performance benefits when used in arrays (although as with most performance issues, this is not entirely clear-cut), and the immutability and copy semantics can make them safer when passing them in to functions—you won't normally introduce side effects by working with a value type because you end up using a copy, rather than modifying shared data that other code might be relying on.

Our polar 3D point seems to comply with the requirements. Any given point is just that: a specific point in 3D space—a good candidate for immutability. (We might want to move a plane to a different point, but we can't change what a particular point means.) It is also no more than three doubles in size, which is small enough for copy semantics. Example 3-28 shows our declaration of this type, which we can add to our project. (As with enum, Visual Studio doesn't offer a template for value types. Again, we can use the Class template, replacing the class with the code we want.)

Example 3-28. A value type

```
struct PolarPoint3D
{
    public PolarPoint3D(double distance, double angle, double altitude)
    {
        Distance = distance;
        Angle = angle;
        Altitude = altitude;
    }

    public double Distance
    {
        get;
        private set;
    }

    public double Angle
    {
        get;
        private set;
```

```
    }

    public double Altitude
    {
        get;
        private set;
    }
}
```

If you think that it looks just like a class declaration, but using the **struct** keyword instead of **class**, you'd be right—these two kinds of types are very similar. However, if we try to compile it, we get an error on the first line of the constructor:

```
The 'this' object cannot be used before all of its fields are assigned to
```

So, although the basic syntax of a **struct** looks just like a **class** there are important differences. Remember that when you allocate an instance of a particular type, it is *always* initialized to some default value. With classes, all fields are initialized to zero (or the nearest equivalent value). But things work slightly differently with value types—we need to do slightly more work.

Anytime we write a **struct**, C# automatically generates a default, parameterless constructor that initializes all of our storage to zero, so if we don't want to write any custom constructors, we won't have any problems. (Unlike with a **class**, we aren't allowed to replace the default constructor. We can define extra constructors, but the default constructor is always present and we're not allowed to write our own—see the sidebar on the next page for details.)

Example 3-28 has hit trouble because we're trying to provide an additional constructor, which initializes the properties to particular values. If we write a constructor in a **struct**, the compiler refuses to let us invoke any methods until we've initialized all the fields. (It doesn't do the normal zero initialization for custom constructors.) This restriction turns out to include properties, because **get** and **set** accessors are methods under the covers. So C# won't let us use our properties until the underlying fields have been initialized, and we can't do that because these are auto properties—the C# compiler has generated hidden fields that we can only access through the properties. This is a bit of a chicken-and-egg bootstrapping problem!

Fortunately, C# gives us a way of calling one of our constructors from another. We can use this to call the default constructor to do the initialization; then our constructor can set the properties to whatever values it wishes. We call the constructor using the **this** keyword, and the standard function calling syntax with any arguments enclosed in parentheses. As Example 3-29 shows, we can invoke the default constructor with an empty argument list.

Value Types and Default Constructors

Why aren't we allowed to define a custom default constructor for a value type, given that we're allowed to do that for a reference type? The short answer is that the specification for the relevant behavior in the .NET Framework doesn't let you. (The specification in question is called the Common Language Infrastructure [CLI], incidentally.)

The slightly longer answer is: for efficiency reasons. By mandating that the default constructor for any value type always initializes everything to zero, large arrays of value types can be constructed very cheaply, just by allocating the required amount of memory and zeroing out the whole array in one step. And similarly, it simplifies the initialization of fields and variables—everything can be initialized to zero.

Example 3-29. Calling one constructor from another

```
public PolarPoint3D(double distance, double angle, double altitude)
    : this()
{
    Distance = distance;
    Angle = angle;
    Altitude = altitude;
}
```

You add the call just before the opening brace for the body of the constructor, and prefix it with a colon. We can also use this technique to avoid writing common initialization code multiple times. Say we wanted to provide another utility constructor that just took the polar coordinates, and initialized the altitude to zero by default. Instead of repeating all the code from the first constructor, we could just add this extra constructor to our definition for `PolarPoint3D`, as shown in Example 3-30.

Example 3-30. Sharing common initialization code

```
public PolarPoint3D(double distance, double angle)
    : this(distance, angle, 0)
{
}

public PolarPoint3D(
    double distance,
    double angle,
    double altitude)
    : this()
{
    Distance = distance;
    Angle = angle;
    Altitude = altitude;
}
```

Incidentally, this syntax for calling one constructor from another works equally well in classes, and is a great way of avoiding code duplication.

Too Many Constructors, Mr. Mozart

You should be careful of adding too many constructors to a **class** or **struct**. It is easy to lose track of which parameters are which, or to make arbitrary choices about which constructors you provide and which you don't.

For example, let's say we wanted to add yet another constructor to **PolarPoint3D** that lets callers pass just the angle and altitude, initializing the distance to a default of zero, as Example 3-31 shows.

Example 3-31. A constructor too far

```
public PolarPoint3D(
    double altitude,
    double angle )
    : this( 0, angle, altitude )
{
}
```

Even before we compile, we can see that there's a problem—we happen to have added the **altitude** parameter so that it is the first in the list, and **angle** stays second. In our main constructor, the altitude comes after the angle. Because they are both just doubles, there's nothing to stop you from accidentally passing the parameters "the wrong way round." This is the exactly the kind of thing that surprises users of your class, and leads to hard-to-find bugs. But while inconsistent parameter ordering is bad design, it's not a showstopper.

However, when we compile, things get even worse. We get another error:

```
Type 'PolarPoint3D' already defines a member called 'PolarPoint3D' with the same
parameter types
```

We have too many constructors. But how many is too many?

Overloading

When we define more than one member in a type with the same name (be it a constructor or, as we'll see later, a method) we call this *overloading*.

Initially, we created two constructors (two overloads of the constructor) for **Polar Point3D**, and they compiled just fine. This is because they took *different sets of parameters*. One took three doubles, the other two. In fact, there was also the third, hidden constructor that took no parameters at all. All three constructors took different numbers of parameters, meaning there's no ambiguity about which constructor we want when we initialize a new **PolarPoint3D**.

The constructor in Example 3-31 seems different: the two doubles have different names. Unfortunately, this doesn't matter to the C# compiler—it only looks at the *types* of the parameters, and the *order* in which they are declared. It does not use names for disambiguation. This should hardly be surprising, because we're not required to provide argument names when we call methods or constructors. If we add the overload in Example 3-31, it's not clear what new `PolarPoint3D(0, 0)` would mean, and that's why we get an error—we've got two members with the same name (`PolarPoint3D`—the constructor), and exactly the same parameter types, in the same order.

Looking at overloaded functions will emphasize that it really is only the method name and the parameters that matter—a function's return type is not considered to be a disambiguating aspect of the member for overload purposes.

That means there's nothing we can do about it: we're going to have to get rid of this third constructor (just delete it); and while we're in the code, we'll finish up the declaration of the data portion of our `Plane` by adding a property for its position, shown in Example 3-32.

Example 3-32. Using our custom value type for a property

```
public PolarPoint3D Position
{
    get;
    set;
}
```

Overloaded Methods and Default Named Parameters

Just as with constructors, we can provide more than one method with the same name, but a different list of parameter types. It is, in general, a bad idea to provide two overloads with the same name if they perform a semantically different operation (again—that's the kind of thing that surprises developers using your class), so the most common reason for overloading is to provide several different ways to do something. We can provide users of our code with flexible methods that take lots of arguments to control different aspects of the code, and we can also provide developers that don't need this flexibility with simpler options by providing overloads that don't need as many arguments.

Suppose we added a method to our `Plane` class enabling messages to be sent to aircraft. Perhaps in our first attempt we define a method whose signature looks like this:

```
public void SendMessage(string messageText)
```

But suppose that as the project progresses, we find that it would be useful to be able to delay transmission of certain messages. We could modify the `SendMessage` method so that it accepts an extra argument. There's a handy type in the framework called `TimeSpan` which lets us specify duration. We could modify the method to make use of it:

```
public void SendMessage(string messageText, TimeSpan delay)
```

Alas! If we already had code in our project depending on the original signature, we'd start to see this compiler error:

```
No overload for method 'SendMessage' takes '1' arguments
```

We've changed the signature of that method, so all our clients are sadly broken. They need to be rewritten to use the new method. That's not great.

A better alternative is to provide both signatures—keep the old single-parameter contract around, but add an overload with the extra argument. And to ensure that the overloads behave consistently (and to avoid duplicating code) we can make the simpler method call the new method as its actual implementation. The old method was just the equivalent of calling the new method with a delay of zero, so we could replace it with the method shown in Example 3-33. This lets us provide the newly enhanced SendMessage, while continuing to support the old, simpler version.

Example 3-33. Implementing one overload in terms of another

```
public void SendMessage(string messageName)
{
    SendMessage(messageName, TimeSpan.Zero);
}
```

(TimeSpan.Zero is a `static` field that returns a duration of zero.)

Until C# 4.0 that's as far as we could go. However, the C# designers noticed that a lot of member overloads were just like this one: facades over an über-implementation, with a bunch of parameters defaulted out to particular values. So they decided to make it easier for us to support multiple variations on the same method. Rather than writing lots of overloads, we can now just specify default values for a method's arguments, which saves us typing a lot of boilerplate, and helps make our default choices more transparent.

Let's take out the single-parameter method overload we just added, and instead change the declaration of our multiparameter implementation, as shown in Example 3-34.

Example 3-34. Parameter with default value

```
public void SendMessage(
    string messageName,
    TimeSpan delay = default(TimeSpan))
```

Even though we've only got one method, which supports two arguments, code that tries to call it with a single argument will still work. That's because default values can fill in for missing arguments. (If we tried to call SendMessage with no arguments at all, we'd get a compiler error, because there's no default for the first argument here.)

But it doesn't end there. Say we had a method with four parameters, like this one:

```
    public void MyMethod(
        int firstOne,
        double secondInLine = 3.1416,
        string thirdHere = "The third parameter",
        TimeSpan lastButNotLeast = default(TimeSpan))
    {
        // ...
    }
```

If we want to call it and specify the first parameter (which we have to, because it has no default), and the third, but *not* the second or the fourth, we can do so by using the names of the parameters, like this:

```
MyMethod(127, thirdHere: "New third parameter");
```

With just one method, we now have many different ways to call it—we can provide all the arguments, or just the first and second, or perhaps the first, second, and third. There are many combinations. Before named arguments and defaults were added in C# 4.0, the only way to get this kind of flexibility was to write an overload for each distinct combination.

Under the Hood with Default Parameters

Default and named parameters are very useful features, but we need to warn you of a subtle potential problem. Although they are more-or-less equivalent to providing a bunch of different function overloads, as far as the syntax for the caller goes, under the covers, they are implemented very differently.

The compiler marks a parameter to indicate that it is optional using the `OptionalAttribute` and there's a `DefaultParameterValueAttribute` to specify a default value. These two attributes have been around for quite a while—they were originally added for the benefit of Visual Basic, long before C# started using them. (Attributes are discussed in Chapter 17.)

When you call a method (or constructor), the C# compiler always emits a complete call—the compiled code passes a full set of arguments to the method, even if your source code left some arguments out. For example, in our `Plane` example, if you wrote:

```
SendMessage("SomeMessage");
```

but the `Plane` class only has the method shown in Example 3-34, the compiler actually generates code equivalent to this:

```
SendMessage("SomeMessage", default(TimeSpan));
```

In other words, it plugs in the default value at compile time. This means if you're using some external library that uses default values, and a newer version of the library comes out that changes the default values for some method or constructor, your code won't pick up those new values unless you recompile your code.

There's also a subtler problem you can run into. Some parts of the .NET Framework require you to provide a particular constructor overload. For example, it you write a custom control for WPF, and you want to use it from Xaml, it must have a default constructor. (WPF and Xaml are described in Chapter 20.) If all your constructors take parameters, then even if you provide default values for all the parameters, that's not good enough. You can write, say, `new MyControl()` in C#, but only because the C# compiler is implicitly passing the missing values for you. Not everything in the world of .NET understands the concept of default arguments. (C# itself didn't until version 4.0.) Sometimes only a genuine no-arguments constructor will do.

This is not just limited to normal methods—you can use this same syntax to provide default values for parameters in your constructors, if you wish.

Being forced to delete the extra constructor we tried to add back in Example 3-31 was a little disappointing—we're constraining the number of ways users of our type can initialize it. Named arguments and default values have helped, but can we do more?

Object Initializers

Until C# 3.0, the only real solution to this was to write one or more *factory methods*. These are described in the sidebar below. But now we have another option.

Factory Methods

A *factory method* is a static method that builds a new object. There's no formal support for this in C#, it's just a common solution to a problem—a *pattern*, as popular idioms are often called in programming. We can get around the overload ambiguity problems by providing factory methods with different names. And the names can make it clear how we're initializing the instance:

```
public static PolarPoint3D FromDistanceAndAngle(
  double distance, double angle)
{
    return new PolarPoint3D(distance, angle, 0);
}

public static PolarPoint3D FromAngleAndAltitude(
  double angle, double altitude)
{
    return new PolarPoint3D(0, angle, altitude);
}
```

We rather like this approach, although some people frown on it as insufficiently *discoverable*. (Most developers aren't expecting to find static methods that act rather like constructors, and if nobody finds these methods, we're wasting our time in providing them.) However, this pattern is used all over the .NET Framework libraries—DateTime, TimeSpan, and Color are popular types that all use this technique.

With C# 3.0 the language was extended to support *object initializers*—an extension to the new syntax that lets us set up a load of properties, by name, as we create our object instance.

Example 3-35 shows how an object initializer looks when we use it in our Main function.

Example 3-35. Using object initializers

```
static void Main(string[] args)
{
    Plane someBoeing777 = new Plane("BA0049")
                        {
                            Direction = DirectionOfApproach.Approaching,
                            SpeedInMilesPerHour = 150
                        };

    Console.WriteLine(
        "Your plane has identifier {0}," +
        " and is traveling at {1:0.00}mph [{2:0.00}kph]",
        // Use the property getter
        someBoeing777.Identifier,
        someBoeing777.SpeedInMilesPerHour,
        someBoeing777.SpeedInKilometersPerHour);

    someBoeing777.SpeedInKilometersPerHour = 140.0;

    Console.WriteLine(
        "Your plane has identifier {0}," +
        " and is traveling at {1:0.00}mph [{2:0.00}kph]",
        // Use the property getter
        someBoeing777.Identifier,
        someBoeing777.SpeedInMilesPerHour,
        someBoeing777.SpeedInKilometersPerHour);

    Console.ReadKey();

}
```

 Object initializers are mostly just a convenient syntax for constructing a new object and then setting some properties. Consequently, this only works with writable properties—you can't use it for immutable types,‡ so this wouldn't work with our PolarPoint3D.

We still use the constructor parameter for the read-only Identifier property; but then we add an extra section in braces, between the closing parenthesis and the semicolon, in which we have a list of property assignments, separated by commas. What's particularly interesting is that the purpose of the constructor parameter is normally identifiable only by the value we happen to assign to it, but the object initializer is "self-documenting"—we can easily see what is being initialized to which values, at a glance.

‡ This is a slight oversimplification. In Chapter 8, we'll encounter anonymous types, which are always immutable, and yet we can use object initializers with those. In fact, we are required to. But anonymous types are a special case.

The job isn't quite done yet, though. While there's nothing technically wrong with using both the constructor parameter and the object initializer, it does look a little bit clumsy. It might be easier for our clients if we allow them to use a default, parameterless constructor, and then initialize *all* the members using this new syntax. As we'll see in Chapter 6, we have other ways of enforcing invariants in the object state, and dealing with incorrect usages. Object initializers are certainly a more expressive syntax, and on the basis that self-documenting and transparent is better, we're going to change how `Plane` works so that we can initialize the whole object with an object initializer.

 As with any design consideration, there is a counter argument. Some classes may be downright difficult to put into a "default" (zero-ish) state that isn't actively dangerous. We're also increasing the size of the public API by the changes we're making—we're adding a public setter. Here, we've decided that the benefits outweigh the disadvantages in this particular case (although it's really a judgment call; no doubt some developers would disagree).

First, as Example 3-36 shows, we'll delete the special constructor from `Plane`, and then make `Identifier` an ordinary read/write property. We can also remove the `_identifier` backing field we added earlier, because we've gone back to using an auto property.

Example 3-36. Modifying Plane to work better with object initializers

```
class Plane
{
    // Remove the constructor that we no longer require
    // public Plane(string newIdentifier)
    // {
    //     Identifier = newIdentifier;
    // }

    public string Identifier
    {
        get;
        // remove the access modifier
        // to make it public
        set;
    }

    // ...
}
```

We can now use the object initializer syntax for all the properties we want to set. As Example 3-37 shows, this makes our code look somewhat neater—we only need one style of code to initialize the object.

Example 3-37. Nothing but object initializer syntax

```
Plane someBoeing777 = new Plane
                    {
                            Identifier = "BA0049",
                            Direction = DirectionOfApproach.Approaching,
                            SpeedInMilesPerHour = 150
                    };
```

Object initializer syntax provides one big advantage over offering lots of specialized constructors: people using your class can provide any combination of properties they want. They might decide to set the `Position` property inline in this object initializer too, as Example 3-38 does—if we'd been relying on constructors, default or named arguments wouldn't have helped if there was no constructor available that accepted a `Position`. We've not had to provide an additional constructor overload to make this possible—developers using our class have a great deal of flexibility. Of course, this approach only makes sense if our type is able to work sensibly with default values for the properties in question. If you absolutely need certain values to be provided on initialization, you're better off with constructors.

Example 3-38. Providing an extra property

```
Plane someBoeing777 = new Plane
                    {
                            Identifier = "BA0049",
                            Direction = DirectionOfApproach.Approaching,
                            SpeedInMilesPerHour = 150,
                            Position = new PolarPoint3D(20, 180, 14500)
                    };
```

So, we've addressed the data part of our `Plane`; but the whole point of a class is that it can encapsulate both state and *operations*. What methods are we going to define in our class?

Defining Methods

When deciding what methods a class might need, we generally scan our specifications or scenarios for verbs that relate to the object of that class. If we look back at the ATC system description at the beginning of this chapter, we can see several plane-related actions, to do with granting permissions to land and permissions to take off. But do we need functions on the `Plane` class to deal with that? Possibly not. It might be better to deal with that in another part of the model, to do with our ground control, runways, and runway management (that, you'll be pleased to hear, we won't be building).

But we will periodically need to update the position of all the planes. This involves changing the state of the plane—we will need to modify its `Position`. And it's a change of state whose details depend on the existing state—we need to take the direction and speed into account. This sounds like a good candidate for a method that the `Plane` class should offer. Example 3-39 shows the code to add inside the class.

Example 3-39. A method

```
public void UpdatePosition(double minutesToAdvance)
{
    double hours = minutesToAdvance / 60.0;
    double milesMoved = SpeedInMilesPerHour * hours;
    double milesToTower = Position.Distance;
    if (Direction == DirectionOfApproach.Approaching)
    {
        milesToTower -= milesMoved;
        if (milesToTower < 0)
        {
            // We've arrived!
            milesToTower = 0;
        }
    }
    else
    {
        milesToTower += milesMoved;
    }
    PolarPoint3D newPosition = new PolarPoint3D(
        milesToTower, Position.Angle, Position.Altitude);
}
```

This method takes a single argument, indicating how much elapsed time the calculation should take into account. It looks at the speed, the direction, and the current position, and uses this information to calculate the new position.

 This code illustrates that our design is some way from being finished. We never change the altitude, which suggests that our planes are going to have a hard time reaching the ground. (Although since this code makes them stop moving when they get directly above the tower, they'll probably reach the ground soon enough...) Apparently our initial specification did not fully and accurately describe the problem our software should be solving. This will not come as astonishing news to anyone who has worked in the software industry. Clearly we need to talk to the client to get clarification, but let's implement what we can for now.

Notice that our code is able to use all of the properties—`SpeedInMilesPerHour`, `Direction`, and so on—without needing to qualify them with a variable. Whereas in Example 3-35 we had to write `someBoeing777.SpeedInMilesPerHour`, here we just write `SpeedInMilesPerHour`. Methods are meant to access and modify an object's state, and so you can refer directly to any member of the method's containing class.

There's one snag with that. It can mean that for someone reading the code, it's not always instantly obvious when the code uses a local variable or argument, and when it uses some member of the class. Our properties use PascalCasing, while we're using camelCasing for arguments and variables, which helps, but what it we wanted to access a field? Those conventionally use camelCasing too. That's why some developers put an underscore in front of their field names—it makes it more obvious when we're doing something with the object's state. But there's an alternative—a more explicit style, shown in Example 3-40.

Example 3-40. Explicit member access

```
public void UpdatePosition(double minutesToAdvance)
{
    double hours = minutesToAdvance / 60;
    double milesMoved = this.SpeedInMilesPerHour * hours;
    double milesToTower = this.Position.Distance;
    if (this.Direction == DirectionOfApproach.Approaching)
    {
        milesToTower -= milesMoved;
        if (milesToTower < 0)
        {
            // We've arrived!
            milesToTower = 0;
        }
    }
    else
    {
        milesToTower += milesMoved;
    }
    PolarPoint3D newPosition = new PolarPoint3D(
        milesToTower,
        this.Position.Angle,
        this.Position.Altitude);
}
```

This is almost the same as Example 3-39, except every member access goes through a variable called this. But we've not defined any such variable—where did that come from?

The UpdatePosition method effectively has an implied extra argument called this, and it's the object on which the method has been invoked. So, if our Main method were to call someBoeing777.UpdatePosition(10), the this variable would refer to whatever object the Main method's someBoeing777 variable referred to.

Methods get a this argument by default, but they can opt out, because sometimes it makes sense to write methods that don't apply to any particular object. The Main method of our Program class is one example—it has no this argument, because the .NET Framework doesn't presume to create an object; it just calls the method and lets us decide what objects, if any, to create. You can tell a method has no this argument because it will be marked with the static keyword—you may recall from Chapter 2 that this means the method can be run without needing an instance of its defining type.

Aside from our Main method, why might we not want a method to be associated with a particular instance? Well, one case comes to mind for our example application.

There's a rather important feature of airspace management that we're likely to need to cope with: ensuring that we don't let two planes hit each other. So, another method likely to be useful is one that allows us to check whether one plane is too close to another one, within some margin of error (say, 5,000 feet). And this method isn't associated with any single plane: it always involves two planes.

Now we could define a method on Plane that accepted another Plane as an argument, but that's a slightly misleading design—it has a lack of symmetry which suggests that the planes play different roles, because you're invoking the method on one while passing in the other as an argument. So it would make more sense to define a static method—one not directly associated with any single plane—and to have that take two Plane objects.

Declaring Static Methods

We'll add the method shown in Example 3-41 to the Plane class. Because it is marked static, it's not associated with a single Plane, and will have no implicit this argument. Instead, we pass in both of the Plane objects we want to look at as explicit arguments, to emphasize the fact that neither of the objects is in any way more significant than the other in this calculation.

Example 3-41. Detecting when Planes are too close

```
public static bool TooClose(Plane first, Plane second, double minimumMiles)
{
    double x1 = first.Position.Distance * Math.Cos(first.Position.Angle);
    double x2 = second.Position.Distance * Math.Cos(second.Position.Angle);
    double y1 = first.Position.Distance * Math.Sin(first.Position.Angle);
    double y2 = second.Position.Distance * Math.Sin(second.Position.Angle);
    double z1 = first.Position.Altitude / feetPerMile;
    double z2 = second.Position.Altitude / feetPerMile;

    double dx = x1 - x2;
    double dy = y1 - y2;
    double dz = z1 - z2;

    double distanceSquared = dx * dx + dy * dy + dz * dz;
    double minimumSquared = minimumMiles * minimumMiles;
    return distanceSquared < minimumSquared;
}
private const double feetPerMile = 5280;
```

We've seen plenty of function declarations like this before, but we'll quickly recap its anatomy. This one returns a bool to indicate whether we're safe (true) or not (false). In its parameter list, we have the references to the two Plane objects, and a double for the margin of error (in miles).

 Because there's no implicit this parameter, any attempt to use nonstatic members of the class without going through an argument or variable such as first and second in Example 3-41 will cause an error. This often catches people out when learning C#. They try adding a method to the Program class of a new program, and they forget to mark it as static (or don't realize that they need to), and then are surprised by the error they get when attempting to call it from Main. Main is a static method, and like any static method, it cannot use nonstatic members of its containing type unless you provide it with an instance.

Example 3-41 performs some calculations to work out how close the planes are. The details aren't particularly important here—we're more interested in how this uses C# methods. But just for completeness, the method converts the position into Cartesian coordinates, and then calculates the sum of the squares of the differences of the coordinates in all three dimensions, which will give us the square of the distance between the two planes. We could calculate the actual distance by taking the square root, but since we only want to know whether or not we're too close, we can just compare with the minimum distance squared. (Computers are much faster at squaring than they are at calculating square roots, so given that we could do it either way, we may as well avoid the square root.)

Static Fields and Properties

It isn't just functions that we can declare as static. Fields and properties can be static, too. In fact, we've already seen a special kind of static field—the const value we defined for the conversion between miles and kilometers. There was only one conversion factor value, however many objects we instantiated.

The only difference between a const field and a static field is that we can modify the static field. (Remember: the const field was immutable.) So, a static property or field effectively lets us get or set data associated with the class, rather than the object. No matter how many objects we create, we are always getting and setting the same value.

Let's look at a trivial illustration, shown in Example 3-42, to explore how it works, before we think about why we might want to use it.

Example 3-42. Static state

```
public class MyClassWithAStaticProperty
{
    public static bool TrueOrFalse
    {
        get;
        set;
    }

    public void SayWhetherTrueOrFalse()
```

```
        {
            Console.WriteLine("Object is {0}", TrueOrFalse);
        }
}


class Program
{
    static void Main(string[] args)
    {
        // Create two objects
        MyClassWithAStaticProperty object1 = new MyClassWithAStaticProperty();
        MyClassWithAStaticProperty object2 = new MyClassWithAStaticProperty();

        // Check how the property looks to each object,
        // and accessed through the class name


        object1.SayWhetherTrueOrFalse();
        object2.SayWhetherTrueOrFalse();
        Console.WriteLine("Class is {0}",
            MyClassWithAStaticProperty.TrueOrFalse);

        // Change the value
        MyClassWithAStaticProperty.TrueOrFalse = true;

        // And see that it has changed everywhere
        object1.SayWhetherTrueOrFalse();
        object2.SayWhetherTrueOrFalse();
        Console.WriteLine("Class is {0}",
            MyClassWithAStaticProperty.TrueOrFalse);

        Console.ReadKey();
    }
}
```

If you compile and run this code in a console application project, you'll see the following output:

```
Object is False
Object is False
Class is False
Object is True
Object is True
Class is True
```

This demonstrates that there's clearly just the one piece of information here, no matter how many different object instances we may try to look at it through. But why might we want this kind of static, class-level data storage?

The principal use for class-level data is to enforce the reality that there is *exactly one* instance of some piece of data throughout the whole system. If you think about it, that's exactly what our miles-to-kilometers value is all about—we only need one instance of that number for the whole system, so we declare it as **const** (which, as we've already seen, is like a special case of `static`). A similar pattern crops up in lots of places in the .NET Framework class library. For example, on a computer running Windows, there is a specific directory containing certain OS system files (typically *C:\Windows\system32*). The class library provides a class called `Environment` which offers, among other things, a `SystemDirectory` property that returns that location, and since there's only one such directory, this is a `static` property.

Another common use for `static` is when we want to cache information that is expensive to calculate, or which is frequently reused by lots of different objects of the same type. To get a benefit when lots of objects use the common data, it needs to be available to all instances.

Static Constructors

We can even apply the `static` keyword to a constructor. This lets us write a special constructor that only runs once for the whole class. We could add the constructor in Example 3-43 to our `Plane` class to illustrate this.

Example 3-43. Static constructor

```
static Plane()
{
    Console.WriteLine("Plane static constructor");
}
```

With this code in place, you would see the message printed out by that constructor just once at the beginning of the program—static constructors run exactly once.

> In case you're wondering, yes, `static` fields can be marked as `readonly`. And just as a normal `readonly` field can only be modified in a constructor, a `static readonly` field can only be modified in a `static` constructor.

But when exactly do static constructors run? We know when regular members get initialized and when normal constructors run—that happens when we **new** up the object. Everything gets initialized to zero, and then our constructor(s) are called to do any other initialization that we need doing. But what about static initialization?

The static constructor will run no later than the first time either of the following happens: you create an instance of the class; you use any static member of the class. There are no guarantees about the exact moment the code will run—it's possible you'll see them running earlier than you would have expected for optimization reasons.

Field initializers for static fields add some slight complication. (Remember, a field initializer is an expression that provides a default value for a field, and which appears in the field declaration itself, rather than the constructor. Example 3-44 shows some examples.) .NET initializes the statics *in the order in which they are declared*. So, if you reference one static field from the initializer for another static field in the same class, you need to be careful, or you can get errors at runtime. Example 3-44 illustrates how this can go wrong. (Also, the .NET Framework is somewhat noncommittal about exactly when field initializers will run—in theory it has more freedom than with a static constructor, and could run them either later or earlier than you might expect, although in practice, it's not something you'd normally need to worry about unless you're writing multithreaded code that depends on the order in which static initialization occurs.)

Example 3-44. Unwise ordering of static field initializers

```
class Bar
{
    public bool myField;
}

// Bad - null reference exception on construction
class Foo
{
    public static bool field2 = field1.myField;
    public static Bar field1 = new Bar();
}

// OK - initialized in the right order
class Foo
{
    public static Bar field1 = new Bar();
    public static bool field2 = field1.myField;
}
```

Summary

We saw how to define *classes* from which we can create instances called *objects*, and that this can be useful when attempting to model real-world entities. We can also define *value types*, using the `struct` keyword, and the main difference is that when we assign variables or pass arguments, value types always copy the whole value, whereas ordinary classes (which are reference types) only copy a reference to the underlying object. We also saw a simpler kind of type: `enum`. This lets us define named sets of constant values, and is useful when we need a value representing a choice from a fixed set of options.

So, now we know how to abstract basic ideas of information storage (through fields and simple properties) and manipulation (through functions and calculated properties), using classes and objects. In the next chapter, we're going to look at how we can extend these ideas further using a concept called *polymorphism* to model a hierarchy of related classes that can extend or refine some basic contract.

CHAPTER 4

Extensibility and Polymorphism

In the previous chapter, we saw how to define various types of classes and specify their members—fields, properties, and functions.

In this chapter, we're going to start by looking at this again in more detail, and try to understand what underlying concepts we're implementing when we use these different coding patterns. We'll then introduce a couple of new concepts—inheritance and polymorphism and the language features that help us implement them.

We've finished our ATC application, by the way. Having gotten a reputation for building robust mission-critical software on time and to spec, we've now been retained by the fire department to produce a training and simulation system for them. Example 4-1 shows what we have so far.

Example 4-1. Classes representing firefighters and fire trucks

```
class Firefighter
{
    public string Name { get; set; }

    public void ExtinguishFire()
    {
        Console.WriteLine("{0} is putting out the fire!", Name);
    }

    public void Drive(Firetruck truckToDrive, Point coordinates)
    {
        if (truckToDrive.Driver != this)
        {
            // We can't drive the truck if we're not the driver
            // But just silently failing is BADBAD
            // What we need is some kind of structured means
            // of telling the client about the failure
            // We'll get to that in Chapter 6
            return;
        }
        truckToDrive.Drive(coordinates);
    }
```

```
}
class Firetruck
{
    public Firefighter Driver { get; set; }
    public void Drive(Point coordinates)
    {
        if (Driver == null)
        {
            // We can't drive if there's no driver
            return;
        }

        Console.WriteLine("Driving to {0}", coordinates);
    }
}
```

We have a model of the Firetruck, which uses a Firefighter as its Driver. The truck can be instructed to drive somewhere (if it has a driver), and you can tell a Firefighter to drive the truck somewhere (if he is the designated driver).

You can think of this as modeling a relationship between a Firetruck and its Driver. That driver has to be a Firefighter. In object-oriented design, we call this relationship between classes an *association*.

Association Through Composition and Aggregation

An *association* is a kind of flexible, "arms length" relationship between two entities in the system. There are no particular constraints about the direction of the relationship: the firefighter can be associated with the truck, or the truck with the firefighter. Or both.

Any particular firefighter may have associations with other types, and we can always assign another driver to the fire truck; there's no exclusivity. For instance, we can do something like this:

```
Firetruck truckOne = new Firetruck();
Firefighter joe = new Firefighter { Name  = "Joe" };
Firefighter frank = new Firefighter { Name = "Frank" };

truckOne.Driver = joe;
// Later...
truckOne.Driver = frank;
```

But what about the 30 foot retractable ladder that we happen to have on the fire truck; what kind of relationship exists between the ladder and the fire truck?

Here's our ladder class:

```
class Ladder
{
    public double Length { get; set; }
}
```

This particular ladder is one of those powered, extensible rotating things that are built right into the truck. So let's add a property to represent that (see Example 4-2).

Example 4-2. Fire truck with integral ladder

```
class Firetruck
{
    public Firefighter Driver { get; set; }

    readonly Ladder ladder = new Ladder { Length = 30.0 };
    public Ladder Ladder
    {
        get
        {
            return ladder;
        }
    }

    // ...
}
```

When we construct the Truck, it creates a 30-foot ladder for itself, with a read-only property to retrieve it.

We call this "made of" association between classes *composition*. The ladder is a built-in part of the fire truck, but the fire truck can never be a part of the ladder, and the truck itself is responsible for the life cycle of its own ladder.

What if we need to manage other equipment on the truck—a detachable coil of hose, for example:

```
class Hose
{
}
```

We could add a property to the Truck to get and set that (modeling a particular coil of hose being connected to the hose system on the truck):

```
public Hose Hose
{
    get;
    set;
}
```

This is another kind of composition relationship—one component of the Truck is a hose, and the truck certainly can't be a part of the hose; but the containing object (the truck) no longer controls the creation and lifetime of its own piece of apparatus. Instead, we say that it *aggregates* the hose.

Of course, there are no hard-and-fast rules about these terms and the code you write; they are just concepts which we use when we are designing systems. The definitions we've used come from the Unified Modeling Language (UML) 2.0, and we're just mapping them to C# language features.

Nonetheless, it is useful to have a common conceptual language for describing our systems and the common characteristics of the code we use to implement them. Equally, when you are looking at someone else's code (remembering that "someone else" includes "past you") it is helpful to be able to translate what was written into these standard modeling concepts.

So we have a software model of the Firetruck, which has a Ladder and a Hose and uses a Firefighter as its Driver. What about the fire chief?

The fire chief is just another firefighter. He can drive a truck. He can put out fires. But he can do other stuff too. For instance, he can delegate responsibility for putting out a fire to another firefighter.

The question we ask ourselves is this: is the FireChief a Firefighter with extra responsibilities? If the answer is yes, we are describing an *is-a* association (the FireChief *is a* Firefighter) which we can represent by an *inheritance* relationship.

Inheritance and Polymorphism

We'll get into the nuances of the question in the preceding paragraph in a minute, but let's assume for the time being that our answer to the question is yes (which, on face value, seems reasonable). Example 4-3 shows how we use inheritance in C#.

Example 4-3. Inheritance in C#

```
class FireChief : Firefighter
{
    public void TellFirefighterToExtinguishFire (Firefighter colleague)
    {
        colleague.ExtinguishFire();
    }
}
```

Notice that we use the colon in the class declaration to indicate that FireChief is a Firefighter. We then say that Firefighter is a *base class* of FireChief. Looking at the relationship from the other direction, we can also say that FireChief is a *derived class* of Firefighter.

We've added the extra function that allows the chief to tell a firefighter to extinguish a fire—which encapsulates that extra responsibility. What we *haven't* had to do is to duplicate all the functionality of the firefighter; that comes along anyway.

We can now use the fire chief just as we would a firefighter, as shown in Example 4-4.

Example 4-4. Using base class functionality inherited by a derived class

```
Firetruck truckOne = new Firetruck();
FireChief bigChiefHarry = new FireChief { Name  = "Harry" };

truckOne.Driver = bigChiefHarry;
bigChiefHarry.Drive(truckOne, new Point(100,300));
```

```
Firefighter joe = new Firefighter { Name = "Joe" };

bigChiefHarry.TellFirefighterToExtinguishFire(joe);
```

Because `bigChiefHarry` is an object of type `FireChief`, and a `FireChief` is a `Fire fighter`, we can assign him to be the driver of a truck and tell him to drive it somewhere. But because he is a `FireChief`, we can also ask him to tell Joe to put out the fire when he gets there.

Wherever we talk about a `FireChief`, we can treat the object as a `Firefighter`. This use of one type as though it were one of its bases is an example of *polymorphism*.

Equally, we could phrase that the other way around: we can successfully substitute an instance of a more-derived class where we expect a base class. This is known as the *Liskov Substitution Principle* (LSP) after computer scientist Barbara Liskov, who articulated the idea in a paper she delivered in 1987.

It is quite possible to derive one class from another in a way that means we *can't* treat the derived class as its base type. The derived class could change the meaning or behavior of a function with the same signature as its base, or throw errors in situations where the base promised that everything would be fine—say, the base accepted parameters in the range 1–10, where the derived class accepts parameters in the range 2–5.

This violates the LSP, which is a very poor design practice, but it is very easy to slip into, especially if the classes evolve independently over time.

What happens if our client doesn't know that Harry is a fire chief, though? What if we refer to the object via a reference typed to `Firefighter` instead?

```
FireChief bigChiefHarry = new FireChief { Name  = "Harry" };
// Another reference to Harry, but as a firefighter
Firefighter stillHarry = bigChiefHarry;

Firefighter joe = new Firefighter { Name = "Joe" };

stillHarry.TellFirefighterToExtinguishFire(joe);
```

You know that `stillHarry` is referencing an object that is a `FireChief`, with that extra method on it. But the compiler produces a long, semicomprehensible error full of useful suggestions if you try to compile and execute this code:

```
'Firefighter' does not contain a definition for
 'TellFirefighterToExtinguishFire' and no extension method
 'TellFirefighterToExtinguishFire' accepting a first argument of type
 'Firefighter' could be found (are you missing a using directive or an
 assembly reference?)
```

The compiler is being rather tactful. It is assuming that you must've forgotten to include some external reference that's got a suitable extension method definition to fix your problem. (We'll be looking at that technique in a later chapter, by the way.)

Unfortunately, the real reason for our bug is hidden in the error's opening salvo: we're trying to talk to a FireChief method through a *variable* that is strongly typed to be a Firefighter, and you can't call on any members of the derived class through a reference typed to a base.

So, if we can't use a derived member from a reference to a base type, is there any way we can refine these classes so that Harry never puts out a fire, but always passes responsibility to his Number One when he's asked to do so, regardless of whether we happen to know that he's a FireChief? After all, *he knows* that he's the boss!

To get started, we'll have to make a few changes to the model to accommodate this idea of the chief's Number One. In other words, we need to create an *association* between the FireChief and his NumberOne. Remember that we typically implement this as a read/write property, which we can add to the FireChief:

```
public Firefighter NumberOne
{
    get;
    set;
}
```

And let's change the main function so that it does what we want (see Example 4-5).

Example 4-5. Using base class methods to keep the compiler happy

```
// A reference to Joe, Harry's number one
Firefighter joe = new Firefighter { Name = "Joe" };

// Firefighter harry is really a firechief, with joe as his NumberOne
Firefighter harry = new FireChief { Name  = "Harry", NumberOne = joe };

// Harry is just a firefighter, so he can extinguish fires
// but we want him to get joe to do the work
harry.ExtinguishFire();
```

But if we compile that, here's the output we get:

```
Harry is putting out the fire!
```

That's not what we want at all. What we want is a different implementation for that ExtinguishFire method if we're *actually* a FireChief, rather than an ordinary Firefighter.

Replacing Methods in Derived Classes

So the implementation for the `ExtinguishFire` method that we want on the `FireChief` looks like this:

```
public void ExtinguishFire()
{
    // Get our number one to put out the fire instead
    TellFirefighterToExtinguishFire(NumberOne);
}
```

What happens if we just add that function to our `FireChief` and compile and run?

Well, it compiles, but when we run it, it still says:

```
Harry is putting out the fire!
```

It seems to have completely ignored our new function!

Let's go back and have a look at that compiler output again. You'll see that although it built and ran, there's a warning (you may have to rebuild to get it to appear again; Choose Rebuild Solution from the Build menu):

```
'FireChief.ExtinguishFire()' hides inherited member
 'Firefighter.ExtinguishFire()'. Use the new keyword if hiding was intended.
```

 It is a good idea to leave all your compiler warnings on and work until you are both error *and* warning free. That way, when something crops up unexpectedly like this, you can spot it easily, rather than burying it in a pile of stuff you're habitually ignoring.

It is telling us that, rather than *replacing* the implementation on the base class, our method (with matching signature) is *hiding* it; and that if this is what we really meant to do, we should add the keyword new to the method.

Hiding Base Members with new

OK, let's do that:

```
public new void ExtinguishFire()
{
    // Get our number one to put out the fire instead
    TellFirefighterToExtinguishFire(NumberOne);
}
```

We typically add the new modifier between the accessibility modifier and the return value.

Compile and run again. You'll notice that we've gotten rid of the warning, but the output hasn't changed:

```
Harry is putting out the fire!
```

What's going on?

This method-hiding approach is actually letting a single object provide different implementations for the ExtinguishFire method. The implementation we get is based on the type of the variable we use, rather than the type of object to which the variable refers. You can see that happening if we use the code in Example 4-6 in our client.

Example 4-6. Different reference type, different method

```
// A reference to Joe, Harry's number one
Firefighter joe = new Firefighter { Name = "Joe" };

// Firefighter harry is really a firechief, with joe as his NumberOne
FireChief harry = new FireChief { Name  = "Harry", NumberOne = joe };
Firefighter harryAsAFirefighter = harry;

// Harry is just a firefighter, so he can extinguish fires
// but as a firechief he gets joe to do the work
harry.ExtinguishFire();
// While as a firefighter he does it himself
harryAsAFirefighter.ExtinguishFire();
```

The output we get now looks like this:

```
Joe is putting out the fire!
Harry is putting out the fire!
```

When we talk to our Harry object through a FireChief reference, he gets Joe to put out the fire. If we talk to the object through a Firefighter reference, he does it himself. Same object, but two completely different implementations.

Why might we want to do that?

Let's say we had multiple fire chiefs on a job, but it is our policy that a chief acting as another chief's Number One is not allowed to delegate the job again. Our code models exactly this behavior, as shown in Example 4-7.

 Of course, whether that's *desirable* behavior is another matter entirely— we've ended up with such radically different approaches to putting out a fire that it might be better to separate them back out into functions with different names.

When you go through a refactoring process such as this, it is a good idea to check that you're still happy with the semantic implications of your code. Ideally, you want to end up with a neat design, but a superficially neat design that makes no sense is not helpful.

Example 4-7. Making twisted use of method hiding

```
// A reference to Joe, Harry's number one
Firefighter joe = new Firefighter { Name = "Joe" };

// FireChief harry has joe as his NumberOne
FireChief harry = new FireChief { Name  = "Harry", NumberOne = joe };
FireChief tom = new FireChief { Name = "Tom", NumberOne = harry };

// Harry is just a firefighter, so he can extinguish fires
// but as a firechief he gets joe to do the work
harry.ExtinguishFire();

// But if Tom is asked to extinguish a fire, he asks Harry to do it
// Our policy dictates that Harry has to do it himself, not delegate to
// Joe this time.
tom.ExtinguishFire();
```

Harry delegates to Joe when he is asked to do it himself, because we are calling through a reference to a `FireChief`.

Tom is also a `FireChief`, and we are calling through a reference to him as a `FireChief`, so he delegates to Harry; but when Harry is asked to do it in his role as a `Firefighter` (remember, the `NumberOne` property is a reference to a `Firefighter`), he does it himself, because we are now calling the method through that reference typed to `Firefighter`.

So our output looks like this:

```
Joe is putting out the fire!
Harry is putting out the fire!
```

That's all very well, but we don't actually want that restriction—the fire chief should be allowed to pass the work off to his subordinate as often as he likes, regardless of who he asked to do it.

There's one big caveat regarding everything we've just shown about method hiding: I can't think of the last time I used this *feature* in a real application, but I see the *warning* from time to time and it usually alerts me to a mistake in my code.

We've wanted to illustrate how method hiding works, but we discourage you from using it. The main reason to avoid method hiding with new is that it tends to surprise your clients, and that, as we've established, is not a good thing. (Would you really expect behavior to change because the type of the variable, not the underlying object, changes?)

While method hiding is absolutely necessary for some corner cases, we usually treat this warning as an error, and think very carefully about what we're doing if it comes up. 9 times out of 10, we've got an inadvertent clash of names.

Replacing Methods with virtual and override

What we actually want to do is to change the implementation based on the type of the object itself, not the variable we're using to get at it. To do that we need to replace or *override* the default implementation in our base class with the one in our derived class. A quick glance at the C# spec shows us that there is a keyword to let us do just that: override.

Let's switch to the override modifier on the FireChief implementation of the ExtinguishFire() method:

```
public override void ExtinguishFire()
{
    // Get our number one to put out the fire instead
    TellFirefighterToExtinguishFire(NumberOne);
}
```

Notice that we removed the new modifier and replaced it with override instead. But if you compile, you'll see that we're not quite done (i.e., we get a compiler error):

```
'FireChief.ExtinguishFire()': cannot override inherited member
'Firefighter.ExtinguishFire()' because it is not marked virtual, abstract,
or override
```

We're not allowed to override the method with our own implementation because *our base class has to say we're allowed to do so*. Fortunately, we wrote the base class, so we can do that (as the compiler error suggests) by marking the method in the base with the virtual modifier:

```
class Firefighter
{
    public virtual void ExtinguishFire()
    {
        Console.WriteLine("{0} is putting out the fire!", Name);
    }

    // ...
}
```

Why do we have this base-classes-opt-in system? Why is everything not virtual by default (like, say, Java)? Arguments continue on this very issue, but the designers of C# chose to go with the nonvirtual-by-default option. There are a couple of reasons for this: one has to do with implicit contracts, and another is related to versioning.

 There is also (potentially) a small performance overhead for virtual function dispatch, but this is negligible in most real-world scenarios. As always, test before optimizing for this!

We already saw how our public API is effectively a contract with our clients. With virtual functions, though, we are defining not only a contract for the caller, as usual, but also a contract for anyone who might choose to override that method. That requires more documentation, and a greater degree of control over *how* you implement the method.

 By declaring a method as virtual, the base class gives derived classes permission to replace whole pieces of its own innards. That's a very powerful but very dangerous technique, rather like organ transplant surgery on an animal you've never seen before. Even a trained surgeon might balk at replacing the kidneys of a dromedary armed with nothing more than developer-quality documentation about the process.

For example, some method in your base class calls its MethodA, then its MethodB, to do some work. You then (perhaps unknowingly) rely on that ordering when you provide overrides for MethodA and MethodB. If a future version of the base class changes that ordering, you will break.

Let's go back to our example to look at that in more detail, because it is really important.

First, let's change the implementation of Firefighter.ExtinguishFire so that it makes use of a couple of helper methods: TurnOnHose and TrainHoseOnFire (see Example 4-8).

Example 4-8. Virtual methods and method ordering

```
class Firefighter
{
    // This calls TrainHoseOnFire and TurnOnHose as part of the
    // process for extinguishing the fire
    public virtual void ExtinguishFire()
    {
        Console.WriteLine("{0} is putting out the fire!", Name);
         TrainHoseOnFire();
         TurnOnHose();
    }

    private void TurnOnHose()
    {
        Console.WriteLine("The fire is going out.");
    }

    private void TrainHoseOnFire()
    {
        Console.WriteLine("Training the hose on the fire.");
    }

    // ...
}
```

Let's also simplify our `Main` function so that we can see what is going on, as shown in Example 4-9.

Example 4-9. Calling a virtual method

```
static void Main(string[] args)
{
    // A reference to Joe, Harry's number one
    Firefighter joe = new Firefighter { Name = "Joe" };
    joe.ExtinguishFire();

    Console.ReadKey();
}
```

If we compile and run, we'll see the following output:

```
Joe is putting out the fire!
Training the hose on the fire.
The fire is going out.
```

All is well so far, but what happens if we add a trainee firefighter into the mix? The trainee is extremely fastidious and follows his instructor's guidelines to the letter. We're going to make a class for him and override the `TurnOnHose` and `TrainHoseOnFire` methods so that the work is done in the trainee's own particular idiom.

Hang on a moment, though! Our helper methods are `private` members. We can't get at them, except from other members of our `Firefighter` class itself.

Before we can do anything, we need to make them accessible to derived classes.

Inheritance and Protection

In the preceding chapter, we mentioned that there were two additional accessibility modifiers that we would deal with later: `protected` and `protected internal`. Well, this is where they come into their own. They make members accessible to derived classes.

If you want a member to be available *either* to derived classes *or* to other classes in your own assembly, you mark that member `protected internal`. It will be visible to other classes in the library, or to clients that derive classes from your base, but inaccessible to other clients who just reference your assembly.

If, on the other hand, you want your class to make certain methods available only to derived classes, you just mark those methods `protected`. In terms of code out there in the wild, this is the most common usage, but it is not necessarily the best one!

 Both `protected internal` and `internal` are much underused access modifiers. They are a very convenient way of hiding away library implementation details from your consumers, and reducing the amount of documentation and surface-area testing you need.

I suspect that they are unpopular (as with most "hidden by default" or "secure by default" schemes) because they can sometimes get in your way. There are a fair number of implementation details of classes in the .NET Framework that are `internal` (or `private`) that people would very much like to access, for example.

A common reason for taking something useful and applying the `internal` modifier is that it was not possible to fully document (or understand the full implications of) the "hook" this would provide into the framework. And rather than open up potential security or reliability problems, they are marked `internal` until a later date: perhaps much, much later, tending toward never. Although there is an intention to revisit these things, real-world pressures mean that they often remain unchanged.

This is another example of the "lock down by default" strategy which helps improve software quality.

That doesn't make it any less irritating when you can't get at the inner workings, though!

So we'll mark those methods in the base class `virtual` and `protected`, as shown in Example 4-10.

Example 4-10. Opening methods up to derived classes

```
protected virtual void TurnOnHose()
{
    Console.WriteLine("The fire is going out.");
}

protected virtual void TrainHoseOnFire()
{
    Console.WriteLine("Training the hose on the fire.");
}
```

We can now create our `TraineeFirefighter` class (see Example 4-11).

Example 4-11. Overriding the newly accessible methods

```
class TraineeFirefighter : Firefighter
{
    private bool hoseTrainedOnFire;
    protected override void TurnOnHose()
    {
        if (hoseTrainedOnFire)
        {
            Console.WriteLine("The fire is going out.");
        }
```

```
        else
        {
            Console.WriteLine("There's water going everywhere!");
        }
    }

    protected override void TrainHoseOnFire()
    {
        hoseTrainedOnFire = true;
        Console.WriteLine("Training the hose on the fire.");
    }
}
```

As you can see, the trainee is derived from `Firefighter`. We added an extra Boolean field to keep track of whether the trainee has actually trained the hose on the fire, and then provided our own implementations of `TrainHoseOnFire` and `TurnOnHose` that make use of that extra field. This is intended to model the detailed but slightly peculiar and occasionally erratic way in which the trainee follows the instructions for these operations in his copy of *How to Be a Firefighter*, rather than allowing common sense to prevail.

We also need a quick update to our main function to use our trainee. Let's add the following code at the end:

```
// A reference to Bill, the trainee
Firefighter bill = new TraineeFirefighter { Name = "Bill" };
bill.ExtinguishFire();
```

If we compile and run, we see the following output:

```
Joe is putting out the fire!
Training the hose on the fire.
The fire is going out.

Bill is putting out the fire!
Training the hose on the fire.
The fire is going out.
```

Well done, Bill; all that training came in handy, exactly as we'd expect.

Although it works, you'll notice that we've duplicated some code from our base class into our derived class—the bit that actually does the work in each of those methods. It would be better if we could just call on our base class implementation to do the job for us. As you'd expect, C# has this in hand, with the **base** keyword.

Calling Base Class Methods

If we ever want to call on the implementation of a member in our base class (bypassing any of our own overrides), we can do so through the special **base** name:

```
base.CallOnTheBase();
```

Using that, we can reimplement our `TraineeFirefighter` and remove that duplicate code, as shown in Example 4-12.

Example 4-12. Avoiding duplication by calling the base class

```
class TraineeFirefighter : Firefighter
{
    private bool hoseTrainedOnFire;
    protected override void TurnOnHose()
    {
        if (hoseTrainedOnFire)
        {
            // Call on the base implementation
            base.TurnOnHose();
        }
        else
        {
            Console.WriteLine("There's water going everywhere!");
        }
    }

    protected override void TrainHoseOnFire()
    {
        hoseTrainedOnFire = true;
        base.TrainHoseOnFire();
    }
}
```

So, what happens if in a later version we change the implementation of the `Extinguish Fire` method on the base class? Maybe we found an optimization that means it is faster to implement it like this:

```
public virtual void ExtinguishFire()
{
    Console.WriteLine("{0} is putting out the fire!", Name);
    // We've swapped these around
    TurnOnHose();
    TrainHoseOnFire();
}
```

Let's imagine that this `Firefighter` class is being implemented by one of our colleagues. She tested the new implementation against her `Firefighter` unit test suite, exactly as required, and everything passed just fine—fires were extinguished. Then she handed it over to us to use (with our new `TraineeFirefighter` class that we're working on).

If we compile and run, we get the following output:

```
Joe is putting out the fire!
Training the hose on the fire.
The fire is going out.

Bill is putting out the fire!
There's water going everywhere!
Training the hose on the fire.
```

So the `Firefighter` code works fine, just as our colleague promised; but our `Trainee` `Firefighter` has made a bit of a mess. This is a shame, as he has not done anything different—we didn't change a single line of our `TraineeFirefighter` code that was working just a moment earlier.

The problem is that, while our documentation for `ExtinguishFire` told us that it would call both of those `virtual` methods it didn't promise to do so in any particular order. And there was no documentation at all on our `protected virtual` methods to tell us *how* we should override them, or whether there were any particular constraints or invariants we should maintain.

 This is a very common combination of problems when designing an inheritance hierarchy—poor documentation on the base class, and insufficiently defensive implementations in a derived class. Creating a class hierarchy is not an easy thing to do. And this is when we're only making selected methods `virtual`—imagine the chaos if all methods were `virtual` by default!

In the next chapter, we're going to look at some alternative ways to vary behavior that are more easily documented and potentially more robust than deriving from a base class.

That's not to say that you shouldn't make use of such a powerful concept as polymorphism; it is just that you should take care when you do so.

Let's just recap the implications of all that, as it is a bit complicated.

Back in Chapter 3, when we designed our first class, we talked about its public contract, and how that encapsulated the implementation details which allowed us to use it as though it was a black box.

With the addition of `public` and `protected virtual` members, we're opening that black box and creating a second contract: for people who derive their own classes, which, as we just saw, is a whole lot more complex.

The designers of C# decided that should be an opt-in complexity: unless we specify that a member is `virtual` we don't have to worry about it. Along the same lines, they've also provided a way to ensure that we don't have to worry about anyone deriving from us at all.

Thus Far and No Farther: sealed

Having got through all of that, you're probably rightly concerned that, simple though it is in theory, the practical implications of inheritance are actually rather complex and require a lot of documentation, testing, and imagining how people might use and abuse your virtual methods. And we have to do that for every class down the hierarchy.

When we designed our FireChief, we happily provided an override for the Extinguish Fire method, without giving a thought for the fact that *someone else might override that method in his own derived class*. In fact, we didn't even consider the possibility that anyone might derive from FireChief at all. No documentation, nothing.

Now there are several members on our own base class that could be overridden by a class that derives from FireChief. Does that have any implications for our own documentation or testing? Can we even tell? And how could we have guessed that was going to happen when we built our FireChief class, since there was only one virtual member on the base at that time? This looks like it has the potential to become a rich future source of bugs and security holes.

Fortunately, we can eliminate this problem at a stroke by saying that we *didn't* design our FireChief to be derived from, and stopping anyone from doing so. We do that by marking the FireChief class sealed. Let's see how that looks:

```
sealed class FireChief : Firefighter
{
    // ...
}
```

We apply the sealed modifier before the class keyword and after any accessibility modifiers if they are present.

So, what happens if we try to derive a new class from FireChief now?

```
class MasterChief : FireChief
{
}
```

Compile it, and you'll see the following error:

```
'MasterChief': cannot derive from sealed type 'FireChief'
```

That's put a stop to that. Let's delete our MasterChief so that everything builds again.

 Not only can sealing classes be very useful (and defensive), but if you decide later that you want to unseal the class and allow people to derive their own types, it doesn't (normally) break binary compatibility for the type. Sealing a previously unsealed class, however, does break compatibility.

We now have three different types of firefighter. Let's remind ourselves how they are related (see Figure 4-1).

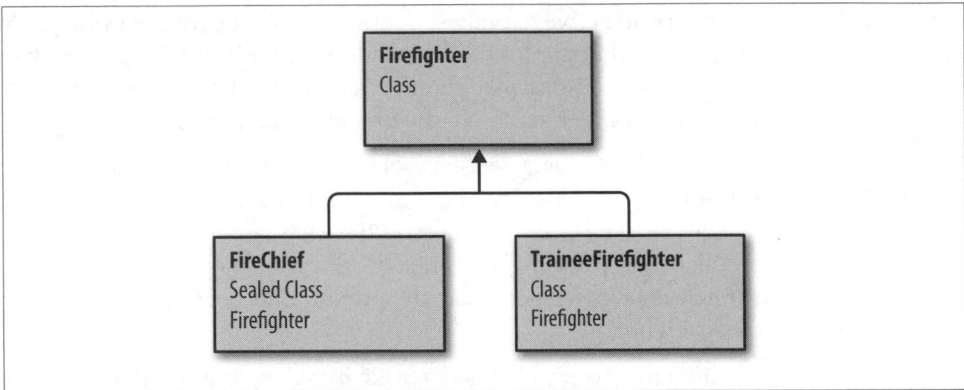

Figure 4-1. Three types of firefighter

Nonvirtual by Default, but Not sealed?

Why, you may ask, if we are nonvirtual by default aren't we also sealed by default, with an "unseal" keyword?

Notice, for instance, that we've been talking about classes so far—value types (`struct`) are sealed (with no opt-out), so you can't derive from them.

There's no performance hit to marking a class sealed. There are potential security advantages to marking a class sealed (no one can sneakily exploit polymorphism to insert code where you weren't expecting it). So why not make them all sealed?

It is certainly much less problematic to present an unsealed class than it is to present a virtual method; if there are no virtual methods, all you can do is to bolt extra bits on, which do no harm to anyone. It also conforms to the expectations of a generation of C++ and Java developers in this regard.

Plenty of people argue that we should have both unsealed-by-default *and* virtual-by-default, and they certainly have a point, particularly with regard to convenience; but the designers of C# took a different view. No doubt, the debate will continue.

Those three types of firefighter basically differ in the strategy that they use for putting out fires. There's a base class that provides a default implementation, and a couple of classes that override the virtual methods to do things differently.

Let's say we wanted to support lots of different types of firefighter, all of whom were expected to have a different approach to fighting fire, from the trainee, to the chief, to Gulliver (who has his own idiosyncratic way of putting out a fire in Lilliput).

We still want the handy `Name` property and the `Drive` method, and we still want anyone to be able to call an `ExtinguishFire` method.

Noticing that our `FireChief`, for example, doesn't make use of the base implementation at all; we don't want to provide a standard for that method. We'll just let all implementers decide for themselves how it is going to work.

We're shooting for something that looks like Figure 4-2.

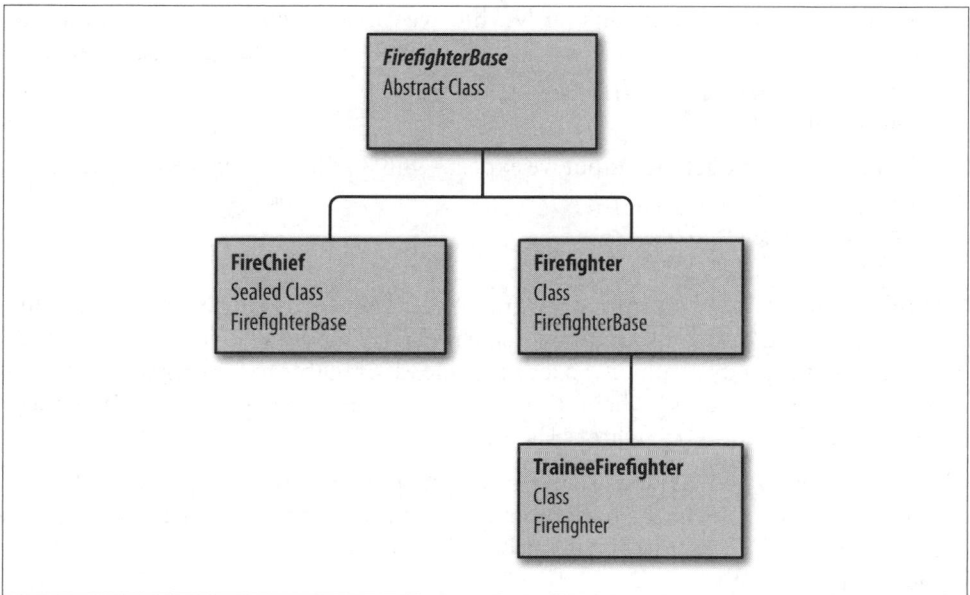

Figure 4-2. Abstract base classes

Requiring Overrides with abstract

An abstract base class is intended to provide the "scaffolding" for a hierarchy of related classes, but it is not intended to be instantiated itself, because it isn't "finished." It *requires* that classes derived from it add in some missing bits.

Let's turn our current firefighter into an abstract base for the others to use, and see how that works.

First, we can add the `abstract` modifier to the class itself, and see what happens:

```
abstract class Firefighter
{
    // ...
}
```

As usual, we add the modifier before the `class` keyword (and after any accessibility modifiers, if present).

If we build, we now get a compiler error:

```
Cannot create an instance of the abstract class or interface 'Firefighter'
```

That's because we're trying to create an instance of the `Firefighter` in our main function:

```
Firefighter joe = new Firefighter { Name = "Joe" };
```

This is no longer allowed, because the `Firefighter` class is now abstract.

OK, we'll comment that out temporarily while we carry on refactoring. We want it to continue to build as we go so that we can see if we've introduced any other errors:

```
//Firefighter joe = new Firefighter { Name = "Joe" };
//joe.ExtinguishFire;
```

Build and run, and we get the output we expect—Bill is still spraying the water around:

```
Bill is putting out the fire!
There's water going everywhere!
Training the hose on the fire.
```

One other thing: if we're creating an abstract base class, we usually name it something such as `FooBase` to distinguish it from a regular class. This is by no means a hard-and-fast rule, but it is pretty common. So let's rename `Firefighter` to `FirefighterBase`, and make sure we change it where it is referenced elsewhere—on the `Firetruck`, `FireChief`, and `TraineeFirefighter` classes.

The easiest way to do that is to use the automatic rename refactoring in the IDE. Just type over the old name in the declaration, click on the Smart Tag that appears, and choose Rename Firefighter to FirefighterBase from the menu. You could do it by hand if you wanted, though.

The whole purpose of this was to get rid of the default implementation we have for putting out fires, so let's turn `Firefighterbase.ExtinguishFire` into an *abstract method*.

Just like the modifier for the class, we use the **abstract** keyword, but this time we also remove the method body and add a semicolon at the end of the declaration:

```
abstract class FirefighterBase
{
    public abstract void ExtinguishFire();
}
```

If you try building again now, you can see that we have a new compiler error:

```
'TraineeFirefighter' does not implement inherited abstract member
'FirefighterBase.ExtinguishFire()'
```

Remember, we are *required* to override an **abstract** method; our class isn't finished until we do so (unlike a **virtual** method, where we are invited to override it, but it will fall back on the base if we don't). While our `FireChief` does override the method, our `TraineeFirefighter` doesn't. So we need to add a suitable implementation:

```
class TraineeFirefighter : FirefighterBase
{
    // Override the abstract method
    public override void ExtinguishFire()
```

```
    {
        // What are we going to put here?
    }
    // ...
}
```

But what are we going to put into that `ExtinguishFire` override? Before, we depended on our base class for the implementation, but our base is now abstract, so we don't have one available anymore!

That's because we've forgotten about our regular `Firefighter`. Let's add a class for him back into the hierarchy:

```
class Firefighter : FirefighterBase
{
    public override void ExtinguishFire()
    {
        Console.WriteLine("{0} is putting out the fire!", Name);
        TurnOnHose();
        TrainHoseOnFire();
    }
}
```

Notice we've given him the "standard firefighter" implementation for `ExtinguishFire`.

If we take one more look at the base class, we can see that we still have those two **virtual** implementation helpers. While everything builds correctly at the moment, they don't really belong there; they are really a part of the `Firefighter` implementation, so let's move them in there. We end up with the code in Example 4-13.

Example 4-13. Refactored base classes

```
abstract class FirefighterBase
{
    public abstract void ExtinguishFire();

    public string Name { get; set; }

    public void Drive(Firetruck truckToDrive, Point coordinates)
    {
        if (truckToDrive.Driver != this)
        {
            // We can't drive the truck if we're not the driver
            return;
        }
        truckToDrive.Drive(coordinates);
    }
}

class Firefighter : FirefighterBase
{
    public override void ExtinguishFire()
    {
        Console.WriteLine("{0} is putting out the fire!", Name);
        TrainHoseOnFire();
```

```
        TurnOnHose();
    }

    protected virtual void TurnOnHose()
    {
        Console.WriteLine("The fire is going out.");
    }

    protected virtual void TrainHoseOnFire()
    {
        Console.WriteLine("Training the hose on the fire.");
    }
}
```

But we're still not quite done! If you build this you'll see another compiler error:

```
'TraineeFirefighter.TurnOnHose()': no suitable method found to override
'TraineeFirefighter.TrainHoseOnFire()': no suitable method found to override
```

Our trainee firefighter really is a kind of firefighter, and depends on those two **virtual** functions we just moved. The error message is telling us that we can't override a method that isn't actually present in the base.

We need to change its base class from `FirefighterBase` to `Firefighter`. This has the advantage that we can also get rid of its duplicate override of the `ExtingushFire` method (see Example 4-14).

Example 4-14. Using the newly refactored base classes

```
class TraineeFirefighter : Firefighter
{
    protected override void TurnOnHose()
    {
        if (hoseTrainedOnFire)
        {
            Console.WriteLine("The fire is going out.");
        }
        else
        {
            Console.WriteLine("There's water going everywhere!");
        }
    }

    private bool hoseTrainedOnFire;
    protected override void TrainHoseOnFire()
    {
        hoseTrainedOnFire = true;
        Console.WriteLine("Training the hose on the fire.");
    }
}
```

We also need to uncomment our two lines about Joe in the `Main` function—everything should work again:

```
Firefighter joe = new Firefighter { Name = "Joe" };
joe.ExtinguishFire();
```

We can build and run to check that. We get the expected output:

```
Joe is putting out the fire!
Training the hose on the fire.
The fire is going out.

Bill is putting out the fire!
There's water going everywhere!
Training the hose on the fire.
```

Let's remind ourselves of the current class hierarchy (see Figure 4-2). Our `FireChief` is no longer an "ordinary" `Firefighter`, with an override for putting out fires, but he does take advantage of our common scaffolding for "firefighters in general" that we modeled as an abstract base class called `FirefighterBase`. Our `Firefighter` also takes advantage of that same scaffolding, but our `TraineeFirefighter` really is a `Firefighter`—just with its own idiosyncratic way of doing some of the internal methods that `Firefighter` uses to get the job done.

Back to the requirements for our fire department application: let's say we want to keep track of who is actually in the fire station at any particular time, just in case there is a fire on the premises and we can take a roll call (health and safety is very important, especially in a fire station).

There are two types of folks in the fire station: the firefighters and the administrators. Example 4-15 shows our new `Administrator` class.

Example 4-15. A class representing administrative staff

```
class Administrator
{
    public string Title { get; set; }
    public string Forename { get; set; }
    public string Surname { get; set; }
    public string Name
    {
        get
        {
            StringBuilder name = new StringBuilder();
            AppendWithSpace(name, Title);
            AppendWithSpace(name, Forename);
            AppendWithSpace(name, Surname);
            return name.ToString();
        }
    }

    void AppendWithSpace(StringBuilder builder, string stringToAppend)
    {
        // Don't do anything if the string is empty
```

```
        if (string.IsNullOrEmpty(stringToAppend))
        {
            return;
        }

        // Add a space if we've got any text already
        if (builder.Length > 0)
        {
            builder.Append(" ");
        }
        builder.Append(stringToAppend);
    }
}
```

If you look at our `Firefighter` class, it had a single `string` property for a `Name`. With the `Administrator`, you can independently get and set the `Title`, `Forename`, and `Surname`. We then provided a special read-only property that returns a single formatted string for the whole `Name`. It uses a framework class called `StringBuilder` to assemble the name from the individual components as efficiently as possible.

`AppendWithSpace` is a utility function that does the actual work of concatenating the substrings. It works out whether it needs to append anything at all using a `static` method on `string` that checks whether it is null or empty, called `IsNullOrEmpty`; finally, it adds an extra space to separate the individual words.

To do the roll call we want to write some code such as that in Example 4-16.

Example 4-16. Using the Administrator class

```
static void Main(string[] args)
{
    FireStation station = new FireStation();

    // A reference to Joe, Harry's number one
    Firefighter joe = new Firefighter { Name = "Joe" };

    // A reference to Bill, the trainee
    FirefighterBase bill = new TraineeFirefighter { Name = "Bill" };

    // Harry is back
    FireChief bigChiefHarry = new FireChief { Name = "Harry"};

    // And here's our administrator - Arthur
    Administrator arthur = new Administrator
    {
        Title = "Mr",
        Forename = "Arthur",
        Surname = "Askey"
    };

    station.ClockIn(joe);
    station.ClockIn(bill);
    station.ClockIn(bigChiefHarry);
    station.ClockIn(arthur);
```

```
        station.RollCall();

        Console.ReadKey();
}
```

 When you are designing a class framework it can often be a good idea to write some example client code. You can then ensure that your design is a good abstract model while supporting clean, simple code at point-of-use.

Clearly, we're going to need a `FireStation` class that is going to let our administrators and firefighters `ClockIn` (registering their presence in the station), and where we can do a `RollCall` (displaying their names). But what type is that `ClockIn` function going to take, given that we haven't specified any common base class that they share?

All Types Are Derived from Object

.NET comes to our rescue again. It turns out that *every type in the system is derived from* `Object`. Every one—value types (`struct`) and reference types (`class`) alike, even the built-in types such as `Int32`.

It is easy to see how that would work for a class declaration in C#. If you don't specify a particular base class, you get `Object` by default.

But what about a `struct`, or `enum`, or the built-in types; what happens if we try to talk to them through their `Object` "base class"?

Boxing and Unboxing Value Types

Let's give it a try. This code snippet will compile and work quite happily:

```
// Int variable
int myIntVariable = 1;
object myObject = myIntVariable;
```

What happens under the covers is that the runtime allocates a new object and puts a copy of the value inside it. This is called *boxing*, and, as you might expect given that it involves allocating objects and copying values, it is relatively expensive when compared to a straightforward assignment.

You can also convert back the other way:

```
// Int variable
int myIntVariable = 1;
object myObject = myIntVariable;
int anotherIntVariable = (int)myObject;
```

Notice how we use the type name in parentheses to perform the conversion back to an int. In general, this sort of conversion from one type to another is known as a "cast," and will work for classes too (although we'll see a more explicit way of doing that later in this chapter).

The runtime looks at that box object for us and checks that it contains a value of the correct type. If so, it will copy the value back out of the box and into the new variable.

 What if it *isn't* of the correct type? The runtime will throw an `Invalid CastException`. You can find out more about exceptions in Chapter 6.

That process is known as unboxing, and is also quite expensive (although not as expensive as boxing, as it doesn't need to allocate the object).

Although these performance costs are individually fairly small, if you are processing large numbers of value types in a way that requires them to be repeatedly boxed and unboxed the costs can add up quite rapidly; so you should be aware of boxing and unboxing when you are profiling your application.

So the only common base of both `Firefighter` and `Administrator` is `Object` at the moment (remember, everything is ultimately derived from `Object`). That seems a bit low level, but it is all we have to go on for now, so we'll make do.

Example 4-17 shows our first pass at a `FireStation`.

Example 4-17. FireStation class

```
class FireStation
{
    List<object> clockedInStaff = new List<object>();

    public void ClockIn(object staffMember)
    {
        if (!clockedInStaff.Contains(staffMember))
        {
            clockedInStaff.Add(staffMember);
        }
    }

    public void RollCall()
    {
        foreach(object staffMember in clockedInStaff)
        {
            // Hmmm... What to do?
        }
    }
}
```

Our ClockIn method is making use of a list of objects to keep track of who is in the station. To do that it is using the generic collection class List<T> we first saw in Chapter 2. Using the List.Contains method, the implementation checks that they weren't already in the station, and adds them if necessary.

Everything is fine so far. Then we reach the RollCall method. We're using foreach to iterate over the clocked-in staff, but we don't actually have a method to call to get their names!

We want a way of indicating that these disparate object types (firefighters, fire chiefs, and administrators) all support giving out their name.

We saw one way of doing that already: we could create a common base class, and move the Name functionality in there. Let's see what happens if we try to do that.

Practically speaking, we have two completely different implementations of the Name property. We saw that we can model that situation with an abstract base class from which Firefighter and Administrator both derive, both implementing the method in their own way.

Here's our NamedPerson base with an abstract property for the Name:

```
abstract class NamedPerson
{
    public abstract string Name
    {
        get;
    }
}
```

There's no problem when we implement this on our Administrator:

```
class Administrator : NamedPerson
{
    public override string Name
    {
        get
        {
            StringBuilder name = new StringBuilder();
            AppendWithSpace(name, Title);
            AppendWithSpace(name, Forename);
            AppendWithSpace(name, Surname);
            return name.ToString();
        }
    }

    // ...
}
```

Notice how we derived from NamedPerson and added the override modifier to our Name property so that it overrides the abstract method in our base.

That's fine so far. What about our `FirefighterBase`? Let's try doing exactly the same thing:

```
abstract class FirefighterBase : NamedPerson
{
    public abstract void ExtinguishFire();

    public override string Name { get; set; }

    // ...
}
```

If we compile that, we get an error:

```
'FirefighterBase.Name.set': cannot override because 'NamedPerson.Name' does
 not have an overridable set accessor
```

We run into difficulty because `FirefighterBase` has *both* a getter and a setter for the `Name` property, but our base allows only a getter.

Properties Under the Hood

We're going to dive into the guts of the thing here, so feel free to skip this if you're not deeply interested in how this works under the covers.

If you *do* look under the hood at the IL code emitted by the compiler, using a tool such as `ildasm`, you can see that properties consist of two pieces: the property metadata, and (either or both of) two functions called `get_PropName` and `set_PropName`, which actually implement the getter/setter. If you've chosen to use the simple property syntax, there's also a field created with a name that is something like `<PropName>k__BackingField`.

At the IL level, there's no difference between a property override and a new property declaration. It is the metadata on the getter and setter functions that determines whether they are `virtual` (and indeed what their accessibility might be).

So the fact that we can't override a property that has a getter in the base class with one that has a getter and a setter in the derived class is a feature of the C# language, not the underlying platform.

Well, we could work around that with another member to set the name; but as you can see in Example 4-18, it is all getting a bit ugly.

Example 4-18. Mounting evidence that all is not well in our class hierarchy

```
abstract class FirefighterBase : NamedPerson
{
    public abstract void ExtinguishFire();

    public override string Name
    {
        get
        {
            return RealName;
```

```
        }
    }

    public string RealName
    {
        get; set;
    }

    // ...
}
```

Not only is it ugly, but we have to replace all our object initializers to refer to our new RealName property, so it is making us do unnecessary work, which is never good:

```
Firefighter joe = new Firefighter { RealName = "Joe" };
```

Are you feeling uncomfortable with this approach yet? Let's push on with it just a little bit further, and see what happens if we want to support a second behavior. Say we had a `SalariedPerson` abstract base that provides us with the contract for getting/setting a person's salary. We're going to need to apply that to both the `FirefighterBase` and the `Administrator`, to tie in with the billing system:

```
abstract class SalariedPerson
{
    public abstract decimal Salary
    {
        get;
        set;
    }
}
```

We're providing a `decimal` property for the `Salary` that must be implemented by any `SalariedPerson`.

So, what happens if we now try to derive from this class for our `Administrator`, as shown in Example 4-19?

Example 4-19. The final straw: Our class hierarchy needs a rethink

```
class Administrator : NamedPerson, SalariedPerson
{
    private decimal salary;
    public override decimal Salary
    {
        get
        {
            return salary;
        }
        set
        {
            salary = value;
        }
    }
    // ...
}
```

C++ developers will be familiar with this syntax for specifying multiple base classes.

Another compiler error:

```
Class 'Administrator' cannot have multiple base classes: 'NamedPerson' and
'SalariedPerson'
```

C# Does Not Support Multiple Inheritance of Implementation

This is a pretty fundamental roadblock! *You cannot derive your class from more than one base class.*

When the designers of .NET were thinking about the platform fundamentals, they looked at this issue of multiple inheritance and how they'd support it across multiple languages, including C#, VB, and C++. They decided that the C++ approach was too messy and prone to error (particularly when you think about how to resolve members that appear in *both* base classes with the same signature). The implications of multiple inheritance were probably just too difficult to come to grips with, and therefore were unlikely to bring net productivity gains. With that view prevailing, single inheritance of implementation is baked into the platform.

In more recent interviews, the .NET team has reflected that perhaps there might have been a way of allowing multiple inheritance of implementation, without introducing all the complexity of C++ multiple inheritance. That's the benefit of 20/20 hindsight; we (or our children) will just have to wait until the next platform generation and see how the argument goes then.

So are we really stymied? No! While we can't support multiple inheritance of implementation, we *can* support multiple inheritance of interface.

C# Supports Multiple Inheritance of Interface

With our abstract base classes in this example, we're not really trying to provide a base implementation for our objects at all. We're trying to mark them as supporting a particular contract that we can then rely on in our client code.

C# provides us with a mechanism for doing exactly that: `interface`. Let's rewrite our `NamedPerson` and `SalariedPerson` classes as interfaces instead, as shown in Example 4-20.

Example 4-20. Defining interfaces

```
interface INamedPerson
{
    string Name
    {
        get;
    }
}

interface ISalariedPerson
{
    decimal Salary
    {
        get;
        set;
    }
}
```

We use much the same syntax as we do for a class definition, but using the keyword `interface` instead.

Notice also that we dropped the abstract modifier on the members; an interface is implicitly without implementation. There are no accessibility modifiers on the members either; an interface member is only ever allowed to be `public`.

The only other change we've made is to prefix our interface name with an **I**. This is not a rule, but another one of those naming conventions to which most people conform.

We can now implement those interfaces on our **Administrator**, as shown in Example 4-21.

Example 4-21. Implementing interfaces

```
class Administrator : INamedPerson, ISalariedPerson
{
    public decimal Salary
    {
        get;
        set;
    }

    public string Name
    {
        get
        {
            StringBuilder name = new StringBuilder();
            AppendWithSpace(name, Title);
            AppendWithSpace(name, Forename);
            AppendWithSpace(name, Surname);
            return name.ToString();
        }
    }
    // ...
}
```

And we can implement them on our `FirefighterBase`, as shown in Example 4-22.

Example 4-22. The same interfaces in a different part of the class hierarchy

```
abstract class FirefighterBase : INamedPerson, ISalariedPerson
{
    public string Name
    {
        get;
        set;
    }

    public decimal Salary
    {
        get;
        set;
    }

    // ...
}
```

Notice that we can happily implement the setter on our `FirefighterBase`, even though the interface only *requires* a getter. The restrictions on how you implement the interface—as long as you conform to the contract it specifies—are much looser than those on overrides of a base class. Also, C# doesn't allow you to use the simple property syntax to define virtual properties or their overrides, but there is no such restriction when you're implementing an interface. So we've been able to use simple property syntax here rather than having to implement using full-blown properties.

We can now make use of this interface in our `FireStation` class. Instead of a list of objects, we can use a list of `INamedPerson`, and call on the `Name` property in our `RollCall` method, as shown in Example 4-23.

Example 4-23. Modifying the FireStation class to use an interface

```
class FireStation
{
    List<INamedPerson> clockedInStaff = new List<INamedPerson>();

    public void ClockIn(INamedPerson staffMember)
    {
        if (!clockedInStaff.Contains(staffMember))
        {
            clockedInStaff.Add(staffMember);
            Console.WriteLine("Clocked in {0}", staffMember.Name);
        }
    }

    public void RollCall()
    {
        foreach (INamedPerson staffMember in clockedInStaff)
        {
            Console.WriteLine(staffMember.Name);
```

```
        }
      }
}
```

 If you've been following through the code in Visual Studio (which I thoroughly recommend), you'll also need to change your object initializers back to this form:

```
Firefighter joe = new Firefighter { Name = "Joe" };
```

If we compile and run, we get the output we hoped for—a roll call of everyone in the station:

```
Clocked in Joe
Clocked in Bill
Clocked in Harry
Clocked in Mr Arthur Askey
Joe
Bill
Harry
Mr Arthur Askey
```

Deriving Interfaces from Other Interfaces

Interfaces support inheritance too, just like classes. If you want, you could create a named, salaried person interface like this:

```
interface INamedSalariedPerson : INamedPerson, ISalariedPerson
{
}
```

What happens if you have conflicting names? Imagine the interface ISettable NamedPerson:

```
interface ISettableNamedPerson
{
    string Name
    {
        get; set;
    }
}
```

What happens if we implement both INamedPerson and ISettableNamedPerson on our FirefighterBase?

```
abstract class FirefighterBase : INamedPerson, ISettableNamedPerson, ISalariedPerson
{
    // ...
}
```

The answer is that everything is just fine! Each interface requires that we implement a **string** property called Name; one requires at least a getter, the other a getter and a setter.

When we access the property through the relevant interface, it can resolve correctly which member we meant; there's no requirement for a *separate* implementation for each interface.

But what if that was actually wrong? What if our `Name` property on `INamedPerson` had entirely different semantics from the one on `ISettableNamedPerson`? Let's suppose that one is intended to allow only letters and numbers with no spaces and the other is just our freeform "any old text" implementation with which we are familiar.

Whenever our client expects an `INamedPerson` we need to provide the second implementation, and whenever the client expects an `ISettableNamedPerson`, the first.

We can do that by *explicitly implementing the interfaces*.

Explicit Interface Implementation

To explicitly implement a particular member of an interface, you drop the accessibility modifier and add the interface name as a prefix, as shown in Example 4-24.

Example 4-24. Explicit interface implementation

```
class AFootInBothCamps : INamedPerson, ISettableNamedPerson
{
    private string settableName;

    string INamedPerson.Name
    {
        get
        {
            Console.WriteLine("Accessed through the INamedPerson interface");
            return settableName;
        }
    }

    string ISettableNamedPerson.Name
    {
        get
        {
            return settableName;
        }
        set
        {
            Console.WriteLine(
            "Accessed through the " +
            "ISettableNamedPerson interface");

            if( settableName != null && settableName.Contains(" ") )
            {
                // You can't set it if it contains the space
                // character
                return;
            }
            settableName = value;
```

```
        }
    }
}
```

Example 4-25 shows how we're going to access them from our main function.

Example 4-25. Calling different interface implementations of the same member name on the same object

```
class Program
{
    static void Main(string[] args)
    {
        AFootInBothCamps both = new AFootInBothCamps();

        ISettableNamedPerson settablePerson = both;
        INamedPerson namedPerson = both;

        settablePerson.Name = "hello";

        Console.WriteLine(settablePerson.Name);
        Console.WriteLine(namedPerson.Name);

        Console.ReadKey();
    }
}
```

Notice how we're creating our object, and then providing two additional references to it: one through a variable of type ISettableNamedPerson and one through INamedPerson.

We then call on the Name property through each of those interfaces, and get the following output:

```
Accessed through the ISettableNamedPerson interface
hello
Accessed through the INamedPerson interface
hello
```

But what if we try to access it through a reference typed to the class itself?

```
Console.WriteLine(both.Name);
```

Add the following line to the main function and compile, and we get a compiler error!

```
'AFootInBothCamps' does not contain a definition for 'Name' and no extension
method 'Name' accepting a first argument of type 'AFootInBothCamps' could be
found (are you missing a using directive or an assembly reference?)
```

We've seen that error before; it means we're trying to talk to a member that doesn't exist. What's happened is that the members that are explicitly implemented *exist only* if we are accessing them through the relevant interfaces.

However, as long as we explicitly implement one of the two (or two of the three, or however many we're stuck with), we can choose one interface as our "default" and implement it using the regular syntax, as shown in Example 4-26.

Example 4-26. Implementing one of the interfaces implicitly

```
class AFootInBothCamps : INamedPerson, ISettableNamedPerson
{
    private string settableName;

    // Regular implementation syntax
    public string Name
    {
        get
        {
            Console.WriteLine("Accessed through the INamedPerson interface");
            return settableName;
        }
    }

    string ISettableNamedPerson.Name
    {
        get
        {
            return settableName;
        }
        set
        {
            Console.WriteLine("Accessed through the ISettableNamedPerson "
                            + "interface");
            if( settableName != null && settableName.Contains(" ") )
            {
                // You can't set it if it contains the space
                // character
                return;
            }
            settableName = value;
        }
    }
}
```

Now we can compile and run, and the default implementation for our class is the one for the INamedPerson interface:

```
Accessed through the ISettableNamedPerson interface
hello
Accessed through the INamedPerson interface
hello
Accessed through the INamedPerson interface
hello
```

 In real life, you don't often come across this need for explicit interface implementation. If you have control over all the code in the application, you should avoid designing in a clash where the names are the same but the semantics are different. Like overloads or overrides with different meanings, it surprises other developers.

The .NET Framework contains a few examples where it uses explicit interface implementation to hide the interface members from the public API of a class, even though there is no clash. The authors are unconvinced that this improves matters.

More often, you will come across this usage where you *don't* have control of the code—with two third-party libraries, for instance, both of which declare interfaces with different semantics but a clash of names. Even then, this is not a problem unless you happen to need to implement both interfaces on one class. Even rarer!

(Abstract) Base Classes Versus Interfaces

We've clearly simplified our code by introducing interfaces into our model. Would we ever want to use abstract base classes rather than an interface?

Well, we've already seen an example where an abstract base class is a good choice—if there's additional implementation scaffolding that we wish to bring along with us, and the abstract members are plumbed into that structure. It would be unnecessary to introduce an interface just for the abstract member.

In general, an interface is a good way of defining *just the contract*, without providing any implementation at all, especially if that contract is shared between different parts of a system.

It also has strict versioning rules: if you add or remove members from an interface and ship your assembly, it is a *different interface* and will *no longer be binary compatible* with code that implements the previous version of the interface (although clients that just call through the interface will still work fine if you haven't removed or changed something on which they depended). With an abstract base class, you can generally add members and it remains binary compatible with older code (although a new abstract member will also break anyone who inherits from it, of course).

Right, let's go back to our `FireStation` class for a minute, and imagine an interface we could create to formalize the contract for clocking in: our billing system might define this contract for us so that we can plug into it.

As it happens, our `FireStation` provides an implementation which can `ClockIn` named people, but our billing system's `IClockIn` contract is much more generic—it can clock in anything of type `Object`, as we had in our original implementation:

```
interface IClockIn
{
    void ClockIn(object item);
}
```

We can now implement `IClockIn` on our `FireStation`, as shown in Example 4-27.

Example 4-27. Implementing the IClockIn interface

```
class FireStation : IClockIn
{
    List<INamedPerson> clockedInStaff = new List<INamedPerson>();

    public void ClockIn(INamedPerson staffMember)
    {
        if (!clockedInStaff.Contains(staffMember))
        {
            clockedInStaff.Add(staffMember);
            Console.WriteLine("Clocked in {0}", staffMember.Name);
        }
    }

    public void RollCall()
    {
        foreach (INamedPerson staffMember in clockedInStaff)
        {
            Console.WriteLine(staffMember.Name);
        }
    }

    public void ClockIn(object item)
    {
        // What to do here
    }

}
```

Our original `ClockIn` method is unchanged, and we've added a new overload that takes an object, and therefore matches the requirement in our interface. But how do we implement that new method? We want to check that the person being clocked in is an `INamedPerson`, and if it is, perform our usual operation. Otherwise, we want to tell the user that we can't clock him in.

In other words, we need a manual check for the type of the object.

The Last Resort: Checking Types at Runtime

C# provides us with a couple of keywords for checking the type of an object: as and is.

Here's how we can use them in our `ClockIn` implementation:

```
public void ClockIn(object item)
{
    if (item is INamedPerson)
    {
        ClockIn(item as INamedPerson);
    }
    else
    {
        Console.WriteLine("We can't check in a '{0}'", item.GetType());
    }
}
```

Notice how we are using the type name to check if the item is of that type. And then we call our *other* overload of `ClockIn` by explicitly converting to a reference of our `INamedPerson` type, using as.

It checks to see if our object would be accessible through a reference of the specified type. It looks at the whole inheritance hierarchy for the object (up and down) to see if it matches, and if it does, it provides us a reference of the relevant type.

What if you don't bother with the is check and just use as? Conveniently, the as operation just converts to a null reference if it can't find a suitable type match:

```
public void ClockIn(object item)
{
    INamedPerson namedPerson = item as INamedPerson;
    if(namedPerson != null)
    {
        ClockIn(namedPerson);
    }
    else
    {
        Console.WriteLine("We can't check in a '{0}'", item.GetType());
    }
}
```

This is the form in which you most often see a test like this, because it is marginally more efficient than the previous example. In the first version, the runtime has to perform the expensive runtime type checking twice: once for the if() statement and once to see whether we can actually perform the conversion, or whether null is required. In the second case, we do the expensive check only once, and then do a simple test for null.

Summary

So far, we've seen how to create classes; to model relationships between instances of those classes through association, composition, and aggregation; and to create relationships between classes by derivation. We also saw how `virtual` functions enable derived classes to replace selected aspects of a base class.

We saw how to use `protected` and `protected internal` to control the visibility of members to derived classes. Then, we saw how we can use either `abstract` classes and methods or interfaces to define public contracts for a class.

Finally, we looked at a means of examining the inheritance hierarchy by hand, and verifying whether an object we are referencing through a base class is, in fact, an instance of a more derived class.

In the next chapter, we are going to look at some other techniques for code reuse and extensibility that don't rely on inheritance.

CHAPTER 5

Composability and Extensibility with Delegates

In the preceding two chapters, we saw how to encapsulate behavior and information with classes. Using the concepts of association, composition, aggregation, and derivation, we modeled relationships between those classes and looked at some of the benefits of polymorphism along with the use and abuse of virtual functions and their implied contracts with derived classes.

In this chapter, we'll look at a *functional* (rather than class-based) approach to composition and extensibility, and see how we can use this to implement some of the patterns that have previously required us to burn our one and only base class and override virtual functions; and all with the added benefit of a looser coupling between classes.

Let's start with another example. This time, we want to build a system that processes incoming (electronic) documents prior to publication. We might want to do an automated spellcheck, repaginate, perform a machine translation for a foreign-language website, or perform one of any other number of operations that our editors will devise during the development process and beyond.

After some business analysis, our platform team has given us a class called Document, which is shown in Example 5-1. This is their baby, and we're not allowed to mess with it.

Example 5-1. The Document class

```
public sealed class Document
{
    // Get/set document text
    public string Text
    {
        get;
        set;
    }

    // Date of the document
```

```
    public DateTime DocumentDate
    {
        get;
        set;
    }

    public string Author
    {
        get;
        set;
    }
}
```

It has simple properties for its Text, the DocumentDate, and the Author, and no other methods.

What Is Coupling?

Two classes are said to be coupled if a change to one requires a change to another. We saw examples of that in the previous chapter. When we created our NamedPerson class, it required changes to the FirefighterBase and the Administrator classes. We therefore say that FirefighterBase and Administrator are *coupled* to NamedPerson.

Of course, any class or function that refers to another class or function is coupled to that class—that's unavoidable (indeed, desirable). But to make testing simpler and systems more reliable, we try to ensure that we *minimize the number of other types* to which any class or function is coupled, and that we *minimize the number of couplings* between any two types. That way, any given change to a class will have a minimal number of knock-on effects elsewhere in the system.

We also try to ensure that we organize classes into conceptual groupings called *layers* so that more tightly coupled classes live together in one layer, and that there are a minimal number of well-controlled couplings between layers. As part of that layered approach, it is usual to try to ensure that most couplings go one-way; classes of a "lower" layer should not depend on classes in a layer above.

That way, we can further limit (and understand) the way changes propagate through the system. The layers act like firewalls, blocking the further impact of a change.

As usual with software design, these disciplines are not hard-and-fast rules, and they are not imposed by the platform or language; but they are common practices that the platform and language are designed to support.

Now we want to be able to process the document. At the very least, we want to be able to Spellcheck, Repaginate, or Translate it (into French, say). Because we can't change the Document class, we'll implement these methods in a static utility class of common processes, as we learned in Chapter 3. Example 5-2 shows this class, although the implementations are obviously just placeholders—we're illustrating how to structure the code here, and trying to write a real spellchecker would be a rather large distraction.

Example 5-2. Some document processing methods

```
static class DocumentProcesses
{
    public static void Spellcheck( Document doc )
    {
        Console.WriteLine("Spellchecked document.");
    }

    public static void Repaginate( Document doc)
    {
        Console.WriteLine("Repaginated document.");
    }

    public static void TranslateIntoFrench( Document doc )
    {
        Console.WriteLine("Document traduit.");
    }

    // ...
}
```

Now we can build a simple example of a document processor that translates, spell-checks, and then repaginates the document (see Example 5-3).

Example 5-3. Processing a document

```
static class DocumentProcessor
{
    public static void Process(Document doc)
    {
        DocumentProcesses.TranslateIntoFrench(doc);
        DocumentProcesses.Spellcheck(doc);
        DocumentProcesses.Repaginate(doc);
    }
}
```

And we can call on it from our main function, to process a couple of documents, as shown in Example 5-4.

Example 5-4. A program to test the document processing classes

```
class Program
{
    static void Main(string[] args)
    {
        Document doc1 = new Document
        {
            Author = "Matthew Adams",
            DocumentDate = new DateTime(2000, 01, 01),
            Text = "Am I a year early?"
        };
        Document doc2 = new Document
        {
            Author = "Ian Griffiths",
```

```
        DocumentDate = new DateTime(2001, 01, 01),
        Text = "This is the new millennium, I promise you."
    };

    Console.WriteLine("Processing document 1");
    DocumentProcessor.Process(doc1);
    Console.WriteLine();
    Console.WriteLine("Processing document 2");
    DocumentProcessor.Process(doc2);

    Console.ReadKey();
  }
}
```

Compile and run that, and you'll see the following output:

```
Processing document 1
Document traduit.
Spellchecked document.
Repaginated document.

Processing document 2
Document traduit.
Spellchecked document.
Repaginated document.
```

We encapsulated a particular set of processing instructions, executed in a particular order, in this (static) DocumentProcessor class so that we can easily reuse it with different client applications that want a standard, reliable means of performing our "translate into French" process. So far, this should all be pretty familiar.

But what about a different set of processing operations, one that leaves the document in its native language and just spellchecks and repaginates?

We could just create a second DocumentProcessor-like class, and encapsulate the relevant method calls in a process function:

```
static class DocumentProcessorStandard
{
    public static void Process(Document doc)
    {
        DocumentProcesses.Spellcheck(doc);
        DocumentProcesses.Repaginate(doc);
    }
}
```

And then we could add some calls to that processor in our Main method:

```
Console.WriteLine();
Console.WriteLine("Processing document 1 (standard)");
DocumentProcessorStandard.Process(doc1);
Console.WriteLine();
Console.WriteLine("Processing document 2 (standard)");
DocumentProcessorStandard.Process(doc2);
```

Nothing is intrinsically wrong with any of this; it clearly works, and we have a nice enough design that neatly encapsulates our processing.

We note that each DocumentProcessor is coupled to the Document class, and also to each method that it calls on the DocumentProcesses class. Our client is coupled to the Document and each DocumentProcessor class that it uses.

If we go back to the specification we showed earlier, we see that we are likely to be creating a lot of different functions to modify the document as part of the production process; they'll slip in and out of use depending on the type of document, other systems we might have to work with, and the business process of the day.

Rather than hardcoding this process in an ever-increasing number of processor classes (and coupling those to an ever-increasing number of DocumentProcesses), it would obviously be better if we could devolve this to the developers on our production team. They could provide an ordered set of processes (of some kind) to the one and only DocumentProcessor class that actually runs those processes.

We can then focus on making the process-execution engine as efficient and reliable as possible, and the production team will be able to create sequences of processes (built by either us, them, contractors, or whoever), without having to come back to us for updates all the time.

Figure 5-1 represents that requirement as a diagram.

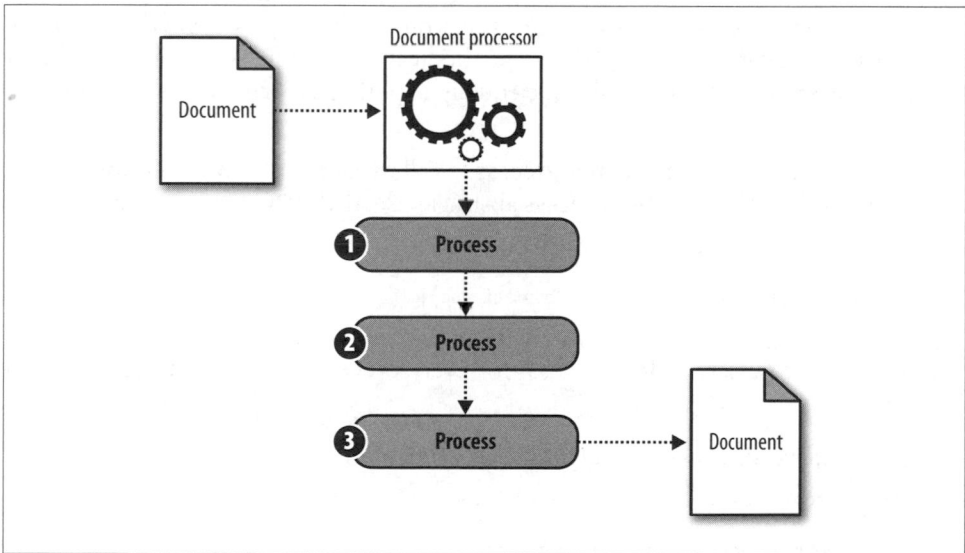

Figure 5-1. Document processor architecture

The document is submitted to the document processor, which runs it through an ordered sequence of processes. The same document comes out at the other end.

OK, let's build a `DocumentProcessor` class that implements that (see Example 5-5).

Example 5-5. An adaptable document processor

```
class DocumentProcessor
{
    private readonly List<DocumentProcess> processes =
        new List<DocumentProcess>();

    public List<DocumentProcess> Processes
    {
        get
        {
            return processes;
        }
    }

    public void Process(Document doc)
    {
        foreach(DocumentProcess process in Processes)
        {
            process.Process(doc);
        }
    }
}
```

Our document processor has a `List` of `DocumentProcess` objects (a hypothetical type we've not written yet). A `List<T>` is an ordered collection—that is to say that the item you `Add` at index 0 stays at index 0, and is first out of the block when you iterate the list, and so on. That means our `Process` method can just iterate over the collection of `DocumentProcess` objects, and call some equally hypothetical `Process` method on each to do the processing.

But what type of thing is a `DocumentProcess`? Well, we already saw a solution we can use—we could create a `DocumentProcess` abstract base, with a `Process` abstract method:

```
abstract class DocumentProcess
{
    public abstract void Process(Document doc);
}
```

We then need to create a derived class for every processing operation, as shown in Example 5-6.

Example 5-6. Implementations of the abstract DocumentProcess

```
class SpellcheckProcess : DocumentProcess
{
    public override void Process(Document doc)
    {
        DocumentProcesses.Spellcheck(doc);
    }
}
```

```
class RepaginateProcess : DocumentProcess
{
    public override void Process(Document doc)
    {
        DocumentProcesses.Repaginate(doc);
    }
}

class TranslateIntoFrenchProcess : DocumentProcess
{
    public override void Process(Document doc)
    {
        DocumentProcesses.TranslateIntoFrench(doc);
    }
}
```

Now we can configure a processor in our client by adding some process objects to the list (see Example 5-7).

Example 5-7. Configuring a document processor with processes

```
static DocumentProcessor Configure()
{
    DocumentProcessor rc = new DocumentProcessor();
    rc.Processes.Add(new TranslateIntoFrenchProcess());
    rc.Processes.Add(new SpellcheckProcess());
    rc.Processes.Add(new RepaginateProcess());
    return rc;
}
```

See how we are adding the processes to the processor in the same order we had in our function calls previously? Our process objects are logically similar to function calls, and the order in which they appear is logically similar to a program, except that they are composed at runtime rather than compile time.

We can then use this configuration method in our client, and call on the processor to process our documents, as shown in Example 5-8.

Example 5-8. Using the dynamically configured processor

```
static void Main(string[] args)
{
    Document doc1 = new Document
    {
        Author = "Matthew Adams",
        DocumentDate = new DateTime(2000, 01, 01),
        Text = "Am I a year early?"
    };
    Document doc2 = new Document
    {
        Author = "Ian Griffiths",
        DocumentDate = new DateTime(2001, 01, 01),
        Text = "This is the new millennium, I promise you."
    };
```

```
DocumentProcessor processor = Configure();

Console.WriteLine("Processing document 1");
processor.Process(doc1);
Console.WriteLine();
Console.WriteLine("Processing document 2");
processor.Process(doc2);

Console.ReadKey();
}
```

If you compile and run, you'll see the same output as before:

```
Processing document 1
Document traduit.
Spellchecked document.
Repaginated document.

Processing document 2
Document traduit.
Spellchecked document.
Repaginated document.
```

This is a very common pattern in object-oriented design—encapsulating a method in an object and/or a process in a sequence of objects.

What's nice about it is that our `DocumentProcessor` is now coupled only to the `Document` class, plus the abstract base it uses as a contract for the individual processes. It is no longer coupled to each and every one of those processes; they can vary without requiring any changes to the processor itself, because they implement the contract demanded by the abstract base class.

Finally, the processing sequence (the "program" for the `DocumentProcessor`) is now the responsibility of the client app, not the processor library; so our different production teams can develop their own particular sequences (and, indeed, new processes) without having to refer back to the core team and change the document processor in any way.

In fact, the only thing that is a bit of a pain about this whole approach is that we have to declare a new class every time we want to wrap up a simple method call. Wouldn't it be easier just to be able to refer to the method call directly?

C# provides us with a tool to do just that: the `delegate`.

Functional Composition with delegate

We just wrote some code that wraps up a method call inside an object. The call itself is wrapped up in another method with a well-known signature.

You can think of a delegate as solving that same sort of problem: it is an object that lets us wrap up a method call on another object (or class).

But while our DocumentProcess classes have their methods hardcoded into virtual function overrides, a *delegate* allows us to reference a specific function (from a given class or object instance) at runtime, then use the delegate to execute that function.

So, in the same way that a variable can be considered to contain a reference to an object, a delegate can be thought to contain a reference to a function (see Figure 5-2).

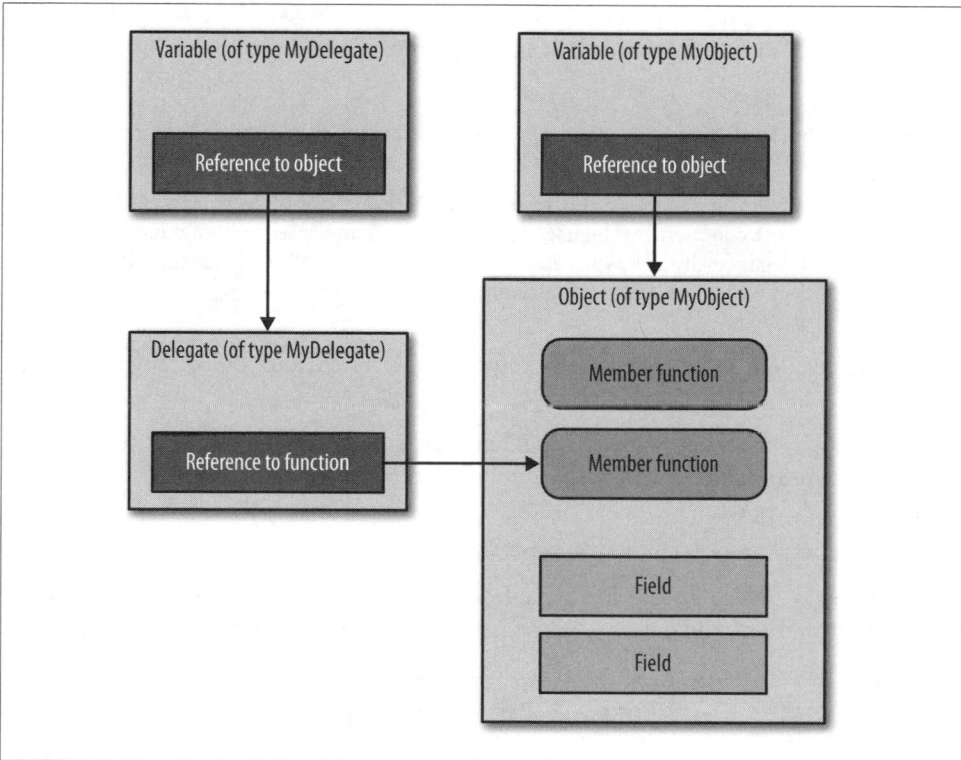

Figure 5-2. Delegates and variables

Before we get into the specific C# syntax, I just want to show you that there isn't anything mystical about a delegate; in fact, there is a class in the .NET Framework called Delegate which encapsulates the behavior for us.

As you might expect, it uses properties to store the reference to the function. There are two, in fact: Method (which indicates which member function to use) and Target (which tells us the object on which the method should be executed, if any).

As you can see, the whole thing is not totally dissimilar in concept from our previous DocumentProcess base class, but we don't need to derive from Delegate to supply the function to call. That ability has moved into a property instead.

That's all there is to a delegate, really.

However, it is such a powerful and useful tool that the C# language designers have provided us with special language syntax to declare new `Delegate` types, assign the appropriate function, and then call it in a much more compact and expressive fashion. It also allows the compiler to check that all the parameter and return types match up along the way, rather than producing errors at runtime if you get it wrong.

It is so compact, expressive, and powerful that you can probably get through your entire C# programming career without ever worrying about the classes the C# compiler emits which derive from that `Delegate` class and implement it all.

> So, why have we just spent a page or so discussing these implementation details, if we're never going to see them again?
>
> While you don't usually need to *use* the `Delegate` class directly, it is easy to get confused by language-specific voodoo and lose track of what a delegate really is: it is just an object, which in turn calls whichever function we like, all specified through a couple of properties.

Let's start by defining a new delegate type to reference our document processing functions.

As I mentioned earlier, rather than using that `Delegate` class, C# lets us define a delegate type using syntax which looks pretty much like a function declaration, prefixed with the keyword `delegate`:

```
delegate void DocumentProcess(Document doc);
```

That defines a delegate type for a method which returns `void`, and takes a single `Document` parameter. The delegate's type name is `DocumentProcess`.

Delegates Under the Hood

Anyone who has sensibly decided not to go any further into the implementation details can skip this sidebar. For those still reading...

When you declare a delegate like this, under the covers C# emits a class called `DocumentProcess`, derived from `MulticastDelegate` (which is a subclass of `Delegate`).

Among other things, that emitted class has a function called `Invoke(int param)` which matches the signature we declared on the delegate.

So how is `Invoke` implemented? Surprisingly, it doesn't have any method body at all! Instead, all of the members of the emitted class are marked as special by the compiler, and the runtime actually provides the implementations so that it can (more or less) optimally dispatch the delegated function.

Having added the delegate, we have two types called `DocumentProcess`, which is not going to work. Let's get rid of our old `DocumentProcess` abstract base class, and the three

---

classes we derived from it. Isn't it satisfying, getting rid of code? There is less to test and you are statistically likely to have fewer bugs.

So how are we going to adapt our DocumentProcessor to use our new definition for the DocumentProcess type? Take a look at Example 5-9.

Example 5-9. Modifying DocumentProcess to use delegates

```
class DocumentProcessor
{
    private readonly List<DocumentProcess> processes =
        new List<DocumentProcess>();
    public List<DocumentProcess> Processes
    {
        get
        {
            return processes;
        }
    }

    public void Process(Document doc)
    {
        foreach(DocumentProcess process in Processes)
        {
          // Hmmm... this doesn't work anymore
            process.Process(doc);
        }
    }
}
```

We're still storing a set of DocumentProcess objects, but those objects are now delegates to member functions that conform to the signature specified by the DocumentProcess delegate.

We can still iterate over the process collection, but we no longer have a Process method on the object. The equivalent function on the delegate type is a method called Invoke which matches the signature of our delegated function:

```
process.Invoke(doc);
```

While this works just fine, it is such a common thing to need to do with a delegate that C# lets us dispense with .Invoke entirely and treat the delegate as though it really was the function to which it delegates:

```
process(doc);
```

Here's the final version of our Process method:

```
    public void Process(Document doc)
    {
        foreach(DocumentProcess process in Processes)
        {
            process(doc);
        }
    }
```

 This can take a bit of getting used to, because our variable names are usually camelCased and our method names are usually PascalCased. Using function call syntax against a camelCased object can cause severe cognitive dissonance. I've still never really gotten used to it myself, and I always feel like I need a sit-down and a cup of coffee when it happens.

Now we need to deal with the `Configure` method that sets up our processes. Rather than creating all those process classes, we need to create the delegate instances instead.

You *can* construct a delegate instance just like any other object, using `new`, and passing the name of the function to which you wish to delegate as a constructor parameter:

```
static DocumentProcessor Configure()
{
    DocumentProcessor rc = new DocumentProcessor();
    rc.Processes.Add(new DocumentProcess(DocumentProcesses.TranslateIntoFrench));
    rc.Processes.Add(new DocumentProcess(DocumentProcesses.Spellcheck));
    rc.Processes.Add(new DocumentProcess(DocumentProcesses.Repaginate));
    return rc;
}
```

However, C# has more syntactic shorthand that can do away with a lot of that boilerplate code. It can work out which delegate type you mean from context, and you only need to provide the method name itself:

```
static DocumentProcessor Configure()
{
    DocumentProcessor rc = new DocumentProcessor();
    rc.Processes.Add(DocumentProcesses.TranslateIntoFrench);
    rc.Processes.Add(DocumentProcesses.Spellcheck);
    rc.Processes.Add(DocumentProcesses.Repaginate);
    return rc;
}
```

Not only have we achieved the same end in much less code, but we've actually reduced coupling between our subsystems still further—our `DocumentProcessor` doesn't depend on any classes other than the `Document` itself; it will work with any class, static or otherwise, that can provide a method that conforms to the appropriate signature, as defined by our delegate.

So far, we've only provided delegates to static functions, but this works just as well for an instance method on a class.

Let's imagine we need to provide a trademark filter for our document, to ensure that we pick out any trademarks in an appropriate typeface. Example 5-10 shows our `TrademarkFilter` class.

Example 5-10. Another processing step

```
class TrademarkFilter
{
    readonly List<string> trademarks = new List<string>();
```

```
public List<string> Trademarks
{
    get
    {
        return trademarks;
    }
}

public void HighlightTrademarks(Document doc)
{
    // Split the document up into individual words
    string[] words = doc.Text.Split(' ', '.', ',');
    foreach( string word in words )
    {
        if( Trademarks.Contains(word) )
        {
            Console.WriteLine("Highlighting '{0}'", word);
        }
    }
}
}
}
```

It maintains a list of `Trademarks` to pick out, and has a `HighlightTrademarks` method that does the actual work. Notice that it is coupled only to the `Document`—it knows nothing about our processor infrastructure. Neither have we burned our base; we didn't have to inherit from any particular class to fit in with the processor framework, leaving it free for, say, our forthcoming "highlighter framework."

Example 5-11 shows how we add it to our configuration code.

Example 5-11. Adding a processing step with a nonstatic method

```
static DocumentProcessor Configure()
{
    DocumentProcessor rc = new DocumentProcessor();
    rc.Processes.Add(DocumentProcesses.TranslateIntoFrench);
    rc.Processes.Add(DocumentProcesses.Spellcheck);
    rc.Processes.Add(DocumentProcesses.Repaginate);

    TrademarkFilter trademarkFilter = new TrademarkFilter();
    trademarkFilter.Trademarks.Add("O'Reilly");
    trademarkFilter.Trademarks.Add("millennium");

    rc.Processes.Add(trademarkFilter.HighlightTrademarks);

    return rc;
}
```

We create our `TrademarkFilter` object and add a few "trademarks" to its list. To specify a delegate to the method *on that instance* we use our reference to the instance and the name of the function on that instance. Notice that the syntax is very similar to a method call on an object, but without the parentheses.

If we compile and run, we get the expected output:

```
Processing document 1
Document traduit.
Spellchecked document.
Repaginated document.

Processing document 2
Document traduit.
Spellchecked document.
Repaginated document.
Highlighting 'millennium'
```

This pattern is very common in object-oriented design: an overall process encapsulated in a class is customized by allowing a client to specify some action or actions for it to execute somewhere within that process. Our DocumentProcess delegate is typical for this kind of action—the function takes a single parameter of some type (the object our client wishes us to process), and returns void.

Because we so often need delegates with this kind of signature, the framework provides us with a generic type that does away with the need to declare the delegate types explicitly, every time.

Generic Actions with Action<T>

Action<T> is a *generic type* for a delegate to a function that returns void, and takes a single parameter of some type T. We used a generic type before: the List<T> (List-of-T) where T represents the type of the objects that can be added to the list. In this case, we have an Action-of-T where T represents the type of the parameter for the function.

So, instead of declaring our own delegate:

```
delegate void DocumentProcess( Document doc );
```

we could just use an Action<> like this:

```
Action<Document>
```

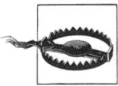

A quick warning: although these are functionally equivalent, you cannot use an Action<Document> polymorphically as a DocumentProcess—they are, of course, different classes under the covers.

We're choosing between an implementation that uses a type we're declaring ourselves, or one supplied by the framework. Although there are sometimes good reasons for going your own way, it is usually best to take advantage of library code if it is an exact match for your requirement.

So, we can delete our own delegate definition, and update our DocumentProcessor to use an Action<Document> instead, as shown in Example 5-12.

Example 5-12. Modifying the processor to use the built-in Action<T> delegate type

```
class DocumentProcessor
{
    private readonly List<Action<Document>> processes =
        new List<Action<Document>>();

    public List<Action<Document>> Processes
    {
        get
        {
            return processes;
        }
    }

    public void Process(Document doc)
    {
        foreach (Action<Document> process in Processes)
        {
            process(doc);
        }
    }
}
```

Compile and run, and you'll see that we still get our expected output.

If you were watching the IntelliSense as you were typing in that code, you will have noticed that there are several Action<> types in the framework: Action<T>, Action<T1,T2>, Action<T1,T2,T3>, and so on. As you might expect, these allow you to define delegates to methods which return void, but which take two, three, or more parameters. .NET 4 provides Action<> delegate types going all the way up to 16 parameters. (Previous versions stopped at four.)

OK, let's suppose that everything we've built so far has been deployed to the integration test environment, and the production folks have come back with a new requirement. Sometimes they configure a processing sequence that fails against a particular document—and it invariably seems to happen three hours into one of their more complex processes. They have some code which would let them do a quick check for some of their more compute-intensive processes and establish whether they are likely to fail. They want to know if we can implement this for them somehow.

One way we might be able to do this is to provide a means of supplying an optional "check" function corresponding to each "action" function. We could then iterate all of the check functions first (they are supposed to be quick), and look at their return values. If any fail, we can give up (see Figure 5-3).

We could implement that by rewriting our DocumentProcessor as shown in Example 5-13.

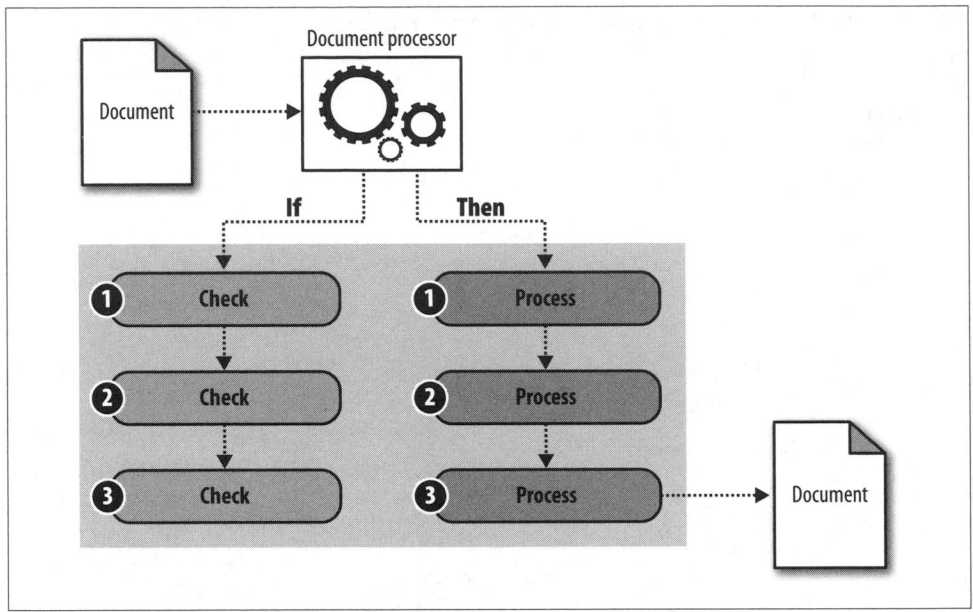

Figure 5-3. Document processor with checking

Example 5-13. Adding quick checking to the document processor

```
class DocumentProcessor
{
    class ActionCheckPair
    {
        public Action<Document> Action { get; set; }
        public Check QuickCheck { get; set; }
    }

    private readonly List<ActionCheckPair> processes = new List<ActionCheckPair>();


    public void AddProcess(Action<Document> action)
    {
        AddProcess(action, null);
    }

    public void AddProcess(Action<Document> action, Check quickCheck)
    {
        processes.Add(
            new ActionCheckPair { Action = action, QuickCheck = quickCheck });
    }

    public void Process(Document doc)
    {
        // First time, do the quick check
        foreach( ActionCheckPair process in processes)
        {
            if (process.QuickCheck != null && !process.QuickCheck(doc))
```

```
        {
            Console.WriteLine("The process will not succeed.");
            return;
        }
    }

    // Then perform the action
    foreach (ActionCheckPair process in processes)
    {
        process.Action(doc);
    }
    }
}
```

There are quite a few new things to look at here.

First, we declared a new class *inside* our DocumentProcessor definition, rather than in the namespace scope. We call this a *nested class*.

We chose to nest the class because it is private to the DocumentProcessor, and we can avoid polluting the namespace with implementation details. Although you can make nested classes publicly accessible, it is unusual to do so and is considered a bad practice.

This nested class just associates a pair of delegates: the Action<Document> that does the work, and the corresponding Check that performs the quick check.

We removed the public property for our list of processes, and replaced it with a pair of AddProcess method overloads. These allow us to add processes to the sequence; one takes both the action and the check, and the other is a convenience overload that allows us to pass the action only.

 Notice how we had to change the public contract for our class because we initially exposed the list of processes directly. If we'd made the list an implementation detail and provided the single-parameter AddProcess method in the first place, we wouldn't now need to change our clients as we'd only be extending the class.

Our new Process function first iterates the processes and calls on the QuickCheck delegate (if it is not null) to see if all is OK. As soon as one of these checks returns false, we return from the method and do no further work. Otherwise, we iterate through the processes again and call the Action delegate.

What type is a Check? We need a delegate to a method that returns a Boolean and takes a Document:

```
delegate bool Check(Document doc);
```

We call this type of "check" method a *predicate*: a function that operates on a set of parameters and returns either true or false for a given input. As you might expect, given the way things have been going so far, this is a sufficiently useful idea for it to appear in the framework (again, as of .NET 3.5).

Generic Predicates with Predicate<T>

Unlike the many variants of Action<>, the framework provides us with a single Predicate<T> type, which defines a delegate to a function that takes a single parameter of type T and returns a Boolean.

 Why only the one parameter? There are good computer-science-philosophical reasons for it. In mathematical logic, a predicate is usually defined as follows:

$$P : X \rightarrow \{ \text{ true, false } \}$$

That can be read as "a Predicate of some entity X maps to 'true' or 'false'". The single parameter in the mathematical expression is an important limitation, allowing us to build more complex systems from the simplest possible building blocks.

This formal notion gives rise to the single parameter in the .NET Predicate<T> class, however pragmatically useful it may be to have more than one parameter in your particular application.

We can delete our Check delegate (Hurrah! More code removed!), and replace it with a Predicate<T> that takes a Document as its type parameter:

    Predicate<Document>

And we can update the DocumentProcessor to make use of Predicate<T>, as shown in Example 5-14.

Example 5-14. DocumentProcessor updated to use Predicate<T>

```
class DocumentProcessor
{
    class ActionCheckPair
    {
        public Action<Document> Action { get; set; }
        public Predicate<Document> QuickCheck { get; set; }
    }

    private readonly List<ActionCheckPair> processes =
        new List<ActionCheckPair>();

    public void AddProcess(Action<Document> action)
    {
        AddProcess(action, null);
    }

    public void AddProcess(Action<Document> action,
```

```
                    Predicate<Document> quickCheck)
    {
        processes.Add(
            new ActionCheckPair { Action = action, QuickCheck = quickCheck });
    }

    // ...
}
```

We can now update our client code to use our new DocumentProcessor API, calling AddProcess now that the list of processes is private (see Example 5-15).

Example 5-15. Updating Configure to use modified DocumentProcessor

```
static DocumentProcessor Configure()
{
    DocumentProcessor rc = new DocumentProcessor();
    rc.AddProcess(DocumentProcesses.TranslateIntoFrench);
    rc.AddProcess(DocumentProcesses.Spellcheck);
    rc.AddProcess(DocumentProcesses.Repaginate);

    TrademarkFilter trademarkFilter = new TrademarkFilter();
    trademarkFilter.Trademarks.Add("Ian");
    trademarkFilter.Trademarks.Add("Griffiths");
    trademarkFilter.Trademarks.Add("millennium");

    rc.AddProcess(trademarkFilter.HighlightTrademarks);

    return rc;
}
```

For the time being, we're using the overload of AddProcess that doesn't supply a quickCheck, so if we compile and run, we get the same output as before:

```
Processing document 1
Document traduit.
Spellchecked document.
Repaginated document.

Processing document 2
Document traduit.
Spellchecked document.
Repaginated document.
Highlighting 'millennium'
```

OK, the idea here was to allow our production team to quickly configure a check to see if the process was likely to fail, before embarking on a resource-intensive task. Let's say DocumentProcesses.TranslateIntoFrench is a very time-consuming function, and they've discovered that any document whose text contains a question mark (?) will fail.

They've raised a bug with the machine translation team, but they don't want to hold up the entire production process until it is fixed—only 1 in 10 documents suffer from this problem.

They need to add a quick check to go with the `TranslateIntoFrench` process. It is only one line of code:

```
return !doc.Contains("?");
```

They could create a static class, with a static utility function to use as their predicate, but the boilerplate code would be about 10 times as long as the actual code itself. That's a barrier to readability, maintenance, and therefore the general well-being of the developer. C# comes to our rescue with a language feature called the *anonymous method*.

Using Anonymous Methods

An anonymous method is just like a regular function, except that it is *inlined* in the code at the point of use.

Let's update the code in our `Configure` function to include a delegate to an anonymous method to perform the check:

```
rc.AddProcess(
    DocumentProcesses.TranslateIntoFrench,
    delegate(Document doc)
        {
            return !doc.Text.Contains("?");
        });
```

The delegate to the anonymous method (i.e., the anonymous delegate) is passed as the second parameter to our `AddProcess` method. Let's pull it out so that we can see it a little more clearly (there's no need to make this change in your code; it is just for clarity):

```
Predicate<Document> predicate =
    delegate(Document doc)
        {
            return !doc.Text.Contains("?");
        }
```

Written like this, it looks recognizably like a function definition, except that we use the `delegate` keyword to let the compiler know we are providing a delegate. There's no need to specify the return type—that is inferred from the context. (In this case, the delegate type is `Predicate<T>`, so the compiler knows the return type is `bool`.) Any parameters in our parameter list are accessible only inside the body of the anonymous method itself.

Why do we call it an anonymous method? Because it doesn't have a name that can be referenced elsewhere! The variable that references the delegate to the anonymous method has a name, but not the anonymous delegate type, or the anonymous method itself.

If you compile and run the code you'll see the new output:

```
Processing document 1
The processing will not succeed
```

```
Processing document 2
Document traduit.
Spellchecked document.
Repaginated document.
```

The production team is happy; but is the job done?

Not quite; although this inline syntax for an anonymous method is a lot more compact than a static class/function declaration, we can get more compact and expressive still, using *lambda expression* syntax, which was added in C# 3.0 (anonymous methods having been around since C# 2.0).

Creating Delegates with Lambda Expressions

In the 1930s (a fertile time for computing theory!) two mathematicians named Church and Kleene devised a formal system for investigating the properties of functions. This was called *lambda calculus*, and (as further developed by Curry and others) it is still a staple part of computational theory for computer scientists.

Fast-forward 70 or so years, and we see just a hint of this theory peeking through in C#'s lambda expressions—only a hint, though, so bear with it.

As we saw before, you can think of a function as an expression that maps a set of inputs (the parameters) to an output (the return value).

Mathematicians sometimes use a notation similar to this to define a function:

$(x,y,z) \rightarrow x + y + z$

You can read this as defining a function that operates on three parameters (x, y, and z). The result of the function is just the sum of the three parameters, and, by definition, it can have *no side effects on the system*. The parameters themselves aren't modified by the function; we just map from the input parameters to a result.

Lambda expressions in C# use syntax very similar to this to define functional expressions. Here's the C# equivalent of that mathematical expression we used earlier:

```
(x,y,z) => x + y + z;
```

 Notice how it rather cutely uses => as the programming language equivalent of →. C++ users should not mistake this for the -> operator—it is quite different!

This defines a lambda expression that takes three parameters and returns the sum of those three parameters.

Some languages enforce the *no side effects* constraint; but in C# there is nothing to stop you from writing a lambda expression such as this one:

```
(x,y,z) =>
{
    SomeStaticClass.CrashAndBurnAndMessWithEverything();
    x.ModifyInternalState();
    return x + y + z;
}
```

(Incidentally, this form of lambda expression, using braces to help define its body, is called a *statement-form lambda*.) In C#, a lambda is really just a concise way to write an anonymous method. We're just writing normal code, so we can include operations that have side effects.

So, although C# brings along some functional techniques with lambda syntax, it is not a "pure" functional language like ML or F#. Nor does it intend to be.

So, what use is a lambda, then?

We'll see some very powerful techniques in Chapter 8 and Chapter 14, where lambdas play an important role in LINQ. Some of the data access features of the .NET Framework use the fact that we can convert lambdas into data structures called *expression trees*, which can be composed to create complex query-like expressions over various types of data.

For now, we're merely going to take advantage of the fact that we can implicitly create a delegate from a lambda, resulting in less cluttered code.

How do we write our anonymous delegate as a lambda? Here's the original:

```
Predicate<Document> predicate =
    delegate(Document doc )
    {
        return !doc.Text.Contains("?");
    }
```

And here it is rewritten using a lambda expression:

```
Predicate<Document> predicate = doc => !doc.Text.Contains("?");
```

Compact, isn't it!

For a lot of developers, this syntax takes some getting used to, because it is completely unlike anything they've ever seen before. Where are the type declarations? Is this taking advantage of some of these dynamic programming techniques we've heard so much about?

The short answer is no (but we'll get to dynamic typing in Chapter 18, don't worry). One of the nicer features of lambda expression syntax is that it takes care of working out what types the various parameters need to be, based on the context. In this case, the compiler knows that it needs to produce a `Predicate<Document>`, so it can infer that the parameter type for the lambda must be a `Document`. You even get full IntelliSense on your lambda parameters in Visual Studio.

 It is well worth getting used to reading and writing lambdas; you'll find them to be a very useful and expressive means of defining short functions, especially when we look at various aspects of the LINQ technologies and expression composition in later chapters.

Most developers, once they get over the initial comprehension hurdles, fall in love with lambdas—I promise!

Delegates in Properties

The delegates we've seen so far have taken one or more parameters, and returned either `void` (an `Action<>`) or a `bool` (a `Predicate<T>`).

But we can define a delegate to any sort of function we like. What if we want to provide a mechanism that allows the client to be notified when each processing step has been completed, and provide the processor with some text to insert into a process log?

Our callback delegate might look like this:

```
delegate string LogTextProvider(Document doc);
```

We could add a property to our `DocumentProcessor` so that we can get and set the callback function (see Example 5-16).

Example 5-16. A property that holds a delegate

```
class DocumentProcessor
{
    public LogTextProvider LogTextProvider
    {
        get;
        set;
    }
    // ...
}
```

And then we could make use of it in our `Process` method, as shown in Example 5-17.

Example 5-17. Using a delegate in a property

```
public void Process(Document doc)
{
    // First time, do the quick check
    foreach (ActionCheckPair process in processes)
    {
        if (process.QuickCheck != null && !process.QuickCheck(doc))
        {
            Console.WriteLine("The process will not succeed.");
            if (LogTextProvider != null)
```

```
        {
            Console.WriteLine(LogTextProvider(doc));
        }
        return;
    }
}

// Then perform the action
foreach (ActionCheckPair process in processes)
{
    process.Action(doc);
    if (LogTextProvider != null)
    {
        Console.WriteLine(LogTextProvider(doc));
    }
}
}
```

Notice that we're checking that our property is not null, and then we use standard delegate syntax to call the function that it references.

Let's set a callback in our client (see Example 5-18).

Example 5-18. Setting a property with a lambda

```
static void Main(string[] args)
{
    // ...

    DocumentProcessor processor = Configure();

    processor.LogTextProvider = (doc => "Some text for the log...");

    // ...
}
```

Here we used a lambda expression to provide a delegate that takes a Document parameter called doc, and returns a string. In this case, it is just a constant string. Later, we'll do some work to emit a more useful message.

Take a moment to notice again how compact the lambda syntax is, and how the compiler infers all those parameter types for us. Remember how much code we had to write to do this sort of thing back in the world of abstract base classes?

Compile and run, and we see the following output:

```
Processing document 1
The processing will not succeed.
Some text for the log...

Processing document 2
Document traduit.
Some text for the log...
Spellchecked document.
Some text for the log...
```

```
Repaginated document.
Some text for the log...
Highlighting 'millennium'
Some text for the log...
```

That's an example of a delegate for a function that returns something other than **void** or a **bool**. As you might have already guessed, the .NET Framework provides us with a generic type so that we don't have to declare those delegates by hand, either.

Generic Delegates for Functions

The .NET Framework exposes a generic class called **Func<T, TResult>**, which you can read as "Func-of T and TResult."

As with **Predicate<T>** and **Action<T>** the first type parameter determines the type of the first parameter of the function referenced by the delegate.

Unlike **Predicate<T>** or **Action<T>** we also get to specify the type of the return value, using the last type parameter: **TResult**.

 Just like Action<T>, there is a whole family of Func<> types which take one, two, three, and more parameters. Before .NET 4, Func<> went up to four parameters, but now goes all the way up to 16.

So we could replace our custom delegate type with a Func<>. We can delete the delegate declaration:

```
delegate string LogTextProvider(Document doc);
```

and update the property:

```
public Func<Document,string> LogTextProvider
{
    get;
    set;
}
```

We can build and run without any changes to our client code because the new property declaration still expects a delegate for a function with the same signature. And we still get a bit of log text:

```
Processing document 1
The processing will not succeed.
Some text for the log...

Processing document 2
Document traduit.
Some text for the log...
Spellchecked document.
Some text for the log...
Repaginated document.
```

```
Some text for the log...
Highlighting 'millennium'
Some text for the log...
```

OK, let's go back and have a look at that log function. As we noted earlier, it isn't very useful right now. We can improve it by logging the name of the file we have processed after each output stage, to help the production team diagnose problems.

Example 5-19 shows an update to the Main function to do that.

Example 5-19. Doing more in our logging callback

```
static void Main(string[] args)
{
    Document doc1 = new Document
    {
        Author = "Matthew Adams",
        DocumentDate = new DateTime(2000, 01, 01),
        Text = "Am I a year early?"
    };
    Document doc2 = new Document
    {
        Author = "Ian Griffiths",
        DocumentDate = new DateTime(2001, 01, 01),
        Text = "This is the new millennium, I promise you."
    };
    Document doc3 = new Document
    {
        Author = "Matthew Adams",
        DocumentDate = new DateTime(2002, 01, 01),
        Text = "Another year, another document."
    };

    string documentBeingProcessed = null;
    DocumentProcessor processor = Configure();

    processor.LogTextProvider = (doc => documentBeingProcessed);

    documentBeingProcessed = "(Document 1)";
    processor.Process(doc1);
    Console.WriteLine();
    documentBeingProcessed = "(Document 2)";
    processor.Process(doc2);
    Console.WriteLine();
    documentBeingProcessed = "(Document 3)";
    processor.Process(doc3);

    Console.ReadKey();
}
```

We added a third document to the set, just so that we can see more get processed. Then we set up a local variable called documentBeingProcessed. As we move through the documents we update that variable to reflect our current status.

How do we get that information into the lambda expression? Simple: we just use it!

Compile and run that code, and you'll see the following output:

```
The processing will not succeed.
(Document 1)

Document traduit.
(Document 2)
Spellchecked document.
(Document 2)
Repaginated document.
(Document 2)
Highlighting 'millennium'
(Document 2)

Document traduit.
(Document 3)
Spellchecked document.
(Document 3)
Repaginated document.
(Document 3)
```

We took advantage of the fact that *an anonymous method has access to variables declared in its parent scope*, in addition to anything in its own scope. For more information about this, see the sidebar below.

Closures

In general, we call an instance of a function and the set of variables on which it operates a *closure*.

In a pure functional language, a closure is typically implemented by taking a snapshot of the values of the variables at the time at which the closure is created, along with a reference to the function concerned, and those values are immutable.

In C#, a similar technique is applied—but the language allows us to modify those variables *after the closure has been created*.

As we see in this chapter, we can use this to our advantage, but we have to be careful to understand and manage the scope of the variables in the closure to avoid peculiar side effects.

We've seen how to read variables in our containing scope, but what about writing back to them? That works too. Let's create a process counter that ticks up every time we execute a process, and add it to our logging function (see Example 5-20).

Example 5-20. Modifying surrounding variables from a nested method

```
static void Main(string[] args)
{
    // ... (document setup)

    DocumentProcessor processor = Configure();
```

```
    string documentBeingProcessed = "(No document set)";
    int processCount = 0;

    processor.LogTextProvider = (doc => {
                                    processCount += 1;
                                    return documentBeingProcessed;
                                });

    documentBeingProcessed = "(Document 1)";
    processor.Process(doc1);
    Console.WriteLine();
    documentBeingProcessed = "(Document 2)";
    processor.Process(doc2);
    Console.WriteLine();
    documentBeingProcessed = "(Document 3)";
    processor.Process(doc3);

    Console.WriteLine();
    Console.WriteLine("Executed " + processCount + " processes.");

    Console.ReadKey();
}
```

We added a processCount variable at method scope, which we initialized to zero. We've switched our lambda expression into the *statement form* with the braces so that we can write multiple statements in the function body. In addition to returning the name of the document being processed, we also increment our processCount.

Finally, at the end of processing, we write out a line that tells us how many processes we've executed. So our output looks like this:

```
The processing will not succeed.
(Document 1)

Document traduit.
(Document 2)
Spellchecked document.
(Document 2)
Repaginated document.
(Document 2)
Highlighting 'millennium'
(Document 2)

Document traduit.
(Document 3)
Spellchecked document.
(Document 3)
Repaginated document.
(Document 3)
(Document 3)

Executed 9 processes.
```

OK, our production team is very happy with all of that, but they have another requirement. Apparently, they have one team working on some diagnostic components that are going to track the time taken to execute some of their processes, and another team developing some real-time display of all the processes as they run through the system. They want to know when a process is about to be executed and when it has completed so that these teams can execute some of their own code.

Our first thought might be to implement a couple of additional callbacks: one called as processing starts, and the other as it ends; but that won't quite meet their needs—they have two separate teams who both want, independently, to hook into it.

We need a pattern for notifying several clients that something has occurred. The .NET Framework steps up with events.

Notifying Clients with Events

An *event* is *raised* (or *sent*) by a *publisher* (or *sender*) when something of interest occurs (such as an action taking place, or a property changing). Clients can *subscribe* to the event by providing a suitable delegate, rather like the callbacks we used previously. The method wrapped by the delegate is called the *event handler*. The neat thing is that *more than one client* can subscribe to the event.

Here's an example of a couple of events that we can add to the `DocumentProcessor` to help our production team:

```
class DocumentProcessor
{
    public event EventHandler Processing;
    public event EventHandler Processed;

    // ...
}
```

Notice that we use the keyword `event` to indicate that what follows is an event declaration. We then specify the delegate type for the event (`EventHandler`) and the name of the event (using PascalCasing). So, this is just like a declaration for a public field of type `EventHandler`, but annotated with the `event` keyword.

What does this `EventHandler` delegate look like? The framework defines it like this:

```
delegate void EventHandler(object sender, EventArgs e);
```

Notice that our delegate takes two parameters. The first is a reference to the publisher of the event so that subscribers can tell who raised it. The second is some data associated with the event. The `EventArgs` class is defined in the framework, and is a placeholder for events that don't need any extra information. We'll see how to customize this later.

 Almost all events follow this two-argument pattern. Technically, they're not required to—you can use any delegate type for an event. But in practice, this pattern is almost universal.

So, how do we raise an event? Well, it really is just like a delegate, so we can use the delegate calling syntax as shown in the OnProcessing and OnProcessed methods in Example 5-21.

Example 5-21. Raising events

```
public void Process(Document doc)
{
    OnProcessing(EventArgs.Empty);
    // First time, do the quick check
    foreach (ActionCheckPair process in processes)
    {
        if (process.QuickCheck != null && !process.QuickCheck(doc))
        {
            Console.WriteLine("The process will not succeed.");
            if (LogTextProvider != null)
            {
                Console.WriteLine(LogTextProvider(doc));
            }
            OnProcessed(EventArgs.Empty);
            return;
        }
    }

    // Then perform the action
    foreach (ActionCheckPair process in processes)
    {
        process.Action(doc);
        if (LogTextProvider != null)
        {
            Console.WriteLine(LogTextProvider(doc));
        }
    }
    OnProcessed(EventArgs.Empty);
}

private void OnProcessing(EventArgs e)
{
    if (Processing != null)
    {
        Processing(this, e);
    }
}

private void OnProcessed(EventArgs e)
{
    if (Processed != null)
    {
        Processed(this, e);
    }
}
```

Notice how we pulled out the code to check for null and execute the delegate into functions called OnXXX. This isn't strictly necessary, but it is a very common practice.

 If we are designing our class as a base, we often mark this kind of method as a `protected virtual` so that derived classes can override the event-raising function instead of subscribing to the event.

This can be more efficient than going through the event, and it allows us (optionally) to decline to raise the event by not calling on the base implementation.

Be careful to document whether derived classes are allowed *not* to call the base, though!

Now we need to subscribe to those events. So let's create a couple of classes to simulate what the production department would need to do (see Example 5-22).

Example 5-22. Subscribing to and unsubscribing from events

```
class ProductionDeptTool1
{
    public void Subscribe ( DocumentProcessor processor )
    {
        processor.Processing += processor_Processing;
        processor.Processed += processor_Processed;
    }

    public void Unsubscribe(DocumentProcessor processor)
    {
        processor.Processing -= processor_Processing;
        processor.Processed -= processor_Processed;
    }

    void processor_Processing(object sender, EventArgs e)
    {
        Console.WriteLine("Tool1 has seen processing.");
    }

    void processor_Processed(object sender, EventArgs e)
    {
        Console.WriteLine("Tool1 has seen that processing is complete.");
    }
}

class ProductionDeptTool2
{
    public void Subscribe( DocumentProcessor processor )
    {
        processor.Processing +=
            (sender, e) => Console.WriteLine("Tool2 has seen processing.");
        processor.Processed +=
            (sender, e) =>
                Console.WriteLine("Tool2 has seen that processing is complete.");
    }
}
```

To subscribe to an event we use the += operator, with a suitable delegate. You can see in ProductionDeptTool1.Subscribe that we used the standard delegate syntax, and in ProductionDeptTool2.Subscribe we used the lambda expression syntax.

 Of course, you don't have to subscribe to events in methods called Subscribe—you can do it anywhere you like!

When you're done watching an event for any reason, you can unsubscribe using the -= operator and another delegate to the same method. You can see that in the ProductionDeptTool1.Unsubscribe method.

When you subscribe to an event your subscriber implicitly holds a reference to the publisher. This means that the garbage collector won't be able to collect the publisher if there is still a rooted reference to the subscriber. It is a good idea to provide a means of unsubscribing from events you are no longer actively observing, to avoid growing your working set unnecessarily.

Let's add some code to our Main method to make use of the two new tools, as shown in Example 5-23.

Example 5-23. Updated Main method

```
static void Main(string[] args)
{
    // ...

    ProductionDeptTool1 tool1 = new ProductionDeptTool1();
    tool1.Subscribe(processor);

    ProductionDeptTool2 tool2 = new ProductionDeptTool2();
    tool2.Subscribe(processor);

    documentBeingProcessed = "(Document 1)";

    // ...

    Console.ReadKey();
}
```

If we compile and run, we now see the following output:

```
Tool1 has seen processing.
Tool2 has seen processing.
The processing will not succeed.
(Document 1)
Tool1 has seen that processing is complete.
Tool2 has seen that processing is complete.

Tool1 has seen processing.
Tool2 has seen processing.
```

```
Document traduit.
(Document 2)
Spellchecked document.
(Document 2)
Repaginated document.
(Document 2)
Highlighting 'millennium'
(Document 2)
Tool1 has seen that processing is complete.
Tool2 has seen that processing is complete.

Tool1 has seen processing.
Tool2 has seen processing.
Document traduit.
(Document 3)
Spellchecked document.
(Document 3)
Repaginated document.
(Document 3)
(Document 3)
Tool1 has seen that processing is complete.
Tool2 has seen that processing is complete.

Executed 9 processes.
```

You might notice that the event handlers have been executed in the order in which we added them. This is *not guaranteed* to be the case, and you cannot depend on this behavior.

If you need deterministic ordering (as we did for our processes, for example) you should not use an event.

Earlier, I alluded to the fact that we can customize the data we send through with the event. We do this by deriving our own class from **EventArgs**, and adding extra properties or methods to it. Let's say we want to send the current document through in the event; we can create a class like the one shown in Example 5-24.

Example 5-24. Custom event arguments class

```
class ProcessEventArgs : EventArgs
{
    // Handy constructor
    public ProcessEventArgs(Document document)
    {
        Document = document;
    }

    // The extra property
    // We don't want subscribers to be able
    // to update this property, so we make
    // it private
    // (Of course, this doesn't prevent them
    // from changing the Document itself)
```

```
    public Document Document
    {
        get;
        private set;
    }
}
```

We also need to create a suitable delegate for the event, one that takes a `ProcessEven`
`tArgs` as its second parameter rather than the `EventArgs` base class. We could do this
by hand, sticking to the convention of calling the first parameter `sender` and the data
parameter `e`:

```
delegate void ProcessEventHandler(object sender, ProcessEventArgs e);
```

Once again, this is such a common thing to need that the framework provides us with
a generic type, `EventHandler<T>`, to save us the boilerplate code. So we can replace the
`ProcessEventHandler` with an `EventHandler<ProcessEventArgs>`.

Let's update our event declarations (see Example 5-25).

Example 5-25. Updated event members

```
public event EventHandler<ProcessEventArgs> Processing;
public event EventHandler<ProcessEventArgs> Processed;
```

and then our helper methods which raise the event that will need to take a `ProcessE`
`ventArgs` (see Example 5-26).

Example 5-26. Updated code for raising events

```
private void OnProcessing(ProcessEventArgs e)
{
    if (Processing != null)
    {
        Processing(this, e);
    }
}

private void OnProcessed(ProcessEventArgs e)
{
    if (Processed != null)
    {
        Processed(this, e);
    }
}
```

And finally, our calls to those methods will need to create an appropriate `ProcessEven`
`tArgs` object, as shown in Example 5-27.

Example 5-27. Creating the event arguments object

```
public void Process(Document doc)
{
    ProcessEventArgs e = new ProcessEventArgs(doc);
    OnProcessing(e);
```

```
    // First time, do the quick check
    foreach (ActionCheckPair process in processes)
    {
        if (process.QuickCheck != null && !process.QuickCheck(doc))
        {
            Console.WriteLine("The process will not succeed.");
            if (LogTextProvider != null)
            {
                Console.WriteLine(LogTextProvider(doc));
            }
            OnProcessed(e);
            return;
        }
    }

    // Then perform the action
    foreach (ActionCheckPair process in processes)
    {
        process.Action(doc);
        if (LogTextProvider != null)
        {
            Console.WriteLine(LogTextProvider(doc));
        }
    }
    OnProcessed(e);
}
```

Notice how we happen to reuse the same event data for each event we raise. That's safe to do because our event argument instance cannot be modified—its only property has a **private** setter. If it were possible for event handlers to change the event argument object, it would be risky to use the same one for both events.

We could offer our colleagues on the production team another facility using these events. We already saw how they need to perform a quick check before each individual process to determine whether they should abort processing. We can take advantage of our **Processing** event to give them the option of canceling the whole process before it even gets off the ground.

The framework defines a class called **CancelEventArgs** which adds a **Boolean** property called **Cancel** to the basic **EventArgs**. Subscribers can set the property to **True**, and the publisher is expected to abort the operation.

Let's add a new **EventArgs** class for that (see Example 5-28).

Example 5-28. A cancelable event argument class

```
class ProcessCancelEventArgs : CancelEventArgs
{
    public ProcessCancelEventArgs(Document document)
    {
        Document = document;
    }

    public Document Document
```

```
    {
        get;
        private set;
    }
}
```

We'll update the declaration of our `Processing` event, and its corresponding helper, as shown in Example 5-29 (but we'll leave the `Processed` event as it is—if the document has already been processed, it's too late to cancel it).

Example 5-29. A cancelable event

```
public event EventHandler<ProcessCancelEventArgs> Processing;

private void OnProcessing(ProcessCancelEventArgs e)
{
    if (Processing != null)
    {
        Processing(this, e);
    }
}
```

Finally, we need to update the `Process` method to create the right kind of event argument object, and to honor requests for cancellation (see Example 5-30).

Example 5-30. Supporting cancellation

```
public void Process(Document doc)
{
    ProcessEventArgs e = new ProcessEventArgs(doc);
    ProcessCancelEventArgs ce = new ProcessCancelEventArgs(doc);
    OnProcessing(ce);
    if (ce.Cancel)
    {
        Console.WriteLine("Process canceled.");
        if (LogTextProvider != null)
        {
            Console.WriteLine(LogTextProvider(doc));
        }
        return;
    }
    // ...
}
```

Now we'll make use of this in one of our production tools, as shown in Example 5-31.

Example 5-31. Taking advantage of cancelability

```
class ProductionDeptTool1
{
    public void Subscribe(DocumentProcessor processor)
    {
        processor.Processing += processor_Processing;
        processor.Processed += processor_Processed;
    }
```

```csharp
    public void Unsubscribe(DocumentProcessor processor)
    {
        processor.Processing -= processor_Processing;
        processor.Processed -= processor_Processed;
    }

    void processor_Processing(object sender, ProcessCancelEventArgs e)
    {
        Console.WriteLine("Tool1 has seen processing, and not canceled.");
    }

    void processor_Processed(object sender, EventArgs e)
    {
        Console.WriteLine("Tool1 has seen that processing is complete.");
    }
}

class ProductionDeptTool2
{
    public void Subscribe(DocumentProcessor processor)
    {
        processor.Processing += (sender, e) =>
            {
                Console.WriteLine("Tool2 has seen processing and canceled it");
                if(e.Document.Text.Contains("document"))
                {
                    e.Cancel = true;
                }
            };
        processor.Processed += (sender, e) =>
            Console.WriteLine("Tool2 has seen that processing is complete.");
    }
}
```

Notice how we don't *have* to update the event data parameter—we can take advantage of polymorphism and just refer to it through its base type, unless we want to take advantage of its new features. In the lambda expression syntax, of course, the new type parameter is inferred and we don't have to change anything; we can just update the handler in `ProductionDeptTool2` to cancel if it sees the text `"document"`.

If we compile and run, we now see the following output:

```
The process will not succeed.
(Document 1)
Tool1 has seen that processing is complete.
Tool2 has seen that processing is complete.

Tool1 has seen processing, and not canceled.
Tool2 has seen processing, and not canceled.
Document traduit.
(Document 2)
Spellchecked document.
(Document 2)
Repaginated document.
```

```
(Document 2)
Highlighting 'millennium'
(Document 2)
Tool1 has seen that processing is complete.
Tool2 has seen that processing is complete.

Tool1 has seen processing, and not canceled.
Tool2 has seen processing and canceled.
Process canceled.
(Document 3)

Executed 6 processes.
```

So we have our cancellation behavior, but we have to be very careful. Notice that
Tool1 happened to see the event first, and it happily executed its handler, before
Tool2 got in and canceled the whole thing. When you write handlers for cancelable
events, you *must* ensure that it doesn't matter if some or all of those handlers never get
called and that they behave correctly if the action they expect never actually occurs.
Cancelable events need very careful documentation to indicate how they relate to the
actions around them, and the exact semantics of cancellation. It is therefore (in general)
a bad idea to do what we have just done, and convert a noncancelable event into a
cancelable one, if your code has already shipped; you stand a very good chance of
breaking any clients that just recompile successfully against the new version.

Exposing Large Numbers of Events

Some classes (particularly those related to user interactions) need to expose a very large
number of events. If you use the normal event syntax shown in the preceding examples,
storage is allocated for every single event you declare, even if the events have no subscribers. This means that objects of this type can get very large, very quickly.

To avoid this situation, C# provides you with the ability to manage storage for the
events yourself, using syntax similar to a property getter and setter, with your own
backing storage:

```
public event EventHandler MyEvent
{
    add
    {
        // Code to add handler here
    }
    remove
    {
        // Code to remove handler here
    }
}
```

Typically, you use a Dictionary<Key,Val> to create the backing storage for the event
only when it gets its first subscriber. (Dictionaries are described in Chapter 9.)

Example 5-32 updates the DocumentProcessor we're developing in this chapter to use a dictionary for the backing storage for its events.

Example 5-32. Custom event storage

```
class DocumentProcessor
{
    private Dictionary<string, Delegate> events;

    public event EventHandler<ProcessCancelEventArgs> Processing
    {
        add
        {
            Delegate theDelegate =
                EnsureEvent("Processing");
            events["Processing"] =
                ((EventHandler<ProcessCancelEventArgs>)
                    theDelegate) + value;
        }
        remove
        {
            Delegate theDelegate =
                EnsureEvent("Processing");
            events["Processing"] =
                ((EventHandler<ProcessCancelEventArgs>)
                    theDelegate) - value;
        }
    }

    public event EventHandler<ProcessEventArgs> Processed
    {
        add
        {
            Delegate theDelegate =
                EnsureEvent("Processed");
            events["Processed"] =
                ((EventHandler<ProcessEventArgs>)
                    theDelegate) + value;
        }
        remove
        {
            Delegate theDelegate =
                EnsureEvent("Processed");
            events["Processed"] =
                ((EventHandler<ProcessEventArgs>)
                    theDelegate) - value;
        }
    }

    private Delegate EnsureEvent(string eventName)
    {
        // Construct the dictionary if it doesn't already
        // exist
        if (events == null)
        {
```

```
            events = new Dictionary<string, Delegate>();
        }
        // Add a placeholder for the delegate if we don't
        // have it already
        Delegate theDelegate = null;
        if (!events.TryGetValue(
                eventName, out theDelegate))
        {
            events.Add(eventName, null);
        }
        return theDelegate;
    }

    private void OnProcessing(ProcessCancelEventArgs e)
    {
        Delegate eh = null;
        if( events != null &&
            events.TryGetValue("Processing", out eh) )
        {
            EventHandler<ProcessCancelEventArgs> pceh =
                eh as EventHandler<ProcessCancelEventArgs>;
            if (pceh != null)
            {
                pceh(this, e);
            }
        }
    }

    private void OnProcessed(ProcessEventArgs e)
    {
        Delegate eh = null;
        if (events != null &&
            events.TryGetValue("Processed", out eh))
        {
            EventHandler<ProcessEventArgs> pceh =
                eh as EventHandler<ProcessEventArgs>;
            if (pceh != null)
            {
                pceh(this, e);
            }
        }
    }

    // ...
}
```

Obviously, that's a lot more complex than the automatic method, and you would not normally use it for a class that exposes just a couple of events, but it can save a lot of working set for classes that are either large in number, or publish a large number of events but have few subscribers.

Summary

In this chapter, we saw how functional techniques provide powerful reuse and extensibility mechanisms for our programs, in ways that can be more flexible and yet simpler than class-based approaches. We also saw how events enabled a publisher-to-multiple-subscribers relationship. In the next chapter, we'll look at how we deal with unexpected situations: errors, failures, and exceptions.

Summary

CHAPTER 6

Dealing with Errors

Errors happen all the time; they're a fact of life:

- Despite the best efforts of Microsoft Word, an army of highly skilled reviewers and editors, and even your authors, it would be surprising if there wasn't a typographical error in a book of this length.

- Although they are relatively few and far between, there are bugs in the .NET Framework—hence the need for occasional service packs.

- You might type your credit card number for an online transaction and accidentally transpose two digits; or forget to type in the expiration date.

Like it or not, we're going to have to face up to the fact that there are going to be errors of all kinds to deal with in our software too. In this chapter, we'll look at various types of errors, the tools that C# and the .NET Framework give us to deal with them, and some strategies for applying those tools.

First, we need to recognize that all errors are not made the same. We've classified a few of the more common ones in Table 6-1.

Table 6-1. A far-from-exhaustive list of some common errors

Error	Description/example
Bug	A failure to implement a contract according to its documentation.
Unexpected behavior	A failure to document a contract properly for all expected input.
Unexpected input	A client passes data to a method that is outside some expected range.
Unexpected data type	A client passes data to a method that is not of the expected type.
Unexpected data format	A client passes data to a method in a format that is not recognized.
Unexpected result	A client receives information from a method that it did not expect for the given input.
Unexpected method call	The class wasn't expecting you to call a particular method at that time—you hadn't performed some required initialization, for example.
Unavailable resource	A method tried to access a resource of some kind and it was not present—a hardware device was not plugged in, for instance.

Error	Description/example
Contended resource	A method tried to access a scarce resource of some kind (memory or a hardware device that cannot be shared), and it was not available because someone else was using it.

Although bugs are probably the most obvious type of error, we won't actually be dealing with them directly in this chapter. We will, however, look at how our error-handling techniques can make it easier (or harder!) to find the bugs that are often the cause of the other, better defined issues.

Let's get started with an example we can use to look at error-handling techniques. We're going to branch out into the world of robotics for this one, and build a turtle-controlling application. The real-world turtle is a rectangular piece of board on which are mounted two motors that can drive two wheels. The wheels are located in the middle of the left and right edges of the board, and there are nondriven castor wheels at the front and back to give it a bit of stability. We can drive the two motors independently: we can move forward, move backward, or stop. And by moving the wheels in different directions, or moving one wheel at time, we can steer it about a bit like a tank.

Let's create a class to model our turtle (see Example 6-1).

Example 6-1. The Turtle class

```
class Turtle
{
    // The width of the platform
    public double PlatformWidth
    {
        get; set;
    }

    // The height of the platform
    public double PlatformHeight
    {
        get; set;
    }

    // The speed at which the motors drive the wheels,
    // in meters per second. For ease, we assume that takes account
    // of the distance traveled by the tires in contact
    // with the ground, and any slipping
    public double MotorSpeed
    {
        get; set;
    }

    // The state of the left motor
    public MotorState LeftMotorState
    {
        get; set;
    }
```

```csharp
    // The state of the right motor
    public MotorState RightMotorState
    {
        get; set;
    }

    // The current position of the turtle
    public Point CurrentPosition
    {
        get; private set;
    }

    // The current orientation of the turtle
    public double CurrentOrientation
    {
        get; private set;
    }
}

// The current state of a motor
enum MotorState
{
    Stopped,
    Running,
    Reversed
}
```

In addition to the motor control, we can define the size of the platform and the speed at which the motors rotate the wheels. We also have a couple of properties that tell us where the turtle is right now, relative to its point of origin, and the direction in which it is currently pointing.

To make our turtle simulator actually do something, we can add a method which makes time pass. This looks at the state of the different motors and applies an appropriate algorithm to calculate the new position of the turtle. Example 6-2 shows our first, somewhat naive, go at it.

Example 6-2. Simulating turtle motion

```csharp
// Run the turtle for the specified duration
public void RunFor(double duration)
{
    if (LeftMotorState == MotorState.Stopped &&
        RightMotorState == MotorState.Stopped)
    {
        // If we are at a full stop, nothing will happen
        return;
    }

    // The motors are both running in the same direction
    // then we just drive
    if ((LeftMotorState == MotorState.Running &&
        RightMotorState == MotorState.Running) ||
        (LeftMotorState == MotorState.Reversed &&
```

```
        RightMotorState == MotorState.Reversed))
    {
        Drive(duration);
        return;
    }

    // The motors are running in opposite directions,
    // so we don't move, we just rotate about the
    // center of the rig
    if ((LeftMotorState == MotorState.Running &&
         RightMotorState == MotorState.Reversed) ||
        (LeftMotorState == MotorState.Reversed &&
         RightMotorState == MotorState.Running))
    {
        Rotate(duration);
        return;
    }
}
```

If both wheels are pointing in the same direction (forward or reverse), we drive (or reverse) in the direction we are pointing. If they are driving in opposite directions, we rotate about our center. If both are stopped, we will remain stationary.

Example 6-3 shows the implementations of **Drive** and **Rotate**. They use a little bit of trigonometry to get the job done.

Example 6-3. Simulating rotation and movement

```
private void Rotate(double duration)
{
    // This is the total circumference of turning circle
    double circum = Math.PI * PlatformWidth;
    // This is the total distance traveled
    double d = duration * MotorSpeed;
    if (LeftMotorState == MotorState.Reversed)
    {
        // And we're going backwards if the motors are reversed
        d *= -1.0;
    }
    // So we've driven it this proportion of the way round
    double proportionOfWholeCircle = d / circum;
    // Once round is 360 degrees (or 2pi radians), so we have traveled
    // this far:
    CurrentOrientation =
        CurrentOrientation + (Math.PI * 2.0 * proportionOfWholeCircle);
}

private void Drive(double duration)
{
    // This is the total distance traveled
    double d = duration * MotorSpeed;
    if (LeftMotorState == MotorState.Reversed)
    {
        // And we're going backwards if the motors are reversed
        d *= -1.0;
```

```
    }
    // Bit of trigonometry for the change in the x,y coordinates
    double deltaX = d * Math.Sin(CurrentOrientation);
    double deltaY = d * Math.Cos(CurrentOrientation);

    // And update the position
    CurrentPosition =
        new Point(CurrentPosition.X + deltaX, CurrentPosition.Y + deltaY);
}
```

Let's write a quick test program to see whether the code we've written actually does what we expect (see Example 6-4).

Example 6-4. Testing the turtle

```
static void Main(string[] args)
{
    // Here's our turtle
    Turtle arthurTheTurtle =
        new Turtle {PlatformWidth = 10.0, PlatformHeight = 10.0, MotorSpeed = 5.0};

    ShowPosition(arthurTheTurtle);

    // We want to proceed forwards
    arthurTheTurtle.LeftMotorState = MotorState.Running;
    arthurTheTurtle.RightMotorState = MotorState.Running;
    // For two seconds
    arthurTheTurtle.RunFor(2.0);

    ShowPosition(arthurTheTurtle);


    // Now, let's rotate clockwise for a bit
    arthurTheTurtle.RightMotorState = MotorState.Reversed;
    // PI / 2 seconds should do the trick
    arthurTheTurtle.RunFor(Math.PI / 2.0);

    ShowPosition(arthurTheTurtle);


    // And let's go into reverse
    arthurTheTurtle.RightMotorState = MotorState.Reversed;
    arthurTheTurtle.LeftMotorState = MotorState.Reversed;

    // And run for 5 seconds
    arthurTheTurtle.RunFor(5);

    ShowPosition(arthurTheTurtle);

    // Then rotate back the other way
    arthurTheTurtle.RightMotorState = MotorState.Running;
    // And run for PI/4 seconds to give us 45 degrees
    arthurTheTurtle.RunFor(Math.PI / 4.0);

    ShowPosition(arthurTheTurtle);
```

```
    // And finally drive backwards for a bit
    arthurTheTurtle.RightMotorState = MotorState.Reversed;
    arthurTheTurtle.LeftMotorState = MotorState.Reversed;
    arthurTheTurtle.RunFor(Math.Cos(Math.PI / 4.0));

    ShowPosition(arthurTheTurtle);

    Console.ReadKey();
}

private static void ShowPosition(Turtle arthurTheTurtle)
{
    Console.WriteLine(
        "Arthur is at ({0}) and is pointing at angle {1:0.00} radians.",
        arthurTheTurtle.CurrentPosition,
        arthurTheTurtle.CurrentOrientation);
}
```

We chose the times for which to run quite carefully so that we end up going through
relatively readable distances and angles. (Hey, someone could design a more usable
facade over this API!) If we compile and run, we see the following output:

```
Arthur is at (0,0) and is pointing at angle 0.00 radians.
Arthur is at (0,10) and is pointing at angle 0.00 radians.
Arthur is at (0,10) and is pointing at angle 1.57 radians.
Arthur is at (-25,10) and is pointing at angle 1.57 radians.
Arthur is at (-25,10) and is pointing at angle 0.79 radians.
Arthur is at (-27.5,7.5) and is pointing at angle 0.79 radians.
```

OK, that seems fine for basic operation. But what happens if we change the width of
the platform to zero?

```
Turtle arthurTheTurtle =
    new Turtle { PlatformWidth = 0.0, PlatformHeight = 10.0, MotorSpeed = 5.0 };
```

Not only does that not make much sense, but the output is not very useful either; clearly
we have divide-by-zero problems:

```
Arthur is at (0,0) and is pointing at angle 0.00 radians.
Arthur is at (0,10) and is pointing at angle 0.00 radians.
Arthur is at (0,10) and is pointing at angle Infinity radians.
Arthur is at (NaN,NaN) and is pointing at angle Infinity radians.
Arthur is at (NaN,NaN) and is pointing at angle NaN radians.
Arthur is at (NaN,NaN) and is pointing at angle NaN radians.
```

Clearly, our real-world turtle could go badly wrong if we told it to rotate through an
infinite angle. At the very least, we'd get bored waiting for it to finish. We should prevent
the user from running it if the PlatformWidth is less than or equal to zero. Previously,
we used the following code:

```
// Run the turtle for the specified duration
public void RunFor(double duration)
{
```

```
    if (PlatformWidth <= 0.0)
    {
        // What to do here?
    }

    // ...
}
```

That detects the problem, but what should we do if our particular turtle is not set up correctly? Previously, we silently ignored the problem, and returned as though everything was just fine. Is that really what we want to do?

For this application it might be perfectly safe, but what if another developer uses our turtle with a paintbrush strapped to its back, to paint the lines on a tennis court? The developer added a few extra moves at the beginning of his sequence, and he didn't notice that he had inadvertently done so before he initialized the PlatformWidth. We could have a squiggly paint disaster on our hands!

Not a Number?

The System.Double type defines a number of constant values that are used to represent some very interesting doubles:

- Double.NaN is the result of dividing zero by zero (e.g., 0.0/0.0).
- Double.NegativeInfinity is the result of dividing a negative number by zero (e.g., -1.0/0.0).
- Double.PositiveInfinity is the result of dividing a positive number by zero (e.g., 1.0/0.0).

They also behave in interesting ways. For example, you can't compare one of these special values with another (e.g., (0.0/0.0 != Double.NaN)).

Instead, you have to use helper methods such as these:

- Double.IsNaN(0.0/0.0)
- Double.IsPositiveInfinity(1.0/0.0)
- Double.IsNegativeInfinity(-1.0/0.0)

If you don't care whether it is a positive or a negative infinity, just some sort of infinity, you can use this helper: Double.IsInfinity(1.0/0.0).

Be very careful when playing with infinities, as you can easily get into trouble!

When and How to Fail

Choosing when and how to fail is one of the big debates in software development. There is a lot of consensus about what we *do*, but things are much less clear-cut when it comes to failures.

You have a number of choices:

1. Try to plow on regardless.
2. Try to make sense of what has happened and work around it.
3. Return an error of some kind to your caller, and hope the caller knows what to do with it.
4. Stop.

At the moment, we're using option 1: try to plow on regardless; and you can see that this might or might not be dangerous. The difficulty is that we can be sure it is safe *only if we know why our client is calling us*. Given that we can't possibly have knowledge of the continuum of all possible clients (and their clients, and their clients' clients), plugging on regardless is, in general, *not safe*. We might be exposing ourselves to all sorts of security problems and data integrity issues of which we *cannot* be aware at this time.

What about option 2? Well, that is really an extension of the contract: we're saying that particular types of data outside the range we previously defined *are* valid, it is just that we'll special-case them to other values. This is quite common with range properties, where we clamp values outside the range to the minimum and maximum permitted values. Example 6-5 shows how we could implement that.

Example 6-5. Range checking

```
class Turtle
{
    // The width of the platform must be between 1.0 and 10.0 inclusive
    // Values outside this range will be coerced into the range.
    private double platformWidth;
    public double PlatformWidth
    {
        get { return platformWidth; }
        set
        {
            platformWidth = value;
            EnsurePlatformSize();
        }
    }

    // The height of the platform must be between 1.0 and 10.0 inclusive
    // Values outside this range will be coerced into the range.
    private double platformHeight;
    public double PlatformHeight
    {
        get { return platformHeight; }
        set
        {
            platformHeight = value;
            EnsurePlatformSize();
        }
    }
```

```
    // The new constructor initializes the platform size appropriately
    public Turtle()
    {
        EnsurePlatformSize();
    }

    // This method enforces the newly documented constraint
    // we added to the contract
    private void EnsurePlatformSize()
    {
        if (PlatformWidth < 1.0)
        {
            PlatformWidth = 1.0;
        }
        if (PlatformWidth > 10.0)
        {
            PlatformWidth = 10.0;
        }
        if (PlatformHeight < 1.0)
        {
            PlatformHeight = 1.0;
        }
        if (PlatformHeight > 10.0)
        {
            PlatformHeight = 10.0;
        }
    }
    // ...
}
```

Here we documented a constraint in our contract, and enforced that constraint first at construction, and then whenever clients attempt to modify the value.

We chose to enforce that constraint at the point when the value can be changed because that makes the effect of the constraint directly visible. If users set an out-of-bounds value and read it back they can immediately see the effect of the constraint on the property. That's not the only choice, of course. We could have done it just before we used it—but if we changed the implementation, or added features, we might have to add lots of calls to EnsurePlatformSize, and you can be certain that we'd forget one somewhere.

When we run the application again, we see the following output:

```
Arthur is at (0,0) and is pointing at angle 0.00 radians.
Arthur is at (0,10) and is pointing at angle 0.00 radians.
Arthur is at (0,10) and is pointing at angle 15.71 radians.
Arthur is at (-1.53075794227797E-14,35) and is pointing at angle 15.71 radians.
Arthur is at (-1.53075794227797E-14,35) and is pointing at angle 7.85 radians.
Arthur is at (-3.53553390593275,35) and is pointing at angle 7.85 radians.
```

Although this is a very useful technique, and it has clearly banished those less-than-useful NaNs, we have to consider: is this the right solution for this particular problem? Let's think about our tennis-court-painting robot again. Would we really want it to paint the court as though it were a 1-meter-wide robot, just because we forgot to initialize it? Looking at the distances traveled and the angles through which it has turned, the answer is clearly no!

 Constraints such as this are useful in lots of cases. We might want to ensure that some UI element not extend off the screen, or grow too big or small, for example. But equally, an online banking application that doesn't permit transactions less than $10 shouldn't just clamp the amount the user entered from $1 to $10 and carry on happily!

So let's backtrack a little and look at another option: returning a value that signifies an error.

Returning Error Values

For many years, programmers have written methods that detect errors, and which report those errors by returning an *error code*. Typically, this is a `Boolean` value of some kind, with `True` representing success and `False` failure. Or you might use either an `int` or an `enum` if you need to distinguish lots of different types of errors.

 Before we add an error return value, we should remove the code we just added that silently enforces the constraints. We can delete `EnsurePlat formSize` and any references to it. (Or if you're following along in Visual Studio and don't want to delete the code, just comment out all the relevant lines.)

So where are we going to return the error from? Our first instinct might be to put it in the `RunFor` method, where we suggested earlier; but look at the code—there's nothing substantive there. The problem actually occurs in `Rotate`. What happens if we change the `Rotate` method later so that it depends on different properties? Do we also update `RunFor` to check the new constraints? Will we remember?

It is `Rotate` that actually uses the properties, so as a rule of thumb we should do the checking there. It will also make the debugging easier later—we can put breakpoints near the origin of the error and *see* what is going wrong.

Let's change the `Rotate` method and see what happens (see Example 6-6).

Example 6-6. Indicating errors through the return value

```
private bool Rotate(double duration)
{
    if (PlatformWidth <= 0.0)
    {
        return false;
    }
```

```
    // This is the total circumference of turning circle
    double circum = Math.PI * PlatformWidth;
    // This is the total distance traveled
    double d = duration * MotorSpeed;
    if (LeftMotorState == MotorState.Reversed)
    {
        // And we're going backwards if the motors are reversed
        d *= -1.0;
    }
    // So we've driven it this proportion of the way round
    double proportionOfWholeCircle = d / circum;
    // Once round is 360 degrees (or 2pi radians), so we have traveled
    CurrentOrientation =
        CurrentOrientation + (Math.PI * 2.0 * proportionOfWholeCircle);
    return true;
}
```

If we compile and run with our all-new error checking added, we see the following output:

```
Arthur is at (0,0) and is pointing at angle 0.00 radians.
Arthur is at (0,10) and is pointing at angle 0.00 radians.
Arthur is at (0,10) and is pointing at angle 0.00 radians.
Arthur is at (0,-15) and is pointing at angle 0.00 radians.
Arthur is at (0,-15) and is pointing at angle 0.00 radians.
Arthur is at (0,-18.5355339059327) and is pointing at angle 0.00 radians.
```

Hmmm; that's not very good. **Rotate** has indeed failed, but we've carried on driving the turtle up and down that line because we didn't do anything with the return value.

 This is the great benefit, and great downside, of error return values: you can just ignore them.

Let's look at where we call **Rotate** and see what we can do with that error (see Example 6-7).

Example 6-7. Detecting failure and then wondering what to do with it

```
// Run the turtle for the specified duration
public void RunFor(double duration)
{
    // ...

    // The motors are running in opposite directions,
    // so we don't move, we just rotate about the
    // center of the rig
    if ((LeftMotorState == MotorState.Running &&
         RightMotorState == MotorState.Reversed) ||
        (LeftMotorState == MotorState.Reversed &&
         RightMotorState == MotorState.Running))
    {
```

```
        if (!Rotate(duration))
        {
            // It failed, so what now?
        }
        return;
    }
}
```

It is simple enough to check to see if it failed, but what are we actually going to do about it? Is there any action we can take? Not surprisingly, the answer is no—we know no more about the needs of our caller than we did when we were discussing the other options. So we are going to have to pass the error on up. Example 6-8 shows an implementation of Run that does that.

Example 6-8. Passing the buck

```
// Run the turtle for the specified duration
// Returns false if there was a failure
// Or true if the run succeeded
public bool RunFor(double duration)
{
    if (LeftMotorState == MotorState.Stopped &&
        RightMotorState == MotorState.Stopped)
    {
        // If we are at a full stop, nothing will happen
        return true;
    }

    // The motors are both running in the same direction
    // then we just drive
    if ((LeftMotorState == MotorState.Running &&
        RightMotorState == MotorState.Running) ||
        (LeftMotorState == MotorState.Reversed &&
        RightMotorState == MotorState.Reversed))
    {
        Drive(duration);
        return true;
    }

    // The motors are running in opposite directions,
    // so we don't move, we just rotate about the
    // center of the rig
    if ((LeftMotorState == MotorState.Running &&
        RightMotorState == MotorState.Reversed) ||
        (LeftMotorState == MotorState.Reversed &&
        RightMotorState == MotorState.Running))
    {
        return Rotate(duration);
    }

    // We didn't expect to get here
    return false;
}
```

Notice that we updated our documentation for the `public` method as we changed the contract. We also have to return values from all of the exit points of our method.

That has exposed another problem with our implementation: we never supported one motor at the stop condition, and the other at the driving or reversing condition. Well, that's fine—we can return an error if we hit those conditions now.

One problem with this contract is that we can't tell *why* our error occurred. Was it due to the state of the motors, or a problem with `Rotate`? We could create an `enum` that lets us distinguish between these error types:

```
enum TurtleError
{
    OK,
    RotateError,
    MotorStateError
}
```

Then we could use the `enum` as shown in Example 6-9.

Example 6-9. Indicating errors with an enum

```
// Run the turtle for the specified duration
// Returns one of the TurtleError values if a failure
// occurs, or TurtleError.OK if it succeeds
public TurtleError RunFor(double duration)
{
    if (LeftMotorState == MotorState.Stopped &&
        RightMotorState == MotorState.Stopped)
    {
        // If we are at a full stop, nothing will happen
        return TurtleError.OK;
    }

    // The motors are both running in the same direction
    // then we just drive
    if ((LeftMotorState == MotorState.Running &&
         RightMotorState == MotorState.Running) ||
        (LeftMotorState == MotorState.Reversed &&
         RightMotorState == MotorState.Reversed))
    {
        Drive(duration);
        return TurtleError.OK;
    }

    // The motors are running in opposite directions,
    // so we don't move, we just rotate about the
    // center of the rig
    if ((LeftMotorState == MotorState.Running &&
         RightMotorState == MotorState.Reversed) ||
        (LeftMotorState == MotorState.Reversed &&
         RightMotorState == MotorState.Running))
    {
        if (!Rotate(duration))
        {
```

```
            return TurtleError.RotateError;
        }
    }
    return TurtleError.MotorStateError;
}
```

OK so far, although it is starting to get a bit tortuous, and we're going up only one call in the stack. But let's build and run anyway:

```
Arthur is at (0,0) and is pointing at angle 0.00 radians.
Arthur is at (0,10) and is pointing at angle 0.00 radians.
Arthur is at (0,10) and is pointing at angle 0.00 radians.
Arthur is at (0,-15) and is pointing at angle 0.00 radians.
Arthur is at (0,-15) and is pointing at angle 0.00 radians.
Arthur is at (0,-18.5355339059327) and is pointing at angle 0.00 radians.
```

Yup; we're no better off than before, because all we've done is to pass the responsibility up to the client, and they are still free to ignore our pleadings. Given that the problem is a result of our oversight in the first place, what is the likelihood that we'll remember to check the error message?

Things would be even worse if this was in a library; we could recompile against this new version, and everything would seem fine, while in the background everything would quietly be going horribly wrong.

It is probably about time we did something with the error message, so let's see what happens in our client code (see Example 6-10).

Example 6-10. Handling an error

```
static void Main(string[] args)
{
    Turtle arthurTheTurtle =
        new Turtle {
            PlatformWidth = 0.0,
            PlatformHeight = 10.0,
            MotorSpeed = 5.0 };

    ShowPosition(arthurTheTurtle);

    // We want to proceed forwards
    arthurTheTurtle.LeftMotorState = MotorState.Running;
    arthurTheTurtle.RightMotorState = MotorState.Running;
    // For two seconds
    TurtleError result = arthurTheTurtle.RunFor(2.0);

    if (result != TurtleError.OK)
    {
        HandleError(result);
        return;
    }

    ShowPosition(arthurTheTurtle);
```

```csharp
    // Now, let's rotate clockwise for a bit
    arthurTheTurtle.RightMotorState = MotorState.Reversed;
    // PI / 2 seconds should do the trick
    result = arthurTheTurtle.RunFor(Math.PI / 2.0);
    if (result != TurtleError.OK)
    {
        HandleError(result);
        return;
    }

    ShowPosition(arthurTheTurtle);


    // And let's go into reverse
    arthurTheTurtle.RightMotorState = MotorState.Reversed;
    arthurTheTurtle.LeftMotorState = MotorState.Reversed;

    // And run for 5 seconds
    result = arthurTheTurtle.RunFor(5);
    if (result != TurtleError.OK)
    {
        HandleError(result);
        return;
    }

    ShowPosition(arthurTheTurtle);

    // Then rotate back the other way
    arthurTheTurtle.RightMotorState = MotorState.Running;
    // And run for PI/4 seconds to give us 45 degrees
    result = arthurTheTurtle.RunFor(Math.PI / 4.0);
    if (result != TurtleError.OK)
    {
        HandleError(result);
        return;
    }

    ShowPosition(arthurTheTurtle);

    // And finally drive backwards for a bit
    arthurTheTurtle.RightMotorState = MotorState.Reversed;
    arthurTheTurtle.LeftMotorState = MotorState.Reversed;
    result = arthurTheTurtle.RunFor(Math.Cos(Math.PI / 4.0));
    if (result != TurtleError.OK)
    {
        HandleError(result);
        return;
    }

    ShowPosition(arthurTheTurtle);

    Console.ReadKey();
}

private static void HandleError(TurtleError result)
```

```
{
    Console.WriteLine("We hit turtle error {0}", result);
    Console.ReadKey();
}
```

Every time we call the RunFor method, we have to stash away the error message that is returned, check it for problems, and then decide what we're going to do.

In this instance, we decided to quit the application, after showing an error message to the user, because it isn't safe to continue.

If we compile and run, here's the output:

```
Arthur is at (0,0) and is pointing at angle 0.00 radians.
Arthur is at (0,10) and is pointing at angle 0.00 radians.
We hit turtle error RotateError
```

From an application point of view, this is *much* better behavior than before: we were able to stop when we hit our first problem. Unfortunately, we had to write quite a lot of boilerplate code to achieve that end, and our code is much less readable than it was before. We also created a huge number of potential exit points out of our function, which decreases its maintainability. So while it is better, I'm not *totally* happy with it; this is catching just one potential error from one function, and we have almost as many lines of code dealing with that as we do our success scenario, scattered throughout our whole program!

Debugging with Return Values

So we finally spotted the problem, and stopped it from causing trouble. How do we find out what is wrong? Well, first we should take a look at the error message. That tells us that it has something to do with rotating the turtle, which gives us a bit of a clue. The easiest way to see what is really going on, though, might be to set a breakpoint in our error handler and see what state the system is in when the error occurs.

To set a breakpoint, we can put the cursor on the line where we want to break into the debugger, and press F9. Figure 6-1 shows the code with a breakpoint set.

```
private static void HandleError(TurtleError result)
{
    Console.WriteLine("We hit turtle error {0}", result);
    Console.ReadKey();
}
```

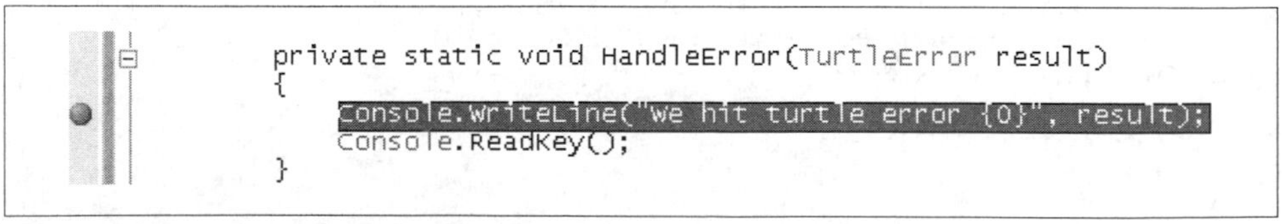

Figure 6-1. Code with a breakpoint set

If we run this now, the application will break into the debugger when we hit our error handler. If we press Ctrl-Alt-C, we can inspect the call stack to see where we went wrong, as shown in Figure 6-2.

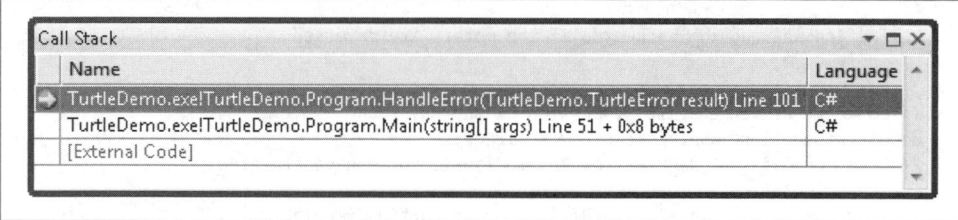

Figure 6-2. Call stack, broken in the error handler

As you can see, there's not an awful lot to help us; we lost context in which the error occurred because we returned out of the method that had the actual problem, and wound back up to our calling function.

It isn't completely useless—we now know which call had the problem (this time), so we can put a breakpoint on the relevant line and run again; but what if this was a hard-to-reproduce, intermittent error? We may have lost our one chance this week to identify and fix the problem!

These are not the only problems with a return-value-based approach to error handling. What if we already need to use the return value on the method? We're heading into the realm of "magic" values that mean an error has occurred, or we could add out or ref parameters to allow our method to return both a useful output and an error code.

And what about property setters; we don't have the option of a return value, but we might well like to return an error of some kind if the value is out of range.

If you're thinking "surely there has to be a better way," you're right. C# (like most modern languages) supports an alternative means of signaling errors: *exceptions*.

Exceptions

Rather than **return** an error code from a method, we can instead **throw** an instance of any type derived from `Exception`. Let's rewrite our `Rotate` method to do that (see Example 6-11).

Example 6-11. Indicating an error with an exception

```csharp
private void Rotate(double duration)
{
    if (PlatformWidth <= 0.0)
    {
        throw new InvalidOperationException(
            "The PlatformWidth must be initialized to a value > 0.0");
    }
    // This is the total circumference of turning circle
    double circum = Math.PI * PlatformWidth;
    // This is the total distance traveled
    double d = duration * MotorSpeed;
    if (LeftMotorState == MotorState.Reversed)
```

```
{
    // And we're going backwards if the motors are reversed
    d *= -1.0;
}
// So we've driven it this proportion of the way round
double proportionOfWholeCircle = d / circum;
// Once round is 360 degrees (or 2pi radians), so we have traveled
CurrentOrientation =
    CurrentOrientation + (Math.PI * 2.0 * proportionOfWholeCircle);
// return true; (This is now redunant, so you can delete it)
}
```

Notice that we changed the return specification back to **void**, and removed the unnecessary return at the end. The interesting bit, though, is in our test at the beginning of the method.

Pre- and Post Conditions: Design by Contract

The quick tests at the beginning of the method are sometimes called "guard clauses" or "guards."

Unless performance is more important to your application than correct operation (and it usually isn't), it is a good idea to check these preconditions before you attempt to execute the method.

Sometimes you will also want a similar set of post-condition tests on exit from the method, to verify that your state is still valid at the end of the operation.

The *design-by-contract* development philosophy requires you to specify these pre- and post conditions as a part of your method contract, and some languages such as Eiffel support declarative specification of these conditions.

Microsoft Research is working on an extension of C# called Spec# which includes some of these design-by-contract features. You can read about it at *http://research.mi crosoft.com/en-us/projects/specsharp/*.

Rather than **return** an instance of an **enum**, we **throw** an instance of the **InvalidOpera tionException** class.

InvalidOperationException is one of several types derived from **Exception**. It is intended to be used when an operation fails because the current state of the object itself doesn't allow the method to succeed (rather than, say, because a parameter passed in to the method was incorrect). That seems to fit this case quite nicely, so we can make use of it.

 Back before C# 3.0, you could throw an instance of any type you liked (e.g., a string). In C# 3.0, a constraint was added that only types derived from **Exception** can be thrown.

If we take a look at the Exception class (see *http://msdn.microsoft.com/library/system .exception*) we'll see that it has a Message property. That's what we're setting with the string we pass to the constructor, and it can be any text we like—preferably something that will help us (or one of our clients) debug the problem in the future.

There's also a property called Data. This is a dictionary of key/value pairs that lets us associate more information with the exception, and it can be extremely useful for debugging or logging purposes.

Replacing the return value with an exception, we will need to perform a bit of surgery on our application to get it to compile.

First, let's change the Turtle.RunFor method so that it no longer returns a value, and delete the TurtleError enumeration (see Example 6-12).

Example 6-12. Passing the buck is no longer required

```
// Run the turtle for the specified duration
public void RunFor(double duration)
{
    if (LeftMotorState == MotorState.Stopped &&
        RightMotorState == MotorState.Stopped)
    {
        // If we are at a full stop, nothing will happen
        return;
    }

    // The motors are both running in the same direction
    // then we just drive
    if ((LeftMotorState == MotorState.Running &&
        RightMotorState == MotorState.Running) ||
        (LeftMotorState == MotorState.Reversed &&
        RightMotorState == MotorState.Reversed))
    {
        Drive(duration);
    }

    // The motors are running in opposite directions,
    // so we don't move, we just rotate about the
    // center of the rig
    if ((LeftMotorState == MotorState.Running &&
        RightMotorState == MotorState.Reversed) ||
        (LeftMotorState == MotorState.Reversed &&
        RightMotorState == MotorState.Running))
    {
        Rotate(duration);

    }
}
```

Then, we can update the calling program, and strip out the code that deals with the return value (see Example 6-13).

Example 6-13. Main no longer checking explicitly for errors

```
static void Main(string[] args)
{
    Turtle arthurTheTurtle = new Turtle {
        PlatformWidth = 0.0, PlatformHeight = 10.0, MotorSpeed = 5.0 };

    ShowPosition(arthurTheTurtle);

    // We want to proceed forwards
    arthurTheTurtle.LeftMotorState = MotorState.Running;
    arthurTheTurtle.RightMotorState = MotorState.Running;
    // For two seconds
    arthurTheTurtle.RunFor(2.0);

    ShowPosition(arthurTheTurtle);


    // Now, let's rotate clockwise for a bit
    arthurTheTurtle.RightMotorState = MotorState.Reversed;
    // PI / 2 seconds should do the trick
    arthurTheTurtle.RunFor(Math.PI / 2.0);

    ShowPosition(arthurTheTurtle);


    // And let's go into reverse
    arthurTheTurtle.RightMotorState = MotorState.Reversed;
    arthurTheTurtle.LeftMotorState = MotorState.Reversed;

    // And run for 5 seconds
    arthurTheTurtle.RunFor(5);

    ShowPosition(arthurTheTurtle);

    // Then rotate back the other way
    arthurTheTurtle.RightMotorState = MotorState.Running;
    // And run for PI/4 seconds to give us 45 degrees
    arthurTheTurtle.RunFor(Math.PI / 4.0);

    ShowPosition(arthurTheTurtle);

    // And finally drive backwards for a bit
    arthurTheTurtle.RightMotorState = MotorState.Reversed;
    arthurTheTurtle.LeftMotorState = MotorState.Reversed;
    arthurTheTurtle.RunFor(Math.Cos(Math.PI / 4.0));

    ShowPosition(arthurTheTurtle);

    Console.ReadKey();
}
```

Finally, we can delete the HandleError method.

OK, what happens if you compile and run (make sure you press F5 or choose Debug→Start Debugging so that you run in the debugger)? Well, you drop very rapidly into the debugger, as you can see in Figure 6-3.

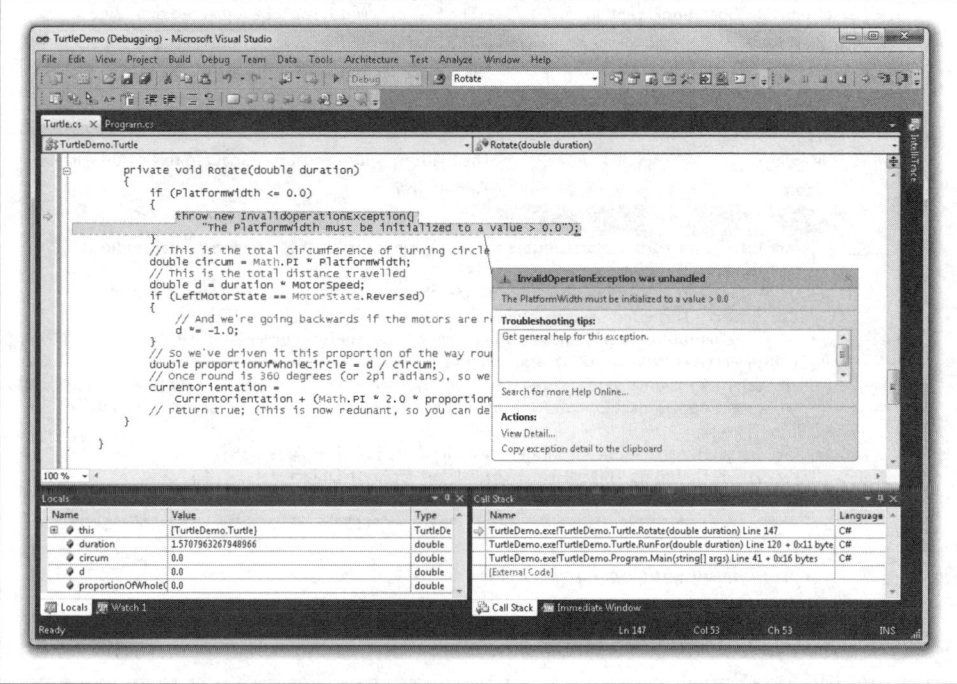

Figure 6-3. An unhandled exception in the debugger

As the debugger implies, we've broken in here because the exception is unhandled; but notice that we've broken right at the point at which the exception actually occurred. Even if we hadn't provided some nice descriptive error text, we can clearly see why we failed, unlike with error codes, where by the time the debugger got involved, we had already lost track of the root cause of the failure.

If we want an even closer look, we can click the View Detail link on the callout. This produces a dialog containing a property grid view of the exception object that was thrown. We can examine this to help us debug the problem. (You can see the Message and Data properties that we previously looked at, and I've popped open the StackTrace for the exception, in the example in Figure 6-4.)

That's already a huge improvement over the return value approach; but are there any obvious downsides to throwing an exception?

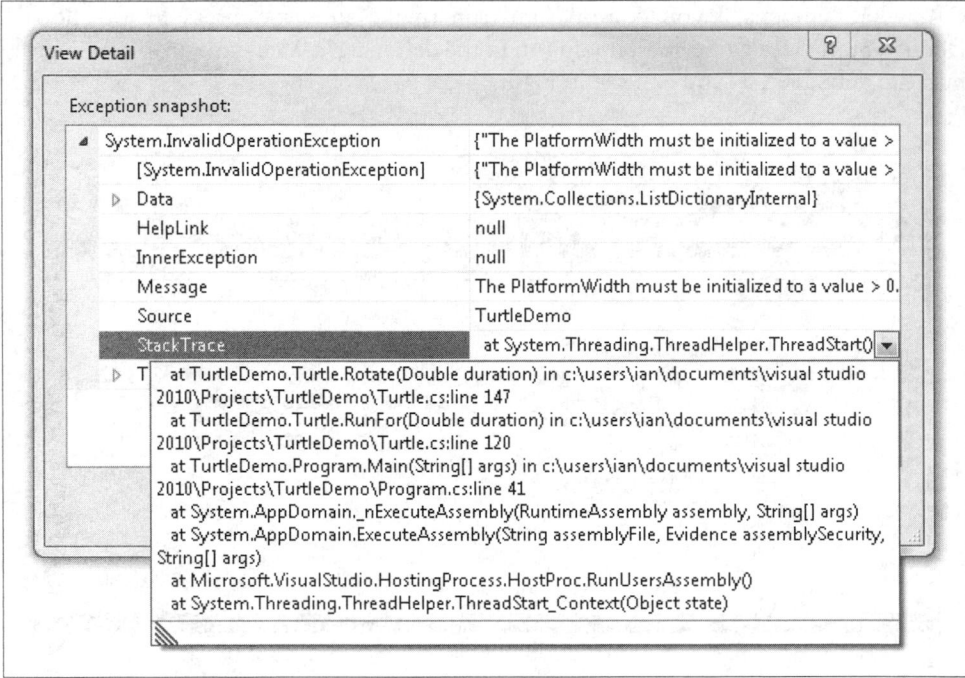

Figure 6-4. Exception detail with stack trace open

Well, the first downside is that throwing an exception is *way more expensive* than simply returning a value. You don't really want to throw an exception just to manage your normal flow of control. Passing parameters and looking at internal state is always going to be a better choice for anything you might call "the success path."

That being said, expense is, of course, relative, and as usual, you should use the best tool for the job. Plus, exceptions are actually *lower cost* than return values if you don't actually throw them. In our previous example, we allocated and copied return values *even if everything was OK*. With the exception model, the success path is basically free.

> The debate about when to use exceptions versus return values continues to rage in our industry. I don't expect it to let up anytime soon. As I said at the beginning of the chapter, it is almost like we're not really on top of the whole error-handling situation.

We've seen what happens if we *don't* handle an exception that we throw (i.e., it percolates up until eventually we crash); and while that behavior is far more satisfactory than the situation when we ignored a return value, we would like to do much better. We want to handle the error and exit gracefully, as we did before.

As you might expect, C# provides us with language features to do just that: `try`, `finally`, and `catch`.

Handling Exceptions

When we handled our return values, we had to propagate them up the call stack by hand, adding appropriate return values to each and every method, checking the result, and either passing it up or transforming and passing it as we go.

Exceptions, on the other hand, propagate up the stack automatically. If we don't want to add a handler, we don't have to, and the next call site up gets its chance instead, until eventually we pop out at the top of `Main` and either break into the debugger or Windows Error Handling steps in.

This means we can take a more structured approach to error handling—identifying points in our application control flow where we want to handle particular types of exceptions, and gathering our error-handling code into easily identified blocks.

The `try`, `catch`, and `finally` keywords help us to define those blocks (along with the ubiquitous braces).

In our example, we have no need to handle the potential errors from each and every call to `RunFor` separately. Instead, we can wrap the whole set into a single set of `try`, `catch`, and `finally` blocks, as shown in Example 6-14.

Example 6-14. Handling exceptions

```
static void Main(string[] args)
{
    Turtle arthurTheTurtle = new Turtle {
        PlatformWidth = 0.0, PlatformHeight = 10.0, MotorSpeed = 5.0 };

    ShowPosition(arthurTheTurtle);

    try
    {
        // We want to proceed forwards
        arthurTheTurtle.LeftMotorState = MotorState.Running;
        arthurTheTurtle.RightMotorState = MotorState.Running;
        // For two seconds
        arthurTheTurtle.RunFor(2.0);

        ShowPosition(arthurTheTurtle);


        // Now, let's rotate clockwise for a bit
        arthurTheTurtle.RightMotorState = MotorState.Reversed;
        // PI / 2 seconds should do the trick
        arthurTheTurtle.RunFor(Math.PI / 2.0);

        ShowPosition(arthurTheTurtle);
```

```
        // And let's go into reverse
        arthurTheTurtle.RightMotorState = MotorState.Reversed;
        arthurTheTurtle.LeftMotorState = MotorState.Reversed;

        // And run for 5 seconds
        arthurTheTurtle.RunFor(5);

        ShowPosition(arthurTheTurtle);

        // Then rotate back the other way
        arthurTheTurtle.RightMotorState = MotorState.Running;
        // And run for PI/4 seconds to give us 45 degrees
        arthurTheTurtle.RunFor(Math.PI / 4.0);

        ShowPosition(arthurTheTurtle);

        // And finally drive backwards for a bit
        arthurTheTurtle.RightMotorState = MotorState.Reversed;
        arthurTheTurtle.LeftMotorState = MotorState.Reversed;
        arthurTheTurtle.RunFor(Math.Cos(Math.PI / 4.0));

        ShowPosition(arthurTheTurtle);
    }
    catch (InvalidOperationException e)
    {
        Console.WriteLine("Error running turtle:");
        Console.WriteLine(e.Message);
    }
    finally
    {
        Console.ReadKey();
    }
}
```

If any of the code in the **try** block throws an exception, the runtime looks to see if there are any `catch` blocks whose exception type matches the type of that exception. It matches successfully if the `catch` parameter is either of the same type, or of a less-derived (base) type than that of the exception.

You can have any number of `catch` blocks for different types of exceptions, and it will look through them in the order they are defined; the first one that matches wins (even if there is a "better" match farther down).

If it doesn't find a suitable match, the exception will be propagated on up the call stack, just as though there was no **try** block.

To see how this works in practice, let's quickly modify the code in Example 6-14 to catch `Exception` as well, as shown in Example 6-15.

Example 6-15. Poorly placed catch block

```
try
{
  ...
}
catch (Exception e2)
{
    Console.WriteLine("Caught generic exception...");
}
catch (InvalidOperationException e)
{
    Console.WriteLine("Error running turtle:");
    Console.WriteLine(e.Message);
}
finally
{
    Console.WriteLine("Waiting in the finally block...");
    Console.ReadKey();
}
```

If you try to compile this, you'll see the following error:

```
A previous catch clause already catches all exceptions of this or of a
super type ('System.Exception')
```

This occurs because Exception is an ancestor of InvalidOperationException, and the clause appears first in the list of catch blocks. If we switch those around, we compile successfully, as shown in Example 6-16.

Example 6-16. Catching exceptions in the right order

```
try
{
  ...
}
catch (InvalidOperationException e)
{
    Console.WriteLine("Error running turtle:");
    Console.WriteLine(e.Message);
}
catch (Exception e2)
{
    Console.WriteLine("Caught generic exception...");
}
finally
{
    Console.WriteLine("Waiting in the finally block...");
    Console.ReadKey();
}
```

Catching Too Much

You should consider very carefully whether you want to catch instances of the base Exception type.

When you do that you are saying "something bad happened, but I don't really know what it was." That degree of uncertainty tends to imply that the app has lost control of its own internal consistency.

It is a common practice to catch Exception in your top-level exception handlers (e.g., in Main or, as we'll see later, in threading worker functions); and when you do, you normally need to terminate the application (or at least restart some subsystem).

Of course, you might know perfectly well what might go wrong, and you're catching Exception because you can't be bothered to list the half dozen exception types you intend to handle in the same way. (Maybe F1 wasn't working so well that day and you couldn't inspect the docs; and someone was pressing you to check in your changes.)

Beware!

What happens if an implementation detail changes in another class on which you depend, such that a new exception is thrown? Your handler will swallow it up and carry on. That *might* be OK, and your game of tic-tac-toe will continue happily. Or it might have unintended consequences, such as data loss or the start of WWIII. You just can't know in advance.

When the flow of control leaves the **try** block successfully, *or* the flow of control exits the last **catch** block if an exception occurred in the **try** block, the code in the **finally** block is executed. In other words, the code in the **finally** block is *always* executed, regardless of whether there was an exception.

If you designed your exception-handling code nicely, you'll almost certainly use far more **finally** blocks than you do **catch** blocks. The **finally** block is a good place for cleaning up your resources, or winding back internal state if an error occurs, to ensure that your pre- and post conditions are still valid, whereas a **catch** block allows you to deal with an error condition you, as a client, understand in some way—even if it is only to present a message to the user (as in this case).

If we compile and run our code again, we'll see the following output:

```
Arthur is at (0,0) and is pointing at angle 0.00 radians.
Arthur is at (0,10) and is pointing at angle 0.00 radians.
Error running turtle:
The PlatformWidth must be initialized to a value > 0.0
Waiting in the finally block...
```

Notice how the error-handling code is now consolidated neatly into clearly defined blocks, rather than scattered throughout our code, and we've been able to cut down substantially on the number of points of return from our method.

At the moment, we're not handling any exceptions in our Turtle itself. Let's imagine that our Turtle is being provided to clients in a library, and we (as the leading vendors of turtle simulators) want the library to do some internal logging when errors occur: maybe we have an opt-in customer experience program that sends telemetry back to our team.

We still want the errors to propagate up to the client for them to deal with; we just want to see them on the way past.

C# gives us the ability to catch, and then transparently rethrow, an exception, as shown in Example 6-17.

Example 6-17. Rethrowing an exception

```
// Run the turtle for the specified duration
public void RunFor(double duration)
{
    try
    {

        if (LeftMotorState == MotorState.Stopped &&
            RightMotorState == MotorState.Stopped)
        {
            // If we are at a full stop, nothing will happen
            return;
        }

        // The motors are both running in the same direction
        // then we just drive
        if ((LeftMotorState == MotorState.Running &&
            RightMotorState == MotorState.Running) ||
            (LeftMotorState == MotorState.Reversed &&
            RightMotorState == MotorState.Reversed))
        {
            Drive(duration);
        }

        // The motors are running in opposite directions,
        // so we don't move, we just rotate about the
        // center of the rig
        if ((LeftMotorState == MotorState.Running &&
            RightMotorState == MotorState.Reversed) ||
            (LeftMotorState == MotorState.Reversed &&
            RightMotorState == MotorState.Running))
        {
            Rotate(duration);

        }
    }
    catch (Exception ex)
    {
        Console.WriteLine("Log message: " + ex.Message);
        // Rethrow
        throw;
```

```
        }
}
```

The first thing to notice is that we caught the base `Exception` type, having just said that we almost never do that. We want to log every exception, and because we're rethrowing rather than eating it, we won't simply ignore exceptions we weren't expecting.

After we execute our handler code (just writing the message to the console in this case), we use the `throw` keyword, without any object, to rethrow the exception we just caught.

If you compile and run that, you'll see the following output:

```
Arthur is at (0,0) and is pointing at angle 0.00 radians.
Arthur is at (0,10) and is pointing at angle 0.00 radians.
Log error: The PlatformWidth must be initialized to a value > 0.0
Error running turtle:
The PlatformWidth must be initialized to a value > 0.0
Waiting in the finally block
```

Notice that we get the output from both of the exception handlers.

That's not the only way to throw from a `catch` block: it is perfectly reasonable to throw any exception from our exception handler! We often do this to wrap up an exception that comes from our implementation in another exception type that is more appropriate for our context. The original exception is not thrown away, but stashed away in the `InnerException` property of the new one, as shown in Example 6-18.

Example 6-18. Wrapping one exception in another

```
// Run the turtle for the specified duration
public void RunFor(double duration)
{
    try
    {

        if (LeftMotorState == MotorState.Stopped &&
            RightMotorState == MotorState.Stopped)
        {
            // If we are at a full stop, nothing will happen
            return;
        }

        // The motors are both running in the same direction
        // then we just drive
        if ((LeftMotorState == MotorState.Running &&
            RightMotorState == MotorState.Running) ||
            (LeftMotorState == MotorState.Reversed &&
            RightMotorState == MotorState.Reversed))
        {
            Drive(duration);
        }

        // The motors are running in opposite directions,
        // so we don't move, we just rotate about the
        // center of the rig
```

```
        if ((LeftMotorState == MotorState.Running &&
             RightMotorState == MotorState.Reversed) ||
            (LeftMotorState == MotorState.Reversed &&
             RightMotorState == MotorState.Running))
        {
            Rotate(duration);

        }
    }
    catch (InvalidOperationException iox)
    {
        throw new Exception("Some problem with the turtle...", iox);
    }
    catch (Exception ex)
    {
        // Log here
        Console.WriteLine("Log message: " + ex.Message);
        // Rethrow
        throw;
    }
}
```

Notice how we passed the exception to be wrapped as a parameter to the new exception when we constructed it. Let's make a quick modification to the exception handler in Main to take advantage of this new feature (see Example 6-19).

Example 6-19. Reporting an InnerException

```
static void Main(string[] args)
{
    Turtle arthurTheTurtle = new Turtle {
        PlatformWidth = 0.0, PlatformHeight = 10.0, MotorSpeed = 5.0 };

    ShowPosition(arthurTheTurtle);

    try
    {
        // ...
    }
    catch (InvalidOperationException e)
    {
        Console.WriteLine("Error running turtle:");
        Console.WriteLine(e.Message);
    }
    catch (Exception e1)
    {
        // Loop through the inner exceptions, printing their messages
        Exception current = e1;
        while (current != null)
        {
            Console.WriteLine(current.Message);
            current = current.InnerException;
        }
    }
    finally
```

```
    {
        Console.WriteLine("Waiting in the finally block");
        Console.ReadKey();
    }
}
```

If we compile and run again, we can see the following output, including the messages from both the outer and inner exceptions:

```
Arthur is at (0,0) and is pointing at angle 0.00 radians.
Arthur is at (0,10) and is pointing at angle 0.00 radians.
Some problem with the turtle has occurred
The PlatformWidth must be initialized to a value > 0.0
Waiting in the finally block
```

Clearly, wrapping an implementation-detail exception with something explicitly documented in our public contract can simplify the range of exception handlers you require. It also helps to encapsulate implementation details, as the exceptions you throw can be considered part of your contract.

On the other hand, are there any disadvantages to throwing a wrapped exception (or indeed rethrowing the original exception explicitly, rather than implicitly with throw;)? As programming tends to be a series of compromises, the answer is, as you might expect, yes.

If you explicitly (re)throw an exception, the call stack in the exception handler starts at the new throw statement, losing the original context in the debugger (although you can still inspect it in the inner exception in the object browser). This makes debugging noticeably less productive.

Because of this, you should consider carefully whether you need to wrap the exception, and always ensure that you implicitly (rather than explicitly) rethrow exceptions that you have caught and then wish to pass through.

When Do finally Blocks Run?

It is worth clarifying exactly when the finally block gets executed, under a few edge conditions.

First, let's see what happens if we run our example application *outside* the debugger. If we do that (by pressing Ctrl-F5) we'll see that Windows Error Handling* materializes, and presents the user with an error dialog *before* we actually hit our finally block at all! It is like the runtime has inserted an extra catch block in our own (top-level) exception handler, rather than percolating up another level (and hence out of our scope, invoking the code in the finally block).

And what happens when exceptions are thrown out of the exception handlers?

---

* Or "Dr. Watson" as the crash handler was more colorfully named on older versions of Windows.

Let's add a `finally` block to our `RunFor` method (see Example 6-20).

Example 6-20. Seeing when finally blocks run

```
// Run the turtle for the specified duration
public void RunFor(double duration)
{
    try
    {
        // ...
    }
    catch (InvalidOperationException iox)
    {
        throw new Exception("Some problem with the turtle has occurred", iox);
    }
    catch (Exception ex)
    {
        // Log here
        Console.WriteLine("Log error: " + ex.Message);
        // Rethrow
        throw;
    }
    finally
    {
        Console.WriteLine("In the Turtle finally block");
    }
}
```

If you compile and run this code, you'll see the following output:

```
Arthur is at (0,0) and is pointing at angle 0.00 radians.
In the Turtle finally block
Arthur is at (0,10) and is pointing at angle 0.00 radians.
In the Turtle finally block
Some problem with the turtle has occurred
The PlatformWidth must be initialized to a value > 0.0
Waiting in the finally block
```

So our `finally` block executes *after* the exception is thrown, but *before* it executes the exception handlers farther up the stack.

Deciding What to Catch

One important question remains: how did we *know* what exception type to catch from our code? Unlike some other languages (e.g., Java) there is no keyword which allows us to specify that a method can throw a particular exception. We have to rely on good developer documentation. The MSDN documentation for the framework itself carefully documents all the exceptions that can be thrown from its methods (and properties), and we should endeavor to do the same.

The .NET Framework provides a wide variety of exception types that you can catch (and often use). Let's revisit Table 6-1 (the common error types) and see what is available for those situations (see Table 6-2).

Table 6-2. *Some common errors and their exception types*

Error	Description	Examples

Unexpected input	A client passes data to a method that is outside some expected range.	`ArgumentException`
		
		`ArgumentNullException`
		
		`ArgumentOutOfRangeException`

Unexpected data type	A client passes data to a method that is not of the expected type.	`InvalidCastException`
Unexpected data format	A client passes data to a method in a format that is not recognized.	`FormatException`
Unexpected result	A client receives information from a method that it did not expect for the given input (e.g., null).	`NullReferenceException`
Unexpected method call	The class wasn't expecting you to call a particular method at that time; you hadn't performed some required initialization, for example.	`InvalidOperationException`
Unavailable resource	A method tried to access a resource of some kind and it failed to respond in a timely fashion; a hardware device was not plugged in, for instance.	`TimeoutException`

Contended resource	A method tried to access a scarce resource of some kind (memory or a hardware device that cannot be shared) and it was not available because someone else was using it.	`OutOfMemoryException`
		
		`TimeoutException`

Obviously, that's a much abbreviated list, but it contains some of the most common exceptions you'll see in real applications. One of the most useful that you'll throw yourself is the `ArgumentException`. You can use that when parameters passed to your methods fail to validate.

Let's make use of that in our `RunFor` method. Say that a "feature" of our turtle hardware is that it crashes and becomes unresponsive if we try to run it for zero seconds. We can work around this in our software by checking for this condition in the `RunFor` method, and throwing an exception if clients try this, as shown in Example 6-21.

Example 6-21. Throwing an exception when arguments are bad

```
public void RunFor(double duration)
{
    if (duration <= double.Epsilon)
    {
        throw new ArgumentException(
            "Must provide a duration greater than 0",
            "duration");
    }
    try
    {
        // ...
    }
    catch (InvalidOperationException iox)
```

```
    {
        throw new Exception("Some problem with the turtle has occurred", iox);
    }
    catch (Exception ex)
    {
        // Log here
        Console.WriteLine("Log error: " + ex.Message);
        // Rethrow
        throw;
    }
    finally
    {
        Console.WriteLine("In the Turtle finally block");
    }
}
```

The second parameter in this constructor should match the name of the parameter that is in error. The first represents the exception message.

 When you come to use `ArgumentNullException` (which you throw when you are erroneously passed a null argument) you'll find that the error message and parameter arguments are swapped around in the constructor. This irritating inconsistency has been with us since .NET 1.0, and too much code depends on it to fix it now.

The code in Example 6-22 updates `Main`, to sneak in an attempt to run it for zero seconds.

Example 6-22. Testing for the expected exception

```
static void Main(string[] args)
{
    Turtle arthurTheTurtle = new Turtle {
        PlatformWidth = 0.0, PlatformHeight = 10.0, MotorSpeed = 5.0 };

    ShowPosition(arthurTheTurtle);

    try
    {
        arthurTheTurtle.RunFor(0.0);
    // ...
    }
    catch (InvalidOperationException e)
    {
        Console.WriteLine("Error running turtle:");
        Console.WriteLine(e.Message);
    }
    catch (Exception e1)
    {
        // Loop through the inner exceptions, printing their messages
        Exception current = e1;
        while (current != null)
```

```
        {
            Console.WriteLine(current.Message);
            current = current.InnerException;
        }
    }
    finally
    {
        Console.WriteLine("Waiting in the finally block");
        Console.ReadKey();
    }
}
```

If we compile and run, we'll see the following output:

```
Arthur is at (0,0) and is pointing at angle 0.00 radians.
Must provide a duration greater than 0
Parameter name: duration
Waiting in the finally block
```

Notice how the error message automatically includes the details of the problem parameter.

Custom Exceptions

You might want to create your own exceptions for a couple of reasons:

- My exception is a special snowflake.
- I want to group my exceptions together for layered exception handling.

The first of these is the most problematic. You should think very carefully about whether your exception is *really* special, or whether you can just reuse an existing exception type.

When you introduce new exceptions, you're asking clients to understand and deal with a new type of problem, and you're expecting them to handle it in a special way. There *are* occasional instances of this, but more often the differences are in the context (i.e., that it was thrown from your code) rather than the exception itself (i.e., something was out of range, invalid, null, or unavailable, or it timed out).

Slightly more often, you provide custom exception types when you want to provide a convenient API over some additional information that comes along with the exception. The Exception.Data property we discussed earlier might be a better solution—it gives you somewhere to put information without needing to add a new kind of exception. But the convenience of a dedicated property might outweigh the costs of introducing a custom exception.

Finally, you might wish to create a custom exception class to allow you to conceptually group some subsystem's exceptions together. DbException is an example of this in the .NET Framework; it represents the various errors that can occur when using a database. There are various specialized errors that derive from this, such as the SqlException thrown by the SQL Server subsystem, but the common base class enables you to write a single `catch` for all database errors, rather than having to handle provider-specific errors.

Again, you should think carefully about this before doing it: what client exception-handling scenarios are you enabling, and why do you need the custom type?

However, having been through all of this, creating your own exception type is very simple. Let's create a `TurtleException` for our exception wrapper (see Example 6-23).

 Whether we really *want* a `TurtleException` is another matter. I'm not sure I really would in these circumstances, but your mileage may vary.

Example 6-23. A custom exception

```
[Serializable]
class TurtleException : Exception
{
    public TurtleException()
    {}

    public TurtleException(string message)
        : base(message)
    { }

    public TurtleException(string message, Exception innerException)
        : base(message, innerException)
    {}

    // For serialization support
    protected TurtleException(SerializationInfo info, StreamingContext context)
        : base(info, context)
    {}
}
```

The first thing to notice is that we derive from `Exception`.

If you've plowed through the MSDN documentation you might have noticed the `ApplicationException` type, which derives from `Exception`, and was provided as a base class for application-defined exceptions. Why, you might ask, are we not deriving from `ApplicationException`?

Well, `ApplicationException` adds no functionality to `Exception`, and the .NET designers could not come up with a scenario where it was useful to catch `ApplicationException` (as opposed to `Exception`). Sadly, they only realized this after .NET 1.0 had shipped, so it is in the library, but it is now deprecated. You should neither derive from nor catch `ApplicationException`.

Also, we provide a bunch of standard constructors: a default parameterless constructor, one that takes a message, and one that takes a message and an inner exception. Even if you add more properties to your own exception that you wish to initialize in the constructor, you should still provide constructors that follow this pattern (including the default, parameterless one).

The final constructor supports *serialization*. We do this because `Exception` itself is marked as a serializable class, which means that derived classes have to be too. This enables exceptions to cross appdomain boundaries.[†] We're just calling the base class's constructor here. Because there is no constructor inheritance in C#, we need to provide a matching constructor which calls the one in our base. If we didn't do this, any code that polymorphically used our `TurtleException` as its base `Exception` might break.

Summary

In this chapter, we reviewed the various types of errors that might occur in our software and looked at several strategies for handling them. These include ignoring the problem, aborting the application, returning errors, and throwing exceptions. We also saw some of the benefits and pitfalls of returning errors, and how exceptions can often provide a more robust and flexible means of alerting your clients to problems. We saw how we can handle exceptions in layers, sometimes catching, using, and then rethrowing an exception, sometimes wrapping an implementation exception in a public exception type, and sometimes allowing exceptions to bubble up to the next layer of handlers. We saw what happens when an unhandled exception pops out at the top of the stack, and how we can use `finally` blocks at each layer to ensure that application state remains consistent, and resources can be released, whether exceptions occur or not. We then took a quick review of some of the most common exceptions provided by the framework, and how we might use them. Finally, we looked at creating our own exception types and why we might (and might not) wish to do so.

We've come a long way in the past few chapters, covering all of the everyday C# programming concepts you'll need. In the next few chapters, we'll look at features of the .NET Framework in more detail, and how we can best use them in C#; starting with the collection classes.

† An appdomain is a kind of process within a process. We'll talk about them a little more in Chapter 11 and Chapter 15, but they're mainly used by systems that need to host code, such as ASP.NET.

CHAPTER 7

Arrays and Lists

Most programs have to deal with multiple pieces of information. Payroll systems need to calculate the salary of every employee in a company; a space battle game has to track the position of all the ships and missiles; a social networking website needs to be able to show all of the user's acquaintances. Dealing with large numbers of items is a task at which computers excel, so it's no surprise that C# has a range of features dedicated to working with collections of information.

Sets of information crop up so often that we've already seen some of what C# has to offer here. So we'll start with a more detailed look at the collection-based features we've already seen, and in the next chapter we'll look at the powerful LINQ (Language Integrated Query) feature that C# offers for finding and processing information in potentially large sets of information.

Arrays

The ability to work with collections is so important that the .NET Framework's type system has a feature just for this purpose: the *array*. This is a special kind of object that can hold multiple items, without needing to declare a field for each individual item. Example 7-1 creates an array of strings, with one entry for each event coming up in one of the authors' calendars over the next few days. You may notice a theme here (although one misfit appears to be a refugee from an earlier chapter's theme, but that's just how the author's weekend panned out; real data is never tidy).

Example 7-1. An array of strings

```
string[] eventNames =
{
    "Swing Dancing at the South Bank",
    "Saturday Night Swing",
    "Formula 1 German Grand Prix",
    "Swing Dance Picnic",
    "Stompin' at the 100 Club"
};
```

Look at the variable declaration on the first line. The square brackets after `string` indicate that `eventNames` is not just a single `string`; it's an array of `string` values. These square brackets tie in with the syntax for accessing individual elements in the array. Example 7-2 prints the first and fifth items in the array. (So this will print out the text "Swing Dancing at the South Bank", followed by "Stompin' at the 100 Club".)

Example 7-2. Using elements in an array

```
Console.WriteLine(eventNames[0]);
Console.WriteLine(eventNames[4]);
```

The number inside the square brackets is called the *index*, and as you can see, C# starts counting array elements from zero. As you may recall from Chapter 2, the index says how far into the array we'd like C# to look—to access the very first element, we don't have to go any distance into the array at all, so its index is 0. Likewise, an index of 4 jumps past the first four items to arrive at the fifth.

To modify an array element you just put the same syntax on the lefthand side of an assignment. For example, noticing that I got one of the event names slightly wrong, I can update it, like so:

```
eventNames[1] = "Saturday Night Swing Club";
```

While you can change any element of an array like this, the number of elements is fixed for the lifetime of the array. (As we'll see later, this limitation is less drastic than it first sounds.)

 If you try to use too high an index or a negative index when accessing an array element, the code will throw an `IndexOutOfRangeException`. Since elements are numbered from zero, the highest acceptable index is one less than the number of elements. For example, `eventNames[4]` is the last item in our five-item array, so trying to read or write `eventNames[5]` would throw an exception.

The .NET Framework supports arrays whose first element is numbered from something other than zero. This is to support languages such as Visual Basic that have historically offered such a construct. However, you cannot use such arrays with the C# index syntax shown here—you would need to use the `Array` class's `GetValue` and `SetValue` helper methods to use such an array.

Since the size of an array is fixed at the moment it is constructed, let's look at the construction process in more detail.

Construction and Initialization

There are two ways you can create a new array in C#. Example 7-1 showed the most straightforward approach—the array variable declaration was followed by a list of the array's contents enclosed in braces, which is called an *initializer list*. But this requires you to know exactly what you want in the array when you write the code. You will often work with information that your program discovers at runtime, perhaps from a database or a web service. So C# offers an alternative mechanism that lets you choose the array's size at runtime.

For example, suppose I decide I'd like to display the events in my calendar as a numbered list. I already have an array of event names, but I'd like to build a new string array that adds a number to the event text. Example 7-3 shows how to do this.

Example 7-3. Creating an array dynamically

```
static string[] AddNumbers(string[] names)
{
    string[] numberedNames = new string[names.Length];
    for (int i = 0; i < names.Length ; ++i)
    {
        numberedNames[i] = string.Format("{0}: {1}", i, names[i]);
    }
    return numberedNames;
}
```

This AddNumbers method doesn't know up front what will be in the array it creates—it's building a modified copy of an existing array. So instead of creating a fixed list of items, it uses this syntax: new *ElementType*[*arrayLength*]. This specifies the two things that are fixed when you create a new array: the type and number of elements.

When you create an array with this minimal syntax, the elements all start out with their default values. With the **string** type used here, the default is **null**; an array of numbers created this way would contain all zeros. So Example 7-3 immediately goes on to populate the newly created array with some useful values. In fact, that's also what happened in Example 7-1—when you provide an array with a list of initial contents, the C# compiler turns it into the sort of code shown in Example 7-4.

Example 7-4. How initializer lists work

```
string[] eventNames = new string[5];
eventNames[0] = "Swing Dancing at the South Bank";
eventNames[1] = "Saturday Night Swing";
eventNames[2] = "Formula 1 German Grand Prix";
eventNames[3] = "Swing Dance Picnic";
eventNames[4] = "Stompin' at the 100 Club";
```

The array initialization syntax in Example 7-1 is really just convenient shorthand—the .NET Framework itself always expects to be told the number and type of elements, so it's just a matter of whether the C# compiler works out the element count for you.

The Example 7-1 shorthand works only at the point at which you declare a variable. If your program decides to put a new array into an existing variable, you'll find that the syntax no longer works (see Example 7-5).

Example 7-5. Where array initializers fail

```
// Won't compile!
eventNames =
{
    "Dean Collins Shim Sham Lesson",
    "Intermediate Lindy Hop Lesson",
    "Wild Times - Social Dancing at Wild Court"
};
```

The reasons for this are somewhat arcane. In general, C# cannot always work out what element type you need for an array, because it may have more than one choice. For example, a list of strings doesn't necessarily have to live in an array of type `string[]`. An array of type `object[]` is equally capable of holding the same data. And as we'll see later, initializer lists don't necessarily have to initialize arrays—this list of strings could initialize a `List<string>`, for example.

As it happens, only one of those choices would work in Example 7-5—we're assigning into the `eventNames` variable, which is of type `string[]`, so you'd think the compiler would know what we want. But since there are some situations which really are ambiguous, Microsoft decided to require you to specify the element type everywhere except for the one special case of initializing a newly declared array variable.

The upshot is not so bad—if you specify the element type, you still get to use the initializer list syntax and have C# count the elements for you. Example 7-6 modifies Example 7-5 by explicitly stating the type of array we'd like before providing its contents. By the way, we could also have added this explicit array type in Example 7-1— it would have worked, it's just more verbose than necessary in that particular case.

Example 7-6. Combining an explicit element type with an initializer list

```
// Will compile!
eventNames = new string[]
{
    "Dean Collins Shim Sham Lesson",
    "Intermediate Lindy Hop Lesson",
    "Wild Times - Social Dancing at Wild Court"
};
```

This syntax works anywhere you need an array-typed expression. For example, we could use this to pass in an array to the `AddNumbers` method in Example 7-3, as shown in Example 7-7.

Example 7-7. Inline array initializer

```
string[] result = AddNumbers(new string[] { "The Jazz Devil", "Jitterbugs" });
```

This inline array technique can occasionally be useful if you need to call a method that demands to be passed an array, and you happen not to have one handy. The `String` class's `Split` method illustrates an interesting twist on this.

Array arguments and the params keyword

The `String.Split` method breaks a string into multiple strings based on separator characters. You tell it which characters to treat as separators by passing a `char` array. Example 7-8 splits on spaces, commas, and periods.

Example 7-8. Array arguments in the class library

```
string[] items = inputString.Split(
    new char[] { ' ', ',', '.' },
    StringSplitOptions.RemoveEmptyEntries);
```

If `inputString` contained `"One,Two Three, Four. Five."`, this would put a five-element array into items containing the strings `"One"`, `"Two"`, `"Three"`, `"Four"`, and `"Five"`.

Example 7-8 asks `Split` to ignore empty items so that when we get both a period and a space in succession we don't get an empty string in the results to represent the fact that there were two separators. If you don't need to skip such things, there's a simpler overload of `Split` that illustrates yet another way to initialize an array:

```
string[] items = inputString.Split(' ', ',', '.');
```

It looks like we've passed three `char` arguments to this method. But there's no such overload of `Split`—this ends up calling an overload that looks like this:

```
public string[] Split(params char[] separator) ...
```

That `params` keyword is significant. When an argument is marked with this keyword, C# lets you use syntax that makes it look like a series of individual arguments, and it will create an array from these for you. (You're free to provide the array explicitly if you prefer.) The `params` keyword can be used on only the very last argument of a method, to avoid potential ambiguity about which values go into arrays and which become arguments in their own right. That's why Example 7-8 had to create the array explicitly.

The examples so far contain nothing but strings. This is a poor way to represent events in a calendar—it would be useful to know when each event occurs. We could add a second array of type `DateTimeOffset[]` whose elements correspond to the event names in the original array. But spreading related data across multiple arrays can make code awkward to write and hard to maintain. Fortunately, there's a better way.

Custom Types in Arrays

You can create an array using any type for the element type—you're not limited to types provided by the .NET Framework class library. You can use a class defined in the way shown in Chapter 3, such as the calendar event type in Example 7-9.

Example 7-9. Custom class to represent events in a calendar

```
class CalendarEvent
{
    public string Title { get; set; }
```

```
    public DateTimeOffset StartTime { get; set; }
    public TimeSpan Duration { get; set; }
}
```

This class holds the event's title, start time, and duration in a single object. We can create an array of these objects, as shown in Example 7-10.

Example 7-10. Creating an array with a custom element type

```
CalendarEvent[] events =
{
    new CalendarEvent
    {
        Title = "Swing Dancing at the South Bank",
        StartTime = new DateTimeOffset (2009, 7, 11, 15, 00, 00, TimeSpan.Zero),
        Duration = TimeSpan.FromHours(4)
    },
    new CalendarEvent
    {
        Title = "Saturday Night Swing",
        StartTime = new DateTimeOffset (2009, 7, 11, 19, 30, 00, TimeSpan.Zero),
        Duration = TimeSpan.FromHours(6.5)
    },
    new CalendarEvent
    {
        Title = "Formula 1 German Grand Prix",
        StartTime = new DateTimeOffset (2009, 7, 12, 12, 10, 00, TimeSpan.Zero),
        Duration = TimeSpan.FromHours(3)
    },
    new CalendarEvent
    {
        Title = "Swing Dance Picnic",
        StartTime = new DateTimeOffset (2009, 7, 12, 15, 00, 00, TimeSpan.Zero),
        Duration = TimeSpan.FromHours(4)
    },
    new CalendarEvent
    {
        Title = "Stompin' at the 100 Club",
        StartTime = new DateTimeOffset (2009, 7, 13, 19, 45, 00, TimeSpan.Zero),
        Duration = TimeSpan.FromHours(5)
    }
};
```

Notice that Example 7-10 uses the new keyword to initialize each object. This highlights an important point about arrays: individual array elements are similar to variables of the same type. Recall from Chapter 3 that a custom type defined with the class keyword, such as the CalendarEvent type in Example 7-9, is a *reference type*. This means that when you declare a variable of that type, the variable does not represent a particular object—it's a storage location that can *refer* to an object. And the same is true of each element in an array if the element type is a reference type. Figure 7-1 shows the objects that Example 7-10 creates: five CalendarEvent objects (shown on the right), and an array object of type `CalendarEvent[]` (shown on the left) where each element in the array refers to one of the event objects.

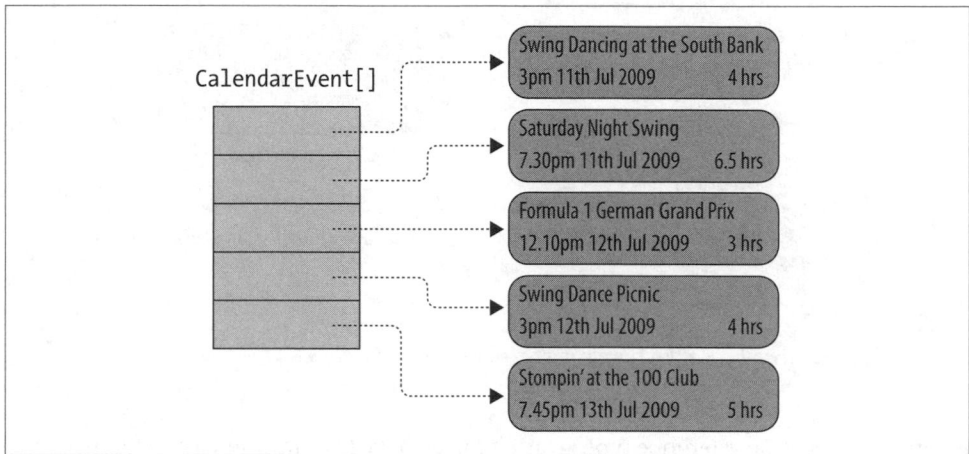

Figure 7-1. An array with reference type elements

As you saw in Chapter 3, with reference types multiple different variables can all refer to the same object. Since elements in an array behave in a similar way to local variables of the element type, we could create an array where all the elements refer to the same object, as shown in Example 7-11.

Example 7-11. Multiple elements referring to the same object

```
CalendarEvent theOnlyEvent = new CalendarEvent
{
    Title = "Swing Dancing at the South Bank",
    StartTime = new DateTimeOffset (2009, 7, 11, 15, 00, 00, TimeSpan.Zero),
    Duration = TimeSpan.FromHours(4)
};

CalendarEvent[] events =
{
    theOnlyEvent,
    theOnlyEvent,
    theOnlyEvent,
    theOnlyEvent,
    theOnlyEvent
};
```

Figure 7-2 illustrates the result. While this particular example is not brilliantly useful, in some situations it's helpful for multiple elements to refer to one object. For example, imagine a feature for booking meeting rooms or other shared facilities—this could be a useful addition to a calendar program. An array might describe how the room will be used today, where each element represents a one-hour slot for a particular room. If the same individual had booked the same room for two different slots, the two corresponding array elements would both refer to the same person.

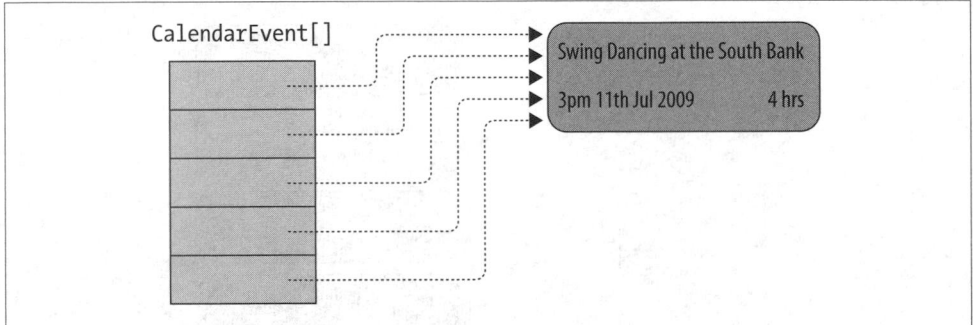

Figure 7-2. An array where all of the elements refer to the same object

Another feature that reference type array elements have in common with reference type variables and arguments is support for polymorphism. As you saw in Chapter 4, a variable declared as some particular reference type can refer to any object of that type, or of any type *derived* from the variable's declared type. This works for arrays too—using the examples from Chapter 4, if an array's type is `FirefighterBase[]`, each element could refer to a `Firefighter`, or `TraineeFirefighter`, or anything else that derives from `FirefighterBase`. (And each element is allowed to refer to an object of a different type, as long as the objects are all compatible with the element type.) Likewise, you can declare an array of any interface type—for example, `INamedPerson[]`, in which case each element can refer to any object of any type that implements that interface. Taking this to extremes, an array of type `object[]` has elements that can refer to any object of any reference type, or any boxed value.

As you will remember from Chapter 3, the alternative to a reference type is a *value type*. With value types, each variable holds its own copy of the value, rather than a reference to some potentially shared object. As you would expect, this behavior carries over to arrays when the element type is a value type. Consider the array shown in Example 7-12.

Example 7-12. An array of integer values

```
int[] numbers = { 2, 3, 5, 7, 11 };
```

Like all the numeric types, `int` is a value type, so we end up with a rather different structure. As Figure 7-3 shows, the array elements are the values themselves, rather than references to values.

Why would you need to care about where exactly the value lives? Well, there's a significant difference in behavior. Given the `numbers` array in Example 7-12, consider this code:

```
int thirdElementInArray = numbers[2];
thirdElementInArray += 1;
Console.WriteLine("Variable: " + thirdElementInArray);
Console.WriteLine("Array element: " + numbers[2]);
```

which would print out the following:

```
Variable: 6
Array element: 5
```

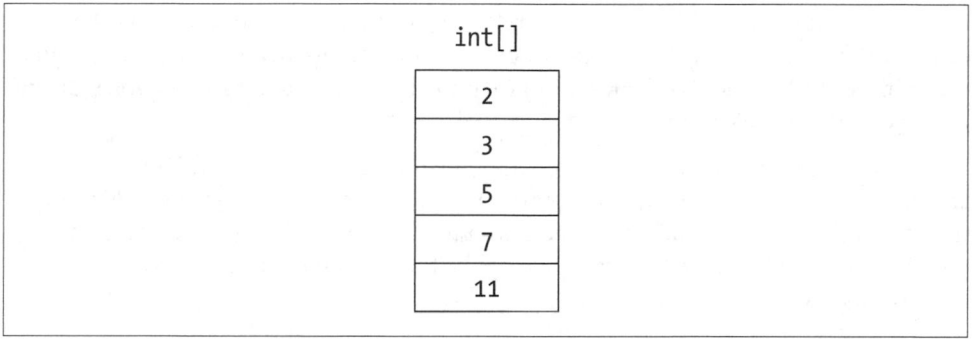

Figure 7-3. An array with value type elements

Because we are dealing with a value type, the `thirdElementInArray` local variable gets a copy of the value in the array. This means that the code can change the local variable without altering the element in the array. Compare that with similar code working on the array from Example 7-10:

```
CalendarEvent thirdElementInArray = events[2];
thirdElementInArray.Title = "Modified title";
Console.WriteLine("Variable: " + thirdElementInArray.Title);
Console.WriteLine("Array element: " + events[2].Title);
```

This would print out the following:

```
Variable: Modified title
Array element: Modified title
```

This shows that we've modified the event's title both from the point of view of the local variable and from the point of view of the array element. That's because both refer to the same `CalendarEvent` object—with a reference type, when the first line gets an element from the array we don't get a copy of the object, we get a copy of the reference to that object. The object itself is not copied.

The distinction between the reference and the object being referred to means that there's sometimes scope for ambiguity—what exactly does it mean to change an element in an array? For value types, there's no ambiguity, because the element *is* the value. The only way to change an entry in the `numbers` array in Example 7-12 is to assign a new value into an element:

```
numbers[2] = 42;
```

But as you've seen, with reference types the array element is just a reference, and we may be able to modify the object it refers to without changing the array element itself. Of course, we can also change the element, it just means something slightly different—we're asking to change which object that particular element refers to. For example, this:

```
events[2] = events[0];
```

causes the third element to refer to the same object as the first. This doesn't modify the object that element previously referenced. (It might cause the object to become inaccessible, though—if nothing else has a reference to that object, overwriting the array element that referred to it means the program no longer has any way of getting hold of that object, and so the .NET Framework can reclaim the memory it occupies during the next garbage collection cycle.)

It's often tempting to talk in terms of "the fourth object in the array," and in a lot of cases, that's a perfectly reasonable approximation in practice. As long as you're aware that with reference types, array elements contain references, not objects, and that what you really mean is "the object referred to by the fourth element in the array" you won't get any nasty surprises.

Regardless of what element type you choose for an array, all arrays provide various useful methods and properties.

Array Members

An array is an object in its own right; distinct from any objects its elements may refer to. And like any object, it has a type—as you've already seen, we write an array type as *SomeType*[]. Whatever type *SomeType* may be, its corresponding array type, *SomeType*[], will derive from a standard built-in type called **Array**, defined in the **System** namespace.

The **Array** base class provides a variety of services for working with arrays. It can help you find interesting items in an array. It can reorder the elements, or move information between arrays. And there are methods for working with the array's size.

Finding elements

Suppose we want to find out if an array of calendar items contains any events that start on a particular date. An obvious way to do this would be to write a loop that iterates through all of the elements in the array, looking at each date in turn (see Example 7-13).

Example 7-13. Finding elements with a loop

```
DateTime dateOfInterest = new DateTime (2009, 7, 12);
foreach (CalendarEvent item in events)
{
    if (item.StartTime.Date == dateOfInterest)
    {
        Console.WriteLine(item.Title + ": " + item.StartTime);
```

```
        }
}
```

 Example 7-13 relies on a useful feature of the `DateTimeOffset` type that makes it easy to work out whether two `DateTimeOffset` values fall on the same day, regardless of the exact time. The `Date` property returns a `DateTime` in which the year, month, and day are copied over, but the time of day is set to the default time of midnight.

Although Example 7-13 works just fine, the `Array` class provides an alternative: its `FindAll` method builds a new array containing only those elements in the original array that match whatever criteria you specify. Example 7-14 uses this method to do the same job as Example 7-13.

Example 7-14. Finding elements with FindAll

```
DateTime dateOfInterest = new DateTime (2009, 7, 12);
CalendarEvent[] itemsOnDateOfInterest = Array.FindAll(events,
    e => e.StartTime.Date == dateOfInterest);

foreach (CalendarEvent item in itemsOnDateOfInterest)
{
    Console.WriteLine(item.Title + ": " + item.StartTime);
}
```

Notice that we're using a lambda expression to tell `FindAll` which items match. That's not mandatory—`FindAll` requires a delegate here, so you can use any of the alternatives discussed in Chapter 5, including lambda expressions, anonymous methods, method names, or any expression that returns a suitable delegate. The delegate type here is `Predicate<T>`, where `T` is the array element type (`Predicate<CalendarEvent>` in this case). We also discussed predicate delegates in Chapter 5, but in case your memory needs refreshing, we just need to supply a function that takes a `CalendarEvent` and returns `true` if it matches, and `false` if it does not. Example 7-14 uses the same expression as the `if` statement in Example 7-13.

This may not seem like an improvement on Example 7-13. We've not written any less code, and we've ended up using a somewhat more advanced language feature—lambda expressions—to get the job done. However, notice that in Example 7-14, we've already done all the work of finding the items of interest before we get to the loop. Whereas the loop in Example 7-13 is a mixture of code that works out what items we need and code that does something with those items, Example 7-14 keeps those tasks neatly separated. And if we were doing more complex work with the matching items, that separation could become a bigger advantage—code tends to be easier to understand and maintain when it's not trying to do too many things at once.

The `FindAll` method becomes even more useful if you want to pass the set of matching items on to some other piece of code, because you can just pass the array of matches it returns as an argument to some method in your code. But how would you do that with the approach in Example 7-13, where the match-finding code is intermingled with the processing code? While the simple `foreach` loop in Example 7-13 is fine for trivial examples, `FindAll` and similar techniques (such as LINQ, which we'll get to in the next chapter) are better at managing the more complicated scenarios likely to arise in real code.

 This is an important principle that is not limited to arrays or collections. In general, you should try to construct your programs by combining small pieces, each of which does one well-defined job. Code written this way tends to be easier to maintain and to contain fewer bugs than code written as one big, sprawling mass of complexity. Separating code that selects information from code that processes information is just one example of this idea.

The `Array` class offers a few variations on the `FindAll` theme. If you happen to be interested only in finding the first matching item, you can just call `Find`. Conversely, `FindLast` returns the very last matching item.

Sometimes it can be useful to know where in the array a matching item was found. So as an alternative to `Find` and `FindLast`, `Array` also offers `FindIndex` and `FindLastIndex`, which work in the same way except they return a number indicating the position of the first or last match, rather than returning the matching item itself.

Finally, one special case for finding the index of an item turns out to crop up fairly often: the case where you know exactly which object you're interested in, and just need to know where it is in the array. You could do this with a suitable predicate, for example:

```
int index = Array.FindIndex(events, e => e == someParticularEvent);
```

But `Array` offers the more specialized `IndexOf` and `LastIndexOf`, so you only have to write this:

```
int index = Array.IndexOf(events, someParticularEvent);
```

Ordering elements

Sometimes it's useful to modify the order in which entries appear in an array. For example, with a calendar, some events will be planned long in advance while others may be last-minute additions. Any calendar application will need to be able to ensure that events are displayed in chronological order, regardless of how they were added, so we need some way of getting items into the right order.

The `Array` class makes this easy with its `Sort` method. We just need to tell it how we want the events ordered—it can't really guess, because it doesn't have any way of knowing whether we consider our events to be ordered by the `Title`, `StartTime`, or `Duration` property. This is a perfect job for a delegate: we can provide a tiny bit of code that looks at two `CalendarEvent` objects and says whether one should appear before the other, and pass that code into the `Sort` method (see Example 7-15).

Example 7-15. Sorting an array

```
Array.Sort(events,
    (event1, event2) => event1.StartTime.CompareTo(event2.StartTime));
```

The `Sort` method's first argument, `events`, is just the array we'd like to reorder. (We defined that back in Example 7-10.) The second argument is a delegate, and for convenience we again used the lambda syntax introduced in Chapter 5. The `Sort` method wants to be able to know, for any two events, whether one should appear before the other, It requires a delegate of type `Comparison<T>`, a function which takes two arguments—we called them `event1` and `event2` here—and which returns a number. If `event1` is before `event2`, the number must be negative, and if it's after, the number must be positive. We return zero to indicate that the two are equal. Example 7-15 just defers to the `StartTime` property—that's a `DateTimeOffset`, which provides a handy `CompareTo` method that does exactly what we need.

It turns out that Example 7-15 isn't changing anything here, because the `events` array created in Example 7-10 happens to be in ascending order of date and time already. So just to illustrate that we can sort on any criteria, let's order them by duration instead:

```
Array.Sort(events,
    (event1, event2) => event1.Duration.CompareTo(event2.Duration));
```

This illustrates how the use of delegates enables us to plug in any number of different ordering criteria, leaving the `Array` class to get on with the tedious job of shuffling the array contents around to match the specified order.

Some data types such as dates or numbers have an intrinsic ordering. It would be irritating to have to tell `Array.Sort` how to work out whether one number comes before or after another. And in fact we don't have to—we can pass an array of numbers to a simpler overload of the `Sort` method, as shown in Example 7-16.

Example 7-16. Sorting intrinsically ordered data

```
int[] numbers = { 4, 1, 2, 5, 3 };
Array.Sort(numbers);
```

As you would expect, this arranges the numbers into ascending order. We would provide a comparison delegate here only if we wanted to sort the numbers into some other order. You might be wondering what would happen if we tried this simpler method with an array of `CalendarEvent` objects:

```
Array.Sort(events); // Blam!
```

If you try this, you'll find that the method throws an `InvalidOperationException`, because `Array.Sort` has no way of working out what order we need. It works only for types that have an intrinsic order. And should we want to, we could make `Calen` `darEvent` self-ordering. We just have to implement an interface called `IComparable<Cal` `endarEvent>`, which provides a single method, `CompareTo`. Example 7-17 implements this, and defers to the `DateTimeOffset` value in `StartTime`—the `DateTimeOffset` type implements `IComparable<DateTimeOffset>`. So all we're really doing here is passing the responsibility on to the property we want to use for ordering, just like we did in Example 7-15. The one extra bit of work we do is to check for comparison with `null`— the `IComparable<T>` interface documentation states that a non-null object should always compare as greater than `null`, so we return a positive number in that case. Without this check, our code would crash with a `NullReferenceException` if `null` were passed to `CompareTo`.

Example 7-17. Making a type comparable

```
class CalendarEvent : IComparable<CalendarEvent>
{
    public string Title { get; set; }
    public DateTimeOffset StartTime { get; set; }
    public TimeSpan Duration { get; set; }


    public int CompareTo(CalendarEvent other)
    {
        if (other == null) { return 1; }
        return StartTime.CompareTo(other.StartTime);
    }
}
```

Now that our `CalendarEvent` class has declared an intrinsic ordering for itself, we are free to use the simplest `Sort` overload:

```
Array.Sort(events);  // Works, now that CalendarEvent is IComparable<T>
```

Getting your array contents in order isn't the only reason for relocating elements, so `Array` offers some slightly less specialized methods for moving data around.

Moving or copying elements

Suppose you want to build a calendar application that works with multiple sources of information—maybe you use several different websites with calendar features and would like to aggregate all the events into a single list. Example 7-18 shows a method that takes two arrays of `CalendarEvent` objects, and returns one array containing all the elements from both.

Example 7-18. Copying elements from two arrays into one big one

```
static CalendarEvent[] CombineEvents(CalendarEvent[] events1,
                                     CalendarEvent[] events2)
{
```

```
CalendarEvent[] combinedEvents =
    new CalendarEvent[events1.Length + events2.Length];
events1.CopyTo(combinedEvents, 0);
events2.CopyTo(combinedEvents, events1.Length);

return combinedEvents;
}
```

This example uses the CopyTo method, which makes a complete copy of all the elements of the source array into the target passed as the first argument. The second argument says where to start copying elements into the target—Example 7-18 puts the first array's elements at the start (offset zero), and then copies the second array's elements directly after that. (So the ordering won't be very useful—you'd probably want to sort the results after doing this.)

You might sometimes want to be a bit more selective—you might want to copy only certain elements from the source into the target. For example, suppose you want to remove the first event. Arrays cannot be resized in .NET, but you could create a new array that's one element shorter, and which contains all but the first element of the original array. The CopyTo method can't help here as it copies the whole array, but you can use the more flexible Array.Copy method instead, as Example 7-19 shows.

Example 7-19. Copying less than the whole array

```
static CalendarEvent[] RemoveFirstEvent(CalendarEvent[] events)
{
    CalendarEvent[] croppedEvents = new CalendarEvent[events.Length - 1];
    Array.Copy(
        events,                 // Array from which to copy
        1,                      // Starting point in source array
        croppedEvents,          // Array into which to copy
        0,                      // Starting point in destination array
        events.Length - 1       // Number of elements to copy
        );
    return croppedEvents;
}
```

The key here is that we get to specify the index from which we want to start copying—1 in this case, skipping over the first element, which has an index of 0.

> In practice, you would rarely do this—if you need to be able to add or remove items from a collection, you would normally use the List<T> type that we'll be looking at later in this chapter, rather than a plain array. And even if you are working with arrays, there's an Array.Resize helper function that you would typically use in reality—it calls Array.Copy for you. However, you often have to copy data between arrays, even if it might not be strictly necessary in this simple example. A more complex example would have obscured the essential simplicity of Array.Copy.

The topic of array sizes is a little more complex than it first appears, so let's look at that in more detail.

Array Size

Arrays know how many elements they contain—several of the previous examples have used the Length property to discover the size of an existing array. This read-only property is defined by the base **Array** class, so it's always present.* That may sound like enough to cover the simple task of knowing an array's size, but arrays don't have to be simple sequential lists. You may need to work with multidimensional data, and .NET supports two different styles of arrays for that: jagged and rectangular arrays.

Arrays of arrays (or jagged arrays)

As we said earlier, you can make an array using any type as the element type. And since arrays themselves have types, it follows that you can have an array of arrays. For example, suppose we wanted to create a list of forthcoming events over the next five days, grouped by day. We could represent this as an array with one entry per day, and since each day may have multiple events, each entry needs to be an array. Example 7-20 creates just such an array.

Example 7-20. Building an array of arrays

```
static CalendarEvent[][] GetEventsByDay(CalendarEvent[] allEvents,
                                        DateTime firstDay,
                                        int numberOfDays)
{
    CalendarEvent[][] eventsByDay = new CalendarEvent[numberOfDays][];

    for (int day = 0; day < numberOfDays; ++day)
    {
        DateTime dateOfInterest = (firstDay + TimeSpan.FromDays(day)).Date;
        CalendarEvent[] itemsOnDateOfInterest = Array.FindAll(allEvents,
            e => e.StartTime.Date == dateOfInterest);

        eventsByDay[day] = itemsOnDateOfInterest;
    }

    return eventsByDay;
}
```

---

* There's also a LongLength, which is a 64-bit version of the property, which theoretically allows for larger arrays than the 32-bit Length property. However, .NET currently imposes an upper limit on the size of any single array: it cannot use more than 2 GB of memory, even in a 64-bit process. So in practice, LongLength isn't very useful in the current version of .NET (4). (You can use a lot more than 2 GB of memory in total in a 64-bit process—the 2 GB limit applies only to individual arrays.)

We'll look at this one piece at a time. First, there's the method declaration:

```
static CalendarEvent[][] GetEventsByDay(CalendarEvent[] allEvents,
                                        DateTime firstDay,
                                        int numberOfDays)
{
```

The return type—`CalendarEvent[][]`—is an array of arrays, denoted by two pairs of square brackets. You're free to go as deep as you like, by the way—it's perfectly possible to have an array of arrays of arrays of arrays of anything.

The method's arguments are fairly straightforward. This method expects to be passed a simple array containing an unstructured list of all the events. The method also needs to know which day we'd like to start from, and how many days we're interested in.

The very first thing the method does is construct the array that it will eventually return:

```
CalendarEvent[][] eventsByDay = new CalendarEvent[numberOfDays][];
```

Just as `new CalendarEvent[5]` would create an array capable of containing five `CalendarEvent` elements, `new CalendarEvent[5][]` would create an array capable of containing five arrays of `CalendarEvent` objects. Since our method lets the caller specify the number of days, we pass that argument in as the size of the top-level array.

Remember that arrays are reference types, and that whenever you create a new array whose element type is a reference type, all the elements are initially null. So although our new `eventsByDay` array is capable of referring to an array for each day, what it holds right now is a `null` for each day. So the next bit of code is a loop that will populate the array:

```
for (int day = 0; day < numberOfDays; ++day)
{
    ...
}
```

Inside this loop, the first couple of lines are similar to the start of Example 7-14:

```
DateTime dateOfInterest = (firstDay + TimeSpan.FromDays(day)).Date;
CalendarEvent[] itemsOnDateOfInterest = Array.FindAll(allEvents,
    e => e.StartTime.Date == dateOfInterest);
```

The only difference is that this example calculates which date to look at as we progress through the loop. So `Array.FindAll` will return an array containing all the events that fall on the day for the current loop iteration. The final piece of code in the loop puts that into our array of arrays:

```
eventsByDay[day] = itemsOnDateOfInterest;
```

Once the loop is complete, we return the array:

```
    return eventsByDay;
}
```

Each element will contain an array with the events that fall on the relevant day.

Code that uses such an array can use the normal element access syntax, for example:

```
Console.WriteLine("Number of events on first day: " + eventsByDay[0].Length);
```

Notice that this code uses just a single index—this means we want to retrieve one of the arrays from our array of arrays. In this case, we're looking at the size of the first of those arrays. Or we can dig further by providing multiple indexes:

```
Console.WriteLine("First day, second event: " + eventsByDay[0][1].Title);
```

This syntax, with its multiple sets of square brackets, fits right in with the syntax used to declare and construct the array of arrays.

So why is an array of arrays sometimes called a *jagged array*? Figure 7-4 shows the various objects you would end up with if you called the method in Example 7-20, passing the events from Example 7-10, asking for five days of events starting from July 11. The figure is laid out to show each child array as a row, and as you can see, the rows are not all the same length—the first couple of days have two items per row, the third day has one, and the last two are empty (i.e., they are zero-length arrays). So rather than looking like a neat rectangle of objects, the rows form a shape with a somewhat uneven or "jagged" righthand edge.

This jaggedness can be either a benefit or a problem, depending on your goals. In this example, it's helpful—we used it to handle the fact that the number of events in our calendar may be different every day, and some days may have no events at all. But if you're working with information that naturally fits into a rectangular structure (e.g., pixels in an image), rows of differing lengths would constitute an error—it would be better to use a data structure that doesn't support such things, so you don't have to work out how to handle such an error.

Moreover, jagged arrays end up with a relatively complicated structure—there are a lot of objects in Figure 7-4. Each array is an object distinct from the objects its element refers to, so we've ended up with 11 objects: the five events, the five per-day arrays (including two zero-length arrays), and then one array to hold those five arrays. In situations where you just don't need this flexibility, there's a simpler way to represent multiple rows: a rectangular array.

Rectangular arrays

A rectangular array[†] lets you store multidimensional data in a single array, rather than needing to create arrays of arrays. They are more regular in form than jagged arrays—in a two-dimensional rectangular array, every row has the same width.

---

† Rectangular arrays are also sometimes called *multidimensional arrays*, but that's a slightly confusing name, because jagged arrays also hold multidimensional data.

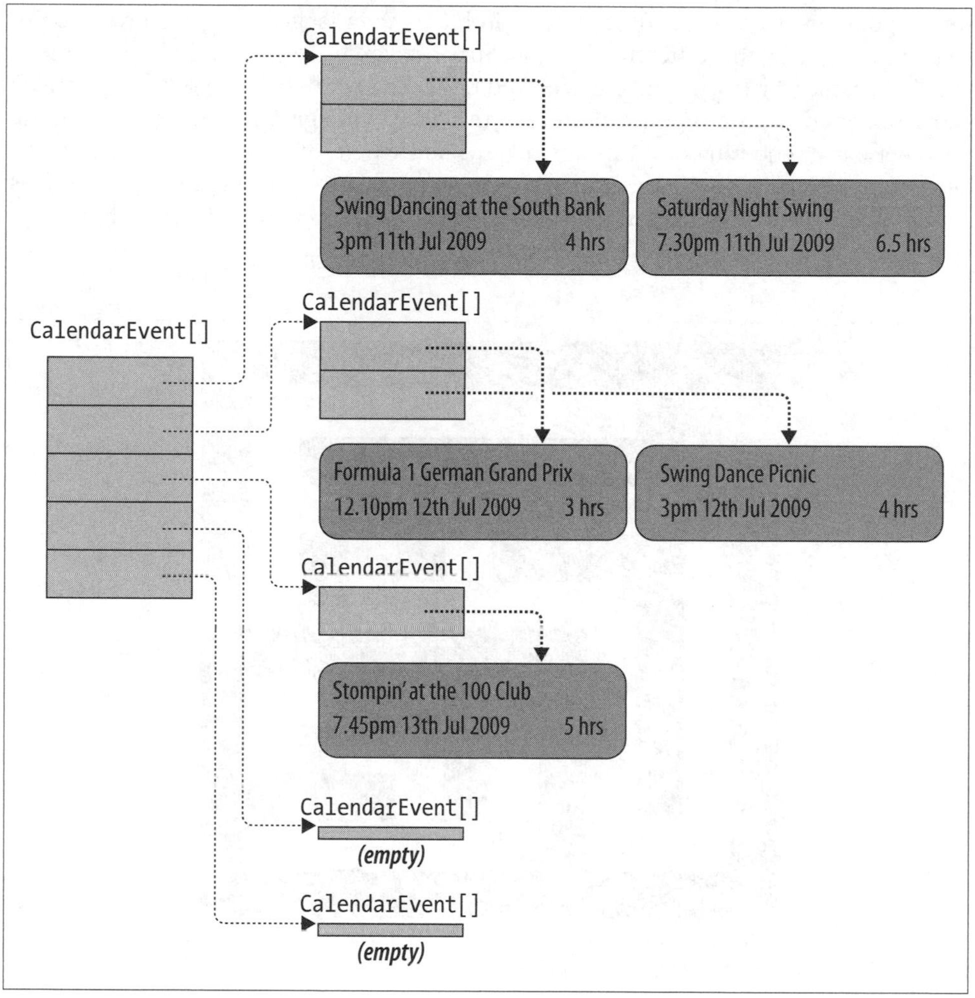

CalendarEvent[]

Swing Dancing at the South Bank
3pm 11th Jul 2009   4 hrs

Saturday Night Swing
7.30pm 11th Jul 2009   6.5 hrs

CalendarEvent[]

CalendarEvent[]

Formula 1 German Grand Prix
12.10pm 12th Jul 2009   3 hrs

Swing Dance Picnic
3pm 12th Jul 2009   4 hrs

CalendarEvent[]

Stompin' at the 100 Club
7.45pm 13th Jul 2009   5 hrs

CalendarEvent[]
(empty)

CalendarEvent[]
(empty)

Figure 7-4. A jagged array

Rectangular arrays are not limited to two dimensions, by the way. Just as you can have arrays of arrays of arrays, so you can have any number of dimensions in a "rectangular" array, although the name starts to sound a bit wrong. With three dimensions, it's a cuboid rather than a rectangle, and more generally the shape of these arrays is always an *orthotope*. Presumably the designers of C# and the .NET Framework felt that this "proper" name was too obscure (as does the spellchecker in Word) and that *rectangular* was more usefully descriptive, despite not being technically correct. Pragmatism beat pedantry here because C# is fundamentally a practical language.

Rectangular arrays tend to suit different problems than jagged arrays, so we need to switch temporarily to a different example. Suppose you were writing a simple game in which a character runs around a maze. And rather than going for a typical modern 3D game rendered from the point of view of the player, imagine something a bit more retro—a basic rendering of a top-down view, and where the walls of the maze all fit neatly onto a grid. If you're too young to remember this sort of thing, Figure 7-5 gives a rough idea of what passed for high-tech entertainment back when your authors were at school.

Figure 7-5. Retro gaming—3D is for wimps

We don't want to get too hung up on the details of the game play, so let's just assume that our code needs to know where the walls are in order to work out where the player can or can't move next, and whether she has a clean shot to take out the baddies chasing her through the maze. We could represent this as an array of numbers, where 0 represents a gap and 1 represents a wall, as Example 7-21 shows. (We could also have used `bool` instead of `int` as the element type, as there are only two possible options: a wall or no wall. However, using `true` and `false` would have prevented each row of data from fitting on a single row in this book, making it much harder to see how Example 7-21 reflects the map in Figure 7-5. Moreover, using numbers leaves open the option to add exciting game features such as unlockable doors, squares of instant death, and other classics.)

Example 7-21. A multidimensional rectangular array

```
int[,] walls = new int[,]
{
    { 1, 1, 1, 1, 1, 1, 1, 1, 1, 1, 1, 1 },
    { 0, 0, 1, 0, 0, 0, 0, 0, 0, 0, 0, 1 },
    { 1, 0, 1, 1, 1, 1, 1, 1, 1, 1, 0, 1 },
    { 1, 0, 0, 0, 0, 0, 0, 1, 0, 0, 0, 1 },
    { 1, 0, 1, 1, 1, 1, 0, 1, 0, 1, 0, 1 },
    { 1, 0, 1, 0, 0, 0, 0, 0, 0, 1, 0, 0 },
    { 1, 0, 1, 0, 1, 1, 1, 1, 1, 1, 1, 1 },
    { 1, 0, 1, 0, 0, 0, 1, 0, 0, 0, 0, 1 },
    { 1, 0, 1, 0, 1, 0, 1, 0, 0, 1, 0, 1 },
    { 1, 0, 1, 0, 1, 0, 1, 0, 1, 1, 1, 1 },
    { 1, 0, 0, 0, 1, 0, 0, 0, 0, 0, 0, 1 },
    { 1, 1, 1, 1, 1, 1, 1, 1, 1, 1, 1, 1 }
};
```

There are a couple of differences between this and previous examples. First, notice that the array type has a comma between the square brackets. The number of commas indicates how many dimensions we want—no commas at all would mean a one-dimensional array, which is what we've been using so far, but the single comma here specifies a two-dimensional array. We could represent a cuboid layout with int[,,], and so on, into as many dimensions as your application requires.

The second thing to notice here is that we've not had to use the new keyword for each row in the initializer list—new appears only once, and that's because this really is just a single object despite being multidimensional. As Figure 7-6 illustrates, this kind of array has a much simpler structure than the two-dimensional jagged array in Figure 7-4.

While Figure 7-6 is accurate in the sense that just one object holds all the values here, the grid-like layout of the numbers is not a literal representation of how the numbers are really stored, any more than the position of the various objects in Figure 7-4 is a literal representation of what you'd see if you peered into your computer's memory chips with a scanning electron microscope.

In reality, multidimensional arrays store their elements as a sequential list just like the simple array in Figure 7-3, because computer memory itself is just a big sequence of storage locations. But the programming model C# presents makes it look like the array really is multidimensional.

The syntax for accessing elements in a rectangular array is slightly different from that of a jagged array. But like a jagged array, the access syntax is consistent with the declaration syntax—as Example 7-22 shows, we use a single pair of square brackets, passing in an index for each dimension, separated by commas.

int[,]

1	1	1	1	1	1	1	1	1	1	1	1
0	0	1	0	0	0	0	0	0	0	0	1
1	0	1	1	1	1	1	1	1	1	0	1
1	0	0	0	0	0	0	1	0	0	0	1
1	0	1	1	1	1	0	1	0	1	0	1
1	0	1	0	0	0	0	0	0	1	0	0
1	0	1	0	1	1	1	1	1	1	1	1
1	0	1	0	0	0	1	0	0	0	0	1
1	0	1	0	1	0	1	0	0	1	0	1
1	0	1	0	1	0	1	0	1	1	1	1
1	0	0	0	1	0	0	0	0	0	0	1
1	1	1	1	1	1	1	1	1	1	1	1

Figure 7-6. A two-dimensional rectangular array

Example 7-22. Accessing an element in a rectangular array

```
static bool CanCharacterMoveDown(int x, int y, int[,] walls)
{
    int newY = y + 1;

    // Can't move off the bottom of the map
    if (newY == walls.GetLength(0)) { return false; }

    // Can only move down if there's no wall in the way
    return walls[newY, x] == 0;
}
```

 If you pass in the wrong number of indexes, the C# compiler will complain. The number of dimensions (or *rank*, to use the official term) is considered to be part of the type: int[,] is a different type than int[,,], and C# checks that the number of indexes you supply matches the array type's rank.

Example 7-22 performs two checks: before it looks to see if there's a wall in the way of the game character, it first checks to see if the character is up against the edge of the map. To do this, it needs to know how big the map is. And rather than assuming a fixed-size grid, it asks the array for its size. But it can't just use the `Length` property we saw earlier—that returns the total number of elements. Since this is a 12 × 12 array, `Length` will be 144. But we want to know the length in the vertical dimension. So instead, we use the `GetLength` method, which takes a single argument indicating which dimension you want—0 would be the vertical dimension and 1 in this case is horizontal.

 Arrays don't really have any concept of horizontal and vertical. They simply have as many dimensions as you ask for, and it's up to your program to decide what each dimension is for. This particular program has chosen to use the first dimension to represent the vertical position in the maze, and the second dimension for the horizontal position.

This rectangular example has used a two-dimensional array of integers, and since `int` is a value type, the values get to live inside the array. You can also create multidimensional rectangular arrays with reference type elements. In that case, you'll still get a single object containing all the elements of the array in all their dimensions, but these individual elements will be null references—you'll need to create objects for them to refer to, just like you would with a single-dimensional array.

While jagged and rectangular multidimensional arrays give us flexibility in terms of how to specify the size of an array, we have not yet dealt with an irritating sizing problem mentioned back at the start of the chapter: an array's size is fixed. We saw that it's possible to work around this by creating new arrays and copying some or all of the old data across, or by getting the `Array.Resize` method to do that work for us. But these are inconvenient solutions, so in practice, we rarely work directly with arrays in C#. There's a far easier way to work with changing collection sizes, thanks to the `List<T>` class.

List<T>

The `List<T>` class, defined in the `System.Collections.Generic` namespace, is effectively a resizable array. Strictly speaking, it's just a generic class provided by the .NET Framework class library, and unlike arrays, `List<T>` does not get any special treatment from the type system or the CLR. But from a C# developer's perspective, it feels very similar—you can do most of the things you could do with an array, but without the restriction of a fixed size.

Generics

`List<T>` is an example of a *generic type*. You do not use a generic type directly; you use it to build new types. For example, `List<int>` is a list of integers, and `List<string>` is a list of strings. These are two types in their own right, built by passing different *type arguments* to `List<T>`. Plugging in type arguments to form a new type is called *instantiating* the generic type.

Generics were added in C# 2.0 mainly to support collection classes such as `List<T>`. Before this, we had to use the `ArrayList` class (which you should no longer use; it's not present in Silverlight, and may eventually be deprecated in the full .NET Framework). `ArrayList` was also a resizable array, but it represented all items as `object`. This meant it could hold anything, but every time you read an element, you were obliged to cast to the type you were expecting, which was messy.

With generics, we can write code that has one or more placeholder type names—the `T` in `List<T>`, for example. We call these *type parameters*. (The distinction between parameters and arguments is the same here as it is for methods: a parameter is a named placeholder, whereas an argument is a specific value or type provided for that parameter at the point at which you use the code.) So you can write code like this:

```
public class Wrapper<T>
{
    public Wrapper(T v) { Value = v; }
    public T Value { get; private set; }
}
```

This code doesn't need to know what type `T` is—and in fact `T` can be any type. If we want a wrapper for an `int`, we can write `Wrapper<int>`, and that generates a class exactly like the example, except with the `T` replaced by `int` throughout.

Some classes take multiple type parameters. Dictionary collections (which are described in Chapter 9) require both a key and a value type, so you would specify, say, `Dictionary<string, MyClass>`. An instantiated generic type is a type in its own right, so you can use one as an argument for another generic type, for example, `Dictionary<string, List<int>>`.

You can also specify a type parameter list for a method. For example, .NET defines an extension method for all collections called `OfType<TResult>`. If you have a `List<object>` that happens to contain a mixture of different kinds of objects, you can retrieve just the items that are of type `string` by calling `myList.OfType<string>()`.

You may be wondering why .NET offers arrays when `List<T>` appears to be more useful. The answer is that it wouldn't be possible for `List<T>` to exist if there were no arrays: `List<T>` uses an array internally to hold its elements. As you add elements, it allocates new, larger arrays as necessary, copying the old contents over. It employs various tricks to minimize how often it needs to do this.

List<T> is one of the most useful types in the .NET Framework. If you're dealing with multiple pieces of information, as programs often do, it's very common to need some flexibility around the amount of information—fixed-size lists are the exception rather than the rule. (An individual's calendar tends to change over time, for example.) So have we just wasted your time with the first half of this chapter? Not at all—not only do arrays crop up a lot in APIs, but List<T> collections are very similar in use to arrays.

We could migrate most of the examples seen so far in this chapter from arrays to lists. Returning to our earlier, nonrectangular example, we would need to modify only the first line of Example 7-10, which creates an array of CalendarEvent objects. That line currently reads:

```
CalendarEvent[] events =
```

It is followed by the list of objects to add to the array, contained within a pair of braces. If you change that line to this:

```
List<CalendarEvent> events = new List<CalendarEvent>
```

the initializer list can remain the same. Notice that besides changing the variable declaration to use the List<T> type (with the generic type argument T set to the element type CalendarEvent, of course) we also need an explicit call to the constructor. (Normally, you'd expect parentheses after the type name when invoking a constructor, but those are optional when using an initializer list.) As you saw earlier, the use of new is optional when assigning a value to a newly declared array, but C# does not extend that courtesy to other collection types.

While we can initialize the list in much the same way as we would an array, the difference is that we are free to add and remove elements later. To add a new element, we can use the Add method:

```
CalendarEvent newEvent = new CalendarEvent
    {
        Title = "Dean Collins Shim Sham Lesson",
        StartTime = new DateTimeOffset (2009, 7, 14, 19, 15, 00, TimeSpan.Zero),
        Duration = TimeSpan.FromHours(1)
    };

events.Add(newEvent);
```

This appends the element to the end of the list. If you want to put the new element somewhere other than at the end, you can use Insert:

```
events.Insert(2, newEvent);
```

The first argument indicates the index at which you'd like the new item to appear—any items at or after this index will be moved down to make space. You can also remove items, either by index, using the RemoveAt method, or by passing the value you'd like to remove to the Remove method (which will remove the first element it finds that contains the specified value).

List<T> does not have a Length property, and instead offers a Count. This may seem like pointless inconsistency with arrays, but there's a reason. An array's Length property is guaranteed not to change. A List<T> cannot make that guarantee, and so the behavior of its Count property is necessarily different from an array's Length. The use of different names signals the fact that the semantics are subtly different.

List<T> also offers AddRange, which lets you add multiple elements in a single step. This makes it much easier to concatenate lists—remember that with arrays we ended up writing the CombineEvents method in Example 7-18 to concatenate a couple of arrays. But with lists, it becomes as simple as the code shown in Example 7-23.

Example 7-23. Adding elements from one list to another

```
events1.AddRange(events2);
```

The one possible downside of List<T> is that this kind of operation modifies the first list. Example 7-18 built a brand-new array, leaving the two input arrays unmodified, so if any code happened still to be using those original arrays, it would carry on working. But Example 7-23 modifies the first list by adding in the events from the second list. You would need to be confident that nothing in your code was relying on the first list containing only its original content. Of course, you could always build a brand-new new List<T> from the contents of two existing lists. (There are various ways to do this, but one straightforward approach is to construct a new List<T> and then call AddRange twice, once for each list.)

You access elements in a List<T> with exactly the same syntax as for an array. For example:

```
Console.WriteLine("List element: " + events[2].Title);
```

As with arrays, a List<T> will throw an IndexOutOfRangeException if you use too high an index, or a negative index. This applies for writes as well as reads—a List<T> will not automatically grow if you write to an index that does not yet exist.

There is a subtle difference between array element access and list element access that can cause problems with custom value types (structs). You may recall that Chapter 3 warned that when writing a custom value type, it's best to make it immutable if you plan to use it in a collection. To understand why, you need to know how List<T> makes the square bracket syntax for element access work.

Custom Indexers

Arrays are an integral part of the .NET type system, so C# knows exactly what to do when you access an array element using the square bracket syntax. However, as List<T> demonstrates, it's also possible to use this same syntax with some objects that are not arrays. For this to work, the object's type needs to help C# out by defining the behavior for this syntax. This takes the form of a slightly unusual-looking property, as shown in Example 7-24.

Example 7-24. A custom indexer

```
class Indexable
{
    public string this[int index]
    {
        get
        {
            return "Item " + index;
        }
        set
        {
            Console.WriteLine("You set item " + index + " to " + value);
        }
    }
}
```

This has the get and set parts we'd expect in a normal property, but the definition line is a little unusual: it starts with the accessibility and type as normal, but where we'd expect to see the property name we instead have this[int index]. The this keyword signifies that this property won't be accessed by any name. It is followed by a parameter list enclosed in square brackets, signifying that this is an indexer property, defining what should happen if we use the square bracket element access syntax with objects of this type. For example, look at the code in Example 7-25.

Example 7-25. Using a custom indexer

```
Indexable ix = new Indexable();
Console.WriteLine(ix[10]);
ix[42] = "Xyzzy";
```

After constructing the object, the next line uses the same element access syntax you'd use to read an element from an array. But this is not an array, so the C# compiler will look for a property of the kind shown in Example 7-24. If you try this on a type that doesn't provide an indexer, you'll get a compiler error, but since this type has one, that ix[10] expression ends up calling the indexer's get accessor. Similarly, the third line has the element access syntax on the lefthand side of an assignment, so C# will use the indexer's set accessor.

 If you want to support the multidimensional rectangular array style of index (e.g., `ix[10, 20]`), you can specify multiple parameters between the square brackets in your indexer. Note that the `List<T>` class does not do this—while it covers most of the same ground as the built-in array types, it does not offer rectangular multidimensional behavior. You're free to create a jagged list of lists, though. For example, `List<List<int>>` is a list of lists of integers, and is similar in use to an `int[][]`.

The indexer in Example 7-24 doesn't really contain any elements at all—it just makes up a value in the `get`, and prints out the value passed into `set` without storing it anywhere. So if you run this code, you'll see this output:

```
Item 10
You set item 42 to Xyzzy
```

It may seem a bit odd to provide array-like syntax but to discard whatever values are "written," but this is allowed—there's no rule that says that indexers are required to behave in an array-like fashion. In practice, most do—the reason C# supports indexers is to make it possible to write classes such as `List<T>` that feel like arrays without necessarily having to be arrays. So while Example 7-24 illustrates that you're free to do whatever you like in a custom indexer, it's not a paragon of good coding style.

What does any of this have to do with value types and immutability, though? Look at Example 7-26. It has a public field with an array and also an indexer that provides access to the array.

Example 7-26. Arrays versus indexers

```csharp
// This class's purpose is to illustrate a difference between
// arrays and indexers. Do not use this in real code!
class ArrayAndIndexer<T>
{
    public T[] TheArray = new T[100];
    public T this[int index]
    {
        get
        {
            return TheArray[index];
        }
        set
        {
            TheArray[index] = value;
        }
    }
}
```

You might think that it would make no difference whether we use this class's indexer, or go directly for the array. And some of the time that's true, as it is in this example:

```
ArrayAndIndexer<int> aai = new ArrayAndIndexer<int>();
aai.TheArray[10] = 42;
Console.WriteLine(aai[10]);
aai[20] = 99;
Console.WriteLine(aai.TheArray[20]);
```

This swaps freely between using the array and the indexer, and as the output shows, items set through one mechanism are visible through the other:

```
42
99
```

However, things are a little different if we make this class store a mutable value type. Here's a very simple modifiable value type:

```
struct CanChange
{
    public int Number { get; set; }
    public string Name { get; set; }
}
```

The Number and Name properties both have setters, so this is clearly not an immutable type. This might not seem like a problem—we can do more or less exactly the same with this type as we did with int just a moment ago:

```
ArrayAndIndexer<CanChange> aai = new ArrayAndIndexer<CanChange>();
aai.TheArray[10] = new CanChange { Number = 42 };
Console.WriteLine(aai[10].Number);
aai[20] = new CanChange { Number = 99, Name = "My item" };
Console.WriteLine(aai.TheArray[20].Number);
```

That works fine. The problem arises when we try to modify a property of one of the values already inside the array. We can do it with the array:

```
aai.TheArray[10].Number = 123;
Console.WriteLine(aai.TheArray[10].Number);
```

That works—it prints out 123 as you'd expect. But this does not work:

```
aai[20].Number = 456;
```

If you try this, you'll find that the C# compiler reports the following error:

```
error CS1612: Cannot modify the return value of
'ArrayAndIndexer<CanChange>.this[int]' because it is not a variable
```

That's a slightly cryptic message. But the problem becomes clear when we think about what we just asked the compiler to do. The intent of this code:

```
aai[20].Number = 456;
```

seems clear—we want to modify the Number property of the item whose index is 20. And remember, this line of code is using our ArrayAndIndexer<T> class's indexer. Looking at Example 7-26, which of the two accessors would you expect it to use here? Since we're modifying the value, you might expect **set** to be used, but a **set** accessor is an all or nothing proposition: calling **set** means you want to replace the whole element. But we're not trying to do that here—we just want to modify the **Number** property of the value, leaving its **Name** property unmodified. If you look at the **set** code in Example 7-26, it simply doesn't offer that as an option—it will completely replace the element at the specified index in the array. The **set** accessor can come into play only when we're providing a whole new value for the element, as in:

```
aai[20] = new CanChange { Number = 456 };
```

That compiles, but we end up losing the **Name** property that the element in that location previously had, because we overwrote the entire value of the element.

Since **set** doesn't work, that leaves **get**. The C# compiler could interpret this code:

```
aai[20].Number = 456;
```

as being equivalent to the code in Example 7-27.

Example 7-27. What the compiler might have done

```
CanChange elem = aai[20];
elem.Number = 456;
```

And in fact, that's what it would have done if we were using a reference type. However, it has noticed that **CanChange** is a value type, and has therefore rejected the code. (The error message says nothing about value types, but you can verify that this is the heart of the problem by changing the **CanChange** type from a **struct** to a **class**. That removes the compiler error, and you'll find that the code **aai[20].Number = 456** works as expected.)

Why has the compiler rejected this seemingly obvious solution? Well, remember that the crucial difference between reference types and value types is that values usually involve copies—if you retrieve a value from an indexer, the indexer returns a copy. So in Example 7-27 the **elem** variable holds a copy of the item at index 20. Setting **elem.Number** to 456 has an effect on only that copy—the original item in the array remains unchanged. This makes clear why the compiler rejected our code—the only thing it can do with this:

```
aai[20].Number = 456;
```

is to call the **get** accessor, and then set the **Number** property on the *copy* returned by the array, leaving the original value unaltered. Since the copy would then immediately be discarded, the compiler has wisely determined that this is almost certainly not what we meant. (If we really want that copy-then-modify behavior, we can always write the code in Example 7-27 ourselves, making the fact that there's a copy explicit. Putting the copy into a named variable also gives us the opportunity to go on and do something with the copy, meaning that setting a property on the copy might no longer be a waste of effort.)

You might be thinking that the compiler could read and modify a copy like Example 7-27, and then write that value back using the **set** indexer accessor. However, as Example 7-24 showed, indexer accessors are not required to work in the obvious way, and more generally, accessors can have side effects. So the C# compiler cannot assume that such a **get**-modify-**set** sequence is necessarily safe.

This problem doesn't arise with reference types, because in that case, the **get** accessor returns a reference rather than a value—no copying occurs because that reference refers to the same object that the corresponding array entry refers to.

But why does this work when we use the array directly? Recall that the compiler didn't have a problem with this code:

```
aai.TheArray[10].Number = 123;
```

It lets that through because it's able to make that behave like we expect. This will in fact modify the **Number** property of the element in the array. And this is the rather subtle difference between an array and an indexer. With an array you really can work directly with the element inside the array—no copying occurs in this example. This works because the C# compiler knows what an array is, and is able to generate code that deals directly with array elements *in situ*. But there's no way to write a custom indexer that offers the same flexibility. (There are reasons for this, but to explain them would require an exploration of the .NET Framework's type safety rules, which would be lengthy and quite outside the scope of this chapter.)

Having established the root of the problem, let's look at what this means for **List<T>**.

Immutability and List<T>

The **List<T>** class gets no special privileges—it may be part of the .NET Framework class library, but it is subject to the same restrictions as your code. And so it has the same problem just described—the following code will produce the same compiler error you saw in the preceding section:

```
List<CanChange> numbers = new List<CanChange> { new CanChange() };
numbers[0].Number = 42;  // Will not compile
```

One way of dealing with this would be to avoid using custom value types in a collection class such as **List<T>**, preferring custom reference types instead. And that's not a bad rule of thumb—reference types are a reasonable default choice for most data types. However, value types do offer one compelling feature if you happen to be dealing with very large volumes of data. As Figure 7-1 showed earlier, an array with reference type elements results in an object for the array itself, and one object for each element in the array. But when an array has value type elements, you end up with just one object—the values live inside the array, as Figure 7-3 illustrates. **List<T>** has similar characteristics because it uses an array internally.

For an array with hundreds of thousands of elements, the simpler structure of Figure 7-3 can have a noticeable impact on performance. For example, I just ran a quick test on my computer to see how long it would take to create a List<CanChange> with 500,000 entries, and then run through the list, adding the Number values together. Example 7-28 shows the code—it uses the Stopwatch class from the System.Diagnostics namespace, which provides a handy way to see how long things are taking.

Example 7-28. Microbenchmarking values versus references in lists

```
Stopwatch sw = new Stopwatch();
sw.Start();
int itemCount = 500000;
List<CanChange> items = new List<CanChange>(itemCount);
for (int i = 0; i < itemCount; ++i)
{
    items.Add(new CanChange { Number = i });
}
sw.Stop();
Console.WriteLine("Creation: " + sw.ElapsedTicks);
sw.Reset();
sw.Start();
int total = 0;
for (int i = 0; i < itemCount; ++i)
{
    total += items[i].Number;
}
sw.Stop();
Console.WriteLine("Total: " + total);
Console.WriteLine("Sum: " + sw.ElapsedTicks);
```

With CanChange as a value type, it takes about 150 ms on my machine to populate the list, and then about 40 ms to run through all the numbers, adding them together. But if I change CanChange from a struct to a class (i.e., make it a reference type) the numbers become more like 600 ms and 50 ms, respectively. So that's about 25 percent longer to perform the calculations but a staggering four times longer to create the collection in the first place. And that's because with CanChange as a reference type, we now need to ask the .NET Framework to create half a million objects for us instead of just one object when we initialize the list. From the perspective of an end user, this is the difference between a tiny hiatus and an annoyingly long delay—when an application freezes for more than half a second, users begin to wonder if it has hung, which is very disruptive.

Please don't take away the message that value types are four times faster than reference types—they aren't. A micro benchmark like this should always be taken with a very strong pinch of salt. All we've really measured here is how long it takes to do something contrived in an isolated and artificial experiment. This example is illuminating only insofar as it demonstrates that the choice between value types and reference types can *sometimes* have a profound effect. It would be a mistake to draw a generalized conclusion from this.

Notice that even in this example we see significant variation: the first part of the code slowed down by a factor of four, but in the second part, the impact was much smaller. In some scenarios, there will be no measurable difference, and as it happens there are situations in which value types can be shown to be slower than reference types.

The bottom line is this: the only important performance measurements are ones you make yourself on the system you are building. If you think your code might get a useful speedup by using a value type instead of a reference type in a large collection, measure the effect of that change, rather than doing it just because some book said it would be faster.

Since the use of value types in a collection can sometimes offer very useful performance benefits, the rule of thumb we suggested earlier—always use reference types—looks too restrictive in practice. So this is where immutability comes into play. As we saw earlier in this section, the fact that a `get` accessor can only return a copy of a value type causes problems if you ever need to modify a value already in a collection. But if your value types are immutable, you will never hit this problem. And as we'll see in Chapter 16, there are other benefits to immutable types.

So we now know how `List<T>` is able to make itself resemble an array. Having understood some of the subtle differences between array element access and custom indexers, let's get back to some of the other functionality of `List<T>`.

Finding and Sorting

Earlier we saw that the `Array` class offers a variety of helper methods for finding elements in arrays. If you try to use these directly on a `List<T>`, it won't work. The following code from Example 7-14 will not compile if `events` is a `List<CalendarEvents>`, for example:

```
DateTime dateOfInterest = new DateTime (2009, 7, 12);
CalendarEvent[] itemsOnDateOfInterest = Array.FindAll(events,
    e => e.StartTime.Date == dateOfInterest);
```

This will cause an error, because `Array.FindAll` expects an array, and we're now giving it a `List<T>`. However, all the finding and sorting functionality we saw earlier is still available; you just have to use the methods provided by `List<T>` instead of `Array`:

```
DateTime dateOfInterest = new DateTime(2009, 7, 12);
List<CalendarEvent> itemsOnDateOfInterest = events.FindAll(
    e => e.StartTime.Date == dateOfInterest);
```

Notice a slight stylistic difference—whereas with arrays, `FindAll` is a static method provided by the `Array` class, `List<T>` chooses to make its `FindAll` method an instance member—so we invoke it as `events.FindAll`. Style aside, it works in exactly the same way. As you might expect, it returns its results as another `List<T>` rather than as an array.

This same stylistic difference exists with all the other techniques we looked at before. `List<T>` provides `Find`, `FindLast`, `FindIndex`, `FindLastIndex`, `IndexOf`, `LastIndexOf`, and `Sort` methods that all work in almost exactly the same way as the array equivalents we looked at earlier, but again, they're instance methods rather than static methods.

Since `List<T>` offers almost everything you're likely to want from an array and more besides, `List<T>` will usually be your first choice to represent a collection of data. (The only common exception is if you need a rectangular array.) Unfortunately, you will sometimes come up against APIs that simply require you to provide an array. In fact, we already wrote some code that does this: the `AddNumbers` method back in Example 7-3 requires its input to be in the form of an array. But even this is easy to deal with: `List<T>` provides a handy `ToArray()` method for just this eventuality, building a copy of the list's contents in array form.

But wouldn't it be better if we could write our code in such a way that it didn't care whether incoming information was in an array, a `List<T>`, or some other kind of collection? It is possible to do exactly this, using the polymorphism techniques discussed in Chapter 4.

Collections and Polymorphism

Polymorphic code is code that is able to work on a variety of different forms of data. The `foreach` keyword has this characteristic. For example:

```
foreach (CalendarEvent ev in events)
{
    Console.WriteLine(ev.Title);
}
```

This code works if `events` is an array—`CalendarEvent[]`—but it works equally well if `events` is a `List<CalendarEvent>`. And in fact, there are many more specialized collection types in the .NET Framework class library that we'll look at in a later chapter that `foreach` can work with. You can even arrange for it to work with custom collection classes you may have written yourself. All this is possible because the .NET Framework defines some standard interfaces for representing collections of things. The `foreach` construct depends on a pair of interfaces: `IEnumerable<T>` and `IEnumerator<T>`. These derive from a couple of nongeneric base interfaces, `IEnumerable` and `IEnumerator`. These interfaces are defined in the class library, and they are reproduced in Example 7-29.

Example 7-29. Enumeration interfaces

```
namespace System.Collections.Generic
{
    public interface IEnumerable<out T> : IEnumerable
    {
        new IEnumerator<T> GetEnumerator();
    }

    public interface IEnumerator<out T> : IDisposable, IEnumerator
    {
        new T Current { get; }
    }
}

namespace System.Collections
{
    public interface IEnumerable
    {
        IEnumerator GetEnumerator();
    }

    public interface IEnumerator
    {
        bool MoveNext();
        object Current { get; }
        void Reset();
    }
}
```

The split between the generic and nongeneric interfaces here is a historical artifact. Versions 1.0 and 1.1 of .NET did not support generics, so only the base `IEnumerable` and `IEnumerator` interfaces existed. When .NET 2.0 shipped in 2005, generics were introduced, making it possible to provide versions of these interfaces that were explicit about what type of objects a collection contains, but in order to maintain backward compatibility the old version 1.x interfaces had to remain. You will normally use the generic versions, because they are easier to work with.

Conceptually, if a type implements `IEnumerable<T>` it is declaring that it contains a sequence of items of type `T`. To get hold of the items, you can call the `GetEnumerator` method, which will return an `IEnumerator<T>`. An enumerator is an object that lets you work through the objects in an enumerable collection one at a time.[‡] The split between enumerables and enumerators makes it possible to have different parts of your program

---

[‡] If you're familiar with C++ and its Standard Template Library, an enumerator is broadly similar in concept to an iterator in the STL.

working their way through the same collection at the same time, without all of them needing to be in the same place. This can be useful in multithreaded applications (although as we'll see in a later chapter, you have to be extremely careful about letting multiple threads use the same data structure simultaneously).

 Some enumerable collections, such as List<T>, can be modified. (.NET defines an IList<T> interface to represent the abstract idea of a modifiable, ordered collection. List<T> is just one implementation IList<T>.) You should avoid modifying a collection while you're in the process of iterating through it. For example, do not call Add on a List<T> in the middle of a foreach loop that uses that list. List<T> detects when this happens, and throws an exception.

Note that unlike IList<T>, IEnumerable<T> does not provide any methods for modifying the sequence. While this provides less flexibility to the consumer of a sequence, it broadens the range of data that can be wrapped as an IEnumerable<T>. For some sources of data it doesn't make sense to provide consumers of that data with the ability to reorder it.

These interfaces make it possible to write a function that uses a collection without having any idea of the collection's real type—you only need to know what type of elements it contains. We could rewrite Example 7-3 so that it works with any IEnumerable<string> rather than just an array of strings, as shown in Example 7-30.

Example 7-30. Using IEnumerable<T> and IEnumerator<T>

```
static string[] AddNumbers(IEnumerable<string> names)
{
    List<string> numberedNames = new List<string>();

    using (IEnumerator<string> enumerator = names.GetEnumerator())
    {
        int i = 0;
        while (enumerator.MoveNext())
        {
            string currentName = enumerator.Current;
            numberedNames.Add(string.Format("{0}: {1}", i, currentName));
            i += 1;
        }
    }
    return numberedNames.ToArray();
}
```

Since List<T> and arrays both implement IEnumerable<T>, this modified code in Example 7-30 will now work with List<string>, as well as arrays, or any other collection class that implements IEnumerable<string>. For more information on the subtleties of type compatibility and enumerations, see the sidebar on the next page.

Enumerations and Variance

Suppose you've written a function that uses an enumeration of elements of some base type, perhaps an `IEnumerable<FirefighterBase>`. (Chapter 4 defined `FirefighterBase` as a base class of various types representing firefighters.) For example:

```
static void ShowNames(IEnumerable<FirefighterBase> people)
{
    foreach (FirefighterBase person in people)
    { Console.WriteLine(person.Name); }
}
```

What would you expect to happen if you tried to pass this method an `IEnumerable<TraineeFirefighter>`, where `TraineeFirefighter` derives from `FirefighterBase`? It seems like it should work—`ShowNames` expects to get a sequence of `FirefighterBase` objects, and since `TraineeFirefighter` derives from `FirefighterBase`, an `IEnumerable<TraineeFirefighter>` will return a sequence of objects that are all of type `FirefighterBase` (as well as being of type `TraineeFirefighter`).

In C# 4.0, this works as you'd expect. But it didn't in previous versions. In general, it's not safe to assume that types are necessarily compatible just because their type arguments happen to be compatible. For example, there's an `IList<T>` interface which defines an **Add** method. `IList<TraineeFirefighter>` cannot safely be converted to `IList<FirefighterBase>`, because the latter's **Add** method would allow anything derived from `FirefighterBase` (e.g., `Firefighter`, `TraineeFirefighter`) to be added, but in practice the implementer of `IList<TraineeFirefighter>` might not allow that—it might accept only the `TraineeFirefighter` type.

`IEnumerable<T>` works here because the `T` type only ever comes out of an enumeration; there's no way to pass instances of `T` into `IEnumerable<T>`. The interface definition states this—as Example 7-29 shows, the type argument is prefixed with the **out** keyword. In the official terminology, this means that `IEnumerable<T>` is *covariant* with `T`. This means that if type `D` derives from type `B` (or is otherwise type-compatible—maybe `B` is an interface that `D` implements), `IEnumerable<D>` is type-compatible with `IEnumerable<B>`.

Generic arguments can also be prefixed with the **in** keyword, meaning that the type is only ever passed in, and will never be returned. The `IComparable<T>` interface we saw earlier happens to work this way. In this case, we say that `IComparable<T>` is *contravariant* with `T`—it works the other way around. You cannot pass an `IComparable<TraineeFirefighter>` to a method expecting an `IComparable<FirefighterBase>`, because that method might pass in a different kind of `FirefighterBase`, such as `Firefighter`. But you can pass an `IComparable<FirefighterBase>` to a method expecting an `IComparable<TraineeFirefighter>` (even though you cannot pass a `FirefighterBase` to a method expecting a `TraineeFirefighter`). An `IComparable<FirefighterBase>` is capable of being compared to any `FirefighterBase`, and is therefore able to be compared with a `TraineeFirefighter`.

By default, generic arguments are neither covariant nor contravariant. C# 4.0 introduced support for variance because the absence of variance with collection interfaces just seemed wrong—`IEnumerable<T>` now works like most developers would expect.

Example 7-30 works much harder than it needs to—it creates the enumerator explicitly, and walks through the objects by calling MoveNext in a loop, retrieving the Current value each time around. (A newly created enumerator needs us to call MoveNext before first reading Current. It doesn't automatically start on the first item because there might not be one—collections can be empty.) As it happens, that's exactly what foreach does, so we can get that to do the work for us. Example 7-31 does the same thing as Example 7-30, but lets the C# compiler generate the code.

Example 7-31. Using an IEnumerable<T> with foreach

```
static string[] AddNumbers(IEnumerable<string> names)
{
    List<string> numberedNames = new List<string>();
    int i = 0;
    foreach (string currentName in names)
    {
        numberedNames.Add(string.Format("{0}: {1}", i, currentName));
        i += 1;
    }
    return numberedNames.ToArray();
}
```

This example only half enters into the spirit of things—it can accept any IEnumerable<string>, but it stubbornly continues to return an array. This isn't necessarily a problem; after all, arrays implement IEnumerable<T>. However, our code is a little inelegant in the way that it creates a List<string> and then converts that into an array at the end. There's a better way—C# makes it very easy to provide a sequence of objects directly as an IEnumerable<T>.

Creating Your Own IEnumerable<T>

Before version 2 of C# (which shipped with Visual Studio 2005), writing your own enumerable types was tedious—you had to write a class that implemented IEnumerator, and that would usually be a separate class from the one that implemented IEnumerable, because multiple enumerators can be active simultaneously for any single collection. It wasn't hugely tricky, but it was enough of a hassle to put most people off. But C# 2 made it extremely easy to provide enumerations. Example 7-32 shows yet another reworking of the AddNumbers method.

Example 7-32. Implementing IEnumerable<T> with yield return

```
static IEnumerable<string> AddNumbers(IEnumerable<string> names)
{
    int i = 0;
    foreach (string currentName in names)
    {
        yield return string.Format("{0}: {1}", i, currentName);
        i += 1;
    }
}
```

Instead of using the normal return statement, this method uses yield return. This special form of return statement can only be used inside a method that returns either an enumerable or an enumerator object—you'll get a compiler error if you try to use it anywhere else. It works rather differently from a normal return. A normal return statement indicates that the method has finished, and would like to return control to the caller (returning a value, if the method's return type was not void). But yield return effectively says: "I want to return this value as an item in the collection, but I might not be done yet—I could have more values to return."

The yield return in Example 7-32 is in the middle of a foreach loop. Whereas a normal return would break out of the loop, in this case the loop is still running, even though the method has returned a value. This leads to some slightly surprising flow of execution. Let's look at the order in which this code runs. Example 7-33 modifies the AddNumbers method from Example 7-32 by adding a few calls to Console.Writeline, so we can see exactly how the code runs. It also includes a Main method with a foreach loop iterating over the collection returned by AddNumbers, again with some Console.WriteLine calls to keep track of what's going on.

Example 7-33. Exploring yield return

```
class Program
{
    static IEnumerable<string> AddNumbers(IEnumerable<string> names)
    {
        Console.WriteLine("Starting AddNumbers");
        int i = 0;
        foreach (string currentName in names)
        {
            Console.WriteLine("In AddNumbers: " + currentName);
            yield return string.Format("{0}: {1}", i, currentName);
            i += 1;
        }
        Console.WriteLine("Leaving AddNumbers");
    }

    static void Main(string[] args)
    {
        string[] eventNames =
        {
            "Swing Dancing at the South Bank",
            "Saturday Night Swing",
            "Formula 1 German Grand Prix",
            "Swing Dance Picnic",
            "Stompin' at the 100 Club"
        };

        Console.WriteLine("Calling AddNumbers");
        IEnumerable<string> numberedNames = AddNumbers(eventNames);
        Console.WriteLine("Starting main loop");
        foreach (string numberedName in numberedNames)
        {
            Console.WriteLine("In main loop: " + numberedName);
```

```
        }
        Console.WriteLine("Leaving main loop");
    }
}
```

Here's the output:

```
Calling AddNumbers
Starting main loop
Starting AddNumbers
In AddNumbers: Swing Dancing at the South Bank
In main loop: 0: Swing Dancing at the South Bank
In AddNumbers: Saturday Night Swing
In main loop: 1: Saturday Night Swing
In AddNumbers: Formula 1 German Grand Prix
In main loop: 2: Formula 1 German Grand Prix
In AddNumbers: Swing Dance Picnic
In main loop: 3: Swing Dance Picnic
In AddNumbers: Stompin' at the 100 Club
In main loop: 4: Stompin' at the 100 Club
Leaving AddNumbers
Leaving main loop
```

Even though the main method calls `AddNumbers` only once, before the start of the loop, you can see from the output that the code flits back and forth between the main loop and `AddNumbers` for each item in the list.

That's how `yield return` works—it returns from the method temporarily. Execution will continue from after the `yield return` as soon as the code consuming the collection asks for the next element. (More precisely, it will happen when the client code calls `MoveNext` on the enumerator.) C# generates some code that remembers where it had got to on the last `yield return` so that it can carry on from where it left off.

 You might be wondering what happens if the consumer abandons the loop halfway through. If that happens, execution will not continue from the `yield return`. However, as you saw in Example 7-30, code that consumes an enumeration should have a `using` statement to ensure that the enumerator is always disposed of—a `foreach` loop will always do this for you. The enumerator generated by C# to implement `yield return` relies on this to ensure that any `using` or `finally` blocks inside your enumerator method run correctly even when the enumeration is abandoned halfway through.

This causes a slight wrinkle in the story regarding exception handling. You'll find that you cannot use `yield return` inside a `try` block that is followed by a `catch` block, for example, because it's not possible for the C# compiler to guarantee that exceptions will be handled consistently in situations where enumerations are abandoned.

This ability to continue from where we left off as the consumer iterates through the loop illustrates a subtler benefit of `yield return`: it doesn't just make the code slightly neater; it lets the code be *lazy*.

Lazy collections

The `AddNumbers` method in Example 7-31 creates all of its output before it returns anything. We could describe it as being *eager*—it does all the work it might need to do right up front. But the modified version in Example 7-32, which uses `yield return`, is not so eager: it generates items only when it is asked for them, as you can see from the output of Example 7-33. This approach of not doing work until absolutely necessary is often referred to as a *lazy* style. In fact, if you look closely at the output you'll see that the `AddNumbers` method in Example 7-33 is *so* lazy, it doesn't seem to run any code at all until we start asking it for items—the `Starting AddNumbers` message printed out at the beginning of the `AddNumbers` method (before it starts its `foreach` loop) doesn't appear when we call `AddNumbers`—as you can see, the `Starting main loop` message appears first, even though `Main` doesn't print that out until after `AddNumbers` returns. This illustrates that none of the code in `AddNumbers` runs at the point when we call `AddNumbers`. Nothing happens until we start retrieving elements.

 Support for lazy collections is the reason that `IEnumerable<T>` does not provide a `Count` property. The only way to find out how many items are in an enumeration is to enumerate the whole lot and see how many come out. Enumerable sequences don't necessarily know how many items they contain until you've asked for all the items.

Lazy enumeration has some benefits, particularly if you are dealing with very large quantities of information. Lazy enumeration makes it possible to start processing data as soon as the first item becomes available. Example 7-34 illustrates this. Its `GetAllFilesInDirectory` returns an enumeration that returns all the files in a folder, including all those in any subdirectories. The `Main` method here uses this to enumerate all the files on the C: drive. (In fact, the `Directory` class can save us from writing all this code—there's an overload of `Directory.EnumerateFiles` that will do a lazy, recursive search for you. But writing our own version is a good way to see how lazy enumeration works.)

Example 7-34. Lazy enumeration of a large, slow data set

```
class Program
{
    static IEnumerable<string> GetAllFilesInDirectory(string directoryPath)
    {
        IEnumerable<string> files = null;
        IEnumerable<string> subdirectories = null;
        try
        {
```

```
            files = Directory.EnumerateFiles(directoryPath);
            subdirectories = Directory.EnumerateDirectories(directoryPath);
        }
        catch (UnauthorizedAccessException)
        {
            Console.WriteLine("No permission to access " + directoryPath);
        }
        if (files != null)
        {
            foreach (string file in files)
            {
                yield return file;
            }
        }
        if (subdirectories != null)
        {
            foreach (string subdirectory in subdirectories)
            {
                foreach (string file in GetAllFilesInDirectory(subdirectory))
                {
                    yield return file;
                }
            }
        }
    }

    static void Main(string[] args)
    {
        foreach (string file in GetAllFilesInDirectory(@"c:\"))
        {
            Console.WriteLine(file);
        }
    }
}
```

If you run this, you'll find it starts printing out filenames immediately, even though it clearly won't have had time to discover every single file on the hard disk. (That's why we're not using the overload of `Directory.GetFiles` that recursively searches subdirectories for us. As you'll see in Chapter 8, the `Directory` class can save us from writing all this code, but it insists on finding all the files before starting to return any of them.)

It's possible to chain enumerations together. For example, we can combine Example 7-34 with the `AddNumbers` function, as shown in Example 7-35.

Example 7-35. Chaining lazy enumerators together

```
IEnumerable<string> allFiles = GetAllFilesInDirectory(@"c:\");
IEnumerable<string> numberedFiles = AddNumbers(allFiles);
foreach (string file in numberedFiles)
{
    Console.WriteLine(file);
}
```

If we're using the version of `AddNumbers` from Example 7-32—the one that uses `yield return`—this will start printing out filenames (with added numbers) immediately. However, if you try it with the version from Example 7-31, you'll see something quite different. The program will sit there for as many minutes as it takes to find all the filenames on the hard disk—it might print out some messages to indicate that you don't have permission to access certain folders, but it won't print out any filenames until it has all of them. And it ends up consuming quite a lot of memory—on my system it uses more than 130 MB of memory, as it builds up a huge `List<string>` containing all of the filenames, whereas the lazy version makes do with a rather more frugal 7 MB.

So in its eagerness to do all of the necessary work up front, Example 7-31 actually slowed us down. It didn't return any information until it had collected all of the information. Ironically, the lazy version in Example 7-32 enabled us to get to work much faster, and to work more efficiently.

 This style of enumeration, in which work is done no sooner than necessary, is sometimes called *deferred execution*. While that's more of a mouthful, it's probably more fitting in cases where the effect is the opposite of what *lazy* suggests.

Lazy enumeration also permits an interesting technique whereby infinite loops aren't necessarily a problem. A method can yield an infinite collection, leaving it up to the caller to decide when to stop. Example 7-36 returns an enumeration of numbers in the Fibonacci series. That's an infinite series, and since this example uses the `BigInteger` type introduced in .NET 4, the quantity of numbers it can return is limited only by space and time—the amount of memory in the computer, and the impending heat death of the universe, respectively (or your computer's next reboot, whichever comes sooner).

Example 7-36. An infinite sequence

```
using System.Numerics; // Required for BigInteger

...

static IEnumerable<BigInteger> Fibonacci()
{
    BigInteger current = 1;
    BigInteger previous = 1;
    yield return 1;
    while (true)
    {
        yield return current;
        BigInteger next = current + previous;
        previous = current;
        current = next;
    }
}
```

Because consumers of enumerations are free to stop enumerating at any time, in practice this sort of enumeration will just keep going until the calling code decides to stop. We'll see some slightly more practical uses for this when we explore parallel execution and multithreading later in the book.

The concept of chaining lazy enumerations together shown in Example 7-35 is a very useful technique—it's the basis of the most powerful feature that was added in version 3 of C#: LINQ. LINQ is such an important topic that the next chapter is devoted to it. But before we move on, let's review what we've seen so far.

Summary

The .NET Framework's type system has intrinsic support for collections of items in the form of arrays. You can make arrays out of any type. They can be either simple single-dimensional lists, nested arrays of arrays, or multidimensional "rectangular" arrays. The size of an array is fixed at the moment you create it, so when we need a bit more flexibility we use the List<T> generic collection class instead. This works more or less like an array, except we can add and remove items at will. (It uses arrays internally, dynamically allocating new arrays and copying elements across as necessary.) Both arrays and lists offer various services for finding and sorting elements. Thanks to the IEnumerable<T> interface, it's possible to write polymorphic code that can work with any kind of collection. And as we're about to see, LINQ takes that idea to a whole new level.

CHAPTER 8

LINQ

LINQ, short for Language Integrated Query, provides a powerful set of mechanisms for working with collections of information, along with a convenient syntax. You can use LINQ with the arrays and lists we saw in the previous chapter—anything that implements `IEnumerable<T>` can be used with LINQ, and there are LINQ providers for databases and XML documents. And even if you have to deal with data that doesn't fit into any of these categories, LINQ is extensible, so in principle, a provider could be written for more or less any information source that can be accessed from .NET. This chapter will focus mainly on LINQ to Objects—the provider for running queries against objects and collections—but the techniques shown here are applicable to other LINQ sources.

Collections of data are ubiquitous, so LINQ can have a profound effect on how you program. Both of your authors have found that LINQ has changed how we write C# in ways we did not anticipate. Pre-LINQ versions of C# now feel like a different and significantly less powerful language. It may take a little while to get your head around how to use LINQ, but it's absolutely worth the effort.

LINQ is not a single language feature—it's the culmination of several elements that were added to version 3.0 of the C# language and version 3.5 of the .NET Framework. (Despite the different version numbers, these did in fact ship at the same time—they were both part of the Visual Studio 2008 release.) So as well as exploring the most visible aspect of LINQ—the query syntax—we'll also examine the other associated language and framework features that contribute to LINQ.

Query Expressions

C# 3.0 added *query expressions* to the language—these look superficially similar to SQL queries in some respects, but they do not necessarily involve a database. For example, we could use the data returned by the `GetAllFilesInDirectory` code from the preceding chapter, reproduced here in Example 8-1. This returns an `IEnumerable<string>` containing the filenames of all the files found by recursively searching the specified directory. In fact, as we mentioned in the last chapter, it wasn't strictly necessary to work that hard. We implemented the function by hand to illustrate some details of how lazy evaluation works, but as Example 8-1 shows, we can get the .NET Framework class library to do the work for us. The `Directory.EnumerateFiles` method still enumerates the files in a lazy fashion when used in this recursive search mode—it works in much the same way as the example we wrote in the previous chapter.

Example 8-1. Enumerating filenames

```
static IEnumerable<string> GetAllFilesInDirectory(string directoryPath)
{
    return Directory.EnumerateFiles(directoryPath, "*",
        SearchOption.AllDirectories);
}
```

Since a LINQ query can work with any enumeration of objects, we can write a query that just returns the files larger than, say, 10 million bytes, as shown in Example 8-2.

Example 8-2. Using LINQ with an enumeration

```
var bigFiles = from file in GetAllFilesInDirectory(@"c:\")
               where new FileInfo(file).Length > 10000000
               select file;

foreach (string file in bigFiles)
{
    Console.WriteLine(file);
}
```

As long as the C# file has a `using System.Linq;` directive at the top (and Visual Studio adds this to new C# files by default) this code will work just fine. Notice that we've done nothing special to enable the use of a query here—the `GetAllFilesInDirectory` method just returns the lazy enumeration provided by the `Directory` class. And more generally, this sort of query works with anything that implements `IEnumerable<T>`.

Let's look at the query in more detail. It's common to assign LINQ query expressions into variables declared with the **var** keyword, as Example 8-2 does:

```
var bigFiles = ...
```

This tells the compiler that we want it to deduce that variable's type for us. As it happens, it will be an `IEnumerable<string>`, and we could have written that explicitly, but as you'll see shortly, queries sometimes end up using anonymous types, at which point the use of **var** becomes mandatory.

The first part of the query expression itself is always a `from` clause. This describes the source of information that we want to query, and also defines a so-called *range variable*:

```
from file in GetAllFilesInDirectory(@"c:\")
```

The source appears on the right, after the `in` keyword—this query runs on the files returned by the `GetAllFilesInDirectory` method. The range variable, which appears between the `from` and `in` keywords, chooses the name by which we'll refer to source items in the rest of the query—`file` in this example. It's similar to the iteration variable in a `foreach` loop.

The next line in Example 8-2 is a `where` clause:

```
where new FileInfo(file).Length > 10000000
```

This is an optional, although very common, LINQ query feature. It acts as a filter—only items for which the expression is true will be present in the results of the query. This clause constructs a `FileInfo` object for the file, and then looks at its `Length` property so that the query only returns files that are larger than the specified size.

The final part of the query describes what information we want to come out of the query, and it must be either a `select` or a `group` clause. Example 8-2 uses a `select` clause:

```
select file;
```

This is a trivial `select` clause—it just selects the range variable, which contains the filename. That's why this particular query ends up producing an `IEnumera ble<string>`. But we can put other expressions in here—for example, we could write:

```
select File.ReadAllLines(file).Length;
```

This uses the `File` class (defined in `System.IO`) to read the file's text into an array with one element per line, and then retrieves that array's `Length`. This would make the query return an `IEnumerable<int>`, containing the number of lines in each file.

You may be wondering exactly how this works. The code in a LINQ query expression looks quite different from most other C# code—it is, by design, somewhat reminiscent of database queries. But it turns out that all that syntax turns into straightforward method calls.

Query Expressions Versus Method Calls

The C# language specification defines a process by which all LINQ query expressions are converted into method invocations. Example 8-3 shows what the query expression in Example 8-2 turns into. Incidentally, C# ignores whitespace on either side of the `.` syntax for member access, so the fact that this example has been split across multiple lines to fit on the page doesn't stop it from compiling.

Example 8-3. LINQ query as method calls

```
var bigFiles = GetAllFilesInDirectory(@"c:\").
    Where(file => new FileInfo(file).Length > 10000000);
```

Let's compare this with the components of the original query:

```
var bigFiles = from file in GetAllFilesInDirectory(@"c:\")
               where new FileInfo(file).Length > 10000000
               select file;
```

The source, which follows the in keyword in the query expression, becomes the starting point—that's the enumeration returned by GetAllFilesInDirectory in this case. The next step is determined by the presence of the where clause—this turns into a call to the Where method on the source enumeration. As you can see, the condition in the where clause has turned into a lambda expression, passed as an argument to the Where method.

The final select clause has turned into...nothing! That's because it's a trivial select— it just selects the range variable and nothing else, in which case there's no need to do any further processing of the information that comes out of the Where method. If we'd had a slightly more interesting expression in the select clause, for example:

```
var bigFiles = from file in GetAllFilesInDirectory(@"c:\")
               where new FileInfo(file).Length > 10000000
               select "File: " + file;
```

we would have seen a corresponding Select method in the equivalent function calls, as Example 8-4 shows.

Example 8-4. Where and Select as methods

```
var bigFiles = GetAllFilesInDirectory(@"c:\").
               Where(file => new FileInfo(file).Length > 10000000).
               Select(file => "File: " + file);
```

A question remains, though: where did the Where and Select methods here come from? GetAllFilesInDirectory returns an IEnumerable<string>, and if you examine this interface (which we showed in the preceding chapter) you'll see that it doesn't define a Where method. And yet if you try these method-based equivalents of the query expressions, you'll find that they compile just fine as long as you have a using System.Linq; directive at the top of the file, and a project reference to the System.Core library. What's going on? The answer is that Where and Select in these examples are extension methods.

Extension Methods and LINQ

One of the language features added to C# 3.0 for LINQ is support for *extension methods*. These are methods bolted onto a type by some other type. You can add new methods to an existing type, even if you can't change that type—perhaps it's a type built into the .NET Framework. For example, the built-in string type is not something we get to change, and it's sealed, so we cannot derive from it either, but that doesn't stop us from adding new methods. Example 8-5 adds a new and not very useful Backwards method that returns a copy of the string with the characters in reverse order.[*]

---

[*] This is even less useful than it sounds. If the string in question contains characters that are required to be used in strict sequence, such as combining characters or surrogates, naively reversing the character order will have peculiar results. But the point here is to illustrate how to add new methods to an existing type, not to explain why it's surprisingly difficult to reverse a Unicode string.

Example 8-5. Adding an extension method to string

```
static class StringAdditions
{
    // Naive implementation for illustrative purposes.
    // DO NOT USE in real code!
    public static string Backwards(this string input)
    {
        char[] characters = input.ToCharArray();
        Array.Reverse(characters);
        return new string(characters);
    }
}
```

Notice the `this` keyword in front of the first argument—that indicates that `Backwards` is an extension method. Also notice that the class is marked as `static`—you can only define extension methods in static classes.

As long as this class is in a namespace that's in scope (either because of a `using` directive, or because it's in the same namespace as the code that wants to use it) you can call this method as though it were a normal member of the `string` class:

```
string stationName = "Finsbury Park";
Console.WriteLine(stationName.Backwards());
```

The `Where` and `Select` methods used in Example 8-4 are extension methods. The `System.Linq` namespace defines a static class called `Enumerable` which defines these and numerous other extension methods for `IEnumerable<T>`. Here's the signature for one of the `Where` overloads:

```
public static IEnumerable<TSource> Where<TSource>(
    this IEnumerable<TSource> source,
    Func<TSource, bool> predicate)
```

Notice that this is a generic method—the method itself takes a type argument, called `TSource` here, and passes that through as the type argument `T` for the first parameter's `IEnumerable<T>`. The result is that this method extends `IEnumerable<T>`, whatever `T` may be. In other words, as long as the `System.Linq` namespace is in scope, all `IEnumerable<T>` implementations appear to offer a `Where` method.

`Select` and `Where` are examples of *LINQ operators*—standard methods that are available wherever LINQ is supported. The `Enumerable` class in `System.Linq` provides all the LINQ operators for `IEnumerable<T>`, but is not the only LINQ provider—it just provides query support for collections in memory, and is sometimes referred to as LINQ to Objects. In later chapters, we'll see sources that support LINQ queries against databases and XML documents. Anyone can write a new provider, because C# neither knows nor cares what the source is or how it works—it just mechanically translates query expressions into method calls, and as long as the relevant LINQ operators are available, it will use them. This leaves different data sources free to implement the various operators in whatever way they see fit. Example 8-6 shows how you could exploit this to provide custom implementations of the `Select` and `Where` operators.

Example 8-6. Custom implementation of some LINQ operators

```
public class Foo
{
    public string Name { get; set; }
    public Foo Where(Func<Foo, bool> predicate)
    {
        return this;
    }

    public TResult Select<TResult>(Func<Foo, TResult> selector)
    {
        return selector(this);
    }
}
```

These are normal methods rather than extension methods—we're writing a custom type, so we can add LINQ operators directly to that type. Since C# just converts LINQ queries into method calls, it doesn't matter whether LINQ operators are normal methods or extension methods. So with these methods in place, we could write the code shown in Example 8-7.

Example 8-7. Confusing but technically permissible use of a LINQ query

```
Foo source = new Foo { Name = "Fred" };
var result = from f in source
             where f.Name == "Fred"
             select f.Name;
```

C# will follow the rules for translating query expressions into method calls, just as it would for any query, so it will turn Example 8-7 into this:

```
Foo source = new Foo { Name = "Fred" };
var result = source.Where(f => f.Name == "Fred").Select(f => f.Name);
```

Since the Foo class provides the Where and Select operators that C# expects, this will compile and run. It won't be particularly useful, because our Where implementation completely ignores the predicate. And it's also a slightly bizarre thing to do—our Foo class doesn't appear to represent any kind of collection, so it's rather misleading to use syntax that's intended to be used with collections. In fact, Example 8-7 has the same effect as:

```
var result = source.Name;
```

So you'd never write code like Example 8-6 and Example 8-7 for a type as simple as Foo in practice—the purpose of these examples is to illustrate that the C# compiler blindly translates query expressions into method calls, and has no understanding or expectation of what those calls might do. The real functionality of LINQ lives entirely in the class library. Query expressions are just a convenient syntax.

let Clauses

Query expressions can contain `let` clauses. This is an interesting kind of clause in that unlike most of the rest of a query, it doesn't correspond directly to any particular LINQ operator. It's just a way of making it easier to structure your query.

You would use a `let` clause when you need to use the same information in more than one place in a query. For example, suppose we want to modify the query in Example 8-2 to return a `FileInfo` object, rather than a filename. We could do this:

```
var bigFiles = from file in GetAllFilesInDirectory(@"c:\")
               where new FileInfo(file).Length > 10000000
               select new FileInfo(file);
```

But this code repeats itself—it creates a `FileInfo` object in the `where` clause and then creates another one in the `select` clause. We can avoid this repetition with a `let` clause:

```
var bigFiles = from file in GetAllFilesInDirectory(@"c:\")
               let info = new FileInfo(file)
               where info.Length > 10000000
               select info;
```

The C# compiler jumps through some significant hoops to make this work. There's no need to know the details to make use of a `let` clause, but if you're curious to know how it works, here's what happens. Under the covers it generates a class containing two properties called `file` and `info`, and ends up generating two queries:

```
var temp = from file in GetAllFilesInDirectory(@"c:\")
           select new CompilerGeneratedType(file, new FileInfo(file));
var bigFiles = from item in temp
               where item.info.Length > 10000000
               select item.info;
```

The purpose of the first query is to produce a sequence in which the range variable is wrapped in the compiler-generated type, alongside any variables declared with a `let` clause. (It's not actually called `CompilerGeneratedType`, of course—the compiler generates a unique, meaningless name.) This allows all these variables to be available in all the clauses of the query.

LINQ Concepts and Techniques

Before we look in detail at the services LINQ offers, there are some features that apply across all of LINQ that you should be aware of.

Delegates and Lambdas

LINQ query syntax makes implicit use of lambdas. The expressions that appear in `where`, `select`, or most other clauses are written as ordinary expressions, but as you've seen, the C# compiler turns queries into a series of method calls, and the expressions become lambda expressions.

Most of the time, you can just write the expressions you need and they work. But you need to be wary of code that has side effects. For example, it would be a bad idea to write the sort of query shown in Example 8-8.

Example 8-8. Unhelpful side effects in a query

```
int x = 10000;
var bigFiles = from file in GetAllFilesInDirectory(@"c:\")
               where new FileInfo(file).Length > x++
               select file;
```

The `where` clause here increments a variable declared outside the scope of the query.

 This is allowed (although it's a bad idea) in LINQ to Objects. Some LINQ providers, such as the ones you would use with databases, will reject such a query at runtime.

This will have the potentially surprising result that the query could return different files every time it runs, even if the underlying data has not changed. Remember, the expression in the `where` clause gets converted into an anonymous method, which will be invoked once for every item in the query's source. The first time this runs, the local `x` variable will be incremented once for every file on the disk. If the query is executed again, that'll happen again—nothing will reset `x` to its original state.

Moreover, queries are often executed sometime after the point at which they are created, which can make code with side effects very hard to follow—looking at the code in Example 8-8 it's not possible to say exactly when `x` will be modified. We'd need more context to know that—when exactly is the `bigFiles` query evaluated? How many times?

In practice, it is important to avoid side effects in queries. This extends beyond simple things such as the `++` operator—you also need to be careful about invoking methods from within a query expression. You'll want to avoid methods that change the state of your application.

It's usually OK for expressions in a query to *read* variables from the surrounding scope, though. A small modification to Example 8-8 illustrates one way you could exploit this (see Example 8-9).

Example 8-9. Using a local variable in a query

```
int minSize = 10000;
var bigFiles = from file in GetAllFilesInDirectory(@"c:\")
               where new FileInfo(file).Length > minSize
               select file;

var filesOver10k = bigFiles.ToArray();
minSize = 100000;
var filesOver100k = bigFiles.ToArray();
minSize = 1000000;
```

```
var filesOver1MB = bigFiles.ToArray();
minSize = 10000000;
var filesOver10MB = bigFiles.ToArray();
```

This query makes use of a local variable as before, but this query simply reads the value rather than modifying it. By changing the value of that variable, we can modify how the query behaves the next time it is evaluated. (The call to `ToArray()` executes the query and puts the results into an array. This is one way of forcing an immediate execution of the query.)

Functional Style and Composition

LINQ operators all share a common characteristic: they do not modify the data they work on. For example, you can get LINQ to sort the results of a query, but unlike `Array.Sort` or `List<T>.Sort`, which both modify the order of an existing collection, sorting in LINQ works by producing a new `IEnumerable<T>` which returns objects in the specified order. The original collection is not modified.

This is similar in style to .NET's `string` type. The `string` class provides various methods that look like they will modify the string, such as `Trim`, `ToUpper`, and `Replace`. But strings are immutable, so all of these methods work by building a new string—you get a modified copy, leaving the original intact.

LINQ never tries to modify sources, so it's able to work with immutable sources. LINQ to Objects relies on `IEnumerable<T>`, which does not provide any mechanism for modifying the contents or order of the underlying collection.

 Of course, LINQ does not *require* sources to be immutable. `IEnumerable<T>` can be implemented by modifiable and immutable classes alike. The point is that LINQ will never attempt to modify its source collections.

This approach is sometimes described as a *functional* style. Functional programming languages such as F# tend to have this characteristic—just as mathematical functions such as addition, multiplication, and trigonometric functions do not modify their inputs, neither does purely functional code. Instead, it generates new information based on its inputs—new enumerations layered on top of input enumerations in the case of LINQ.

C# is not a purely functional language—it's possible and indeed common to write code that modifies things—but that doesn't stop you from using a functional style, as LINQ shows.

Functional code is often highly composable—it tends to lead to APIs whose features can easily be combined in all sorts of different ways. This in turn can lead to more maintainable code—small, simple features are easier to design, develop, and test than complex, monolithic chunks of code, but you can still tackle complex problems by combining smaller features. Since LINQ works by passing a sequence to a method that transforms its input into a *new* sequence, you can plug together as many LINQ operators as you like. The fact that these operators never modify their inputs simplifies things. If multiple pieces of code are all vying to modify some data, it can become difficult to ensure that your program behaves correctly. But with a functional style, once data is produced it never changes—new calculations yield new data instead of modifying existing data. If you can be sure that some piece of data will never change, it becomes much easier to understand your code's behavior, and you'll have a better chance of making it work. This is especially important with multithreaded code.

Deferred Execution

Chapter 7 introduced the idea of lazy enumeration (or *deferred execution*, as it's also sometimes called). As we saw, iterating over an enumeration such as the one returned by `GetAllFilesInDirectory` does the necessary work one element at a time, rather than processing everything up front. The query in Example 8-2 preserves this characteristic—if you run the code, you won't have to wait for `GetAllFilesInDirectory` to finish before you see any results; it will start printing filenames immediately. (Well, almost immediately—it depends on how far it has to look before finding a file large enough to get through the `where` clause.) And in general, LINQ queries will defer work as much as possible—merely having executed the code that defines the query doesn't actually do anything. So in our example, this code:

```
var bigFiles = from file in GetAllFilesInDirectory(@"c:\")
               where new FileInfo(file).Length > 10000000
               select file;
```

does nothing more than *describe* the query. No work is done until we start to enumerate the `bigFiles` result with a `foreach` loop. And at each iteration of that loop, it does the minimum work required to get the next item—this might involve retrieving multiple results from the underlying collection, because the `where` clause will keep fetching items until it either runs out or finds one that matches the condition. But even so, it does no more work than necessary.

The picture may change a little as you use some of the more advanced features described later in this chapter—for example, you can tell a LINQ query to sort your data, in which case it will probably have to look at all the results before it can work out the correct order. (Although even that's not a given—it's possible to write a source that knows all about ordering, and if you have special knowledge about your data source, it may be possible to write a source that delivers data in order while still fetching items lazily. We'll see providers that do this when we look at how to use LINQ with databases in a later chapter.)

Although deferred execution is almost always a good thing, there's one gotcha to bear in mind. Because the query doesn't run up front, it will run *every time* you evaluate it. LINQ doesn't keep a copy of the results when you execute the query, and there are good reasons you wouldn't want it to—it could consume a lot of memory, and would prevent you from using the technique in Example 8-9. But it does mean that relatively innocuous-looking code can turn out to be quite expensive, particularly if you're using a LINQ provider for a database. Inadvertently evaluating the query multiple times could cause multiple trips to the database server.

LINQ Operators

There are around 50 standard LINQ operators. The rest of this chapter describes the most important operators, broken down by the main areas of functionality. We'll show how to use them both from a query expression (where possible) and with an explicit method call.

Sometimes it's useful to call the LINQ query operator methods explicitly, rather than writing a query expression. Some operators offer overloads with advanced features that are not available in a query expression. For example, sorting strings is a locale-dependent operation—there are variations on what constitutes alphabetical ordering in different languages. The query expression syntax for ordering data always uses the current thread's default culture for ordering. If you need to use a different culture for some reason, or you want a culture-independent order, you'll need to call an overload of the OrderBy operator explicitly instead of using an orderby clause in a query expression.

There are even some LINQ operators that don't have an equivalent in a query expression. So understanding how LINQ uses methods is not just a case of looking at implementation details. It's the only way to access some more advanced LINQ features.

Filtering

You already saw the main filtering feature of LINQ. We illustrated the where clause and the corresponding Where operator in Example 8-2 and Example 8-3, respectively. Another filter operator worth being aware of is called OfType. It has no query expression equivalent, so you can use it only with a method call. OfType is useful when you have a collection that could contain a mixture of types, and you only want to look at the elements that have a particular type. For example, in a user interface you might want to get hold of control elements (such as buttons), ignoring purely visual elements such as images or drawings. You could write this sort of code:

```
var controls = myPanel.Children.OfType<Control>();
```

If `myPanel.Children` is a collection of objects of some kind, this code will ensure that `controls` is an enumeration that only returns objects that can be cast to the `Control` type.

Although `OfType` has no equivalent in a query expression, that doesn't stop you from using it in conjunction with a query expression—you can use the result of `OfType` as the source for a query:

```
var controlNames = from control in myPanel.Children.OfType<Control>()
                   where !string.IsNullOrEmpty(control.Name)
                   select control.Name;
```

This uses the `OfType` operator to filter the items down to objects of type `Control`, and then uses a `where` clause to further filter the items to just those with a nonempty `Name` property.

Ordering

Query expressions can contain an **orderby** clause, indicating the order in which you'd like the items to emerge from the query. In queries with no **orderby** clause, LINQ does not, in general, make any guarantees about the order in which items emerge. LINQ to Objects happens to return items in the order in which they emerge from the source enumeration if you don't specify an order, but other LINQ providers will not necessarily define a default order. (In particular, database LINQ providers typically return items in an unpredictable order unless you explicitly specify an order.)

So as to have some data to sort, Example 8-10 brings back the `CalendarEvent` class from Chapter 7.

Example 8-10. Class representing a calendar event

```
class CalendarEvent
{
    public string Title { get; set; }
    public DateTimeOffset StartTime { get; set; }
    public TimeSpan Duration { get; set; }
}
```

When examples in this chapter refer to an **events** variable, assume that it was initialized with the data shown in Example 8-11.

Example 8-11. Some example data

```
List<CalendarEvent> events = new List<CalendarEvent>
{
    new CalendarEvent
    {
        Title = "Swing Dancing at the South Bank",
        StartTime = new DateTimeOffset (2009, 7, 11, 15, 00, 00, TimeSpan.Zero),
        Duration = TimeSpan.FromHours(4)
    },
    new CalendarEvent
    {
```

```
        Title = "Saturday Night Swing",
        StartTime = new DateTimeOffset (2009, 7, 11, 19, 30, 00, TimeSpan.Zero),
        Duration = TimeSpan.FromHours(6.5)
    },
    new CalendarEvent
    {
        Title = "Formula 1 German Grand Prix",
        StartTime = new DateTimeOffset (2009, 7, 12, 12, 10, 00, TimeSpan.Zero),
        Duration = TimeSpan.FromHours(3)
    },
    new CalendarEvent
    {
        Title = "Swing Dance Picnic",
        StartTime = new DateTimeOffset (2009, 7, 12, 15, 00, 00, TimeSpan.Zero),
        Duration = TimeSpan.FromHours(4)
    },
    new CalendarEvent
    {
        Title = "Stompin' at the 100 Club",
        StartTime = new DateTimeOffset (2009, 7, 13, 19, 45, 00, TimeSpan.Zero),
        Duration = TimeSpan.FromHours(5)
    }
};
```

Example 8-12 shows a LINQ query that orders these events by start time.

Example 8-12. Ordering items with LINQ

```
var eventsByStartTime = from ev in events
                        orderby ev.StartTime
                        select ev;
```

By default, the items will be sorted into ascending order. You can be explicit about this if you like:

```
var eventsByStartTime = from ev in events
                        orderby ev.StartTime ascending
                        select ev;
```

And, of course, you can sort into descending order too:

```
var eventsByStartTime = from ev in events
                        orderby ev.StartTime descending
                        select ev;
```

The expression in the **orderby** clause does not need to correspond directly to a property of the source object. It can be a more complex expression. For example, we could extract just the time of day to produce the slightly confusing result of events ordered by what time they start, regardless of date:

```
var eventsByStartTime = from ev in events
                        orderby ev.StartTime.TimeOfDay
                        select ev;
```

You can specify multiple criteria. Example 8-13 sorts the events: first by date (ignoring the time) and then by duration.

Example 8-13. Multiple sort criteria

```
var eventsByStartDateThenDuration = from ev in events
                                    orderby ev.StartTime.Date, ev.Duration
                                    select ev;
```

Four LINQ query operator methods correspond to the **orderby** clause. Most obviously, there's **OrderBy**, which takes a single ordering criterion as a lambda:

```
var eventsByStartTime = events.OrderBy(ev => ev.StartTime);
```

That code has exactly the same effect as Example 8-12. Of course, like most LINQ operators, you can chain this together with other ones. So we could combine that with the **Where** operator:

```
var longEvents = events.OrderBy(ev => ev.StartTime).
                        Where(ev => ev.Duration > TimeSpan.FromHours(2));
```

This is equivalent to the following query:

```
var longEvents = from ev in events
                 orderby ev.StartTime
                 where ev.Duration > TimeSpan.FromHours(2)
                 select ev;
```

You can customize the comparison mechanism used to sort the items by using an overload that accepts a comparison object—it must implement **IComparer<TKey>**[†] where **TKey** is the type returned by the ordering expression. So in these examples, it would need to be an **IComparer<DateTimeOffset>**, since that's the type of the **StartTime** property we're using to order the data. There's not a lot of scope for discussion about what order dates come in, so this is not a useful example for plugging in an alternate comparison. However, string comparisons do vary a lot—different languages have different ideas about what order letters come in, particularly when it comes to letters with accents. The .NET Framework class library offers a **StringComparer** class that can provide an **IComparer<string>** implementation for any language and culture supported in .NET. The following example uses this in conjunction with an overload of the **OrderBy** operator to sort the events by their title, using a string sorting order appropriate for the French-speaking Canadian culture, and configured for case insensitivity:

```
CultureInfo cult = new CultureInfo("fr-CA");
// 2nd argument is true for case insensitivity
StringComparer comp = StringComparer.Create(cult, true);
var eventsByTitle = events.OrderBy(ev => ev.Title, comp);
```

There is no equivalent query expression—if you want to use anything other than the default comparison for a type, you must use this overload of the **OrderBy** operator.

[†] This is very similar to IComparable<T>, introduced in the preceding chapter. But while objects that implement IComparable<T> can themselves be compared with other objects of type T, an IComparer<T> compares two objects of type T—the objects being compared are separate from the comparer.

The `OrderBy` operator method always sorts in ascending order. To sort in descending order, there's an `OrderByDescending` operator.

If you want to use multiple sort criteria, as in Example 8-13, a different operator comes into play: you need to use either `ThenBy` or `ThenByDescending`. This is because the `OrderBy` and `OrderByDescending` operators discard the order of incoming elements and impose the specified order from scratch—that's the whole point of those operators. Refining an ordering by adding further sort criteria is a different kind of operation, hence the different operators. So the method-based equivalent of Example 8-13 would look like this:

```
var eventsByStartTime = events.OrderBy(ev => ev.StartTime).
                               ThenBy(ev => ev.Duration);
```

Ordering will cause LINQ to Objects to iterate through the whole source collection before returning any elements—it can only sort items once it has seen all of the items.

Concatenation

Sometimes you'll end up wanting to combine two sequences of values into one. LINQ provides a very straightforward operator for this: `Concat`. There is no equivalent in the query expression syntax. If you wanted to combine two lists of events into one, you would use the code in Example 8-14.

Example 8-14. Concatenating two sequences

```
var allEvents = existingEvents.Concat(newEvents);
```

Note that this does not modify the inputs. This builds a new enumeration object that returns all the elements from `existingEvents`, followed by all the elements from `newEvents`. So this can be safer than the `List<T>.AddRange` method shown in Chapter 7, because this doesn't modify anything. (Conversely, if you were expecting Example 8-14 to modify `existingEvents`, you will be disappointed.)

 This is a good illustration of how LINQ uses the *functional* style described earlier. Like mathematical functions, most LINQ operators calculate their outputs without modifying their inputs. For example, if you have two `int` variables called x and y, you would expect to be able to calculate x+y without that calculation changing either x or y. Concatenation works the same way—you can produce a sequence that is the concatenation of two inputs without changing those inputs.

As with most LINQ operators, concatenation uses deferred evaluation—it doesn't start asking its source enumerations for elements in advance. Only when you start to iterate through the contents of `allEvents` will this start retrieving items from `existingEvents`. (And it won't start asking for anything from `newEvents` until it has retrieved all the elements from `existingEvents`.)

Grouping

LINQ provides the ability to take flat lists of data and group them. As Example 8-15 shows, we could use this to write a LINQ-based alternative to the `GetEventsByDay` method shown in Chapter 7.

Example 8-15. Simple LINQ grouping

```
var eventsByDay = from ev in events
                  group ev by ev.StartTime.Date;
```

This will arrange the objects in the `events` source into one group for each day.

The `eventsByDay` variable here ends up with a slightly different type than anything we've seen before. It's an `IEnumerable<IGrouping<DateTimeOffset, CalendarEvent>>`. So `eventsByDay` is an enumeration, and it returns an item for each group found by the `group` clause. Example 8-16 shows one way of using this. It iterates through the collection of groupings, and for each grouping it displays the `Key` property—the value by which the items have been grouped—and then iterates through the items in the group.

Example 8-16. Iterating through grouped results

```
foreach (var day in eventsByDay)
{
    Console.WriteLine("Events for " + day.Key);
    foreach (var item in day)
    {
        Console.WriteLine(item.Title);
    }
}
```

This produces the following output:

```
Events for 7/11/2009 12:00:00 AM
Swing Dancing at the South Bank
Saturday Night Swing
Events for 7/12/2009 12:00:00 AM
Formula 1 German Grand Prix
Swing Dance Picnic
Events for 7/13/2009 12:00:00 AM
Stompin' at the 100 Club
```

This illustrates that the query in Example 8-15 has successfully grouped the events by day, but let's look at what returned in a little more detail. Each group is represented as an `IGrouping<TKey, TElement>`, where `TKey` is the type of the expression used to group the data—a `DateTimeOffset` in this case—and `TElement` is the type of the elements making up the groups—`CalendarEvent` in this example. `IGrouping<TKey, TElement>` derives from `IEnumerable<TElement>`, so you can enumerate through the contents of a group like you would any other enumeration. (In fact, the only thing `IGrouping<TKey, TElement>` adds is the `Key` property, which is the grouping value.) So the query in Example 8-15 returns a sequence of sequences—one for each group (see Figure 8-1).

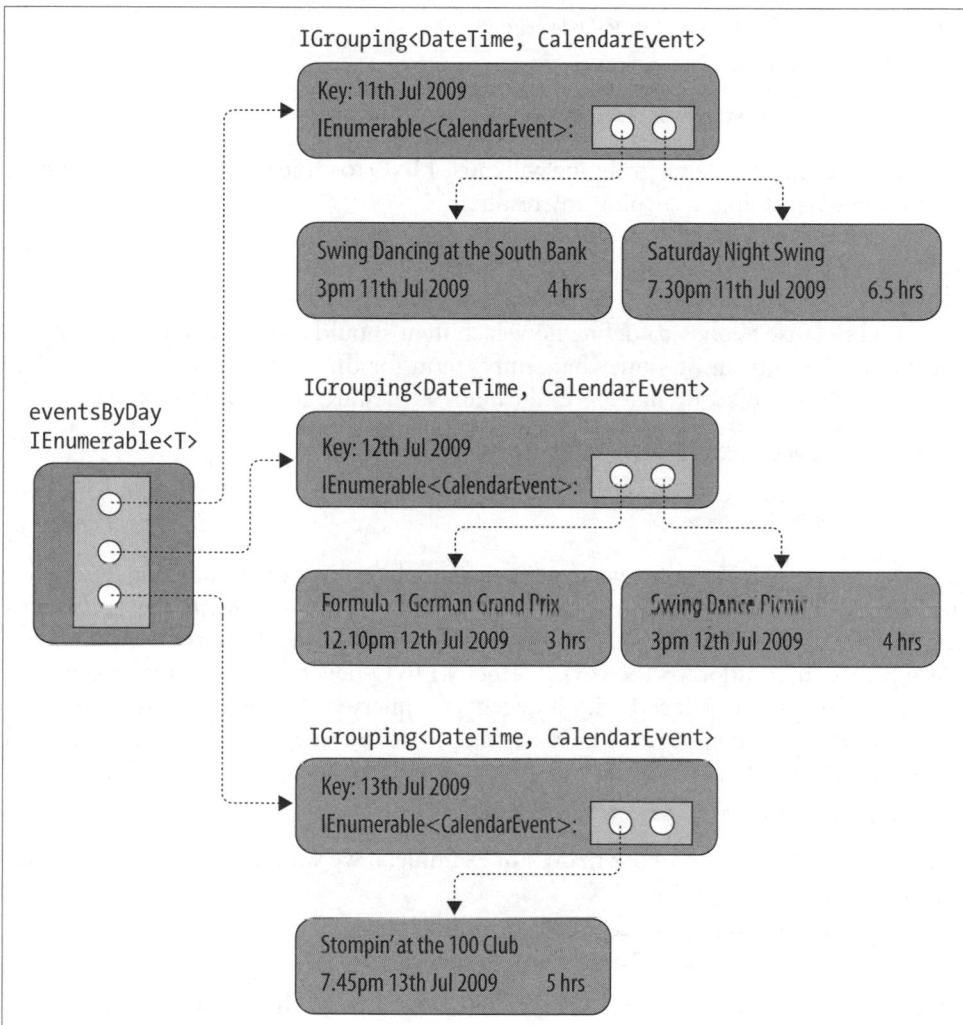

Figure 8-1. Result of groupby query

While a LINQ query expression is allowed to end with a group clause, as Example 8-15 does, it doesn't have to finish there. If you would like to do further processing, you can add an into keyword on the end, followed by an identifier. The continuation of the query after a group … into clause will iterate over the groups, and the identifier effectively becomes a new range variable. Example 8-17 uses this to convert each group into an array. (Calling ToArray on an IGrouping effectively discards the Key, and leaves you with just an array containing that group's contents. So this query ends up producing an IEnumerable<CalendarEvent[]>—a collection of arrays.)

Example 8-17. Continuing a grouped query with into

```
var eventsByDay = from ev in events
                  group ev by ev.StartTime.Date into dayGroup
                  select dayGroup.ToArray();
```

Like the ordering operators, grouping will cause LINQ to Objects to evaluate the whole source sequence before returning any results.

Projections

The select clause's job is to define how each item should look when it comes out of the query. The official (if somewhat stuffy) term for this is *projection*. The simplest possible kind of projection just leaves the items as they are, as shown in Example 8-18.

Example 8-18. Trivial projection

```
var projected = from ev in events
                select ev;
```

Earlier, you saw this kind of trivial select clause collapsing away to nothing. However, that doesn't happen here, because this is what's called a *degenerate query*—it contains nothing but a trivial projection. (Example 8-2 was different, because it contained a where clause in addition to the trivial select.) LINQ never reduces a query down to nothing at all, so when faced with a degenerate query, it leaves the trivial select in place, even though it appears to have nothing to do. So Example 8-18 becomes a call to the Select LINQ operator method:

```
var projected = events.Select(ev => ev);
```

But projections often have work to do. For example, if we want to pick out event titles, we can write this:

```
var projected = from ev in events
                select ev.Title;
```

Again, this becomes a call to the Select LINQ operator method, with a slightly more interesting projection lambda:

```
var projected = events.Select(ev => ev.Title);
```

We can also calculate new values in the select clause. This calculates the end time of the events:

```
var projected = from ev in events
                select ev.StartTime + ev.Duration;
```

You can use any expression you like in the select clause. In fact, there's not even any obligation to use the range variable, although it's likely to be a bit of a waste of time to construct a query against a data source if you ultimately don't use any data from that source. But C# doesn't care—any expression is allowed. The following slightly silly code generates one random number for each event, in a way that is entirely unrelated to the event in question:

```
Random r = new Random();
var projected = from ev in events
                select r.Next();
```

You can, of course, construct a new object in the select clause. There's one interesting variation on this that often crops up in LINQ queries, which occurs when you want the query to return multiple pieces of information for each item. For example, we might want to display calendar events in a format where we show both the start and the end times. This is slightly different from how the CalendarEvent class represents things—it stores the duration rather than the end time. We could easily write a query that calculates the end time, but it wouldn't be very useful to have just that time. We'd want all the details—the title, the start time, and the end time.

In other words, we'd be transforming the data slightly. We'd be taking a stream of objects where each item contains Title, StartTime, and Duration properties, and producing one where each item contains a Title, StartTime, and EndTime. Example 8-19 does exactly this.

Example 8-19. Select clause with anonymous type

```
var projected = from ev in events
                select new
                {
                    Title = ev.Title,
                    StartTime = ev.StartTime,
                    EndTime = ev.StartTime + ev.Duration
                };
```

This constructs a new object for each item. But while the new keyword is there, notice that we've not specified the name of a type. All we have is the object initialization syntax to populate various properties—the list of values in braces after the new keyword. We haven't even defined a type anywhere in these examples that has a Title, a StartTime, and an EndTime property. And yet this compiles. And we can go on to use the results as shown in Example 8-20.

Example 8-20. Using a collection with an anonymous item type

```
foreach (var item in projected)
{
    Console.WriteLine("Event {0} starts at {1} and ends at {2}",
        item.Title, item.StartTime, item.EndTime);
}
```

These two examples are using the *anonymous type* feature added in C# 3.0.

Anonymous types

If we want to define a type to represent some information in our application, we would normally use the `class` or `struct` keyword as described in Chapter 3. Typically, the type definition would live in its own source file, and in a real project we would want to devise unit tests to ensure that it works as expected. This might be enough to put you off the idea of defining a type for use in a very narrow context, such as having a convenient container for the information coming out of a query. But it's often useful for the `select` clause of a query just to pick out a few properties from the source items, possibly transforming the data in some way to get it into a convenient representation.

> Extracting just the properties you need can become important when using LINQ with a database—database providers are typically able to transform the projection into an equivalent SQL `SELECT` statement. But if your LINQ query just fetches the whole row, it will end up fetching every column whether you need it or not, placing an unnecessary extra load on the database and network.

There's a trade-off here. Is the effort of creating a type worth the benefits if you're only going to use it to hold the results of a query? If your code immediately does further processing of the data, the type will be useful to only a handful of lines of code. But if you don't create the type, you have to deal with a compromise—you might not be able to structure the information coming out of your query in exactly the way you want.

C# 3.0 shifts the balance in favor of creating a type in this scenario, by removing most of the effort required, thanks to anonymous types. This is another language feature added mainly for the benefit of LINQ, although you can use it in other scenarios if you find it useful. An anonymous type is one that the C# compiler writes for you, based on the properties in the object initializer list. So when the compiler sees this expression from Example 8-19:

```
new
{
    Title = ev.Title,
    StartTime = ev.StartTime,
    EndTime = ev.StartTime + ev.Duration
};
```

it knows that it needs to supply a type, because we've not specified a type name after the `new` keyword. It will create a new class definition, and will define properties for each entry in the initializer. It will work out what types the properties should have from the types of the expressions in the initializer. For example, the `ev.Title` expression evaluates to a string, so it will add a property called `Title` of type `string`.

Before generating a new anonymous type, the C# compiler checks to see if it has already generated one with properties of the same name and type, specified in the same order elsewhere in your project. If it has, it just reuses that type. So if different parts of your code happen to end up creating identical anonymous types, the compiler is smart enough to share the type definition. (Normally, the order in which properties are defined has no significance, but in the case of anonymous types, C# considers two types to be equivalent only if the properties were specified in the same order.)

The nice thing about this is that when we come to use the items in a collection based on an anonymous type (such as in Example 8-20) IntelliSense and compile-time checking work exactly as they always do—it's just like working with a normal type, but we didn't have to write it.

From the point of view of the .NET Framework, the type generated by the C# compiler is a perfectly ordinary type like any other. It neither knows nor cares that the compiler wrote the class for us. It's anonymous only from the point of view of our C# code—the generated type does in fact have a name, it's just a slightly odd-looking one. It'll be something like this:

```
<>f__AnonymousType0`3
```

The C# compiler deliberately picks a name for the type that would be illegal as a C# class name (but which is still legal as far as .NET is concerned) in order to stop us from trying to use the class by its name—that would be a bad thing to do, because the compiler doesn't guarantee to keep the name the same from one compilation to the next.

The anonymity of the type name means that anonymous types are only any use within a single method. Suppose you wanted to return an anonymous type (or an IEnumera ble<SomeAnonymousType>) from a method—what would you write as the return type if the type in question has no name? You could use Object, but the properties of the anonymous type won't be visible. The best you could do is use dynamic, which we describe in Chapter 18. This would make it possible to access the properties, but without the aid of compile-time type checking or IntelliSense. So the main purpose of anonymous types is simply to provide a convenient way to get information from a query to code later in the same method that does something with that information.

Anonymous types would not be very useful without the var keyword, another feature introduced in C# 3.0. As we saw earlier, when you declare a local variable with the var keyword, the compiler works out the type from the expression you use to initialize the variable. To see why we need this for anonymous types to be useful, look at Example 8-19—how would you declare the projected local variable if we weren't using var? It's going to be some sort of IEnumerable<T>, but what's T here? It's an anonymous type, so by definition we can't write down its name. It's interesting to see how Visual

Studio reacts if we ask it to show us the type by hovering our mouse pointer over the variable—Figure 8-2 shows the resultant data tip.

Visual Studio chooses to denote anonymous types with names such as `'a`, `'b`, and so forth. These are not legal names—they're just placeholders, and the data tip pop up goes on to show the structure of the anonymous types they represent.

Whether or not you're using anonymous types in your projections, there's an alternative form of projection that you will sometimes find useful when dealing with multiple sources.

```
(local variable) IEnumerable<'a> projected

Anonymous Types:
    'a is new { string Title, DateTimeOffset StartTime, DateTimeOffset EndTime }
```

Figure 8-2. How Visual Studio shows anonymous types

Using multiple sources

Earlier, Example 8-15 used a `groupby` clause to add some structure to a list of events— the result was a list containing one group per day, with each group itself containing a list of events. Sometimes it can be useful to go in the opposite direction—you may have structured information that you would like to flatten into a single list. You can do this in a query expression by writing multiple `from` clauses, as Example 8-21 shows.

Example 8-21. Flattening lists using multiple from clauses

```
var items = from day in eventsByday
            from item in day
            select item;
```

You can think of this as having roughly the same effect as the following code:

```
List<CalendarEvent> items = new List<CalendarEvent>();
foreach (IGrouping<DateTime, CalendarEvent> day in eventsByDay)
{
    foreach (CalendarEvent item in day)
    {
        items.Add(item);
    }
}
```

That's not exactly how it works, because the LINQ query will use deferred execution— it won't start iterating through the source items until you start trying to iterate through the query. The `foreach` loops, on the other hand, are eager—they build the entire flattened list as soon as they run. But lazy versus eager aside, the set of items produced is the same—for each item in the first source, every item in the second source will be processed.

 Notice that this is very different from the concatenation operator shown earlier. That also works with two sources, but it simply returns all the items in the first source, followed by all the items in the second source. But Example 8-21 will iterate through the source of the second `from` clause once for every item in the source of the first `from` clause. (So concatenation and flattening are as different as addition and multiplication.) Moreover, the second `from` clause's source expression typically evaluates to a different result each time around.

In Example 8-21, the second `from` clause uses the range variable from the first `from` clause as its source. This is a common technique—it's what enables this style of query to flatten a grouped structure. But it's not mandatory—you can use any LINQ-capable source you like; for example, any `IEnumerable<T>`. Example 8-22 uses the same source array for both `from` clauses.

Example 8-22. Alternative use of multiple from clauses

```
int[] numbers = { 1, 2, 3, 4, 5 };
var multiplied = from x in numbers
                 from y in numbers
                 select x * y;
foreach (int n in multiplied)
{
    Console.WriteLine(n);
}
```

The source contains five numbers, so the resultant `multiplied` sequence contains 25 elements—the second `from` clause counts through all five numbers for each time around the first `from` clause.

The LINQ operator method for flattening multiple sources is called `SelectMany`. The equivalent of Example 8-22 looks like this:

```
var multiplied = numbers.SelectMany(
    x => numbers,
    (x, y) => x * y);
```

The first lambda is expected to return the collection over which the nested iteration will be performed—the collection for the second `from` clause in the LINQ query. The second lambda is the projection from the `select` clause in the query. In queries with a trivial final projection, a simpler form is used, so the equivalent of Example 8-21 is:

```
var items = days.SelectMany(day => day);
```

Whether you're using a multisource `SelectMany` or a simple single-source projection, there's a useful variant that lets your projection know each item's position, by passing a number into the projection.

Numbering items

The `Select` and `SelectMany` LINQ operators both offer overloads that make it easy to number items. Example 8-23 uses this to build a list of numbered event names.

Example 8-23. Adding item numbers

```
var numberedEvents = events.
        Select((ev, i) => string.Format("{0}: {1}", i + 1, ev.Title));
```

If we iterate over this, printing out each item:

```
foreach (string item in numberedEvents)
{
    Console.WriteLine(item);
}
```

the results look like this:

```
1: Swing Dancing at the South Bank
2: Formula 1 German Grand Prix
3: Swing Dance Picnic
4: Saturday Night Swing
5: Stompin' at the 100 Club
```

This illustrates how LINQ often makes for much more concise code than was possible before C# 3.0. Remember that in Chapter 7, we wrote a function that takes an array of strings and adds a number in a similar fashion. That required a loop with several lines of code, and it worked only if we already happened to have a collection of strings. Here we've turned a collection of `CalendarEvents` into a collection of numbered event titles with just a single method call.

As you get to learn LINQ, you'll find this happens quite a lot—situations in which you might have written a loop, or a series of loops, can often turn into fairly simple LINQ queries.

Zipping

The `Zip` operator is useful when you have two related sequences, where each element in one sequence is somehow connected with the element at the same position in the other sequence. You can unite the two sequences by *zipping* them back into one. Obviously, the name has nothing to do with the popular ZIP compression format. This operator is named after zippers of the kind used in clothing.

This might be useful with a race car telemetry application of the kind we discussed in Chapter 2. You might end up with two distinct series of data produced by two different measurement sources. For example, fuel level readings and lap time readings could be two separate sequences, since such readings would likely be produced by different instruments. But if you're getting one reading per lap in each sequence, it might be useful to combine these into a single sequence with one element per lap, as Example 8-24 shows.

Example 8-24. Zipping two sequences into one

```
IEnumerable<TimeSpan> lapTimes = GetLapTimes();
IEnumerable<double> fuelLevels = GetLapFuelLevels();

var lapInfo = lapTimes.Zip(fuelLevels, (time, fuel) =>
    new
    {
        LapTime = time,
        FuelLevel = fuel
    });
```

You invoke the `Zip` operator on one of the input streams, passing in the second stream as the first argument. The second argument is a projection function—it's similar to the projections used with the `Select` operator, except it is passed two arguments, one for each stream. So the `lapInfo` sequence produced by Example 8-24 will contain one item per lap, where the items are of an anonymous type, containing both the `LapTime` and the `FuelLevel` in a single item.

Since the two sequences are of equal length here—the number of laps completed—it's clear how long the output sequence will be, but what if the input lengths differ? The `Zip` operator stops as soon as either one of the input sequences stops, so the shorter of the two determines the length. Any spare elements in the longer stream will not be used.

Getting Selective

Sometimes you won't want to work with an entire collection. For example, in an application with limited screen space, you might want to show just the next three events on the user's calendar. While there is no way to do this directly in a query expression, LINQ defines a `Take` operator for this purpose. As Example 8-25 shows, you can still use the query syntax for most of the query, using the `Take` operator as the final stage.

Example 8-25. Taking the first few results of a query

```
var eventsByStart = from ev in events
                    orderby ev.StartTime
                    where ev.StartTime > DateTimeOffset.Now
                    select ev;

var next3Events = eventsByStart.Take(3);
```

LINQ also defines a `Skip` operator which does the opposite of `Take`—it drops the first three items (or however many you ask it to drop) and then returns all the rest.

If you're interested in only the very first item, you may find the `First` operator more convenient. If you were to call `Take(1)`, the method would still return a collection of items. So this code would not compile:

```
CalendarEvent nextEvent = eventsByStart.Take(1);
```

You'd get the following compiler error:

```
CS0266: Cannot implicitly convert type 'System.Collections.Generic.IEnumerable<
CalendarEvent>' to CalendarEvent'. An explicit conversion exists (are you
missing a cast?)
```

In other words, Take always returns an IEnumerable<CalendarEvent>, even if we ask for only one object. But this works:

```
CalendarEvent nextEvent = eventsByStart.First();
```

First gets the first element from the enumeration and returns that. (It then abandons the enumerator—it doesn't iterate all the way to the end of the sequence.)

You may run into situations where the list might be empty. For example, suppose you want to show the user's next appointment for today—it's possible that there are no more appointments. If you call First in this scenario, it will throw an exception. So there's also a FirstOrDefault operator, which returns the default value when there are no elements (e.g., null, if you're dealing with a reference type). The Last and LastOrDefault operators are similar, except they return the very last element in the sequence, or the default value in the case of an empty sequence.

A yet more specialized case is where you are expecting a sequence to contain no more than one element. For example, suppose you modify the CalendarEvent class to add an ID property intended to be used as a unique identifier for the event. (Most real calendar systems have a concept of a unique ID to provide an unambiguous way of referring to a particular calendar entry.) You might write this sort of query to find an item by ID:

```
var matchingItem = from ev in events
                   where ev.ID == theItemWeWant
                   select ev;
```

If the ID property is meant to be unique, we would hope that this query returns no more than one item. The presence of two or more items would point to a problem. If you use either the First or the FirstOrDefault operator, you'd never notice the problem—these would pick the first item and silently ignore any more. As a general rule, you don't want to ignore signs of trouble. In this case, it would be better to use either Single or SingleOrDefault. Single would be the right choice in cases where failure to find a match would be an error, while SingleOrDefault would be appropriate if you do not necessarily expect to find a match. Either will throw an InvalidOperationException if the sequence contains more than one item. So given the previous query, you could use the following:

```
CalendarEvent item = matchingItem.SingleOrDefault();
```

If a programming error causes multiple different calendar events to end up with the same ID, this code will detect that problem. (And if your code contains no such problem, this will work in exactly the same way as FirstOrDefault.)

Testing the Whole Collection

You may need to discover at runtime whether certain characteristics are true about any or every element in a collection. For example, if the user is adding a new event to the calendar, you might want to warn him if the event overlaps with any existing items. First, we'll write a helper function to do the date overlap test:

```
static bool TimesOverlap(DateTimeOffset startTime1, TimeSpan duration1,
    DateTimeOffset startTime2, TimeSpan duration2)
{
    DateTimeOffset end1 = startTime1 + duration1;
    DateTimeOffset end2 = startTime2 + duration2;

    return (startTime1 < startTime2) ?
        (end1 > startTime2) :
        (startTime1 < end2);
}
```

Then we can use this to see if any events overlap with the proposed time for a new entry:

```
DateTimeOffset newEventStart = new DateTimeOffset(2009, 7, 20, 19, 45, 00,
    TimeSpan.Zero);
TimeSpan newEventDuration = TimeSpan.FromHours(5);
bool overlaps = events.Any(
        ev => TimesOverlap(ev.StartTime, ev.Duration,
                        newEventStart, newEventDuration));
```

The Any operator looks to see if there is at least one item for which the condition is true, and it returns true if it finds one and false if it gets to the end of the collection without having found a single item that meets the condition. So if overlaps ends up false here, we know that events didn't contain any items whose time overlapped with the proposed new event time.

There's also an All operator that returns true only if all of the items meet the condition. We could also have used this for our overlap test—we'd just need to invert the sense of the test:

```
bool noOverlaps = events.All(
        ev => !TimesOverlap(ev.StartTime, ev.Duration,
                        newEventStart, newEventDuration));
```

 The All operator returns true if you apply it to an empty sequence. This surprises some people, but it's difficult to say what the right behavior is—what does it mean to ask if some fact is true about all the elements if there are no elements? This operator's definition takes the view that it returns false if and only if at least one element does not meet the condition. And while there is some logic to that, you would probably feel misled if a company told you "All our customers think our widgets are the best they've ever seen" but neglected to mention that it has no customers.

There's an overload of the `Any` operator that doesn't take a condition. You can use this to ask the question: is there anything in this sequence? For example:

```
bool doIHaveToGetOutOfBedToday = eventsForToday.Any();
```

 The `Any` and `All` operators are technically known as *quantifiers*. More specifically, they are sometimes referred to as the *existential quantifier* and the *universal quantifier*, respectively. You may also have come across the common mathematical notation for these.

The existential quantifier is written as a backward E (∃), and is conventionally pronounced "there exists." This corresponds to the `Any` operator—it's true if at least one item exists in the set that meets the condition.

The universal quantifier is written as an upside down A (∀), and is conventionally pronounced "for all." It corresponds to the `All` operator, and is true if all the elements in some set meet the condition. The convention that the universal quantifier is true for any empty set (i.e., that `All` returns `true` when you give it no elements, regardless of the condition) has a splendid mathematical name: it is called a *vacuous truth*.

Quantifiers are special cases of a more general operation called *aggregation*—aggregation operators perform calculations across all the elements in a set. The quantifiers are singled out as special cases because they have the useful property that the calculation can often terminate early: if you're testing to see whether something is true about all the elements in the set, and you find an element for which it's not true, you can stop right there. But for most whole-set operations that's not true, so there are some more general-purpose aggregation operators.

Aggregation

Aggregation operators perform calculations that involve every single element in a collection, producing a single value as the result. This can be as simple as counting the number of elements—this involves all the elements in the sense that you need to know how many elements exist to get the correct count. And if you're dealing with an `IEnumerable<T>`, it is usually necessary to iterate through the whole collection because in general, enumerable sources don't know how many items they contain in advance. So the `Count` operator iterates through the entire collection, and returns the number of elements it found.

 LINQ to Objects has optimizations for some special cases. It looks for an implementation of a standard `ICollection<T>` interface, which defines a `Count` property. (This is distinct from the `Count` operator, which, like all LINQ operators, is a method, not a property.) Collections such as arrays and `List<T>` that know how many items they contain implement this interface. So the `Count` operator may be able to avoid having to enumerate the whole collection by using the `Count` property. And more generally, the nature of the `Count` operator depends on the source—database LINQ providers can arrange for the database to calculate the correct value for `Count`, avoiding the need to churn through an entire table just to count rows. But in cases where there's no way of knowing the count up front, such as the file enumeration in Example 8-1, `Count` can take a long time to complete.

LINQ defines some specialized aggregation operators for numeric values. The `Sum` operator returns the sum of the values of a given expression for all items in a collection. For example, if you want to find out how many hours of meetings you have in a collection of events, you could do this:

```
double totalHours = events.Sum(ev => ev.Duration.TotalHours);
```

`Average` calculates the same sum, but then divides the result by the number of items, returning the mean value. `Min` and `Max` return the lowest and highest of the values calculated by the expression.

There's also a general-purpose aggregation operator called `Aggregate`. This lets you perform any operation that builds up some value by performing some calculation on each item in turn. In fact, `Aggregate` is all you really need—the other aggregation operators are simply more convenient.[‡] For instance, Example 8-26 shows how to implement `Count` using `Aggregate`.

Example 8-26. Implementing Count with Aggregate

```
int count = events.Aggregate(0, (c, ev) => c + 1);
```

The first argument here is a *seed* value—it's the starting point for the value that will be built up as the aggregation runs. In this case, we're building up a count, so we start at 0. You can use any value of any type here—`Aggregate` is a generic method that lets you use whatever type you like.

The second argument is a delegate that will be invoked once for each item. It will be passed the current aggregated value (initially the seed value) and the current item. And then whatever this delegate returns becomes the new aggregated value, and will be passed in as the first argument when that delegate is called for the next item, and so

---

‡ That's true for LINQ to Objects. However, database LINQ providers may implement `Sum`, `Average`, and so on using corresponding database query features. They might not be able to do this optimization if you use the general-purpose `Aggregate` operator.

on. So in this example, the aggregated value starts off at 0, and then we add 1 each time around. The final result is therefore the number of items.

Example 8-26 doesn't look at the individual items—it just counts them. If we wanted to implement Sum, we'd need to add a value from the source item to the running total instead of just adding 1:

```
double hours = events.Aggregate(0.0,
                           (total, ev) => total + ev.Duration.TotalHours);
```

Calculating an average is a little more involved—we need to maintain both a running total and the count of the number of elements we've seen, which we can do by using an anonymous type as the aggregation value. And then we can use an overload of Aggregate that lets us provide a separate delegate to be used to determine the final value—that gives us the opportunity to divide the total by the count:

```
double averageHours = events.Aggregate(
    new { TotalHours = 0.0, Count = 0 },
    (agg, ev) => new
                {
                    TotalHours = agg.TotalHours + ev.Duration.TotalHours,
                    Count = agg.Count + 1
                },
    (agg) => agg.TotalHours / agg.Count);
```

Obviously, it's easier to use the specialized Count, Sum, and Average operators, but this illustrates the flexibility of Aggregate.

 While LINQ calls this mechanism Aggregate, it is often known by other names. In functional programming languages, it's sometimes called *fold* or *reduce*. The latter name in particular has become slightly better known in recent years thanks to Google's much-publicized use of a programming system called map/reduce. (LINQ's name for *map* is Select, incidentally.) LINQ's names weren't chosen to be different for the sake of it—they are more consistent with these concepts' names in database query languages. Most professional developers are currently likely to have rather more experience with SQL than, say, Haskell or LISP.

Set Operations

LINQ provides operators for some common set-based operations. If you have two collections, and you want to discover all the elements that are present in both collections, you can use the Intersect operator:

```
var inBoth = set1.Intersect(set2);
```

It also offers a Union operator, which provides all the elements from both input sets, but when it comes to the second set it will skip any elements that were already returned because they were also in the first set. So you could think of this as being like Concat, except it detects and removes duplicates. In a similar vein, there's the `Distinct` operator—this works on a single collection, rather than a pair of collections. `Distinct` ensures that it returns any given element only once, so if your input collection happens to contain duplicate entries, `Distinct` will skip over those.

Finally, the `Except` operator returns only those elements from the first set that do not also appear in the second set.

Joining

LINQ supports joining of sources, in the sense typically associated with databases—given two sets of items, you can form a new set by combining the items from each set that have the same value for some attribute. This is a feature that tends not to get a lot of use when working with object models—relationships between objects are usually represented with references exposed via properties, so there's not much need for joins. But joins can become much more important if you're using LINQ with data from a relational database. (Although the Entity Framework, which we describe in a later chapter, is often able to represent relationships between tables as object references. It'll use joins at the database level under the covers, but you may not need to use them explicitly in LINQ all that often.)

Even though joins are typically most useful when working with data structured for storage in a relational database, you can still perform joins across objects—it's possible with LINQ to Objects even if it's not all that common.

In our hypothetical calendar application, imagine that you want to add a feature where you can reconcile events in the user's local calendar with events retrieved from his phone's calendar, and you need to try to work out which of the imported events from the phone correspond to items already in the calendar. You might find that the only way to do this is to look for events with the same name that occur at the same time, in which case you might be able to use a join to build up a list of events from the two sources that are logically the same events:

```
var pairs = from localEvent in events
            join phoneEvent in phoneEvents
            on new { Title = localEvent.Title, Start = localEvent.StartTime }
            equals new { Title = phoneEvent.Name, Start = phoneEvent.Time }
            select new { Local = localEvent, Phone = phoneEvent };
```

A LINQ join expects to be able to compare just a single object in order to determine whether two items should be joined. But we want to join items only when both the title and the time match. So this example builds an anonymously typed object to hold both values in order to be able to provide LINQ with the single object it expects. (You can use this technique for the grouping operators too, incidentally.) Note that this example also illustrates how you would deal with the relevant properties having different names. You can imagine that the imported phone events might use different property names because you might need to use some third-party import library, so this example shows how the code would look if it called the relevant properties `Name` and `Time` instead of `Title` and `StartTime`. We fix this by mapping the properties from the two sources into anonymous types that have the same structure.

Conversions

Sometimes it's necessary to convert the results of a LINQ query into a specific collection type. For example, you might have code that expects an array or a `List<T>`. You can still use LINQ queries when creating these kinds of collections, thanks to the standard `ToArray` and `ToList` operators. Example 8-17 used `ToArray` to convert a grouping into an array of objects. We could extend that further to convert the query into an array of arrays, just like the original example from Chapter 7:

```
var eventsByDay = from ev in events
                  group ev by ev.StartTime.Date into dayGroup
                  select dayGroup.ToArray();

CalendarEvent[][] arrayOfEventsByDay = eventsByDay.ToArray();
```

In this example, `eventsByDay` is of type `IEnumerable<CalendarEvent[]>`. The final line then turns the enumeration into an array of arrays—a `CalendarEvent[][]`.

Remember that LINQ queries typically use deferred execution—they don't start doing any work until you start asking them for elements. But by calling `ToList` or `ToArray`, you will fully execute the query, because it builds the entire list or array in one go.

As well as providing conversion operators for getting data out of LINQ and into other data types, there are some operators for getting data into LINQ's world. Sometimes you will come across types that provide only the old .NET 1.x-style nongeneric `IEnumerable` interface. This is problematic for LINQ because there's no way for it to know what kinds of objects it will find. You might happen to know that a collection will always contain `CalendarEvent` objects, but this would be invisible to LINQ if you are working with a library that uses old-style collections. So to work around this, LINQ defines a `Cast` operator—you can use this to tell LINQ what sort of items you believe are in the collection:

```
IEnumerable oldEnum = GetCollectionFromSomewhere();
var items = from ev in oldEnum.Cast<CalendarEvent>()
            orderby ev.StartTime
            select ev;
```

As you would expect, this will throw an `InvalidCastException` if it discovers any elements in the collection that are not of the type you said. But be aware that like most LINQ operators, `Cast` uses deferred execution—it casts the elements one at a time as they are requested, so any mismatch will not be discovered at the point at which you call `Cast`. The exception will be thrown at the point at which you reach the first non-matching item while enumerating the query.

Summary

LINQ provides a convenient syntax for performing common operations on collections of data. The query expression syntax is reminiscent of database query languages, and can be used in conjunction with databases, as later chapters will show. But these queries are frequently used on objects in memory. The compiler transforms the query syntax into a series of method calls, meaning that the choice of LINQ implementation is determined by context—you can write your own custom LINQ provider, or use a built-in provider such as LINQ to Objects, LINQ to SQL, or LINQ to XML.

All providers implement standard operators—methods with well-known names and signatures that implement various common query features. The features include filtering, sorting, grouping, and the ability to transform data through a projection. You can also perform test and aggregation operations across entire sets. Queries can be composed—most operators' output can be used as input to other operators. LINQ uses a functional style to maximize the flexibility of composition.

CHAPTER 9

Collection Classes

In the preceding two chapters we saw how to store information in arrays and lists, and how to sort, search, and process that information using LINQ. Important as sequential lists and rectangular arrays are, they don't accommodate every possible requirement you could have for storing and structuring data. So in this final chapter on working with collections, we'll look at some of the other collection classes offered by the .NET Framework.

Dictionaries

A *dictionary* is a collection that enables you to look up information associated with some kind of value. .NET calls this sort of collection a dictionary because it is reminiscent of a traditional printed dictionary: the information is structured to make it easy to find the entry for a particular word—if you know what word you're looking for, you can find it very quickly even among tens of thousands of definitions. The information you find when you've looked up the word depends on the sort of dictionary you bought—it might provide a definition of the word, but other kinds exist, such as dictionaries of quotations, or of etymology.

Likewise, a .NET dictionary collection is structured to enable quick and easy lookup of entries. The syntax looks very similar to array access, but where you'd expect to see a number, the index can be something else, such as a string, as shown in Example 9-1.

Example 9-1. Looking up an entry in a dictionary

```
string definition = myDictionary["sea"];
```

Just as printed dictionaries vary in what you get when you look up a word, so can .NET dictionaries. The `Dictionary` type in the `System.Collections.Generic` namespace is a generic type, letting you choose the type for both the *key*—the value used for the index—and the *value* associated with the index. (Note that there are some restrictions regarding the key type—see the sidebar on the next page.) Example 9-1, which models a traditional printed dictionary, uses strings for the index, and expects a string as the result, so `myDictionary` in that example would be defined as shown in Example 9-2.

Example 9-2. A dictionary with string keys and string values

```
Dictionary<string, string> myDictionary = new Dictionary<string, string>();
```

Keys, Comparison, and Hashes

To be able to look up entries quickly, dictionaries impose a couple of requirements on keys. First, a dictionary entry's key must not change in a way that affects comparisons. (This often just means that you should never change a key. However, it's technically possible to build a type for which certain kinds of changes have no impact on comparisons performed by the `Equals` methods. Such changes are invisible to the dictionary.) Second, it should provide a good hash function.

To understand the first requirement—that for comparison purposes, keys must not change—consider what changing a key would mean in a printed dictionary. Suppose you look up the entry for *bug* in your dictionary, and then you cross out the word *bug* and write *feature* in its place. The usual way of looking up words will now fail for this entry—the entry was positioned in exactly the right place for when the key was *bug*. Anyone looking up *feature* will not think to look in the location for your amended item. And it's the same with a dictionary collection—to enable fast lookup, dictionaries create an internal structure based on the keys items had when they were added to the dictionary. It has no way of knowing when you've changed a key value. If you really need to do this, you should remove the entry, and then add it back with the new key— this gives the dictionary a chance to rebuild its internal lookup data structures.

This requirement is most easily met by using an immutable type, such as `string`, or any of the built-in numeric types.

The second requirement—that key types should have a good hash function—is a bit less obvious, and has to do with how dictionary collections implement fast lookup. The base `System.Object` class defines a virtual method called `GetHashCode`, whose job is to return an `int` whose value loosely represents the value of the object. `GetHashCode` is required to be consistent with the `Equals` method (also defined by `System.Object`)— two objects or values that are equal according to `Equals` are required to return the same hash code. Those are the rules, and dictionaries will not work if you break them.

This means that if you override `Equals`, you are required to override `GetHashCode`, and vice versa.

The rules about hash codes for items that are not equal are more flexible. Ideally, non-equal items should return nonequal hash codes, but clearly that's not always possible: a `long` can have any of several quintillion distinct values, but a hash code is an `int`, which has merely a few billion possible values. So inevitably there will be *hash collisions*—nonequal values that happen to have equal hash codes. For example, `long` returns the same hash code for the values 4,294,967,296 and 1.

`GetHashCode` implementations should try to minimize hash collisions. The reason is that dictionaries use the hash code to work out where to put the entry—in the printed

---

dictionary analogy the hash code effectively tells it on which page the entry belongs. Hash collisions mean dictionary entries share a page, and the dictionary has to spend time scanning through the entries to find the right one. The fewer hash collisions you have, the faster dictionaries work.

If you use built-in numeric types such as `int` as keys, or if you use `string`, you can safely ignore all of this because these types provide good hash codes. You need to care about this only if you plan to use a custom type which defines its own notion of equality (i.e., that overrides `Equals`).

When you start using collection types that require multiple generic type arguments such as this, specifying the full type name in the variable declaration and then again in the constructor starts to look a bit verbose, so if you're using a dictionary with a local variable, you might prefer to use the `var` keyword introduced in C# 3.0, as shown in Example 9-3.

Example 9-3. Avoiding repetitive strain injury with var

```
var myDictionary = new Dictionary<string, string>();
```

Remember, the `var` keyword simply asks C# to work out the variable's type by looking at the expression you're using to initialize the variable. So Example 9-3 is exactly equivalent to Example 9-2.

Just as arrays and other lists can be initialized with a list of values in braces, you can also provide an initializer list for a dictionary. As Example 9-4 shows, you must provide both a key and a value for each entry, so each entry is contained within nested braces to keep the key/value grouping clear.

Example 9-4. Dictionary initializer list

```
var myDictionary = new Dictionary<string, string>()
{
    { "dog", "Not a cat." },
    { "sea", "Big blue wobbly thing that mermaids live in." }
};
```

Storing individual items in a dictionary also uses an array-like syntax:

```
myDictionary["sea"] = "Big blue wobbly thing that mermaids live in.";
```

As you may already have guessed, dictionaries exploit the C# *indexer* feature we saw in Chapter 8.

Common Dictionary Uses

Dictionaries are extremely useful tools, because the situations they deal with—anyplace something is associated with something else—crop up all the time. They are so widely used that it's helpful to look at some common concrete examples.

Looking up values

Computer systems often use inscrutable identifiers where people would normally use a name. For example, imagine a computer system for managing patients in a hospital. This system would need to maintain a list of appointments, and it would be useful for the hospital's reception staff to be able to tell arriving patients where to go for their appointment. So the system would need to know about things such as buildings and departments—radiography, physiotherapy, and so on.

The system will usually have some sort of unique identifier for entities such as these in order to avoid ambiguity and ensure data integrity. But users of the system will most likely want to know that an appointment is in the Dr. Marvin Munroe Memorial Building, rather than, say, the building with ID 49. So the user interface will need to convert the ID to text.

The information about which ID corresponds to which building typically belongs in a database, or possibly a configuration file. You wouldn't want to bake the list into a big `switch` statement in the code, as that would make it hard to support multiple customers, and would also need a new software release anytime a building is built or renamed.

The user interface could just look up the name in the database every time it needs to display an appointment's information, but there are a few problems with this. First, the computer running the UI might not have access to the database—if the UI is written as a client-side application in WPF or Windows Forms, there's a good chance that it won't—a lot of companies put databases behind firewalls that restrict access even on the internal network. And even if it did, making a request to the server for each ID-based field takes time—in a form with several such fields, you could easily end up causing a noticeable delay. And this would be unnecessary for data that's not expected to change from day to day.

A dictionary can provide a better solution here. When the application starts up, it can load a dictionary to go from an ID to a name. Translating an ID to a displayable name then becomes as simple as this:

```
string buildingName = buildingIdToNameMap[buildingId];
```

As for how you would load this dictionary in the first place, that'll depend on where the data is stored. Whether it's coming from a file, a database, a web service, or somewhere else, you can use LINQ to initialize a dictionary—we'll see how to do that in "Dictionaries and LINQ."

Caching

Dictionaries are often used to cache information that is slow to fetch or create. Information can be placed in a dictionary the first time it is loaded, allowing an application to avoid that cost the next time the information is required. For example, suppose a doctor is with a patient, and wants to look at information regarding recent tests or medical procedures the patient has undergone. This will typically involve requesting records from some server to describe these patient encounters, and you might find that the application can be made considerably more responsive by keeping hold of the records on the client side after they have been requested so that they don't have to be looked up again and again as the doctor scrolls through a list of records.

This is a very similar idea to the lookup usage we described earlier, but there are two important differences. First, caches usually need some sort of policy that decides when to remove data from the cache—if we add every record we load into the cache and never clear out old ones, the cache will consume more memory over time, slowing the program down, which is the opposite of the intended effect. The appropriate policy for removing items from a cache will be application-specific. In a patient record viewing application, the best approach might be to clear the cache as soon as the doctor starts looking up information for a new patient, since that suggests the doctor has moved on to a new appointment and therefore won't be looking at the previous patient's details anytime soon. But that policy works only because of how this particular system is used—other systems may require other mechanisms. Another popular heuristic is to set an upper limit on either the number of entries or the total size of the data in a cache, and to remove items based on when they were last retrieved.

The second difference between using a dictionary to cache data rather than to look up preloaded data is that in caching scenarios, the data involved is often more dynamic. A list of known countries won't change very often, but patient records might change while in use, particularly if the patient is currently in the hospital. So when caching copies of information locally in a dictionary, you need to have some way of dealing with the fact that the information in the cache might be stale. (For example, although caching patient records locally would be useful, your application might need to deal with the possibility that new test results become available while the patient is with the doctor.) As with removal policy, detection of stale data requires application-specific logic.

For example, some data might never change—accounting data usually works this way, because even when data is discovered to be incorrect, it's not usually modified. Legal auditing requirements usually mean you have to fix problems by adding a new accounting record that corrects the old one. So for this sort of entry, you know that a cache of any given record will never be stale. (Newer records might exist that supersede the cached record you have, but the cache of that record will still be consistent with whatever is in the database for that entry.)

Sometimes it might be possible to perform a relatively cheap test to discover whether the cached record is consistent with the information on a server. HTTP supports this— a client can send a request with an If-Modified-Since header, containing the date at which the cached information was known to be up-to-date. If the server has no newer information, it sends a very short reply to confirm this, and will not send a new copy of the data. Web browser caches use this to make web pages you've previously visited load faster, while ensuring that you always see the most recent version of the page.

But you may simply have to guess. Sometimes the best staleness heuristic available to you might be something such as "If the cached record we have is more than 20 minutes old, let's get a fresh copy from the server." But you need to be careful with this approach. Guesswork can sometimes lead to a cache that offers no useful performance improvements, or which produces data that is too stale to be useful, or both.

Regardless of the precise details of your cache removal and staleness policies, the approach will look something like Example 9-5. (The Record type in this example is not a class library type, by the way. It's just for illustration—it would be the class for whatever data you want to cache.)

Example 9-5. Using a dictionary for caching

```
class RecordCache
{
    private Dictionary<int, Record> cachedRecords =
        new Dictionary<int, Record>();

    public Record GetRecord(int recordId)
    {
        Record result;
        if (cachedRecords.TryGetValue(recordId, out result))
        {
            // Found item in cache, but is it stale?
            if (IsStale(result))
            {
                result = null;
            }
        }

        if (result == null)
        {
            result = LoadRecord(recordId);
            // Add newly loaded record to cache
            cachedRecords[recordId] = result;
        }
        DiscardAnyOldCacheEntries();

        return result;
    }

    private Record LoadRecord(int recordId)
    {
        ... Code to load the record would go here ...
    }

    private bool IsStale(Record result)
    {
        ... Code to work out whether the record is stale would go here ...
    }
```

```
    private void DiscardAnyOldCacheEntries()
    {
        ... Cache removal policy code would go here ...
    }
}
```

Notice that this code does not use the indexer to look up a cache entry. Instead, it uses a method called `TryGetValue`. You use this when you're not sure if the dictionary will contain the entry you're looking for—in this case, the entry won't be present the first time we look it up. (The dictionary would throw an exception if we use the indexer to look up a value that's not present.) `TryGetValue` returns `true` if an entry for the given key was found, and `false` if not. Notice that its second argument uses the `out` qualifier and it uses this to return the item when it's found, or a null reference when it's not found.

 You might be wondering why `TryGetValue` doesn't just use a `null` return value to indicate that a record wasn't found, rather than this slightly clumsy arrangement with a `bool` return value and an `out` argument. But that wouldn't work with value types, which cannot be null. Dictionaries can hold either reference types or value types.

Dynamic properties

Another common use for a dictionary is when you want something that works like a property, but where the set of available properties is not necessarily fixed. For example, WCF is designed to send and receive messages over a wide range of network technologies, each of which may have its own unique characteristics. So WCF defines some normal properties and methods to deal with aspects of communication that are common to most scenarios, but also provides a dictionary of dynamic properties to handle transport-specific scenarios.

For example, if you are using WCF with HTTP-based communication, you might want your client code to be able to modify the `User-Agent` header. This header is specific to HTTP, and so WCF doesn't provide a property for this as part of its programming model, because it wouldn't do anything for most network protocols. Instead, you control this with a dynamic property, added via the WCF `Message` type's `Properties` dictionary, as Example 9-6 shows.

Example 9-6. Setting a dynamic property on a WCF message

```
Message wcfMessage = CreateMessageSomehow();

HttpRequestMessageProperty reqProps = new HttpRequestMessageProperty();
reqProps.Headers.Add(HttpRequestHeader.UserAgent, "my user agent");

wcfMessage.Properties[HttpRequestMessageProperty.Name] = reqProps;
```

 C# 4.0 introduces an alternative way to support dynamic properties, through the `dynamic` keyword (which we will describe in Chapter 18). This makes it possible to use normal C# property access syntax with properties whose availability is determined at runtime. So you might think `dynamic` makes dictionaries redundant. In practice, `dynamic` is normally used only when interacting with dynamic programming systems such as scripting languages, so it's not based on .NET's dictionary mechanisms.

Sparse arrays

The final common scenario we'll look at for dictionaries is to provide efficient storage for a *sparse array*. A sparse array is indexed by an integer, like a normal array, but only a tiny fraction of its elements contain anything other than the default value. For a numeric element type that would mean the array is mostly zeros, while for a reference type it would be mostly nulls.

As an example of where this might be useful, consider a spreadsheet. When you create a new spreadsheet, it appears to be a large expanse of cells. But it's not really storing information for every cell. I just ran Microsoft Excel, pressed Ctrl-G to go to a particular cell and typed in `$XFD$1000000`, and then entered a value for that cell. This goes to the 16,384th column (which is as wide as Excel 2007 can go), and the 1 millionth row. Yet despite spanning more than 16 billion cells, the file is only 8 KB. And that's because it doesn't really contain all the cells—it only stores information for the cells that contain something.

The spreadsheet is sparse—it is mostly empty. And it uses a representation that makes efficient use of space when the data is sparse.

If you try to create a rectangular array with 16,384 columns and 1 million rows, you'll get an exception as such an array would go over the .NET 4 upper size limit for any single array of 2 GB. A newly created array always contains default values for all of its elements, so the information it contains is always sparse to start with—sparseness is a characteristic of the data, rather than the storage mechanism, but the fact that we simply cannot create a new, empty array this large demonstrates that a normal array doesn't store sparse information efficiently.

There is no built-in type designed specifically for storing sparse data, but we can use a dictionary to make such a thing. Example 9-7 uses a dictionary to provide storage for a single-dimensional sparse array of `double` elements. It uses `long` as the index argument type to enable the array to grow to a logical size that is larger than would be possible with an `int`, which tops out at around 2.1 billion.

Example 9-7. A sparse array of numbers

```
class SparseArray
{
    private Dictionary<long, double> nonEmptyValues =
```

```
                        new Dictionary<long, double>();

    public double this[long index]
    {
        get
        {
            double result;
            nonEmptyValues.TryGetValue(index, out result);
            return result;
        }
        set
        {
            nonEmptyValues[index] = value;
        }
    }
}
```

Notice that this example doesn't bother to check the return value from `TryGetValue`. That's because when it fails to find the entry, it sets the result to the default value, and in the case of a `double`, that means 0. And 0 is what we want to return for an entry whose value has not been set yet.

The following code uses the `SparseArray` class:

```
SparseArray big = new SparseArray();
big[0] = 123;
big[10000000000] = 456;

Console.WriteLine(big[0]);
Console.WriteLine(big[2]);
Console.WriteLine(big[10000000000]);
```

This sets the value of the first element, and also the element with an index of 10 billion—this simply isn't possible with an ordinary array. And yet it works fine here, with minimal memory usage. The code prints out values for three indexes, including one that hasn't been set. Here are the results:

```
123
0
456
```

Reading the value that hasn't been set returns the default value of 0, as required.

 Some arrays will be sparser than others, and there will inevitably come a point of insufficient sparseness at which this dictionary-based approach will end up being less efficient than simply using a large array. It's hard to predict where the dividing line between the two techniques will fall, as it will depend on factors such as the type and quantity of data involved, and the range of index values. As with any implementation choice made on the grounds of efficiency, you should compare the performance against the simpler approach to find out whether you're getting the benefit you hoped for.

IDictionary<TKey, TValue>

The examples we've seen so far have all used the `Dictionary` type defined in the `System.Collections.Generic` namespace. But that's not the only dictionary. As we saw a couple of chapters ago, the `IEnumerable<T>` type lets us write polymorphic code that can work with any sequential collection class. We can do the same with a dictionary—the .NET Framework class library defines an interface called `IDictionary<TKey, TValue>`, which is reproduced in Example 9-8.

Example 9-8. IDictionary<TKey, TValue>

```
namespace System.Collections.Generic
{
    public interface IDictionary<TKey, TValue> :
        ICollection<KeyValuePair<TKey, TValue>>,
        IEnumerable<KeyValuePair<TKey, TValue>>,
        IEnumerable
    {

        void Add(TKey key, TValue value);
        bool ContainsKey(TKey key);
        bool Remove(TKey key);
        bool TryGetValue(TKey key, out TValue value);

        TValue this[TKey key] { get; set; }
        ICollection<TKey> Keys { get; }
        ICollection<TValue> Values { get; }
    }
}
```

You can see the indexer—`TValue this[TKey]`—and the `TryGetValue` method that we already looked at. But as you can see, dictionaries also implement other useful standard features.

The `Add` method adds a new entry to the dictionary. This might seem redundant because you can add new entries with the indexer, but the difference is that the indexer will happily overwrite an existing value. But if you call `Add`, you are declaring that you believe this to be a brand-new entry, so the method will throw an exception if the dictionary already contained a value for the specified key.

There are members for helping you discover what's already in the dictionary—you can get a list of all the keys and values from the `Keys` and `Values` properties. Both of these implement `ICollection<T>`, which is a specialized version of `IEnumerable<T>` that adds in useful members such as `Count`, `Contains`, and `CopyTo`.

Notice also that `IDictionary<TKey, TValue>` derives from `IEnumerable<KeyPairValue<TKey, TValue>>`. This means it's possible to enumerate through the contents of a dictionary with a `foreach` loop. The `KeyPairValue<TKey, TValue>` items returned by the enumeration just package the key and associated value into a single struct. We could add the method in Example 9-9 to the class in Example 9-7, in order to print out just those elements with a nondefault value.

Example 9-9. Iterating through a dictionary's contents

```
public void ShowArrayContents()
{
    foreach (var item in nonEmptyValues)
    {
        Console.WriteLine("Key: '{0}', Value: '{1}'",
            item.Key, item.Value);
    }
}
```

Remember, the presence of `IEnumerable<T>` is all that LINQ to Objects needs, so we can use dictionaries with LINQ.

Dictionaries and LINQ

Because all `IDictionary<TKey, TValue>` implementations are also enumerable, we can run LINQ queries against them. Given the `RecordCache` class in Example 9-5, we might choose to implement the cache item removal policy as shown in Example 9-10.

Example 9-10. LINQ query with dictionary source

```
private void DiscardAnyOldCacheEntries()
{
    // Calling ToList() on source in order to query a copy
    // of the enumeration, to avoid exceptions due to calling
    // Remove in the foreach loop that follows.
    var staleKeys = from entry in cachedRecords.ToList()
                    where IsStale(entry.Value)
                    select entry.Key;
    foreach (int staleKey in staleKeys)
    {
        cachedRecords.Remove(staleKey);
    }
}
```

But it's also possible to create new dictionaries with LINQ queries. Example 9-11 illustrates how to use the standard `ToDictionary` LINQ operator.

Example 9-11. LINQ's ToDictionary operator

```
IDictionary<int, string> buildingIdToNameMap =
    MyDataSource.Buildings.ToDictionary(
        building => building.ID,
        building => building.Name);
```

This example presumes that `MyDataSource` is some data source class that provides a queryable collection containing a list of buildings. Since this information would typically be stored in a database, you would probably use a database LINQ provider such as LINQ to Entities or LINQ to SQL. The nature of the source doesn't greatly matter, though—the mechanism for extracting the resources into a dictionary object are the same in any case. The `ToDictionary` operator needs to be told how to extract the key from each item in the sequence. Here we've provided a lambda expression that retrieves the `ID` property—again, this property would probably be generated by a database mapping tool such as the ones provided by the Entity Framework or LINQ to SQL. (We will be looking at data access technologies in a later chapter.) This example supplies a second lambda, which chooses the value—here we pick the `Name` property. This second lambda is optional—if you don't provide it, `ToDictionary` will just use the entire source item from the stream as the value—so in this example, leaving out the second lambda would cause `ToDictionary` to return an `IDictionary<int, `*Building*`>` (where *Building* is whatever type of object `MyDataSource.Buildings` provides).

The code in Example 9-11 produces the same result as this:

```
var buildingIdToNameMap = new Dictionary<int, string>();
foreach (var building in MyDataSource.Buildings)
{
    buildingIdToNameMap.Add(building.ID, building.Name);
}
```

HashSet and SortedSet

`HashSet<T>` is a collection of distinct values. If you add the same value twice, it will ignore the second **add**, allowing any given value to be added only once. You could use this to ensure uniqueness—for example, imagine an online chat server. If you wanted to make sure that usernames are unique, you could maintain a `HashSet<string>` of usernames used so far, and check that a new user's chosen name isn't already in use by calling the hash set's `Contains` method.

 You might notice that `List<T>` offers a `Contains` method, and so with a little extra code, you could implement a uniqueness check using `List<T>`. However, `HashSet<T>` uses the same hash-code-based fast lookup as a dictionary, so `HashSet<T>` will be faster for large sets than `List<T>`.

`HashSet<T>` was added in .NET 3.5. Prior to that, people tended to use a dictionary with nothing useful in the value as a way of getting fast hash-code-based uniqueness testing.

.NET 4 adds `SortedSet<T>`, which is very similar to `HashSet<T>`, but adds the feature that if you iterate through the items in the set, they will come out in order. (You can provide an `IComparer<T>` to define the required order, or you can use self-ordering types.) Obviously, you could achieve the same effect by applying the `OrderBy` LINQ operator to a `HashSet<T>`, but `SortedSet<T>` sorts the items as they are added, meaning that they're already sorted by the time you want to iterate over them.

Both HashSet<T> and SortedSet<T> offer various handy set-based methods. You can determine whether an IEnumerable<T> is a subset of (i.e., all its elements are also found in) a set with the IsSubsetOf, for example. The available methods are defined by the common ISet<T> interface, reproduced in Example 9-12.

Example 9-12. ISet<T>

```
namespace System.Collections.Generic
{
    public interface ISet<T> : ICollection<T>, IEnumerable<T>, IEnumerable
    {
        bool Add(T item);
        void ExceptWith(IEnumerable<T> other);
        void IntersectWith(IEnumerable<T> other);
        bool IsProperSubsetOf(IEnumerable<T> other);
        bool IsProperSupersetOf(IEnumerable<T> other);
        bool IsSubsetOf(IEnumerable<T> other);
        bool IsSupersetOf(IEnumerable<T> other);
        bool Overlaps(IEnumerable<T> other);
        bool SetEquals(IEnumerable<T> other);
        void SymmetricExceptWith(IEnumerable<T> other);
        void UnionWith(IEnumerable<T> other);
    }
}
```

Queues

Queue<T> is a handy collection type for processing entities on a first come, first served basis. For example, some doctors' general practice surgeries operate an appointment-free system. Since the time taken to see each patient in these scenarios can vary wildly depending on the problem at hand, seeing patients in turn can end up being a lot more efficient than allocating fixed-length appointment slots.

We could model this with a Queue<Patient> (where Patient is some class defined by our application). When a patient arrives, she would be added to a queue by calling its Enqueue method:

```
    private Queue<Patient> waitingPatients = new Queue<Patient>();

    ...

    public void AddPatientToQueue(Patient newlyArrivedPatient)
    {
        waitingPatients.Enqueue(newlyArrivedPatient);
    }
```

When a doctor has finished seeing one patient and is ready to see the next, the Dequeue method will return the patient who has been in the queue longest, and will then remove that patient from the queue:

```
    Patient nextPatientToSee = waitingPatients.Dequeue();
```

 While this example perfectly matches how `Queue<T>` works, you probably wouldn't use a `Queue<T>` here in practice. You'd want to handle crashes and power failures gracefully in this application, which means that in practice, you'd probably store the list of waiting patients in a database, along with something such as a ticket number indicating their place in the queue.

In-memory queues tend to show up more often in multithreaded servers for keeping track of outstanding work. But since we haven't gotten to either the networking or the threading chapters yet, an example along those lines would be premature.

`Queue<T>` implements `IEnumerable<T>`, so you can use LINQ queries across items in the whole queue. It also implements `ICollection<T>`, so you can discover whether the queue is currently empty by inspecting its `Count` property.

`Queue<T>` operates in strict first in, first out (FIFO) order, which is to say that `Dequeue` will return items in exactly the same order in which they were added with `Enqueue`. That might be fine for general practice, but it wouldn't work so well for the emergency room.

Linked Lists

If you've ever had to visit a hospital emergency room, you'll know that waiting in a queue is one of the defining features of the experience unless you were either very lucky or very unlucky. If you were lucky, the queue will have been empty and you will not have had to wait. Alternatively, if you were unlucky, your condition may have been sufficiently perilous that you got to jump to the head of the queue.

In medical emergencies, a triage system will be in place to work out where each arriving patient should go in the queue. A similar pattern crops up in other scenarios—frequent fliers with gold cards may be allocated standby seats at the last minute even though others have been waiting for hours; celebrities might be able to walk right into a restaurant for which the rest of us have to book a table weeks in advance.

The `LinkList<T>` class is able to model these sorts of scenarios. At its simplest, you could use it like a `Queue<T>`—call `AddLast` to add an item to the back of the queue (as `Enqueue` would), and `RemoveFirst` to take the item off the head of the queue (like `Dequeue` would). But you can also add an item to the front of the queue with `AddFirst`. Or you can add items anywhere you like in the queue with the `AddBefore` and `AddAfter` methods. Example 9-13 uses this to place new patients into the queue.

Example 9-13. Triage in action

```
private LinkedList<Patient> waitingPatients = new LinkedList<Patient>();

...

LinkedListNode<Patient> current = waitingPatients.First;
```

```
while (current != null)
{
    if (current.Value.AtImminentRiskOfDeath)
    {
        current = current.Next;
    }
    else
    {
        break;
    }
}
if (current == null)
{
    waitingPatients.AddLast(newPatient);
}
else
{
    waitingPatients.AddBefore(current, newPatient);
}
```

This code adds the new patient after all those patients in the queue whose lives appear to be at immediate risk, but ahead of all other patients—the patient is presumably either quite unwell or a generous hospital benefactor. (Real triage is a little more complex, of course, but you still insert items into the list in the same way, no matter how you go about choosing the insertion point.)

Note the use of LinkedListNode<T>—this is how LinkedList<T> presents the queue's contents. It allows us not only to see the item in the queue, but also to navigate back and forth through the queue with the Next and Previous properties.

Stacks

Whereas Queue<T> operates a FIFO order, Stack<T> operates a last in, first out (LIFO) order. Looking at this from a queuing perspective, it seems like the height of unfairness—latecomers get priority over those who arrived early. However, there are some situations in which this topsy-turvy ordering can make sense.

A performance characteristic of most computers is that they tend to be able to work faster with data they've processed recently than with data they've not touched lately. CPUs have caches that provide faster access to data than a computer's main memory can support, and these caches typically operate a policy where recently used data is more likely to stay in the cache than data that has not been touched recently.

If you're writing a server-side application, you may consider throughput to be more important than fairness—the total rate at which you process work may matter more than how long any individual work item takes to complete. In this case, a LIFO order may make the most sense—work items that were only just put into a queue are much more likely to still live in the CPU's cache than those that were queued up ages ago, and so you'll get better throughput during high loads if you process newly arrived items first. Items that have sat in the queue for longer will just have to wait for a lull.

Like `Queue<T>`, `Stack<T>` offers a method to add an item, and one to remove it. It calls these `Push` and `Pop`, respectively. They are very similar to the queue's `Enqueue` and `Dequeue`, except they both work off the same end of the list. (You could get the same effect using a `LinkedList`, and always calling `AddFirst` and `RemoveFirst`.)

A stack could also be useful for managing navigation history. The Back button in a browser works in LIFO order—the first page it shows you is the last one you visited. (And if you want a Forward button, you could define a second stack—each time the user goes Back, `Push` the current page onto the Forward stack. Then if the user clicks Forward, `Pop` a page from the Forward stack, and `Push` the current page onto the Back stack.)

Summary

The .NET Framework class library provides various useful collection classes. We saw `List<T>` in an earlier chapter, which provides a simple resizable linear list of items. Dictionaries store entries by associating them with keys, providing fast key-based lookup. `HashSet<T>` and `SortedSet<T>` manage sets of unique items, with optional ordering. Queues, linked lists, and stacks each manage a queue of items, offering various strategies for how the order of addition relates to the order in which items come out of the queue.

Strings

Chapter 10 is all about strings. A bit late, you might think: we've had about nine chapters of string-based action already! Well, yes, you'd be right. That's not terribly surprising, though: text is probably the single most important means an application has of communicating with its users. That is especially true as we haven't introduced any graphical frameworks yet. I suppose we could have beeped the system speaker in Morse, although even that can be considered a text-based operation.

Even with a graphical UI framework where we have pictures and buttons and graphs and sounds, they almost always have textual labels, descriptions, comments, or tool tips.

Users who have difficulty reading (perhaps because they have a low-vision condition) may have that text transformed into sound by accessibility tools, but the application is still processing text strings under the covers.

Even when we are dealing with integers or doubles internally within an algorithm, there comes a time when we need to represent them to humans, and preferably in a way that is meaningful to us. We usually do that (at least in part) by converting them into strings of one form or another.

Strings are surprisingly complex and sophisticated entities, so we're going to take some time to explore their properties in this chapter.

First, we'll look at what we're really doing when we initialize a literal string. Then, we'll see a couple of techniques which let us convert from other types to a string representation and how we can control the formatting of that conversion.

Next, we'll look at various different techniques we can use to process a string. This will include composition, splitting, searching and replacing content, and what it means to compare strings of various kinds.

Finally, we will look at how .NET represents strings internally, how that differs from other representations in popular use in the world, and how we can convert between those representations by using an Encoding.

What Is a String?

A string is an ordered sequence of characters:

We could consider this sentence to be a string.

We start with the first character, which is W. Then we continue on in order from left to right:

'W', 'e', ' ', 'c', 'o', 'u', 'l', 'd'

And so on.

A string doesn't have to be a whole sentence, of course, or even anything meaningful. Any ordered sequence of characters is a string. Notice that each character might be an uppercase letter, lowercase letter, space, punctuation mark, number (or, in fact, any other textual symbol). It doesn't even have to be an English letter. It could be Arabic, for example:

العربية

Here we have the following characters:

'ة' ,'ي' ,'ب' ,'ر' ,'ع' ,'ل' ,'ا'

If you look carefully, you'll notice that the string is ordered the other way round—the first character is the rightmost one, and the last character is the leftmost one. This is because Arabic scripts read right to left and not left to right; but the string is still ordered, character by character.

A quick reminder: a font is a particular visual design for an entire set of characters. Historically, it was a box containing a set of moveable type in a specific design at a certain size, but we've come to blur the meanings of font family, typeface, and font in popular usage, and people tend to use these terms interchangeably now.

I think it is interesting to note that only a few years ago, fonts were the sole purview of designers and printers; but they've now become commonplace, thanks to the ubiquity of the word processor.

Just in case you have been on the moon since 1968, here are three examples taken from different fonts:

Times New Roman

Arial

Arial Black

You'll also notice that the "joined up" cursive form of the characters is visually quite different from their form when separated out individually. This is normal; the ultimate visual representation of the character in the string is entirely separate from the string itself. We're just so used to the characters of our own language that we don't tend to think of them as abstract symbols, and tend to discount any visual differences down to the choice of font or other typographical niceties when we are interpreting them.

We could happily design a font where the character e looks like **Q** and the character f looks like **A**. All our text processing would continue as normal: searching and sorting would be just fine (words starting with f wouldn't start appearing in the dictionary before words starting with e), because the data in the string is unchanged; but when we drew it on the screen, it would look more than a bit confusing.[*]

The take-home point is that there are a bunch of layers between the .NET runtime's representation of a string as data in memory, and its final visual appearance on a screen, in a file, or in another application (such as *notepad.exe*, for example). As we go through this chapter, we'll unpick those layers as we come across them, and point out some of the common pitfalls.

Let's get on and see how the .NET Framework presents a string to us.

The String and Char Types

It will come as no surprise that the .NET Framework provides us with two types that correspond with strings and characters: String and Char. In fact, as we've seen before, these are such important types that C# even provides us with keywords that correspond to the underlying types: string and char.

String needs to provide us with that "ordered sequence of characters" behavior. It does so by implementing IEnumerable<char>, as Example 10-1 illustrates.

Example 10-1. Iterating through the characters in a string

```
string myString = "I've gone all vertical.";

foreach (char theCharacter in myString)
{
    Console.WriteLine(theCharacter);
}
```

---

[*] In fact, I don't think that this particular typeface would catch on.

If you create a console application for this code, you'll see output like this when it runs:

```
I
'
v
e

g
o
n
e

a
l
l

v
e
r
t
i
c
a
l
.
```

What exactly does that code do? First, it initializes a variable called `myString` which we will use to hold the reference to our string object (because `String` is a reference type).

We then enumerate the string, yielding every `Char` in turn, and we output each `Char` to the console on its own separate line. `Char` is a value type, so we're actually getting a *copy* of the character from the string itself.

The string object is created using a *literal string*—a sequence of characters enclosed in double quotes:

```
"I've gone all vertical."
```

We're already quite familiar with initializing a string with a literal—we probably do it without a second thought; but let's have a look at these literals in a little more detail.

Literal Strings and Chars

The simplest literal string is a set of characters enclosed in double quotes, shown in the first line of Example 10-2.

Example 10-2. A string literal

```
string myString = "Literal string";
Console.WriteLine(myString);
```

This produces the output:

```
Literal string
```

You can also initialize a string from a `char[]`, using the appropriate constructor. One way to obtain a `char` array is by using `char` literals. A `char` literal is a single character, wrapped in single quotes. Example 10-3 constructs a string this way.

Example 10-3. Initializing a string from char literals

```
string myString = new string(new []
    { 'H', 'e', 'l', 'l', 'o', ' ', '"', 'w', 'o', 'r', 'l', 'd', '"' });
Console.WriteLine(myString);
```

If you compile and run this, you'll see the following output:

```
Hello "world"
```

Notice that we've got double-quote marks in our output. That was easy to achieve with this `char[]`, because the delimiter for an individual character is the single quote; but how could we include double quotes in the string, without resorting to a literal `char` array? Equally, how could we specify the single-quote character as a literal `char`?

Escaping Special Characters

The way to deal with troublesome characters in string and char literals is to *escape* them with the backslash character. That means that you precede the quote with a \, and it interprets the quote as part of the string, rather than the end of it. Like this:[†]

```
"Literal \"string\""
```

If you build and run with this change, you'll see the output, with quotes in place:

```
Literal "string"
```

There are several other special characters that you can escape in this way. You can find some common ones listed in Table 10-1.

Table 10-1. Common escaped characters for string literals

Escaped character	Purpose
\"	Include a double quote in a string literal.
\'	Include a single quote in a char literal.
\\	Insert a backslash.
\n	New line.
\r	Carriage return.
\t	Tab.

There are also some rather uncommon ones, listed in Table 10-2. In general, you don't need to worry about them, but they are quite interesting.

---

† We'll just show the string literal from here on, rather than repeating the boilerplate code each time. Just replace the string initializer with the example.

Table 10-2. Less common escape characters for string literals

Escaped character	Purpose
\0	The character represented by the char with value zero (not the character 'o').
\a	Alert or "Bell". Back in the dim and distant past, terminals didn't really have sound, so you couldn't play a great big .*wav* file beautifully designed by Robert Fripp every time you wanted to alert the user to the fact that he had done something a bit wrong. Instead, you sent this character to the console, and it beeped at you, or even dinged a real bell (like the line-end on a manual typewriter). It still works today, and on some PCs there's still a separate speaker just for making this old-school beep. Try it, but be prepared for unexpected retro-side effects like growing enormous sideburns and developing an obsession with disco.
\b	Backspace. Yes, you can include backspaces in your string.
	Write:
	`"Hello world\b\b\b\b\bdolly"`
	to the console, and you'll see:
	`Hello dolly`
	Not all rendering engines support this character, though. You can see the same string rendered in a WPF application in Figure 10-1. Notice how the backspace characters have been ignored.
	Remember: output mechanisms can interpret individual characters differently, even though they're the *same* character, in the *same* string.
\f	Form feed. Another special character from yesteryear. This used to push a whole page worth of paper through the printer. This is somewhat less than useful now, though. Even the console doesn't do what you'd expect.
	If you write:
	`"Hello\fworld"`
	to the console, you'll see something like:
	`Hello♀world`
	Yes, that is the symbol for "female" in the middle there. That's because the original IBM PC defined a special character mapping so that it could use some of these characters to produce graphical symbols (like male, female, heart, club, diamond, and spade) that weren't part of the regular character set. These mappings are sometimes called *code pages*, and the default code page for the console (at least for U.S. English systems) incorporates those original IBM definitions. We'll talk more about code pages and encodings later.
\v	Vertical quote. This one looks like a "male" symbol (♂) in the console's IBM-emulating code page.

The first character in Table 10-2 is worth a little attention: character value 0, sometimes also referred to as the *null character*, although it's not the same as a null reference—char is a value type, so it's more like the char equivalent of the number 0. In a lot of programming systems, this character is used to mark the end of a string—C and C++ use this convention, as do many Windows APIs. However, in .NET, and therefore in C#, string objects contain the length as a separate field, and so you're free to put null characters in your strings if you want. However, you may need to be careful—if those

Figure 10-1. WPF ignoring control characters

strings end up being passed to Windows APIs, it's possible that Windows will ignore everything after the first null.

There's one more escape form that's a little different from all the others, because you can use it to escape *any* character. This escape sequence begins with \u and is then followed by four hexadecimal digits, letting you specify the exact numeric value for a character. How can a textual character have a numeric value? Well, we'll get into that in detail in the "Encoding Characters" on page 360 section, but roughly speaking, each possible character can be identified by number. For example, the uppercase letter A has the number 65, B is 66, and so on. In hexadecimal, those are 41 and 42, respectively. So we can write this string:

```
"\u0041\u0042\u0043"
```

which is equivalent to:

```
"ABC"
```

Of course, if that's the string you want, you'd normally just write that second form. The \u escape sequence is more useful when you need a particular character that's not on your keyboard. For example, \u00A9 is the copyright symbol: ©.

Sometimes you'll have a block of text that includes a lot of these special characters (like carriage returns, for instance) and you want to just paste it out of some other application straight into your code as a literal string without having to add lots of backslashes.

> While it can be done, you might question the wisdom of large quantities of text in your C# source files. You might want to store the text in a separate resource file, and load it up on demand.

If you prefix the opening double-quote mark with the @ symbol, the compiler will then interpret every subsequent character (including any whitespace such as newlines, and tabs) as part of the string, until it sees a matching double-quote mark to close the string. Example 10-4 exploits this to embed new lines and indentation in a string literal.

Example 10-4. Avoiding backslashes with @-quoting

```
    string multiLineString =
@"Lots of
lines and
        tabs!";
    Console.WriteLine(multiLineString);
```

This code will produce the following output:

```
    Lots of
    lines and
            tabs!
```

Notice how it respects the whitespace between the double quotes.

 The @ prefix can be especially useful for literal file paths. You don't need to escape all those backslashes. So instead of writing `"C:\\some\\path"` you can write just `@"c:\some\path"`.

Formatting Data for Output

So, we know how to initialize literal strings, which is terribly useful; but what about our other data? How do we display an `Int32` or `DateTime` or whatever?

We've already met one way of converting any object to a string—the virtual `ToString` method, which Example 10-5 uses.

Example 10-5. Converting numbers to strings with ToString

```
int myValue = 45;
string myString = myValue.ToString();

Console.WriteLine(myString);
```

This will produce the output you might expect:

```
    45
```

What if we try a `decimal`? Example 10-6 shows this.

Example 10-6. Calling ToString on a decimal

```
decimal myValue = 45.65M;
string myString = myValue.ToString();
Console.WriteLine(myString);
```

Again, we get the expected output:

```
    45.65
```

OK, what if we have some decimals in something like an accounting ledger, and we want to format them all to line up properly, with a preceding dollar sign?

Well, there's an overload of `ToString` on each of the numeric types that takes an additional parameter—a format string.

Standard Numeric Format Strings

In most instances, we're not dreaming up a brand-new format for our numeric strings; if we were, people probably wouldn't understand what we meant. Consequently, the framework provides us with a whole bunch of standard numeric format strings, for everyday use. Let's have a look at them in action.

Currency

Example 10-7 shows how we format a decimal as a currency value, using an overload of the standard `ToString` method.

Example 10-7. Currency format

```
decimal dollarAmount = 123165.4539M;
string text = dollarAmount.ToString("C");

Console.WriteLine(text);
```

The capital `C` indicates that we want the decimal formatted as if it were a currency value; and here's the output:

```
$123,165.45
```

Notice how it has rounded to two decimal places (rounding down in this case), added a comma to group the digits, and inserted a dollar sign for us.

> Actually, I've lied to you a bit. On my machine the output looked like this:
>
> ```
> £123,165.45
> ```
>
> That's because it is configured for UK English, not U.S. English, and my default currency symbol is the one for pounds sterling. We'll talk about formatting and globalization a little later in this chapter.

That's the simplest form of this "currency" format. We can also add a number after the `C` to indicate the number of decimal places we want to use, as Example 10-8 shows.

Example 10-8. Specifying decimal places with currency format

```
decimal dollarAmount = 123165.4539M;
string text = dollarAmount.ToString("C3");

Console.WriteLine(text);
```

This will produce three decimal places in the output:

```
$123,165.454
```

Notice that it is again rounding the result. If you want to truncate, or always round up, you'll need to round the original value before you convert to a string.

This formatting style is available on all of the numeric types. (We'll see some later that apply to only particular types.)

Decimal

Decimal formatting is a bit confusingly named, as it actually applies to *integer* types, not the decimal type. It gets its name from the fact that it displays the number as a string of decimal digits (0–9), with a preceding minus sign (-) if necessary. Example 10-9 uses this format.

Example 10-9. Decimal format, with explicit precision

```
int amount = 1654539;
string text = amount.ToString("D9");
```

We're asking for nine digits in the output string, and it pads with leading zeros:

```
001654539
```

If you don't supply a qualifying number of decimal digits, as Example 10-10 shows, it just uses as many as necessary.

Example 10-10. Decimal format with unspecified precision

```
int amount = -2895729;
string text = amount.ToString("D");
```

This produces:

```
-2895729
```

Hexadecimal

Another one for integer types, hexadecimal formatting, shown in Example 10-11, represents numbers as a string of hex digits (0–9, A–F).

Example 10-11. Hexadecimal format

```
int amount = 256;
string text = amount.ToString("X");
```

This produces the output:

```
100
```

As with the decimal format string, you can specify a number to indicate the total number of digits to which to pad the number, as shown in Example 10-12.

Example 10-12. Hexadecimal format with explicit precision

```
int amount = 256;
string text = amount.ToString("X4");
```

This produces the output:

```
0100
```

Notice that the method doesn't prepend a 0x or similar; so there is nothing to distinguish this as a hex string, if you happen to hit a value that does not include the digits A–F. (The convention of preceding hexadecimal values with 0x is common in C family languages, which is why C# supports it for numeric constants, but it's not universal. VB.NET uses the prefix &H, for example. All .NET languages share the same numeric types and formatting services, so if they printed hex numbers with a C# prefix, that would be annoying for users of other languages. If you want a prefix, you have to add it yourself.)

Exponential form

All numeric types can be expressed in *exponential form*. You will probably be familiar with this notation. For example, 1.05×10^3 represents the number 1050, and 1.05×10^{-3} represents the number 0.00105.

Developers use plain text editors, which don't support formatting such as superscript, so there's a convention for representing exponential numbers with plain, unformatted text. We can write those last two examples as 1.05E+003 and 1.05E-003, respectively. C# recognizes this convention for literal floating-point values. But we can also use it when printing out numbers.

To display this form, we use the format string E, with the numeric specifier determining how many decimal places of precision we use.

 It will always format the result with one digit to the left of the decimal point, so you could also think of the precision specified as "one less than the number of significant figures."

Example 10-13 asks for exponential formatting with four digits of precision.

Example 10-13. Exponential format

```
double amount = 254.23875839484;
string text = amount.ToString("E4");
```

And here's the string it produces:

```
2.5424E+002
```

If you don't provide a precision specifier, as in Example 10-14, you get six digits to the right of the decimal point (or fewer, if the trailing digits would be zero).

 We'll see later how these defaults can be controlled by the framework's globalization features

Example 10-14. Exponential format without precision

```
double amount = 254.23875839484;
string text = amount.ToString("E");
```

This produces:

```
2.542388E+002
```

Fixed point

Another format string that applies to all numeric types, the fixed-point format provides the ability to display a number with a specific number of digits after the decimal point. As usual, it rounds the result, rather than truncating. Example 10-15 asks for four digits after the decimal point.

Example 10-15. Fixed-point format

```
double amount = 152.68385485;
string text = amount.ToString("F4");
```

This produces:

```
152.6839
```

The output will be padded with trailing zeros if necessary. Example 10-16 causes this by asking for four digits where only two are required.

Example 10-16. Fixed-point format causing trailing zeros

```
double amount = 152.68;
string text = amount.ToString("F4");
```

So, the output in this case is:

```
152.6800
```

General

Sometimes you want to use fixed point, if possible, but if an occasional result demands a huge number of leading zeros, you'd prefer to fall back on the exponential form (rather than display it as zero, for instance). The "general" format string, illustrated in Example 10-17, will provide you with this behavior. It is available on all numeric types.

Example 10-17. General format

```
double amount = 152.68;
string text = amount.ToString("G4");
Console.WriteLine(text);

double amount2 = 0.00000000000015268;
text = amount2.ToString("G4");
Console.WriteLine(text);
```

This will produce the following output:

```
152.7
1.527E-13
```

Note that the precision string determines the number of significant figures in either case, not the number of decimal places (as per the fixed-point and exponential forms). As usual, rounding is used if there are more digits than the precision allows. And if you do not specify the precision (i.e., you just use "G") it chooses the number of digits based on the precision of the data you're using—float will show fewer digits than double, for example.

 If you don't specify a particular format string, the default is as though you had specified "G".

Numeric

The numeric format, shown in Example 10-18, is very similar to the fixed-point format, but adds a "group" separator for values with enough digits (just as the currency format does). The precision specifier can be used to determine the number of decimal places, and rounding is applied if necessary.

Example 10-18. Numeric format

```
double amount = 1520494.684848;
string text = amount.ToString("N4");
Console.WriteLine(text);
```

This will produce the following output:

```
1,520,494.6848
```

Percent

Very often you need to display a number as a percentage. However, it's common to maintain values which represent a percentage using one of the floating-point types, predivided by 100 for ease of future manipulation.

The more mathematically minded among you probably rail against people calling the value 0.58 "a percentage" when they really mean 58%; but it is, unfortunately, a somewhat common convention in computer circles. Worse, it's not consistently applied, making it hard to know whether you are dealing with predivided values, or "true" percentages. It can get especially confusing when you are frequently dealing with values less than 1 percent:

```
double interestRatePercent = 0.2;
```

Is that supposed to be 0.2 percent (like I get on my savings) or 20 percent APR (like my credit card)? One way to avoid ambiguity is to avoid mentioning "percent" in your variable names and always to store values as fractions, representing 100 percent as 1.0, converting into a percentage only when you come to display the number.

The percent format is useful if you follow this convention: it will multiply by 100, enabling you to work with ratios internally, but to display them as percentages where necessary. It displays numbers in a fixed-point format, and adds a percentage symbol for you. The precision determines the number of decimal places to use, with the usual rounding method applied. Example 10-19 asks for four decimal places.

Example 10-19. Percent format

```
double amount = 0.684848;
string text = amount.ToString("P4");
Console.WriteLine(text);
```

This will produce:

```
68.4848 %
```

Note that this format works with any numeric type—including the integer types. There's no special treatment for an `Int32` or `Int16`, for example. They are multiplied up by 100, in just the same way as the floating-point types. This means that you can't format values in increments of less than 100 percent with an integer. For instance, 0 × 100 implies 0 percent, 1 × 100 implies 100 percent, and so on.

Round trip

The last of the standard numeric format strings we're going to look at is the *round-trip* format. This is used when you are expecting the string value to be converted back into its numeric representation at some point in the future, and you want to guarantee no loss of precision.

This format has no use for a precision specifier, because by definition, we always want full precision. (You can provide one if you like, because all the standard numeric formats follow a common pattern, including an optional precision. This format supports the common syntax rules, it just ignores the precision.) The framework will use the most compact form it can to achieve the round-trip behavior. Example 10-20 shows this format in use.

Example 10-20. Round-trip format

```
double amount = 0.684848;
string text = amount.ToString("R");
Console.WriteLine(text);
```

This produces the following output:

```
0.684848
```

Custom Numeric Format Strings

You are not limited to the standard forms discussed in the preceding section. You can provide your own custom numeric format strings for additional control over the final output.

The basic building blocks of a custom numeric format string are as follows:

- The # symbol, which represents an optional digit placeholder; if the digit in this position would have been a leading or trailing 0, it will be omitted.
- The 0 symbol, which represents a required digit placeholder; the string is padded with a 0 if the place is not needed.
- The . (dot) symbol, which represents the location of the decimal point.
- The , (comma) symbol, which performs two roles: it can enable digit grouping, and it can also scale the number down.

Look at Example 10-21.

Example 10-21. Custom numeric formats

```
double value = 12.3456;
Console.WriteLine(value.ToString("00.######"));

value = 1.23456;
Console.WriteLine(value.ToString("00.000000"));

Console.WriteLine(value.ToString("##.000000"));
```

We see the following output:

```
12.3456
01.234560
1.234560
```

You don't actually have to put all the # symbols you require before the decimal place—a single one will suffice; but the placeholders after the decimal point, as shown in Example 10-22, are significant.

Example 10-22. Placeholders after the decimal point

```
double value = 1234.5678;
text = value.ToString("#.###");
Console.WriteLine(text);
```

This produces:

```
1234.568
```

Notice how it is rounding the result in the usual way.

The # symbol will never produce a leading or trailing zero. Take a look at Example 10-23.

Example 10-23. Placeholders and leading or trailing zeros

```
double value = 0.46;
string text = value.ToString("#.###");
Console.WriteLine(text);
```

The preceding example will produce the following output:

```
.46
```

The comma serves two purposes, depending on where you put it. First, it can introduce a separator for showing digits in "groups" of three (so you can easily see the thousands, millions, billions, etc.). We get this behavior when we put a comma between a couple of digit placeholders (the placeholders being either # or 0), as Example 10-24 shows.

Example 10-24. Comma for grouping digits

```
int value = 12345678;
string text = value.ToString("#,#");
Console.WriteLine(text);
```

Our output string now looks like this:

```
12,345,678
```

On the other hand, commas placed just to the left of the decimal point act as a scale on the number. Each comma divides the result by 1,000. Example 10-25 shows two commas, dividing the output by 1,000,000. (It also includes a comma for grouping, although that will not have any effect with this particular value.)

Example 10-25. Comma for scaling down output

```
int value = 12345678;
string text = value.ToString("#,#,,.");
Console.WriteLine(text);
```

This produces:

```
12
```

Format strings don't have to have a decimal point, but you can still use commas to scale the number down even when there's no decimal point for the commas to be to the left of—they just appear at the end of the format string instead. In effect, there's an implied decimal point right at the end of the string if you leave it off, so in Example 10-26, the commas are still considered to be to the left of the point even though you can't see it.

Example 10-26. Implied decimal point

```
int value = 12345678;
string text = value.ToString("#,#,,");
Console.WriteLine(text);
```

Again, this produces:

```
12
```

The division rounds the result, so 12745638 would produce 13 with the same formatting.

You can also add your own arbitrary text to be included "as is" in the format string, as Example 10-27 shows.

Example 10-27. Arbitrary text in a custom format string

```
int value = 12345678;
string text = value.ToString("###-### but ###");
Console.WriteLine(text);
```

This time, the output is:

```
12-345 but 678
```

Notice how it includes the extra characters we included (the - and the but).

Were you expecting the output to be 123-456 but 78?

The framework applies the placeholder rule for the lefthand side of the decimal point, so it drops the first nonrequired placeholder, not the last one. Remember that this is a numeric conversion, not something like a telephone-number format. The behavior may be easier to understand if you replace each # with 0. In that case, we'd get 012-345 but 678. Using # just loses the leading zero.

If you want to include one of the special formatting characters, you can do so by escaping it with a backslash. Don't forget that the C# compiler will attempt to interpret backslash as an escape character in a literal string, but in this case, we don't want that—we want to include a backslash in the string that we pass to ToString. So unless you are using the @ symbol as a literal string prefix, you'll need to escape the escape character as Example 10-28 shows.

Example 10-28. Escaping characters in a custom format string

```
int value = 12345678;
string text = value.ToString("###-### \\# ###");
Console.WriteLine(text);
```

Example 10-29 shows the @-quoted equivalent.

Example 10-29. @-quoting a custom format string

```
int value = 12345678;
string text = value.ToString(@"###-### \# ###");
Console.WriteLine(text);
```

Both will produce this output:

```
12-345 # 678
```

You can also include literal strings (with or without special characters), by wrapping them in single quotes as Example 10-30 shows.

Example 10-30. Literal string in a custom format string

```
int value = 12345678;
string text = value.ToString(@"###-### \# ### 'is a number'");
Console.WriteLine(text);
```

This produces the output:

```
12-345 # 678 is a number
```

Finally, you can also get the multiply-by-100 behavior for predivided percentage values using the % symbol, as shown in Example 10-31.

Example 10-31. Percentage in a custom format string

```
double value = 0.95;
string text = value.ToString("#0.##%");
Console.WriteLine(text);
```

Notice that this also includes the percentage symbol in the output:

```
95%
```

 There is also a per-thousand (per-mille) symbol (‰), which is Unicode character 2030. You can use this in the same way as the percentage symbol, but it multiplies up by 1,000. We'll learn more about Unicode characters later in this chapter.

Dates and Times

It is not just numeric types that support formatting when they are converted to strings. The `DateTime`, `DateTimeOffset`, and `TimeSpan` types follow a similar pattern.

`DateTimeOffset` is generally the preferred way to represent a particular point in time inside a program, because it builds in information about the time zone (and daylight saving if applicable), leaving no scope for ambiguity regarding the time it represents. However, `DateTime` is a more natural way to present times to users, partly because it has *more* scope for ambiguity. People very rarely explicitly say what time zone they're thinking of—we're used to learning that a shop opens at 9:00 a.m., or that our flight is due to arrive at 8:30 p.m. `DateTime` lives in this same slightly fuzzy world, where 9:00 a.m. is, in some sense, the same time before and after daylight saving comes into effect. So if you have a `DateTimeOffset` that you wish to display, unless you want to show the time zone information in the user interface, you will most likely convert it to a `DateTime` that's relative to the local time zone, as Example 10-32 shows.

Example 10-32. Preparing to present a DateTimeOffset to the user

```
DateTimeOffset tmo = GetTimeFromSomewhere();
DateTime localDateTime = tmo.ToLocalTime().DateTime;
```

There are two benefits to this. First, this gets the time into a representation likely to align with how end users normally think of times, that is, relative to whatever time zone they're in right now. Second, `DateTime` makes formatting slightly easier than `DateTimeOffset`: `DateTimeOffset` supports the same `ToString` formats as `DateTime`, but `DateTime` offers some additional convenient methods.

First, `DateTime` offers an overload of the `ToString` method which can accept a range of standard format strings. Some of the more popular ones (such as `d`, the short date format, and `D`, the long date format) are also exposed as methods. Example 10-33 illustrates this.

Example 10-33. Showing the date in various formats

```
DateTime time = new DateTime(2001, 12, 24, 13, 14, 15, 16);
Console.WriteLine(time.ToString("d"));
Console.WriteLine(time.ToShortDateString());
Console.WriteLine(time.ToString("D"));
Console.WriteLine(time.ToLongDateString());
```

This produces:

```
12/24/2001
12/24/2001
24 December 2001
24 December 2001
```

There are also format strings and methods for the time part only, as Example 10-34 shows.

Example 10-34. Getting just the time

```
DateTime time = new DateTime(2001, 12, 24, 13, 14, 15, 16);
Console.WriteLine(time.ToString("t"));
Console.WriteLine(time.ToShortTimeString());
Console.WriteLine(time.ToString("T"));
Console.WriteLine(time.ToLongTimeString());
```

This will result in:

```
13:14
13:14
13:14:15
13:14:15
```

Or, as Example 10-35 shows, you can combine the two.

Example 10-35. Getting both the time and date

```
DateTime time = new DateTime(2001, 12, 24, 13, 14, 15, 16);
Console.WriteLine(time.ToString("g"));
Console.WriteLine(time.ToString("G"));
Console.WriteLine(time.ToString("f"));
Console.WriteLine(time.ToString("F"));
```

Notice how the upper- and lowercase versions of all these standard formats are used to choose between the short and long time formats:

```
24/12/2001 13:14
24/12/2001 13:14:15
24 December 2001 13:14
24 December 2001 13:14:15
```

Another common format is the "round trip" shown in Example 10-36. As for the numeric types, this is designed for scenarios where you expect to convert both to and from strings, without loss of precision.

Example 10-36. Round-trip DateTime format

```
DateTime time = new DateTime(2001, 12, 24, 13, 14, 15, 16);
Console.WriteLine(time.ToString("O"));
```

This produces:

```
2001-12-24T13:14:15.0160000
```

(If you use a `DateTimeOffset`, this last format will add the time zone on the end; for example, +01:00 would indicate that the time is from a zone one hour ahead of UTC.) This round-trip format is sortable using standard string precedence rules. Another format with that characteristic is the universal sortable form, shown in Example 10-37. This converts from local time to UTC before doing the format.

Example 10-37. Universal sortable format

```
DateTime time = new DateTime(2001, 12, 24, 13, 14, 15, 16);
Console.WriteLine(time.ToString("u"));
```

Because I am currently in the GMT time zone, and daylight saving is not in operation, I am at an offset of zero from UTC, so no apparent conversion takes place. But note the suffix Z which indicates a UTC time:

```
2001-12-24 13:14:15Z
```

 Dealing with dates and times is notoriously difficult, especially if you have to manage multiple time zones in a single application. There is no "silver bullet" solution. Even using `DateTimeOffset` internally and converting to local time for output is not necessarily a complete solution. You must beware of hidden problems like times that don't exist (because we skipped forward an hour when we applied daylight saving time), or exist twice (because we skipped back an hour when we left daylight saving time).

As with the numeric conversions, you also have the option of custom format strings.

The key components are:

d: day
M: month (note that this is uppercase to distinguish it from m for minute)
y: year
h: hour (12-hour format)
H: hour (24-hour format)
m: minute
s: seconds
f: fractions of a second

The / character will be substituted with the appropriate date separator for your locale, and : with the time separator.

You can repeat the substitution character to obtain shorter/longer forms of the relevant part of the date or time.

For example, you can format the day part like Example 10-38 does.

Example 10-38. Formatting the day

```
DateTime time = new DateTime(2001, 12, 24, 13, 14, 15, 16);
Console.WriteLine(time.ToString("dddd"));
Console.WriteLine(time.ToString("ddd"));
Console.WriteLine(time.ToString("dd"));
```

This will produce:

```
Monday
Mon
24
```

(As you saw in Example 10-33, a single d means something else: it shows the whole date, in short form.) Other useful formatting characters include:

z: offset from UTC (with zzz providing hours and minutes)
tt: the a.m./p.m. designator

As with the numeric formats, you can also include string literals, escaping special characters in the usual way.

Going the Other Way: Converting Strings to Other Types

Now that we know how to control the formatting of various types when we convert them to a string, let's take a step aside for a moment to look at converting back. If we've got a string, how do we convert that to a numeric type, for instance?

Probably the easiest way is to use the static methods on the `Convert` class, as Example 10-39 shows.

Example 10-39. Converting a string to an int

```
int converted = Convert.ToInt32("35");
```

This class also supports numeric conversions from a variety of different bases (specifically 2, 8, 10, and 16), shown in Example 10-40.

Example 10-40. Converting hexadecimal strings to ints

```
int converted = Convert.ToInt32("35", 16);
int converted = Convert.ToInt32("0xFF", 16);
```

Although we get to specify the base as a number, only binary, octal, decimal, and hexadecimal are actually supported. If you request any other base (e.g., 7) the method will throw an `ArgumentException`.

What happens if we pass a string that doesn't represent an instance of the type to which we want to convert, as Example 10-41 does?

Example 10-41. Attempting to convert a nonnumeric string to a number

```
double converted = Convert.ToDouble("Well, what do you think?");
```

As this string cannot be converted to a double, we see a `FormatException`.

Throwing (and catching) exceptions is a relatively expensive operation, and sometimes we want to try a particular conversion, then, if it fails, try another. We'd rather not pay for the exception if we don't have to.

Fortunately, the individual numeric types (and `DateTime`) give us the means to do this. Instead of using `Convert`, we can use the various `TryParse` methods they provide.

Rather than returning the parsed value, it returns a bool which indicates whether the parse was successful. The parsed value is retrieved via an `out` parameter. Example 10-42 shows that in use.

Example 10-42. Avoiding exceptions with TryParse

```
int parsed;
if (!int.TryParse("Well, how about that", out parsed))
{
    Console.WriteLine("That didn't parse");
}
```

For each of the `TryParse` methods, there is an equivalent `Parse`, which throws a `FormatException` on failure and returns the parsed value on success. For many applications, you can use these as an alternative to the `Convert` methods.

Some parse methods can also offer you additional control over the process. `DateTime.ParseExact`, for example, allows you to provide an exact format specification for the date/time string, as Example 10-43 shows.

Example 10-43. DateTime.ParseExact

```
DateTime dt =
    DateTime.ParseExact("12^04^2008","dd^MM^yyyy",CultureInfo.CurrentCulture);
```

This can be useful if you expect a nonstandard format for your string, coming from a legacy system, perhaps.

Composite Formatting with String.Format

The previous examples have all turned exactly one piece of information into a single string (or vice versa). Very often, though, we need to compose multiple pieces of information into our final output string, with different conversions for each part. We could do that by composing strings (something we'll look at later in this chapter), but it is often more convenient to use a helper method: `String.Format`. Example 10-44 shows a basic example.

Example 10-44. Basic use of String.Format

```
int val1 = 32;
double val2 = 123.457;
DateTime val3 = new DateTime(1999, 11, 1, 17, 22, 25);
string formattedString = String.Format("Val1: {0}, Val2: {1}, Val3: {2}",
                                        val1, val2, val3);
Console.WriteLine(formattedString);
```

This method takes a format string, plus a variable number of additional parameters. Those additional parameters are substituted into the format string where indicated by a *format item*. At its simplest, a format item is just an index into the additional parameter array, enclosed in braces (e.g., {0}). The preceding code will therefore produce the following output:

```
Val1: 32, Val2: 123.457, Val3: 01/11/1999 17:22:25
```

A specific format item can be referenced multiple times, and in any order in the format string. You can also apply the standard and custom formatting we discussed earlier to any of the individual format items. Example 10-45 shows that in action.

Example 10-45. Using format strings from String.Format

```
int first = 32;
double second = 123.457;
DateTime third = new DateTime(1999, 11, 1, 17, 22, 25);
```

```
string output = String.Format(
    "Date: {2:d}, Time: {2:t}, Val1: {0}, Val2: {1:#.##}",
    first, second, third);
Console.WriteLine(output);
```

Notice the colon after the index, followed by the simple or custom formatting string, which transforms the output:

```
Date: 01/11/1999, Time: 17:22, Val1: 32, Val2: 123.46
```

`String.Format` is a very powerful technique, but you should be aware that there is some overhead in its use with value types. The additional parameters take the form of an array of objects (so that we can pass in any type for each format item). This means that the values passed in are boxed, and then unboxed. For many applications this overhead will be irrelevant, but, as always, you should measure and be aware of the hidden cost.

Culture Sensitivity

Up to this point, we've quietly ignored a significantly complicating factor in string manipulation: the fact that the rules for text vary considerably among cultures.

There are also lots of different types of rules in operation, from the characters to use for particular types of separators, to the natural sorting order for characters and strings. I've already called out an example where the output on my UK English machine was different from that on a U.S. English computer. As another very simple example, the decimal number we write as 1.8 in U.S. or UK English would be written 1,8 in French. For the .NET Framework, these rules are encapsulated in an object of the type `System.Globalization.CultureInfo`.

The `CultureInfo` class makes certain commonly used cultures accessible through static properties. `CurrentCulture` returns the default culture, used by all the culture-sensitive methods if you don't supply a specific culture to a suitable overload. This value can be controlled on a per-thread basis, and defaults to the Windows default user locale. Another per-thread value is the `CurrentUICulture`. By default, this is based on the current user's personally selected preferred language, falling back on the operating system default if the user hasn't selected anything. This culture determines which resources the system uses when looking up localized resources such as strings.

 `CurrentCulture` and `CurrentUICulture` may sound very similar, but are often different. For example, Microsoft does not provide a version of Windows translated into British English—Windows offers British users "Favorites" and "Colors" despite a national tendency to spell those words as "Favourites" and "Colours." But we do have the option to ask for UK conventions for dates and currency, in which case `CurrentCulture` and `CurrentUICulture` will be British English and U.S. English, respectively.

Finally, it's sometimes useful to ensure that your code always behaves the same way, regardless of the user's culture settings. For example, if you're formatting (or parsing) text for persistent storage, you might need to read the text on a machine configured for a culture other than that on which it was created, and you will want to ensure that it is interpreted correctly. If you rely on the current culture, dates written out on a UK machine will be processed incorrectly on U.S. machines because the month and day are reversed. (In the UK, 3/12/2010 is a date in December.) The `InvariantCulture` property returns a culture with rules which will not vary with different installed or user-selected cultures.

 If you've been looking at the IntelliSense as we've been building the string format examples in this chapter, you might have noticed that none of the obviously culture-sensitive methods seem to offer an overload which takes a `CultureInfo`. However, on closer examination, you'll notice that `CultureInfo` also implements the `IFormatProvider` interface. All of the formatting methods we've looked at *do* provide an overload which takes an instance of an object which implements `IFormatProvider`. Problem solved!

You can also create a `CultureInfo` object for a specific culture, by providing that culture's canonical name to the `CreateSpecificCulture` method on the `CultureInfo` object.

But what are the canonical names? You may have come across some of them in the past. UK English, for instance, is `en-GB`, and French is `fr`. Example 10-46 gets a list of all the known canonical names by calling another method on `CultureInfo` that lists all the cultures the system knows about: `GetCultures`.

Example 10-46. Showing available cultures

```
var cultures = CultureInfo.GetCultures(CultureTypes.AllCultures).
                          OrderBy(c => c.EnglishName);
foreach (var culture in cultures)
{
    Console.WriteLine("{0} : {1}", culture.EnglishName, culture.Name);
}
```

We won't reproduce the output here, because it is a bit long. This is a short excerpt:

```
English (United Kingdom) : en-GB
English (United States) : en-US
English (Zimbabwe) : en-ZW
Estonian : et
Estonian (Estonia) : et-EE
Faroese : fo
Faroese (Faroe Islands) : fo-FO
Filipino : fil
Filipino (Philippines) : fil-PH
Finnish : fi
Finnish (Finland) : fi-FI
French : fr
```

Notice that we're showing the English version of the name, followed by the canonical name for the culture.

Example 10-47 illustrates a difference in string formatting between two different cultures.

Example 10-47. Formatting numbers for different cultures

```
CultureInfo englishUS = CultureInfo.CreateSpecificCulture("en-US");
CultureInfo french = CultureInfo.CreateSpecificCulture("fr");

double value = 1.8;

Console.WriteLine(value.ToString(englishUS));
Console.WriteLine(value.ToString(french));
```

This will produce the output we'd expect:

```
1.8
1,8
```

Exploring Formatting Rules

If you look at the `CultureInfo` class, you'll see numerous properties, some of which define the culture's rules for formatting particular kinds of information. For example, there are the `DateTimeFormat` and `NumberFormat` properties. These are instances of `Date TimeFormatInfo` and `NumberFormatInfo`, respectively, and expose a large number of properties with which you can control the formatting rules for the relevant types.

These types also implement `IFormatProvider`, so you can use these types to provide your own custom formatting rules to the string formatting methods we looked at earlier. Example 10-48 formats a number in an unusual way.

Example 10-48. Modifying the decimal separator

```
double value = 1.8;
NumberFormatInfo nfi = new NumberFormatInfo();
nfi.NumberDecimalSeparator = "^";

Console.WriteLine(value.ToString(nfi));
```

Here we use the `NumberFormatInfo` to change the decimal separator to the circumflex (hat) symbol. The resultant output is:

```
1^8
```

You can use this to control all sorts of features of the formatting engine, such as the default precision, percentage and positive/negative symbols, and separators.

Now that we know how to format strings of various kinds, we'll go back to looking at some of the features of the string itself. In particular, we'll look at how to slice and dice an existing string in various ways.

Accessing Characters by Index

Earlier, we saw how to enumerate the characters in a string; however, we often want to be able to retrieve a character at a particular offset into the string. `String` defines an *indexer*, so we can do just that. Example 10-49 uses the indexer to retrieve the character at a particular (zero-based) index in the string.

Example 10-49. Retrieving characters with a string's indexer

```
string myString = "Indexing";
char theThirdCharacter = myString[2];
Console.WriteLine(theThirdCharacter);
```

If you execute that code in a console application, you'll see:

```
d
```

What if we try to use the indexer to assign a value (i.e., to replace the character at that location in the string) as in Example 10-50?

Example 10-50. Trying to assign a value with a string's indexer

```
string myString = "Indexing";
myString[2] = 'f';  // Will fail to compile
```

Well, that doesn't compile. We get an error:

```
Property or indexer 'string.this[int]' cannot be assigned to -- it is read only
```

So, the indexer is read-only. This is a part of a very important constraint on a `String` object.

Strings Are Immutable

Once a string has been created, it is *immutable*. You can't slice it up into substrings, trim characters off it, add characters to it, or replace one character or substring with another.

"What?" I hear you ask. "Then how are we supposed to do our string processing?" Don't worry, you can still do all of those things, but they don't affect the original string—copies (of the relevant pieces) are made instead.

Why did the designers of the .NET Framework make strings immutable? All that copying is surely going to be an overhead. Well, yes, it is, and sometimes you need to be aware of it.

That being said, there are balancing performance *improvements* when dealing with unchanging strings. The framework can store a single instance of a string and then any variables that reference that particular sequence of characters can reference the same instance. This can actually save on allocations and reduce your working set. And in multithreaded scenarios, the fact that strings never change means it's safe to use them without the cross-thread coordination that is required when accessing modifiable data. As usual, "performance" considerations are largely a compromise between the competing needs of various possible scenarios.

In our view, an overridingly persuasive argument for immutability relates to the safe use of strings as keys. Consider the code in Example 10-51.

Example 10-51. Using strings as keys in a dictionary

```
string myKey = "TheUniqueKey";
Dictionary<string, object> myDictionary = new Dictionary<string, object>();

myDictionary.Add(myKey, new object());

// Imagine you could do this...
myKey[2] = 'o';
```

Remember, a string is a reference type, so the `myKey` variable references a string object which is initialized to `"TheUniqueKey"`. When we add our object to the dictionary, we pass a reference to that same string object, which the dictionary will use as a key. If you cast your mind back to Chapter 9, you'll remember that the dictionary relies on the hash code for the key object when storing dictionary entries, which can then be disambiguated (if necessary) by the actual value of the key itself.

Now, imagine that we *could* modify the original string object, using the reference we hold in that `myKey` variable. One characteristic of a (useful!) hash algorithm is that its output changes for any change in the original data. So all of a sudden our key's hash code has changed. The hash for `"TheUniqueKey"` is different from the one for `"ThoUnique Key"`. Sadly, the dictionary has no way of knowing that the hash for that key has changed; so, when we come to look up the value using our original reference to our key, it will no longer find a match.

This can (and does!) cause all sorts of subtle bugs in applications built on runtimes that allow mutable strings. But since .NET strings are immutable, this problem cannot occur if you use strings as keys.

Another, related, benefit is that you avoid the buffer-overrun issues so prevalent on other runtimes. Because you can't modify an existing string, you can't accidentally run over the end of your allocation and start stamping on other memory, causing crashes at best and security holes at worst. Of course, immutable strings are not the only way the .NET designers could have addressed this problem, but they do offer a very simple solution that helps the developer fall naturally into doing the right thing, without having to think about it. We think that this is a very neat piece of design.

So, we can obtain (i.e., read) a character at a particular index in the string, using the square-bracket indexer syntax. What about slicing and dicing the string in other ways?

Getting a Range of Characters

You can obtain a contiguous range of characters within a string by using the Substring method. There are a couple of overloads of this method, and Example 10-52 shows them in action.

Example 10-52. Using Substring

```
string myString = "This is the silliest stuff that ere I heard.";
string subString = myString.Substring(5);
string anotherSubString = myString.Substring(12, 8);
Console.WriteLine(subString);
Console.WriteLine(anotherSubString);
```

Notice that both of these overloads return a new string, containing the relevant portion of the original string. The first overload starts with the character at the specified index, and returns the rest of the string (regardless of how long it might be). The second starts at the specified index, and returns as many characters as are requested.

A very common requirement is to get the last few characters from a string. Many platforms have this as a built-in function, or feature of their strings, but the .NET Framework leaves you to do it yourself. To do so depends on us knowing how many characters there are in the string, subtracting the offset from the end, and using that as our starting index, as Example 10-53 shows.

Example 10-53. Getting characters from the righthand end of a string

```
static string Right(string s, int length)
{
    int startIndex = s.Length - length;
    return s.Substring(startIndex);
}
```

Notice how we're using the Length property on the string to determine the total number of characters in the string, and then returning the substring from that offset (to the end). We could then use this method to take the last six characters of our string, as Example 10-54 does.

Example 10-54. Using our Right method

```
string myString =
    "This is the silliest stuff that ere I heard.";
string subString = Right(myString, 6);
Console.WriteLine(subString);
```

If you build and run this sample, you'll see the following output:

```
heard.
```

Extension Methods for String

You will probably build up an armory of useful methods for dealing with strings. It can be helpful to aggregate them together into a set of extension methods.

Here's an example implementing the `Right` method that we've used as an example in this chapter, but modifying it to work as an extension method, and also providing an equivalent to the version of `Substring` that takes both a start position and a length:

```
public static class StringExtensions
{
    public static string Right(this string s,
                               int length)
    {
        int startIndex = s.Length - length;
        return s.Substring(startIndex);
    }

    public static string Right(this string s,
                               int offset, int length)
    {
        int startIndex = s.Length - offset;
        return s.Substring(startIndex, length);
    }
}
```

By implementing them as extension methods, we can now write code like this:

```
string myString =
        "This is the silliest stuff that ere I heard.";
string subString = myString.Right(6);
string subString2 = myString.Right(6, 5);
Console.WriteLine(subString);
Console.WriteLine(subString2);
```

This will produce output like the following:

```
heard.
heard
```

Notice that the `Length` of the string is the total number of *characters* in the string—much as the length of an array is the total number of entities in the array, not the number of bytes allocated to it (for example).

Composing Strings

You can create a new string by composing one or more other strings. Example 10-55 shows one way to do this.

Example 10-55. Concatenating strings

```
string fragment1 = "To be, ";
string fragment2 = "or not to be.";
string composedString = fragment1 + fragment2;
Console.WriteLine(composedString);
```

Here, we've used the + operator to *concatenate* two strings. The C# compiler turns this into a call to the `String` class's static method `Concat`, so Example 10-56 shows the equivalent code.

Example 10-56. Calling String.Concat explicitly

```
string composedString2 = String.Concat(fragment1, fragment2);
Console.WriteLine(composedString2);
```

 Don't forget—we're taking the first two strings, and then creating a new string that is `fragment1.Length` + `fragment2.Length` characters long. The original strings remain unchanged.

There are several overloads of `Concat`, all taking various numbers of strings—this enables you to concatenate multiple strings in a single step without producing intermediate strings. One of the overloads, used in Example 10-57, can concatenate an entire array of strings.

Example 10-57. Concatenating an array of strings

```
static void Main(string[] args)
{
    string[] strings = Soliloquize();
    string output = String.Concat(strings);
    Console.WriteLine(output);
    Console.ReadKey();
}

private static string[] Soliloquize()
{
    return new string[] {
        "To be, or not to be--that is the question:",
        "Whether 'tis nobler in the mind to suffer",
        "The slings and arrows of outrageous fortune",
        "Or to take arms against a sea of troubles",
        "And by opposing end them." };
}
```

If we build and run that example, we'll see some output like this:

```
To be, or not to be--that is the question:Whether 'tis nobler in the mind to suf
ferThe slings and arrows of outrageous fortuneOr to take arms against a sea of t
roublesAnd by opposing end them.
```

That's probably not quite what we meant. We've been provided with each line of Hamlet's soliloquy, and we really want the single output string to have breaks after each line.

Instead of using `String.Concat`, we can instead use `String.Join` to concatenate all of the strings as shown in Example 10-58. This lets us insert the string of our choice between each string.

Example 10-58. String.Join

```
static void Main(string[] args)
{
    string[] strings = Soliloquize();
    string output = String.Join(Environment.NewLine, strings);
    Console.WriteLine(output);
    Console.ReadKey();
}
```

Here we're using the `Environment.NewLine` constant to get the line-break string appropriate for our platform (rather than explicitly using "\n" or "\r" or "\r\n").

 For historical reasons, not all operating systems use the same sequence of characters to represent the end of a line. Windows (like DOS before it) mimics old-fashioned printers, where you had to send two control characters: a *carriage return* (ASCII value 13, or \r in a string or character literal) would cause the print head to move back to the beginning of the line, and then a *line feed* (ASCII 10, or \n) would advance the paper up by one line. This meant you could send a text file directly to a printer without modification and it would print correctly, but it produced the slightly clumsy situation of requiring two characters to denote the end of a line. Unix conventionally uses just a single line feed to mark the end of a line. `Environment.NewLine` is offered so that you don't have to assume that you're running on a particular platform. That being said, `Console` is flexible, and treats either convention as a line end. But this can matter if you're saving files to disk.

If we build and run, we'll see the following output:

```
To be, or not to be--that is the question:
Whether 'tis nobler in the mind to suffer
The slings and arrows of outrageous fortune
Or to take arms against a sea of troubles
And by opposing end them.
```

Splitting It Up Again

As well as joining text up, we can also split it up into smaller pieces at a particular breaking string or character. For example, we could split the final concatenated string back up at whitespace or punctuation as in Example 10-59.

Example 10-59. Splitting a string

```
string[] strings = Soliloquize();
string output = String.Join(Environment.NewLine, strings);

string[] splitStrings = output.Split(
    new char[] { ' ', '\t', '\r', '\n', ',', '-', ':' });

bool first = true;
```

```
foreach (string splitBit in splitStrings)
{
    if( first )
    {
        first = false;
    }
    else
    {
        Console.Write(", ");
    }
    Console.Write(splitBit);
}
```

If we run again, we see the following output:

```
To, be, , or, not, to, be, , that, is, the, question, , , Whether, 'tis, nobler,
 in, the, mind, to, suffer, , The, slings, and, arrows, of, outrageous, fortune,
 , Or, to, take, arms, against, a, sea, of, troubles, , And, by, opposing, end,
them.
```

Notice how our separation characters were not included in the final output, but we do seem to have some "blanks" (which are showing up here as multiple commas in a row with nothing in between). These empty entries occur when you have multiple consecutive separation characters, and, most often, you would rather not have to deal with them. The `Split` method offers an overload that takes an additional parameter of type `StringSplitOptions`, shown in Example 10-60, which lets us eliminate these empty entries.

Example 10-60. Eliminating empty strings in String.Split

```
string[] splitStrings = output.Split(
    new char[] { ' ', '\t', '\r', '\n', ',', '-', ':' },
    StringSplitOptions.RemoveEmptyEntries);
```

Our output is now the more manageable:

```
To, be, or, not, to, be, that, is, the, question, Whether, 'tis, nobler, in, the
, mind, to, suffer, The, slings, and, arrows, of, outrageous, fortune, Or, to, t
ake, arms, against, a, sea, of, troubles, And, by, opposing, end, them.
```

Upper- and Lowercase

Some of the words in that output list originally appeared at the beginning of a line, and therefore have an initial uppercase letter, while others were in the body of a line, and are therefore entirely lowercase. In our output, it might be nicer if we represented them all consistently (in lower case, for example).

This is easily achieved with the `ToUpper` and `ToLower` members of `String`. We can change our output line to the code shown in Example 10-61.

Example 10-61. Forcing strings to lowercase

```
Console.Write(splitBit.ToLower());
```

Our output is now consistently lowercase:

```
to, be, or, not, to, be, that, is, the, question, whether, 'tis, nobler, in, the
, mind, to, suffer, the, slings, and, arrows, of, outrageous, fortune, or, to, t
ake, arms, against, a, sea, of, troubles, and, by, opposing, end, them.
```

 Upper- and lowercase rules vary considerably among cultures, and you should be cautious when using ToUpper and ToLower for this purpose. For culture-insensitive scenarios, there are also methods called ToUpper Invariant and ToLowerInvariant whose results are not affected by the current culture. MSDN provides a considerable amount of resources devoted to culture-sensitive string operations. A good starting point can be found here:

http://msdn.microsoft.com/en-us/library/5bz7d2f8

Manipulating Text

The result of the preceding section was nice and neat; but what if our array of strings had come from a user? Users have a tendency to whack the Return key a few times before they write anything at all, and add spurious spaces and tabs to the beginning and end of lines, particularly when copying and pasting between applications. They might also add commas or periods or something like that, again in the interest of tidiness. They might spell things incorrectly. There's no accounting for what users might do. Let's simulate that with a new function shown in Example 10-62.

Example 10-62. Simulating messy input

```
private static string[] SoliloquizeLikeAUser()
{
    return new string[] {
        "",
        null,
        "   ",
        String.Empty,
        "    To be, or not to be--that is the question: ",
        "Whether 'tis nobelr in the mind to suffer,",
        "\tThe slings and arrows of outrageous fortune ,",
        "",
        "\tOr to take arms against a sea of troubles, ",
        "And by opposing end them.",
        "",
        "",
        "",
        "",
        ""};
}
```

Notice their extensive use of the Return key, the tendency to put the odd comma at the end of the line, and the occasional whack of the Tab key at the beginning of lines.

Sadly, if we use this function and then print the output using `String.Concat` like we did in Example 10-57, we end up with output like this:

```
        To be, or not to be--that is the question:
    Whether 'tis nobelr in the mind to suffer,
            The slings and arrows of outrageous fortune ,
            Or to take arms against a sea of troubles,
    And by opposing end them.
```

We can write some code to tidy this up. We can build up our output string, concatenating the various strings, and cleaning it up as we go. This is going to involve iterating through our array of strings, inspecting them, perhaps transforming them, and then appending them to our resultant string. Example 10-63 shows how we could structure this, although it does not yet include any of the actual cleanup code.

Example 10-63. Cleaning up input

```
string[] strings = SoliloquizeLikeAUser();
string output = String.Empty; // This is equivalent to ""
foreach (string line in strings)
{
    // Do something to look at the line...
    // then...
    output = output + line + Environment.NewLine;
}
Console.WriteLine(output);
```

This would work just fine; but look at what happens every time we go round the loop. We create a new string and store a reference to it in `output`, throwing away whatever was in `output` before. That's potentially very wasteful of resources, if we do this a lot.

Fortunately, the .NET Framework provides us with another type we can use for precisely these circumstances: `StringBuilder`.

Mutable Strings with StringBuilder

Having said that a `String` is immutable, we are now going to look at a class that is very, very much like a string, and yet it can be modified. Example 10-64 shows it in action.

Example 10-64. Building up strings with StringBuilder

```
string[] strings = SoliloquizeLikeAUser();
StringBuilder output = new StringBuilder();
foreach (string line in strings)
{
    // Do something to look at the line...
    // then...
    output.AppendLine(line);
}
Console.WriteLine(output.ToString());
```

After we've retrieved our array of strings, we create an (empty) instance of a `StringBuilder`. For each string in our array, we then call the `AppendLine` method to append the string, along with a suitable line-end character. Notice that we don't keep creating new instances of the `StringBuilder` as we go along. Instead, it automatically handles the job of allocating an appropriate amount of internal storage and appending each new string we pass it.

When we construct the `StringBuilder`, it allocates a chunk of memory in which we can build the string—initially it allocates enough space for 16 characters. If we append something that would make the string too long to fit, it allocates a new chunk of memory. Crucially, it allocates more than it needs, the idea being to have enough spare space to satisfy a few more appends without needing to allocate yet another chunk of memory. The precise details of the allocation strategy are not documented, but we'll see it in action shortly.

In an ideal world, we would avoid overallocating, *and* avoid repeatedly having to allocate more space. If we have some way of knowing in advance how long the final string will be, we can do this, because we can specify the initial capacity of the `StringBuilder` in its constructor. Example 10-65 illustrates the effect.

Example 10-65. Capacity versus Length

```
StringBuilder builder1 = new StringBuilder();
StringBuilder builder2 = new StringBuilder(1024);

Console.WriteLine(builder1.Capacity);
Console.WriteLine(builder1.Length);

Console.WriteLine(builder2.Capacity);
Console.WriteLine(builder1.Length);
```

This would produce the output:

```
16
0
1024
0
```

Notice how we're using the `Capacity` to see how many characters we *could* have in the `StringBuilder`, and the `Length` to determine how many we *do* have. We can now append some content to these two strings, as Example 10-66 shows.

Example 10-66. Exploring capacity

```
StringBuilder builder1 = new StringBuilder();
StringBuilder builder2 = new StringBuilder(1024);

Console.WriteLine(builder1.Capacity);
Console.WriteLine(builder1.Length);
Console.WriteLine(builder2.Capacity);
Console.WriteLine(builder2.Length);

builder1.Append('A', 24);
builder2.Append('A', 24);

Console.WriteLine(builder1.Capacity);
Console.WriteLine(builder1.Length);
Console.WriteLine(builder2.Capacity);
Console.WriteLine(builder2.Length);
```

We're using a different overload of the `Append` method on `StringBuilder`. This one takes a `char` as its first parameter, and then a repeat count. So, in each case, we append a string with 24 As.

If we run this, we get the output:

```
16
0
1024
0
32
24
1024
24
```

The first four lines are the same as before, but now we see that the capacity of the first `StringBuilder` has increased to 32 characters, and the string it holds is 24 characters long. The second `StringBuilder` has retained its capacity of 1,024 characters, because that was plenty to hold the 24 characters we appended.

What if we append another 12 characters to that first `StringBuilder`, as Example 10-67 shows?

Example 10-67. Appending more text

```
builder1.Append('B', 12);
Console.WriteLine(builder1.Capacity);
Console.WriteLine(builder1.Length);
```

The additional two lines of output look like this:

```
64
36
```

We've gone from a capacity of 16 to 32 to 64 characters. OK; can you guess what happens if we append another 30 characters (to push ourselves over the 64-character limit) as Example 10-68 does?

Example 10-68. Appending yet more text

```
builder1.Append('C', 30);
Console.WriteLine(builder1.Capacity);
Console.WriteLine(builder1.Length);
```

Yup, the last two lines of output now read:

```
128
66
```

There is a geometric progression—the capacity is doubling each time we exceed its previous capacity. It does this in an attempt to minimize the amount of allocation it has to do, but in order to prevent things from getting totally out of hand, overallocation will never grow the capacity by more than 8,000 characters (in the current version of the framework, at least). Of course, if you append a string that is longer than 8,000 characters, `StringBuilder` will have to allocate enough space, but it won't overallocate in that case.

 You may have noticed that in the preceding examples, the `String Builder` had to reallocate each time we called `Append`. How is that any better than just appending strings? Well, it isn't, but that's only because we deliberately contrived the examples to show what happens when you exceed the capacity. You won't usually see such optimally bad behavior—in practice, you'll see fewer allocations than appends.

If we know we're going to need a particular amount of space, we can manually ensure that the builder has appropriate capacity, as shown in Example 10-69.

Example 10-69. Ensuring capacity

```
builder1.EnsureCapacity(32000);
Console.WriteLine(builder1.Capacity);
Console.WriteLine(builder1.Length);
```

The last two lines of output indicate that it has complied with our wishes:

```
32000
66
```

What if we then call `EnsureCapacity` with a smaller number? Example 10-70 tries to do this.

Example 10-70. Attempting to reduce capacity

```
builder1.EnsureCapacity(70);
Console.WriteLine(builder1.Capacity);
Console.WriteLine(builder1.Length);
```

Here's the output:

```
32000
66
```

Nope—it doesn't reduce the capacity. `EnsureCapacity` only guarantees that the capacity is *at least* what you ask for, so it does nothing if there's more than you need.

OK, so `StringBuilder` is going to accumulate the string for us, making sure there's enough space as we go along. What about finishing off the method we were writing so that it tidies up that user input as it goes along?

The first thing we'd like to do is to correct that mistake where the user seems to have misspelled "nobler" as "nobelr".

Finding and Replacing Content

Find-and-replace is a very common requirement when processing strings. Fortunately, the .NET Framework provides us with a couple of options.

If we just want to find a piece of text we can use one of several overloads of the `IndexOf` method. This takes some text for which to look, and an index at which to start looking. By calling the method repeatedly, using the last index returned as the basis of the start index for the next search, we can find all instances of the relevant text in the input string, as Example 10-71 shows.

Example 10-71. Searching for text

```
string inputString =
    "If a dog and a man go into a bar, " +
    "is it necessarily the beginning of a joke?";
int index = -1;
do
{
    index += 1;
    index = inputString.IndexOf(" a ", index);
    Console.WriteLine(index);
}
while (index >= 0);
```

This produces the output:

```
2
12
26
68
-1
```

Notice how the method returns -1 when it cannot find a further match.

That's finding content. What we really want to be able to do is to replace content, though. As you might expect, `string` also offers us a `Replace` function, which is shown in Example 10-72.

Example 10-72. Replacing text

```
string original = "Original text.";
string replaced = original.Replace("Original", "Replaced");
Console.WriteLine(original);
Console.WriteLine(replaced);
```

This takes any match for the first parameter found in the source, and replaces it with the text in the second parameter. In this case, the output looks like this:

```
Original text.
Replaced text.
```

As you know, strings are immutable, so `Replace` creates a new string containing our substitutions.

`Replace` offers no control over how many replacements to make, and from where to start the replacement; both of these are common requirements in text processing. Fortunately, `StringBuilder` has a family of `Replace` methods which address all of these issues, performing an in-place replace with optional start index and number of replacements to make.

Remember that we had the code shown in Example 10-73.

Example 10-73. Code from earlier for tidying up the text

```
string[] strings = SoliloquizeLikeAUser();
StringBuilder output = new StringBuilder();
foreach (string line in strings)
{
    // Do something to look at the line...
    // then...
    output.AppendLine(line);
}
Console.WriteLine(output.ToString());
```

We can now add our replacement line, by adding the code in Example 10-74 just before the final output to the console.

Example 10-74. Fixing a specific typo

```
output.Replace("nobelr", "nobler");
Console.WriteLine(output.ToString());
```

The relevant line now appears without the spelling error:

```
Whether 'tis nobler in the mind to suffer
```

OK, the next thing we'd like to do is to ignore completely blank lines.

All Sorts of "Empty" Strings

Let's start by leaving out lines that have no content at all. There's a special constant for the empty string; we saw it earlier: `String.Empty`. Let's see what happens if we use the code in Example 10-75, which writes the line to the console only if it is not equal to `String.Empty`.

Example 10-75. Detecting empty strings

```
foreach (string line in strings)
{
    if (line != String.Empty)
    {
        output.AppendLine(line);
    }
    else
    {
        System.Diagnostics.Debug.WriteLine("Found a blank line");
    }
}
```

You might be wondering exactly how string comparisons are performed. Some languages base string comparison on object identity so that `"Abc"` is not equal to a different string object that also contains `"Abc"`. (That may seem weird, but in one sense it's consistent: comparing reference types always means asking "do these two variables refer to the same thing?") But in C#, when you have distinct string objects, it performs a "character-like" comparison between strings, so any two strings containing the same sequence of characters are equal. This is different from how most reference types work, but by treating strings as a special case, the result is closer to what most people would expect. (Or at least to what most people who hadn't already become accustomed to the oddities of another language might expect.)

 Because not all languages use by-value string comparison, the .NET Framework supports the by-identity style too. Consequently, you get by-value comparison only if the C# compiler knows it's dealing with strings. If you store two strings in variables of type `object`, the C# compiler loses track of the fact that they are strings, so if you compare these variables with the `==` operator, it doesn't know it should provide the string-specific by-value comparison, and will instead do the default by-identity comparison you get for most reference types.

For the sake of working out what is going on, we're also writing a message to the debug output each time we find a blank line.

If we build and run, the output to the console looks like this:

```
    To be, or not to be--that is the question:
  Whether 'tis nobelr in the mind to suffer,
        The slings and arrows of outrageous fortune ,
```

```
        Or to take arms against a sea of troubles,
    And by opposing end them.
```

The debug output indicates that the code found and removed eight blank lines. (If you can't see the Output panel in Visual Studio, you can show it with the View→Output menu item. Ensure that the "Show output from" drop down has Debug selected.) But apparently it missed some, judging by the output.

So which are the eight "blank" lines—that is, the lines that are the equivalent of `String.Empty`? If you single-step through the debugger, you'll see that they are the ones that look like "" and `String.Empty`.

The ones that contain just whitespace account for some of the remaining blanks in the output. While visibly blank, these are clearly not "empty"—they contain whitespace characters. We'll deal with that in a minute. The other line that looks "empty" but isn't is the `null` string.

As we said earlier, strings are reference types. There is, therefore, a considerable difference between a null reference to a string, and an empty string, as far as the .NET runtime is concerned. However, a lot of applications don't care about this distinction, so it can sometimes be useful to treat a null string in much the same way as an empty string. The `String` class offers a static method that lets us test for nullness-or-emptiness with a single call, which Example 10-76 uses.

Example 10-76. Testing for either blank or null

```
foreach (string line in strings)
{
    if (!String.IsNullOrEmpty(line))
    {
        output.AppendLine(line);
    }
    else
    {
        System.Diagnostics.Debug.WriteLine("Found a blank line");
    }
}
```

Notice we have to use the ! operator, as the static method returns `true` if the string *is* null or empty. Our output is now stripped of "blank" lines except the one that contains just whitespace. If you check the debug output panel, you'll see that nine lines have been ignored:

```
    To be, or not to be--that is the question:
Whether 'tis nobelr in the mind to suffer,
        The slings and arrows of outrageous fortune ,
        Or to take arms against a sea of troubles,
    And by opposing end them.
```

So, what can we do about that remaining blank line at the start? We can deal with this by stripping out spurious whitespace, and then looking to see whether anything is left.

Not only will this fix our blank-line problem, but it will also remove any whitespace that the user has left at the start and end of the line.

Trimming Whitespace

You often (but not always) want to trim whitespace from the beginning and/or end of a piece of text; especially user-provided text. When storing data in a SQL database, for example, it is frequently desirable to trim this whitespace.

With that in mind, the framework provides us with the `Trim`, `TrimStart`, and `TrimEnd` methods. Example 10-77 uses `Trim` to remove the whitespace at the start *and* end of every line.

Example 10-77. Trimming whitespace

```
foreach (string line in strings)
{
    if (line != null)
    {
        string trimmedLine = line.Trim();
        if (trimmedLine.Length != 0)
        {
            output.AppendLine(trimmedLine);
        }
        else
        {
            System.Diagnostics.Debug.WriteLine(
                "Found a blank line (after trimming)");
        }
    }
    else
    {
        System.Diagnostics.Debug.WriteLine("Found a null line");
    }
}
```

Notice how we're trimming the line once, and storing a reference to the result in a variable, then using that trimmed string in our subsequent tests. Because we're calling a method on our string instance, we need to test it for nullness *before* we do that, or we'll get a null reference exception. This means that we don't need to call `IsNullOr Empty` in our later test. We know that it cannot be null. Instead, we do a quick test for emptiness. It turns out that the most efficient way to do this is not to compare against `String.Empty` but to check the `Length` of our string.

If we build and run this, we see the following output:

```
To be, or not to be--that is the question:
Whether 'tis nobler in the mind to suffer,
The slings and arrows of outrageous fortune ,
Or to take arms against a sea of troubles,
And by opposing end them.
```

And in the output window:

```
Found a blank line (after trimming)
Found a null line
Found a blank line (after trimming)
Found a blank line (after trimming)
Found a blank line (after trimming)
Found a blank line (after trimming)
Found a blank line (after trimming)
Found a blank line (after trimming)
Found a blank line (after trimming)
```

You'll notice that `Trim` has successfully removed all the whitespace at the beginning and end of each line, both spaces and tab characters, but left the whitespace in the middle of the line alone.

`Trim` isn't limited to removing whitespace characters, though. Another overload allows us to specify the array of characters we want to trim from the beginning or end of the line. We could use this to get rid of those spurious commas, too, using the code in Example 10-78.

Example 10-78. Trimming specific characters

```
string trimmedLine = line.Trim(' ', '\t', ',');
```

This overload of `Trim` uses the parameter array syntax, so we can specify the characters we want to trim as a simple parameter list. In this case, we tell it to trim spaces, tabs, and commas.

Our output, then, looks like this:

```
To be, or not to be--that is the question:
Whether 'tis nobler in the mind to suffer
The slings and arrows of outrageous fortune
Or to take arms against a sea of troubles
And by opposing end them.
```

Of course, although the output is correct for this particular input, it isn't quite the same as the original `Trim` function—it isn't removing *all possible* whitespace characters, just the ones we happened to remember to list. There are a surprising number of different characters that represent whitespace—as well as your basic ordinary space, .NET recognizes a character for an *en space* (one the same width as the letter *N*), an *em space* (the same width as *M*), a *thin space*, and a *hair space*, to name just a few. There are more than 20 of the things!

Example 10-79 shows a function that will trim all whitespace, plus any additional characters we specify.

Example 10-79. Trimming any whitespace and specific additional characters

```
private static string TrimWhitespaceAnd(
    string inputString,
    params char[] characters)
```

```csharp
{
    int start = 0;
    while (start < inputString.Length)
    {
        // If it is neither whitespace nor a character from our list
        // then we've hit the first non-trimmable character, so we can stop
        if (!char.IsWhiteSpace(inputString[start]) &&
            !characters.Contains(inputString[start]))
        {
            break;
        }
        // Work forward a character
        start++;
    }
    // Work backwards from the end
    int end = inputString.Length -1;
    while (end >= start)
    {
        // If it is neither whitespace nor a character from our list
        // then we've hit the first non-trimmable character
        if (!char.IsWhiteSpace(inputString[end]) &&
            !characters.Contains(inputString[end]))
        {
            break;
        }
        // Work back a character
        end--;
    }
    // Work out how long our string is for the
    // substring function
    int length = (end - start) + 1;
    if (length == inputString.Length)
    {
        // If we didn't trim anything, just return the
        // input string (don't create a new one
        return inputString;
    }
    // If the length is zero, then return the empty string
    if (length == 0)
    {
        return string.Empty;
    }
    return inputString.Substring(start, length);
}
```

This method works by iterating through our string, examining each character and checking to see whether it should be trimmed. If so, then we increment the start position by one character, and check the next one, until we hit a character that should not be trimmed, or the end of the string. We then do the same thing starting from the end of the string, and reversing character by character until we reach the start point.

 If you wanted to write the equivalent of TrimStart or TrimEnd you would just optionally leave out the end or start checking, respectively.

Finally, we create our new output string, by using the Substring method we looked at earlier. Notice how we've avoided creating strings unnecessarily; we don't build up the results as we go along, and we don't create new strings in the "no change" and "empty" cases. (We could have written a much shorter function if we weren't worried about this: inputString.Trim().Trim(characters) would have done the whole job! However, with two calls to Trim, we end up generating two new strings instead of one. You'd need to measure your code's performance in realistic test scenarios to find out whether the more complex code in Example 10-79 is worth the effort. We're showing it mainly to illustrate how to dig around inside a string.)

The interesting new bit of code, though, is that char.IsWhitespace method.

Checking Character Types

We're generally familiar with the idea that characters might be numbers, letters, whitespace, or punctuation. This is formalized in the .NET Framework, and char provides us with a bunch of static helper functions to do the categorization for us.

Several are fairly self-explanatory:

IsWhitespace, IsLetter, IsDigit, IsLetterOrDigit, IsPunctuation

There are also a couple of useful items for testing whether a character is upper- or lowercase:

IsUpper, IsLower

Then there are a few less intuitively obvious items:

IsNumber (you might wonder whether there was a difference between this and IsDigit?)

IsSeparator, IsControl

IsHighSurrogate, IsLowSurrogate

Even the self-explanatory items turn out to be a little more complicated than you might think. These categories come from Unicode, and to understand that, we need to delve a little more deeply into the way that characters are encoded.

Encoding Characters

When we give a char variable the value 'A', what exactly is that value?

We've already alluded to the fact that there is some kind of encoding going on—remember that we mentioned the IBM-derived Latin1 scheme when we were discussing escaped character literals.

Computers work with binary values, typically made up of one or more bytes, and we clearly need some kind of mapping between the binary values in these bytes and the characters we want them to represent. We've all got to agree on what the binary values mean, or we can't exchange information. To that end, the American Standards Association convened a committee in the 1960s which defined (and then redefined, tweaked, and generally improved over subsequent decades) a standard called ASCII (pronounced ass‡-key): the American Standard Code for Information Interchange.

This defined 128 characters, represented using 7 bits of a byte. The first 32 values from 0x00–0x19, and also the very last value, 0x7F, are called *control characters*, and include things like the tab character (0x09), backspace (0x09), bell (0x07), and delete (0x7F).

The rest are called the *printable characters*, and include space (0x20), which is not a control character, but a "blank" printable character; all the upper and lowercase letters; and most of the punctuation marks in common use in English.

This was a start, but it rapidly became apparent that ASCII did not have enough characters to deal with a lot of the common Western ("Latin") scripts; the accented characters in French, or Spanish punctuation marks, for example. It also lacked common characters like the international copyright symbol ©, or the registered trademark symbol ®.

Since ASCII uses only 7 bits, and most computers use 8-bit bytes, the obvious solution was to put the necessary characters into byte values not used by ASCII. Unfortunately, different mappings between byte values and characters emerged in different countries. These mappings are called *code pages*. If you bought a PC in, say, Norway, it would use a code page that offered all of the characters required to write in Norwegian, but if you tried to view the same file on a PC bought in Greece, the non-ASCII characters would look like gibberish because the PC would be configured with a Greek code page. IBM defined *Latin-1* (much later updated and standardized as ISO-8859-1) as a single code page that provides most of what is required by most of the European languages that use Latin letters. Microsoft defined the *Windows-1252* code page, which is mostly (but not entirely) compatible. Apple defined the *Mac-Roman* encoding, which has the same goal, but is completely different again.

All of these encodings were designed to provide a single solution for Western European scripts, but they all fall short in various different ways—Dutch, for example, is missing some of its diphthongs. This is largely because 8 bits just isn't enough to cover all possible characters in all international languages. Chinese alone has well over 100,000 characters.

---

‡ A sort of donkey, before anyone complains.

In the late 1980s and early 1990s, standardization efforts were underway to define an internationally acceptable encoding that would allow characters from all scripts to be represented in a reasonably consistent manner. This became the *Unicode* standard, and is the one that is in use in the .NET Framework.

Unicode is a complex standard, as might be expected from something that is designed to deal with all current (and past) human languages, and have sufficient flexibility to deal with most conceivable future changes, too. It uses numbers to define more than 1 million *code points* in a *codespace*. A code point is roughly analogous to a character in other encodings, including formal definitions of special *categories* such as *graphic characters*, *format characters*, and *control characters*. It's possible to represent a sequence of code points as a sequence of 16-bit values.

You might be wondering how we can handle more than 1 million characters, when there are only 65,536 different values for 16-bit numbers. The answer is that we can team up pairs of characters. The first is called a *high surrogate*; if this is then followed by a *low surrogate*, it defines a character outside the normal 16-bit range.

Unicode also defines complex ways of combining characters. Characters and their diacritical marks can appear consecutively in a string, with the intention that they become combined in their ultimate visual representation; or you can use multiple characters to define special ligatures (characters that are joined together, like Æ).

The .NET Framework `Char`, then, is a 16-bit value that represents a Unicode code point.

 This encoding is called UTF-16, and is the common in-memory representation for strings in most modern platforms. Throughout the Windows API, this format is referred to as "Unicode". This is somewhat imprecise, as there are numerous different Unicode formats. But since none were in widespread use at the time Windows first introduced Unicode support, Microsoft apparently felt that "UTF-16" was an unnecessarily confusing name. But in general, when you see "Unicode" in either Windows or the .NET Framework, it means UTF-16.

From that, we can see that those `IsNumber`, `IsLetter`, `IsHighSurrogate`, and `IsLowSurrogate` methods correspond to tests for particular Unicode categories.

Why Encodings Matter

You may ask: why do we need to know about encodings when "it just works"? That's all very well for our in-memory representation of a string, but what happens when we save some text to disk, encrypt it, or send it across the Web as HTML? We may not want the 16-bit Unicode encoding we've got in memory, but something else. These encodings are really information interchange standards, as much as they are internal choices about how we represent strings.

Most XML documents, for example, are encoded using the UTF-8 encoding. This is an encoding that lets us represent any character in the Unicode codespace, and is compatible with ASCII for the characters in the 7-bit set. It achieves this by using variable-length characters: a single byte for the ASCII range, and two to six bytes for the rest. It takes advantage of special marker values (with the high bit set) to indicate the start of two to six byte sequences.

> While UTF-8 and ASCII are compatible in the sense that any file that contains ASCII text happens to be a valid UTF-8 file (and has the same meaning whether you interpret it as ASCII or UTF-8), there are two caveats. First, a lot of people are sloppy with their terminology and will describe any old 8-bit text encoding as ASCII, which is wrong. ASCII is strictly 7-bit. Latin1 text that uses characters from the top-bit-set range is not valid UTF-8. Second, it's possible to construct a valid UTF-8 file that only uses characters from the 7-bit range, and yet is not a valid ASCII file. (For example, if you save a file from Windows Notepad as UTF-8, it will not be valid ASCII.) That's because UTF-8 is allowed to contain certain non-ASCII features. One is the so-called BOM (Byte Order Mark), which is a sequence of bytes at the start of the file unambiguously representing the file as UTF-8. (The bytes are 0xEF, 0xBB, 0xBF.) The BOM is optional, but Notepad always adds it if you save as UTF-8, which is likely to confuse any program that only understands how to process ASCII.

We're not going to look at any more details of these specific encodings. If you're writing an encoder or decoder by hand, you'll want to refer to the relevant specifications and vast bodies of work on their interpretation.

Fortunately, for the rest of us mortals, the .NET Framework provides us with standard implementations of most of the encodings, so we can convert between the different representations fairly easily.

Encoding and Decoding

Encoding is the process of turning a text string into a sequence of bytes. Conversely, *decoding* is the process of turning a byte sequence into a text string. The .NET APIs for encoding and decoding represents these sequences as byte arrays.

Let's look at the code in Example 10-80 that illustrates this. First, we'll encode some text using the UTF-8 and ASCII encodings, and write the byte values we see to the console.

Example 10-80. Encoding text

```
static void Main(string[] args)
{
    string listenUp = "Listen up!";
```

```
    byte[] utf8Bytes = Encoding.UTF8.GetBytes(listenUp);
    byte[] asciiBytes = Encoding.ASCII.GetBytes(listenUp);

    Console.WriteLine("UTF-8");
    Console.WriteLine("-----");
    foreach (var encodedByte in utf8Bytes)
    {
        Console.Write(encodedByte);
        Console.Write(" ");
    }

    Console.WriteLine();
    Console.WriteLine();

    Console.WriteLine("ASCII");
    Console.WriteLine("-----");
    foreach (var encodedByte in asciiBytes)
    {
        Console.Write(encodedByte);
        Console.Write(" ");
    }

    Console.ReadKey();
}
```

The framework provides us with the Encoding class. This has a set of static properties that provide us with specific instances of an Encoding object for a particular scheme. In this case, we're using UTF8 and ASCII, which actually return instances of UTF8Encoding and ASCIIEncoding, respectively.

 Under normal circumstances, you do not need to know the actual type of these instances; you can just talk to the object returned through its Encoding base class.

GetBytes returns us the byte array that corresponds to the actual in-memory representation of a string, encoded using the relevant scheme.

If we build and run this code, we see the following output:

```
UTF-8
-----
76 105 115 116 101 110 32 117 112 33

ASCII
-----
76 105 115 116 101 110 32 117 112 33
```

Notice that our encodings are identical in this case, just as promised. For basic Latin characters, UTF-8 and ASCII are compatible. (Unlike Notepad, the .NET UTF8Encoding does not choose to add a BOM by default, so unless you use characters outside the

ASCII range this will in fact produce files that can be understood by anything that knows how to process ASCII.)

Let's make a quick change to the string we're trying to change, and translate it into French. Replace the first line inside the `Main` method with Example 10-81. Notice that we've got a capital *E* with an acute accent at the beginning.

Example 10-81. Using a nonASCII character

```
string listenUp = "Écoute-moi!";
```

If you don't have a French keyboard and you're wondering how to insert that E-acute character, there are a number of ways to do it.

If you know the decimal representation of the Unicode code point, you can hold down the Alt key and type the number on the numeric keypad (and then release the Alt key). So Alt-0163 will insert the symbol for the UK currency, £, and Alt-0201 produces É. This doesn't work for the normal number keys, though, so if you don't have a numeric keypad—most laptops don't—this isn't much help.

Possibly the most fun, though, is to run the *charmap.exe* application. The program icon for it in the Start menu is buried pretty deeply, so it's easier to type charmap into a command prompt, the Start→Run box, or the Windows 7 Start menu search box. This is very instructive, and allows you to explore the various different character sets and (if you check the "Advanced view" box) encodings. You can see an image of it in Figure 10-2.

Alternatively, you could just escape the character—the string literal `"\u00C9coutez moi"` will produce the same result. And this has the advantage of not requiring non-ASCII values in your source file. Visual Studio is perfectly able to edit various file encodings, including UTF-8, so you can put non-ASCII characters in strings without having to escape them, and you can even use them in identifiers. But some text-oriented tools are not so flexible, so there may be advantages in keeping your source code purely ASCII.

Now, when we run again, we get the following output:

```
UTF-8
-----
195 137 99 111 117 116 101 45 109 111 105 33

ASCII
-----
63 99 111 117 116 101 45 109 111 105 33
```

We've quite clearly *not* got the same output in each case. The UTF-8 case starts with 195, 137, while the ASCII starts with 63. After this preamble, they're again identical.

So, let's try *decoding* those two byte arrays back into strings, and see what happens.

Insert the code in Example 10-82 before the call to `Console.ReadKey`.

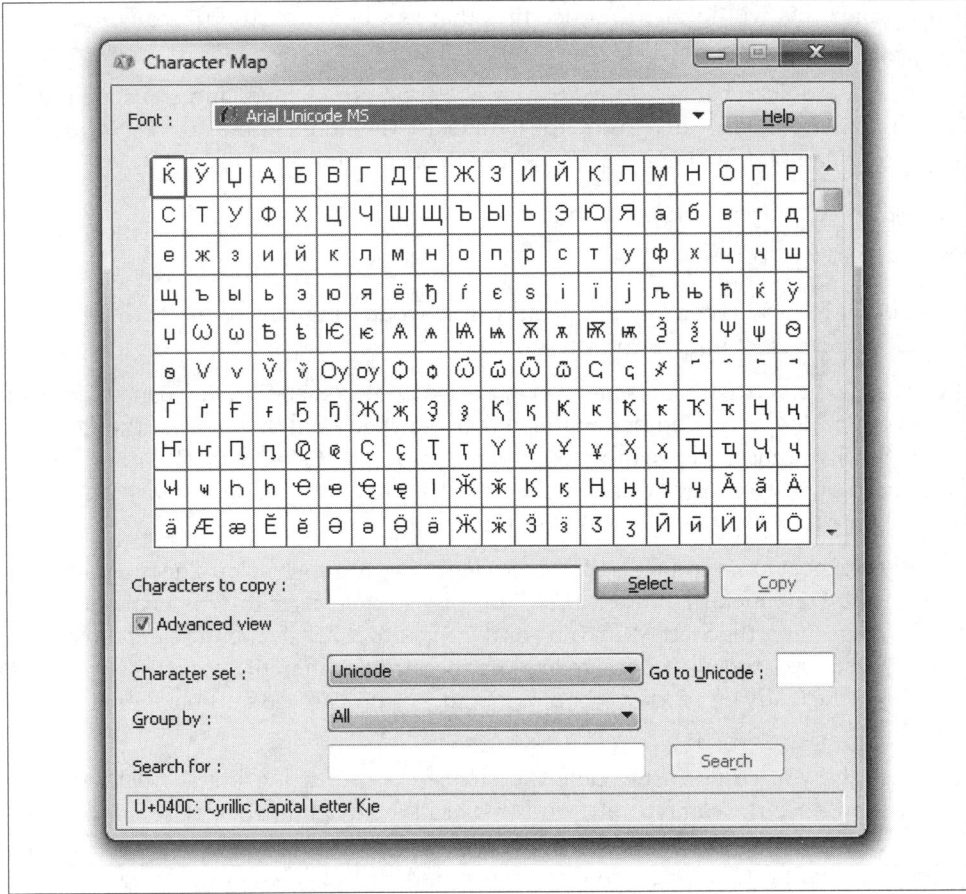

Figure 10-2. Charmap.exe in action

Example 10-82. Decoding text

```
string decodedUtf8 = Encoding.UTF8.GetString(utf8Bytes);
string decodedAscii = Encoding.ASCII.GetString(asciiBytes);

Console.WriteLine();
Console.WriteLine();

Console.WriteLine("Decoded UTF-8");
Console.WriteLine("-------------");
Console.WriteLine(decodedUtf8);

Console.WriteLine();
Console.WriteLine();

Console.WriteLine("Decoded ASCII");
Console.WriteLine("-------------");
Console.WriteLine(decodedAscii);
```

We're now using the `GetString` method on our `Encoding` objects, to *decode* the byte array back into a string. Here's the output:

```
UTF-8
-----
195 137 99 111 117 116 101 45 109 111 105 33

ASCII
-----
63 99 111 117 116 101 45 109 111 105 33

Decoded UTF-8
-------------
Écoute-moi!

Decoded ASCII
-------------
?coute-moi!
```

The UTF-8 bytes have decoded back to our original string. This is because the UTF-8 encoding supports the E-acute character, and it does so by inserting *two* bytes into the array: `195 137`.

On the other hand, our ASCII bytes have been decoded and we see that the first character has become a question mark.

If you look at the encoded bytes, you'll see that the first byte is 63, which (if you look it up in an ASCII table somewhere) corresponds to the question mark character. So this isn't the fault of the decoder. The *encoder*, when faced with a character it didn't understand, inserted a question mark.

 So, you need to be careful that any encoding you choose is capable of supporting the characters you are using (or be prepared for the information loss if it doesn't).

OK, we've seen an example of the one-byte-per-character ASCII representation, and the at-least-one-byte-per-character UTF-8 representation. Let's have a look at the underlying at-least-two-bytes-per-character UTF-16 encoding that the framework uses internally—Example 10-83 uses this.

Example 10-83. Using UTF-16 encoding

```
static void Main(string[] args)
{
    string listenUpFR = "Écoute-moi!";

    byte[] utf16Bytes = Encoding.Unicode.GetBytes(listenUpFR);

    Console.WriteLine("UTF-16");
    Console.WriteLine("-----");
    foreach (var encodedByte in utf16Bytes)
    {
```

```
            Console.Write(encodedByte);
            Console.Write(" ");
        }

        Console.ReadKey();
    }
```

Notice that we're using the `Unicode` encoding this time.

If we compile and run, we see the following output:

```
UTF-16
-----
201 0 99 0 111 0 117 0 116 0 101 0 45 0 109 0 111 0 105 0 33 0
```

It is interesting to compare this with the ASCII output we had before:

```
ASCII
-----
63 99 111 117 116 101 45 109 111 105 33
```

The first character is different, because UTF-16 can encode the E-acute correctly;
thereafter, every other byte in the UTF-16 array is zero, and the next byte corresponds
to the ASCII value. As we said earlier, the Unicode standard is highly compatible with
ASCII, and each 16-bit value (i.e., pair of bytes) corresponds to the equivalent 7-bit
value in the ASCII encoding.

There's one more note to make about this byte array, which has to do with the order
of the bytes. This is easier to see if we first update the program to show the values in
hex, using the formatting function we learned about earlier, as Example 10-84 shows.

Example 10-84. Showing byte values of encoded text

```csharp
static void Main(string[] args)
{
    string listenUpFR = "Écoute-moi!";

    byte[] utf16Bytes = Encoding.Unicode.GetBytes(listenUpFR);

    Console.WriteLine("UTF-16");
    Console.WriteLine("-----");
    foreach (var encodedByte in utf16Bytes)
    {
        Console.Write(string.Format("{0:X2}", encodedByte));
        Console.Write(" ");
    }

    Console.ReadKey();
}
```

If we run again, we now see our bytes written out in hex format:

```
UTF-16
-----
C9 00 63 00 6F 00 75 00 74 00 65 00 2D 00 6D 00 6F 00 69 00 21 00
```

But remember that each UTF-16 code point is represented by a 16-bit value, so we need to think of each pair of bytes as a character. So, our second character is 63 00. This is the 16-bit hex value 0x0063, represented in the *little-endian* form. That means we get the *least-significant byte* (LSB) first, followed by the *most-significant byte* (MSB).

For good (but now largely historical) reasons of engineering efficiency, the Intel x86 family is natively a little-endian architecture. It always expects the LSB followed by the MSB, so the default Unicode encoding is little-endian. On the other hand, platforms like the 680x0 series used in "classic" Macs are big-endian—they expect the MSB, followed by the LSB. Some chip architectures (like the later versions of the ARM chip used in most phones) can even be switched between flavors!

 Another historical note: one of your authors is big-endian (he used the Z80 and 68000 when he was a baby developer) and the other is little endian (he used the 6502, and early pre-endian-switching versions of the ARM when he was growing up).

Consequently, one of us has felt like every memory dump he's looked at since about 1995 has been "backwards". The other takes the contrarian position that it's so-called "normal" numbers that are written backwards. So take a deep breath and count to 01.

Should you need to communicate with something that expects its UTF-16 in a big-endian byte array, you can ask for it. Replace the line in Example 10-84 that initializes the utf16Bytes variable with the code in Example 10-85.

Example 10-85. Using big-endian UTF-16

```
byte[] utf16Bytes = Encoding.BigEndianUnicode.GetBytes(listenUpFR);
```

As you might expect, we get the following output:

```
UTF-16
------
00 C9 00 63 00 6F 00 75 00 74 00 65 00 2D 00 6D 00 6F 00 69 00 21
```

And let's try it once more, but with Arabic text, as Example 10-86 shows.

Example 10-86. Big-endian Arabic

```
static void Main(string[] args)
{
    string listenUpArabic = "أنصت إلىّ";

    byte[] utf16Bytes = Encoding.BigEndianUnicode.GetBytes(listenUpArabic);

    Console.WriteLine("UTF-16");
    Console.WriteLine("-----");
    foreach (var encodedByte in utf16Bytes)
    {
        Console.Write(string.Format("{0:X2}", encodedByte));
```

```
        Console.Write(" ");
    }

    Console.ReadKey();
}
```

And our output is:

```
UTF-16
-----
06 23 06 46 06 35 06 2A 00 20 06 25 06 44 06 4A 06 51
```

(Just to prove that you do get values bigger than 0xFF in Unicode!)

Why Represent Strings As Byte Sequences?

In the course of the chapters on file I/O (Chapter 11) and networking (Chapter 13), we're going to see a number of communications and storage APIs that deal with writing arrays of bytes to some kind of target device. The byte format in which those strings go down the wires is clearly very important, and, while the framework default choices are often appropriate, knowing how (and why) you might need to choose a different encoding will ensure that you're equipped to deal with mysterious bugs—especially when wrangling text in a language other than your own, or to/from a non-Windows platform.§

Summary

In this chapter, we delved into the workings of strings, looking at the difference between the immutable String and its mutable cousin, StringBuilder. We saw how to convert other data types to and from strings, and how to control that formatting, especially when we consider cultures and languages other than our own.

We saw the various ways in which we can compose strings, and the performance trade-offs of each technique. Finally, we looked at how strings are actually represented in memory, and how we may need to convert between different encodings for different applications, platforms, and configurations.

---

§ Yes, other platforms do exist.

CHAPTER 11

Files and Streams

Almost all programmers have to deal with storing, retrieving, and processing information in files at some time or another. The .NET Framework provides a number of classes and methods we can use to find, create, read, and write files and directories In this chapter we'll look at some of the most common.

Files, though, are just one example of a broader group of entities that can be opened, read from, and/or written to in a sequential fashion, and then closed. .NET defines a common contract, called a *stream*, that is offered by all types that can be used in this way. We'll see how and why we might access a file through a stream, and then we'll look at some other types of streams, including a special storage medium called *isolated storage* which lets us save and load information even when we are in a lower-trust environment (such as the Silverlight sandbox). Finally, we'll look at some of the other stream implementations in .NET by way of comparison. (Streams crop up in all sorts of places, so this chapter won't be the last we see of them—they're important in networking, for example.)

Inspecting Directories and Files

We, the authors of this book, have often heard our colleagues ask for a program to help them find duplicate files on their system. Let's write something to do exactly that. We'll pass the names of the directories we want to search on the command line, along with an optional switch to determine whether we want to recurse into subdirectories or not. In the first instance, we'll do a very basic check for similarity based on filenames and sizes, as these are relatively cheap options. Example 11-1 shows our `Main` function.

Example 11-1. Main method of duplicate file finder

```
static void Main(string[] args)
{
    bool recurseIntoSubdirectories = false;

    if (args.Length < 1)
    {
```

```
        ShowUsage();
        return;
    }

    int firstDirectoryIndex = 0;

    if (args.Length > 1)
    {
        // see if we're being asked to recurse
        if (args[0] == "/sub")
        {
            if (args.Length < 2)
            {
                ShowUsage();
                return;
            }
            recurseIntoSubdirectories = true;
            firstDirectoryIndex = 1;
        }
    }

    // Get list of directories from command line.
    var directoriesToSearch = args.Skip(firstDirectoryIndex);

    List<FileNameGroup> filesGroupedByName =
        InspectDirectories(recurseIntoSubdirectories, directoriesToSearch);

    DisplayMatches(filesGroupedByName);

    Console.ReadKey();
}
```

The basic structure is pretty straightforward. First we inspect the command-line arguments to work out which directories we're searching. Then we call `InspectDirectories` (shown later) to build a list of all the files in those directories. This groups the files by filename (without the full path) because we do not consider two files to be duplicates if they have different names. Finally, we pass this list to `DisplayMatches`, which displays any potential matches in the files we have found. `DisplayMatches` refines our test for duplicates further—it considers two files with the same name to be duplicates only if they have the same size. (That's not foolproof, of course, but it's surprisingly effective, and we will refine it further later in the chapter.)

Let's look at each of these steps in more detail.

The code that parses the command-line arguments does a quick check to see that we've provided at least one command-line argument (in addition to the /sub switch if present) and we print out some usage instructions if not, using the method shown in Example 11-2.

Example 11-2. Showing command line usage

```
private static void ShowUsage()
{
    Console.WriteLine("Find duplicate files");
    Console.WriteLine("====================");
    Console.WriteLine(
        "Looks for possible duplicate files in one or more directories");
    Console.WriteLine();
    Console.WriteLine(
        "Usage: findduplicatefiles [/sub] DirectoryName [DirectoryName] ...");
    Console.WriteLine("/sub - recurse into subdirectories");
    Console.ReadKey();
}
```

The next step is to build a list of files grouped by name. We define a couple of classes for this, shown in Example 11-3. We create a `FileNameGroup` object for each distinct filename. Each `FileNameGroup` contains a nested list of `FileDetails`, providing the full path of each file that has that name, and also the size of that file.

Example 11-3. Types used to keep track of the files we've found

```
class FileNameGroup
{
    public string FileNameWithoutPath { get; set; }
    public List<FileDetails> FilesWithThisName { get; set; }
}

class FileDetails
{
    public string FilePath { get; set; }
    public long FileSize { get; set; }
}
```

For example, suppose the program searches two folders, *c:\One* and *c:\Two*, and suppose both of those folders contain a file called *Readme.txt*. Our list will contain a `FileNameGroup` whose `FileNameWithoutPath` is Readme.txt. Its nested `FilesWithThis Name` list will contain two `FileDetails` entries, one with a `FilePath` of c:\One \Readme.txt and the other with c:\Two\Readme.txt. (And each `FileDetails` will contain the size of the relevant file in `FileSize`. If these two files really are copies of the same file, their sizes will, of course, be the same.)

We build these lists in the `InspectDirectories` method, which is shown in Example 11-4. This contains the meat of the program, because this is where we search the specified directories for files. Quite a lot of the code is concerned with the logic of the program, but this is also where we start to use some of the file APIs.

Example 11-4. InspectDirectories method

```
private static List<FileNameGroup> InspectDirectories(
    bool recurseIntoSubdirectories,
    IEnumerable<string> directoriesToSearch)
{
    var searchOption = recurseIntoSubdirectories ?
        SearchOption.AllDirectories : SearchOption.TopDirectoryOnly;

    // Get the path of every file in every directory we're searching.
    var allFilePaths = from directory in directoriesToSearch
                       from file in Directory.GetFiles(directory, "*.*",
                                                       searchOption)
                       select file;

    // Group the files by local filename (i.e. the filename without the
    // containing path), and for each filename, build a list containing the
    // details for every file that has that filename.
    var fileNameGroups = from filePath in allFilePaths
                         let fileNameWithoutPath = Path.GetFileName(filePath)
                         group filePath by fileNameWithoutPath into nameGroup
                         select new FileNameGroup
                         {
                             FileNameWithoutPath = nameGroup.Key,
                             FilesWithThisName =
                              (from filePath in nameGroup
                               let info = new FileInfo(filePath)
                               select new FileDetails
                               {
                                   FilePath = filePath,
                                   FileSize = info.Length
                               }).ToList()
                         };

    return fileNameGroups.ToList();
}
```

To get it to compile, you'll need to add:

```
using System.IO;
```

The parts of Example 11-4 that use the `System.IO` namespace to work with files and directories have been highlighted. We'll start by looking at the use of the `Directory` class.

Examining Directories

Our `InspectDirectories` method calls the static `GetFiles` method on the `Directory` class to find the files we're interested in. Example 11-5 shows the relevant code.

Example 11-5. Getting the files in a directory

```
var searchOption = recurseIntoSubdirectories ?
    SearchOption.AllDirectories : SearchOption.TopDirectoryOnly;

// Get the path of every file in every directory we're searching.
var allFilePaths = from directory in directoriesToSearch
                   from file in Directory.GetFiles(directory, "*.*",
                                                       searchOption)
                   select file;
```

The overload of `GetFiles` we're calling takes the directory we'd like to search, a filter (in the standard command-line form), and a value from the `SearchOption` enumeration, which determines whether to recurse down through all the subfolders.

 We're using LINQ to Objects to build a list of all the files we require. As you saw in Chapter 8, a query with multiple `from` clauses works in a similar way to nested `foreach` loops. The code in Example 11-5 will end up calling `GetFiles` for each directory passed on the command line, and it will effectively concatenate the results of all those calls into a single list of files.

The `GetFiles` method returns the full path for each file concerned, but when it comes to finding matches, we just want the filename. We can use the `Path` class to get the filename from the full path.

Manipulating File Paths

The `Path` class provides methods for manipulating strings containing file paths. Imagine we have the path *c:\directory1\directory2\MyFile.txt*. Table 11-1 shows you how you can slice that with various different `Path` methods.

Table 11-1. The effect of various Path methods

Method name	Result
GetDirectoryName	c:\directory1\directory2
GetExtension	.txt (note the leading ".")
GetFileName	MyFile.txt
GetFileNameWithoutExtension	MyFile
GetFullPath	c:\directory1\directory2\MyFile.txt
GetPathRoot	c:\

What if we use a network path? Table 11-2 shows the results of the same methods when applied to this path:

```
\\MyPC\Share1\directory2\MyFile.txt
```

Table 11-2. *The effect of various Path methods with a network path*

Method name	Result
GetDirectoryName	\\MyPC\Share1\directory2
GetExtension	.txt
GetFileName	MyFile.txt
GetFileNameWithoutExtension	MyFile
GetFullPath	\\MyPC\Share1\directory2\MyFile.txt
GetPathRoot	\\MyPC\Share1

Notice how the path root includes the network hostname and the share name.

What happens if we don't use a full path, but one relative to the current directory? And what's the current directory anyway?

Path and the Current Working Directory

The framework maintains a process-wide idea of the *current working directory*, which is the root path relative to which any file operations that *do not* fully qualify the path are made. The `Directory` class (as you might imagine) gives us the ability to manipulate it. Rather than a static property, there are two static methods to query and set the current value: `GetCurrentDirectory` and `SetCurrentDirectory`. Example 11-6 shows a call to the latter.

Example 11-6. Setting the current directory

```
Directory.SetCurrentDirectory(@"c:\");
```

Table 11-3 shows the results we'd get if we passed `@"directory2\MyFile.txt"` to the various `Path` methods after having run the code in Example 11-6. As you can see, most of the results reflect the fact that we've not provided a full path, but there's one exception: `GetFullPath` uses the current working directory if we provide it with a relative path.

Table 11-3. *The effect of various Path methods with a relative path*

Method name	Result
GetDirectoryName	directory2
GetExtension	.txt
GetFileName	MyFile.txt
GetFileNameWithoutExtension	MyFile
GetFullPath	c:\directory2\MyFile.txt
GetPathRoot	<blank>

 Path doesn't check that the named file exists. It only looks at the input string and, in the case of GetFullPath, the current working directory.

OK, in our example, we just want the filename without the path, so we use Path.Get FileName to retrieve it. Example 11-7 shows the relevant piece of Example 11-4.

Example 11-7. Getting the filename without the full path

```
var fileNameGroups = from filePath in allFilePaths
                     let fileNameWithoutPath = Path.GetFileName(filePath)
                     group filePath by fileNameWithoutPath into nameGroup
                     select ...
```

We then use the LINQ group operator (which was described in Chapter 8) to group all of the files by name.

Path contains a lot of other useful members that we'll need a little bit later; but we can leave it for the time being, and move on to the other piece of information that we need for our matching code: the file size. The .NET Framework provides us with a class called FileInfo that contains a whole bunch of members that help us to discover things about a file.

Examining File Information

The various functions from the System.IO classes we've dealt with so far have all been static, but when it comes to retrieving information such as file size, we have to create an instance of a FileInfo object, passing its constructor the path of the file we're interested in. That path can be either an absolute path like the ones we've seen already, or a path relative to the current working directory. FileInfo has a lot of overlapping functionality with other classes. For example, it provides a few helpers similar to Path to get details of the directory, filename, and extension.

However, the only method we're really interested in for our example is its Length property, which tells us the size of the file. Every other member on FileInfo has a functional equivalent on other classes in the framework. Even Length is duplicated on the stream classes we'll come to later, but it is simpler for us to use FileInfo if we don't intend to open the file itself.

We use FileInfo in the final part of InspectDirectories, to put the file size into the per-file details. Example 11-8 shows the relevant excerpt from Example 11-4.

Example 11-8. Getting the file size

```
...
select new FileNameGroup
{
    FileNameWithoutPath = nameGroup.Key,
    FilesWithThisName =
```

```
    (from filePath in nameGroup
     let info = new FileInfo(filePath)
     select new FileDetails
     {
         FilePath = filePath,
         FileSize = info.Length
     }).ToList()
};
```

We're now only one method short of a sort-of-useful program, and that's the one that trawls through this information to find and display matches: DisplayMatches, which is shown in Example 11-9.

Example 11-9. DisplayMatches

```
private static void DisplayMatches(
    IEnumerable<FileNameGroup> filesGroupedByName)
{
    var groupsWithMoreThanOneFile = from nameGroup in filesGroupedByName
                                    where nameGroup.FilesWithThisName.Count > 1
                                    select nameGroup;

    foreach (var fileNameGroup in groupsWithMoreThanOneFile)
    {
        // Group the matches by the file size, then select those
        // with more than 1 file of that size.
        var matchesBySize = from file in fileNameGroup.FilesWithThisName
                            group file by file.FileSize into sizeGroup
                            where sizeGroup.Count() > 1
                            select sizeGroup;

        foreach (var matchedBySize in matchesBySize)
        {
            string fileNameAndSize = string.Format("{0} ({1} bytes)",
                fileNameGroup.FileNameWithoutPath, matchedBySize.Key);
            WriteWithUnderlines(fileNameAndSize);
            // Show each of the directories containing this file
            foreach (var file in matchedBySize)
            {
                Console.WriteLine(Path.GetDirectoryName(file.FilePath));
            }
            Console.WriteLine();
        }
    }
}

private static void WriteWithUnderlines(string text)
{
    Console.WriteLine(text);
    Console.WriteLine(new string('-', text.Length));
}
```

We start with a LINQ query that looks for the filenames that crop up in more than one folder, because those are the only candidates for being duplicates. We iterate through each such name with a **foreach** loop. Inside that loop, we run another LINQ query that groups the files of that name by size—see the first emphasized lines in Example 11-9. If **InspectDirectories** discovered three files called *Program.cs*, for example, and two of them were 278 bytes long while the other was 894 bytes long, this **group** clause would separate those three files into two groups. The **where** clause in the same query removes any groups that contain only one file.

So the **matchesBySize** variable refers to a query that returns a group for each set of two or more files that have the same size (and because we're inside a loop that iterates through the names, we already know they have the same name). Those are our duplicate candidates. We then write out the filename and size (and an underline separator of the same length). Finally, we write out each file location containing candidate matches using **Path.GetDirectoryName**.

If we compile and run that lot, we'll see the following output:

```
Find duplicate files
=====================
Looks for possible duplicate files in one or more directories

Usage: findduplicatefiles [/sub] DirectoryName [DirectoryName] ...
/sub - recurse into subdirectories
```

We haven't given it anywhere to look! How are we going to test our application? Well, we could provide it with some command-line parameters. If you open the project properties and switch to the **Debug** tab, you'll see a place where you can add command-line arguments (see Figure 11-1).

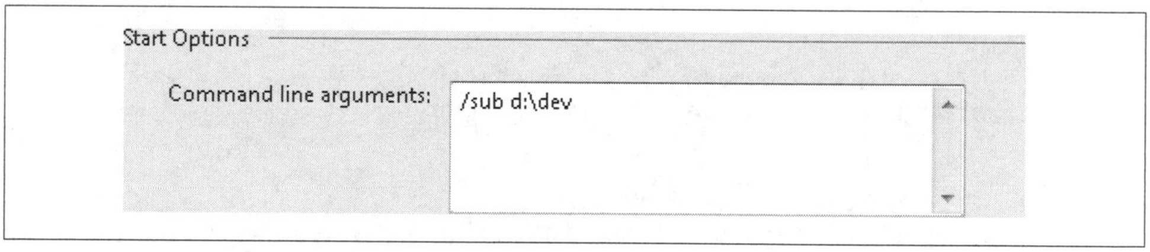

Figure 11-1. Setting command-line arguments

However, we could do a bit better for test purposes. Example 11-10 shows a modified **Main** that supports a new **/test** command-line switch, which we can use to create test files and exercise the function.

Example 11-10. Adding a /test switch

```
static void Main(string[] args)
{
    bool recurseIntoSubdirectories = false;

    if (args.Length < 1)
    {
        ShowUsage();
```

```
        return;
    }

    int firstDirectoryIndex = 0;
    IEnumerable<string> directoriesToSearch = null;
    bool testDirectoriesMade = false;

    try
    {
        // Check to see if we are running in test mode
        if (args.Length == 1 && args[0] == "/test")
        {
            directoriesToSearch = MakeTestDirectories();
            testDirectoriesMade = true;
            recurseIntoSubdirectories = true;
        }
        else
        {
            if (args.Length > 1)
            {
                // see if we're being asked to recurse
                if (args[0] == "/sub")
                {
                    if (args.Length < 2)
                    {
                        ShowUsage();
                        return;
                    }
                    recurseIntoSubdirectories = true;
                    firstDirectoryIndex = 1;
                }
            }

            // Get list of directories from command line.
            directoriesToSearch = args.Skip(firstDirectoryIndex);
        }

        List<FileNameGroup> filesGroupedByName =
            InspectDirectories(recurseIntoSubdirectories, directoriesToSearch);

        DisplayMatches(filesGroupedByName);
        Console.ReadKey();
    }
    finally
    {
        if( testDirectoriesMade )
        {
            CleanupTestDirectories(directoriesToSearch);
        }
    }
}
```

In order to operate in test mode, we've added an alternative way to initialize the variable that holds the list of directories (`directoriesToSearch`). The original code, which initializes it from the command-line arguments (skipping over the `/sub` switch if present), is still present. However, if we find the `/test` switch, we initialize it to point at some test directories we're going to create (in the `MakeTestDirectories` method). The rest of the code can then be left as it was (to avoid running some completely different program in our test mode). Finally, we add a bit of cleanup code at the end to remove any test directories if we created them.

So, how are we going to implement `MakeTestDirectories`? We want to create some temporary files, and write some content into them to exercise the various matching possibilities.

Creating Temporary Files

A quick look at `Path` reveals the `GetTempFileName` method. This creates a file of zero length in a directory dedicated to temporary files, and returns the path to that file.

 It is important to note that the file is actually created, whether you use it or not, and so you are responsible for cleaning it up when you are done, even if you don't make any further use of it.

Let's create another test console application, just to try out that method. We can do that by adding the following to our main function:

```
string fileName = Path.GetTempFileName();
// Display the filename
Console.WriteLine(fileName);
// And wait for some input
Console.ReadKey();
```

But wait! If we just compile and run that, we'll leave the file we created behind on the system. We should make sure we delete it again when we're done. There's nothing special about a temporary file. We create it in an unusual way, and it ends up in a particular place, but once it has been created, it's just like any other file in the filesystem. So, we can delete it the same way we'd delete any other file.

Deleting Files

The `System.IO` namespace provides the `File` class, which offers various methods for doing things with files. Deleting is particularly simple: we just use the static `Delete` method, as Example 11-11 shows.

Example 11-11. Deleting a file

```
string fileName = Path.GetTempFileName();
try
{
    // Use the file
    // ...
    // Display the filename
    Console.WriteLine(fileName);
    // And wait for some input
    Console.ReadKey();
}
finally
{
    // Then clean it up
    File.Delete(fileName);
}
```

Notice that we've wrapped the code in which we (could) manipulate the file further in a **try** block, and deleted it in a **finally** block. This ensures that whatever happens, we'll always attempt to clean up after ourselves.

If you compile and run this test project now, you'll see some output like this:

```
C:\Users\yourusername\AppData\Local\Temp\tmpCA8F.tmp
```

The exact text will depend on your operating system version, your username, and (of course) the random filename that was created for you. If you browse to that path, you will see a zero-length file of that name.

If you then press a key, allowing `Console.ReadKey` to return, it will drop through to the **finally** block, where we delete the temporary file, using the static `Delete` method on the `File` class.

There are lots of scenarios where this sort of temporary file creation is just fine, but it doesn't really suit our example application's needs. We want to create multiple temporary files, in multiple different directories. `GetTempFileName` doesn't really do the job for us.

If we look at `Path` again, though, there's another likely looking method: `GetRandomFileName`. This returns a random string of characters that can be used as either a file or a directory name. It uses a cryptographically strong random number generator (which can be useful in some security-conscious scenarios), and is statistically likely to produce a unique name, thus avoiding clashes. Unlike `GetTempFileName` it doesn't actually create the file (or directory); that's up to us.

If you run the code in Example 11-12:

Example 11-12. Showing a random filename

```
Console.WriteLine(Path.GetRandomFileName());
```

you'll see output similar to this:

```
xnicz3rs.juc
```

(Obviously, the actual characters you see will, hopefully, be different, or the statistical uniqueness isn't all that unique!)

So, we can use that method to produce our test file and directory names. But where are we going to put the files? Perhaps one of the various "well-known folders" Windows offers would suit our needs.

Well-Known Folders

Most operating systems have a bunch of well-known filesystem locations, and Windows is no exception. There are designated folders for things like the current user's documents, pictures, or desktop; the program files directory where applications are installed; and the system folder.

The .NET Framework provides a class called `Environment` that provides information about the world our program runs in. Its static method `GetFolderPath` is the one that interests us right now, because it will return the path of various well-known folders. We pass it one of the `Environment.SpecialFolder` enumeration values. Example 11-13 retrieves the location of one of the folders in which applications can store per-user data.

Example 11-13. Getting a well-known folder location

```
string path = Environment.GetFolderPath(Environment.SpecialFolder.ApplicationData);
```

Table 11-4 lists all of the well-known folders that `GetFolderPath` can return, and the location they give on the installed copy of Windows 7 (64-bit) belonging to one of the authors.

Table 11-4. Special folders

Enumeration	Example location	Purpose
ApplicationData	*C:\Users\mwa\ AppData\Roaming*	A place for applications to store their own private information for a particular user; this may be located on a shared server, and available across multiple logins for the same user, on different machines, if the user's domain policy is configured to do so.
CommonApplicationData	*C:\ProgramData*	A place for applications to store their own private information accessible to all users.
CommonProgramFiles	*C:\Program Files\Common Files*	A place where shared application components can be installed.
Cookies	*C:\Users\mwa\ AppData\Roaming*	The location where Internet cookies are stored for this user; another potentially roaming location.

Enumeration	Example location	Purpose
	Microsoft\Windows\Cookies	
Desktop	*C:\Users\mwa*	The current user's desktop (virtual) folder.
	Desktop	
DesktopDirectory	*C:\Users\mwa*	The physical directory where filesystem objects on the desktop are stored (currently, but not necessarily, the same as Desktop).
	Desktop	
Favorites	*C:\Users\mwa*	The directory containing the current user's favorites links.
	Favorites	
History	*C:\Users\mwa*	The directory containing the current user's Internet history.
	AppData\Local	
	Microsoft\Windows	
	History	
InternetCache	*C:\Users\mwa*	The directory that contains the current user's Internet cache.
	AppData\Local	
	Microsoft\Windows	
	Temporary Internet Files	
LocalApplicationData	*C:\Users\mwa*	A place for applications to store their private data associated with the current user. This is guaranteed to be on the local machine (as opposed to `ApplicationData` which may roam with the user).
	AppData\Local	
MyComputer	<blank>	This is always an empty string because there is no real folder that corresponds to My Computer.
MyDocuments	*C:\Users\mwa*	The folder in which the current user's documents (as opposed to private application datafiles) are stored.
	Documents	
MyMusic	*C:\Users\mwa*	The folder in which the current user's music files are stored.
	Music	
MyPictures	*C:\Users\mwa*	The folder in which the current user's picture files are stored.
	Pictures	
Personal	*C:\Users\mwa*	The folder in which the current user's documents are stored (synonymous with MyDocuments).
	Documents	
ProgramFiles	*C:\Program Files*	The directory in which applications are installed. Note that there is no special folder enumeration for the 32-bit applications directory on 64-bit Windows.
Programs	*C:\Users\mwa*	The location where application shortcuts in the Start menu's Programs section are stored for the current user. This is another potentially roaming location.
	AppData\Roaming	
	Microsoft\Windows	

Enumeration	Example location	Purpose
	Start Menu\Programs	
Recent	*C:\Users\mwa*	The folder where links to recently used documents are stored for the current user. This is another potentially roaming location.
	AppData\Roaming	
	Microsoft\Windows	
	Recent	
SendTo	*C:\Users\mwa*	The location that contains the links that form the Send To menu items in the shell. This is another potentially roaming location.
	AppData\Roaming	
	Microsoft\Windows	
	SendTo	
StartMenu	*C:\Users\mwa*	The folder that contains the Start menu items for the current user. This is another potentially roaming location.
	AppData\Roaming	
	Microsoft\Windows	
	Start Menu	
Startup	*C:\Users\mwa*	The folder that contains links to programs that will run each time the current user logs in. This is another potentially roaming location.
	AppData\Roaming	
	Microsoft\Windows	
	Start Menu\Programs	
	\Startup	
System	*C:\Windows*	The Windows system folder.
	system32	
Templates	*C:\Users\mwa*	A location in which applications can store document templates for the current user. Again, this is a potentially roaming location.
	AppData\Roaming	
	Microsoft\Windows	
	Templates	

Notice that this doesn't include all of the well-known folders we have these days, because the set of folders grows with each new version of Windows. Things like Videos, Games, Downloads, Searches, and Contacts are all missing. It also doesn't support Windows 7 libraries in any meaningful sense. This is (sort of) by design. The method provides a lowest common denominator approach to finding useful folders on the system, in a way that works across all supported versions of the framework (including Windows Mobile).

So, we need to choose a path in which our current user is likely to have permission to create/read/write and delete files and directories. It doesn't have to be one that the user can see under normal circumstances. In fact, we're going to create files with extensions that are not bound to any applications and we should not do that in a place that's visible to the user if we want our application to be a good Windows citizen.

 If you create a file in a place that's visible to the user, like Documents or Desktop, you should ensure that it always has a default application associated with it.

There are two candidates for this in Table 11-4: `LocalApplicationData` and `ApplicationData`. Both of these offer places for applications to store files that the user wouldn't normally see. (Of course, users can find these folders if they look hard enough. The goal here is to avoid putting our temporary test files in the same folders as the user's documents.)

The difference between these two folders is that if the user has a roaming profile, files in the latter folder will be copied around the network as they move from one machine to another, while files in the former folder remain on the machine on which they were created. We're building temporary files for test purposes, so `LocalApplicationData` looks like the right choice.

So, let's return to our demo application, and start to implement the `MakeTestDirecto ries` method. The first thing we need to do is to create a few test directories. Example 11-14 contains some code to do that.

Example 11-14. Creating test directories

```
private static string[] MakeTestDirectories()
{
    string localApplicationData = Path.Combine(
        Environment.GetFolderPath(
            Environment.SpecialFolder.LocalApplicationData),
        @"Programming CSharp\FindDuplicates");

    // Let's make three test directories
    var directories = new string[3];
    for (int i = 0; i < directories.Length; ++i)
    {
        string directory = Path.GetRandomFileName();
        // Combine the local application data with the
        // new random file/directory name
        string fullPath = Path.Combine(localApplicationData, directory);
        // And create the directory
        Directory.CreateDirectory(fullPath);
        directories[i] = fullPath;
        Console.WriteLine(fullPath);
    }
    return directories;
}
```

First, we use the `GetFolderPath` method to get the `LocalApplicationData` path. But we don't want to work directly in that folder—applications are meant to create their own folders underneath this. Normally you'd create a folder named either for your company or for your organization, and then an application-specific folder inside that—we've used *Programming CSharp* as the organization name here, and *FindDuplicates* as the application name. We then use a `for` loop to create three directories with random names inside that. To create these new directories, we've used a couple of new methods: `Path.Combine` and `Directory.CreateDirectory`.

Concatenating Path Elements Safely

If you've written any code that manipulates paths before, you'll have come across the leading/trailing slash dilemma. Does your path fragment have one or not? You also need to know whether the path fragment you're going to append really is a relative path—are there circumstances under which you might need to deal with a fully qualified path instead? `Path.Combine` does away with all that anxiety. Not only will it check all those things for you and do the right thing, but it will even check that your paths contain only valid path characters.

Table 11-5 contains some example paths, and the result of combining them with `Path.Combine`.

Table 11-5. Example results of Path.Combine

Path 1	Path 2	Combined
`C:\hello\`	`world`	`C:\hello\world`
`C:\hello`	`world`	`C:\hello\world`
`C:\hello\`	`\world`	`C:\hello\world`
`hello`	`world`	`hello\world`
`C:\hello`	`world.exe`	`c\hello\world.exe`
`\\mybox\hello`	`world`	`\\mybox\hello\world`
`world`	`C:\hello`	`C:\hello`

The last entry in that table is particularly interesting: notice that the second path is absolute, and so the combined path is "optimized" to just that second path.

In our case, Example 11-14 combines the well-known folder with a subfolder name to get a folder location specific to this example. And then it combines that with our new temporary folder names, ready for creation.

Creating and Securing Directory Hierarchies

`Directory.CreateDirectory` is very straightforward: it does exactly what its name suggests. In fact, it will create any directories in the whole path that do not already exist, so you can create a deep hierarchy with a single call. (You'll notice that Example 11-14 didn't bother to create the *Programming CSharp\FindDuplicates* folder—those will get created automatically the first time we run as a result of creating the temporary folders inside them.) A side effect of this is that it is safe to call it if all of the directories in the path already exist—it will just do nothing.

In addition to the overload we've used, there's a second which also takes a `Directory Security` parameter:

```
Directory.CreateDirectory(string path, DirectorySecurity directorySecurity)
```

The `DirectorySecurity` class allows you to specify filesystem access controls with a relatively simple programming model. If you've tried using the Win32 ACL APIs, you'll know that it is a nightmare of GUIDs, SSIDs, and lists sensitive to item ordering. This model does away with much of the complexity.

Let's extend our create function to make sure that *only* our current user has read/write/modify permissions on these directories. Example 11-15 modifies the previous example by explicitly granting the current user full control of the newly created folders. The new or changed lines are highlighted.

Example 11-15. Configuring access control on new directories

```csharp
private static string[] MakeTestDirectories()
{
    string localApplicationData = Path.Combine(
        Environment.GetFolderPath(
            Environment.SpecialFolder.LocalApplicationData),
        @"Programming CSharp\FindDuplicates");

    // Get the name of the logged in user
    string userName = WindowsIdentity.GetCurrent().Name;
    // Make the access control rule
    FileSystemAccessRule fsarAllow =
        new FileSystemAccessRule(
            userName,
            FileSystemRights.FullControl,
            AccessControlType.Allow);
    DirectorySecurity ds = new DirectorySecurity();
    ds.AddAccessRule(fsarAllow);

    // Let's make three test directories
    var directories = new string[3];
    for (int i = 0; i < directories.Length; ++i)
    {
        string directory = Path.GetRandomFileName();
        // Combine the local application data with the
        // new random file/directory name
```

```
        string fullPath = Path.Combine(localApplicationData, directory);

        // And create the directory
        Directory.CreateDirectory(fullPath, ds);

        directories[i] = fullPath;
        Console.WriteLine(fullPath);
    }
    return directories;
}
```

You'll need to add a couple of using directives to the top of the file before you can compile this code:

```
using System.Security.AccessControl;
using System.Security.Principal;
```

What do these changes do? First, we make use of a type called WindowsIdentity to find the current user, and fish out its name. If you happen to want to specify the name explicitly, rather than get the current user programmatically, you can do so (e.g., *MYDOMAIN\SomeUserId*).

Then, we create a FileSystemAccessRule, passing it the username, the FileSystem Rights we want to set, and a value from the AccessControlType enumeration which determines whether we are allowing or denying those rights.

If you take a look at the FileSystemRights enumeration in MSDN, you should recognize the options from the Windows security permissions dialog in the shell. You can combine the individual values (as it is a Flags enumeration), or use one of the precanned sets as we have here.

If you compile this application, and modify the debug settings to pass just the /test switch as the only command-line argument, when you run it you'll see output similar to the following (but with your user ID, and some different random directory names):

```
C:\Users\yourId\AppData\Local\Programming CSharp\FindDuplicates\yzwOiw3p.ysq
C:\Users\yourId\AppData\Local\Programming CSharp\FindDuplicates\qke5k2ql.5et
C:\Users\yourId\AppData\Local\Programming CSharp\FindDuplicates\5hkhspqa.osc
```

If we take a look at the folder in Explorer, you should see your new directories (something like Figure 11-2).

If you right-click on one of these and choose Properties, then examine the Security tab, you should see something like Figure 11-3.

Notice how the *only* user with permissions on this directory is the currently logged on user (in this case ian, on a domain called idg.interact). All of the usual inherited permissions have been overridden. Rather than the regular read/modify/write checkboxes, we've apparently got *special permissions*. This is because we set them explicitly in the code.

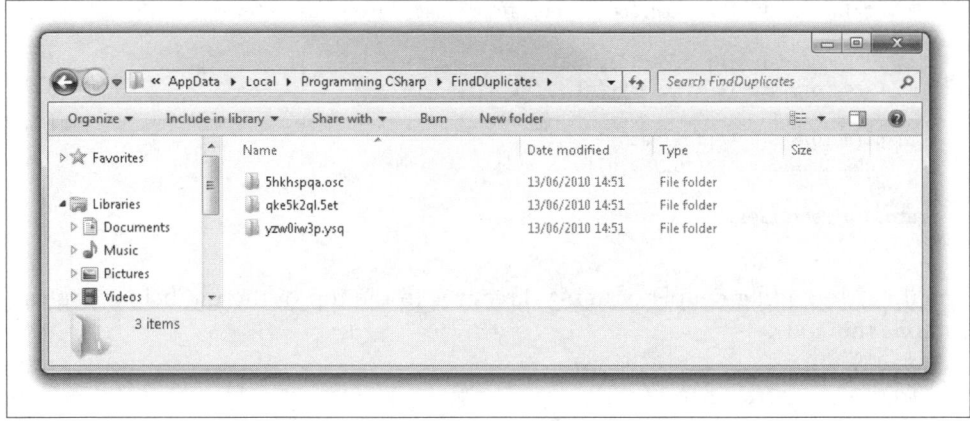

Figure 11-2. Newly created folders

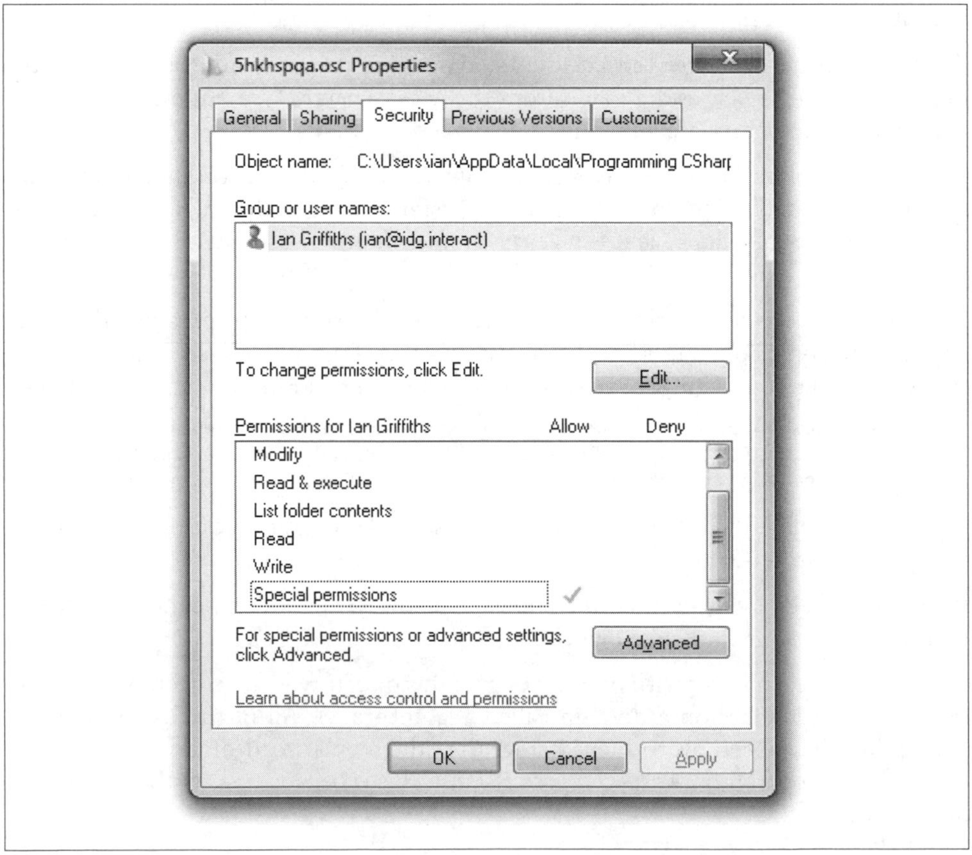

Figure 11-3. Permissions on the new directory

We can have a look at that in more detail if we click the Advanced button, and switch to the Effective Permissions tab. Click the Select button to pick a user (see Figure 11-4). First, let's look at the effective permissions for the local administrator (this is probably *MachineName*\Administrator, unless you've changed your default administrator name to try to make things slightly harder for an attacker).

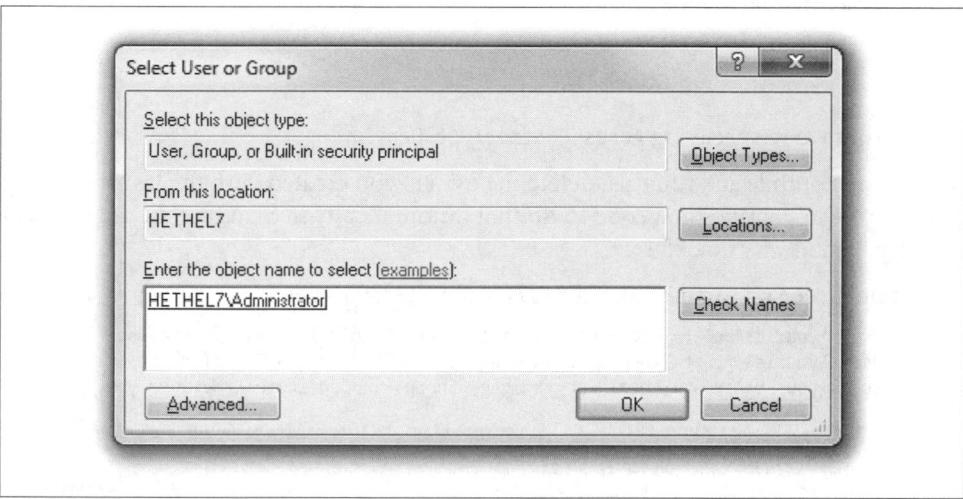

Figure 11-4. Selecting a user

If you click OK, you'll see the effective permissions for Administrator on that folder (Figure 11-5).

You can scroll the scroll bar to prove it for yourself, but you can see that even Administrator cannot actually access your folder! (This is not, of course, strictly true. Administrators can take ownership of the folder and mess with the permissions themselves, but they cannot access the folder without changing the permissions first.) Try again with your own user ID. You will see results similar to Figure 11-6—we have full control. Scroll the list and you'll see that everything is ticked.

What if we wanted "not quite" full control? Say we wanted to deny the ability to write extended attributes to the file. Well, we can update our code and add a second `FileSystemAccessRule`. Example 11-16 shows the additional code required.

Example 11-16. Denying permissions

```
private static string[] MakeTestDirectories()
{
    // ...
    FileSystemAccessRule fsarAllow =
        new FileSystemAccessRule(
            userName,
            FileSystemRights.FullControl,
            AccessControlType.Allow);
```

```
    ds.AddAccessRule(fsarAllow);

    FileSystemAccessRule fsarDeny =
        new FileSystemAccessRule(
            userName,
            FileSystemRights.WriteExtendedAttributes,
            AccessControlType.Deny);
    ds.AddAccessRule(fsarDeny);

    // ...
}
```

Notice that we're specifying `AccessControlType.Deny`.

Before you compile and run this, delete the folders you created with the last run, using Explorer—we'll write some code to do that automatically in a minute, because it will get very boring very quickly!

You should see very similar output to last time (just with some new directory names):

```
C:\Users\yourId\AppData\Local\Programming CSharp\FindDuplicates\slhwbtgo.sop
C:\Users\yourId\AppData\Local\Programming CSharp\FindDuplicates\bsfndkgn.ucm
C:\Users\yourId\AppData\Local\Programming CSharp\FindDuplicates\tayf1uvg.y4y
```

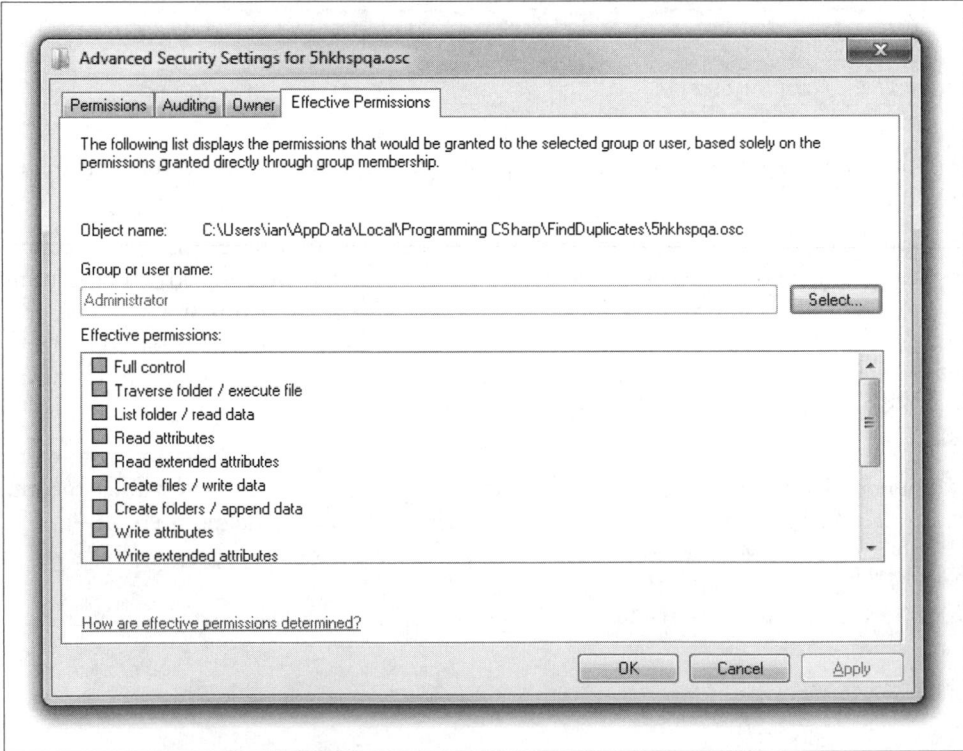

Figure 11-5. Effective permissions for Administrator on the new folder

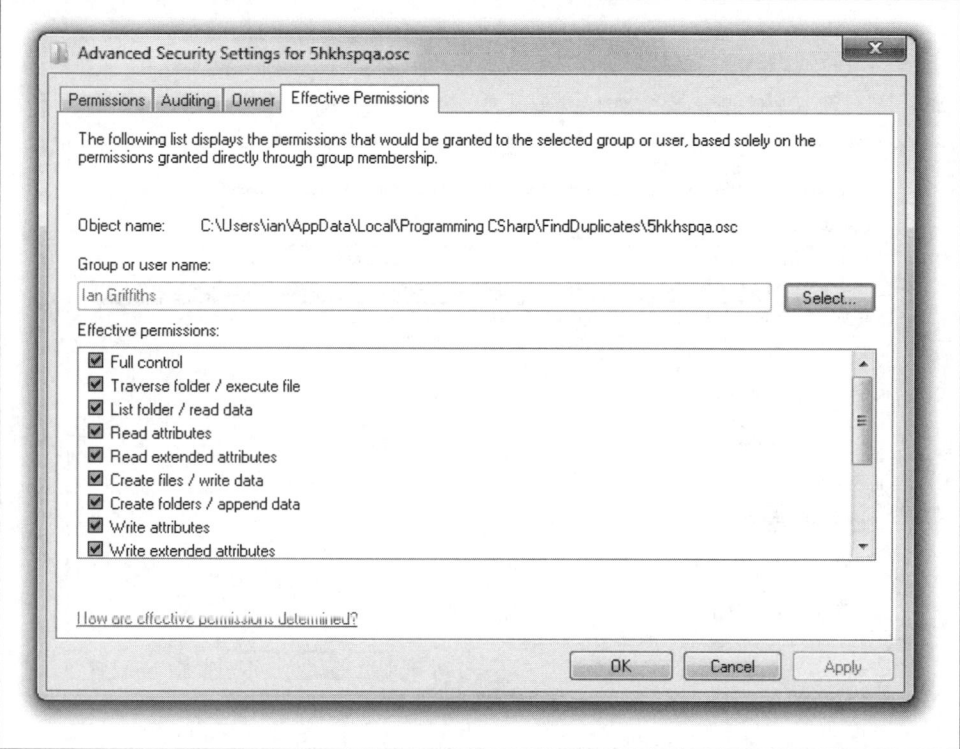

Figure 11-6. Effective permissions for the current user on the new folder

If you look at the permissions, you will now see both the *Allow* and the new *Deny* entries (Figure 11-7).

As a double-check, take a look at the effective permissions for your current user (see Figure 11-8).

In Figure 11-8 you can see that we've no longer got `Full control`, because we've been specifically denied `Write extended attributes`. Of course, we could always give that permission back to ourselves, because we've been allowed `Change permissions`, but that's not the point!

Although that isn't the point, security permissions of all kinds are a complex affair. If your users have local or domain administrator permissions, they can usually work around any other permissions you try to manage. You should always try to abide by the principle of least permission: don't grant people more privileges than they really need to do the job. Although that will require a little more thinking up front, and can sometimes be a frustrating process while you try to configure a system, it is much preferable to a wide-open door.

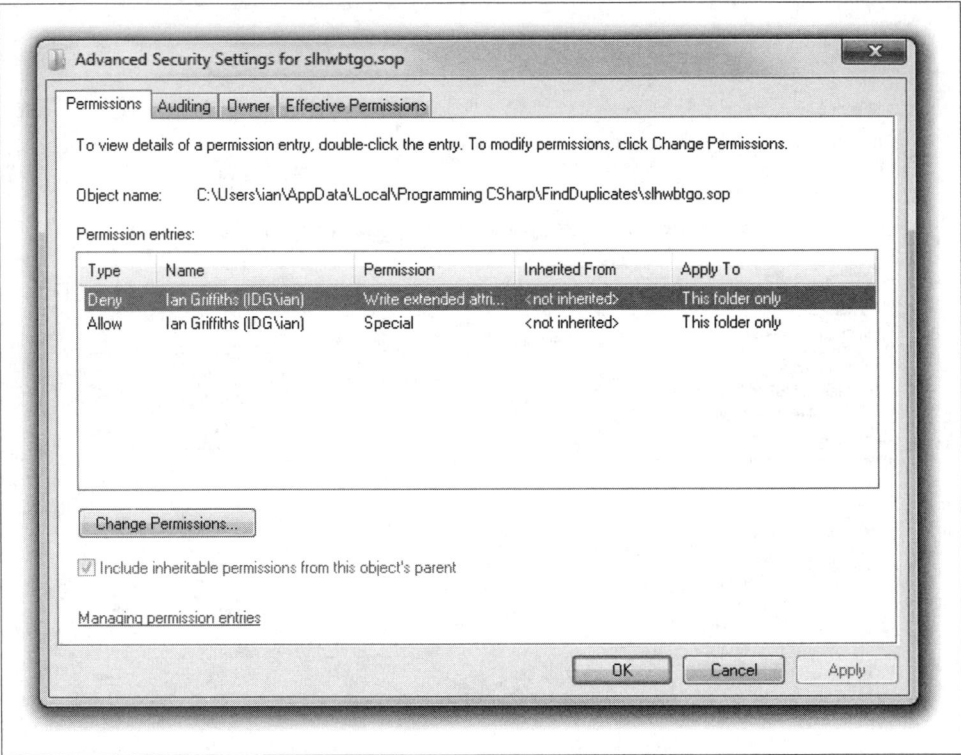

Figure 11-7. Permissions now that we've denied write extended attributes

OK, delete those new directories using Explorer, and we'll write some code to clean up after ourselves. We need to delete the directories we've just created, by implementing our `CleanupTestDirectories` method.

Deleting a Directory

You're probably ahead of us by now. Yes, we can delete a directory using `Directory.Delete`, as Example 11-17 shows.

Example 11-17. Deleting a directory

```
private static void CleanupTestDirectories(IEnumerable<string> directories)
{
    foreach (var directory in directories)
    {
        Directory.Delete(directory);
    }
}
```

We're just iterating through the set of new directories we stashed away earlier, deleting them.

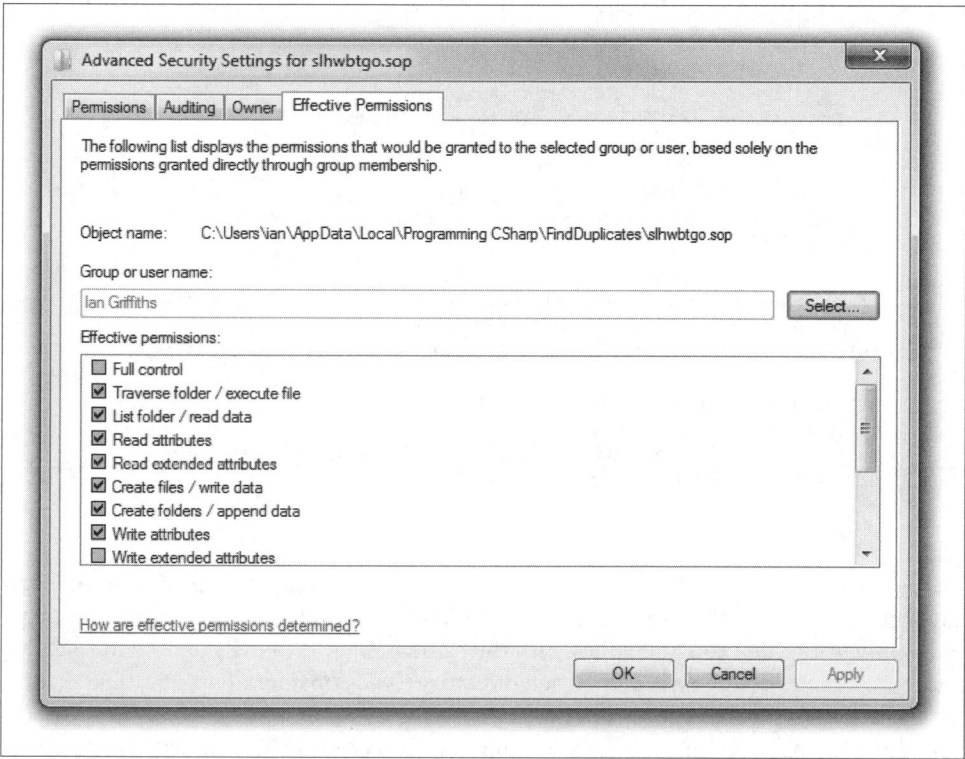

Figure 11-8. *Effective permissions with write extended attributes denied*

OK, we've got our test directories. We'd now like to create some test files to use. Just before we return from `MakeTestDirectories`, let's add a call to a new method to create our files, as Example 11-18 shows.

Example 11-18. *Creating files in the test directories*

```
...
CreateTestFiles(directories);
return directories;
```

Example 11-19 shows that method.

Example 11-19. *The CreateTestFiles method*

```
private static void CreateTestFiles(IEnumerable<string> directories)
{
    string fileForAllDirectories = "SameNameAndContent.txt";
    string fileSameInAllButDifferentSizes = "SameNameDifferentSize.txt";

    int directoryIndex = 0;
    // Let's create a distinct file that appears in each directory
    foreach (string directory in directories)
```

```
    {
        directoryIndex++;

        // Create the distinct file for this directory
        string filename = Path.GetRandomFileName();
        string fullPath = Path.Combine(directory, filename);
        CreateFile(fullPath, "Example content 1");

        // And now the one that is in all directories, with the same content
        fullPath = Path.Combine(directory, fileForAllDirectories);
        CreateFile(fullPath, "Found in all directories");

        // And now the one that has the same name in
        // all directories, but with different sizes
        fullPath = Path.Combine(directory, fileSameInAllButDifferentSizes);

        StringBuilder builder = new StringBuilder();
        builder.AppendLine("Now with");
        builder.AppendLine(new string('x', directoryIndex));
        CreateFile(fullPath, builder.ToString());
    }
}
```

As you can see, we're running through the directories, and creating three files in each. The first has a different, randomly generated filename in each directory, and remember, our application only considers files with the same names as being possible duplicates, so we expect the first file we add to each directory to be considered unique. The second file has the same filename and content (so they will all be the same size) in every folder. The third file has the same name every time, but its content varies in length.

Well, we can't put off the moment any longer; we're going to have to create a file, and write some content into it. There are lots and lots and lots (and lots) of different ways of doing that with the .NET Framework, so how do we go about picking one?

Writing Text Files

Our first consideration should always be to "keep it simple," and use the most convenient method for the job. So, what is the job? We need to create a file, and write some text into it. `File.WriteAllText` looks like a good place to start.

Writing a Whole Text File at Once

The `File` class offers three methods that can write an entire file out in a single step: `WriteAllBytes`, `WriteAllLines`, and `WriteAllText`. The first of these works with binary, but our application has text. As you saw in Chapter 10, we could use an `Encoding` to convert our text into bytes, but the other two methods here will do that for us. (They all use UTF-8.)

WriteAllLines takes a collection of strings, one for each line, but our code in Example 11-19 prepares content in the form of a single string. So as Example 11-20 shows, we use WriteAllText to write the file out with a single line of code. (In fact, we probably didn't need to bother putting this code into a separate method. However, this will make it easier for us to illustrate some of the alternatives later.)

Example 11-20. Writing a string into a new file

```
private static void CreateFile(string fullPath, string contents)
{
    File.WriteAllText(fullPath, contents);
}
```

The path can be either relative or absolute, and the file will be created if it doesn't already exist, and overwritten if it does.

This was pretty straightforward, but there's one problem with this technique: it requires us to have the entire file contents ready at the point where we want to start writing text. This application already does that, but this won't always be so. What if your program performs long and complex processing that produces very large volumes of text? Writing the entire file at once like this would involve having the whole thing in memory first. But there's a slightly more complex alternative that makes it possible to generate gigabytes of text without consuming much memory.

Writing Text with a StreamWriter

The File class offers a CreateText method, which takes the path to the file to create (either relative or absolute, as usual), and creates it for you if it doesn't already exist. If the file is already present, this method overwrites it. Unlike the WriteAllText method, it doesn't write any data initially—the newly created file will be empty at first. The method returns an instance of the StreamWriter class, which allows you to write to the file. Example 11-21 shows the code we need to use that.

Example 11-21. Creating a StreamWriter

```
private static void CreateFile(string fullPath, string p)
{
    using (StreamWriter writer = File.CreateText(fullPath))
    {
        // Use the stream writer here
    }
}
```

We're no longer writing the whole file in one big lump, so we need to let the StreamWriter know when we're done. To make life easier for us, StreamWriter implements IDisposable, and closes the underlying file if Dispose is called. This means that we can wrap it in a using block, as Example 11-21 shows, and we can be assured that it will be closed even if an exception is thrown.

So, what is a StreamWriter? The first thing to note is that even though this chapter has "Stream" in the title, this isn't actually a Stream; it's a wrapper around a Stream. It derives from a class called TextWriter, which, as you might guess, is a base for types which write text into things, and a StreamWriter is a TextWriter that writes text into a Stream. TextWriter defines lots of overloads of Write and WriteLine methods, very similar to those we've been using on Console in all of our examples so far.

If it is so similar in signature, why doesn't Console derive from Text Writer? TextWriter is intended to be used with some underlying resource that needs proper lifetime management, so it implements IDisposable. Our code would be much less readable if we had to wrap every call on Console with a using block, or remember to call Dispose—especially as it isn't really necessary. So, why make TextWriter implement IDisposa ble? We do that so that our text-writing code can be implemented in terms of this base class, without needing to know exactly what sort of TextWriter we're talking to, and still handle the cleanup properly.

The File class's CreateText method calls a constructor on StreamWriter which opens the newly created file, and makes it ready for us to write; something like this:

```
return new StreamWriter(fullPath, false);
```

There's nothing to stop you from doing this yourself by hand, and there are many situations where you might want to do so; but the helper methods on File tend to make your code smaller, and more readable, so you should consider using those first. We'll look at using Stream Writer (and its partner, StreamReader) in this way later in the chapter, when we're dealing with different sorts of underlying streams.

Hang on, though. We've snuck a second parameter into that constructor. What does that Boolean mean? When you create a StreamWriter, you can choose to overwrite any existing file content (the default), or append to what is already there. The second Boolean parameter to the constructor controls that behavior. As it happen, passing false here means we want to overwrite.

This is a great example of why it's better to define nicely named enumerations, rather than controlling this sort of thing with a bool. If the value had not been false, but some mythical value such as OpenBehav ior.Overwrite, we probably wouldn't have needed to explain what it did. C# 4.0 added the ability to use argument names when calling methods, so we could have written new StreamWriter(fullPath, append: false), which improves matters slightly, but doesn't help you when you come across code that hasn't bothered to do that.

So, now we can easily complete the implementation of our `CreateFile` method, as shown in Example 11-22.

Example 11-22. Writing a string with StreamWriter

```
private static void CreateFile(string fullPath, string p)
{
    using (StreamWriter writer = File.CreateText(fullPath))
    {
        writer.Write(p);
    }
}
```

We just write the string we've been provided to the file. In this particular application, Example 11-22 isn't an improvement on Example 11-20—we're just writing a single string, so `WriteAllText` was a better fit. But `StreamWriter` is an important technique for less trivial scenarios.

StreamReader/Writer and Text Encodings

We learned in Chapter 10 that there are a number of different encodings that can be used for text characters (like ASCII, UTF-8, and Unicode). Those encodings determine exactly what sequence of bytes represents any particular character. `StreamWriter` (and `StreamReader`) need to take account of those encodings when they write or read data from a stream.

By default, writers use a UTF-8 encoding, while readers attempt to determine the encoding from the content of the file, but you can override that and provide your own `Encoding` to the constructor. Likewise, the `File.WriteAllText` method used in Example 11-20 defaults to UTF-8, but it too offers an overload that accepts an `Encoding`.

OK, let's build and run this code again (press F5 to make sure it runs in the debugger). And everything seems to be going very well. We see the output we'd hoped for:

```
C:\Users\mwa\AppData\Local\up022gsm.241
C:\Users\mwa\AppData\Local\gdovysqk.cqn
C:\Users\mwa\AppData\Local\xyhazu3n.4pw
SameNameAndContent.txt
----------------------
C:\Users\mwa\AppData\Local\up022gsm.241
C:\Users\mwa\AppData\Local\gdovysqk.cqn
C:\Users\mwa\AppData\Local\xyhazu3n.4pw
```

That is to say, one file is found duplicated in three directories. All the others have failed to match, exactly as we'd expect.

Unfortunately, almost before we'd had a chance to read that, the debugger halted execution to report an unhandled exception. It crashes in the code we added in Example 11-17 to delete the directories, because the directories are not empty.

For now, we're going to have to clean up those directories by hand again, and make another change to our code. Clearly, the problem is that the `Directory.Delete` method doesn't delete the files and directories *inside* the directory itself.

This is easily fixed, because there is another overload of that method which does allow us to delete the files recursively—you just pass a Boolean as the second parameter (`true` for recursive deletes, and `false` for the default behavior).

Don't add this parameter unless you're absolutely sure that the code is working correctly, looking only at the test directory, and not executing this code in nontest mode. We don't want a host of emails appearing telling us that we deleted your entire, non-backed-up source and document tree because you followed this next instruction, having deviated slightly from the earlier instructions.

If you want to avoid having to clean up the directories by hand, though, and you're *really, really sure* everything is fine, you *could* add this, at your own risk:

```
Directory.Delete(directory, true);
```

So far, we have quietly ignored the many, many things that can go wrong when you're using files and streams. Now seems like a good time to dive into that murky topic.

When Files Go Bad: Dealing with Exceptions

Exceptions related to file and stream operations fall into three broad categories:

- The usual suspects you might get from any method: incorrect parameters, null references, and so on
- I/O-related problems
- Security-related problems

The first category can, of course, be dealt with as normal—if they occur (as we discussed in Chapter 6) there is usually some bug or unexpected usage that you need to deal with.

The other two are slightly more interesting cases. We should expect problems with file I/O. Files and directories are (mostly) system-wide shared resources. This means that *anyone* can be doing something with them while you are trying to use them. As fast as you're creating them, some other process might be deleting them. Or writing to them; or locking them so that you can't touch them; or altering the permissions on them so that you can't see them anymore. You might be working with files on a network share, in which case different computers may be messing with the files, or you might lose connectivity partway through working with a file.

This "global" nature of files also means that you have to deal with concurrency problems. Consider this piece of code, for example, that makes use of the (almost totally redundant) method `File.Exists`, shown in Example 11-23, which determines whether a file exists.

Example 11-23. The questionable File.Exists method

```
if (File.Exists("SomeFile.txt"))
{
    // Play with the file
}
```

Is it safe to play with the file in there, on the assumption that it exists?

No.

In another process, even from another machine if the directory is shared, someone could nip in and delete the file or lock it, or do something even more nefarious (like substitute it for something else). Or the user might have closed the lid of his laptop just after the method returns, and may well be in a different continent by the time he brings it out of sleep mode, at which point you won't necessarily have access to the same network shares that seemed to be visible just one line of code ago.

So you have to code extremely defensively, and *expect* exceptions in your I/O code, even if you checked that everything looked OK before you started your work.

Unlike most exceptions, though, abandoning the operation is not always the best choice. You often see transient problems, like a USB drive being temporarily unavailable, for example, or a network glitch temporarily hiding a share from us, or aborting a file copy operation. (Transient network problems are particularly common after a laptop resumes from suspend—it can take a few seconds to get back on the network, or maybe even minutes if the user is in a hotel and has to sign up for an Internet connection before connecting back to the office VPN. Abandoning the user's data is not a user-friendly response to this situation.)

When an I/O problem occurs, the framework throws one of several exceptions derived from `IOException` (or, as we've already seen, `IOException` itself) listed here:

`IOException`

>   This is thrown when some general problem with I/O has occurred. This is the base for all of the more specific exception types, but it is sometimes thrown in its own right, with the `Message` text describing the actual problem. This makes it somewhat less useful for programmatic interpretation; you usually have to allow the user to intervene in some way when you catch one of these.

`DirectoryNotFoundException`

>   This is thrown when an attempt is made to access a directory that does not exist. This commonly occurs because of an error in constructing a path (particularly when relative paths are in play), or because some other process has moved or deleted a directory during an operation.

DriveNotFoundException

> This is thrown when the root drive in a path is no longer available. This could be because a drive letter has been mapped to a network location which is no longer available, or a removable device has been removed. Or because you typed the wrong drive letter!

FileLoadException

> This is a bit of an anomaly in the family of IOExceptions, and we're including it in this list only because it can cause some confusion. It is thrown by the runtime when an assembly cannot be loaded; as such, it has more to do with assemblies than files and streams.

FileNotFoundException

> This is thrown when an attempt is made to access a file that does not exist. As with DirectoryNotFoundException, this is often because there has been some error in constructing a path (absolute or relative), or because something was moved or deleted while the program was running.

PathTooLongException

> This is an awkward little exception, and causes a good deal of confusion for developers (which is one reason correct behavior in the face of long paths is a part of Microsoft's Designed For Windows test suite). It is thrown when a path provided is too long. But what is "too long"? The maximum length for a path in Windows used to be 260 characters (which isn't very long at all). Recent versions allow paths up to about (but not necessarily exactly) 32,767 characters, but making use of that from .NET is awkward. There's a detailed discussion of Windows File and Path lengths if you fall foul of the problem in the MSDN documentation at *http://msdn .microsoft.com/library/aa365247*, and a discussion of the .NET-specific issues at *http://go.microsoft.com/fwlink/?LinkID=163666*.

If you are doing anything with I/O operations, you will need to think about most, if not all, of these exceptions, deciding where to catch them and what to do when they occur.

Let's look back at our example again, and see what we want to do with any exceptions that might occur. As a first pass, we could just wrap our main loop in a try/catch block, as Example 11-24 does. Since our application's only job is to report its findings, we'll just display a message if we encounter a problem.

Example 11-24. A first attempt at handling I/O exceptions

```
try
{
    List<FileNameGroup> filesGroupedByName =
        InspectDirectories(recurseIntoSubdirectories, directoriesToSearch);

    DisplayMatches(foundFiles);
    Console.ReadKey();
}
```

```
catch (PathTooLongException ptlx)
{
    Console.WriteLine("The specified path was too long");
    Console.WriteLine(ptlx.Message);
}
catch (DirectoryNotFoundException dnfx)
{
    Console.WriteLine("The specified directory was not found");
    Console.WriteLine(dnfx.Message);
}
catch (IOException iox)
{
    Console.WriteLine(iox.Message);
}
catch (UnauthorizedAccessException uax)
{
    Console.WriteLine("You do not have permission to access this directory.");
    Console.WriteLine(uax.Message);
}
catch (ArgumentException ax)
{
    Console.WriteLine("The path provided was not valid.");
    Console.WriteLine(ax.Message);
}
finally
{
    if (testDirectoriesMade)
    {
        CleanupTestDirectories(directoriesToSearch);
    }
}
```

We've decided to provide specialized handling for the `PathTooLongException` and `DirectoryNotFoundException` exceptions, as well as generic handling for `IOException` (which, of course, we have to catch after the exceptions derived from it).

In addition to those `IOException`-derived types, we've also caught `UnauthorizedAccessException`. This is a security exception, rather than an I/O exception, and so it derives from a different base (`SystemException`). It is thrown if the user does not have permission to access the directory concerned.

Let's see that in operation, by creating an additional test directory and denying ourselves access to it. Example 11-25 shows a function to create a directory where we deny ourselves the `ListDirectory` permission.

Example 11-25. Denying permission

```
private static string CreateDeniedDirectory(string parentPath)
{
    string deniedDirectory = Path.GetRandomFileName();
    string fullDeniedPath = Path.Combine(parentPath, deniedDirectory);
    string userName = WindowsIdentity.GetCurrent().Name;
    DirectorySecurity ds = new DirectorySecurity();
    FileSystemAccessRule fsarDeny =
```

```
        new FileSystemAccessRule(
            userName,
            FileSystemRights.ListDirectory,
            AccessControlType.Deny);
    ds.AddAccessRule(fsarDeny);

    Directory.CreateDirectory(fullDeniedPath, ds);
    return fullDeniedPath;
}
```

We can call it from our `MakeTestDirectories` method, as Example 11-26 shows (along with suitable modifications to the code to accommodate the extra directory).

Example 11-26. Modifying MakeTestDirectories for permissions test

```
private static string[] MakeTestDirectories()
{
    // ...
    // Let's make three test directories
    // and leave space for a fourth to test access denied behavior
    var directories = new string[4];
    for (int i = 0; i < directories.Length - 1; ++i)
    {
        ... as before ...
    }

    CreateTestFiles(directories.Take(3));

    directories[3] = CreateDeniedDirectory(localApplicationData);

    return directories;
}
```

But hold on a moment, before you build and run this. If we've denied ourselves permission to look at that directory, how are we going to delete it again in our cleanup code? Fortunately, because we own the directory that we created, we can modify the permissions again when we clean up.

Finding and Modifying Permissions

Example 11-27 shows a method which can give us back full control over any directory (providing we have the permission to change the permissions). This code makes some assumptions about the existing permissions, but that's OK here because we created the directory in the first place.

Example 11-27. Granting access to a directory

```
private static void AllowAccess(string directory)
{
    DirectorySecurity ds = Directory.GetAccessControl(directory);

    string userName = WindowsIdentity.GetCurrent().Name;
```

```
    // Remove the deny rule
    FileSystemAccessRule fsarDeny =
        new FileSystemAccessRule(
            userName,
            FileSystemRights.ListDirectory,
            AccessControlType.Deny);
    ds.RemoveAccessRuleSpecific(fsarDeny);

    // And add an allow rule
    FileSystemAccessRule fsarAllow =
        new FileSystemAccessRule(
            userName,
            FileSystemRights.FullControl,
            AccessControlType.Allow);
    ds.AddAccessRule(fsarAllow);

    Directory.SetAccessControl(directory, ds);
}
```

Notice how we're using the `GetAccessControl` method on `Directory` to get hold of the directory security information. We then construct a filesystem access rule which matches the deny rule we created earlier, and call `RemoveAccessRuleSpecific` on the `DirectorySecurity` information we retrieved. This matches the rule up exactly, and then removes it if it exists (or does nothing if it doesn't).

Finally, we add an *allow* rule to the set to give us full control over the directory, and then call the `Directory.SetAccessControl` method to set those permissions on the directory itself.

Let's call that method from our cleanup code, compile, and run. (Don't forget, we're deleting files and directories, and changing permissions, so take care!)

Here's some sample output:

```
C:\Users\mwa\AppData\Local\ufmnho4z.h5p
C:\Users\mwa\AppData\Local\5chw4maf.xyu
C:\Users\mwa\AppData\Local\s1ydovhu.0wk
You do not have permission to access this directory.
Access to the path 'C:\Users\mwa\AppData\Local\byjijkza.3cj\' is denied.
```

These methods make it relatively easy to manage permissions when you create and manipulate files, but they don't make it easy to decide what those permissions should be! It is always tempting just to make everything available to anyone—you can get your code compiled and "working" much quicker that way; but only for "not very secure" values of "working," and that's something that has to be of concern for every developer.

 Your application could be the one that miscreants decide to exploit to turn your users' PCs to the dark side.

I warmly recommend that you crank UAC up to the maximum (and put up with the occasional security dialog), run Visual Studio as a nonadministrator (as far as is possible), and think at every stage about the least possible privileges you can grant to your users that will still let them get their work done. Making *your* app more secure benefits everyone: not just your own users, but everyone who doesn't receive a spam email or a hack attempt because the bad guys couldn't exploit your application.

We've now handled the exception nicely—but is stopping really the best thing we could have done? Would it not be better to log the fact that we were unable to access particular directories, and carry on? Similarly, if we get a `DirectoryNotFoundException` or `FileNot FoundException`, wouldn't we want to just carry on in this case? The fact that someone has deleted the directory from underneath us shouldn't matter to us.

If we look again at our sample, it might be better to catch the `DirectoryNotFoundExcep tion` and `FileNotFoundException` inside the `InspectDirectories` method to provide a more fine-grained response to errors. Also, if we look at the documentation for `FileInfo`, we'll see that it may actually throw a base `IOException` under some circumstances, so we should catch that here, too. And in all cases, we need to catch the security exceptions.

We're relying on LINQ to iterate through the files and folders, which means it's not entirely obvious where to put the exception handling. Example 11-28 shows the code from `InspectDirectories` that iterates through the folders, to get a list of files. We can't put exception handling code into the middle of that query.

Example 11-28. Iterating through the directories

```
var allFilePaths = from directory in directoriesToSearch
                   from file in Directory.GetFiles(directory, "*.*",
                                                   searchOption)
                   select file;
```

However, we don't have to. The simplest way to solve this is to put the code that gets the directories into a separate method, so we can add exception handling, as Example 11-29 shows.

Example 11-29. Putting exception handling in a helper method

```
private static IEnumerable<string> GetDirectoryFiles(
    string directory, SearchOption searchOption)
{
    try
    {
        return Directory.GetFiles(directory, "*.*", searchOption);
    }
    catch (DirectoryNotFoundException dnfx)
    {
        Console.WriteLine("Warning: The specified directory was not found");
        Console.WriteLine(dnfx.Message);
    }
    catch (UnauthorizedAccessException uax)
```

```
    {
        Console.WriteLine(
            "Warning: You do not have permission to access this directory.");
        Console.WriteLine(uax.Message);
    }

    return Enumerable.Empty<string>();
}
```

This method defers to `Directory.GetFiles`, but in the event of one of the expected errors, it displays a warning, and then just returns an empty collection.

 There's a problem here when we ask `GetFiles` to search recursively: if it encounters a problem with even just one directory, the whole operation throws, and you'll end up not looking in any directories. So while Example 11-29 makes a difference only when the user passes multiple directories on the command line, it's not all that useful when using the /sub option. If you wanted to make your error handling more fine-grained still, you could write your own recursive directory search. The `GetAllFilesInDirectory` example in Chapter 7 shows how to do that.

If we modify the LINQ query to use this, as shown in Example 11-30, the overall progress will be undisturbed by the error handling.

Example 11-30. Iterating in the face of errors

```
var allFilePaths = from directory in directoriesToSearch
                   from file in GetDirectoryFiles(directory,
                                                  searchOption)
                   select file;
```

And we can use a similar technique for the LINQ query that populates the `fileNameGroups`—it uses `FileInfo`, and we need to handle exceptions for that. Example 11-31 iterates through a list of paths, and returns details for each file that it was able to access successfully, displaying errors otherwise.

Example 11-31. Handling exceptions from FileInfo

```
private static IEnumerable<FileDetails> GetDetails(IEnumerable<string> paths)
{
    foreach (string filePath in paths)
    {
        FileDetails details = null;
        try
        {
            FileInfo info = new FileInfo(filePath);
            details = new FileDetails
            {
                FilePath = filePath,
                FileSize = info.Length
            };
```

```
        }
        catch (FileNotFoundException fnfx)
        {
            Console.WriteLine("Warning: The specified file was not found");
            Console.WriteLine(fnfx.Message);
        }
        catch (IOException iox)
        {
            Console.Write("Warning: ");
            Console.WriteLine(iox.Message);
        }
        catch (UnauthorizedAccessException uax)
        {
            Console.WriteLine(
                "Warning: You do not have permission to access this file.");
            Console.WriteLine(uax.Message);
        }

        if (details != null)
        {
            yield return details;
        }
    }
}
```

We can use this from the final LINQ query in `InspectDirectories`. Example 11-32
shows the modified query.

Example 11-32. Getting details while tolerating errors

```
var fileNameGroups = from filePath in allFilePaths
                     let fileNameWithoutPath = Path.GetFileName(filePath)
                     group filePath by fileNameWithoutPath into nameGroup
                     select new FileNameGroup
                     {
                         FileNameWithoutPath = nameGroup.Key,
                         FilesWithThisName = GetDetails(nameGroup).ToList()
                     };
```

Again, this enables the query to process all accessible items, while reporting errors for
any problematic files without having to stop completely. If we compile and run again,
we see the following output:

```
C:\Users\mwa\AppData\Local\dcyx0fv1.hv3
C:\Users\mwa\AppData\Local\0nf2wqwr.y3s
C:\Users\mwa\AppData\Local\kfilxte4.exy
Warning: You do not have permission to access this directory.
Access to the path 'C:\Users\mwa\AppData\Local\r2gl4q1a.ycp\' is denied.
SameNameAndContent.txt
---------------------
C:\Users\mwa\AppData\Local\dcyx0fv1.hv3
C:\Users\mwa\AppData\Local\0nf2wqwr.y3s
C:\Users\mwa\AppData\Local\kfilxte4.exy
```

We've dealt cleanly with the directory to which we did not have access, and have continued with the job to a successful conclusion.

Now that we've found a few candidate files that may (or may not) be the same, can we actually check to see that they are, in fact, identical, rather than just coincidentally having the same name and length?

Reading Files into Memory

To compare the candidate files, we could load them into memory. The `File` class offers three likely looking static methods: `ReadAllBytes`, which treats the file as binary, and loads it into a byte array; `File.ReadAllText`, which treats it as text, and reads it all into a string; and `File.ReadLines`, which again treats it as text, but loads each line into its own string, and returns an array of all the lines. We could even call `File.OpenRead` to obtain a `StreamReader` (equivalent to the `StreamWriter`, but for reading data—we'll see this again later in the chapter).

Because we're looking at all file types, not just text, we need to use one of the binary-based methods. `File.ReadAllBytes` returns a `byte[]` containing the entire contents of the file. We could then compare the files byte for byte, to see if they are the same. Here's some code to do that.

First, let's update our `DisplayMatches` function to do the load and compare, as shown by the highlighted lines in Example 11-33.

Example 11-33. Updating DisplayMatches for content comparison

```
private static void DisplayMatches(
    IEnumerable<FileNameGroup> filesGroupedByName)
{
    var groupsWithMoreThanOneFile = from nameGroup in filesGroupedByName
                                    where nameGroup.FilesWithThisName.Count > 1
                                    select nameGroup;

    foreach (var fileNameGroup in groupsWithMoreThanOneFile)
    {
        // Group the matches by the file size, then select those
        // with more than 1 file of that size.
        var matchesBySize = from match in fileNameGroup.FilesWithThisName
                            group match by match.FileSize into sizeGroup
                            where sizeGroup.Count() > 1
                            select sizeGroup;

        foreach (var matchedBySize in matchesBySize)
        {
            List<FileContents> content = LoadFiles(matchedBySize);
            CompareFiles(content);
        }
    }
}
```

Notice that we want our `LoadFiles` function to return a `List` of `FileContents` objects. Example 11-34 shows the `FileContents` class.

Example 11-34. File content information class

```
internal class FileContents
{
    public string FilePath { get; set; }
    public byte[] Content { get; set; }
}
```

It just lets us associate the filename with the contents so that we can use it later to display the results. Example 11-35 shows the implementation of `LoadFiles`, which uses `ReadAllBytes` to load in the file content.

Example 11-35. Loading binary file content

```
private static List<FileContents> LoadFiles(IEnumerable<FileDetails> fileList)
{
    var content = new List<FileContents>();
    foreach (FileDetails item in fileList)
    {
        byte[] contents = File.ReadAllBytes(item.FilePath);
        content.Add(new FileContents
        {
            FilePath = item.FilePath,
            Content = contents
        });
    }
    return content;
}
```

We now need an implementation for `CompareFiles`, which is shown in Example 11-36.

Example 11-36. CompareFiles method

```
private static void CompareFiles(List<FileContents> files)
{
    Dictionary<FileContents, List<FileContents>> potentiallyMatched =
        BuildPotentialMatches(files);

    // Now, we're going to look at every byte in each
    CompareBytes(files, potentiallyMatched);

    DisplayResults(files, potentiallyMatched);
}
```

This isn't exactly the most elegant way of comparing several files. We're building a big dictionary of all of the potential matching combinations, and then weeding out the ones that don't actually match. For large numbers of potential matches of the same size this could get quite inefficient, but we'll not worry about that right now! Example 11-37 shows the function that builds those potential matches.

Example 11-37. Building possible match combinations

```
private static Dictionary<FileContents, List<FileContents>>
    BuildPotentialMatches(List<FileContents> files)
{
    // Builds a dictionary where the entries look like:
    //   { 0, { 1, 2, 3, 4, ... N } }
    //   { 1, { 2, 3, 4, ... N }
    // ...
    //   { N - 1, { N } }
    // where N is one less than the number of files.
    var allCombinations = Enumerable.Range(0, files.Count - 1).ToDictionary(
        x => files[x],
        x => files.Skip(x + 1).ToList());

    return allCombinations;
}
```

This set of potential matches will be whittled down to the files that really are the same by `CompareBytes`, which we'll get to momentarily. The `DisplayResults` method, shown in Example 11-38, runs through the matches and displays their names and locations.

Example 11-38. Displaying matches

```
private static void DisplayResults(
    List<FileContents> files,
    Dictionary<FileContents, List<FileContents>> currentlyMatched)
{
    if (currentlyMatched.Count == 0) { return; }

    var alreadyMatched = new List<FileContents>();

    Console.WriteLine("Matches");

    foreach (var matched in currentlyMatched)
    {
        // Don't do it if we've already matched it previously
        if (alreadyMatched.Contains(matched.Key))
        {
            continue;
        }
        else
        {
            alreadyMatched.Add(matched.Key);
        }
        Console.WriteLine("-------");
        Console.WriteLine(matched.Key.FilePath);
        foreach (var file in matched.Value)
        {
            Console.WriteLine(file.FilePath);
            alreadyMatched.Add(file);
        }
    }
    Console.WriteLine("-------");
}
```

This leaves the method shown in Example 11-39 that does the bulk of the work, comparing the potentially matching files, byte for byte.

Example 11-39. Byte-for-byte comparison of all potential matches

```
private static void CompareBytes(
    List<FileContents> files,
    Dictionary<FileContents, List<FileContents>> potentiallyMatched)
{
    // Remember, this only ever gets called with files of equal length.
    int fileLength = files[0].Content.Length;
    var sourceFilesWithNoMatches = new List<FileContents>();
    for (int fileByteOffset = 0; fileByteOffset < fileLength; ++fileByteOffset)
    {
        foreach (var sourceFileEntry in potentiallyMatched)
        {
            byte[] sourceContent = sourceFileEntry.Key.Content;
            for (int otherIndex = 0; otherIndex < sourceFileEntry.Value.Count;
                                                        ++otherIndex)
            {
                // Check the byte at i in each of the two files, if they don't
                //  match, then we remove them from the collection
                byte[] otherContent =
                    sourceFileEntry.Value[otherIndex].Content;
                if (sourceContent[fileByteOffset] != otherContent[fileByteOffset])
                {
                    sourceFileEntry.Value.RemoveAt(otherIndex);
                    otherIndex -= 1;
                    if (sourceFileEntry.Value.Count == 0)
                    {
                        sourceFilesWithNoMatches.Add(sourceFileEntry.Key);
                    }
                }
            }
        }
        foreach (FileContents fileWithNoMatches in sourceFilesWithNoMatches)
        {
            potentiallyMatched.Remove(fileWithNoMatches);
        }
        // Don't bother with the rest of the file if
        // there are no further potential matches
        if (potentiallyMatched.Count == 0)
        {
            break;
        }
        sourceFilesWithNoMatches.Clear();
    }
}
```

We're going to need to add a test file that differs only in the content. In `CreateTest Files` add another filename that doesn't change as we go round the loop:

```
string fileSameSizeInAllButDifferentContent =
    "SameNameAndSizeDifferentContent.txt";
```

Then, inside the loop (at the bottom), we'll create a test file that will be the same length, but varying by only a single byte:

```
// And now one that is the same length, but with different content
fullPath = Path.Combine(directory, fileSameSizeInAllButDifferentContent);

builder = new StringBuilder();
builder.Append("Now with ");
builder.Append(directoryIndex);
builder.AppendLine(" extra");
CreateFile(fullPath, builder.ToString());
```

If you build and run, you should see some output like this, showing the one identical file we have in each file location:

```
C:\Users\mwa\AppData\Local\e33yz4hg.mjp
C:\Users\mwa\AppData\Local\ung2xdgo.k1c
C:\Users\mwa\AppData\Local\jcpagntt.ynd
Warning: You do not have permission to access this directory.
Access to the path 'C:\Users\mwa\AppData\Local\cmoof2kj.ekd\' is denied.
Matches
-------
C:\Users\mwa\AppData\Local\e33yz4hg.mjp\SameNameAndContent.txt
C:\Users\mwa\AppData\Local\ung2xdgo.k1c\SameNameAndContent.txt
C:\Users\mwa\AppData\Local\jcpagntt.ynd\SameNameAndContent.txt
-------
```

Needless to say, this isn't exactly very efficient; and it is unlikely to work so well when you get to those DVD rips and massive media repositories. Even your 64-bit machine probably doesn't have quite that much memory available to it.[*] There's a way to make this more memory-efficient. Instead of loading the file completely into memory, we can take a *streaming* approach.

Streams

You can think of a stream like one of those old-fashioned news ticker tapes. To write data onto the tape, the bytes (or characters) in the file are typed out, one at a time, on the continuous stream of tape.

We can then wind the tape back to the beginning, and start reading it back, character by character, until either we stop or we run off the end of the tape. Or we could give the tape to someone else, and she could do the same. Or we could read, say, 1,000 characters off the tape, and copy them onto another tape which we give to someone to work on, then read the next 1,000, and so on, until we run out of characters.

---

[*] In fact, it is slightly more constrained than that. The .NET Framework limits arrays to 2 GB, and will throw an exception if you try to load a larger file into memory all at once.

Once upon a time, we used to store programs and data in exactly this way, on a stream of paper tape with holes punched in it; the basic technology for this was invented in the 19th century. Later, we got magnetic tape, although that was less than useful in machine shops full of electric motors generating magnetic fields, so paper systems (both tape and punched cards) lasted well into the 1980s (when disk systems and other storage technologies became more robust, and much faster).

The concept of a machine that reads data items one at a time, and can step forward or backward through that stream, goes back to the very foundations of modern computing. It is one of those highly resilient metaphors that only really falls down in the face of highly parallelized algorithms: a single input stream is often the choke point for scalability in that case.

To illustrate this, let's write a method that's equivalent to `File.ReadAllBytes` using a stream (see Example 11-40).

Example 11-40. Reading from a stream

```
private static byte[] ReadAllBytes(string filename)
{
    using (FileStream stream = File.OpenRead(filename))
    {
        long streamLength = stream.Length;
        if (streamLength > 0x7fffffffL)
        {
            throw new InvalidOperationException(
                "Unable to allocate more than 0x7fffffffL bytes" +
                "of memory to read the file");
        }
        // Safe to cast to an int, because
        // we checked for overflow above
        int bytesToRead = (int) stream.Length;
        // This could be a big buffer!
        byte[] bufferToReturn = new byte[bytesToRead];
        // We're going to start at the beginning
        int offsetIntoBuffer = 0;
        while (bytesToRead > 0)
        {
            int bytesRead = stream.Read(bufferToReturn,
                                        offsetIntoBuffer,
                                        bytesToRead);
            if (bytesRead == 0)
            {
                throw new InvalidOperationException(
                    "We reached the end of file before we expected..." +
                    "Has someone changed the file while we weren't looking?");
            }
            // Read may return fewer bytes than we asked for, so be
            // ready to go round again.
            bytesToRead -= bytesRead;
            offsetIntoBuffer += bytesRead;
```

```
        }

    return bufferToReturn;
    }
}
```

The call to `File.OpenRead` creates us an instance of a `FileStream`. This class derives from the base `Stream` class, which defines most of the methods and properties we're going to use.

First, we inspect the stream's `Length` property to determine how many bytes we need to allocate in our result. This is a `long`, so *it* can support truly enormous files, even if *we* can allocate only 2 GB of memory.

 If you try using the `stream.Length` argument as the array size without checking it for size first, it will compile, so you might wonder why we're doing this check. In fact, C# converts the argument to an `int` first, and if it's too big, you'll get an `OverflowException` at runtime. By checking the size explicitly, we can provide our own error message.

Then (once we've set up a few variables) we call `stream.Read` and ask it for all of the data in the stream. It is entitled to give us any number of bytes it likes, up to the number we ask for. It returns the actual number of bytes read, or `0` if we've hit the end of the stream and there's no more data.

 A common programming error is to assume that the stream will give you as many bytes as you asked for. Under simple test conditions it usually will if there's enough data. However, streams can and sometimes do return you less in order to give you *some* data as soon as possible, even when you might think it should be able to give you everything. If you need to read a certain amount before proceeding, you need to write code to keep calling `Read` until you get what you require, as Example 11-40 does.

Notice that it returns us an `int`. So even if .NET did let us allocate arrays larger than 2 GB (which it doesn't) a stream can only tell us that it has read 2 GB worth of data at a time, and in fact, the third argument to `Read`, where we tell it how much we want, is also an `int`, so 2 GB is the most we can ask for. So while `FileStream` is able to work with larger files thanks to the 64-bit `Length` property, it will split the data into more modest chunks of 2 GB or less when we read. But then one of the main reasons for using streams in the first place is to avoid having to deal with all the content in one go, so in practice we tend to work with much smaller chunks in any case.

So we always call the Read method in a loop. The stream maintains the current read position for us, but we need to work out where to write it in the destination array (offsetIntoBuffer). We also need to work out how many more bytes we have to read (bytesToRead).

We can now update the call to ReadAllBytes in our LoadFile method so that it uses our new implementation:

```
byte[] contents = ReadAllBytes(item.Filename);
```

 If this was all you were going to do, you wouldn't actually implement ReadAllBytes yourself; you'd use the one in the framework! This is just by way of an example. We're going to make more interesting use of streams shortly.

Build and run again, and you should see output with exactly the same form as before:

```
C:\Users\mwa\AppData\Local\1ssoimgj.wqg
C:\Users\mwa\AppData\Local\cjiymq5b.bfo
C:\Users\mwa\AppData\Local\diss5tgl.zae
Warning: You do not have permission to access this directory.
Access to the path 'C:\Users\mwa\AppData\Local\u1wOrjOo.2xe\' is denied.
Matches
-------
C:\Users\mwa\AppData\Local\1ssoimgj.wqg\SameNameAndContent.txt
C:\Users\mwa\AppData\Local\cjiymq5b.bfo\SameNameAndContent.txt
C:\Users\mwa\AppData\Local\diss5tgl.zae\SameNameAndContent.txt
-------
```

That's all very well, but we haven't actually improved anything. We wanted to avoid loading all of those files into memory. Instead of loading the files, let's update our FileContents class to hold a stream instead of a byte array, as Example 11-41 shows.

Example 11-41. FileContents using FileStream

```
internal class FileContents
{
    public string FilePath { get; set; }
    public FileStream Content { get; set; }
}
```

We'll have to update the code that creates the FileContents too, in our LoadFiles method from Example 11-35. Example 11-42 shows the change required.

Example 11-42. Modifying LoadFiles

```
content.Add(new FileContents
            {
                FilePath = item.FilePath,
                Content = File.OpenRead(item.FilePath)
            });
```

(You can now delete our ReadAllBytes implementation, if you want.)

Because we're opening all of those files, we need to make sure that we always close them all. We can't implement the using pattern, because we're handing off the references outside the scope of the function that creates them, so we'll have to find somewhere else to call Close.

DisplayMatches (Example 11-33) ultimately causes the streams to be created by calling LoadFiles, so DisplayMatches should close them too. We can add a try/finally block in that method's innermost foreach loop, as Example 11-43 shows.

Example 11-43. Closing streams in DisplayMatches

```
foreach (var matchedBySize in matchesBySize)
{
    List<FileContents> content = LoadFiles(matchedBySize);
    try
    {
        CompareFiles(content);
    }
    finally
    {
        foreach (var item in content)
        {
            item.Content.Close();
        }
    }
}
```

The last thing to update, then, is the CompareBytes method. The previous version, shown in Example 11-39, relied on loading all the files into memory upfront. The modified version in Example 11-44 uses streams.

Example 11-44. Stream-based CompareBytes

```
private static void CompareBytes(
    List<FileContents> files,
    Dictionary<FileContents, List<FileContents>> potentiallyMatched)
{
    // Remember, this only ever gets called with files of equal length.
    long bytesToRead = files[0].Content.Length;
    // We work through all the files at once, so allocate a buffer for each.
    Dictionary<FileContents, byte[]> fileBuffers =
        files.ToDictionary(x => x, x => new byte[1024]);

    var sourceFilesWithNoMatches = new List<FileContents>();
    while (bytesToRead > 0)
    {
        // Read up to 1k from all the files.
        int bytesRead = 0;
        foreach (var bufferEntry in fileBuffers)
        {
            FileContents file = bufferEntry.Key;
            byte[] buffer = bufferEntry.Value;
```

```
        int bytesReadFromThisFile = 0;
        while (bytesReadFromThisFile < buffer.Length)
        {
            int bytesThisRead = file.Content.Read(
                buffer, bytesReadFromThisFile,
                buffer.Length - bytesReadFromThisFile);
            if (bytesThisRead == 0) { break; }
            bytesReadFromThisFile += bytesThisRead;
        }
        if (bytesReadFromThisFile < buffer.Length
         && bytesReadFromThisFile < bytesToRead)
        {
            throw new InvalidOperationException(
                "Unexpected end of file - did a file change?");
        }
        bytesRead = bytesReadFromThisFile; // Will be same for all files
    }
    bytesToRead -= bytesRead;

    foreach (var sourceFileEntry in potentiallyMatched)
    {
        byte[] sourceFileContent = fileBuffers[sourceFileEntry.Key];

        for (int otherIndex = 0; otherIndex < sourceFileEntry.Value.Count;
                                                        ++otherIndex)
        {
            byte[] otherFileContent =
                fileBuffers[sourceFileEntry.Value[otherIndex]];
            for (int i = 0; i < bytesRead; ++i)
            {
                if (sourceFileContent[i] != otherFileContent[i])
                {
                    sourceFileEntry.Value.RemoveAt(otherIndex);
                    otherIndex -= 1;
                    if (sourceFileEntry.Value.Count == 0)
                    {
                        sourceFilesWithNoMatches.Add(sourceFileEntry.Key);
                    }
                    break;
                }
            }
        }
    }
    foreach (FileContents fileWithNoMatches in sourceFilesWithNoMatches)
    {
        potentiallyMatched.Remove(fileWithNoMatches);
    }
    // Don't bother with the rest of the file if there are
    // not further potential matches
    if (potentiallyMatched.Count == 0)
    {
        break;
    }
    sourceFilesWithNoMatches.Clear();
```

```
        }
}
```

Rather than reading entire files at once, we allocate small buffers, and read in 1 KB at a time. As with the previous version, this new one works through all the files of a particular name and size simultaneously, so we allocate a buffer for each file.

We then loop round, reading in a buffer's worth from each file, and perform comparisons against just that buffer (weeding out any nonmatches). We keep going round until we either determine that none of the files match or reach the end of the files.

Notice how each stream remembers its position for us, with each Read starting where the previous one left off. And since we ensure that we read exactly the same quantity from all the files for each chunk (either 1 KB, or however much is left when we get to the end of the file), all the streams advance in unison.

This code has a somewhat more complex structure than before. The all-in-memory version in Example 11-39 had three loops—the outer one advanced one byte at a time, and then the inner two worked through the various potential match combinations. But because the outer loop in Example 11-44 advances one chunk at a time, we end up needing an extra inner loop to compare all the bytes in a chunk. We could have simplified this by only ever reading a single byte at a time from the streams, but in fact, this chunking has delivered a significant performance improvement. Testing against a folder full of source code, media resources, and compilation output containing 4,500 files (totaling about 500 MB), the all-in-memory version took about 17 seconds to find all the duplicates, but the stream version took just 3.5 seconds! Profiling the code revealed that this performance improvement was entirely a result of the fact that we were comparing the bytes in chunks. So for this particular application, the additional complexity was well worth it. (Of course, you should always measure your own code against representative problems—techniques that work well in one scenario don't necessarily perform well everywhere.)

Moving Around in a Stream

What if we wanted to step forward or backward in the file? We can do that with the Seek method. Let's imagine we want to print out the first 100 bytes of each file that we reject, for debug purposes. We can add some code to our CompareBytes method to do that, as Example 11-45 shows.

Example 11-45. Seeking within a stream

```
if (sourceFileContent[i] != otherFileContent[i])
{
    sourceFileEntry.Value.RemoveAt(otherIndex);
    otherIndex -= 1;
    if (sourceFileEntry.Value.Count == 0)
    {
        sourceFilesWithNoMatches.Add(sourceFileEntry.Key);
```

```
    }
#if DEBUG
    // Remember where we got to
    long currentPosition = sourceFileEntry.Key.Content.Position;
    // Seek to 0 bytes from the beginning
    sourceFileEntry.Key.Content.Seek(0, SeekOrigin.Begin);
    // Read 100 bytes from
    for (int index = 0; index < 100; ++index)
    {
        var val = sourceFileEntry.Key.Content.ReadByte();
        if (val < 0) { break; }
        if (index != 0) { Console.Write(", "); }
        Console.Write(val);
    }
    Console.WriteLine();
    // Put it back where we found it
    sourceFileEntry.Key.Content.Seek(currentPosition, SeekOrigin.Begin);
#endif
    break;
}
```

We start by getting hold of the current position within the stream using the `Position` property. We do this so that the code doesn't lose its place in the stream. (Even though we've detected a mismatch here, remember we're comparing lots of files here—perhaps this same file matches one of the other candidates. So we're not necessarily finished with it yet.)

The first parameter of the `Seek` method tells us how far we are going to seek from our origin—we're passing `0` here because we want to go to the beginning of the file. The second tells us what that origin is going to be. `SeekOrigin.Begin` means the beginning of the file, `SeekOrigin.End` means the end of the file (and so the offset counts backward—you don't need to say `-100`, just `100`).

There's also `SeekOrigin.Current` which allows you to move relative to the current position. You could use this to read 10 bytes ahead, for example (maybe to work out what you were looking at in context), and then seek back to where you were by calling `Seek(-10, SeekOrigin.Current)`.

 Not all streams support seeking. For example, some streams represent network connections, which you might use to download gigabytes of data. The .NET Framework doesn't remember every single byte just in case you ask it to seek later on, so if you attempt to rewind such a stream, `Seek` will throw a `NotSupportedException`. You can find out whether seeking is supported from a stream's `CanSeek` property.

Writing Data with Streams

We don't just have to use streaming APIs for reading. We can write to the stream, too.

One very common programming task is to copy data from one stream to another. We use this kind of thing all the time—copying data, or concatenating the content of several files into another, for example. (If you want to copy an entire file, you'd use `File.Copy`, but streams give you the flexibility to concatenate or modify data, or to work with nonfile sources.)

Example 11-46 shows how to read data from one stream and write it into another. This is just for illustrative purposes—.NET 4 added a new `CopyTo` method to `Stream` which does this for you. In practice you'd need Example 11-46 only if you were targeting an older version of the .NET Framework, but it's a good way to see how to write to a stream.

Example 11-46. Copying from one stream to another

```
private static void WriteTo(Stream source, Stream target, int bufferLength)
{
    bufferLength = Math.Max(100, bufferLength);
    var buffer = new byte[bufferLength];
    int bytesRead;

    do
    {
        bytesRead = source.Read(buffer, 0, buffer.Length);
        if (bytesRead != 0)
        {
            target.Write(buffer, 0, bytesRead);
        }
    } while (bytesRead > 0);
}
```

We create a buffer which is at least 100 bytes long. We then `Read` from the source and `Write` to the target, using the buffer as the intermediary. Notice that the `Write` method takes the same parameters as the read: the buffer, an offset into that buffer, and the number of bytes to write (which in this case is the number of bytes read from the source buffer, hence the slightly confusing variable name). As with `Read`, it steadily advances the current position in the stream as it writes, just like that ticker tape. Unlike `Read`, `Write` will always process as many bytes as we ask it to, so with `Write`, there's no need to keep looping round until it has written all the data.

Obviously, we need to keep looping until we've *read* everything from the source stream. Notice that we keep going until `Read` returns 0. This is how streams indicate that we've reached the end. (Some streams don't know in advance how large they are, so you can rely on the `Length` property for only certain kinds of streams such as `FileStream`. Testing for a return value of 0 is the most general way to know that we've reached the end.)

Reading, Writing, and Locking Files

So, we've seen how to read and write data to and from streams, and how we can move the current position in the stream by seeking to some offset from a known position. Up until now, we've been using the `File.OpenRead` and `File.OpenWrite` methods to create our file streams. There is another method, `File.Open`, which gives us access to some extra features.

The simplest overload takes two parameters: a string which is the path for the file, and a value from the `FileMode` enumeration. What's the `FileMode`? Well, it lets us specify exactly what we want done to the file when we open it. Table 11-6 shows the values available.

Table 11-6. FileMode enumeration

FileMode	Purpose
CreateNew	Creates a brand new file. Throws an exception if it already existed.
Create	Creates a new file, deleting any existing file and overwriting it if necessary.
Open	Opens an existing file, seeking to the beginning by default. Throws an exception if the file does not exist.
OpenOrCreate	Opens an existing file, or creates a new file if it doesn't exist.
Truncate	Opens an existing file, and deletes all its contents. The file is automatically opened for writing only.
Append	Opens an existing file and seeks to the end of the file. The file is automatically opened for writing only. You can seek in the file, but only within any information you've appended—you can't touch the existing content.

If you use this two-argument overload, the file will be opened in read/write mode. If that's not what you want, another overload takes a third argument, allowing you to control the access mode with a value from the `FileAccess` enumeration. Table 11-7 shows the supported values.

Table 11-7. FileAccess enumeration

FileAccess	Purpose
Read	Open read-only.
Write	Open write-only.
ReadWrite	Open read/write.

All of the file-opening methods we've used so far have locked the file for our exclusive use until we close or `Dispose` the object—if any other program tries to open the file while we have it open, it'll get an error. However, it is possible to play nicely with other users by opening the file in a *shared* mode. We do this by using the overload which specifies a value from the `FileShare` enumeration, which is shown in Table 11-8. This is a flags enumeration, so you can combine the values if you wish.

Table 11-8. FileShare enumeration

FileShare	Purpose
None	No one else can open the file while we've got it open.
Read	Other people can open the file for reading, but not writing.
Write	Other people can open the file for writing, but not reading (so read/write will fail, for example).
ReadWrite	Other people can open the file for reading or writing (or both). This is equivalent to Read | Write.
Delete	Other people can delete the file that you've created, even while we've still got it open. Use with care!

You have to be careful when opening files in a shared mode, particularly one that permits modifications. You are open to all sorts of potential exceptions that you could normally ignore (e.g., people deleting or truncating it from underneath you).

If you need even more control over the file when you open it, you can create a FileStream instance directly.

FileStream Constructors

There are two types of FileStream constructors—those for *interop* scenarios, and the "normal" ones. The "normal" ones take a string for the file path, while the interop ones require either an IntPtr or a SafeFileHandle. These wrap a Win32 file handle that you have retrieved from somewhere. (If you're not already using such a thing in your code, you don't need to use these versions.) We're not going to cover the interop scenarios here.

If you look at the list of constructors, the first thing you'll notice is that quite a few of them duplicate the various permutations of FileShare, FileAccess, and FileMode overloads we had on File.Open.

You'll also notice equivalents with one extra int parameter. This allows you to provide a hint for the system about the size of the internal buffer you'd like the stream to use. Let's look at buffering in more detail.

Stream Buffers

Many streams provide *buffering*. This means that when you read and write, they actually use an intermediate in-memory buffer. When writing, they may store your data in an internal buffer, before periodically *flushing* the data to the actual output device. Similarly, when you read, they might read ahead a whole buffer full of data, and then return to you only the particular bit you need. In both cases, buffering aims to reduce the number of I/O operations—it means you can read or write data in relatively small increments without incurring the full cost of an operating system API call every time.

There are many layers of buffering for a typical storage device. There might be some memory buffering on the actual device itself (many hard disks do this, for example), the filesystem might be buffered (NTFS always does read buffering, and on a client operating system it's typically write-buffered, although this can be turned off, and is off by default for the server configurations of Windows). The .NET Framework provides stream buffering, and you can implement your own buffers (as we did in our example earlier).

These buffers are generally put in place for performance reasons. Although the default buffer sizes are chosen for a reasonable trade-off between performance and robustness, for an I/O-intensive application, you may need to hand-tune this using the appropriate constructors on `FileStream`.

 As usual, you can do more harm than good if you don't measure the impact on performance carefully on a suitable range of your target systems. Most applications will not need to touch this value.

Even if you don't need to tune performance, you still need to be aware of buffering for robustness reasons. If either the process or the OS crashes before the buffers are written out to the physical disk, you run the risk of data loss (hence the reason write buffering is typically disabled on the server). If you're writing frequently to a `Stream` or `StreamWriter`, the .NET Framework will flush the write buffers periodically. It also ensures that everything is properly flushed when the stream is closed. However, if you just stop writing data but you leave the stream open, there's a good chance data will hang around in memory for a long time without getting written out, at which point data loss starts to become more likely.

In general, you should close files as early as possible, but sometimes you'll want to keep a file open for a long time, yet still ensure that particular pieces of data get written out. If you need to control that yourself, you can call `Flush`. This is particularly useful if you have multiple threads of execution accessing the same stream. You can synchronize writes and ensure that they are flushed to disk before the next worker gets in and messes things up! Later in this chapter, we'll see an example where explicit flushing is extremely important.

Setting Permissions During Construction

Another parameter we can set in the constructor is the `FileSystemRights`. We used this type earlier in the chapter to set filesystem permissions. `FileStream` lets us set these directly when we create a file using the appropriate constructor. Similarly, we can also specify an instance of a `FileSecurity` object to further control the permissions on the underlying file.

Setting Advanced Options

Finally, we can optionally pass another enumeration to the `FileStream` constructor, `FileOptions`, which contains some advanced filesystem options. They are enumerated in Table 11-9. This is a flags-style enumeration, so you can combine these values.

Table 11-9. FileOptions enumeration

FileOptions	Purpose
None	No options at all.
WriteThrough	Ignores any filesystem-level buffers, and writes directly to the output device. This affects only the O/S, and not any of the other layers of buffering, so it's still your responsibility to call `Flush`.
RandomAccess	Indicates that we're going to be seeking about in the file in an unsystematic way. This acts as a hint to the OS for its caching strategy. We might be writing a video-editing tool, for example, where we expect the user to be leaping about through the file.
SequentialScan	Indicates that we're going to be sequentially reading from the file. This acts as a hint to the OS for its caching strategy. We might be writing a video player, for example, where we expect the user to play through the stream from beginning to end.
Encrypted	Indicates that we want the file to be encrypted so that it can be decrypted and read only by the user who created it.
DeleteOnClose	Deletes the file when it is closed. This is very handy for temporary files. If you use this option, you never hit the problem where the file still seems to be locked for a short while even after you've closed it (because its buffers are still flushing asynchronously).
Asynchronous	Allows the file to be accessed asynchronously.

The last option, `Asynchronous`, deserves a section all to itself.

Asynchronous File Operations

Long-running file operations are a common bottleneck. How many times have you clicked the Save button, and seen the UI lock up while the disk operation takes place (especially if you're saving a large file to a network location)?

Developers commonly resort to a background thread to push these long operations off the main thread so that they can display some kind of progress or "please wait" UI (or let the user carry on working). We'll look at that approach in Chapter 16; but you don't necessarily have to go that far. You can use the asynchronous mode built into the stream instead. To see how it works, look at Example 11-47.

Example 11-47. Asynchronous file I/O

```
static void Main(string[] args)
{
    string path = "mytestfile.txt";
    // Create a test file
    using (var file = File.Create(path, 4096, FileOptions.Asynchronous))
```

```
    {
        // Some bytes to write
        byte[] myBytes = new byte[] { 0, 1, 2, 3, 4, 5, 6, 7, 8, 9, 10 };
        IAsyncResult asyncResult = file.BeginWrite(
            myBytes,
            0,
            myBytes.Length,
            // A callback function, written as an anonymous delegate
            delegate(IAsyncResult result)
            {
                // You *must* call EndWrite() exactly once
                file.EndWrite(result);
                // Then do what you like
                Console.WriteLine(
                    "Called back on thread {0} when the operation completed",
                    System.Threading.Thread.CurrentThread.ManagedThreadId);
            },
            null);

        // You could do something else while you waited...
        Console.WriteLine(
            "Waiting on thread {0}...",
            System.Threading.Thread.CurrentThread.ManagedThreadId);
        // Waiting on the main thread
        asyncResult.AsyncWaitHandle.WaitOne();
        Console.WriteLine(
            "Completed {0} on thread {1}...",
            asyncResult.CompletedSynchronously ?
                "synchronously" : "asynchronously",
            System.Threading.Thread.CurrentThread.ManagedThreadId);
        Console.ReadKey();
        return;
    }
}
```

If you put this code in a new console application, and then compile and run, you'll get output similar to this (the actual thread IDs will vary from run to run):

```
Waiting on thread 10...
Completed asynchronously on thread 10...
Called back on thread 6 when the operation completed
```

So, what is happening?

When we create our file, we use an overload on `File.Create` that takes the `FileOptions` we discussed earlier. (Yes, back then we showed that by constructing the `FileStream` directly, but the `File` class supports this too.) This lets us open the file with asynchronous behavior enabled.

Then, instead of calling `Write`, we call `BeginWrite`. This takes two additional parameters. The first is a delegate to a callback function of type `AsyncCallback`, which the framework will call when it has finished the operation to let us know that it has completed. The second is an object that we can pass in, that will get passed back to us in the callback.

This *user state* object is common to a lot of asynchronous operations, and is used to get information from the calling site to callbacks from the worker thread. It has become less useful in C# with the availability of lambdas and anonymous methods which have access to variables in their enclosing state.

We've used an anonymous method to provide the callback delegate. The first thing we do in that method is to call `file.EndWrite`, passing it the `IAsyncResult` we've been provided in the callback. You *must* call `EndWrite` exactly once for every time you call `BeginWrite`, because it cleans up the resources used to carry out the operation asynchronously. It doesn't matter whether you call it from the callback, or on the main application thread (or anywhere else, for that matter). If the operation has not completed, it will block the calling thread until it does complete, then do its cleanup. Should you call it twice with the same `IAsyncResult` for any reason the framework will throw an exception.

In a typical Windows Forms or WPF application, we'd probably put up some progress dialog of some kind, and just process messages until we got our callback. In a server-side application we're more likely to want to kick off several pieces of work like this, and then wait for them to finish. To do this, the `IAsyncResult` provides us with an `AsyncWaitHandle`, which is an object we can use to block our thread until the work is complete.

So, when we run, our main thread happens to have the ID **10**. It blocks until the operation is complete, and then prints out the message about being done. Notice that this was, as you'd expect, on the same thread with ID **10**. But *after* that, we get a message printed out from our callback, which was called by the framework on another thread entirely.

It is important to note that your system may have behaved differently. It is possible that the callback might occur *before* execution continued on the main thread. You have to be extremely careful that your code doesn't depend on these operations happening in a particular order.

We'll discuss these issues in a lot more detail in Chapter 16. We recommend you read that before you use any of these asynchronous techniques in production code.

Remember that we set the `FileOptions.Asynchronous` flag when we opened the file to get this asynchronous behavior? What happens if we don't do that? Let's tweak the code so that it opens with `FileOptions.None` instead, and see. Example 11-48 shows the statements from Example 11-47 that need to be modified

Example 11-48. Not asking for asynchronous behavior

```
...
// Create a test file
using (var file = File.Create(path, 4096, FileOptions.None))
{
...
```

If you build and run that, you'll see some output similar to this:

```
Waiting on thread 9...
Completed asynchronously on thread 9...
Called back on thread 10 when the operation completed
```

What's going on? That all still seemed to be asynchronous!

Well yes, it was, but under the covers, the problem was solved in two different ways. The first one used the underlying support Windows provides for asynchronous I/O in the filesystem to handle the asynchronous file operation. In the second case, the .NET Framework had to do some work for us to grab a thread from the thread pool, and execute the read operation on that to deliver the asynchronous behavior.

 That's true right now, but bear in mind that these are implementation details and could change in future versions of the framework. The principle will remain the same, though.

So far, everything we've talked about has been related to files, but we can create streams over other things, too. If you're a Silverlight developer, you've probably been skimming over all of this a bit—after all, if you're running in the web browser you can't actually read and write files in the filesystem. There is, however, another option that you *can* use (along with all the other .NET developers out there): *isolated storage*.

Isolated Storage

In the duplicate file detection application we built earlier in this chapter, we had to go to some lengths to find a location, and pick filenames for the datafiles we wished to create in test mode, in order to guarantee that we don't collide with other applications. We also had to pick locations that we knew we would (probably) have permission to write to, and that we could then load again.

Isolated storage takes this one stage further and gives us a means of saving and loading data in a location unique to a particular piece of executing code. The physical location itself is abstracted away behind the API; we don't need to know where the runtime is actually storing the data, just that the data is stored safely, and that we can retrieve it again. (Even if we want to know where the files are, the isolated storage API won't tell us.) This helps to make the isolated storage framework a bit more operating-system-agnostic, and removes the need for full trust (unlike regular file I/O). Hence it can be used by Silverlight developers (who can target other operating systems such as Mac OS X) as well as those of us building server or desktop client applications for Windows.

This compartmentalization of the information by characteristics of the executing code gives us a slightly different security model from regular files. We can constrain access to particular assemblies, websites, and/or users, for instance, through an API that is much simpler (although much less sophisticated) than the regular file security.

 Although isolated storage provides you with a simple security model to use from managed code, it does not secure your data effectively against unmanaged code running in a relatively high trust context and trawling the local filesystem for information. So, you should not trust sensitive data (credit card numbers, say) to isolated storage. That being said, if someone you cannot trust has successfully run unmanaged code in a trusted context on your box, isolated storage is probably the least of your worries.

Stores

Our starting point when using isolated storage is a *store* and you can think of any given store as being somewhat like one of the well-known directories we dealt with in the regular filesystem. The framework creates a folder for you when you first ask for a store with a particular set of isolation criteria, and then gives back the same folder each time you ask for the store with the same criteria. Instead of using the regular filesystem APIs, we then use special methods on the store to create, move, and delete files and directories within that store.

First, we need to get hold of a store. We do that by calling one of several static members on the `IsolatedStorageFile` class. Example 11-49 starts by getting the user store for a particular assembly. We'll discuss what that means shortly, but for now it just means we've got some sort of a store we can use. It then goes on to create a folder and a file that we can use to cache some information, and retrieve it again on subsequent runs of the application.

Example 11-49. Creating folders and files in a store

```
static void Main(string[] args)
{
    IsolatedStorageFile store = IsolatedStorageFile.GetUserStoreForAssembly();
    // Create a directory - safe to call multiple times
    store.CreateDirectory("Settings");
    // Open or create the file
    using (IsolatedStorageFileStream stream = store.OpenFile(
                           "Settings\\standardsettings.txt",
                           System.IO.FileMode.OpenOrCreate,
                           System.IO.FileAccess.ReadWrite))
    {
        UseStream(stream);
    }
```

```
    Console.ReadKey();
}
```

We create a directory in the store, called *Settings*. You don't have to do this; you could put your file in the root directory for the store, if you wanted. Then, we use the `OpenFile` method on the store to open a file. We use the standard file path syntax to specify the file, relative to the root for this store, along with the `FileMode` and `FileAc cess` values that we're already familiar with. They all mean the same thing in isolated storage as they do with normal files. That method returns us an `IsolatedStorageFile Stream`. This class derives from `FileStream`, so it works in pretty much the same way.

So, what shall we do with it now that we've got it? For the purposes of this example, let's just write some text into it if it is empty. On a subsequent run, we'll print the text we wrote to the console.

Reading and Writing Text

We've already seen `StreamWriter`, the handy wrapper class we can use for writing text to a stream. Previously, we got hold of one from `File.CreateText`, but remember we mentioned that there's a constructor we can use to wrap any `Stream` (not just a `FileStream`) if we want to write text to it? Well, we can use that now, for our `Isolated StorageFileStream`. Similarly, we can use the equivalent `StreamReader` to read text from the stream if it already exists. Example 11-50 implements the `UseStream` method that Example 11-49 called after opening the stream, and it uses both `StreamReader` and `StreamWriter`.

Example 11-50. Using StreamReader and StreamWriter with isolated storage

```
static void UseStream(Stream stream)
{
    if (stream.Length > 0)
    {
        using (StreamReader reader = new StreamReader(stream))
        {
            Console.WriteLine(reader.ReadToEnd());
        }
    }
    else
    {
        using (StreamWriter writer = new StreamWriter(stream))
        {
            writer.WriteLine(
                "Initialized settings at {0}", DateTime.Now.TimeOfDay);
            Console.WriteLine("Settings have been initialized");
        }
    }
}
```

In the case where we're writing, we construct our `StreamWriter` (in a `using` block, be-cause we need to `Dispose` it when we're done), and then use the `WriteLine` method to write our content. Remember that `WriteLine` adds an extra new line on the end of the text, whereas `Write` just writes the text provided.

In the case where we are reading, on the other hand, we construct a `StreamReader` (also in a `using` block), and then read the entire content using `ReadToEnd`. This reads the entire content of the file into a single string.

So, if you build and run this once, you'll see some output that looks a lot like this:

```
Settings have been initialized
```

That means we've run through the write path. Run a second (or subsequent) time, and you'll see something more like this:

```
Initialized settings at 10:34:47.7014833
```

That means we've run through the read path.

 When you run this, you'll notice that we end up outputting an extra blank line at the end, because we've read a whole line from the file—we called `writer.WriteLine` when generating the file and then used `Console.WriteLine`, which adds *another* end of line after that. You have to be a little careful when manipulating text like this, to ensure that you don't end up with huge amounts of unwanted whitespace because everyone in some processing chain is generously adding new lines or other whitespace at the end!

This is a rather neat result. We can use all our standard techniques for reading and writing to an `IsolatedStorageFileStream` once we've acquired a suitable file: the other I/O types such as `StreamReader` don't need to know what kind of stream we're using.

Defining "Isolated"

So, what makes isolated storage "isolated"? The .NET Framework partitions information written into isolated storage based on some characteristics of the executing code.

Several types of isolated store are available to you:

- Isolation by user and assembly (optionally supporting roaming)
- Isolation by user, domain, and assembly (optionally supporting roaming)
- Isolation by user and application (optionally supporting roaming)
- Isolation by user and site (only on Silverlight)
- Isolation by machine and assembly
- Isolation by machine, domain, and assembly
- Isolation by machine and application

Silverlight supports only two of these: by user and site, and by user and application.

Isolation by user and assembly

In Example 11-50, we acquired a store isolated by user and assembly, using the static method `IsolatedStorageFile.GetUserStoreForAssembly`. This store is unique to a particular user, and the assembly in which the calling code is executing. You can try this out for yourself. If you log in to your box as a user other than the one under which you've already run our example app, and run it again, you'll see some output like this:

```
Settings have been initialized
```

That means our settings file doesn't exist (for this user), so we must have been given a new store.

As you might expect, the user is identified by the authenticated principal for the current thread. Typically, this is the logged-on user that ran the process; but this could have been changed by impersonation (in a web application, for example, you might be running in the context of the web user, rather than that of the ASP.NET process that hosts the site).

Identifying the assembly is slightly more complex. If you have signed the assembly, it uses the information in that signature (be it a strong name signature, or a software publisher signature, with the software publishing signature winning if it has both).

If, on the other hand, the assembly is not signed, it will use the URL for the assembly. If it came from the Internet, it will be of the form:

```
http://some/path/to/myassembly.dll
```

If it came from the local filesystem, it will be of the form:

```
file:///C:/some/path/to/myassembly.dll
```

Figure 11-9 illustrates how multiple stores get involved when you have several users and several different assemblies. User 1 asks *MyApp.exe* to perform some task, which asks for user/assembly isolated storage. It gets Store 1. Imagine that User 1 then asks *MyApp.exe* to perform some other task that requires the application to call on *MyAssembly.dll* to carry out the work. If that in turn asks for user/assembly isolated storage, it will get a different store (labeled Store 2 in the diagram). We get a different store, because they are different assemblies.

When a different user, User 2, asks *MyApp.exe* to perform the first task, which then asks for user/assembly isolated storage, it gets a different store again—Store 3 in the diagram—because they are different users.

OK, what happens if we make two copies of *MyApp.exe* in two different locations, and run them both under the same user account? The answer is that it depends....

If the applications are *not signed* the assembly identification rules mean that they *don't match*, and so we get two *different* isolated stores.

If they *are signed* the assembly identification rules mean that they *do match*, so we get the *same* isolated store.

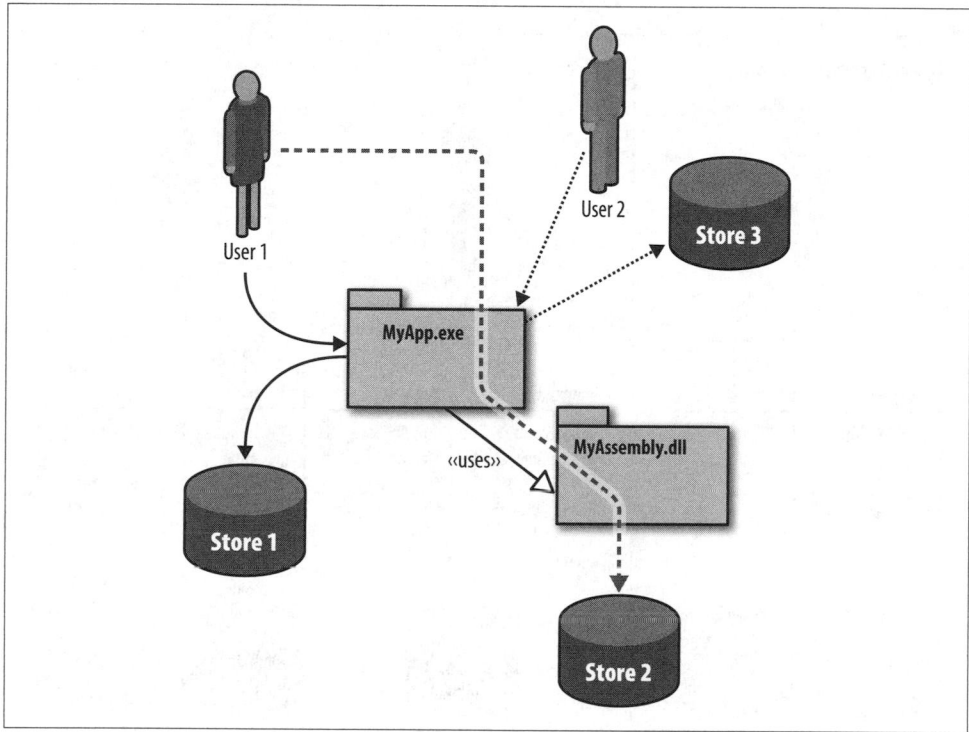

Figure 11-9. User and assembly isolation

Our app isn't signed, so if we try this experiment, we'll see the standard "first run" output for our second copy.

 Be very careful when using isolated storage with signed assemblies. The information used from the signature includes the Name, Strong Name Key, and *Major Version* part of the version info. So, if you rev your application from 1.x to 2.x, all of a sudden you're getting a different isolated storage scope, and all your existing data will "vanish." One way to deal with this is to use a distinct DLL to access the store, and keep its version numbers constant.

Isolation by user, domain, and assembly

Isolating by domain means that we look for some information about the application domain in which we are running. Typically, this is the full URL of the assembly if it was downloaded from the Web, or the local path of the file.

Notice that this is the same rule as for the assembly identity if we didn't sign it! The purpose of this isolation model is to allow a single signed assembly to get different stores if it is run from different locations. You can see a diagram that illustrates this in Figure 11-10.

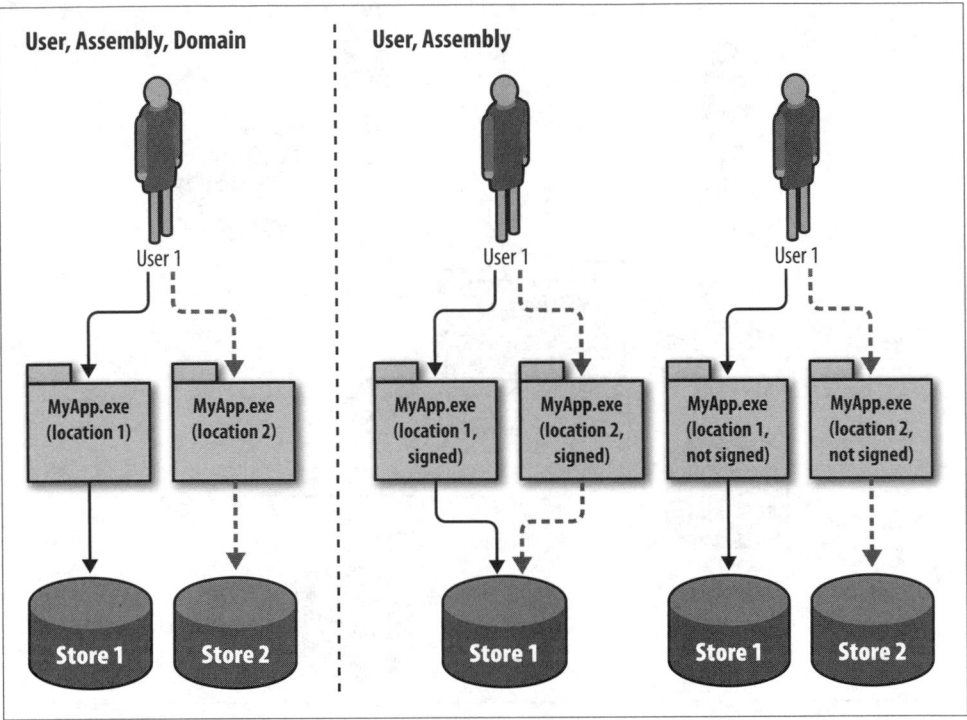

Figure 11-10. Assembly and domain isolation compared

To get a store with this isolation level, we can call the `IsolatedStorageFile` class's `GetUserStoreForDomain` method.

Isolation by user and application

A third level of isolation is by user and application. What defines an "application"? Well, you have to sign the whole lot with a publisher's (Authenticode) signature. A regular strong-name signature won't do (as that will identify only an individual assembly).

 If you want to try this out quickly for yourself, you can run the Click-Once Publication Wizard on the Publish tab of your example project settings. This will generate a suitable test certificate and sign the app.

To get a store with user and application isolation, we call the `IsolatedStorageFile` class's `GetUserStoreForApplication` method.

 If you haven't signed your application properly, this method will throw an exception.

So, it doesn't matter which assembly you call from; as long as it is a part of the same application, it will get the same store. You can see this illustrated in Figure 11-11.

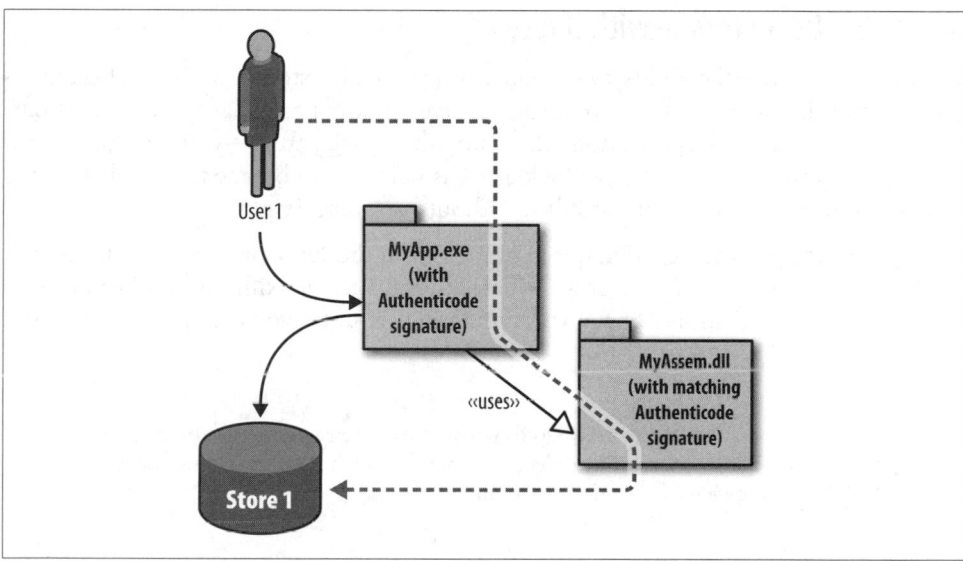

Figure 11-11. Application isolation

 This can be particularly useful for settings that might be shared between several different application components.

Machine isolation

What if your application or component has some data you want to make available to all users on the system? Maybe you want to cache common product information or imagery to avoid a download every time you start the app. For these scenarios you need *machine isolation*.

As you saw earlier, there is an isolation type for the machine which corresponds to each isolation type for the user. The same resolution rules apply in each case. The methods you need are:

```
GetMachineStoreForApplication
GetMachineStoreForDomain
GetMachineStoreForAssembly
```

Managing User Storage with Quotas

Isolated storage has the ability to set *quotas* on particular storage scopes. This allows you to limit the amount of data that can be saved in any particular store. This is particularly important for applications that run with partial trust—you wouldn't want Silverlight applications automatically loaded as part of a web page to be able to store vast amounts of data on your hard disk without your permission.

You can find out a store's current quota by looking at the `Quota` property on a particular `IsolatedStorageFile`. This is a `long`, which indicates the maximum number of bytes that may be stored. This is not a "bytes remaining" count—you can use the `Available FreeSpace` property for that.

 Your available space will go down slightly when you create empty directories and files. This reflects the fact that such items consume space on disk even though they are nominally empty.

The quota can be increased using the `IncreaseQuotaTo` method, which takes a `long` which is the new number of bytes to which to limit the store. This *must* be larger than the previous number of bytes, or an `ArgumentException` is thrown. This call may or may not succeed—the user will be prompted, and may refuse your request for more space.

 You cannot reduce the quota for a store once you've set it, so take care!

Managing Isolated Storage

As a user, you might want to look at the data stored in isolated storage by applications running on your machine. It can be complicated to manage and debug isolated storage, but there are a few tools and techniques to help you.

First, there's the *storeadm.exe* tool. This allows you to inspect isolated storage for the current user (by default), or the current machine (by specifying the **/machine** option) or current roaming user (by specifying **/roaming**).

So, if you try running this command:

```
storeadm /MACHINE /LIST
```

you will see output similar to this (listing the various stores for this machine, along with the evidence that identifies them):

```
Microsoft (R) .NET Framework Store Admin 4.0.30319.1
Copyright (c) Microsoft Corporation.  All rights reserved.

Record #1
[Assembly]
<StrongName version="1"
Key="002400000480000094000000060200000024000052534131000400000100010 0A5FE84898F
190EA6423A7D7FFB1AE778141753A6F8F8235CBC63A9C5D04143C7E0A2BE1FC61FA6EBB52E7FA9B
48D22BAF4027763A12046DB4A94FA3504835ED9F29CD031600D5115939066AABE59A4E61E932AEF
0C24178B54967DD33643FDE04AE50786076C1FB32F64915E8200729301EB912702A8FDD40F63DD5
A2DE218C7"
Name="ConsoleApplication7"
Version="1.0.0.0"/>

        Size : 0
Record #2
[Domain]
<StrongName version="1"
Key="002400000480000094000000060200000024000052534131000400000100010 0A5FE84898F
190EA6423A7D7FFB1AE778141753A6F8F8235CBC63A9C5D04143C7E0A2BE1FC61FA6EBB52E7FA9B
48D22BAF4027763A12046DB4A94FA3504835ED9F29CD031600D5115939066AABE59A4E61E932AEF
0C24178B54967DD33643FDE04AE50786076C1FB32F64915E8200729301EB912702A8FDD40F63DD5
A2DE218C7"
Name="ConsoleApplication7"
Version="1.0.0.0"/>

[Assembly]
<StrongName version="1"
Key="002400000480000094000000060200000024000052534131000400000100010 0A5FE84898F
190EA6423A7D7FFB1AE778141753A6F8F8235CBC63A9C5D04143C7E0A2BE1FC61FA6EBB52E7FA9B
48D22BAF4027763A12046DB4A94FA3504835ED9F29CD031600D5115939066AABE59A4E61E932AEF
0C24178B54967DD33643FDE04AE50786076C1FB32F64915E8200729301EB912702A8FDD40F63DD5
A2DE218C7"
Name="ConsoleApplication7"
Version="1.0.0.0"/>

        Size : 0
```

Notice that there are two stores in that example. One is identified by some assembly evidence (the strong name key, name, and major version info). The other is identified by both domain and assembly evidence. Because the sample application is in a single assembly, the assembly evidence for both stores happens to be identical!

 You can also add the /REMOVE parameter which will delete all of the isolated storage in use at the specified scope. Be *very careful* if you do this, as you may well delete storage used by another application entirely.

That's all very well, but you can't see the place where those files are stored. That's because the actual storage is intended to be abstracted away behind the API. Sometimes, however, it is useful to be able to go and pry into the actual storage itself.

 Remember, this is an implementation detail, and it could change between versions. It has been consistent since the first version of the .NET Framework, but in the future, Microsoft could decide to store it all in one big file hidden away somewhere, or using some mystical API that we don't have access to.

We can take advantage of the fact that the debugger can show us the private innards of the `IsolatedStorageFile` class. If we set a breakpoint on the `store.CreateFile` line in our sample application, we can inspect the `IsolatedStorageFile` object that was returned by `GetUserStoreForApplication` in the previous line. You will see that there is a private field called `m_RootDir`. This is the actual root directory (in the real filesystem) for the store. You can see an example of that as it is on my machine in Figure 11-12.

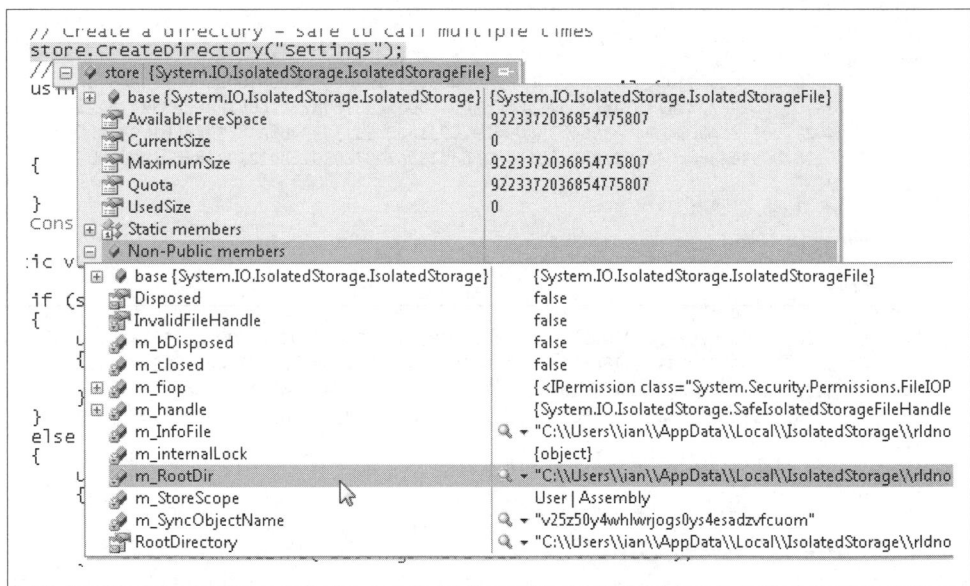

Figure 11-12. IsolatedStorageFile internals

If you copy that path and browse to it using Windows Explorer, you'll see something like the folder in Figure 11-13.

There's the *Settings* directory that we created! As you might expect, if you were to look inside, you'd see the *standardsettings.txt* file our program created.

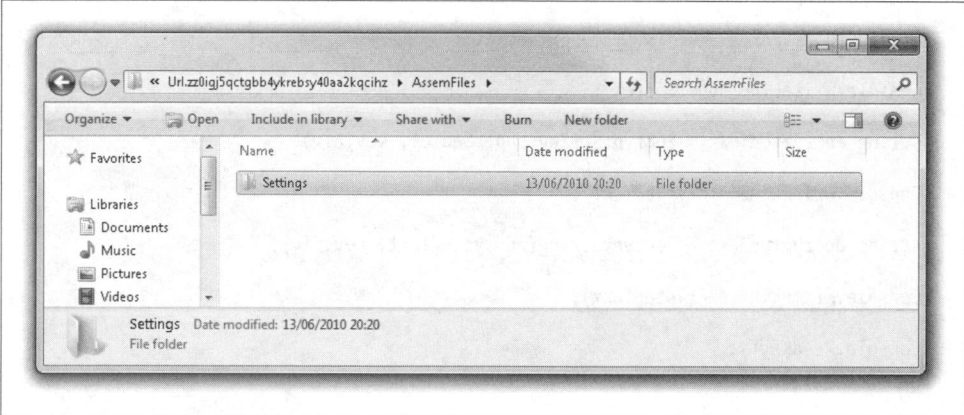

Figure 11-13. An isolated storage folder

As you can see, this is a very useful debugging technique, allowing you to inspect and modify the contents of files in isolated storage, and identify exactly which store you have for a particular scope. It does rely on implementation details, but since you'd only ever do this while debugging, the code you ultimately ship won't depend on any non public features of isolated storage.

OK. So far, we've seen two different types of stream; a regular file, and an isolated storage file. We use our familiar stream tools and techniques (like `StreamReader` and `StreamWriter`), regardless of the underlying type.

So, what other kinds of stream exist? Well, there are lots; several subsystems in the .NET framework provide stream-based APIs. We'll see some networking ones in Chapter 13, for example. Another example is from the .NET Framework's security features: `CryptoStream` (which is used for encrypting and decrypting a stream of data). There's also a `MemoryStream` in `System.IO` which uses memory to store the data in the stream.

Streams That Aren't Files

In this final section, we'll look at a stream that is not a file. We'll use a stream from .NET's cryptographic services to encrypt a string. This encrypted string can be decrypted later as long as we know the key. The test program in Example 11-51 illustrates this.

Example 11-51. Using an encryption stream

```
static void Main(string[] args)
{
    byte[] key;
    byte[] iv;

    // Get the appropriate key and initialization vector for the algorithm
    SelectKeyAndIV(out key, out iv);
```

```
    string superSecret = "This is super secret";

    Console.WriteLine(superSecret);

    string encryptedText = EncryptString(superSecret, key, iv);

    Console.WriteLine(encryptedText);

    string decryptedText = DecryptString(encryptedText, key, iv);

    Console.WriteLine(decryptedText);

    Console.ReadKey();
}
```

It is going to write a message to the console, encrypt it, write the encrypted text to the console, decrypt it, and write the result of that back to the console. All being well, the first line should be the same as the last, and the middle line should look like gibberish!

 Of course, it's not very useful to encrypt and immediately decrypt again. This example illustrates all the parts in one program—in a real application, decryption would happen in a different place than encryption.

The first thing we do is get a suitable *key* and *initialization vector* for our cryptographic algorithm. These are the two parts of the secret key that are shared between whoever is encrypting and decrypting our sensitive data.

A detailed discussion of cryptography is somewhat beyond the scope of this book, but here are a few key points to get us going. Unenciphered data is known as the *plain text*, and the encrypted version is known as *cipher text*. We use those terms even if we're dealing with nontextual data. The key and the initialization vector (IV) are used by a cryptographic algorithm to encrypt the unenciphered data. A cryptographic algorithm that uses the same key and IV for both encryption and decryption is called a *symmetric algorithm* (for obvious reasons). Asymmetric algorithms also exist, but we won't be using them in this example.

Needless to say, if an unauthorized individual gets hold of the key and IV, he can happily decrypt any of your cipher text, and you no longer have a communications channel free from prying eyes. It is therefore extremely important that you take care when sharing these secrets with the people who need them, to ensure that no one else can intercept them. (This turns out to be the hardest part—key management and especially human factors turn out to be security weak points far more often than the technological details. This is a book about programming, so we won't even attempt to solve that problem. We recommend the book *Secrets and Lies: Digital Security in a Networked World* by Bruce Schneier [John Wiley & Sons] for more information.)

We're calling a method called `SelectKeyAndIV` to get hold of the key and IV. In real life, you'd likely be sharing this information between different processes, usually even on different machines; but for the sake of this demonstration, we're just creating them on the fly, as you can see in Example 11-52.

Example 11-52. Creating a key and IV

```
private static void SelectKeyAndIV(out byte[] key, out byte[] iv)
{
    var algorithm = TripleDES.Create();
    algorithm.GenerateIV();
    algorithm.GenerateKey();

    key = algorithm.Key;
    iv = algorithm.IV;
}
```

`TripleDES` is an example of a symmetric algorithm, so it derives from a class called `SymmetricAlgorithm`. All such classes provide a couple of methods called `GenerateIV` and `GenerateKey` that create cryptographically strong random byte arrays to use as an initialization vector and a key. See the sidebar below for an explanation of why we need to use a particular kind of random number generator when cryptography is involved.

How Random Are Random Numbers?

What does "cryptographically strong" mean when we're talking about random numbers? Well, it turns out that most random number generators are not all that random. The easiest way to illustrate this is with a little program that seeds the standard .NET Framework random number generator with an arbitrary integer (3), and then displays some random numbers to the console:

```
static void Main(string[] args)
{
    Random random = new Random(3);
    for (int i = 0; i < 5; ++i)
    {
        Console.WriteLine(random.Next());
    }
    Console.ReadKey();
}
```

If you compile and run, you should see this output:

```
630327709
1498044246
1857544709
426253993
1203643911
```

No, I'm not Nostradamus. It is just that the "random" algorithm is actually entirely predictable, given a particular seed. Normally that seed comes from `Environment.Tick Count`, which means that you normally see different behavior each time. Thus, we have the illusion of "randomness." But this isn't good enough for encryption purposes;

---

encryption schemes have been broken in the past because attackers were able to guess a computer's tick count.

Then there's the question of how uniformly distributed those "random" numbers are, or whether the algorithm has a tendency to generate clusters of random numbers. Getting a smooth, unpredictable stream of random numbers from an algorithm is a very hard problem, and the smoother you want it the more expensive it gets (in general).

Lack of randomness (i.e., predictability) in your random number generator can significantly reduce the strength of a cryptographic algorithm based on its results.

The upshot of this is that you shouldn't use System.Random if you are particularly sensitive to the randomness of your random numbers. This isn't just limited to security applications—you might want to think about your approach if you were building an online casino application, for example.

OK, with that done, we can now implement our EncryptString method. This takes the plain text string, the key, and the initialization vector, and returns us an encrypted string. Example 11-53 shows an implementation.

Example 11-53. Encrypting a string

```
private static string EncryptString(string plainText, byte[] key, byte[] iv)
{
    // Create a crypto service provider for the TripleDES algorithm
    var serviceProvider = new TripleDESCryptoServiceProvider();

    using (MemoryStream memoryStream = new MemoryStream())
    using (var cryptoStream = new CryptoStream(
                                memoryStream,
                                serviceProvider.CreateEncryptor(key, iv),
                                CryptoStreamMode.Write))
    using (StreamWriter writer = new StreamWriter(cryptoStream))
    {
        // Write some text to the crypto stream, encrypting it on the way
        writer.Write(plainText);
        // Make sure that the writer has flushed to the crypto stream
        writer.Flush();
        // We also need to tell the crypto stream to flush the final block out to
        // the underlying stream, or we'll
        // be missing some content...
        cryptoStream.FlushFinalBlock();

        // Now, we want to get back whatever the crypto stream wrote to our memory
        // stream.
        return GetCipherText(memoryStream);
    }
}
```

We're going to write our plain text to a CryptoStream, using the standard Stream Writer adapter. This works just as well over a CryptoStream as any other, but instead of coming out as plain text, it will be enciphered for us. How does that work?

An Adapting Stream: CryptoStream

CryptoStream is quite different from the other streams we've met so far. It doesn't have any underlying storage of its own. Instead, it wraps around another Stream, and then uses an ICryptoTransform either to transform the data written to it from plain text into cipher text before writing it to that output stream (if we put it into CryptoStream Mode.Write), or to transform what it has read from the underlying stream and turning it back into plain text before passing it on to the reader (if we put it into CryptoStream Mode.Read).

So, how do we get hold of a suitable ICryptoTransform? We're making use of a *factory class* called TripleDESCryptoServiceProvider. This has a method called CreateEncryp tor which will create an instance of an ICryptoTransform that uses the TripleDES algorithm to encrypt our plain text, with the specified key and IV.

 A number of different algorithms are available in the framework, with various strengths and weaknesses. In general, they also have a number of different configuration options, the defaults for which can vary between versions of the .NET Framework and even versions of the operating system on which the framework is deployed. To be successful, you're going to have to ensure that you match not just the key and the IV, but also the choice of algorithm and all its options. In general, you should carefully set everything up by hand, and avoid relying on the defaults (unlike this example, which, remember, is here to illustrate streams).

We provide all of those parameters to its constructor, and then we can use it (almost) like any other stream.

In fact, there is a proviso about CryptoStream. Because of the way that most cryptographic algorithms work on blocks of plain text, it has to buffer up what is being written (or read) until it has a full block, before encrypting it and writing it to the underlying stream.

This means that, when you finish writing to it, you might not have filled up the final block, and it might not have been flushed out to the destination stream. There are two ways of ensuring that this happens:

- Dispose the CryptoStream.
- Call FlushFinalBlock on the CryptoStream.

In many cases, the first solution is the simplest. However, when you call Dispose on the CryptoStream it will also Close the underlying stream, which is not always what you want to do. In this case, we're going to use the underlying stream some more, so we don't want to close it just yet. Instead, we call Flush on the StreamWriter to ensure that it has flushed all of its data to the CryptoStream, and then FlushFinalBlock on the

`CryptoStream` itself, to ensure that the encrypted data is all written to the underlying stream.

We can use any sort of stream for that underlying stream. We could use a file stream on disk, or one of the isolated storage file streams we saw earlier in this chapter, for example. We could even use one of the network streams we're going to see in Chapter 13. However, for this example we'd like to do everything in memory, and the framework has just the class for us: the `MemoryStream`.

In Memory Alone: The MemoryStream

`MemoryStream` is very simple in concept. It is just a stream that uses memory as its backing store. We can do all of the usual things like reading, writing, and seeking. It's very useful when you're working with APIs that require you to provide a `Stream`, and you don't already have one handy.

If we use the default constructor (as in our example), we can read and write to the stream, and it will automatically grow in size as it needs to accommodate the data being written. Other constructors allow us to provide a start size suitable for our purposes (if we know in advance what that might be).

We can even provide a block of memory in the form of a `byte[]` array to use as the underlying storage for the stream. In that case, we are no longer able to resize the stream, and we will get a `NotSupportedException` if we try to write too much data. You would normally supply your own `byte[]` array when you already have one and need to pass it to something that wants to *read* from a stream.

We can find out the current size of the underlying block of memory (whether we allocated it explicitly, or whether it is being automatically resized) by looking at the stream's `Capacity` property. Note that this is *not* the same as the maximum number of bytes we've ever written to the stream. The automatic resizing tends to overallocate to avoid the overhead of constant reallocation when writing. In general, you can determine how many bytes you've actually written to by looking at the `Position` in the stream at the beginning and end of your write operations, or the `Length` property of the `MemoryStream`.

Having used the `CryptoStream` to write the cipher text into the stream, we need to turn that into a string we can show on the console.

Representing Binary As Text with Base64 Encoding

Unfortunately, the cipher text is not actually text at all—it is just a stream of bytes. We can't use the `UTF8Encoding.UTF8.GetString` technique we saw in Chapter 10 to turn the bytes into text, because these bytes don't represent UTF-8 encoded characters.

Instead, we need some other sort of text-friendly representation if we're going to be able to print the encrypted text to the console. We could write each byte out as hex digits. That would be a perfectly reasonable string representation.

However, that's not very compact (each byte is taking five characters in the string!):

```
0x01 0x0F 0x03 0xFA 0xB3
```

A much more compact textual representation is Base64 encoding. This is a very popular textual encoding of arbitrary data. It's often used to embed binary in XML, which is a fundamentally text-oriented format.

And even better, the framework provides us with a convenient static helper method to convert from a `byte[]` to a Base64 encoded string: `Convert.ToBase64String`.

 If you're wondering why there's no `Encoding` class for Base64 to correspond to the Unicode, ASCII, and UTF-8 encodings we saw in Chapter 10, it's because Base64 is a completely different kind of thing. Those other encodings are mechanisms that define binary representations of textual information. Base64 does the opposite—it defines a textual representation for binary information.

Example 11-54 shows how we make use of that in our `GetCipherText` method.

Example 11-54. Converting to Base64

```
private static string GetCipherText(MemoryStream memoryStream)
{
    byte[] buffer = memoryStream.ToArray();
    return System.Convert.ToBase64String(buffer, 0, buffer.Length);
}
```

We use a method on `MemoryStream` called `ToArray` to get a `byte[]` array containing all the data written to the stream.

 Don't be caught out by the `ToBuffer` method, which also returns a `byte[]` array. `ToBuffer` returns the whole buffer including any "extra" bytes that have been allocated but not yet used.

Finally, we call `Convert.ToBase64String` to get a string representation of the underlying data, passing it the `byte[]`, along with a start offset into that buffer of zero (so that we start with the first byte), and the length.

That takes care of encryption. How about decryption? That's actually a little bit easier. Example 11-55 shows how.

Example 11-55. Decryption

```
private static string DecryptString(string cipherText, byte[] key, byte[] iv)
{
    // Create a crypto service provider for the TripleDES algorithm
    var serviceProvider = new TripleDESCryptoServiceProvider();

    // Decode the cipher-text bytes back from the base-64 encoded string
```

```
        byte[] cipherTextBytes = Convert.FromBase64String(cipherText);

        // Create a memory stream over those bytes
        using (MemoryStream memoryStream = new MemoryStream(cipherTextBytes))
        // And create a cryptographic stream over the memory stream,
        // using the specified algorithm
        // (with the provided key and initialization vector)
        using (var cryptoStream =
                    new CryptoStream(
                        memoryStream,
                        serviceProvider.CreateDecryptor(key, iv),
                        CryptoStreamMode.Read))
        // Finally, create a stream reader over the stream, and recover the
        // original text
        using (StreamReader reader = new StreamReader(cryptoStream))
        {
            return reader.ReadToEnd();
        }
    }
}
```

First, we use `Convert.FromBase64String` to convert our Base64 encoded string back to an array of bytes. We then construct a `MemoryStream` over that `byte[]` by passing it to the appropriate constructor.

As before, we wrap the `MemoryStream` with a `CryptoStream`, this time passing it the `ICryptoTransform` created by a call to `CreateDecryptor` on our `TripleDESCryptoService Provider`, and putting it into `CryptoStreamMode.Read`.

Finally, we construct our old friend the `StreamReader` over the `CryptoStream`, and read the content back as a string.

So, what's actually happening here?

`CryptoStream` uses the `ICryptoTransform` to take care of turning the cipher text in the `MemoryStream` back into plain text. If you remember, that plain text is actually the set of UTF-8 encoded bytes we originally wrote to the stream with the `StreamWriter` back in the encryption phase. So, the `StreamReader` takes those and converts them back into a string for us. You can see that illustrated in Figure 11-14.

This is a very powerful example of how we can plug together various components in a kind of pipeline to achieve quite complex processing, from simple, easily understood building blocks that conform to a common pattern, but which have no dependencies on each other's implementation details. The `Stream` abstraction is the key to this flexibility.

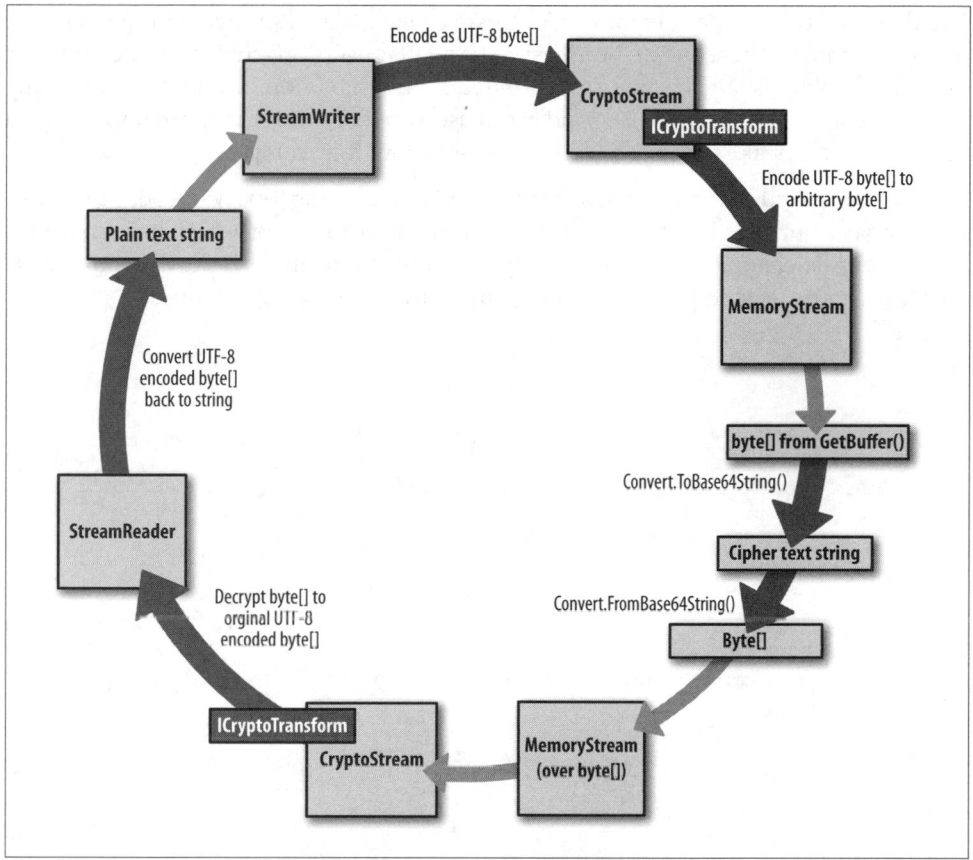

Figure 11-14. Encryption and decryption pipeline using streams

Summary

In this chapter we looked at the classes in the `System.IO` namespace that relate to files and streams. We saw how we can use static methods on the `File`, `Directory`, and `Path` classes to manage and manipulate files and folders in the filesystem, including creating, deleting, appending, and truncating data, as well as managing their access permissions.

We saw how to use `StreamReader` and `StreamWriter` to deal with reading and writing text from files, and how we can also read and write binary data using the underlying `Stream` objects themselves, including the ability to `Seek` backward and forward in the file.

We then looked at a special type of file stream called *isolated storage*. This gives us the ability to manage the scope of file access to particular users, machines, applications, or even assemblies. We gain control over *quotas* (the maximum amount of space any particular store is allowed to use), and get to use local file storage in normally restricted security contexts like that of a Silverlight application, for example.

Finally, we looked at some streams that aren't files, including `MemoryStream`, which uses memory as its underlying storage mechanism, and `CryptoStream`, which has no storage of its own, delegating that responsibility to another stream. We showed how these patterns can be used to plug streams together into a processing pipeline.

CHAPTER 12

XML

XML (the eXtensible Markup Language) provides an industry-standard method for encoding structured information. It defines syntactic and structural rules that enable software applications to process XML files even when they don't understand all of the data.

XML specifications are defined and maintained by the World Wide Web Consortium (W3C). The latest version is XML 1.1 (Second Edition). However, XML 1.0 (currently in its fifth edition) is the most popular version, and is supported by all XML parsers. W3C states that:

> You are encouraged to create or generate XML 1.0 documents if you do not need the new features in XML 1.1; XML Parsers are expected to understand both XML 1.0 and XML 1.1 (see *http://www.w3.org/xml/core/#publications/*).

This chapter will introduce XML 1.0 only, and in fact, will focus on just the most commonly used XML features. We'll introduce you to the `XDocument` and `XElement` classes first, and you'll learn how to create and manipulate XML documents.

Of course, once you have a large document, you'll want to be able to find substrings, and we'll show you two different ways to do that, using LINQ. The .NET Framework also allows you to serialize your objects as XML, and deserialize them at their destination. We'll cover those methods at the end of the chapter.

XML Basics (A Quick Review)

XML is a markup language, not unlike HTML, except that it is *extensible*—that is, applications that use XML can (and do) create new kinds of elements and attributes.

Elements

In XML, a document is a hierarchy of *elements*. An element is typically defined by a pair of *tags*, called the start and end tags. In the following example, `FirstName` is an element:

```
<FirstName>Orlando</FirstName>
```

A start tag contains the element name surrounded by a pair of angle brackets:

```
<FirstName>
```

An end tag is similar, except that the element name is preceded by a forward slash:

```
</FirstName>
```

An element may contain *content* between its start and end tags. In this example, the element contains text, but content can also contain *child elements*. For example, this `Customer` element has three child elements:

```
<Customer>
  <FirstName>Orlando</FirstName>
  <LastName>Gee</LastName>
  <EmailAddress>orlandoO@hotmail.com</EmailAddress>
</Customer>
```

The top-level element in an XML document is called its *root element*. Every document has exactly one root element.

An element does not have to contain content, but every element (except for the root element) has exactly one *parent element*. Elements with the same parent element are called sibling elements.

In this example, `Customers` (plural) is the root. The children of the root element, `Customers`, are the three `Customer` (singular) elements:

```
<Customers>
  <Customer>
    <FirstName>Orlando</FirstName>
    <LastName>Gee</LastName>
    <EmailAddress>orlandoO@hotmail.com</EmailAddress>
  </Customer>
  <Customer>
    <FirstName>Keith</FirstName>
    <LastName>Harris</LastName>
    <EmailAddress>keithO@hotmail.com</EmailAddress>
  </Customer>
  <Customer>
    <FirstName>Donna</FirstName>
    <LastName>Carreras</LastName>
    <EmailAddress>donnaO@hotmail.com</EmailAddress>
  </Customer>
  <Customer>
    <FirstName>Janet</FirstName>
    <LastName>Gates</LastName>
    <EmailAddress>janet1@hotmail.com</EmailAddress>
```

```
    </Customer>
    <Customer>
      <FirstName>Lucy</FirstName>
      <LastName>Harrington</LastName>
      <EmailAddress>lucyO@hotmail.com</EmailAddress>
    </Customer>
  </Customers>
```

Each `Customer` has one parent (`Customers`) and three children (`FirstName`, `LastName`, and `EmailAddress`). Each of these, in turn, has one parent (`Customer`) and zero children.

When an element has no content—no child elements and no text—you can optionally use a more compact representation, where you write just a single tag, with a slash just before the closing angle bracket. For example, this:

```
<Customers/>
```

means exactly the same as this:

```
<Customers></Customers>
```

This *empty element tag* syntax is the only syntax in which an element is represented by just a single tag. Unless you are using this form, it is illegal to omit the closing tag.

XHTML

XHTML is an enhanced standard of HTML that follows the stricter rules of XML validity. The two most important XML rules that make XHTML different from plain HTML follow:

- No elements may overlap, though they may nest. So this is legal, because the elements are nested:

  ```
  <element 1>
    <element2>
      ...
    </element 2>
  </element 1>
  ```

  You may *not* write:

  ```
  <element 1>
    <element2>
      ...
    </element 1>
  </element 2>
  ```

  because in the latter case, `element2` overlaps `element1` rather than being neatly nested within it. (Ordinary HTML allows this.)

- Every element must be closed, which means that for each opened element, you must have a closing tag (or the element tag must be self-closing). So while plain old HTML permits:

  ```
  <br>
  ```

in XHTML we must either write this:

```
<br></br>
```

or use the empty element tag form:

```
<br />
```

X Stands for eXtensible

The key point of XML is to provide an *extensible* markup language. Here's an incredibly short pop-history lesson: HTML was derived from the Standard Generalized Markup Language (SGML). HTML has many wonderful attributes (if you'll pardon the pun), but if you want to add a new element to HTML, you have two choices: apply to the W3C and wait, or strike out on your own and be "nonstandard."

There was a strong need for the ability for two organizations to get together and specify tags that they could use for data exchange. Hey! Presto! XML was born as a more general-purpose markup language that allows users to *define their own tags*. This is the critical distinction of XML.

Creating XML Documents

Because XML documents are structured text documents, you can create them using a text editor and process them using string manipulation functions. To paraphrase David Platt, you can also have an appendectomy through your mouth, but it takes longer and hurts more.

To make the job easier, .NET implements classes and utilities that provide XML functionality. There are several to choose from. There are the streaming XML APIs (which support `XmlReader` and `XmlWriter`), which never attempt to hold the whole document in memory—you work one element at a time, and while that enables you to handle very large documents without using much memory, it can be tricky to code for. So there are simpler APIs that let you build an object model that represents an XML document. Even here, you have a choice. One set of XML APIs is based on the XML Document Object Model (DOM), a standard API implemented in many programming systems, not just .NET. However, the DOM is surprisingly cumbersome to work with, so .NET 3.5 introduced a set of APIs that are easier to use from .NET. These are designed to work well with LINQ, and so they're often referred to as LINQ to XML. These are now the preferred XML API if you don't need streaming. (Silverlight doesn't even offer the XML DOM APIs, so LINQ to XML is your only nonstreaming option there.)

Despite the name, it's not strictly necessary to use LINQ when using the LINQ to XML classes—Example 12-1 uses this API to write a list of customers to an XML document.

Example 12-1. Creating an XML document

```
using System;
using System.Collections.Generic;
using System.Xml.Linq;

namespace Programming_CSharp
{
    // Simple customer class
    public class Customer
    {
        public string FirstName { get; set; }
        public string LastName { get; set; }
        public string EmailAddress { get; set; }
    }

    // Main program
    public class Tester
    {
        static void Main()
        {
            List<Customer> customers = CreateCustomerList();

            var customerXml = new XDocument();
            var rootElem = new XElement("Customers");
            customerXml.Add(rootElem);
            foreach (Customer customer in customers)
            {
                // Create new element representing the customer object.
                var customerElem = new XElement("Customer");

                // Add element representing the FirstName property
                // to the customer element.
                var firstNameElem = new XElement("FirstName",
                    customer.FirstName);
                customerElem.Add(firstNameElem);

                // Add element representing the LastName property
                // to the customer element.
                var lastNameElem = new XElement("LastName",
                    customer.LastName);
                customerElem.Add(lastNameElem);

                // Add element representing the EmailAddress property
                // to the customer element.
                var emailAddress = new XElement("EmailAddress",
                    customer.EmailAddress);
                customerElem.Add(emailAddress);

                // Finally add the customer element to the XML document
                rootElem.Add(customerElem);
            }

            Console.WriteLine(customerXml.ToString());
            Console.Read();
        }
```

```
        // Create a customer list with sample data
        private static List<Customer> CreateCustomerList()
        {
            List<Customer> customers = new List<Customer>
                {
                    new Customer { FirstName = "Orlando",
                                   LastName = "Gee",
                                   EmailAddress = "orlando0@hotmail.com"},
                    new Customer { FirstName = "Keith",
                                   LastName = "Harris",
                                   EmailAddress = "keith0@hotmail.com" },
                    new Customer { FirstName = "Donna",
                                   LastName = "Carreras",
                                   EmailAddress = "donna0@hotmail.com" },
                    new Customer { FirstName = "Janet",
                                   LastName = "Gates",
                                   EmailAddress = "janet1@hotmail.com" },
                    new Customer { FirstName = "Lucy",
                                   LastName = "Harrington",
                                   EmailAddress = "lucy0@hotmail.com" }
                };
            return customers;
        }
    }
}
```

The program will produce this output:

```
<Customers>
  <Customer>
    <FirstName>Orlando</FirstName>
    <LastName>Gee</LastName>
    <EmailAddress>orlando0@hotmail.com</EmailAddress>
  </Customer>
  <Customer>
    <FirstName>Keith</FirstName>
    <LastName>Harris</LastName>
    <EmailAddress>keith0@hotmail.com</EmailAddress>
  </Customer>
  <Customer>
    <FirstName>Donna</FirstName>
    <LastName>Carreras</LastName>
    <EmailAddress>donna0@hotmail.com</EmailAddress>
  </Customer>
  <Customer>
    <FirstName>Janet</FirstName>
    <LastName>Gates</LastName>
    <EmailAddress>janet1@hotmail.com</EmailAddress>
  </Customer>
  <Customer>
    <FirstName>Lucy</FirstName>
    <LastName>Harrington</LastName>
    <EmailAddress>lucy0@hotmail.com</EmailAddress>
  </Customer>
</Customers>
```

 As it happens, this example would have needed less code if we had used LINQ, but for this first example, we wanted to keep things simple. We'll show the LINQ version shortly.

In .NET, the `System.Xml.Linq` namespace contains the LINQ to XML classes we can use to create and process XML documents.

The `Customer` class and the `CreateCustomerList` function in the main `Tester` class contain straightforward code to give us some data to work with, so we will not go over them. The main attraction in this example is the XML creation in the `Main` function. First, we create a new XML document object:

```
var customerXml = new XDocument();
```

Next, we create the root element and add it to the document:

```
var rootElem = new XElement("Customers");
customerXml.Add(rootElem);
```

After these two operations, the `customerXml` object represents an XML document containing an empty element, which might look either like this:

```
<Customers></Customers>
```

or like this:

```
<Customers />
```

LINQ to XML tends to use the empty element tag form where possible, so if you were to call `ToString()` on `customerXml` at this point, it would produce that second version.

Of course, you may already have an XML document, and you may want to turn that into an `XDocument` object. Example 12-2 shows how to load a string into a new `XDocument`.

Example 12-2. Loading XML from a string

```
XDocument doc = XDocument.Parse("<Customers><Customer /></Customers>");
```

There's also a `Load` method, which has several overloads. You can pass in a URL, in which case it will fetch the XML from there and then parse it. You can also pass in a `Stream` or a `TextReader`, the abstract types from the `System.IO` namespace that represent a stream of bytes (such as a file), or a source of text (such as a file of some known character encoding).

XML Elements

With the root element in hand, you can add each customer as a child node:

```
foreach (Customer customer in customers)
{
    // Create new element representing the customer object.
    var customerElem = new XElement("Customer");
```

In this example, we make each property of the customer object a child element of the customer element:

```
// Add element representing the FirstName property to the Customer element.
var firstNameElem = new XElement("FirstName", customer.FirstName);
cstomerElem.Add(firstNameElem);
```

This adds the `FirstName` child element. We're passing the customer's first name as the second constructor argument, which will make that the content of the element. The result will look like this:

```
<FirstName>Orlando</FirstName>
```

The other two properties, `LastName` and `EmailAddress`, are added to the customer element in exactly the same way. Here's an example of the complete customer element:

```
<Customer>
  <FirstName>Orlando</FirstName>
  <LastName>Gee</LastName>
  <EmailAddress>orlando0@hotmail.com</EmailAddress>
</Customer>
```

Finally, the newly created customer element is added to the XML document as a child of the root element:

```
        // Finally add the customer element to the XML document
        rootElem.Add(customerElem);
    }
```

Once all customer elements are created, this example prints the XML document:

```
Console.WriteLine(customerXml.ToString());
```

When you call `ToString()` on any of the LINQ to XML objects (whether they represent the whole document, as in this case, or just some fragment of a document such as an `XElement`), it produces the XML text, and it formats it with indentation, making it easy to read. There are ways to produce more compact representations—if you're sending the XML across a network to another computer, size may be more important than readability. To see a terser representation, we could do this:

```
Console.WriteLine(customerXml.ToString(SaveOptions.DisableFormatting));
```

That will print the XML as one long line with no spaces.

XML Attributes

An XML element may have a set of *attributes*, which store additional information about the element. An attribute is a key/value pair contained in the start tag of an XML element:

```
<Customer FirstName="Orlando" LastName="Gee"></Customer>
```

If you're using an empty element tag, the attributes appear in the one and only tag:

```
<Customer FirstName="Orlando" LastName="Gee" />
```

The next example demonstrates how you can mix the use of child elements and attributes. It creates customer elements with the customer's name stored in attributes and the email address stored as a child element:

```
<Customer FirstName="Orlando" LastName="Gee">
  <EmailAddress>orlandoO@hotmail.com</EmailAddress>
</Customer>
```

The only difference between this and Example 12-1 is that we create XAttribute objects for the FirstName and LastName properties instead of XElement objects:

```
// Add an attribute representing the FirstName property
// to the customer element.
var firstNameAttr = new XAttribute("FirstName", customer.FirstName);
customerElem.Add(firstNameAttr);
// Add an attribute representing the LastName property
// to the customer element.
var lastNameAttr = new XAttribute("LastName", customer.LastName);
customerElem.Add(lastNameAttr);
```

As with elements, we just add the attribute to the parent element. Example 12-3 shows the complete sample code and output.

Example 12-3. Creating an XML document containing elements and attributes

```
using System;
using System.Collections.Generic;
using System.Xml.Linq;

namespace Programming_CSharp
{
    // Simple customer class
    public class Customer
    {
        // Same as in Example 12-1
    }

    // Main program
    public class Tester
    {
        static void Main()
        {
            List<Customer> customers = CreateCustomerList();

            var customerXml = new XDocument();
            var rootElem = new XElement("Customers");
            customerXml.Add(rootElem);
            foreach (Customer customer in customers)
            {
                // Create new element representing the customer object.
                var customerElem = new XElement("Customer");

                // Add an attribute representing the FirstName property
                // to the customer element.
                var firstNameAttr = new XAttribute("FirstName",
```

```
                                        customer.FirstName);
                customerElem.Add(firstNameAttr);


                // Add an attribute representing the LastName property
                // to the customer element.
                var lastNameAttr = new XAttribute("LastName",
                                        customer.LastName);
                customerElem.Add(lastNameAttr);

                // Add element representing the EmailAddress property
                // to the customer element.
                var emailAddress = new XElement("EmailAddress",
                    customer.EmailAddress);
                customerElem.Add(emailAddress);

                // Finally add the customer element to the XML document
                rootElem.Add(customerElem);
            }

            Console.WriteLine(customerXml.ToString());
            Console.Read();
        }

        // Create a customer list with sample data
        private static List<Customer> CreateCustomerList()
        {
            List<Customer> customers = new List<Customer>
                {
                    new Customer { FirstName = "Orlando",
                                   LastName = "Gee",
                                   EmailAddress = "orlando0@hotmail.com"},
                    new Customer { FirstName = "Keith",
                                   LastName = "Harris",
                                   EmailAddress = "keith0@hotmail.com" },
                    new Customer { FirstName = "Donna",
                                   LastName = "Carreras",
                                   EmailAddress = "donna0@hotmail.com" },
                    new Customer { FirstName = "Janet",
                                   LastName = "Gates",
                                   EmailAddress = "janet1@hotmail.com" },
                    new Customer { FirstName = "Lucy",
                                   LastName = "Harrington",
                                   EmailAddress = "lucy0@hotmail.com" }
                };
            return customers;
        }
    }
}

Output:
<Customers>
  <Customer FirstName="Orlando" LastName="Gee">
    <EmailAddress>orlando0@hotmail.com</EmailAddress>
  </Customer>
```

```
<Customer FirstName="Keith" LastName="Harris">
  <EmailAddress>keith0@hotmail.com</EmailAddress>
</Customer>
<Customer FirstName="Donna" LastName="Carreras">
  <EmailAddress>donna0@hotmail.com</EmailAddress>
</Customer>
<Customer FirstName="Janet" LastName="Gates">
  <EmailAddress>janet1@hotmail.com</EmailAddress>
</Customer>
<Customer FirstName="Lucy" LastName="Harrington">
  <EmailAddress>lucy0@hotmail.com</EmailAddress>
</Customer>
</Customers>
```

While it's often convenient to be able to create and add elements and attributes one step at a time, these classes offer constructors that allow us to do more work in a single step. If we know exactly what we want to put in an element, this can lead to neater looking code. For example, we can replace the `foreach` loop with the code in Example 12-4.

Example 12-4. Constructing an XElement all at once

```
foreach (Customer customer in customers)
{
    // Create new element representing the customer object.
    var customerElem = new XElement("Customer",
        new XAttribute("FirstName", customer.FirstName),
        new XAttribute("LastName", customer.LastName),
        new XElement("EmailAddress", customer.EmailAddress)
        );

    // Finally add the customer element to the XML document
    rootElem.Add(customerElem);
}
```

The only difference is that we're passing all the `XAttribute` and `XElement` objects to the containing `XElement` constructor, rather than passing them to `Add` one at a time. As well as being more compact, it's pretty easy to see how this code relates to the structure of the XML element being produced. We can also use this technique in conjunction with LINQ.

Putting the LINQ in LINQ to XML

We've seen several examples that construct an `XElement`, passing the name as the first argument, and the content as the second. We've passed strings, child elements, and attributes, but we can also provide an implementation of `IEnumerable<T>`. So if we add a `using System.Linq;` directive to the top of our file, we could use a LINQ query as the second constructor argument as Example 12-5 shows.

Example 12-5. Generating XML elements with LINQ

```
var customerXml = new XDocument(new XElement("Customers",
    from customer in customers
    select new XElement("Customer",
        new XAttribute("FirstName", customer.FirstName),
        new XAttribute("LastName", customer.LastName),
        new XElement("EmailAddress", customer.EmailAddress)
        )));
```

This generates the whole of the XML document in a single statement. So the work that took 25 lines of code in Example 12-1 comes down to just seven. Example 12-6 shows the whole example, with its much simplified `Main` method.

Example 12-6. Building XML with LINQ

```
using System;
using System.Collections.Generic;
using System.Linq;
using System.Xml.Linq;

namespace Programming_CSharp
{
    // Simple customer class
    public class Customer
    {
        // Same as in Example 12-1
    }

    // Main program
    public class Tester
    {
        static void Main()
        {
            List<Customer> customers = CreateCustomerList();

            var customerXml = new XDocument(new XElement("Customers",
                from customer in customers
                select new XElement("Customer",
                    new XAttribute("FirstName", customer.FirstName),
                    new XAttribute("LastName", customer.LastName),
                    new XElement("EmailAddress", customer.EmailAddress)
                    )));

            Console.WriteLine(customerXml.ToString());
            Console.Read();
        }

        // Create a customer list with sample data
        private static List<Customer> CreateCustomerList()
        {
            List<Customer> customers = new List<Customer>
                {
                    new Customer { FirstName = "Orlando",
                                   LastName = "Gee",
```

```
                            EmailAddress = "orlando0@hotmail.com"},
            new Customer { FirstName = "Keith",
                           LastName = "Harris",
                           EmailAddress = "keith0@hotmail.com" },
            new Customer { FirstName = "Donna",
                           LastName = "Carreras",
                           EmailAddress = "donna0@hotmail.com" },
            new Customer { FirstName = "Janet",
                           LastName = "Gates",
                           EmailAddress = "janet1@hotmail.com" },
            new Customer { FirstName = "Lucy",
                           LastName = "Harrington",
                           EmailAddress = "lucy0@hotmail.com" }
        };
        return customers;
    }
  }
}
```

We're not really doing anything special here—this LINQ query is just relying on plain old LINQ to Objects—the same techniques we already saw in Chapter 8. But this is only half the story. LINQ to XML is not just about creating XML. It also supports reading XML.

Being able to create XML documents to store data to be processed or exchanged is great, but it would not be of much use if you could not find information in them easily. LINQ to XML lets you use the standard LINQ operators to search for information in XML documents.

Searching in XML with LINQ

We'll need an example document to search through. Here's the document from Example 12-3, reproduced here for convenience:

```
<Customers>
  <Customer FirstName="Orlando" LastName="Gee">
    <EmailAddress>orlando0@hotmail.com</EmailAddress>
  </Customer>
  <Customer FirstName="Keith" LastName="Harris">
    <EmailAddress>keith0@hotmail.com</EmailAddress>
  </Customer>
  <Customer FirstName="Donna" LastName="Carreras">
    <EmailAddress>donna0@hotmail.com</EmailAddress>
  </Customer>
  <Customer FirstName="Janet" LastName="Gates">
    <EmailAddress>janet1@hotmail.com</EmailAddress>
  </Customer>
  <Customer FirstName="Lucy" LastName="Harrington">
    <EmailAddress>lucy0@hotmail.com</EmailAddress>
  </Customer>
</Customers>
```

Example 12-7 lists the code for the example.

Example 12-7. Searching an XML document using LINQ

```
using System;
using System.Collections.Generic;
using System.Linq;
using System.Xml.Linq;

namespace Programming_CSharp
{
    public class Customer
    {
        public string FirstName { get; set; }
        public string LastName { get; set; }
        public string EmailAddress { get; set; }
    }

    public class Tester
    {
        private static XDocument CreateCustomerListXml()
        {
            List<Customer> customers = CreateCustomerList();
            var customerXml = new XDocument(new XElement("Customers",
                from customer in customers
                select new XElement("Customer",

                new XAttribute("FirstName", customer.FirstName),
                new XAttribute("LastName", customer.LastName),
                new XElement("EmailAddress", customer.EmailAddress)
                )));

            return customerXml;
        }

        private static List<Customer> CreateCustomerList()
        {
            List<Customer> customers = new List<Customer>
                {
                    new Customer {FirstName = "Douglas",
                                    LastName = "Adams",
                                    EmailAddress = "dAdams@foo.com"},
                    new Customer {FirstName = "Richard",
                                    LastName = "Dawkins",
                                    EmailAddress = "rDawkins@foo.com"},
                    new Customer {FirstName = "Kenji",
                                    LastName = "Yoshino",
                                    EmailAddress = "kYoshino@foo.com"},
                    new Customer {FirstName = "Ian",
                                    LastName = "McEwan",
                                    EmailAddress = "iMcEwan@foo.com"},
                    new Customer {FirstName = "Neal",
                                    LastName = "Stephenson",
                                    EmailAddress = "nStephenson@foo.com"},
                    new Customer {FirstName = "Randy",
```

```
                              LastName = "Shilts",
                              EmailAddress = "rShilts@foo.com"},
              new Customer {FirstName = "Michelangelo",
                              LastName = "Signorile ",
                              EmailAddress = "mSignorile@foo.com"},
              new Customer {FirstName = "Larry",
                              LastName = "Kramer",
                              EmailAddress = "lKramer@foo.com"},
              new Customer {FirstName = "Jennifer",
                              LastName = "Baumgardner",
                              EmailAddress = "jBaumgardner@foo.com"}
      };
      return customers;
}

static void Main()
{
    XDocument customerXml = CreateCustomerListXml();

    Console.WriteLine("Search for single element...");
    var query =
       from customer in
              customerXml.Element("Customers").Elements("Customer")
       where customer.Attribute("FirstName").Value == "Douglas"
       select customer;
    XElement oneCustomer = query.SingleOrDefault();

    if (oneCustomer != null)
    {
        Console.WriteLine(oneCustomer);
    }
    else
    {
        Console.WriteLine("Not found");
    }


    Console.WriteLine("\nSearch using descendant axis... ");
    query = from customer in customerXml.Descendants("Customer")
            where customer.Attribute("FirstName").Value == "Douglas"
            select customer;
    oneCustomer = query.SingleOrDefault();
    if (oneCustomer != null)
    {
        Console.WriteLine(oneCustomer);
    }
    else
    {
        Console.WriteLine("Not found");
    }

    Console.WriteLine("\nSearch using element values... ");
    query = from emailAddress in
                customerXml.Descendants("EmailAddress")
            where emailAddress.Value == "dAdams@foo.com"
```

```
                    select emailAddress;
        XElement oneEmail = query.SingleOrDefault();
        if (oneEmail != null)
        {
            Console.WriteLine(oneEmail);
        }
        else
        {
            Console.WriteLine("Not found");
        }

        Console.WriteLine("\nSearch using child element values... ");
        query = from customer in customerXml.Descendants("Customer")
                where customer.Element("EmailAddress").Value
                    == "dAdams@foo.com"
                select customer;
        oneCustomer = query.SingleOrDefault();
        if (oneCustomer != null)
        {
            Console.WriteLine(oneCustomer);
        }
        else
        {
            Console.WriteLine("Not found");
        }

    }       // end main
  }         // end class
}           // end namespace


Output:
Search for single element...
<Customer FirstName="Douglas" LastName="Adams">
  <EmailAddress>dAdams@foo.com</EmailAddress>
</Customer>

Search using descendant axis...
<Customer FirstName="Douglas" LastName="Adams">
  <EmailAddress>dAdams@foo.com</EmailAddress>
</Customer>

Search using element values...
<EmailAddress>dAdams@foo.com</EmailAddress>

Search using child element values...
<Customer FirstName="Douglas" LastName="Adams">
  <EmailAddress>dAdams@foo.com</EmailAddress>
</Customer>
```

This example refactors Example 12-3 by extracting the creation of the sample customer list XML document into the CreateCustomerListXml() method. You can now simply call this function in the Main() function to create the XML document.

Searching for a Single Node

The first search in Example 12-7 is to find a customer whose first name is "Douglas":

```
var query =
  from customer in
        customerXml.Element("Customers").Elements("Customer")
  where customer.Attribute("FirstName").Value == "Douglas"
  select customer;
XElement oneCustomer = query.SingleOrDefault();

if (oneCustomer != null)
{
    Console.WriteLine(oneCustomer);
}
else
{
    Console.WriteLine("Not found");
}
```

In general, you will have some ideas about the structure of XML documents you are going to process; otherwise, it will be difficult to find the information you want. Here we know the node we are looking for sits just one level below the root element. So the source of the LINQ query—the part after the in keyword—fetches the root Customers element using the singular Element method, and then asks for all of its children called Customers by using the plural Elements method:

```
from customer in
        customerXml.Element("Customers").Elements("Customer")
```

We specify the search conditions with a where clause, as we would do in any LINQ query. In this case, we want to search on the value of the FirstName attribute:

```
where customer.Attribute("FirstName").Value == "Douglas"
```

The select clause is trivial—we just want the query to return all matching elements. Finally, we execute the query using the standard LINQ SingleOrDefault operator, which, as you may recall, returns the one result of the query, unless it failed to match anything, in which case it will return null. (And if there are multiple matches, it throws an exception.) We therefore test the result against null before attempting to use it:

```
if (oneCustomer != null)
{
    Console.WriteLine(oneCustomer);
}
else
{
    Console.WriteLine("Not found");
}
```

In this example, the method is successful, and the resultant element is displayed.

Search Axes

In practice, you don't always know exactly where the information you require will be in the XML document when you write the code. For these cases, LINQ to XML provides the ability to search in different ways—if you are familiar with the XPath query language[*] for XML, this is equivalent to the XPath concept of a search *axis*. This specifies the relationship between the element you're starting from and the search target nodes.

The `Element` and `Elements` methods we used earlier only ever search one level—they look in the children of whatever object you call them on. But we can instead use the `Descendants` method to look not just in the children, but also in their children's children, and so on. So the source for the next query in Example 12-7 looks for all elements called `Customer` anywhere in the document. This is more compact, but also less precise.

```
query = from customer in customerXml.Descendants("Customer")
```

Other methods available for querying along different axes include `Parent`, `Ancestors`, `ElementsAfterSelf`, `ElementsBeforeSelf`, and `Attributes`. The first two look up the tree and are similar to `Elements` and `Descendants`, in that `Parent` looks up just one level, while `Ancestors` will search up through the document all the way to the root. `ElementsBefor eSelf` and `ElementsAfterSelf` search for elements that have the same parent as the current item, and which appear either before or after it in the document. `Attributes` searches in an element's attributes rather than its child elements. (If you are familiar with XPath, you will know that these correspond to the `parent`, `ancestor`, `following-sibling`, `preceding-sibling`, and `attribute` axes.)

Where Clauses

The first query in Example 12-7 included a `where` clause that looked for a particular attribute value on an element. You can, of course, use other criteria. The third query looks at the content of the element itself—it uses the `Value` property to extract the content as text:

```
where emailAddress.Value == "dAdams@foo.com"
```

You can get more ambitious, though—the `where` clause can dig further into the structure of the XML. The fourth query's `where` clause lets through only those elements whose child `EmailAddress` element has a particular value:

```
where customer.Element("EmailAddress").Value == "dAdams@foo.com"
```

---

[*] XPath is supported by both LINQ to XML and the DOM APIs. (Unless you're using Silverlight, in which case the DOM API is missing entirely, and the XPath support is absent from LINQ to XML.) So if you prefer that, you can use it instead, or you can use a mixture of LINQ and XPath.

XML Serialization

So far, our code has constructed the objects representing the Customer XML elements by hand. As XML is becoming popular, especially with the increasingly widespread use of web services, it can be useful to automate this process. If you expect to work with XML elements that always have a particular structure, it can be convenient to serialize objects to or from XML. Working with conventional objects can be a lot easier than using lots of explicit XML code.

The .NET Framework provides a built-in serialization mechanism to reduce the coding efforts by application developers. The System.Xml.Serialization namespace defines the classes and utilities that implement methods required for serializing and deserializing objects. Example 12-8 illustrates this.

Example 12-8. Simple XML serialization and deserialization

```
using System;
using System.IO;
using System.Xml.Serialization;

namespace Programming_CSharp
{
    // Simple customer class
    public class Customer
    {
        public string FirstName { get; set; }
        public string LastName { get; set; }
        public string EmailAddress { get; set; }

        // Overrides the Object.ToString() to provide a
        // string representation of the object properties.
        public override string ToString()
        {
            return string.Format("{0} {1}\nEmail:   {2}",
                        FirstName, LastName, EmailAddress);
        }
    }

    // Main program
    public class Tester
    {
        static void Main()
        {
            Customer c1 = new Customer
                        {
                            FirstName = "Orlando",
                            LastName = "Gee",
                            EmailAddress = "orlando0@hotmail.com"
                        };

            XmlSerializer serializer = new XmlSerializer(typeof(Customer));
            StringWriter writer = new StringWriter();
```

```
        serializer.Serialize(writer, c1);
        string xml = writer.ToString();
        Console.WriteLine("Customer in XML:\n{0}\n", xml);

        Customer c2 = serializer.Deserialize(new StringReader(xml))
                as Customer;
        Console.WriteLine("Customer in Object:\n{0}", c2.ToString());

        Console.ReadKey();
    }
  }
}
```

```
Output:
Customer in XML:
<?xml version="1.0" encoding="utf-16"?>
<Customer xmlns:xsi="http://www.w3.org/2001/XMLSchema-instance"
xmlns:xsd="http://www.w3.org/2001/XMLSchema">
  <FirstName>Orlando</FirstName>
  <LastName>Gee</LastName>
  <EmailAddress>orlando0@hotmail.com</EmailAddress>
</Customer>

Customer in Object:
Orlando Gee
Email:   orlando0@hotmail.com
```

To serialize an object using .NET XML serialization, you need to create an
XmlSerializer object:

```
XmlSerializer serializer = new XmlSerializer(typeof(Customer));
```

You must pass in the type of the object to be serialized to the XmlSerializer constructor.
If you don't know the object type at design time, you can discover it by calling its
GetType() method:

```
XmlSerializer serializer = new XmlSerializer(c1.GetType());
```

You also need to decide where the serialized XML document should be stored. In this
example, you simply send it to a StringWriter:

```
StringWriter writer = new StringWriter();

serializer.Serialize(writer, c1);
string xml = writer.ToString();
Console.WriteLine("Customer in XML:\n{0}\n", xml);
```

The resultant XML string is then displayed on the console:

```
<?xml version="1.0" encoding="utf-16"?>
<Customer xmlns:xsi="http://www.w3.org/2001/XMLSchema-instance"
xmlns:xsd="http://www.w3.org/2001/XMLSchema">
  <FirstName>Orlando</FirstName>
  <LastName>Gee</LastName>
  <EmailAddress>orlando0@hotmail.com</EmailAddress>
</Customer>
```

The first line is an XML declaration. This is to let the consumers (human users and software applications) of this document know that this is an XML file, the official version to which this file conforms, and the encoding format used. This is optional in XML, but this code always produces one.

The root element here is the Customer element, with each property represented as a child element. The xmlns:xsi and xmlns:xsd attributes relate to the XML Schema specification. They are optional, and don't do anything useful in this example, so we will not explain them further. If you are interested, please read the XML specification or other documentation, such as the MSDN Library, for more details.

Aside from those optional parts, this XML representation of the Customer object is equivalent to the one created in Example 12-1. However, instead of writing numerous lines of code to deal with the XML specifics, you need only three lines using .NET XML serialization classes.

Furthermore, it is just as easy to reconstruct an object from its XML form:

```
Customer c2 = serializer.Deserialize(new StringReader(xml))
            as Customer;
Console.WriteLine("Customer in Object:\n{0}", c2.ToString());
```

All it needs is to call the XmlSerializer.Deserialize method. It has several overloaded versions, one of which takes a TextReader instance as an input parameter. Because StringReader is derived from TextReader, you just pass an instance of StringReader to read from the XML string. The Deserialize method returns an object, so it is necessary to cast it to the correct type.

Of course, there's a price to pay. XML serialization is less flexible than working with the XML APIs directly—with serialization you decide exactly what XML elements and attributes you expect to see when you write the code. If you need to be able to adapt dynamically to elements whose names you only learn at runtime, you will need to stick with the XML-aware APIs.

Customizing XML Serialization Using Attributes

By default, all public read/write properties are serialized as child elements. You can customize your classes by specifying the type of XML node you want for each of your public properties, as shown in Example 12-9.

Example 12-9. Customizing XML serialization with attributes

```
using System;
using System.IO;
using System.Xml.Serialization;

namespace Programming_CSharp
{
    // Simple customer class
    public class Customer
```

```csharp
    {
        [XmlAttribute]
        public string FirstName { get; set; }

        [XmlIgnore]
        public string LastName { get; set; }

        public string EmailAddress { get; set; }

        // Overrides the Object.ToString() to provide a
        // string representation of the object properties.
        public override string ToString()
        {
            return string.Format("{0} {1}\nEmail:   {2}",
                        FirstName, LastName, EmailAddress);
        }
    }

    // Main program
    public class Tester
    {
        static void Main()
        {
            Customer c1 = new Customer
                        {
                            FirstName = "Orlando",
                            LastName = "Gee",
                            EmailAddress = "orlando0@hotmail.com"
                        };

            //XmlSerializer serializer = new XmlSerializer(c1.GetType());
            XmlSerializer serializer = new XmlSerializer(typeof(Customer));
            StringWriter writer = new StringWriter();

            serializer.Serialize(writer, c1);
            string xml = writer.ToString();
            Console.WriteLine("Customer in XML:\n{0}\n", xml);

            Customer c2 = serializer.Deserialize(new StringReader(xml)) as
                        Customer;
            Console.WriteLine("Customer in Object:\n{0}", c2.ToString());

            Console.ReadKey();
        }
    }
}
```

Output:

```
Customer in XML:
<?xml version="1.0" encoding="utf-16"?>
<Customer xmlns:xsi="http://www.w3.org/2001/XMLSchema-instance"
          xmlns:xsd="http://www.w3.org/2001/XMLSchema"
          FirstName="Orlando">
  <EmailAddress>orlando0@hotmail.com</EmailAddress>
</Customer>
```

```
Customer in Object:
Orlando
Email:    orlando0@hotmail.com
```

The only changes in this example are a couple of XML serialization attributes added in the Customer class:

```
[XmlAttribute]
public string FirstName { get; set; }
```

The first change is to specify that you want to serialize the FirstName property into an attribute of the Customer element by adding the XmlAttributeAttribute to the property:

```
[XmlIgnore]
public string LastName { get; set; }
```

The other change is to tell XML serialization that you in fact do not want the Last Name property to be serialized at all. You do this by adding the XmlIgnoreAttribute to the property. As you can see from the sample output, the Customer object is serialized without LastName, exactly as we asked.

However, you have probably noticed that when the object is deserialized, its Last Name property is lost. Because it is not serialized, the XmlSerializer is unable to assign it any value. Therefore, its value is left as the default, which is an empty string. So in practice, you would exclude from serialization only those properties you don't need or can compute or can retrieve in other ways.

Summary

In this chapter, we saw how to use the LINQ to XML classes to build objects representing the structure of an XML document, which can then be converted into an XML document, and we saw how the same classes can be used to load XML from a string or file back into memory as objects. These classes support LINQ, both for building new XML documents and for searching for information in existing XML documents. And we also saw how XML serialization can hide some of the details of XML handling behind ordinary C# classes in situations where you know exactly what structure of XML to expect.

CHAPTER 13

Networking

Most interesting computer systems are distributed these days—it's increasingly unusual for a program to run in isolation on a single machine. So .NET provides various ways to communicate across networks. The array of networking options looks a little bewildering at first: there are 10 namespaces whose names start with System.Net containing more than 250 classes, and that's not even the complete set—there's an even bigger API for producing and consuming web services.

Fortunately, it's simpler than this makes it seem—despite the large API surface area most of the options fall into three categories. There's WCF—the Windows Communication Foundation, a framework for building and using web services. There are lower-level APIs for working directly with web protocols. Or you can use sockets if you need very low-level control. We'll start by discussing how to choose the most appropriate style of communication for your application, and then we'll look at these three options in more detail.

Choosing a Networking Technology

The first step in choosing the right networking API is to decide on the nature of the communication your application requires. There are many different styles of distributed applications. Perhaps you are building a public-facing web service designed to be used by a diverse range of clients. Conversely, you might be writing client code that uses someone else's web service. Or maybe you're writing software that runs at both ends of the connection, but even then there are some important questions. Are you connecting a user interface to a service in a tightly controlled environment where you can easily deploy updates to the client and the server at the same time? Or perhaps you have very little control over client updates—maybe you're selling software to thousands of customers whose own computers will connect back to your service, and you expect to have many different versions of the client program out there at any one time. Maybe it doesn't even make sense to talk about clients and servers—you might be creating a peer-to-peer system. Or maybe your system is much simpler than that, and has just two computers talking to each other.

The variations are endless, so no single approach can work well for all systems. The next few sections will look at some common scenarios, and discuss the pros and cons of the various networking options .NET offers. Even within a specific scenario there will often be more than one way to make things work. There are no hard-and-fast rules, because each project has different requirements. So this section won't tell you what to do—it'll just describe the issues you'll need to consider. Ultimately, only you can decide on the right solution for your system. We'll start with a very common web-based scenario.

Web Application with Client-Side Code

Web user interfaces have been getting smarter lately. A few years ago, most of a web application's logic would live on the server, with client-side code in the web browser typically doing little more than making buttons light up and menus fly out in response to the mouse. But now, we expect more from our web user interfaces. Whether you use *AJAX* (Asynchronous JavaScript and XML), or a *RIA* (Rich Internet Application) technology such as Silverlight or Flash, web applications often communicate constantly with the web server, and not just when navigating between pages.

If you're writing the server-side parts of this sort of application in C#, you will typically use ASP.NET to provide a web user interface. But what should you use for programmatic communication—the messages that flow between the web UI and the server once a page is already loaded?

WCF is a flexible choice here, because as Figure 13-1 illustrates, you can make a single set of remote services accessible to many common browser-based user interface technologies. A WCF service can be configured to communicate in several different ways simultaneously. You could use JSON (JavaScript Object Notation), which is widely used in AJAX-based user interfaces because it's is a convenient message format for JavaScript client code. Or you could use XML-based web services. Note that using WCF on the server does not require WCF on the client. These services could be used by clients written in other technologies such as Java, as long as they also support the same web service standards as WCF.

Looking specifically at the case where your web application uses C# code on the *client* side, this would mean using either Silverlight or WPF. (You can put WPF in a web page by writing an *XBAP*—a Xaml Browser Application. This will work only if the end user has WPF installed.) If you're using C# on both the client and the server, the most straightforward choice is likely to be WCF on both ends.

What if your server isn't running .NET, but you still want to use .NET on the web client? There are some restrictions on WCF in this scenario. Silverlight's version of WCF is much more limited than the version in the full .NET Framework—whereas the full version can be configured to use all manner of different protocols, Silverlight's WCF supports just two options. There's the so-called *basic profile* for web services, in which only a narrow set of features is available, and there's a binary protocol unique to WCF, which offers the same narrow set of features but makes slightly more efficient use of network bandwidth than the XML-based basic profile. So if you want a Silverlight client to use WCF to communicate with a non-.NET web service, as Figure 13-2 illustrates, this will work only if your service supports the basic profile.

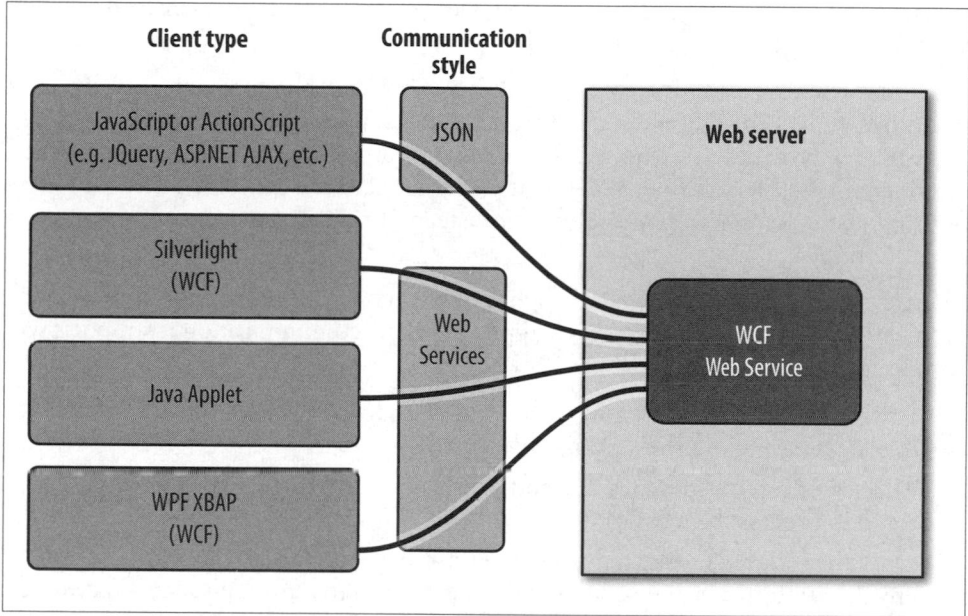

Figure 13-1. Web application clients and a WCF service

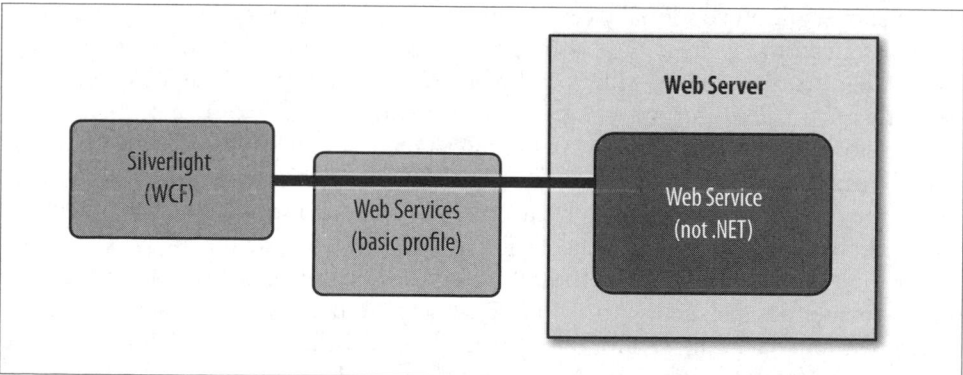

Figure 13-2. Silverlight client and non-.NET web service

More surprisingly, similar restrictions exist with a WPF XBAP. Even though XBAPs use the full version of the .NET Framework, certain features of WCF are disabled for security purposes—client code in web browsers shouldn't have complete freedom to connect to anywhere on the Internet, because that would make life too easy for hackers.

So WCF offers only a very limited version of its services to .NET applications running inside web browsers, meaning that XBAPs have similar WCF limitations to Silverlight.

If you're writing a Silverlight client and you want to talk to a service that does not conform to the web services basic profile, that's not necessarily a showstopper. It just rules out WCF—you will need to use the lower-level web-based APIs instead, or even the socket APIs, depending on the service.

Note that while WCF is usually a good default choice on the server side for web applications with client-side code, there are a few cases where you might not want to use it. ASP.NET provides its own mechanism for supporting AJAX clients, and while it's considerably less flexible than WCF, you might not need the flexibility. The simplicity of using just one framework on the server instead of two might end up looking like a better option.

There's a subtler reason why WCF might not always be the best fit: the style of communication. If you use WCF in a web application, the communication it supports will tend to involve the following steps:

1. Some code in the client (browser script, C# code, or Flash ActionScript) decides to send a message to the server.

2. The server receives the message and runs some code that does whatever it needs to do to process the message.

3. Once the code has finished, the server sends a message back to the client containing any data returned by the code (or if there is no data to return, just a message to say the work is complete).

This is, in effect, a remote method invocation—it's a way for the client to ask the server to run some code and optionally get a return value. (WCF is more flexible than this in general, but in the context of a web application, your communication patterns are constrained because clients will typically be behind a firewall.) That's likely to be a perfectly good pattern for operations such as looking up a stock price or retrieving a weather forecast. However, if you are building a photograph browser application, this would not be a great way to retrieve pictures. You could make it work, but it's easier to use the mechanisms already built into the web browser for downloading images— you'd almost certainly want to make the bitmaps available for download via HTTP rather than using WCF. HTML and Silverlight have UI elements that know how to render images downloaded with HTTP. Browsers are usually able to start rendering images without having to wait for the download to finish, and that's difficult to achieve with a method invocation idiom. And by using normal HTTP image download, you'd also get to take advantage of standard HTTP caching in your web browser and any caching proxies you may be using. Plain old HTTP works better here than trying to fetch a bitmap using something resembling a method call.

More generally, if the information your client code works with looks like a set of resources that might be identified with URIs (Uniform Resource Identifiers; for instance, *http://oreilly.com/*) and accessed via HTTP you might want to stick with ordinary HTTP rather than using WCF. Not only do you get the benefits of normal HTTP caching when reading data, but it may also simplify security—you might be able to take whatever mechanism you use to log people into the website and secure access to web pages, and use it to secure the resources you fetch programmatically.

 A service that presents a set of resources identified by URIs to be accessed via standard HTTP mechanisms is sometimes described as a RESTful service. *REST*, short for *Representational State Transfer*, is an architectural style for distributed systems. More specifically, it's the style used by the World Wide Web. The term comes from the PhD thesis of one of the authors of the HTTP specification (Roy Fielding). REST is a much misunderstood concept, and many people think that if they're doing HTTP they must be doing REST, but it's not quite that straightforward. It's closer to the truth to say that REST means using HTTP in the spirit in which HTTP was meant to be used. For more information on the thinking behind REST, we recommend the book *RESTful Web Services (http://oreilly.com/catalog/9780596529260/)* by Sam Ruby and Leonard Richardson, (O'Reilly).

Using WCF typically requires less effort than designing a RESTful service—you can get up and running with a good deal less thought and forward planning (although you might not consider a lack of thought and planning to be a good thing for your particular application). But if the communication you require with your server doesn't sound like it fits well into a method-call-like style, you'll probably want to consider alternatives to WCF.

Occasionally, neither WCF nor plain HTTP will be the best approach when connecting a web UI to a service. With Silverlight, you have the option to use TCP or UDP sockets from the web browser. (The UDP support is somewhat constrained. Silverlight 4, the current version at the time of writing this, only supports UDP for multicast client scenarios.) This is a lot more work, but it can support more flexible communication patterns—you're not constrained to the request/response style offered by HTTP. Games and chat applications might need this flexibility, because it provides a way for the server to notify the client anytime something interesting happens. Sockets can also offer lower communication latency than HTTP, which can be important for games.

.NET Client and .NET Server

Fashionable though web applications are, they're not the only kind of distributed system. Traditional Windows applications built with WPF or Windows Forms are still widely used, as they can offer some considerable advantages over web applications for both users and developers. Obviously, they're an option only if all your end users are running Windows, but for many applications that's a reasonable assumption. Assuming clients are running Windows, the main downside of this kind of application is that it's hard to control deployment compared to a web application. With web applications, you only have to update an application on the server, and all your clients will be using the new version the next time they request a new page.

 Out-of-browser Internet applications could well blur this distinction. Both Silverlight and Flash make it possible for Internet applications to have parts that are installed on the user's machine and run like normal applications outside the web browser. So the considerations in this section could apply if that's the sort of web application you're building.

To update a classic Windows application, you need to somehow get a new version of the program onto the end users' machines. Since it's rarely practical to install a new version on every single user's machine simultaneously, you need to handle the possibility of having several different versions of the client software all trying to talk to your server. The extent to which this can cause problems will depend on how much control you have over the client computers.

Tightly controlled deployment

Some applications are deployed in tightly controlled environments. For example, suppose you're writing a line-of-business application in WPF that will only ever be deployed to machines owned by your business. If your IT department has an iron grip on the company's computers, you might be able to exert considerable control over what versions of your application are out there. Network administrators could forcibly upgrade users to the latest version. So new versions might overlap with old versions for only a day or so. You could even go further and arrange for your application to check for updates and refuse to continue running when a newer version is available.

This is a happy situation for a developer, because it makes it much easier to introduce changes to your server. Chances are that at some point you'll want to add new services to support new features in your application. You might also want to modify existing services, which is usually more problematic than completely new features—if you're using WCF, it's not easy to modify the way an existing service works without breaking that service for older clients. It's possible, but it's hard, and it's often easier to run multiple versions of the service simultaneously during the transition period. The nice thing about having sufficient control to remove old versions of the application is that you can know when you've reached the end of a transition period and can shut down the older version of the service. This won't be the case if you can't force that sort of change on the client.

Weakly controlled deployment

If your application's customers don't all work for your company, life becomes more complex, because it's harder to force upgrades on your customers. It's not impossible— for example, Microsoft's Windows Live Messenger program occasionally tells you that if you don't upgrade you won't be able to carry on using the service. Mind you, it's a free service, so it gets to dictate its terms of use; you might find that paying customers won't put up with that, insisting that the product they've bought carries on working without needing to install regular upgrades.

The implication is that you might need to support old versions of your service indefinitely. At this point, WCF might not look like such a good choice. One of the attractive features of WCF is that it does a lot of work for you under the covers, but that's a double-edged sword—it works really well when both ends of the connection evolve simultaneously, but it can become a burden over time if the two ends do not move forward in tandem. If you want a service to be able to evolve while the client does not, you end up needing to understand exactly how WCF presents your service, and how the changes you have in mind might affect its operation. For example, if you decide that a method in your service requires an extra argument, what happens when an old client invokes the operation without that new argument? In practice, it might actually be easier just to work directly with HTTP and XML, because that way you have complete control over what messages go across the network.

That's not to say that WCF is definitely the wrong choice here. You could deal with the problem described by maintaining multiple versions of the service, or by dropping down to WCF's lower-level messaging API, for example. But the trade-off between WCF and HTTP is altered by the nature of your deployment. In a tightly controlled deployment, WCF is likely to be a good choice, but when you have less control, the lower-level APIs can start to look like they're worth the extra effort.

Regardless of how much control you have over deployment, as with the web application case there are some specialized scenarios in which neither WCF-based web services nor web APIs are the best fit. If you need communication patterns that don't fit well with HTTP, be aware that with this style of application, you can use the full range of communication styles offered by WCF—as we'll see, it supports more than just the typical web communication patterns. This means that sockets are an even more unusual choice in this scenario, and would typically be useful only if you need very precise control over the way in which messages are constructed and delivered.

.NET Client and External Party Web Service

You won't necessarily write the code at both ends of a connection. You might build a .NET client which talks to a web service provided by someone else. For example, you could write a WPF frontend to an online social media site such as Twitter, or a Silverlight client that accesses an external site such as Digg.

In this case, your choice of communication technology will be determined largely by the service you're connecting to. If it presents information in a way that WCF is able to consume, use WCF. How would you know that this is the case? You could try asking the service provider's support staff if their service works with WCF, but if they're not sure, it'll be down to the nature of the service. If your service provider uses the so-called WS-* family of web service standards, there's a good chance WCF will be able to talk to the service.

 If you were hoping for something more definitive than "a good chance," you're out of luck. The mere fact that two systems have both opted to use the same set of standards is no guarantee that they'll be able to communicate successfully, even if both ends conform strictly to the standards. If this information is news to you, welcome to the world of systems integration!

If WCF works in your scenario, that's great, but when it is not an option, use .NET's HTTP-based APIs. Unless, of course, the service in question is not HTTP-based, and requires you to work directly with TCP or UDP, in which case you would use sockets. In short, you're at the mercy of the server, and you'll just have to pick whichever option happens to work.

Note that because Silverlight's version of WCF is considerably more limited than the full .NET Framework version, a Silverlight client is more likely to have to drop down to the HTTP APIs than a full .NET client.

External Client and .NET Web Service

If you are writing a web service in .NET that you would like to be accessible to client programs written by people other than you, the choice of technology will be determined by two things: the nature of the service and the demands of your clients.[*] If it's something that fits very naturally with HTTP—for example, you are building a service for retrieving bitmaps—writing it as an ordinary ASP.NET application may be the best bet (in which case, refer to Chapter 21). But for services that feel more like a set of remotely invocable methods, WCF is likely to be the best bet. You can configure WCF to support a wide range of different network protocols even for a single service, thus supporting a wide range of clients.

As with the other application types, you would use sockets only if your application has unusual requirements that cannot easily be met using the communication patterns offered by HTTP.

So having looked at some common scenarios and seen which communication options are more or less likely to fit, let's look at how to use those options.

---

[*] More accurately, the demands to which you feel inclined to accede.

WCF

WCF is a framework for building and using remotely accessible services. It's particularly well suited to XML-based web standards, although it's not limited to these. It provides a programming model that supports many different underlying communication mechanisms; as well as supporting numerous web service standards, WCF also offers high-performance proprietary protocols that you can use in end-to-end .NET systems, and it's extensible, so support for other protocols can be added. WCF's design makes many of these details a matter of configuration—you write services and clients in the same way no matter what communication mechanisms are in use.

To explore WCF, we'll build a very simple instant messaging application to allow multiple users to chat with one another. So that we can focus on the communication code, the client will be a simple console application.

Creating a WCF Project

We'll start with the server for our chat application. If you want to build your own copy of the project as you read, open Visual Studio's New Project dialog (Ctrl-Shift-N) and in the template list on the left, select Visual C#→WCF. Choose the WCF Service Library project template. Call the project ChatServerLibrary. Ensure that the "Create directory for solution" checkbox is checked, and call the solution WcfChat.

This project will produce a DLL as its output, because the WCF Service Library project template doesn't commit to hosting the WCF service in any particular container application. WCF can run inside IIS, a Windows Service, a console application, or indeed pretty much any .NET application. If you want to use a particular kind of host, you can just create the relevant type of project—for example, instead of creating a WCF Service Library, you could create an ASP.NET web application project if you wanted to host your WCF service in there. (You can add a WCF service as a new item to an existing web project, so you don't need a WCF-specific project type.) But there are a couple of benefits to this library-based template: as you'll see shortly, it provides an easy way to do simple manual testing of the service. Also, it means you can host the service in multiple different host applications, which can be useful for automated testing—you can test the service without having to deploy it into its intended environment.

Visual Studio will have added a single service to the project, called Service1. This contains some example code that does things we don't need in our chat application, so we'll ignore that. (Feel free to delete them if you're building your own version as you read this.) We'll add a new WCF Service item to the project with the Add New Item dialog, called ChatService. Visual Studio adds two files to the project: *ChatService.cs* and *IChatService.cs*. This reflects the fact that WCF makes a distinction between the code that implements a service, and the *contract* for that service.

WCF Contracts

When two systems communicate over a network, they need to agree on what information is to be sent back and forth. WCF formalizes this with what it calls *contracts*. So the IChatService interface added by the wizard represents a *service contract*. The service contract defines the operations the service offers. As Example 13-1 shows, the interface is marked with a ServiceContract attribute to make it clear that it's a contract definition.

Example 13-1. A service contract

```
[ServiceContract]
public interface IChatService
{
    [OperationContract]
    void DoWork();
}
```

Each method in the interface that defines an operation offered by the service must be marked with an OperationContract. You might have thought that it would be enough that the interface is marked as ServiceContract—why do we also need to annotate each method? WCF requires you to be explicit so that it's always obvious when you're defining some aspect of your system that will be visible across the network. A method call to a local object is a quite different kind of operation than using a remote service—the performance and reliability characteristics are poles apart—so it's important for such boundaries to be clearly visible in the code.

> Although we're defining a method for each operation, ultimately the contract defines what *messages* can go in and out of the service. To invoke an operation, a client will need to send a message to the server over the network. When you add a method marked with OperationContract to an interface marked with ServiceContract, you are really defining the logical structure of the message that will be sent to invoke that operation, and also of the message that will be sent back to the client when the operation is complete. WCF lets you represent these message formats as method signatures because it's a convenient abstraction for developers.
>
> WCF supports other ways of defining message formats—you can write a contract in WSDL, the Web Service Definition Language, and then generate types from that. This approach is beyond the scope of this book.

Our service is designed to let people chat, so it will need to provide clients with a way to send a short bit of text, which we'll refer to as a *note*. (A more obvious name would be *message*, but that would introduce ambiguity—WCF sends messages to and from the server for every operation, so to call one of the pieces of information that crops up in certain messages a message would be confusing.) To keep things simple, we'll just have one big chat room where everyone can see every note; we're not going to support private conversations. To support sending notes, we'll get rid of the DoWork method provided by Visual Studio, and replace it with the code in Example 13-2.

Example 13-2. Modifying the contract

```
[OperationContract]
void PostNote(string from, string note);
```

If you attempt to build your project in Visual Studio, you'll get a compiler error:

```
error CS0535: 'ChatServerLibrary.ChatService' does not implement interface
  member 'ChatServerLibrary.IChatService.PostNote(string, string)'
```

Remember that Visual Studio added two files: *IChatService.cs* (the contract) and *Chat-Service.cs* (the service implementation). The compiler is pointing out to us that our service implementation no longer conforms to the contract for the service. So in *Chat-Service.cs*, we need to replace the DoWork method with this code:

```
public void PostNote(string from, string note)
{
    Debug.WriteLine("{0}: {1}", from, note);
}
```

For this to compile, you'll need to add a using System.Diagnostics; directive to the top of your file.

 There's an obvious security question with this service: how do we know that the note comes from the person it claims to come from? The answer is that we don't—identification is a complex topic, with many possible solutions. The appropriate choice of solution would depend on the context in which the application will be used—on a corporate network, integrated Windows security might be best, but that wouldn't work for a public-facing Internet application. The way to solve these problems is currently an area of debate, and could easily fill a chapter. Since this example just illustrates the basic mechanics of WCF, we are using the naïve trust model for identity: users can claim to be whoever they want to be, and our application will believe them.

WCF Test Client and Host

You can now build and run the application—either press F5 or choose Debug→Start Debugging. Normally, you'd get an error if you tried to run a library project, because you can't run a DLL. However, Visual Studio knows this is a WCF project, and it has a special feature for running and testing WCF libraries. When you run the project, you'll see a balloon pop up in the taskbar notification area, as Figure 13-3 shows.

Figure 13-3. WCF test service host

The WCF Service Host (or WcfSvcHost, as it's abbreviated in the pop up) is a program provided by Visual Studio that loads your WCF DLL and makes its services available for local access for debugging purposes. Visual Studio also launches a second program, the WCF Test Client—this is a Windows application that provides a UI for invoking operations on your service to try it out. As Figure 13-4 shows, it presents a tree view listing all the services defined by your project, and all the operations available in each service. (If you've deleted the unwanted IService1 mentioned earlier in your code, you'll only see one service.)

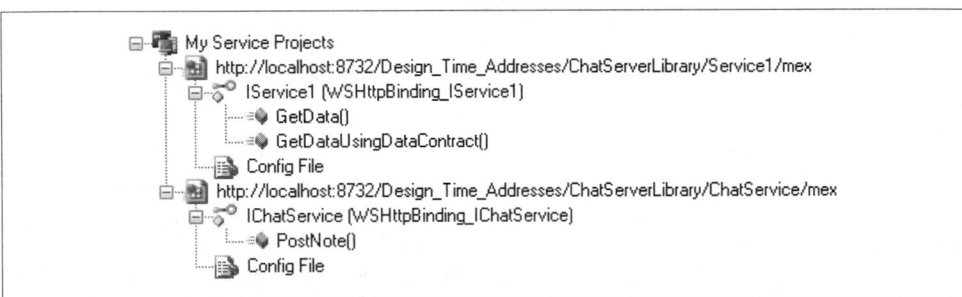

Figure 13-4. Services listed in the WCF Test Client

The test client has found both the original Service1 service that we chose to ignore and the ChatService we added. Double-clicking on the PostNote item that represents the operation we defined for the chat service shows a tab on the right that lets us try out the service—the test client's job is to let us try invoking service operations without having to write a whole program just to do that. Figure 13-5 shows this tab with arguments. If you look at the Value column, you'll see arguments for the from and note parameters of the PostNote operation—you can just type these directly into the Value column.

Clicking the Invoke button invokes the PostNote operation on the service. We can verify that the information typed into the WCF Test Client made it through, by looking in Visual Studio's Output window—that's where text sent to Debug.WriteLine appears. (There's an item on the View menu to make the Output window visible, if it's not already open.) The Output window gets fairly busy, so you might have to look quite carefully, but somewhere in the noise, you'll see that the `from` and `note` argument values are both shown, for example:

```
Ian: Hello, world
```

 If you're trying this yourself, it's possible you'll see an error back in the WCF Test Client if you set breakpoints in Visual Studio—the client program will time out if you spend too long suspended at a breakpoint. It's common with networking systems to give up after a certain length of time. If a client doesn't get a response, all manner of things could be wrong—there may be a network problem, perhaps locally, or maybe at the server end, or somewhere in between. Maybe the server is offline, or just too busy to respond to the request. The client can't easily tell— all it knows is it's not getting a response. So by default, WCF gives up after a minute and throws an exception. The WCF Test Client reports this with an error dialog.

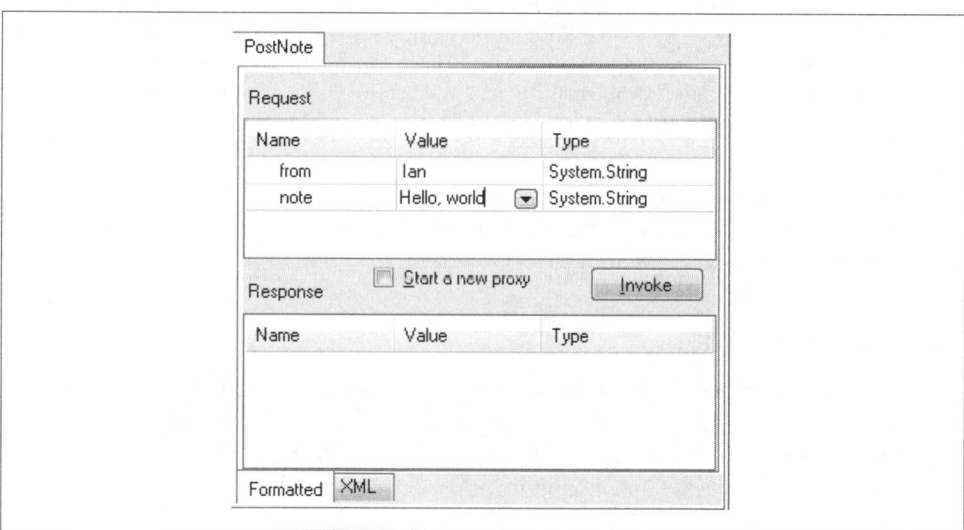

Figure 13-5. Passing arguments with the WCF Test Client

Once the test client has received a response from the service, it indicates this in the bottom half of the tab. Our `PostNote` operation has a return type of `void`, which means that it sends back an empty response. (It still sends a response to report that the operation has finished. It just contains no data.)

You may be curious to know what the messages being sent between the client and the server look like. And if you're not, we'd recommend becoming curious about such things. It's difficult to design good, nontrivial distributed systems (and impossible to diagnose problems with them) if you don't know what the messages they send look like. Sadly, some developers are happy to be ignorant about this sort of thing, but they frequently get stuck and have to ask for help from people who know what they're doing anytime something goes wrong. If you'd rather be one of the wizards who can fix these problems, you need to learn what the messages that go over the network really look like. You can see the messages in the WCF Test Client by clicking on the XML tab at the bottom. It's beyond the scope of this book about C# to explain the structure of these WCF messages in detail, but it's easy to see where the data you sent ended up in this example. If you want to learn more, the book *Learning WCF (http://oreilly.com/catalog/9780596101626/)* by Michele Leroux Bustamante (O'Reilly) would be a good place to start, or for a more advanced treatment, you could try *Programming WCF Services (http://oreilly.com/catalog/9780596526993/)* by Juval Lowy (O'Reilly).

 If you plan to do any real work with network communications, one of the most useful things you can do is get familiar with a tool that lets you inspect the contents of the messages being sent and received by your computer's network card. Microsoft's Network Monitor program is available for free, as is the open source Wireshark (*http://www.wireshark.org/*). They can seem a little intimidating at first because of the sheer level of detail they offer, but they're an indispensable tool for diagnosing communication problems, because they show you exactly what messages were sent and what they contained.

The WCF Service Host and Test Client are useful for very simple interactive testing, but a real, useful service needs to be hosted somewhere more permanent. So next, we'll look at how .NET programs can host WCF services.

Hosting a WCF Service

WCF services are flexible about their location—any ordinary .NET application can host WCF services, so there's no such thing as a specialized WCF Service Host project template in Visual Studio. You can host WCF services inside ASP.NET web applications, Windows Services, console applications, or even applications with GUIs built with Windows Forms or WPF. Any process that can accept incoming network connections should work, so about the only place you can't host a WCF service is in a process where security constraints prevent inbound connections, such as a web browser. (For example, Silverlight clients can make outbound WCF connections, but they can't host a service that accepts incoming connections.)

ASP.NET web applications are a particularly popular host environment for WCF services, because ASP.NET solves a lot of the problems you need to solve for an online service. Web applications automatically become available when a machine starts up—there's no need for anyone to log in and start a program. ASP.NET provides a robust hosting environment—it's able to restart after errors, and integrate into diagnostic management systems so that system administrators can discover when problems occur.

There are well-understood ways to load-balance web applications across multiple servers. ASP.NET can make use of IIS security features such as integrated authentication.

However, ASP.NET is not always the right choice. A WCF service hosted in a web application can't use the full range of protocols supported by WCF—incoming messages have to arrive by HTTP. Also, web applications usually get to run code only while they are actively handling a request from a client. If you need to perform long-running work that continues even when there are no clients connected right now, a web application host might be a bad idea, because in some configurations ASP.NET will restart web applications from time to time, or may even shut them down completely when they've had no incoming requests lately. So in some situations it might make more sense to write your own host. A Windows Service might be a good bet, as it can start automatically when the machine starts.

Sometimes it's useful to host a WCF service inside a normal Windows application. Imagine a WPF application providing some sort of advertising display on a screen in a shop window—it could be useful to build a WCF service into this to enable the display to be controlled without needing physical access to the machine.

The techniques for hosting look much the same in all cases. And since we won't be getting on to ASP.NET until later in the book, we'll keep it simple by hosting our service in a console application. It'll be easy enough to move it into different hosting environments later because the service itself is in a separate DLL project—we could just add it to a Windows Service or a web application.

Regardless of the type of host, one of the most important parts of WCF hosting is the configuration file.

WCF configuration

If you look in the `ChatServerLibrary` project, you'll find an *App.config* file. You'll find one of these, or its web equivalent, *web.config*, in lots of different kinds of .NET applications, but an *App.config* in a library project is something of an anomaly—application configuration files configure *applications*, and a library is not an application. Normally, adding an *App.config* file to a project that builds a DLL does nothing useful, but WCF projects are an exception because of the WCF Service Host we saw earlier. The test host loads the contents of this file into its own application configuration. Normally, application configuration files must go either into projects that build executable applications, or into web projects.

 The *App.config* in a WCF Service Library project is used only by the WCF Service Host. You will always need to copy the configuration into your real service host application.

So that we can have an application to configure, we'll add a console application called ChatHost to our WcfChat solution. This console application will host our WCF service, so we'll add a reference to the ChatServerLibrary. And since we'll be using this console application as the host from now on instead of WcfSvcHost, we'll need to copy the configuration in the ChatServerLibrary project's *App.config* into the ChatHost project's *App.config*. (Once we've done this, we can delete the *App.config* in the ChatServerLibrary project.)

We'll look at each of the *App.config* file's sections to understand how the file works. Everything lives inside the root <configuration> element—all *App.config* and *web.config* files have one of these, no matter what sort of application you're writing. The first child element will be this:

```
<system.web>
  <compilation debug="true" />
</system.web>
```

Our example doesn't need this, so it's safe to delete it. The WCF Service Library template adds this in case you are planning to host the project in a web application—this enables debugging in web apps. But since we're not writing a web application, it's not needed here.

Next is a <system.serviceModel> element—in fact, all the remaining contents of the *App.config* file are inside this element. This is where all WCF configuration lives, regardless of the type of host application.

The first element inside the WCF configuration is <services>. This contains a <service> element for each service the program will host. Visual Studio has added two: one for the Service1 service that we're not using, and one for the ChatService we wrote. Since we don't need the Service1 service, we can delete that first <service> element and everything it contains. This leaves the <service> element for our ChatService. It begins:

```
<service name="ChatServerLibrary.ChatService">
```

The name attribute is the name of the class that implements the service, including the namespace. Inside the <service> element we find some <endpoint> elements. Remember that earlier we said WCF can make a single service implementation accessible through multiple communication mechanisms. You do that by adding one endpoint for each mechanism you wish to support. Here's the first endpoint Visual Studio added for us:

```
<endpoint address=""
          binding="wsHttpBinding"
          contract="ChatServerLibrary.IChatService">
  <identity>
    <dns value="localhost" />
  </identity>
</endpoint>
```

An endpoint is defined by three things: an *address*, a *binding*, and a *contract*—sometimes referred to collectively as the ABC of WCF. The address is typically a URL—it's the address a client would use to connect to the service. In this case the address is blank, which means WCF will deduce the address for us—we'll see how in a moment.

The binding determines the communication technology that WCF will use on this endpoint. Here we've used one of the built-in bindings called wsHttpBinding. The "ws" denotes that this uses the various web service standards that begin with WS-. So this binding supports standards such as WS-ADDRESSING and WS-SECURITY. This is a feature-rich binding, and it may use features that some clients don't understand—it's not supported by Silverlight, for example. If you wanted to use the basic profile that Silverlight clients support, you'd specify basicHttpBinding here instead. But for this application, you can leave the binding as it is.

Finally, the contract attribute here contains the name of the interface type that defines the operation contract for our service. We already looked at contracts—this refers to the interface we saw in Example 13-1 and modified in Example 13-2.

Inside the <endpoint> element you'll see an <identity> element. This is intended for scenarios where the service needs to be able to identify itself securely to a client—for example, in a banking application you'd want to be confident that you're really talking to your bank. But we're not going to get into security in this example, so we can delete the <identity> element and its contents.

Visual Studio added a second endpoint to the *App.config* when we created the ChatService:

```
<endpoint address="mex"
          binding="mexHttpBinding"
          contract="IMetadataExchange" />
```

This enables something called *metadata exchange*—this endpoint doesn't provide a way to use the service, and instead makes it possible to get a *description* of the service. We'll be using this later when we build a client for our service.

Finally, after the two <endpoint> elements, you'll see a <host> element, as Example 13-3 shows. (This contains a very long line, which has been split across two lines here to make it fit on the page.) This <host> element is still inside the <service> element, so like the two <endpoint> elements, this entry is still describing one particular service—our ChatService.

Example 13-3. Host element with default base address

```
<host>
  <baseAddresses>
    <add baseAddress=
"http://localhost:8732/Design_Time_Addresses/ChatServerLibrary/ChatService/" />
  </baseAddresses>
</host>
```

This element contains hosting information that applies to all of this service's endpoints—this is how WCF works out what address to use for each endpoint. The baseAddress attribute is combined with the contents of the address attribute for each <endpoint> element to work out the effective address for that endpoint. Since the first endpoint's address is empty, that endpoint's address will be the baseAddress specified here. The second endpoint's address was mex, so that endpoint for the service will be available at:

```
http://localhost:8732/Design_Time_Addresses/ChatServerLibrary/ChatService/mex
```

If you're wondering why Visual Studio chose this slightly peculiar-looking address as the default base address for our service, see the sidebar below.

Endpoints, Security, and Administrative Privileges

Any process that hosts WCF services needs to be able to accept incoming network messages. If you're using an HTTP-based binding such as the default wsHttpBinding, or the basic-profile-compatible basicHttpBinding, your service host is likely not to be the only program on the machine that wants to receive incoming HTTP requests. Windows has a mechanism for working out which HTTP requests should be handled by which applications—programs can register to listen for requests on particular URLs, or URLs that begin with a particular prefix.

However, programs are not necessarily allowed to listen on any old address. Some programs may reserve certain URL prefixes, preventing other programs from handling them. For example, if you have an edition of Windows that includes Windows Media Center, your system will enable media center extenders (such as an Xbox 360) to connect to http://<yourmachine>:10243/WMPNSSv4/, and Media Center reserves this address using a security feature of Windows: you can apply an *access control list* (ACL) to a URL prefix to say which accounts are allowed to listen for incoming requests on any URL that starts with the reserved string. Only a program running with the special user account used by the Windows Media services will get to use this URL prefix. You can see which URLs are reserved for which user accounts by running the following command from a command prompt:

```
netsh http show urlacl
```

(If you're running Windows 2003, Windows XP, or earlier, you'll need to track down a different program, called httpcfg, but on Windows Vista or later netsh is the command to use.)

Unless you're running with administrative rights enabled, attempting to listen on a URL that your user account hasn't been granted access to (i.e., most URLs) will fail. Running with admin rights enabled is akin to running with scissors, so you wouldn't want to do that, but this seems like it might present a problem for developers writing WCF services. When you deploy your application for real, its installer can configure a suitable ACL for the URL on the target machine to ensure that the program is able to listen correctly, but what do you do on a development machine?

To make life easy for developers, Visual Studio's installer sets up a special range of addresses with an ACL that makes it open for any user logged in to the machine. Listening on anything starting with *http://localhost:8732/Design_Time_Addresses/* will work, even if you're logged on with a nonadministrative account. That's why Visual Studio chooses the base address you see in Example 13-3—it means you don't need to run with elevated privileges.

After the `<services>` element you'll see a `<behaviors>` element in your *App.config*, containing a `<serviceBehaviors>` element which contains a `<behavior>` element. This section allows various WCF features to be switched on or off. You might wonder why these settings don't just go into the `<services>` section. The reason is that you might want to host multiple services, all of which share common behavior configuration. You can define a single named `<behavior>` element, and then point multiple `<service>` elements' `behaviorConfiguration` attributes at that behavior, reducing clutter in your configuration file. Or, as in this case, you can create an unnamed `<behavior>` element, which defines default behavior that applies to all services in this host process. Since we're hosting only one service here, this doesn't offer much advantage, but this separation can be useful when hosting multiple services.

The `<behavior>` element that Visual Studio provides has some comments telling you what you might want to change and why, but paring it down to the essential content leaves just this:

```
<behaviors>
  <serviceBehaviors>
    <behavior>
      <serviceMetadata httpGetEnabled="True" />
      <serviceDebug includeExceptionDetailInFaults="False" />
    </behavior>
  </serviceBehaviors>
</behaviors>
```

This configures a couple of optional features. The first is related to the metadata exchange mentioned earlier—it just ensures that the service description can be fetched in a certain way. Again, we'll come back to metadata when we get to the client, so you can ignore that for now.

The second behavior here—the `serviceDebug` element—doesn't have any effect, because it sets the `includeExceptionDetailInFaults` property to its default value, `False`. Nothing would change if you removed this. The only reason Visual Studio puts this here at all is to help you out when debugging—sometimes it's useful to set this to `True` temporarily, and putting this entry in the file saves you from having to look up the name of the setting. Making this `True` will mean that if your service throws an exception, the full exception details including stack trace will be sent back to the client in the response.

Generally speaking, you should *never do this*, because sending stack traces to your clients reveals implementation details about your system. If some of your clients are evil hackers, this might make it easier for them to break into your system. (Technically, if your system is completely secure, a stack trace won't help them, but when did you last hear about a computer system that was completely secure? It's safe to presume that everything has security flaws, so the less help you give hackers the better—this is often described as reducing the *attack surface area* of your system.) While you don't normally want to send stack traces over the network, doing so can sometimes make it easier to diagnose problems during development. So you might switch this setting on temporarily to make your life easier. *But remember to turn it off before you ship!*

That's everything Visual Studio put into our configuration file. This shows just a tiny fraction of all the settings we could put in there, but this isn't a book about WCF, so that'll do for now.

After all that, our program still isn't ready to host the service. As well as putting configuration entries into the application configuration file, our program needs to make an API call to tell WCF that it wants to host services. (If we were writing a web application, we wouldn't need to do this—having the configuration in the *web.config* file would be enough. But for other application types, we need to do this one last step.)

So we need to add a reference to the `System.ServiceModel` component—that's the main .NET Framework class library DLL for WCF—and we also need to add `using System.ServiceModel;` and `using ChatServerLibrary;` directives to the top of the *Program.cs* file in our `ChatHost` project. We can then write our `Main` method to look like Example 13-4.

Example 13-4. Hosting a WCF service

```
static void Main(string[] args)
{
    using (ServiceHost host = new ServiceHost(typeof(ChatService)))
    {
        host.Open();

        Console.WriteLine("Service ready");
        Console.ReadKey();
    }
}
```

This creates a `ServiceHost` object that will make the `ChatService` available. WCF will load the configuration from our *App.config* file to work out how to host it. And we need to make sure our program hangs around—the service will be available only for as long as the program that hosts it. So we leave the program running until a key is pressed.

If you want to try this out, you'll need to make sure the host console application is the program Visual Studio runs by default—right now it won't be because the `ChatServer Library` is still set as the default. You'll need to right-click on `ChatHost` in the Solution Explorer and select Set as Startup Project. Now pressing F5 will run the program, and a console window will appear showing the message "Service ready" once the `ServiceHost` is ready.

 If you didn't delete the *App.config* file in the `ChatServerLibrary` project earlier, you'll now get an error. Even when you set `ChatHost` as the startup application, Visual Studio will still attempt to launch the WCF Service Host for the `ChatServerLibrary` project. That would be useful in a solution that has just a WCF client and a service DLL. It's unhelpful here because we end up with two programs trying to host the same server on the same URL—whichever one gets there second will fail.

If you don't want to delete the *App.config* in that project, you can disable the WCF Service Host by opening the `ChatServerLibrary` project's Properties, going to the WCF Options tab, and unchecking the relevant checkbox.

Now what? We no longer have the WCF Test Client, because Visual Studio thinks we're running a normal console application. Since the default `wsHttpBinding` for our service endpoint uses HTTP we could try pointing a web browser at it. Remember, the service is running on the address in the configuration file:

```
http://localhost:8732/Design_Time_Addresses/ChatServerLibrary/ChatService/
```

Strictly speaking, the service isn't really designed to support a web browser. This chapter is all about enabling programs to communicate with one another, not how to build web user interfaces. However, WCF is rather generous here—it notices when we connect with a web browser, and decides to be helpful. It generates a web page that patiently explains that the thing we've connected to is a service, and shows how to write code that could talk to the service. And that's exactly what we're going to do next.

Writing a WCF Client

We need to create a client program to talk to our service. Again, to keep things simple we'll make it a console application. We'll add this to the same solution, calling the project `ChatClient`. (Obviously, you'll need to stop the `ChatHost` program first if you're trying this out and it's still running in the debugger.)

When you right-click on a project's References item in Visual Studio's Solution Explorer, you're offered an Add Service Reference menu item as well as the normal Add Reference entry. We're going to use that to connect our client to our server via WCF.

The Add Service Reference dialog offers a Discover button (shown in Figure 13-6) which attempts to locate services in your current solution. Disappointingly, if we were to click it with our code as it is now, it would report that it didn't find any services. That's because we wrote all the hosting code by hand for `ChatHost`—Visual Studio doesn't realize that our console application is hosting services. It usually looks only in web projects—if we'd hosted the service in an ASP.NET web application, it would have found it. But with the approach we're taking here, it needs a little help.

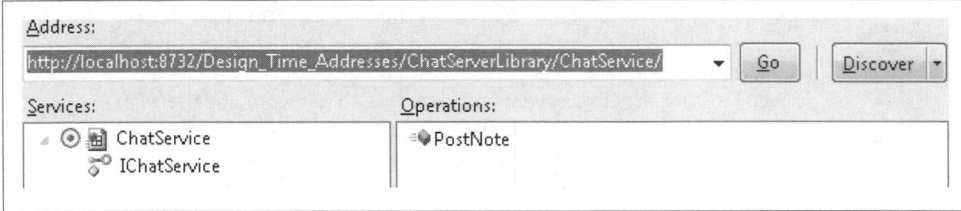

Figure 13-6. Add Service Reference

 If you left the *App.config* file in place in the `ChatServerLibrary` project, it would find that and would launch the WCF Service Host for you when you click Discover. But be careful—`ChatHost` is our real service, and when we start modifying settings in its *App.config* (which we'll do later) it's important that the Add Service Reference dialog is talking to the right service. That's why we suggested deleting the *App.config* from the DLL project earlier—it avoids any possibility of accidentally configuring your client for the wrong service host.

For Visual Studio to be able to connect to our console-hosted service we need the service to be up and running before the Add Service Reference dialog is open. The easiest way to do this is to run the project, *without* debugging it. Instead of pressing F5, we choose Debug→Start Without Debugging, or we press Ctrl-F5. This runs the `ChatHost` program without debugging, leaving Visual Studio free for other tasks, such as adding a service reference.

We'll need the address of the service handy, and since it's quite long, it's easiest to open our host's *App.config* and copy the service address to the clipboard. (It's the `baseAddress` attribute in the `<host>` section.) Then we can go to the `ChatClient` project and add a Service Reference. If we paste the address of the service into the Address box and then click the Go button, after a few seconds we'll see the Services panel on the left display a `ChatService` entry. Expanding this shows an `IChatService` item representing the contract, and selecting this shows the one operation available in our contract, `PostNote`, as Figure 13-6 shows.

While the list of services, contracts, and operations in the Add Service Reference dialog is useful for verifying that we have the service we wanted, the significance of the information here goes a little deeper—it's part of an important feature of how systems communicate in WCF. Remember that we defined a contract earlier, to describe the operations our service provides to its clients. For the client to communicate successfully with the server, it also needs a copy of that contract. So the best way to think of the Add Service Reference dialog is that it's a tool for getting hold of the contract from a service.

This is the purpose of the metadata exchange entry we saw earlier when we looked at the configuration Visual Studio generated for our WCF service. Metadata exchange is just a fancy way of saying that a service provides a way for a client to discover the contract and related information about the service. The Add Service Reference dialog uses this information to configure a client application to communicate with the service, and to provide it with a copy of the contract.

To see the results of this, we'll finish with this dialog. In the Namespace text box near the bottom, we'll type `ChatService`—Visual Studio will put the contract and any other types relating to this service into this namespace. When we click OK a Service References item appears in the project in the Solution Explorer, and it will contain an entry called `ChatService`. (Now that we've done this, we can stop the service host console window we ran earlier.)

Visual Studio generates some code when adding a service reference. By default, it hides this, but we can take a look at it. At the top of the Solution Explorer, there's a toolbar, and if you hover your mouse pointer over the buttons you'll find that one has a tool tip of Show All Files. This button toggles each time you click it. When it's pressed in, the `ChatService` service reference can be expanded, as Figure 13-7 shows.

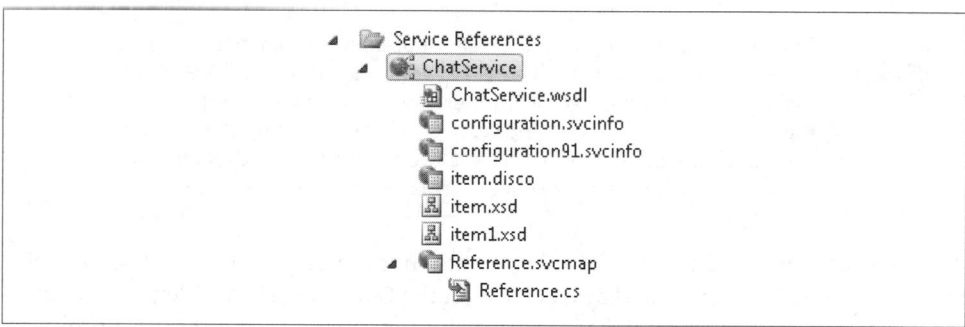

Figure 13-7. Generated files in a service reference

The most interesting file in here is *Reference.cs*, inside the `Reference.svcmap` item. Inside this file, near the top, there's a copy of `IChatService`—the contract we wrote earlier:

```
[System.CodeDom.Compiler.GeneratedCodeAttribute("System.ServiceModel",
                                                "4.0.0.0")]
[System.ServiceModel.ServiceContractAttribute(
        ConfigurationName="ChatService.IChatService")]
public interface IChatService
{

    [System.ServiceModel.OperationContractAttribute(
        Action="http://tempuri.org/IChatService/PostNote",
        ReplyAction="http://tempuri.org/IChatService/PostNoteResponse")]
    void PostNote(string from, string note);
}
```

It looks a little more complex than the original, because Visual Studio has annotated it with various attributes, but it's simply being explicit about the values that WCF fills in by default.† Aside from these extra details, you can see that it is essentially a copy of the original contract.

Sharing contracts

You might wonder why we jumped through all these hoops rather than just copying `IChatService` from the service project to the client. In fact, that would have worked, and we could even have written a separate DLL project to define the contract interface and shared that DLL across the two projects. As you'll see shortly, Visual Studio generated a few other useful things for us as part of this Add Service Reference process, but as it happens, sharing the contract definition directly is sometimes a perfectly reasonable thing to do—you're not obliged to use metadata exchange.

Of course, you won't always own the code at both ends. If you need to connect to a service on the Internet provided by someone else, metadata exchange becomes more important—it provides a way to get hold of a contract you didn't write. And since the metadata exchange mechanisms are standards-based, this can work even when the service is not written in .NET.

 Metadata exchange is not universally supported. In practice, contract discovery can happen in all sorts of ways, including (and we're not making this up) being faxed a printout showing samples of the messages the service expects to send and receive.‡ If you're getting the contract through that kind of informal channel, you'll need to write an interface (by hand) in your client program to represent the service contract.

The process of metadata import also highlights an important point about service evolution. You might modify the `ChatService` after the `ChatClient` has added its reference. If these modifications involve changing the contract, it's clear that there's a problem: the client's copy of the contract is out of date. You might think that sharing the interface directly through a common DLL would be a good way to avoid this problem, but it might only make the problem harder to see: what if you've already deployed a version of the client? If you then modify the contract the modified code might run fine on your machine, but if you deploy an update to the service with this changed contract any copies of the old client out there will now be in trouble because they're still working with an old copy of the contract. Explicitly going through the metadata exchange

---

† In fact, it has revealed a small problem: the `tempuri.org` that appears in the URL indicates something temporary that we're supposed to fill in—the `ServiceContract` attribute on the original service definition has a `Namespace` attribute, and we're supposed to pick a URI that is unique to our service. It's not mandatory in this particular scenario because everything works with the default, but a temporary-looking URI doesn't look entirely professional.

‡ It could be worse. See *http://www.neopoleon.com/home/blogs/neo/archive/2003/09/29/5458 .aspx*.

doesn't make this problem any easier to solve, of course, but it makes it less likely for changes to creep in by accident and go undetected. A complete solution to the problem of service evolution is beyond the scope of this book, so for now, just be aware that changing a contract should not be undertaken lightly.

 Michele Leroux Bustamante's *Learning WCF (http://oreilly.com/catalog/ 9780596101626/)* (O'Reilly) discusses versioning of service contracts.

Proxy

Looking further through the *Reference.cs* file generated by adding the service reference, the next most interesting feature after the contract is a class called `ChatServiceClient`. This implements `IChatService`, because it acts as a *proxy* for the service. If we want to communicate with the service, all we need to do is create an instance of this proxy and invoke the method representing the operation we'd like to perform. So if we add a `using ChatClient.ChatService;` directive to the top of *Program.cs* in `ChatClient`, we can then modify its `Main` method as shown in Example 13-5.

Example 13-5. Invoking a web service with a WCF proxy

```
static void Main(string[] args)
{
    using (ChatServiceClient chatProxy = new ChatServiceClient())
    {

        chatProxy.PostNote("Ian", "Hello again, world");
    }
}
```

Notice the `using` statement—it's important to ensure that you dispose of WCF proxies when you have finished using them. When the client calls this method on the proxy, WCF builds a message containing the inputs, and it sends that to the service. Over in the service (which is running in a separate process, perhaps on a different machine) WCF will receive that message, unpack the inputs, and pass them to the `PostNote` method in the `ChatService` class.

To try this out, we're going to need to run both the client and the server simultaneously. This means configuring the solution in Visual Studio a little differently. If you right-click on the `WcfChat` solution in the Solution Explorer and select Set Startup Projects, the dialog that opens offers three radio buttons. If you select the Multiple Startup Projects radio button, you can choose which of your projects you'd like to run when debugging. In this case, we want to change the Action for both the `ChatClient` and `ChatHost` projects from None to Start. (We leave the `ChatServerLibrary` Action as None—we don't need to run that project, because our `ChatHost` project hosts the server library.) Also, we want to give the service a head start so that it's running before the client tries to use it, so select ChatHost and click the up arrow next to the list, to tell Visual Studio to run it first. (In theory, this is not a reliable technique, because there's no guarantee that the server will get enough of a head start. In practice, it appears to work well enough for this sort of debugging exercise.) Figure 13-8 shows how these settings should look.

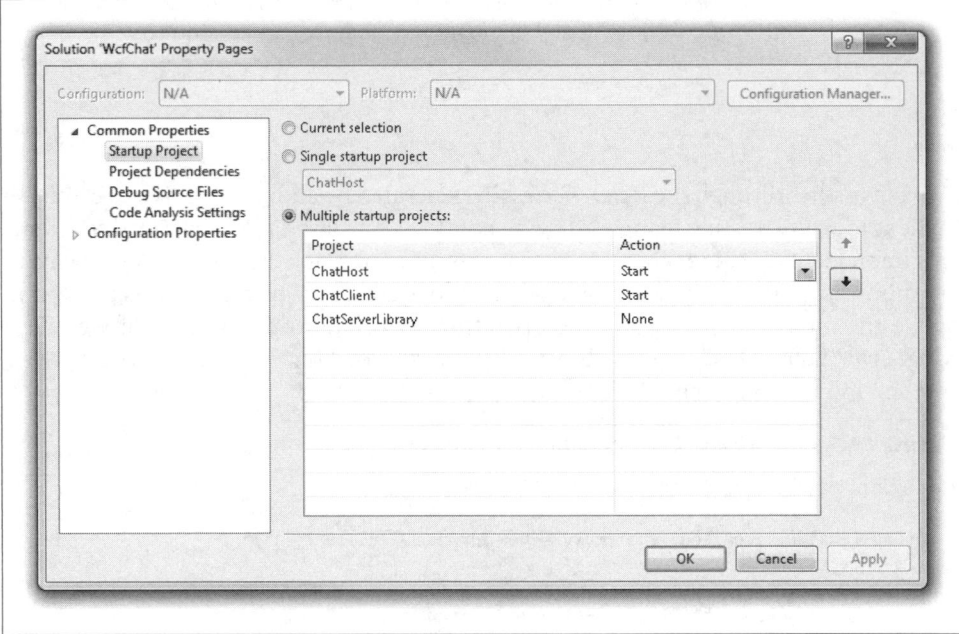

Figure 13-8. Starting multiple projects simultaneously

If we run the program by pressing F5, two console windows will open, one for the client and one for the service.

 If you're following along, it's possible that you'll see an AddressAlrea dyInUseException with an error message complaining that "Another application has already registered this URL with HTTP.SYS." This usually means you have a copy of ChatHost still running—somewhere on your desktop you'll find a console window running the service host. Or possibly, the WCF Service Host is still running. This error occurs when you launch a second copy of the service because it tries to listen on the same address as the first, and only one program can receive requests on a particular URL at any one time.

Visual Studio displays the message in its Output window because of the call to Debug.WriteLine in PostNote, just like it did when using the WCF Test Client earlier, verifying that the proxy was able to invoke an operation on the service. (You might need to look carefully to see this—the message can get buried among the various other notifications that appear in the Output window.)

Notice that in Example 13-5 we didn't need to tell the proxy what address to use. That's because the Add Service Reference dialog imported more than just the contract definition. It adds information to the ChatClient project's *App.config* file, shown in all its gory detail in Example 13-6.

Example 13-6. Generated client-side App.config

```xml
<?xml version="1.0" encoding="utf-8" ?>
<configuration>
    <system.serviceModel>
        <bindings>
            <wsHttpBinding>
                <binding name="WSHttpBinding_IChatService"
                    closeTimeout="00:01:00" openTimeout="00:01:00"
                    receiveTimeout="00:10:00" sendTimeout="00:01:00"
                    bypassProxyOnLocal="false" transactionFlow="false"
                    hostNameComparisonMode="StrongWildcard"
                    maxBufferPoolSize="524288" maxReceivedMessageSize="65536"
                    messageEncoding="Text" textEncoding="utf-8"
                    useDefaultWebProxy="true"
                    allowCookies="false">
                    <readerQuotas maxDepth="32" maxStringContentLength="8192"
                        maxArrayLength="16384"
                        maxBytesPerRead="4096" maxNameTableCharCount="16384" />
                    <reliableSession ordered="true"
                        inactivityTimeout="00:10:00" enabled="false" />
                    <security mode="Message">
                        <transport clientCredentialType="Windows"
                            proxyCredentialType="None" realm="" />
                        <message clientCredentialType="Windows"
                            negotiateServiceCredential="true"
                            algorithmSuite="Default" />
                    </security>
                </binding>
            </wsHttpBinding>
        </bindings>
        <client>
            <endpoint address="http://localhost:8732/Design_Time_Addresses/
                                ChatServerLibrary/ChatService/"
                binding="wsHttpBinding"
                bindingConfiguration="WSHttpBinding_IChatService"
                contract="ChatService.IChatService"
                name="WSHttpBinding_IChatService">
                <identity>
                    <userPrincipalName value="ian@idg.interact" />
                </identity>
            </endpoint>
        </client>
    </system.serviceModel>
</configuration>
```

Like the service configuration we examined earlier, this also has an `<endpoint>` element with an address, binding, and contract, although being on the client side, this `<endpoint>` appears inside a `<client>` element instead of a `<service>` element. The proxy gets the address from this endpoint definition.

 You can provide the proxy with an address from code if you want to. It offers various constructor overloads, some of which accept a URL. But if you don't provide one, it will look in the configuration file.

Notice that the endpoint also has a `bindingConfiguration` attribute—this refers to a `<binding>` element earlier in the file that contains information on exactly how the `wsHttpBinding` should be configured. There was nothing like this in the service, because we were just using the defaults. But the Add Service Reference dialog always generates a binding configuration entry, even if you happen to be using the defaults.

Our "chat" application is demonstrating the ability for the client to send a note to the server, but it's not complete yet. The client needs a couple of extra features. To make our conversation a bit less one-sided, we should be able to see notes written by other people. And unless our conversations are all going to be exceptionally brief, we need to be able to type in more than just one note.

We'll fix that second problem by modifying the code in Example 13-5. We'll put the call to the proxy inside a loop, and we'll also ask for the user's name, so we can support notes from people who may not be called Ian (see Example 13-7).

Example 13-7. Client with input loop

```
static void Main(string[] args)
{
    ChatServiceClient chatProxy = new ChatServiceClient();

    Console.WriteLine("Please enter your name:");
    string name = Console.ReadLine();
    while (true)
    {
        Console.WriteLine("Type a note (or hit enter to quit):");
        string note = Console.ReadLine();
        if (string.IsNullOrEmpty(note))
        {
            break;
        }
        chatProxy.PostNote(name, note);
    }
}
```

We'll also modify the server so that it prints out the note, rather than sending it to the debug output—that'll make it a bit easier to see when notes are coming in. So change PostNote in ChatService to this:

```
public void PostNote(string from, string note)
{
    Console.WriteLine("{0}: {1}", from, note);
}
```

If you run both programs again by pressing F5, the client program will ask you to type in your name, and will then let you type in as many notes as you like. Each new note will be sent to the server, and you should see the notes appear in the server console window.

This is an improvement, but there's still no way for the client to find out when other users have typed notes. For this, we'll need to add bidirectional communication.

Bidirectional Communication with Duplex Contracts

The contract for our chat service is a one-sided affair—it's all about the notes the client sends to the server. But WCF supports *duplex* contracts, which provide a means for the server to call the client back. (Note that there are some issues with HTTP that can make duplex communication tricky—see the sidebar on the next page.) A duplex contract involves two interfaces—as well as an interface that the server implements, we also define an interface that the client must implement if it wants to use the service. In our example, the service wants to notify clients whenever any user posts a note. So the client-side interface, shown in Example 13-8, looks pretty similar to our current server interface.

Example 13-8. Callback interface for duplex contract

```
public interface IChatClient
{
    [OperationContract]
    void NotePosted(string from, string note);
}
```

Notice that while methods in a callback interface require the usual OperationContract attribute, the interface itself does not need to be marked with ServiceContract. That's because this callback interface is not a contract in its own right—it's one half of a duplex contract. So we need to modify the existing IChatService to associate it with this new callback interface (see Example 13-9).

Duplex Communication, HTTP, and Firewalls

Bidirectional communication is problematic on the Internet today. The vast majority of computers are behind firewalls. Firewalls are usually configured to reject most incoming connections. There will be exceptions for machines such as web servers and mail servers—administrators set up firewalls to allow certain kinds of traffic through to such machines—but the default presumption is that any incoming attempts to connect to a service should be blocked unless the firewall has been explicitly told to leave it open.

This is a good default from a security perspective, because the vast majority of unexpected incoming connections are from hackers. Any machine connected directly to the Internet without a firewall will be subject to a continuous stream of traffic from hackers looking for machines that they might try to break into. Typical firewall configuration insulates machines from this stream of attacks, providing an extra line of defense, just in case you get behind on installing OS updates or some hacker uses a so-called *zero-day* attack that exploits a bug which hasn't yet been fixed.

One problem with this is that it makes bidirectional communication difficult if you're using HTTP. HTTP operations can be initiated only by the computer that opened the connection in the first place—there's no way to open a connection to a web server and then wait for it to send a message to you. HTTP is asymmetric, in that nothing happens until the client sends a request. (The lower-level protocol that HTTP runs on top of [TCP] is more flexible than this, by the way—that's one reason for using sockets. Either party in a TCP connection is free to send data at any time regardless of which end originally initiated the connection.)

To enable full bidirectional communication over HTTP, you need both ends to be running an HTTP server. When using duplex communication with WCF in conjunction with an HTTP-based binding, WCF runs what is effectively a miniature web server in the client process. Of course, this is only any use if the server is able to connect back to that client-side mini server.

If both the client and the server are behind the same firewall, that won't be a problem. But if the server is on the Internet, publicly accessible to anyone, it almost certainly won't be able to connect back to most clients. So the technique that is shown in Example 13-8 works only for private networks. To make a chat program that works over the Internet requires the use of either TCP and sockets, or some slightly hacky HTTP tricks that are beyond the scope of this book.

The upshot of this is that you'll want to avoid duplex contracts for Internet-facing applications.

Example 13-9. Duplex contract

```
[ServiceContract(
    CallbackContract=typeof(IChatClient),
    SessionMode=SessionMode.Required)]
public interface IChatService
{
```

```
[OperationContract]
bool Connect(string name);

[OperationContract]
void PostNote(string note);

[OperationContract]
void Disconnect();
}
```

By setting the `ServiceContract` attribute's `CallbackContract` property, we've declared that this is a duplex contract, and have identified the interface that defines the client side of the contract. Example 13-9 also makes a couple of other changes that turn out to be necessary for our service to work as intended: we've set the `SessionMode` property of the `ServiceContract` attribute, and we've added a couple of extra methods to enable clients to connect and disconnect. We've also removed the string name argument from `PostNote`—as you'll see, this will turn out to be redundant. All of these changes are related to *sessions*.

Session-based communication

The `ServiceContract` attribute's `SessionMode` property determines the nature of the relationship between the server and any particular client. By default, the relationship is presumed to be transient, not necessarily lasting any longer than a single operation. This reflects the fact that WCF is designed to support web services, and HTTP does not offer any idea of a connection between the client and the server that lasts longer than a single request.

> It's true that HTTP *allows* a single TCP connection to be reused across multiple requests, but this is just a performance optimization, and nothing is allowed to depend on it. Either the client or the server is free to close the connection at the end of a request, forcing a new one to be established for the next operation, without changing the semantics of the operations. (And even if the client and server both want to keep the connection alive between requests, a proxy in the middle is free to over-rule them.) Logically speaking, each HTTP request is completely disassociated from the ones that came before or after.

This connectionless behavior is very useful for scalability and robustness—it means you can load-balance across large numbers of web servers, and it doesn't greatly matter whether all of a particular client's requests are handled by the same machine. It's often possible to take a single machine in a web farm out of service without disrupting any of the clients. However, the absence of connections is sometimes unhelpful—some applications need some sort of session concept. For example, it would be annoying to have to type in your username and password every time you move from one page to another in a website—once you've logged in to a website, you want it to remember who you are. Likewise, if our chat application is going to be able to call clients back to notify them that notes have arrived, that implies that the application needs to know which clients are currently connected.

Although HTTP has no standard way to represent a session, various ad hoc systems have been developed to add such a feature. Websites typically use cookies. (Cookies are not part of the HTTP specification, but they are supported by all popular web browsers. Some users disable them, though, so they're not necessarily universally available.) The web service standards supported by WCF prefer a slightly different solution—it's similar to how cookies work, but it puts the relevant information in the messages being sent, rather than in the HTTP headers.§

Since our contract is now duplex, it requires the ability to maintain a connection between each client and the server. We tell WCF this by setting the `SessionMode` property to `SessionMode.Required`. Note that this doesn't actually switch on sessions; it merely says that anything that wants to communicate using this contract had better do so with sessions enabled. Remember, the contract is separate from implementations that conform to the contract. The effect of this setting is that WCF will produce an error if you try to use this contract without enabling sessions; we'll see how to enable sessions by modifying the client and server configuration files once we've finished modifying the code.

A session will be established the first time a client connects to a service, which presents our application with another problem. WCF won't send a message until it has something to send, so our chat client will first connect to the service when we send our first note. (Creating an instance of the `ChatServiceProxy` does *not* connect—nothing goes over the network until the first time you try to invoke an operation.) But we want clients to be able to receive notes straight away, without being required to post one first. So we need a way for clients to announce their presence to the service without sending a note. That's why Example 13-9 adds a `Connect` method. And we've also provided a `Disconnect` method for clients to announce that they are leaving so that the chat server doesn't attempt to send notes to clients that are no longer there. (Without this, the server would get an exception the next time it tried to send a message. Although it would notice that the clients had gone, an explicit disconnect is a bit neater—it also makes it possible to tell the difference between users who deliberately leave the conversation and users who get cut off due to problems.)

We now need to update the server to implement the modified contract, and to track the clients.

§ In general, the WS-* family of web service protocols avoids depending on HTTP. This may seem like a peculiar tendency for *web* service standards, but a lot of the organizations involved in creating these specifications wanted the message formats to be useful in message-queue-based systems as well as HTTP. So in general, they tend to avoid transport-specific mechanisms.

Calling the client from the server

Our service is going to need to maintain a list of connected clients so that it can notify every client when it receives each note. We can store the list as private data in our service class, but since that one list needs to be available across all sessions, we need to tell WCF that we only ever want it to create one instance of that class.

WCF offers several different modes for creating instances of your service class. It can create one per client session—that's useful when you want per-session state. But in our case, all notes get sent to everyone, so the only interesting state is global. Since our application state is global, we don't have much use for per-client instances here. WCF can also create a new instance of your service class for every single request—if you don't hold any state in the service class itself this is a reasonable thing to do. But in our case, we want one instance for the lifetime of the service. We can indicate this like so:

```
[ServiceBehavior(
    InstanceContextMode=InstanceContextMode.Single,
    ConcurrencyMode=ConcurrencyMode.Reentrant)]
public class ChatService : IChatService
{
```

We added a `ServiceBehavior` attribute to the code to specify this single-instance behavior. Notice that we also asked for a `ConcurrencyMode` of `Reentrant`. This tells WCF to have our service work on requests for only one session at a time—if requests from multiple clients come in simultaneously, WCF will service them one after another. This is convenient as it means that as long as any single client does only one thing at a time, we don't need to write any code to ensure the thread safety of our state handling.

An alternative to the single-instance context mode would have been to store our state in a `static` field. This would share the data across all clients, which is what we need. But then we'd be on our own for thread safety. The `ConcurrencyMode` property applies only to any particular instance of the service, so if you don't choose the single-instance mode, WCF will let different instances of your service execute simultaneously.

In practice, real applications are likely to need to do their own thread synchronization. Here we're relying on clients making only one call at a time, which might work in a small, controlled example but is a risky thing to do if you don't completely trust your client machines. (Even with only one session at a time, a single client session could invoke multiple operations simultaneously.) You may be wondering why we didn't use `ConcurrencyMode.Single`, which enforces a completely strict one-at-a-time model. Unfortunately, that turns out to prevent you from calling back into clients while you're in the middle of handling a call from a client—a blocking outbound call from a nonreentrant single-threaded context presents an opportunity for deadlocks, so WCF forbids it.

Next, we'll add a field to hold the state—a collection of currently connected clients:

```
private Dictionary<IChatClient, string> clientsAndNames =
    new Dictionary<IChatClient, string>();
```

This is a dictionary where the key type is the client callback interface we defined earlier. The value is the client's name. To see how this gets used, here's the Connect implementation:

```
public bool Connect(string name)
{
    if (clientsAndNames.ContainsValue(name))
    {
        // Name already in use, so refuse connection
        return false;
    }

    IChatClient clientCallback =
        OperationContext.Current.GetCallbackChannel<IChatClient>();

    // clientsAndNames is shared state, but we're not locking
    // here, because we're relying on ConcurrentMode.Reentrant
    // to give us messages one at a time.
    clientsAndNames.Add(clientCallback, name);
    Console.WriteLine(name + " connected");

    return true;
}
```

The first thing we do is check that the username is unique. Now that we're maintaining a list of connected clients, we're in a position to prevent multiple users from picking the same name. If a new user is trying to sign up with a duplicate name, we return false. (A return code here makes more sense than an exception because this isn't really an exceptional condition.)

If the name looks OK, we retrieve the client callback interface with the following expression:

```
OperationContext.Current.GetCallbackChannel<IChatClient>()
```

OperationContext is a WCF class whose Current property provides information about the operation that your code is handling right now. One of the services it provides is the ability to retrieve the callback interface when a duplex contract is in use. GetCallbackChannel returns a proxy object similar to the one the client uses to talk to the service, but this proxy goes in the other direction—it invokes operations on the client that called our Connect method. We just add this to the dictionary of connected clients, associating it with the client's chosen name, and then return true to indicate that we're happy that the user's name wasn't previously in use and that we have accepted the user's connection.

Next, let's look at the modified PostNote:

```
public void PostNote(string note)
{
    IChatClient clientCallback =
        OperationContext.Current.GetCallbackChannel<IChatClient>();
    string name = clientsAndNames[clientCallback];

    Console.WriteLine("{0}: {1}", name, note);

    // ToArray() makes copy of the collection. This avoids an
    // exception due to the collection being modified if we have
    // to disconnect a client part way through the loop.
    KeyValuePair<IChatClient, string>[] copiedNames =
        clientsAndNames.ToArray();
    foreach (KeyValuePair<IChatClient, string> client in copiedNames)
    {
        // Avoid sending the message back to the client that just sent
        // it - they already know what they just typed.
        if (client.Key != clientCallback)
        {
            Console.WriteLine("Sending note to {0}", client.Value);
            try
            {
                client.Key.NotePosted(name, note);
            }
            catch (Exception x)
            {
                Console.WriteLine("Error: {0}", x);
                DisconnectClient(client.Key);
            }
        }
    }
}
```

Again, we begin by retrieving the callback interface for the current client. Remember, our chat server will usually have multiple clients attached, and this lets us discover which particular one is sending a note. The next line looks up the callback interface in the dictionary to find out what name this user originally passed to Connect—this is why we were able to remove the argument we previously had on this method in which the caller passed her name. We remember her name from before—we have to remember it to guarantee uniqueness—and since we're remembering it, there's no need to make the client pass in the name every single time.

This code then iterates through all the connected clients in the clientsAndNames dictionary, to deliver the new note to each client. It calls the NotePosted on the proxy. Notice that we wrapped this in exception-handling code. If a client becomes inaccessible because of a network failure, a crash, a machine failure, or a programming error that caused it to exit without remembering to call Disconnect, the proxy's NotePosted method will throw an exception. Our code catches this and removes the client from the list, to avoid trying to send it any more notes.

This code is a little simplistic, for two reasons. First, we might want to be a little more lenient with errors—perhaps we should give the client a chance to recover before giving up on it entirely. One way to do this would be to have a second collection of connections to act as a kind of sin bin—you could give failed clients another chance after a certain amount of time. (Another strategy would be to require that the client attempt to reconnect in the event of a failure, in which case the server's error handling is just fine as it is.)

Second, calling each client in turn using a loop will perform poorly as the number of clients gets large, or if some clients are on slow connections. This code will be OK for small groups on a private network, but for a larger scale, an asynchronous approach would work better. WCF provides full support for asynchronous use of proxies, but the chapter on threading and asynchronous programming is coming later, so we can't show you that just yet.

The code to disconnect clients is in a separate method, because it's shared by the error-handling code and the Disconnect method that's part of the new contract. Here's the common code:

```
private void DisconnectClient(IChatClient clientCallback)
{
    string name = clientsAndNames[clientCallback];
    Console.WriteLine(name + " disconnected");
    clientsAndNames.Remove(clientCallback);
}
```

This just removes the client from the dictionary. This makes the Disconnect method very simple:

```
public void Disconnect()
{
    IChatClient clientCallback =
        OperationContext.Current.GetCallbackChannel<IChatClient>();
    DisconnectClient(clientCallback);
}
```

Once again, we get hold of the callback interface, and then call the same disconnection helper as the error-handling code.

We have one more modification to make on the server: the wsHttpBinding we're using doesn't support the duplex behavior we require, so we need to modify the ChatHost program's configuration.

Server configuration for duplex and sessions

As we mentioned earlier, WCF lets us change the communication mechanism we're using by configuring a different *binding*. We don't need to change any code to do this. We just need to modify our host project's *App.config* file, specifically the <endpoint> tag:

```
<endpoint address=""
          binding="wsHttpBinding"
          contract="ChatServerLibrary.IChatService">
</endpoint>
```

We change that `binding` attribute's value to `wsDualHttpBinding`. This binding is very similar to `wsHttpBinding`; it just adds support for callbacks. It also enables sessions automatically. (Sessions are available with `wsHttpBinding`, but they are off by default, so you'd need to add further configuration to switch them on if you wanted sessions without duplex communication.)

Our server is now ready to work in duplex mode, so next we need to update the client.

Duplex client

We've made several changes to the contract: we modified the one existing method, added two new methods, and turned it into a duplex contract. We also changed the binding. Any one of these changes would need the client to be updated, because each has an impact on the work done by the Add Service Reference operation. (All these things change the contract, the configuration, or both.) However, we don't need to completely redo the work of adding the service reference. If you right-click on an item in a client's Service References in the Solution Explorer, you'll see an Update Service Reference item. This modifies the generated source code and application configuration, saving you from having to build it all again from scratch. This refetches the metadata, so the service needs to be running when you do this, just as when adding the reference in the first place.

Once we've updated the reference, rebuilding the solution now produces two compiler errors. The call to `PostNote` fails, because we're passing in two arguments where the new contract requires only one. And we also see the following error on the line where we construct the `ChatServiceClient` proxy:

```
error CS1729: 'ChatClient.ChatService.ChatServiceClient' does not contain
a constructor that takes 0 arguments
```

Because the service now has a duplex contract, the generated proxy insists that the client implement its half of the contract—we need to provide an implementation of the callback interface and pass that to the proxy. Example 13-10 shows a straightforward implementation of the interface.

Example 13-10. Implementing the client-side callback interface

```
[CallbackBehavior(ConcurrencyMode=ConcurrencyMode.Reentrant)]
class ChatCallback : IChatServiceCallback
{
    public void NotePosted(string from, string note)
    {
        Console.WriteLine("{0}: {1}", from, note);
    }
}
```

 The callback interface seems to have changed names. We called it IChat Client on the server, but here it's IChatServiceCallback. This is the normal if slightly surprising behavior when using metadata exchange through Visual Studio's Add Service Reference feature. It's nothing to worry about. As far as WCF is concerned, a contract has only one name (IChatService in this case), even when it happens to be split into server-side and client-side pieces. WCF considers the name of the client-side interface to be irrelevant, and doesn't advertise it through metadata exchange. When you add or update a reference to a service with a duplex contract, Visual Studio just makes up the client-side interface name by appending Callback to the contract name.

Notice the CallbackBehavior attribute—it specifies a ConcurrencyMode just like on the server. Again, we've specified Reentrant—this means that this particular callback handler expects to be dealing with just one session at a time, but can cope with being called back by the server while it's waiting for the server to do something. We need this so that the server can send notifications to the client inside its PostNote implementation.

We need to provide WCF with an instance of this callback implementation, so we modify the code at the start of Main from Example 13-7 that creates the proxy:

```
ChatCallback callbackObject = new ChatCallback();
InstanceContext clientContext = new InstanceContext(callbackObject);
ChatServiceClient chatProxy = new ChatServiceClient(clientContext);
```

This wraps the callback object in an InstanceContext—this represents the session, and is essentially the client-side counterpart of the object returned by OperationContext.Current on the server. It provides various utility members for managing the session, but here the only thing we need it for is to pass our callback object to the proxy—the proxy won't take the callback directly and demands that we wrap it in an instance context.

We have a few more modifications to make. Remember that the client now needs to tell the server that it wants to connect, so we can do that directly after asking for the user's name:

```
Console.WriteLine("Please enter your name:");
bool ok = false;
while (!ok)
{
    string name = Console.ReadLine();
    ok = chatProxy.Connect(name);
    if (!ok)
    {
        Console.WriteLine("That name is taken. Please try another.");
    }
}
```

This checks the return code to see if the name we entered was already in use, and asks for a different name if it was. The end user can go through the relevant legal procedures to change her name, and then try again.

The line that calls `PostNote` no longer needs to pass our name each time, because the server now remembers our name based on our session:

```
chatProxy.PostNote(note);
```

And finally, we should add a line of code at the very end of `Main` to let the server know we're going away:

```
chatProxy.Disconnect();
```

We're now ready to test the application. We can run the client and service as before, but we want an extra client or two, to test out this multiuser chat service. Visual Studio doesn't provide a way to debug two instances of the same application, so we need to run the extra instances manually. We can do this by finding the folder where the compiled program lives. This will be in a subfolder of the project folder—the program will be in a *bin\debug* subfolder. Running a couple of instances of the client we can type in some different names, and we see notes appear in the service's console window as the users connect:

```
Service ready
Ian connected
Matthew connected
```

When we type a note in one of the clients, it appears in all of the client console windows, as well as the server.

Our application's user interface has a long way to go before it'll become the new live chat tool of choice, but we have now demonstrated a complete, if rather basic, WCF-based application. We have only scratched the surface of WCF, of course—it's a large enough technology to warrant a book in its own right. *Learning WCF*, a book we already mentioned a couple of times, is a good choice if you'd like to learn more about what WCF can do. Next, we're going to look at how to work directly with HTTP.

HTTP

The .NET Framework class library provides various classes for working directly with HTTP. Some of these are for client scenarios, and are useful when you need to fetch resources from a web server such as bitmaps, or if you need to use an HTTP-based service that WCF cannot easily work with. You can also provide server-side HTTP support. You would normally do that by writing an ASP.NET web application, which we'll look at in a later chapter. But there is a class that enables other program types to receive incoming HTTP requests, called `HttpListener`. (We won't be covering that, and we mention it mainly for completeness—it's more normal to use ASP.NET, to which we have devoted a whole chapter.)

WebClient

The most common starting point for client-side HTTP code is the `WebClient` class in the `System.Net` namespace. It offers a few ways of working with HTTP, starting from very simple but inflexible methods, through to relatively complex mechanisms that give you complete control over detailed aspects of HTTP. We'll start with the simplest ones.

 Although the examples in this section are HTTP-based, `WebClient` supports other protocols, including `https:`, `ftp:`, and `file:` URLs. It is extensible, so in principle you can adapt it to support any protocol that has a URL scheme.

Downloading resources

Example 13-11 illustrates one of the simplest ways of using the `WebClient` class. We construct an instance, and then use its `DownloadString` method to fetch data at a particular URL. (You can specify the URL as either a string or a `Uri` object.)

URLs, URIs, and the Uri Class

HTTP resources are identified by *Uniform Resource Locators* (URLs), strings which contain enough information for a computer to work out where to find the resource. The specification for URLs defines them as being a special kind of *Uniform Resource Identifier* (URI). A URI is a slightly more general idea—URIs give something a name, and that name may or may not have anything to say about where the resource can be found. All URLs are URIs, but only URIs that indicate a resource's location are URLs.

These two kinds of identifiers have a common syntax, so .NET provides just one class to deal with them: the `Uri` class, which is defined in the `System` namespace. It defines helper properties that give you access to the various parts of the URI. Consider this example:

```
Uri blog =
    new Uri("http://www.interact-sw.co.uk/iangblog/");
```

This represents the URL for one of the authors' blogs. Its `Scheme` property's value is `"http"`, its `Host` is `"www.interact-sw.co.uk (http://www.interact-sw.co.uk)"`, and there are properties for all the other syntactic elements found in URIs.

Methods and properties in the .NET Framework class library that require a URL will have a signature that accepts a `Uri` object. (Some APIs also offer overloads that accept a string.)

Incidentally, there's a peculiarly persistent and mistaken belief that the plural of URI is URI. (Apparently this is on the basis that some Latin words have plurals that end in *i*, but that conclusion requires an almost heroic misunderstanding of etymology.) Sir Tim Berners-Lee calls them URIs and he would know, since he invented them (and, not coincidentally, invented the World Wide Web too).

Example 13-11. Fetching content with WebClient

```
WebClient client = new WebClient();
string pageContent = client.DownloadString("http://oreilly.com/");

Console.WriteLine(pageContent);
```

Of course, `DownloadString` succeeds only if the URL you're fetching happens to contain textual content. The URL in Example 13-11 is an HTML web page, which is a text-based format, so it works just fine, but what if you're fetching a bitmap, or a ZIP? In that case, there's `DownloadData`, which works in the same way, except it returns an array of bytes instead of a string:

```
byte[] data =
    client.DownloadData("http://oreilly.com/images/oreilly/oreilly_large.gif");
```

There's a third easy method for fetching data, `DownloadFile`. This downloads the resource into a local file:

```
client.DownloadFile("http://oreilly.com/", @"c:\temp\oreilly.html");
```

These three methods will *block*—they don't return until they have finished fetching the data you asked for (or they have tried and failed, in which case they'll throw some kind of exception). This could take awhile. You might be on a slow network, or talking to a busy server, or just downloading a particularly large resource. If you're building a GUI, it's a bad idea to call blocking APIs.‖ Fortunately, `WebClient` offers asynchronous versions of all these methods. You use these by attaching an event handler to the relevant completion event, for example:

```
client.DownloadFileCompleted += OnDownloadComplete;
client.DownloadFileAsync(new Uri ("http://oreilly.com/"), @"c:\temp\");

...

static void OnDownloadComplete(object sender, AsyncCompletedEventArgs e)
{
    MessageBox.Show("Download complete");
}
```

The `DownloadXxxAsync` methods all return straight away. `WebClient` raises the relevant `DownloadXxxCompleted` event once the data has been fetched. (This means that you'll need to ensure that your application hangs around long enough for that to happen; if you were to use these asynchronous techniques in a console application, you'd need to take steps to make sure the program doesn't exit before the work completes.) Of course, `DownloadStringAsync` and `DownloadDataAsync` cannot provide the fetched data as a return value, unlike their blocking counterparts, so they provide it as the `Result` argument of their completion event argument.

‖ If it's a multithreaded application, it's usually OK to call a blocking API on a worker thread. It's a bad idea only if you're on the UI thread, but that's the thread that all the interesting UI stuff happens on, so it's an easy mistake to make.

If you're writing a Silverlight client, you'll find that `WebClient` offers *only* the asynchronous versions. And in general, that's true of all of Silverlight's networking support—since Silverlight is designed just for building user interfaces, it doesn't even offer you the blocking forms.

As well as providing completion event notifications, `WebClient` also offers progress notifications through its `DownloadProgressChanged` event. This is raised from time to time during asynchronous downloads, regardless of which of the three methods you used. It provides two properties, `BytesReceived` and `TotalBytesToReceive`, which tell you how far the download has gotten and how far it has to go.

If you use these asynchronous methods in a GUI built with either WPF or Windows Forms, you don't need to worry about threading issues. As you'll see in later chapters, that is not true for all asynchronous APIs, but these automatically take care of UI threading for you—as long as you start asynchronous operations from the UI thread, `WebClient` will raise completion and progress events on the UI thread.

Uploading resources

`WebClient` offers the `UploadString`, `UploadData`, and `UploadFile` methods. These correspond directly to the `DownloadString`, `DownloadData`, and `DownloadFile` methods, but instead of fetching data with an HTTP `GET`, they send data to the server, typically using an HTTP `POST`, although overloads are available that let you specify other verbs, such as `PUT`.

Stream-based uploads and downloads

Lots of APIs in the .NET Framework work with the `Stream` abstraction defined in the `System.IO` namespace. The XML classes can load data from a `Stream`, or write data into one, for example. The bitmap decoding and encoding classes in WPF can also work with streams. The first three lines of Example 13-12 obtain a stream for an Atom feed# from a `WebClient` and use it to initialize an `XDocument`. The code then uses LINQ to XML to extract the list of titles and links advertised by this particular feed.

Example 13-12. From HTTP to LINQ to XML via a Stream

```
WebClient client = new WebClient();
Stream feedStm = client.OpenRead("http://feeds.feedburner.com/oreilly/news");
XDocument feedXml = XDocument.Load(feedStm);

string ns = "http://www.w3.org/2005/Atom";
var entries = from entryElement in feedXml.Descendants(XName.Get("entry", ns))
```

#Atom is a common format for representing sets of items, such as blog entries or news articles. It's similar to RSS, but tries to avoid some of RSS's inconsistencies and limitations.

```
            select new
            {
                Title = entryElement.Element(XName.Get("title", ns)).Value,
                Link = entryElement.Element(XName.Get("link", ns)).
                            Attribute("href").Value
            };
foreach (var entry in entries)
{
    Console.WriteLine("{0}: {1}", entry.Title, entry.Link);
}
```

For sending data there's an `OpenWrite` method. With HTTP or HTTPS, this defaults to `POST`, but as with the `Upload` methods, you can call an overload that takes the verb as well as the URL.

You can use streams asynchronously. Following the same pattern as the other methods we've looked at so far, you'll find `OpenReadAsync` and `OpenWriteAsync` methods, with corresponding completion events. But streams add an extra dimension: the `Stream` abstract base class also offers both synchronous and asynchronous operation. For example, if you're reading data, you can call either `Read` or `BeginRead`. You are free to use the `Stream` in either mode, regardless of whether you obtained it from the `WebClient` synchronously or asynchronously. But bear in mind that if you are trying to avoid blocking in order to keep your user interface responsive, you'll most likely want to get hold of the stream asynchronously (e.g., use `OpenReadAsync`) *and* use the stream asynchronously. When you open a stream asynchronously, the completion notification tells you that the `WebClient` is ready to *start* reading (or writing) data, but that's no guarantee that you'll be able to finish reading data immediately. For example, if you use `OpenReadAsync` to fetch a 1 GB file by HTTP, `WebClient` won't wait until it has downloaded the whole 1 GB before giving you a stream. You'll get an `OpenReadCompleted` event when it has begun to fetch data so that you can start processing it straight away, but if you try to read data from the stream faster than your network connection can download it, you'll be made to wait. So if you want nonblocking behavior for the whole download, you'll need to use the `Stream` asynchronously too.

 While the asynchronous methods offered by `WebClient` will call you back on the correct thread in a GUI application, the asynchronous stream methods will not, and you'll have to deal with threading issues yourself.

The `WebClient` class's most powerful mechanism is accessed through its `GetWebRequest` and `GetWebResponse` methods. But these turn out to be wrappers around another set of classes altogether—`WebClient` just provides these wrappers as convenient helpers. So we'll move on to the classes that do the real work for these methods.

WebRequest and WebResponse

WebRequest and WebResponse are abstract base classes for a family of classes that provide the most detailed level of control over web requests. The concrete HttpWebRequest and HttpWebResponse classes add details specific to HTTP, and .NET also offers specialized FtpWebRequest/Response and FileWebRequest/Response classes. This section will mainly focus on the HTTP classes.

The main limitation with the WebClient-based mechanisms we've explored so far is that they focus on the content of the request or the response. They don't provide any way to work with standard HTTP features such as the content type header, the UserAgent string, cache settings, or proxy configuration. But if you use HttpWebRequest and HttpWebResponse, all the detailed aspects of HTTP are available to you.

The cost of this power is additional verbosity. The main difference is that you end up with one object to represent the request and one to represent the response, in addition to streams representing the data being sent or received. Moreover, the only way to access the data with these classes is through streams. To do the same job as Example 13-11—fetching the data from a particular URL into a string—requires the rather more complex code shown in Example 13-13.

Example 13-13. Fetching a string with HttpWebRequest and HttpWebResponse

```
HttpWebRequest req = (HttpWebRequest) WebRequest.Create("http://oreilly.com/");
using (HttpWebResponse resp = (HttpWebResponse) req.GetResponse())
using (Stream respStream = resp.GetResponseStream())
using (StreamReader reader = new StreamReader(respStream))
{
    string pageContent = reader.ReadToEnd();
    Console.WriteLine(pageContent);
}
```

The two casts on the first two lines of Example 13-13 are a little messy, but are, unfortunately, usually necessary. The WebRequest family of classes is extensible to multiple protocols, so most of the methods are declared as returning the abstract base types, rather than the concrete types—the exact type returned depends on the kind of URL you use. So if you need access to a protocol-specific feature, you end up with a cast. In fact, Example 13-13 isn't using anything protocol-specific, so we could have avoided the casts by declaring req and resp as WebRequest and WebResponse, respectively. However, the usual reason for using these classes is that you do in fact want access to HTTP-specific information. For example, you might want to simulate a particular web browser by setting the user agent string, as shown in Example 13-14.

Example 13-14. Changing the user agent header with HttpWebRequest

```
HttpWebRequest req = (HttpWebRequest) WebRequest.Create("http://oreilly.com/");
req.UserAgent = "Mozilla/5.0 (iPod; U; CPU iPhone OS 2_2_1 like Mac OS X; en-us)
AppleWebKit/525.18.1 (KHTML, like Gecko) Mobile/5H11a";

... as before
```

This code has been split across multiple lines, as the user agent string is too wide to fit. This would let you discover what response a website would send if the request came from an Apple iPhone. (Many websites adapt their content for different devices.)

As you'd expect, asynchronous operation is available so that you can avoid blocking the current thread while waiting for network operations to complete. But it looks slightly different from the `WebClient` mechanisms we've seen so far, because of the way in which the methods you call can change when the request gets sent. No network communication happens at the point where you create the request, so there is no asynchronous method for that. Remember, the request object represents all the settings you'd like to use for your HTTP request, so it won't actually attempt to send anything until you've finished setting the request's properties and tell it you're ready to proceed.

There are two ways in which you can cause an `HttpWebRequest` to send the request. Asking for the response object will cause this, but so will asking for a request stream— the request's `GetStream` method returns a write-only stream that can be used to supply the body of the request for `POST` or similar verbs (much like `WebClient.OpenWrite`). This stream will start sending data over the network as soon as your code writes data into the stream—it doesn't wait until you close the stream to send the data all in one go. (For all it knows, you might be planning to send gigabytes of data.) This means that by the time it returns the stream, it needs to be ready to start sending data, which means that the initial phases of the HTTP request must be complete—for example, if the request is going to fail for some reason (e.g., the server is down, or the client machine has lost its network connection), there's no point in attempting to provide the data for the request. So you'll be notified of failures of this kind when you ask for the stream.

The upshot of all this is that `GetStream` is a blocking method—it won't return until the server has been contacted and the request is underway. So there's an asynchronous version of this. But `WebRequest` doesn't support the event-based pattern that `WebClient` uses. Instead, it uses the more complex but slightly more flexible method-based Asynchronous Programming Model, in which you call `BeginGetRequestStream`, passing in a delegate to a method that the request will call back once it's ready to proceed, at which point you call `EndGetRequestStream`. This Begin/End pattern is very common in .NET and will be discussed in Chapter 16.

The second way in which the sending of the request can be triggered is to ask for the response object—if you haven't already asked for the request stream (e.g., because you're doing a `GET`, so there is no request body) the request will be sent at this point. So `GetResponse` also has an asynchronous option. Again, this uses the method-based asynchronous pattern. Example 13-15 shows a version of Example 13-13 modified to get the response object asynchronously.

Example 13-15. Obtaining a response asynchronously

```
HttpWebRequest req = (HttpWebRequest) WebRequest.Create("http://oreilly.com/");
req.BeginGetResponse(delegate(IAsyncResult asyncResult)
{
```

```
    using (HttpWebResponse resp = (HttpWebResponse)
                                  req.EndGetResponse(asyncResult))
    using (Stream respStream = resp.GetResponseStream())
    using (StreamReader reader = new StreamReader(respStream))
    {
        string pageContent = reader.ReadToEnd();
        Console.WriteLine(pageContent);
    }
}, null);
```

This example uses an anonymous method as the completion callback, which allows the code to retain a similar structure to the original, synchronous version. But you need to be mindful that the code that handles the response in Example 13-15 is now a separate method, and could run some considerable length of time after the call to `BeginGetResponse` returns, and probably on a different thread. So as with the event-based pattern, you'll need to ensure that your application runs for long enough for the operation to complete—having some outstanding asynchronous operations in progress will not keep your process alive if all of the nonbackground threads exit.

 This asynchronous pattern does *not* take care of UI threading issues (unlike the event-based pattern seen previously). The completion callback will usually occur on some random thread, and attempting to update the user interface from that code will fail. We'll see how to handle this in Chapter 16.

Example 13-14 shows just one of the HTTP protocol features you can customize—the `UserAgent` string. Many similar settings are available, many of which are quite obscure, so we won't go through all of them here. That's what the MSDN reference is for. But we will cover the most common cases.

Authentication

HTTP defines various ways for a client to authenticate itself to the server. Note that most public-facing websites don't actually use any of these—a website that presents a login UI where you type a username and password directly into fields in the web page itself isn't using HTTP authentication at all, and is usually relying on cookies instead (more on this later). HTTP authentication gets involved in two main scenarios. The most visible scenario is when the browser opens a small window asking for credentials before it navigates to the web page—this is less common than logging in via a form on a web page, but a few websites work this way. Slightly more subtly, HTTP authentication is used for integrated security scenarios—for example, when a client machine belongs to a Windows domain, and the user's identity is automatically available to an intranet web server on the same domain. In this case, you don't need to log in explicitly to an intranet site, and yet it knows exactly who you are—this is thanks to implicit use of HTTP authentication.

By default, HttpWebRequest will not attempt to authenticate the client to the server, even in integrated authentication scenarios. (So it has a different default policy than Internet Explorer—IE will automatically authenticate you to servers on your local network with integrated authentication, but HttpWebRequest will not.) If you're writing client code and you want it to identify the user to the server, you must set the request's Credentials property.

For integrated authentication, there's a special credentials object to represent the user's identity, provided by the CredentialCache class. Example 13-16 shows how to use this to enable integrated authentication. (Obviously, this will only do anything if the server is prepared to use it—so this code merely tells HttpWebRequest that we're happy to use integrated authentication if the server asks for it. If the server turns out not to require authentication at all, you won't see an error.)

Example 13-16. Enabling the use of integrated authentication

```
HttpWebRequest request =
    (HttpWebRequest) WebRequest.Create("http://intraweb/");
request.Credentials = CredentialCache.DefaultCredentials;

...
```

HTTP authentication isn't always integrated with Windows security. It also supports username- and password-based authentication. The HTTP specification supports two ways of using this. *Basic authentication* just sends your username and password as part of the request, so unless you're using HTTPS, that's not very secure. The alternative, *digest authentication*, is better, but seems to be rarely used. In practice, basic authentication over HTTPS seems to be the popular choice. For either kind of authentication, you specify the username and password in the way shown in Example 13-17.

Example 13-17. Providing credentials for basic or digest authentication

```
HttpWebRequest request =
    (HttpWebRequest) WebRequest.Create("https://intraweb/");
request.Credentials = new NetworkCredential("user1", "p@ssw0rd");

...
```

This approach doesn't let you specify whether to use basic or digest authentication because the server gets to choose. Since you therefore don't know whether the password will be sent in the clear, you should normally provide credentials this way only when using HTTPS. You can force the use of digest authentication by wrapping the Network Credential in a CredentialCache object, which lets you specify the authentication schemes you want to support. Even so, you might want to be wary of using digest authentication without HTTPS—although digest authentication can be secure, some servers implement it in an unsecure way.

Working with proxies

By default, web requests will look at the Internet Explorer settings to determine whether a web proxy should be used. But you might not want this default behavior, so there are a couple of ways you can change it.

 Prior to .NET 2.0, IE proxy settings weren't honored, so you may occasionally come across code that goes to some lengths to work out whether it needs to use a proxy. Usually such code is either old or written by someone who didn't know that .NET 2.0 fixed this issue.

You can add entries to your *App.config* file to modify the default proxy behavior. Example 13-18 stops web requests using the configured default proxy by default.

Example 13-18. Configuring default proxy behavior

```
<configuration>
  <system.net>
    <defaultProxy enabled="false" />
  </system.net>
</configuration>
```

The default behavior, in the absence of any configuration, specifies that the use of the default proxy is enabled, but the application will not use the user's credentials to identify the user to the proxy server. (Authenticating the user to a proxy happens independently of authenticating the user to the web server.) Some companies require users to authenticate with the proxy in order to access the Internet, in which case you would need to change the configuration, setting the `<defaultProxy>` element's `useDefaultCredentials` attribute to `true`.

You can also modify the behavior in code. The `HttpWebRequest` class has a `Proxy` property, and you can set this to `null` to disable the use of a proxy. Or you can set it to a `WebProxy` object specifying a specific proxy and settings, as Example 13-19 shows.

Example 13-19. Setting an explicit proxy

```
HttpWebRequest request =
    (HttpWebRequest) WebRequest.Create("https://intraweb/");
request.Proxy = new WebProxy("http://corpwebproxy/");
```

Controlling cache behavior

Windows maintains a per-user cache of web resources, to avoid having to download frequently used bitmaps, CSS, JavaScript, HTML pages, and other content again and again. Internet Explorer uses this cache, but it's also accessible to .NET code. By default, your programs won't use the cache, but you can enable caching by setting the request's `CachePolicy`, as Example 13-20 shows.

Example 13-20. Setting cache policy

```
HttpRequestCachePolicy cachePolicy = new HttpRequestCachePolicy(
    HttpRequestCacheLevel.CacheIfAvailable);
HttpWebRequest request =
    (HttpWebRequest) WebRequest.Create("https://intraweb/");
request.CachePolicy = cachePolicy;
```

The default policy is BypassCache, which means that not only will requests not look in the cache, but any resources you fetch will not be added to the cache. Example 13-20, on the other hand, will use a cached copy of the resource if one is available, and if not, it will add the resource it downloads to the cache (unless headers in the HTTP response indicate that it's not a cacheable resource).

The HttpRequestCacheLevel enumeration supports various other caching options. If you want to force the resource to be fetched anew, but would like the result to be added to the cache, you can specify Reload. You can also force a check for freshness—HTTP allows clients to tell the server that they have a cached version and that they want to download the resource only if a newer version is available, and you can enable this behavior with Revalidate. (Some more obscure options are also available, for developers who are familiar with the full complexities of HTTP caching and want complete control.)

Using cookies

As far as the HTTP specification is concerned, each request is entirely unconnected with any previous requests from the same client. But it's often useful for a website to be able to recognize a series of requests as having come from the same client, and so a common mechanism to support this, called cookies, is widely used.[*] Cookies underpin features such as shopping baskets, where a web application needs to maintain per-user state—I expect to see only the things that I've put in my basket, and not the items that any other users who are logged in right now have put in theirs. Cookies are also commonly used for managing logins—once the user has typed in his username and password in an HTML form, a cookie is often used, in effect, to authenticate the user from then on.

If you're using a web browser, cookies just work without needing any intervention (unless you've disabled them, of course). But if you're writing code, you need to take specific steps to use them—by default, .NET will not use cookies at all, and does not have access to the cookie store for Internet Explorer.[†] Nor does it implement a cookie store of its own.

---

[*] Cookies are so widely supported that although they're not technically part of the HTTP specification, they might as well be.

[†] Silverlight applications are an exception. They rely on the web browser to make HTTP requests, and so your requests will send whatever cookies the containing browser would normally send.

Often, ignoring cookies doesn't cause any problems. But you may find that you sometimes need to write code that accesses a site that depends on cookies to work, in which case you'll need to write code on the client side to make that happen.

The basic idea behind cookies is that when a client receives a response from a server, that response may include information that the server would like the client to remember and to pass back the next time that client makes a request. The client isn't expected to do anything other than pass the information back verbatim—there's no useful information that the client can extract from the cookie. (Or at least there shouldn't be, although there are some infamous cases where people got this wrong. For example, one online store made the mistake of putting prices of shopping basket entries into a cookie, enabling devious customers to grant themselves discounts by manually editing their cookies.) The client is just expected to hold onto the cookies it receives. (See Example 13-21.)

Example 13-21. Getting the cookies from a response

```
CookieContainer container = new CookieContainer();

Uri address = new Uri("http://amazon.com/");
HttpWebRequest req = (HttpWebRequest) WebRequest.Create(address);
HttpWebResponse resp = (HttpWebResponse) req.GetResponse();

CookieCollection cookies = resp.Cookies;
container.Add(address, cookies);
```

We're using the `CookieContainer` class provided by .NET to remember which cookies we've seen from the various servers we've been talking to, and which addresses they are associated with. When we come to make our next request, we can then supply this container:

```
Uri address = new Uri("http://oreilly.com/");
HttpWebRequest newReq = (HttpWebRequest) WebRequest.Create(address);
newReq.CookieContainer = container;
```

Anytime we get a response, the server is allowed to return new cookies, or to modify the value of existing cookies, so you would need to make sure you updated your cookie container anytime you get a response, using the code in Example 13-21.

That's it for HTTP. Finally, we'll take a look at sockets.

Sockets

Sockets are the most powerful networking mechanism available in .NET—HTTP is layered on top of sockets, and in most cases WCF is too. Sockets provide more or less direct access to the underlying TCP/IP network services—they effectively let you speak the native language of the network. This can offer some flexibility and performance benefits over HTTP-based communications, but the downside is that you need to do more work. Also, in corporate environments, communication with the outside world with ad hoc use of sockets is often blocked, as firewalls may be configured to let through only the traffic they understand and expect. But in cases where those restrictions do not apply, and if the flexibility or (relatively small) performance benefits are worth the effort, sockets are a useful tool.

The basic idea of a socket has been around for decades, and appears in many operating systems. The central concept is to present network communication through the same abstractions as file I/O. We already saw something like that with WebClient—it can provide Stream support. However, those streams are concerned with the body of an HTTP request or response. With sockets, the streams are at a lower level, encompassing all the data. (If you used a socket-based stream to connect to a web server, you'd see all of the details of the HTTP protocol in the stream, not just the body.)

Besides the file-like abstraction, socket APIs also have a standard set of operations for establishing connections, and for controlling aspects of those connections' behavior.

To understand sockets, you need some familiarity with the network protocols they depend on, so as well as introducing the API features the next section incorporates a very quick overview of the TCP/IP family of protocols. If you already know TCP/IP, please feel free to skim through the next section and just look at the examples that illustrate usage.

 Sockets can be used with some other protocols besides those in the TCP/IP family. For example, you can use sockets for IrDA (Infrared) or Bluetooth communications to communicate with local devices. There are other network protocols too, but the TCP/IP family is the most widely used.

IP, IPv6, and TCP

The Internet uses a family of protocols typically known collectively as TCP/IP. The lowest level is IP, which is short for *Internet Protocol*. This is the means by which all network traffic flows across the Internet—when you buy an Internet connection, you're buying the ability to deliver information from your computer to the Internet, and vice versa, via IP.

IP's main job is the ability to get *packets* (as individual messages are called in networking) of data between different computer networks (hence *inter*net). For example, data sent by a web server in a data center out of its network port somehow needs to make its way to your home WiFi network. These networks are connected together by *routers*, whose job is to work out where to send IP packets next; there are well-defined rules for how they should do this, ensuring that data ends up at the machine it's meant for. This process depends on the *IP address*—a number that identifies a machine in a way that makes it possible for routers to work out how to route messages to that machine.

If you're using sockets, you will need to work with IP addresses because they're how you identify the machine you'd like to communicate with. You can typically just treat them as opaque identifiers, wrapped by the `IPAddress` class in the `System.Net` namespace. But there's one aspect of IP addressing that it's worth being aware of: the distinction between IPv4 and IPv6 addresses. See the sidebar below.

IPv4 and IPv6

There are two kinds of IP addresses because there are two versions of IP in use today. Version 4 is the most widely used. (Previous version numbers were used only in the Internet's early experimental days, and you never see them on the Internet today.) IPv4 has a problem: its addresses are 32-bit numbers, meaning that there are only enough unique addresses for around 4 billion computers. That may sound like a lot, but it's not enough, given how many computers and devices have Internet access and the rate at which new ones are coming online. We are already using ungainly hacks to enable multiple machines to share addresses, and limited IP address space is a big problem.

In IPv6, an address is a 128-bit number, which provides sufficient address space for the foreseeable future, but there's a problem. Old computers and routers don't support IPv6. Computers can often be fixed with software upgrades—Windows XP can have IPv6 support installed (and it's built into Windows Vista and later versions). But OS support is not the whole story—applications may also need to be updated.

There's a bigger problem for routers—a lot of them have the structure of IPv4 baked into their hardware, so they need to be replaced to get IPv6 support. This makes IPv6 seem like an unattractive choice—would you want your web server to have an address that will be inaccessible to anyone who hasn't upgraded her network and Internet connection to IPv6?

In fact, it's not quite that bad, because there's a special class of IPv6 addresses that are effectively equivalent to IPv4 addresses, so it's possible to provide an IPv6-based server that's accessible to IPv4 clients. But that means any public service you're likely to want to use will be accessible from IPv4, so there's not a whole lot of incentive for end users or corporate network administrators to throw out perfectly good IPv4 routers to upgrade to IPv6, and it means that phone companies don't have many customers demanding IPv6-capable DSL routers. Consequently, the transition to IPv6 is happening incredibly slowly. Nonetheless, the IPv4 address space problem isn't going to go away, so you will need to write your software in a way that's able to work with both IPv4 and IPv6 addresses if you want it to continue to work as IPv6 adoption gradually picks up.

.NET tries to make this relatively easy in practice. Its `IPAddress` class can hold either kind of address. For most applications, client-side code doesn't even need to be aware of which kind is in use. But occasionally, you'll need to work with an IP address in its numeric form, at which point the distinction matters.

While the Internet protocol uses numbers to identify machines, users are more familiar with names such as oreilly.com (*http://oreilly.com*) and www.microsoft.com (*http://www.microsoft.com*). The Internet has a system called the Domain Name Service

(DNS)—your Internet service provider gives you access to this as part of your connection—whose job is to convert these textual names into the IP addresses required to communicate with the machines (or *hosts*, as the entities associated with IP addresses are conventionally called). Example 13-22 uses the `Dns` class in the `System.Net` namespace to look up the IP addresses for a particular hostname. DNS can associate multiple addresses with a name; for example, a DNS name may have both an IPv4 and an IPv6 address. This code loops through all the addresses, printing their type and value. (If you call `ToString()` on an `IPAddress`, which is what `Console.WriteLine` will do in Example 13-22, it'll return the standard string representation for the numeric address.)

Example 13-22. Getting the IP addresses for a hostname

```
IPHostEntry hostDnsEntry = Dns.GetHostEntry("localhost");
foreach(IPAddress address in hostDnsEntry.AddressList)
{
    Console.WriteLine("Type: {0}, Address: {1}", address.AddressFamily,
                                                 address);
}
```

This example looks up the special hostname `localhost`, which always refers to the local machine on which the program is running. Both IPv4 and IPv6 define special addresses that are reserved to refer to the local machine, so if you run Example 13-22, you'll see that it prints out two addresses, one for IPv6 and one for IPv4:

```
Type: InterNetworkV6, Address: ::1
Type: InterNetwork, Address: 127.0.0.1
```

 For years, IPv4 was the only IP version in use, so it's often not qualified with a version number, which is why this IPv4 address's `AddressFam` `ily` property is just displayed as `InterNetwork`, and not `InterNetworkV4`.

Many DNS entries don't have an IPv6 address, and if you modify Example 13-22 to look up such an address (e.g., at the time of this writing, w3.org has only an IPv4 address) you'll see just one address back from `GetHostEntry`:

```
Type: InterNetwork, Address: 128.30.52.45
```

Armed with an IP address for the machine we want to talk to, we now have enough information for the Internet to deliver IP packets to the target machine. But there are a couple of issues to resolve. First, there's the question of how the receiving machine will know what to do with the packet when it arrives. Second, there's the problem that the Internet is fundamentally unreliable. TCP (the *Transmission Control Protocol*) offers a solution to both of these problems.

The Internet does not guarantee to deliver all IP packets. It can't. Suppose you are using a machine connected to the Internet with a 100 Mbps connection and you try to send data at full speed to a machine that is connected with a 56 Kb modem. (Remember those? In some parts of the world, they're still used. If you get a chance, try using a modern website via a 56 Kb dial-up connection, and then marvel at the fact that 56 kbps modems were once considered really fast.) As we send data to this bandwidth-impoverished machine, the routers between us and them will initially try to manage the speed difference—a router connecting a fast network to a slower network will store incoming packets from the fast network in its memory, and they queue up while it plays them out in slow motion to the target network. But eventually it'll run out of memory, at which point it'll just start discarding packets.

At busy times of the day, packets may get discarded even if both ends of the connection can operate at the same speed—perhaps the route the traffic needs to take through the Internet between the two networks includes busy links that just don't have the bandwidth to support all the traffic that all of the ISP's customers are trying to send. So network congestion can also cause packet loss, even in the absence of speed mismatches.

The upshot of this is that IP is not a reliable protocol—you get what's sometimes called a *best effort* service. In attempting to deliver your data, the Internet will give it its best shot, but there are no guarantees. (You may have a service level agreement with your ISP that makes statistical guarantees about the proportion of data it will successfully deliver to and from the boundaries of the ISP's network infrastructure, but there are no guarantees for any single packet, nor can your ISP guarantee what will happen to your data once it has been passed off to someone else's network.)

To add to the fun, IP doesn't even guarantee to deliver messages in the same order you sent them. ISPs might have multiple routes through their network to ensure reliability in the face of individual link failures, or just to ensure enough bandwidth to cope with high loads. So if you send a series of IP packets to the same computer, not all of those packets will necessarily take the same route—they might be split across two or more routes. Some of those routes may prove to be quicker, meaning that the packets can arrive at their destination in a different order than you sent them.

Writing networked applications can be challenging if you have no idea whether any particular message will be received, nor any way of knowing in what order the ones that do arrive will turn up. So to make life easier, we have the Transmission Control Protocol—the TCP in TCP/IP. This is a protocol that sits on top of IP and adds some useful features. It provides support for connections—rather than each packet being handled in isolation, each transmission is part of the sequence of communication occurring over the connection. TCP puts sequence numbers into each IP packet so that it can detect when packets arrived out of order. And finally, the receiving machine acknowledges receipt of each message. Clients use this to work out how fast the messages are getting through, which enables them to send data at a rate that matches the network's ability to deliver, avoiding problems with mismatched network speeds and network congestion. And clients also use this to work out when data didn't get through and needs to be resent.

These features enable TCP to offer a data transmission service that sends data in order, at a rate that will not try to exceed the capacity of the network routes available and in a fashion that is reliable in the face of occasional packet loss. A socket is usually just an API on top of a TCP connection that presents a stream-style API—your program can write data into a socket stream, and the TCP/IP networking code running on the computers at both ends uses TCP to ensure that the program at the receiving end has another socket stream from which it can read the exact same sequence of bytes you wrote into the stream. The programs don't need to know about out-of-order delivery or packet loss. As long as the networks are not hopelessly lossy, it looks like there is perfectly reliable in-order transmission. TCP sockets are symmetrical, in that both ends can send and receive data. And the directions are independent—communication can be full duplex, so there's no need for the two ends to take it in turns.

TCP also solves the problem of how the receiving computer knows what it's supposed to do with incoming data. A single computer may offer many network services—a small company might run the intranet web server, file server, and email server on the same computer, for example. So TCP adds the concept of *port numbers*. A service on a target machine will be associated with a particular number. There's a central administrative body called IANA—the Internet Assigned Numbers Authority—which (among other things) assigns and publishes port numbers for common services. For example, IANA has designated port 80 as the TCP port on which HTTP servers usually accept incoming requests. When a web browser (or the WebClient class we saw earlier) fetches a resource via HTTP, it does so by opening a TCP connection to port 80.

 A single client computer might open several simultaneous connections to the same service—web browsers often do this in order to download the various pictures, CSS, and JavaScript files concurrently, so as to be able to display the web page sooner. To distinguish between them, each connection has a client-side port number as well as a server-side port. But while you need to know the server port in order to connect, the client port number is usually picked for you dynamically by the OS.

Let's look at a real example. We're going to connect to a service using a very old and very simple protocol called *Daytime Protocol*. This hasn't changed since its specification was published in 1983—you can find its definition in a document called RFC867 at *http://www.faqs.org/rfcs/rfc867.html*. It's remarkably simple: clients open a TCP connection to port 13 on a server that offers the daytime service, and the server will send back the time of day as text and then close the connection. The specification is pretty vague about the format—it says this:

```
There is no specific syntax for the daytime.  It is recommended that
    it be limited to the ASCII printing characters, space, carriage
    return, and line feed.  The daytime should be just one line.
```

It then goes on to give examples of a couple of popular formats, but servers are free to do pretty much anything they like.

This is a service that cannot be accessed with the `WebClient` or any of the `WebRequest` family of classes—those types expect data to be layered inside HTTP (or sometimes another higher-level protocol such as FTP), but Daytime Protocol just makes very basic, direct use of plain TCP. So we need to use sockets if we want to access such a service.

The U.S. government's National Institute of Standards and Technology (NIST) lists a few servers that offer this daytime service. Once such machine, located in Redmond, Washington, has the DNS name of `time-nw.nist.gov`. We'll use that. To start with, we need to look up its IP address, which we'll do using a similar technique to Example 13-22:

```
IPHostEntry hostDnsEntry = Dns.GetHostEntry("time-nw.nist.gov");
IPAddress serverIp = hostDnsEntry.AddressList[0];
```

Next, we need to open a TCP connection to port 13 (the daytime service port) on that machine. To do this, we'll need a `Socket` object.

Connecting to Services with the Socket Class

The `System.Net.Sockets` namespace defines the `Socket` class, which makes the socket features of the underlying operating system available from .NET. We use a `Socket` when we want to open a TCP connection to a remote service:

```
Socket daytimeSocket = new Socket(
    serverIp.AddressFamily,
    SocketType.Stream,
    ProtocolType.Tcp);
```

 `Socket` implements `IDisposable`, so you will need to call `Dispose` at some point. And while we would normally write a `using` statement to handle that, that's somewhat unusual with sockets, because they often have a longer lifetime than any particular method. There isn't one right way to handle this, because the right moment to dispose a socket will depend on the way in which your application uses the socket. The next few examples therefore don't show disposal, because we are illustrating aspects of the API that will be the same no matter how you are using sockets. But be aware that you will always need to find a suitable place to call `Dispose`.

The `Socket` constructor needs three pieces of information. It needs to know the address family we will use to identify the server (e.g., IPv4 or IPv6). It also needs to know what style of communication we're expecting—we're asking for stream-like communication. (Some protocols support some other styles of communication, but with TCP you always specify `Stream` here.) Finally, we specify the specific protocol we'd like to use—TCP in this case.

 If this constructor seems more complex than necessary, it's because sockets aren't just for TCP/IP. The underlying Windows socket API (WinSock) was introduced before TCP/IP had become the dominant protocol, so it supports numerous protocols. Windows even supports custom providers that add socket support for new protocols.

Note that we don't specify where we're connecting to yet. That information doesn't go in the constructor because not all sockets work the same way—some protocols support transmission patterns other than simple point-to-point connections. So the Socket class requires that we first say what sort of socket we want before going on to say what we're trying to communicate with. We supply that information when we connect to the service:

```
daytimeSocket.Connect(serverIp, 13);
```

Remember, port 13 is the port number allocated by IANA for the daytime service. We're going to retrieve the time of day as text from this service, so we declare a variable to hold the result:

```
string data;
```

Sockets represent all data as bytes. (Or more precisely, *octets*, which are 8-bit bytes. Back in the old days, some computers used other byte sizes, and you occasionally come across evidence of this—for example, some parts of the Internet email system guarantee to transfer 8-bit bytes, and may truncate your data to seven bits per byte.) The Daytime Protocol specification says that the service will return text using the ASCII encoding, so we need something that can convert a stream of bytes containing ASCII into a .NET string. Example 13-23 does this.

Example 13-23. Retrieving ASCII data from a TCP socket

```
using (Stream timeServiceStream = new NetworkStream(daytimeSocket, true))
using (StreamReader timeServiceReader = new StreamReader(timeServiceStream,
                                                Encoding.ASCII))
{
    data = timeServiceReader.ReadToEnd();
}
```

A few things are going on here. First, we constructed a NetworkStream—this class derives from Stream, and it's how .NET lets us treat a socket-based connection in the same way as any other Stream. In general, the use of streams is optional because the Socket class provides methods that let you read and write data directly. But in this example, getting an actual Stream object is useful because we can plug it into a StreamReader. Stream Reader takes a stream that contains text and can convert the bytes in that stream into string objects. Example 13-23 uses the StreamReader class's ReadToEnd method—this asks to read all of the data in the stream to the very end and to return it as a single string.

Socket Read Granularity

Beware of a classic rookie mistake with TCP sockets. Developers often observe that if they write, say, 20 bytes into a socket, and then on the receiving end they perform a read operation that asks for more bytes (e.g., 1,000), that read usually returns 20 bytes rather than waiting for the requested number of bytes to arrive. Many people mistakenly assume this means TCP guarantees that data will arrive in chunks of the same size in which it was sent. In practice, if a client sends a 20-byte chunk of data, the receiving end may well return six bytes of that chunk from the first read, then another 13 in the next, and then the last byte in the next read. Or even better, it might decide to aggregate that final byte onto the front of the next lump of data sent by the client.

TCP sockets only attempt to deliver all the bytes in the order in which they were originally sent. Your code cannot make any assumptions about the granularity in which the socket will return incoming data. TCP has no idea of a message or a frame—it offers just a linear sequence of bytes. Your code needs to be ready to cope with data coming out of the socket in arbitrarily sized lumps. (Asking the socket for data one byte at a time is a way of simplifying this, although for high-bandwidth communications that might not be the most efficient solution—you may get better throughput if you let the socket give you data in slightly larger chunks.)

Notice that the first line of Example 13-23 passes `true` as a second argument to the `NetworkStream` constructor. This tells the `NetworkStream` that we'd like it to take ownership of the `Socket` object—once we are done with the `NetworkStream` and call `Dispose` on it, it will shut down the `Socket` object for us. That'll happen at the end of the block for the `using` statement here. This is important: we must close connections when we have finished with them, because otherwise, we could end up hogging resources on the server unnecessarily.

Having fetched the data and closed the socket, we finally print out the data:

```
Console.WriteLine(data);
```

Example 13-24 shows the whole example.

Example 13-24. Using a Socket to fetch data from a daytime server

```
IPHostEntry hostDnsEntry = Dns.GetHostEntry("time-nw.nist.gov");
IPAddress serverIp = hostDnsEntry.AddressList[0];

Socket daytimeSocket = new Socket(
    serverIp.AddressFamily,
    SocketType.Stream,
    ProtocolType.Tcp);

daytimeSocket.Connect(serverIp, 13);
string data;
using (Stream timeServiceStream = new NetworkStream(daytimeSocket, true))
using (StreamReader timeServiceReader = new StreamReader(timeServiceStream))
{
```

```
    data = timeServiceReader.ReadToEnd();
}
Console.WriteLine(data);
```

If you run the program, you'll see something like this:

```
    55059 09-08-16 06:29:42 50 0 0 912.5 UTC(NIST) *
```

It's not strictly relevant to the use of sockets, but if you're interested, here's what the numbers this particular server returns all mean. The first number is the number of days that have elapsed since midnight on November 17, 1858. (If you're curious to know why anyone might find that useful, search the Web for "Modified Julian Date".) The set of three numbers that follows are the year, month, and date (2009, August 16 in this example), followed by the time of day as UTC (time zone zero, or as we British authors like to call it, Greenwich Mean Time). The 50 signifies that daylight saving time is in effect where the server is located, and the following two zeros indicate respectively that no leap second will be added this month and that the server believes it is not currently experiencing any problems. The next number indicates that the server is deliberately advancing times by 912.5 ms to compensate for transmission delays in the Internet.

That's all you need to do to use a service with sockets—construct a suitably configured socket, call Connect, and then read data. If the service you're using expects to be sent data, you can also write data into the NetworkStream. Obviously, you need to be prepared for errors—the Connect method will throw an exception if it is unable to connect to the service, and you should also be prepared to get errors anytime you try to read or write data with a socket; even if you connect successfully, parts of the network may later fail, severing the connection to the service. Again, .NET indicates this by throwing exceptions.

We've looked at only half of the story so far—what if you wanted to write a program that implements a service like the daytime service? You can do this with the Socket class too, but it's a little more involved.

Implementing Services with the Socket Class

To implement a TCP-based service, we need to make sure our program is ready to receive requests when they come in. If a computer receives an incoming TCP connection request for some port number and no programs are currently listening for connections on that port number, it will simply reject the request. So the first thing we need to do is create a socket that listens for incoming connections (see Example 13-25).

Example 13-25. Listening for incoming TCP connections

```
using (Socket daytimeListener = new Socket(
    AddressFamily.InterNetworkV6,
    SocketType.Stream,
    ProtocolType.Tcp))
{
```

```
daytimeListener.SetSocketOption(
    SocketOptionLevel.IPv6, (SocketOptionName) 27, 0);

IPEndPoint daytimeEndpoint = new IPEndPoint(IPAddress.IPv6Any, 13);
daytimeListener.Bind(daytimeEndpoint);

daytimeListener.Listen(20);
...
```

As with the client side, we create a Socket object, once again specifying the address family, socket type, and protocol. (In this particular example, the lifetime we require for the Socket happens to be the same as the lifetime of our Main method, so a using statement is an appropriate way to manage the socket's disposal.) Whereas with the client we could just use whichever IP address type came back from Dns.GetHostEntry, when we write a server we need to state which sort of address we want to listen on. Example 13-25 chooses the InterNetworkV6 family to enable the use of IPv6. If you want to support just IPv4 you can specify InterNetwork. In fact, this example supports both kinds of address—the call to SetSocketOption after the constructor puts this socket into *dual mode*, meaning that it's able to accept connections through either IPv4 or IPv6. (The magic number 27 that appears in the call corresponds to a value defined by the Windows SDK that doesn't currently have an equivalent entry in the SocketOption Name enumeration. So unfortunately, this is just a magic incantation that you need to know in order to enable a socket to accept incoming connections on either IP version.)

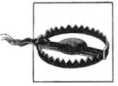 Dual-mode sockets are supported only on Windows Vista or later versions of Windows. If you want to accept incoming connections on both IPv4 and IPv6 on earlier versions of Windows, you'll need to create two sockets and listen for connections on both.

Next, we call Bind—this is how our application claims ownership of a particular TCP port number. We've built an IPEndPoint object that specified port 13—the port number for the daytime service—and also indicates which of the local machine's addresses we'd like to listen on. Machines often have multiple addresses—in fact, a connected machine usually has at least two IPv4 and two IPv6 addresses. Earlier we saw the special machine name localhost, and this corresponds to special IPv4 and IPv6 addresses. Even a completely disconnected machine has these addresses—the IPv4 address 127.0.0.1 and the IPv6 address ::1 always refer to the local machine. On top of this, a machine usually gets both an IPv4 and an IPv6 address when it connects to a network.

It's possible to create sockets that listen on only the local addresses. That might not sound very useful, as it means that you cannot connect to those sockets over the network. In fact, this is quite handy for software developers. You can run services on your machine that are inaccessible over the network but which programs running locally on your machine can still connect to. This may allay the concerns of your IT administrators who don't like the idea of desktop machines running web servers or other services because they (quite reasonably) consider such things to be a security risk. If you configure a service to listen on only these local addresses, it won't be visible on the network, making it less likely to be a security liability. The test web server that Visual Studio can set up for ASP.NET web projects works this way—it uses only a local address, so it is accessible only to browsers running on the same machine. Note that this technique is not very useful outside of a developer machine. A local socket cannot be secured, so it will be accessible to any user logged in to the machine. For a developer box that's fine, but on server systems, this might constitute a security risk. So you should avoid using local sockets.

Example 13-25 chooses the special address `IPAddress.IPv6Any`, which means that the socket will accept incoming connections directed to any of the computer's IPv6 addresses. And since we've configured this to be a dual-mode socket, it will also accept incoming connections for any of the computer's IPv4 addresses too.

If some other program on the computer is already using TCP port 13, the call to `Bind` will throw an exception—any particular port number can be owned by only one process on the machine at any one time. If `Bind` succeeds the port is now ours, and so we can call `Listen` to indicate that we're ready for incoming connection requests.

As you can see from the last line of Example 13-25, `Listen` takes a single argument. This indicates the maximum *backlog* for this socket. The backlog allows for the situation where new connections arrive faster than our server can handle them. As you'll see shortly, we need to execute some code to accept each incoming connection, and at busy times, we might lag behind—if a new connection request comes in before we've managed to accept the last one, that new request goes into the backlog queue. If the number of requests in the backlog gets as high as the number we pass to `Listen`, the OS will start rejecting any further requests until our application catches up.

Our socket is now in a *listening* state, which means that if client programs start trying to connect to our computer on port 13, the OS knows those connections are destined for our program. The next thing our code has to do is *accept* those connections. Example 13-26 does this in a loop so that it can keep accepting connection requests for as long as the program runs.

Example 13-26. Accepting incoming connections

```
while (true)
{
    Socket incomingConnection = daytimeListener.Accept();
    using (NetworkStream connectionStream =
                        new NetworkStream(incomingConnection, true))
    using (StreamWriter writer = new StreamWriter(connectionStream))
    {
        writer.WriteLine(DateTime.Now);
    }
}
```

This code calls `Accept` on the listening `Socket`. If there are currently no clients trying to connect to the service, this call will block—it won't return until there's a client. Once at least one client is attempting to use the service, this will return, handing back another `Socket` object. The `Socket` API is designed to allow multiple simultaneous connections to a single service, and so each call to `Accept` returns a new `Socket`. Your server will end up with one `Socket` object for each distinct connected client, plus the one listening `Socket`.

 You never actually send or receive data on the listening socket. It doesn't represent a TCP connection—its only job is to return a new socket for each incoming TCP connection you accept. Arguably it's a little weird to use the same `Socket` class for both jobs, because accepting incoming connections feels like a pretty different kind of activity than representing an active TCP connection. But that's how sockets have worked for decades. .NET is merely continuing the slightly eccentric tradition.

Example 13-26 chooses to deal with the clients one at a time—the loop accepts a single connection, sends a response, closes the connection, and then moves on to the next client. So this particular server will have up to two active `Socket` objects at any one time—the one for the client connection it's currently handling, and the one `Socket` that is listening for incoming connections. You don't need to do this—it's very common to accept new connections on a listening socket when you already have open connections that came from the same socket. (For example, a web server does not insist on finishing the processing of whatever request it's handling at the moment before starting work on the next one. It's common for a server to have hundreds of inbound connections open simultaneously.) But since this particular service can do all the work it needs to do and then close the connection immediately, it doesn't have any particular reason to open several connections simultaneously.

The code that does the work here is pretty similar to the client code we saw in Example 13-24. As before, we create a `NetworkStream`, passing `true` to indicate that we want to close the `Socket` when we dispose the stream. This time we create a `StreamWriter` instead of a `StreamReader`, because we're now implementing the server, and it's going to be sending data rather than receiving it. We call the writer's `WriteLine` method, passing the current date and time, which, as you may recall, was the whole point of this service in the first place. Example 13-27 shows the completed code.

Example 13-27. The complete daytime service

```
using (Socket daytimeListener = new Socket(
    AddressFamily.InterNetworkV6,
    SocketType.Stream,
    ProtocolType.Tcp))
{
    daytimeListener.SetSocketOption(SocketOptionLevel.IPv6,
                            (SocketOptionName) 27, 0);

    IPEndPoint daytimeEndpoint = new IPEndPoint(IPAddress.IPv6Any, 13);
    daytimeListener.Bind(daytimeEndpoint);
```

```
daytimeListener.Listen(20);

while (true)
{
    Socket incomingConnection = daytimeListener.Accept();
    using (NetworkStream connectionStream =
                        new NetworkStream(incomingConnection, true))
    using (StreamWriter writer = new StreamWriter(connectionStream,
                                                 Encoding.ASCII))
    {
        writer.WriteLine(DateTime.Now);
    }
}
}
```

The first time you run this code, you can expect to see the warning dialog shown in Figure 13-9 (unless you've disabled your Windows Firewall). By default, the Windows Firewall will notify you when programs start listening for incoming network connections out of the blue. Typically, a program that has a legitimate need to accept connections will register itself with the firewall when it's installed, so when a program that the firewall knows nothing about suddenly starts listening for incoming connections, that's likely to be a sign of trouble—it's exactly the sort of thing that malware would do if it wanted to make your machine available to hackers for distributing spam or launching distributed denial of service attacks. Of course, in this case, you know that the code is legitimate because you just wrote it, and the reason your program hasn't gone through the official route of registering itself during installation is that you only just wrote the code, and you haven't written the Windows Installer *.msi* yet. So as a developer, you expect to see this sort of warning for your own programs when they listen for incoming connections. (You didn't see this for the WCF example earlier because it was using the specially reserved design-time address space that Visual Studio sets up when you install it. But that works only for HTTP—there's no equivalent for sockets.) You just need to click Unblock, and you shouldn't see this warning again for this particular program.

To test this program, you can use the client program you wrote earlier. The simplest approach will be to run two copies of Visual Studio, one for the client and one for the server. (Or you could configure Visual Studio to run both projects, as we did earlier.) Run the server first. Then go to the client, modify the line that specifies the machine name—replace time-nw.nist.gov with localhost—and then run the client. It should print out the current time and date. The format will be different from the one used by the NIST server—it'll be the default used by the DateTime type. But that's fine, because the Daytime Protocol specification says we're free to use any format we like as long as it's ASCII and it fits on a single line.

And that's it for basic socket use. Sockets also support asynchronous versions of all the methods—in fact, they support both the event-based and the method-based asynchronous styles we encountered earlier. Since you've already seen this kind of code in action,

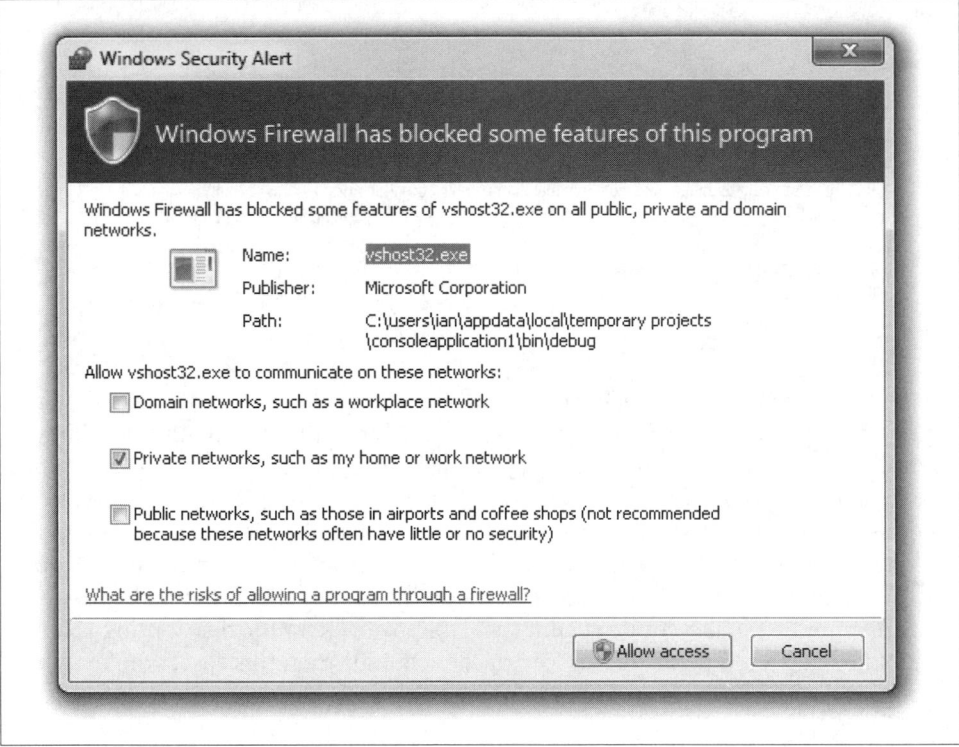

Figure 13-9. Firewall warning when listening for connections

we won't show it again here, but we'll come back to asynchronous programming techniques later in the book.

Other Networking Features

This chapter has touched on the most widely used networking types, but for completeness we should mention that some more specialized networking APIs are available. For example, the `System.Net.Mail` namespace provides types for sending email through an SMTP relay, and the related `System.Net.Mime` namespace supports MIME features, which are the standard way to represent attachments for emails. The `System.Net.Peer` `ToPeer` namespaces provide access to the peer-to-peer networking features of Windows. (There are also WCF bindings that support this system.) The `System.Net.NetworkIn` `formation` namespace provides types for discovering network status, through network interface information, and TCP/IP ICMP mechanisms such as ping. The TLS/SSL infrastructure that enables HTTPS to send encrypted data is also available for you to use directly, through the `System.Net.Security` namespace.

Summary

We looked at three approaches to networked communication in this chapter. WCF works at a fairly high level, enabling us to write servers that offer operations that can be invoked by clients, modeling these remote invocations as method calls. We also looked at the support for HTTP operations provided by the `WebClient`, `HttpWebRequest`, and `HttpWebResponse` classes. And finally, we looked at how to work at a very low level, dealing directly with the bytes sent across the network with TCP, by using the `Socket` class. There's one particularly common form of communication that we've not yet looked at: many applications need to talk to a database. We'll look at this in the next chapter.

CHAPTER 14

Databases

Databases are one of computing's most important inventions. They allow applications to store massive quantities of information, with the ability to search through millions of items and retrieve the ones you need in a fraction of a second. A high-quality database can scale to large numbers of concurrent end users, while providing very reliable storage, even in the face of system crashes. And even if you don't need the scalability, databases still look compelling if your program needs to remember data for any length of time—applications that store valuable information usually rely on databases.

The .NET Framework provides several different ways to communicate with databases. We will mainly be looking at its most recently introduced data access mechanism, the Entity Framework, and how that works with the LINQ features of C#. But first, we'll take a quick look at all of the database features of the .NET Framework, to put the Entity Framework in context.

The .NET Data Access Landscape

The main focus of this chapter, the Entity Framework, was first released as part of Service Pack 1 for Visual Studio 2008, which emerged less than a year after the initial (pre-Service-Pack) release of Visual Studio 2008. This was remarkable, since that first release had already introduced a brand-new data access feature, LINQ to SQL, but then Microsoft has released a lot of data access technologies over the years.

While the pace of change can sometimes seem daunting, each new piece has been a useful advance, and despite the new APIs, the data access services that appeared in .NET v1.0 are still relevant today. So we're not in a state of continuous revolution— new features mostly add layers of functionality. This means it's useful to understand all the parts in order to know what to choose for your applications, so we'll review what each is for and how the pieces build on one another.

Classic ADO.NET

.NET v1 provided a set of data access services called ADO.NET.* In more recent years, ADO.NET seems to have grown into an umbrella term—as new data access features have been added, most (but not all) appear in the ADO.NET section of the documentation. But to understand the layers, it's worth starting with the two parts that were in the first version: interfaces for querying and updating databases, and classes that support disconnected use of data.

IDataReader and friends

ADO.NET defines a family of interfaces that provide a uniform way to perform basic operations such as executing queries, inserting new rows into database tables, and updating or deleting existing rows. Some data access features are common to many different programming systems—if you're familiar with ODBC, or with Java's JDBC, you could think of these ADO.NET interfaces as being the .NET equivalent of those APIs.

These interfaces provide the most direct and efficient way to access the basic services offered by relational databases, which is why the other data access features we'll be looking at in this chapter do not replace this part of ADO.NET. They build on this low-level feature to provide higher-level services.

Because it's not the main focus of this chapter, we won't go into too much detail on how this part of ADO.NET works, and will instead just provide a quick taste. Table 14-1 shows the main ADO.NET base classes that represent the various things needed to get a database to do some work.

Table 14-1. ADO.NET basic data access abstract base classes

Class	Represents
DbConnection	Connection to a database
DbCommand	Command to be executed by a database
DbParameter	Parameter for a command
DbDataRecord	Single row of data returned by a query; alternatively, the IDataRecord interface represents the same concept
DbDataReader	Iterator over the full results returned by a query (potentially many rows and many row sets); implements IDataRecord
DbTransaction	Database transaction

---

* The name is a little confusing. In a sense, ADO.NET is a successor to ADO (ActiveX Data Objects), a data access system that was around before .NET. So ADO.NET does for . NET what ADO did for Visual Basic 6. But they are quite different technologies—ADO.NET makes no use of ADO, or ActiveX. ADO.NET can use OLE DB, the technology underpinning ADO, but native ADO.NET providers are preferred—the OLE DB provider is mainly for legacy sources.

Example 14-1 shows the typical pattern of communication. It starts by creating a connection object—a `SqlConnection` here because this code connects to SQL Server, but for other databases you'd use other types derived from `DbConnection`, such as `Oracle Connection`. Next, it builds a command object, setting its `CommandText` to the SQL we want the database to execute. This particular example is a parameterized command—it selects addresses from a specified state, so we supply the command with a parameter object specifying the state. Then we execute the command by calling `ExecuteReader`, using the data reader object it returns to iterate through the rows produced by the query, and we print out the values. (This particular example assumes you have a SQL Server instance called `.\SQLEXPRESS`. If you installed the full edition or developer edition of SQL Server, specify just `.` instead of `.\SQLEXPRESS`. See "Getting up and running with SQL Server 2008 Express" on page 547 for information on getting the samples installed.)

Example 14-1. Basic data access with ADO.NET

```
string sqlConnectionString = @"Data Source=.\sqlexpress;" +
    "Initial Catalog=AdventureWorksLT2008;Integrated Security=True";
string state = "California";

using (DbConnection conn = new SqlConnection(sqlConnectionString))
using (DbCommand cmd = conn.CreateCommand())
{
    cmd.CommandText =
        "SELECT AddressLine1, AddressLine2, City FROM SalesLT.Address WHERE " +
        "StateProvince=@state";
    DbParameter stateParam = cmd.CreateParameter();
    stateParam.ParameterName = "@state";
    stateParam.Value = state;
    cmd.Parameters.Add(stateParam);

    conn.Open();
    using (DbDataReader reader = cmd.ExecuteReader())
    {
        while (reader.Read())
        {
            string addressLine1 = reader.GetString(0);
            // AddressLine2 is nullable, so we need to be prepared to get
            // back either a string or a DBNull
            string addressLine2 = reader.GetValue(1) as string;
            string city = reader.GetString(2);

            Console.WriteLine(addressLine1);
            Console.WriteLine(addressLine2);
            Console.WriteLine(city);
        }
    }
}
```

You might be wondering why we're fiddling around with parameter objects when it would have been simpler to just put the state directly into the SQL string. This particular example hardcodes the state, so that would have worked, but the technique here would be important if the value was picked at runtime. In general, building SQL queries with string concatenation is a dangerous thing to do—if any of the text comes from outside your code (e.g., from a form on a web page, or part of a URL) your code will be vulnerable to a *SQL injection* attack. Imagine that Example 14-1 was part of a web application, and state here came from part of a URL such as *http://example.com/show-info?state=California*. Users are free to modify URLs—you can just type them into the address bar—so a malicious user might decide to modify that part of the URL. If the code just took the string from the URL and concatenated it directly into the SQL, we would effectively be giving anyone with an Internet connection the ability to run arbitrary SQL commands on our database—SQL queries can contain multiple commands, so users would be able to add extra commands to run after the SELECT. Parameters are one way to avoid this, because the value of a parameter will not be treated as SQL. So it's a good idea to get in the habit of using parameters whenever some part of the query needs to change at runtime.

The API we used here directly reflects the steps needed to communicate with a database, so we have to write a lot of code to bridge between the queries, parameters, and columns of the database world and the world of C#. Just as a sneak preview, Example 14-2 shows the equivalent code using the Entity Framework. Notice that instead of having to build a parameter object for a parameterized query, we've just been able to use a LINQ where clause and the C# == comparison syntax. (The Entity Framework performs a parameterized query under the covers, so this is safe from SQL injection attacks.) Also notice that all the database columns are available as object properties, so we don't have to call GetString or similar helpers to retrieve column values.

Example 14-2. LINQ to Entities versus ADO.NET

```
string state = "California";
using (var context = new AdventureWorksLT2008Entities())
{
    var addresses = from address in context.Addresses
                    where address.StateProvince == state
                    select address;

    foreach (var address in addresses)
    {
        Console.WriteLine(address.AddressLine1);
        Console.WriteLine(address.AddressLine2);
        Console.WriteLine(address.City);
    }
}
```

Example 14-1 has one obvious benefit in exchange for the complexity: we have complete control over the SQL query. You can't see the SQL in Example 14-2 because it gets generated for you. In general, the low-level ADO.NET API gives us more direct access to database features—for example, with SQL Server you can arrange to be no-tified when a query you executed earlier will now return different results due to changes in the database. (This can be useful in caching systems—ASP.NET's cache can take advantage of this. It needs to be used with care, however, because it requires you to keep a database connection open at all times, which can cause severe scaling problems.)

Another potential benefit is that Example 14-1 does not require the application to commit to the Entity Framework's way of doing things. Not all applications necessarily want to use databases in the way the Entity Framework chooses to.

The use of this old-style part of ADO.NET usually comes down to a need for control over some specific aspects of data access, or occasionally because it offers performance benefits in certain specialized scenarios. But for the majority of developers, this style of data access will be unnecessarily low-level and verbose.

These interfaces are not the only part of ADO.NET v1—it has another piece whose job is to manage data after the query that fetched it has completed.

ADO.NET data sets

ADO.NET defines the `DataSet` class, which is a collection of `DataTable` objects. A `DataTable` is an in-memory copy of some tabular data. Typically, this would be fetched from a database table or view, although it's possible to build up a `DataTable` from any information source—it provides methods for creating new rows from scratch.

A `DataSet` can be a convenient way of loading a small subset of a database's contents into client-side code, enabling information to be browsed locally using data binding. It also supports some basic client-side processing of a kind that might normally be done in the database—you can perform searching, filtering, and sorting, for example. In Windows GUIs, moving this sort of work to the client side can improve responsiveness—the user doesn't have to wait for the database to respond to see results. This is what's meant by *disconnected* operation—you can still work with the data even after closing the connection to the database.

`DataSet` objects are serializable, so it's possible to save one to disk or send it across a network. It can use an XML representation, which in theory makes it possible for non-.NET code to access the information in a `DataSet`. However, while it's certainly workable, in practice this seems not to be a popular technique. This may be because the XML representation is relatively complex and unique to the `DataSet`, so there's not much support for it outside of the .NET Framework.

Visual Studio is able to generate derived classes to build a so-called *strongly typed* `DataSet`, whose tables offer row objects with .NET properties representing columns in the corresponding database table. Strongly typed `DataSet`s are often used to reduce the amount of code required to bridge between C# and the database. However, since LINQ to SQL and LINQ to Entities came along, this use of `DataSet`s has become less popular, because the LINQ-based approaches offer the same benefit but are typically easier to use. So DataSets are somewhat out of favor today.

The low-level ADO.NET data access interfaces were the main way to access data in .NET right up until .NET 3.5 and Visual Studio 2008 shipped, bringing LINQ.

LINQ and Databases

As we saw in Chapter 8, LINQ lets you perform tasks with collections of data including filtering, sorting, and grouping. In that chapter, we were working only with objects, but these are exactly the jobs that databases are good at. Moreover, one of the motivations behind LINQ's design was to make it easier to use databases from code. As you can see in Example 14-2, LINQ blends data access seamlessly into C# code—this database example looks very similar to the object examples we saw in the earlier chapter.

Database LINQ Providers

Database LINQ providers work very differently from the LINQ to Objects provider, even though queries use the same syntax for both. In LINQ to Objects, a where clause does all of its work inside the .NET Framework—it's similar in action to a loop with an if statement. But trying that with a database would be a disaster—if your where clause is designed to select a single row out of 20 million, you absolutely don't want C# code to iterate through all 20 million rows! You want the database to do the filtering so that it can use its indexes to locate the row efficiently.

And it works exactly as you'd want—the LINQ where clause in Example 14-2 is effectively translated into a SQL WHERE clause. As you may recall, C# converts a LINQ query expression into a series of method calls, and those method calls just end up building a query object that knows how to return the results. LINQ uses *deferred execution*—the query doesn't start returning results until you ask for them. LINQ providers for databases do something similar, but instead of working directly with IEnumerable<T>, they use a specialized type that derives from IEnumerable<T>, called IQueryable<T>. Since IQueryable<T> derives from IEnumerable<T>, you can still enumerate its contents in the usual ways, but it's only when you do this that it generates a suitable database query; it won't touch the database until you start asking to see elements. So we still have deferred execution, but crucially, when you finally execute the query the complete chain of processing that your LINQ query represents is turned into a single SQL query so that the database can do all the work.

In short, whereas LINQ to Objects enumerates all the objects from the source and runs the chain of processing inside your .NET application, database LINQ providers push the processing to the database.

Example 14-2 uses LINQ to Entities—a LINQ provider for the Entity Framework. The Entity Framework didn't appear until Service Pack 1 of Visual Studio 2008, and there's an older database LINQ provider called LINQ to SQL that appeared in the first Visual Studio 2008 release.

LINQ to SQL works only with SQL Server and SQL Server Compact 3.5, and has a fairly narrow goal. It aims to reduce the overhead involved in writing data access code by providing a convenient C# syntax for working with the data in a SQL Server database.

The Entity Framework is similar, but it adds a couple of additional features. First, it is designed to support multiple database vendors—it has an open provider model, enabling support to be written for any database, and you can get providers for most popular databases. Second, the Entity Framework allows the .NET representation to have a different structure from your database schema if necessary. You can define a conceptual model whose entities do not necessarily correspond directly to rows of particular tables—an entity might include data that spans multiple tables in the database itself. This entity can then be represented as a single object.

Of course, it's possible to have your conceptual model correspond exactly to your database model—you're free to create a straightforward mapping where one entity represents one row in one table. Used in this way the Entity Framework, in conjunction with LINQ to Entities, makes LINQ to SQL look redundant. So why do we have both?

The main reason LINQ to SQL exists is that it was ready when Visual Studio 2008 shipped, whereas Microsoft hadn't finished the Entity Framework at that point. LINQ was a major part of that release, and since one of the main motivations behind LINQ was data access, shipping without a LINQ-based data access feature would have been a bit of a letdown. LINQ to SQL was developed by a different team (it came from the LINQ team, and not the data access group), and it was ready earlier, due no doubt in part to its less ambitious goals.

Microsoft has stated that while both technologies are fully supported, the Entity Framework is where the majority of its efforts will now be focused. Visual Studio 2010 adds a few new LINQ to SQL features, but LINQ to Entities will see more development in the long run.

That's why this chapter's focus is the Entity Framework (although a lot of the concepts here apply equally to both technologies). That being said, both authors really like LINQ to SQL. In scenarios where we're using SQL Server and where we don't need the conceptual model and mapping features of the Entity Framework, we're both more inclined to use LINQ to SQL because of its simplicity and because we've already learned how to use it. But if you learn only one data access technology for .NET, the Entity Framework looks like the better choice for the long term.

Non-Microsoft Data Access Technologies

By the time Microsoft shipped the Entity Framework, various third-party options for mapping relational data into object models had been around for a while. We're not going to talk about them in this book, but it's useful to be aware that the Entity Framework isn't the only game in town.

Perhaps the best known alternative is NHibernate (*http://nhforge.org/*). This is a .NET version of Hibernate, a popular Java ORM (Object Relational Mapper). NHibernate had already been around for a few years by the time the Entity Framework emerged (and its Java progenitor is considerably older). So in many respects it's a more mature and more fully featured ORM than the Entity Framework. On the other hand, NHibernate predates LINQ (and Java currently has nothing resembling LINQ), so at the time of this writing, its LINQ support is somewhat limited.

Many other ORMs are available for .NET, some free and some commercial. They are too numerous to mention here, as a quick web search will confirm.

WCF Data Services

Most communication with databases happens over specialized, vendor-specific protocols. Firewalls are usually configured not to let such protocols through, and with good reason: from a security perspective, making your database directly accessible on the Internet tends to look like a very bad idea. Nonetheless, some people want to do this, and there are scenarios in which it's not the terrible idea it might first seem, particularly if you can exercise sufficient control over what gets exposed.

With WCF Data Services, you can present a relational data store over HTTP and XML or JSON. You can be selective about what data you expose and to whom. Moreover, the model you present doesn't necessarily have to be the same as your underlying database structure. In fact, there doesn't have to be a database involved at all—there's a provider model that enables you to present any data through this mechanism, as long as you can find a way to make it look like relational data.

You will normally use WCF Data Services in conjunction with the Entity Framework—you can define the entities you'd like to present over HTTP, and use the framework's mapping services to bridge between that and the underlying data store. So we'll be looking at these services in more detail later in the chapter, once we've finished exploring the Entity Framework.

The focus of WCF Data Services is different than for the other data access features we've discussed so far—it's mainly about presenting data on the network, where everything else has been about consuming data. However, there's also a client-side component that provides LINQ-based querying for such services. While it's part of the WCF Data Services technology, it's optional—you're not obliged to use it on the client. And this client doesn't strictly require WCF Data Services on the server—the client-side parts could be used against any service that exposes data in the same way.

Silverlight and Data Access

Silverlight uses a seriously trimmed down version of the .NET Framework to keep its download size and install time tolerably small. It doesn't have much data access support. In fact, size is not the only reason—it wouldn't normally make sense for a

Silverlight client application to attempt to connect directly to a database, because Silverlight is a client-side web technology and most system administrators work to ensure that their databases are not accessible via their native protocols over the Internet.

Of course, a direct connection to a database server might be an option in an intranet scenario, but it's not supported. Silverlight offers LINQ, but neither the LINQ to SQL nor the LINQ to Entity Framework providers are available, because the underlying database access mechanisms that these providers use are missing. The only supported database access mechanism in Silverlight is the WCF Data Services client.

Databases

The full .NET Framework is designed to work with a wide range of databases. The simple ADO.NET data access we started with uses interfaces to allow database vendors to supply their own database-specific implementations. Likewise, the Entity Framework is database-agnostic—it has an open provider model designed to allow support for any relational database to be added. Of course, Microsoft ships a provider for its own database, SQL Server, but other suppliers offer providers for various databases, including Oracle, MySQL, PostgreSQL, SQLite, Sybase, and DB2.

In this book, we will use SQL Server. The examples work with SQL Server, which is available for free. (Some editions of Visual Studio will automatically install SQL Server 2008 Express for you by default.) The Express edition of SQL Server is the same database engine as the "real" versions, but with some limits on database size and with some of the more advanced features missing. Despite being a trimmed down version, it's easily capable of supporting substantial websites. It can also be used on client applications written with WPF or Windows Forms, to support client-side data stores or caching, although it can complicate the installation process for such an application—installing a SQL Server instance is not a trivial task.

Getting up and running with SQL Server 2008 Express

If you want to follow the examples in this chapter, not only will you need a copy of SQL Server 2008 Express installed, but you'll also need to install a sample database. We'll be using the lightweight version of the Adventure Works database available from *http://msftdbprodsamples.codeplex.com/*.

Getting this sample up and running is slightly fiddly, because there are numerous different versions of the Adventure Works sample—there are full and lightweight versions for both SQL Server 2005 and SQL Server 2008, and each version of SQL Server comes in various editions, not all of which put their datafiles in the same place. Because of all the variations, it's quite easy to find that the sample database has failed to appear even though the installation appeared to proceed without error.

Moreover, the steps required to install the database change from time to time, as new versions are released. We had been planning to provide detailed steps here, but while we were writing this book, changes to the database installer rendered the first set of instructions we had produced useless. Since that could well happen again between us finishing the book and you reading it, we're providing the instructions as part of the sample code you can download for this book from the O'Reilly website so that we can update them when necessary. You can find these at *http://oreilly.com/catalog/9780596159832/.*

Now that we've finished a quick survey of the data access features available in .NET and we've seen how to get the sample database installed, let's look at the Entity Framework in more detail. We'll start with the model at the heart of the framework.

The Entity Data Model

The main goal of the Entity Framework (or EF for short) is to make it easier for your code to work with data in the database. C# objects are quite different in nature than the information stored in a relational database, and the process of managing these differences, and transferring data between these two worlds, is called *mapping.* (So the Entity Framework is a kind of ORM.) As Figure 14-1 illustrates, mapping happens in both directions. As information is fetched from the database, it is loaded into objects. And if your C# code modifies these objects or creates new ones, you can arrange for the database to be correspondingly updated.

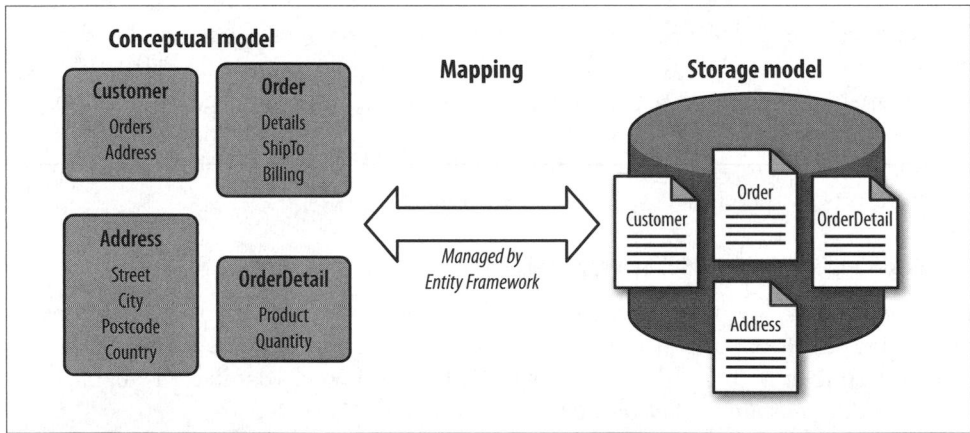

Figure 14-1. Models and mapping in the Entity Framework

The design of a database doesn't always correspond directly to data structures convenient for our application code. There are many reasons we might want our code to work with a model that looks slightly different from the data. The database may contain information not required by the part of the application we're writing, so we may need only a subset. Information about a particular entity may have been split across multiple tables for performance reasons. Naming conventions in the database might not suit our code.

So the Entity Framework allows us to control the mapping. We can define a *conceptual model* that describes the entities as we'd like to work with them from C#, along with *mappings* that describe how that model maps onto the underlying storage. The EF also requires us to provide a *store schema*, which is a definition of the structure we expect it to find in the database. This may seem redundant—after all, the database knows its own schema, so why would the EF need a copy? There are a couple of reasons. First, it's possible to define the model before you create the database—you can generate a database schema from the store schema. Second, you can configure aspects of how the Entity Framework uses the database, such as whether it uses queries or stored procedures to access particular tables. Settings that are associated with the database itself rather than what the EF does with data belong in the store schema rather than the mappings or conceptual schema.

The three parts shown in Figure 14-1—the conceptual model, the storage model, and the mappings between them—are collectively known as the *Entity Data Model*, or EDM.

 There are many constraints on the conceptual model, because the model is useful only if you can construct a successful mapping. There are limits on what mappings are able to do, so your existing database structure will impose some restrictions on the model. Developers who are new to the Entity Framework often find that they have a lot less freedom in the design of the conceptual model than they first presumed. We'll see what mappings are possible in due course, but for now, do not imagine that the EF is able to take any arbitrary conceptual model and bridge it to any old database structure—there is necessarily a close relationship between the database and the conceptual model.

If you use the EF in the simplest way possible, your conceptual model will be the same as your storage model, and the mapping will be very straightforward. If you use Visual Studio's wizard for adding EF support to a project, you'll end up with exactly this sort of direct mapping, with one entity type for each table or view you import. But you can then tweak things to suit your needs. We'll walk through the wizard now even though it produces a straightforward mapping where the conceptual model matches the storage model, it still has to generate a complete set of model and mapping definitions, so it's instructive to look at what it produces.

You can add EF support to any .NET project (except for Silverlight projects). We'll use a console application for the examples. In the Add New Item dialog, we'll select Visual C# Items→Data, and then choose the ADO.NET Entity Data Model item template, calling the new file "AdventureWorksModel".

When you add an Entity Data Model to your project, Visual Studio asks whether you want to start from scratch or base your model on an existing database. We'll choose that simpler second option. If you've previously told Visual Studio about any databases you're using—either via the Server Explorer toolbar or by using this or other data-related wizards—it will show them in a drop down, but you can provide Visual Studio with new connection details from within the wizard. For this walkthrough, we're going to connect to the AdventureWorksLT2008 sample database.

 The wizard uses the name of your connection for one of the types that it generates. You'll see the identifier `AdventureWorksLT2008Entities` cropping up in various examples later. If you happen to give your connection a different name in Visual Studio, you'll need to use that name in the code.

Once you've chosen a database, Visual Studio will show a tree view of all the tables, views, and stored procedures—you can use these as the starting point for your model. For each item you select, it will add corresponding items to the store schema, the conceptual schema, and the mappings. When you complete the wizard, it will generate an *.edmx* file that defines the generated entity model. Visual Studio opens a graphical view of this file—Figure 14-2 shows the conceptual model that appears if you select the `Customer`, `SalesOrderHeader`, and `SalesOrderDetail` tables in the wizard and then click Finish.

This view shows only the conceptual model. You can see slightly more of the EDM in the Model Browser, shown in Figure 14-3. This will normally appear by default when you open an EDM, but if you rearrange your windows and lose track of it, you can right-click on the background of the model and choose Model Browser from the context menu. The browser lists both the conceptual schema (under the `AdventureWorksLT2008Model` node here) and the store schema (under `Adventure WorksLT2008Model.Store`). The three selected tables are visible in both, and if you were to expand them, you'd see that the properties of each entity in the conceptual model correspond directly to the columns of the tables in the store schema.

Even the Model Browser doesn't show the complete picture, as the Entity Data Model has three parts: the conceptual schema, the store schema, and the mappings. To see the mappings, you can select either entities or properties of entities. When you do this in either the main *.edmx* editor view (Figure 14-2) or the Model Browser (Figure 14-3), the Mapping Details window, shown in Figure 14-4, will display the mappings for the selected item. The Mapping Details panel should appear automatically, but if you don't see it, you can open it with the View→Other Windows→Entity Data Model Mapping Details menu item.

As Figure 14-4 shows, the generated mapping is pretty simple. On the left you can see each column from the table definition in the store schema, and on the right you can see which entity property it is mapped to. Since the store schema and conceptual model were generated directly from the database schema, there's nothing complicated going on—the same names appear on either side, and the only difference is that the lefthand side shows data types from the database world such as `nvarchar` and `bit`, while the righthand side shows .NET data types such as `String` and `Boolean`.

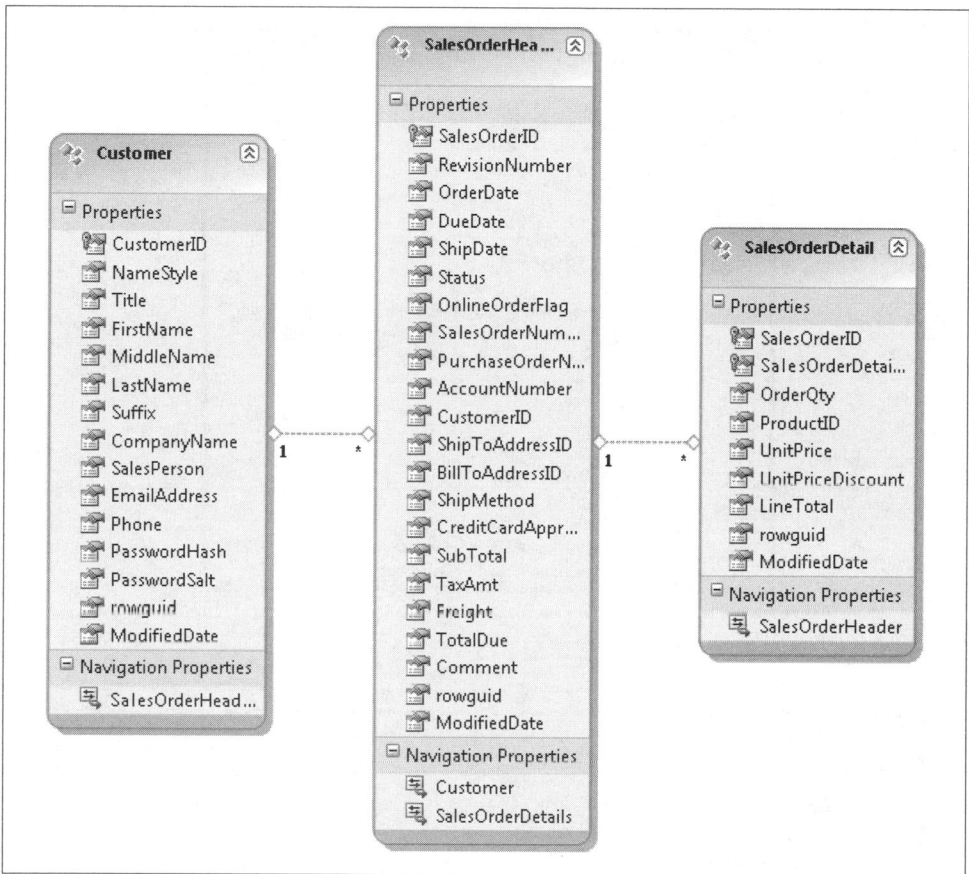

Figure 14-2. Conceptual model with three entities

Generated Code

Visual Studio puts the whole Entity Data Model definition in an *.edmx* file, which is just XML. The wizards and editor windows we've seen so far are just convenient views into that XML. If you look directly at the XML in the *.edmx*, you'll see it contains sections corresponding to the three parts of the model—storage schema, conceptual schema, and mappings. But the whole point of this exercise was to make it easier to use data from code. So Visual Studio generates code based on the contents of any *.edmx* files in your project.

For each entity type you define, a corresponding .NET class will be generated. These classes provide normal properties for each property in the entity type's definition. So when you create and edit entity types, you are in effect defining .NET types that you can use from your C# code.

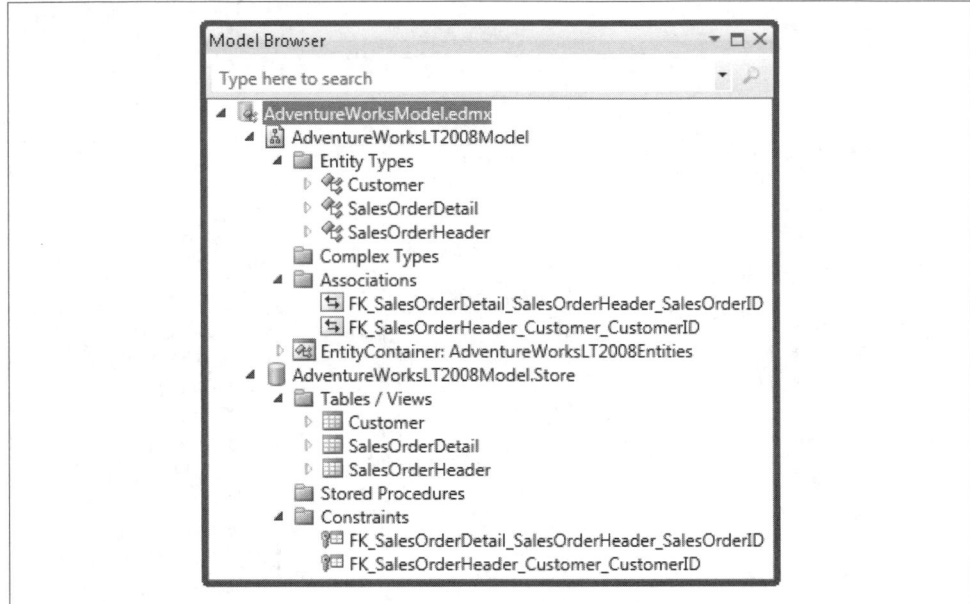

Figure 14-3. EDM in the Model Browser

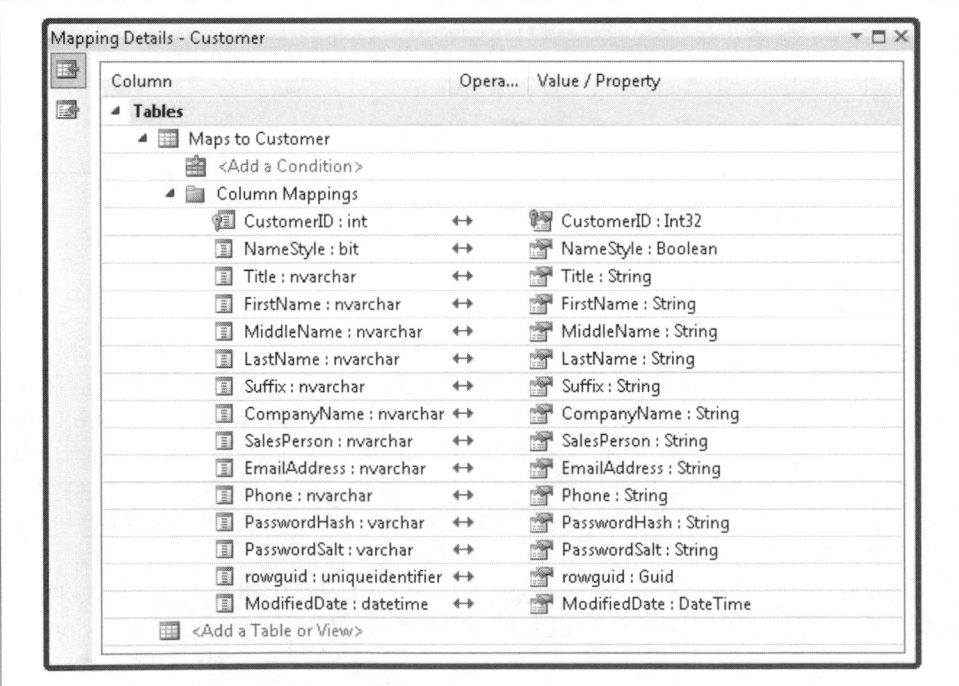

Figure 14-4. The EDM Mapping Details window

 The generated types derive from `EntityObject`, a base class that enables the object to participate in the Entity Framework. This includes features such as change tracking so that the framework can know when it needs to write updates to the database. The first version of the EF required entities to derive from this base class or to implement certain EF interfaces, but .NET 4 introduced so-called *POCO* (Plain Old CLR Object) support, which makes it possible to use an existing class hierarchy with the Entity Framework without having to modify those classes (as long as you can create a successful mapping). There's more work to do that way—if you don't derive from `EntityObject` you need to write extra supporting code to provide the EF with enough information to know how it should handle change tracking, identity, and relationships for your objects. Here we're sticking with the simpler approach of letting the wizard generate classes that derive from the EF's base type.

Visual Studio also generates one extra class representing something called the *object context*. You use this to obtain entity objects representing data already in the database and it's also where you go to add new data. And as we'll see later, this object provides other services for managing the data access operations. This type derives from `ObjectContext`, and sometimes it's just referred to as the context. Example 14-3 uses this generated context type to retrieve rows from the `SalesOrderHeader` table for a particular date.

Example 14-3. Using generated entity types

```
using (var dbContext = new AdventureWorksLT2008Entities())
{
    DateTime orderDate = new DateTime(2004, 6, 1);
    var orders = from order in dbContext.SalesOrderHeaders
                 where order.OrderDate == orderDate
                 select order;

    foreach (SalesOrderHeader order in orders)
    {
        Console.WriteLine(order.TotalDue);
    }
}
```

Notice that this example wraps the context in a `using` statement—the object context is a disposable resource because it does a lot of work behind the scenes, and it needs to tidy up once you no longer need the state it builds up. So it's important that you dispose it when you're done with it.

The object context's type here is `AdventureWorksLT2008Entities`. By default, Visual Studio will just append the word *Entities* to your database connection name. You can change this by selecting the `EntityContainer` item in the Model Browser—you can see this in the middle of Figure 14-3—and then use the Properties panel to choose its name. But we'll keep the default name in the examples.

Notice that the LINQ query in Example 14-3 uses the context's `SalesOrderHeaders` property as the query source. That's not quite the same as the table name—the wizard has added an *s*. By default, the Entity Framework wizard will attempt to pluralize and depluralize words as appropriate—in general, it gives entity types singular names while properties that return collections of entities are plural. (The names in our conceptual model can differ slightly from our storage model thanks to the Entity Data Model's mapping.) If you don't like this plural handling, there's a checkbox to turn it off when you import tables with the wizard.

Example 14-3 also uses the `SalesOrderHeader` class generated for the entity type of the same name. The `order` range variable in the LINQ query is of this type, as is the `order` iteration variable in the loop.

It's this generated entity class that enables us to refer to database columns using normal C# syntax. The LINQ query's `where` clause uses that entity class's `OrderDate` property to build a query that uses the `OrderDate` column of the corresponding database table. Likewise, the loop uses normal C# property syntax to retrieve `TotalDue`, which represents the column of the same name in the database.

If this seems rather uneventful, well, that's the idea. Compare this to the much more fiddly code in Example 14-1—by mapping database columns to properties, the Entity Framework reduces the amount of friction involved in writing data access code.

 You can find the generated source code for the entities in the Solution Explorer by expanding the *.edmx* file—you'll find a file with a similar name, but with *.Designer.cs* in place of *.edmx* (so *AdventureWorks.Designer.cs* in this case). As with all generated code you should avoid modifying it—Visual Studio tends to regenerate code from scratch each time any setting changes. But if you'd like to add features to these generated classes, that's easily done—all the classes are generated with the `partial` keyword, meaning that you can put additional members in separate source files. You can add another class definition with the same name as an entity type, marked with the `partial` keyword, to any source file. The C# compiler will effectively merge your partial class with the generated partial class.

Changing the Mapping

Let's change things a bit, so the mapping has something to do. Most of the column names in this example database happen to fit the usual .NET conventions for property names, but there's an exception: the `rowguid` column in `SalesOrderHeader` is not capitalized in the usual way. (This column exists to support SQL Server replication, so it's fairly unusual to want to use it from code, but in this example it's the only column with a funny-looking name.) If you change this name to `RowGuid` in the designer (either by double-clicking on the property or by using the Properties panel) Visual Studio will update the mapping, and the Mapping Details panel will show that the `rowguid` column in the table is mapped to the RowGuid property of the entity. (If you'd prefer a less subtle change, you could rename the Customer entity's ModifiedDate to, say, LastChanged. The mapping lets you use any names you like.)

Restrictions on Removing Mapped Properties

You might look at the large number of properties in the SalesOrderHeader entity and decide that you'd like to remove some properties completely. While you can do this, be aware that the EF requires certain columns to be mapped. For example, it needs the columns that form the primary key to be mapped, because these are necessary to identify an object as representing a particular row in the database. Less obviously, the EF also demands that you provide a mapping for any nonnullable columns that don't have default values, because without them it would be impossible to create new instances of the entity. The database will insist that the INSERT statement the EF generates for creating the new row provides values for all nonnullable columns that don't have default values. The EF therefore requires that you provide mappings for such columns so that it's able to generate a valid INSERT.

This can be frustrating if you don't actually need to create new items. For example, your code might only need to read data that was added by some other part of the system. It's possible to create read-only entities as a way around this, but it's not straightforward—you need to define either a *query view* or a *defining query*, both of which are advanced topics beyond the scope of a one-chapter description of the Entity Framework.

Changing the names of a few columns isn't very exciting. (And with this particular example database it's not even very useful, although if you're dealing with more idiosyncratic naming schemes, renaming becomes more important.) So let's look at one of the more interesting mapping features: the way in which the EF handles relationships between entities.

Relationships

Databases usually have relationships between tables. In the Adventure Works example, the Customer table has a foreign key relationship with the SalesOrderHeader table. Both tables have a CustomerID column. This is the primary key of the Customer table, and the database schema includes a constraint enforcing that the CustomerID column in the SalesOrderHeader can contain only a value for which a corresponding Customer row exists. Or to put it more simply, each SalesOrderHeader row must be related to a specific Customer row.

This has nothing to do with the *relations* in a *relational* database, incidentally. The *relational* name comes from the set theory underpinning databases, and a relation is not the same thing as a relationship here. A relation effectively corresponds to a table.

Visual Studio's EDM wizard looks for foreign key constraints in the database schema to discover the relationships between tables. In the EDM, it turns these into *associations*. (The distinction between a relationship and an association is somewhat subtle. An association is a named item in the Entity Data Model representing a particular relationship. The main reason this distinction exists is that relationships are a slightly more general concept—associations are capable of modeling only certain kinds of relationships.) Just as tables added with the wizard end up appearing in all three parts of the EDM—a table will appear in the store schema, a corresponding entity will be added to the conceptual schema, and there will be a mapping between the two—a similar process occurs for associations. If a foreign key constraint indicates that there's a relationship between two database tables added through the wizard, Visual Studio will add an association to the EDM's store schema and also to the conceptual schema, and it will set up a suitable mapping between these two associations. And on top of this, it will add *navigation properties* to the related entities in the conceptual model.

In previous versions of the Entity Framework, foreign key columns represented with navigation properties would not get scalar properties providing direct access to the key values—there would have been no `CustomerID` property on the `SalesOrderHeader` type, for example. This proved awkward in practice, so starting with .NET 4 relationships are represented both as the underlying foreign key value and also as a navigation property.

Navigation properties

Associations represent relationships between entities, and the most natural way to present them in the world of objects is through properties. For example, you'd expect an object representing a sales order to provide a property that refers to the related customer. That's exactly what the EF does, and it also works in reverse: the customer object provides a property that holds a collection of references to all the customer's orders. Example 14-4 shows a LINQ query that gets the number of `SalesOrderHeader` rows associated with each customer. It fetches one property from the `Customer` entity class that maps to a column in the database (`CustomerID`) and also uses a property called `SalesOrderHeader`, which represents the customer's orders.

Example 14-4. Using a navigation property

```
using (var dbContext = new AdventureWorksLT2008Entities())
{
    var customerOrderCounts = from cust in dbContext.Customers
```

```
                              select new
                              {
                                  cust.CustomerID,
                                  OrderCount = cust.SalesOrderHeaders.Count
                              };
          foreach (var customerInfo in customerOrderCounts)
          {
              Console.WriteLine("Customer {0} has {1} orders",
                  customerInfo.CustomerID, customerInfo.OrderCount);
          }
      }
}
```

The database table that the `Customer` entity class represents does not have a column called `SalesOrderHeader`. The Entity Framework wizard added this property to represent the relationship between the `Customer` and `SalesOrderHeader` tables. This is not an ordinary property—in Figure 14-2 you can see that it appears separately, under Navigation Properties.

From C# code, a navigation property looks like a collection. Example 14-4 just retrieves the `Count` property, but we could do more advanced things. The query in Example 14-5 has a nested query for each customer that looks for all shipped orders (those with a `Status` of 5), and for each one it reads the total due for that order and a count of all the `SalesOrderDetails` rows associated with that order. So this uses two navigation properties—the one representing the relationship between customers and orders, and the one representing the relationship between orders and order details.

Example 14-5. Traversing multiple relationships with navigation properties

```
var info = from cust in dbContext.Customers
           select new
           {
               cust.CustomerID,
               Orders = from order in cust.SalesOrderHeaders
                        where order.Status == 5
                        select new
                        {
                            order.TotalDue,
                            ItemCount - order.SalesOrderDetails.Count
                        }
           };
```

There's a reason we've used LINQ in these last two examples—it happens to avoid an issue with navigation properties. How does the EF decide how many entities to load for us, and when? In Example 14-4, the LINQ query just retrieves two pieces of information for each customer—the `CustomerID` and the order count—and while Example 14-5 is more complex, it's still circumscribed, so the EF can inspect the query to work out exactly what it needs to retrieve. But when we're not using LINQ, how does the EF know what to do? For instance, consider the code in Example 14-6.

Example 14-6. Following an association after the initial query

```
Customer myCustomer = dbContext.Customers.Single(
    cust => cust.CustomerID == 29531);
Console.WriteLine(myCustomer.SalesOrderHeaders.Count);
```

This fetches the entity for a specific customer, and then tries to get the number of `SalesOrderHeader` entities to which this item is related. Prior to .NET 4, this did not work—it would print out `0`, even though the example database has one related order for this customer. In .NET 3.5 SP1, the Entity Framework would initialize navigation properties such as the `Customer` object's `SalesOrderHeaders` property with an empty collection, and would load the related objects only if we ask it to, using the `Load` method shown in Example 14-7.

Example 14-7. Explicitly loading entities for an association

```
Customer myCustomer = dbContext.Customers.Single(
    cust => cust.CustomerID == 29531);
myCustomer.SalesOrderHeaders.Load();
Console.WriteLine(myCustomer.SalesOrderHeaders.Count);
```

.NET 4 adds an alternative way to do this, called *lazy loading*. Rather than having to call `Load` explicitly, the EF can automatically load related objects at the point at which you access them. The context has a property to control this:

```
dbContext.ContextOptions.LazyLoadingEnabled = false;
```

This is `true` by default; setting it to `false` reverts to the pre-.NET 4 behavior. With this option switched on, Example 14-6 is equivalent to Example 14-7, because the EF will call `Load` for us when we first try to use the navigation property. (The collection ignores calls to `Load` if the entities are already loaded, so requesting multiple loads is not a problem.)

In either case, the EF has to make an extra trip to the database. The call to `Single` will fetch the customer from the database before returning, which means that a second request is required when we later ask it (either explicitly or implicitly) to fetch the related rows, because the EF didn't know we were going to use these items until we asked for them. This might not be a problem, but in general, the more trips you make to the database, the slower things go.

 Be wary of enabling lazy loading, because it can sometimes result in a lot of unnecessary database requests. For example, one author was involved with a project that had some diagnostic code that "helpfully" wrote a snapshot of certain objects into a log, including the value of all their properties. Unfortunately, this code was recursive—if a property referred to another object, it would display that too, and if a property referred to a collection of objects, it would show all of them. This logging code had cycle detection, so it wouldn't get stuck in an infinite loop, but otherwise it wouldn't stop until it had showed every object reachable from the starting point. Unfortunately, lazy loading was enabled, so when this code was given an entity, it ended up fetching all entities that were related, no matter how distantly, to the first object at hand, so it hammered the database with thousands of requests each time a log entry was generated.

Modern databases are surprisingly fast—it's possible for this sort of problem to go unnoticed on development machines with their own local database instance. But you probably don't want it happening on a busy live server.

To get consistent results you'd want to make sure the initial query and subsequent lazy loads happen as part of a transaction (as shown later), but to ensure scalability in a busy system you want to minimize the number of requests made in any single transaction. So you can tell the EF that you want certain related entities to be fetched at the same time as the main result. You do this with the `Include` method shown in Example 14-8, which is available on any of the entity sets provided by the context.

Example 14-8. Specifying relationships to preload

```
var customersWithOrderDetails = dbContext.Customers.
    Include("SalesOrderHeaders.SalesOrderDetails");
Customer myCustomer = customersWithOrderDetails.Single(
    cust => cust.CustomerID == 29531);
Console.WriteLine(myCustomer.SalesOrderHeaders.Count);
```

This call to `Include` asks to load related entities available through the `Customer` entity's `SalesOrderHeaders` property. (These will be loaded regardless of the lazy loading setting.) It also says that for each of those related entities, the EF should load any related entities visible through the `SalesOrderDetails` property. In other words, this tells the EF that we would like it to fetch all of the orders for this customer and all of the details for those orders. It will generate a single query that fetches all of the necessary information in one request.

If you're wondering why it doesn't just prefetch all related items all of the time, consider the performance implications. In some circumstances, aggressively prefetching all related items might amount to attempting to copy a significant fraction of your database into memory! But even in more circumscribed cases, fetching more data than you need can slow your system down or reduce scalability.

So far we have seen only so-called one-to-many relationships—one customer can be related to many orders, one order can be related to many order details. But there are other kinds of relationships.

Multiplicity

The multiplicity of a relationship refers to the number of participants at either end of the association. In the Entity Framework, an association's multiplicity determines the nature of the navigation properties that represent the relationship.

In the Entity Framework, there are always two ends to an association, regardless of the multiplicity. For example, we have customers at one end of a relationship and orders at the other end. The multiplicity describes how many items may be at a particular end, not how many ends there are.

You will sometimes want to represent more complex relationships—for example, a so-called *ternary* relationship involves three kinds of parties. This is a different concept from multiplicity and is called *degree*. For example, consider a teaching arrangement in a college, where a student is taught a subject by a teacher; this relationship involves three entities (student, subject, and teacher). These higher-degree relationships are typically modeled in the database by having a table just for the relationship itself. Likewise, the EDM does not directly support relationships with a degree of more than two, so you would represent such a relationship with a distinct entity type in the conceptual model, adding associations between that entity and all the participants in the relationship.

For each end of a relationship, you can specify a multiplicity of either 1, 0..1, or *. The first, 1, means what it says—there is always one item at that end of the association. The last, *, means any number—there can be zero, one, or several items at that end. A multiplicity of 0..1 means zero or one—this indicates that the association is optional, but where present, there is just one entity at this end.

In a *one-to-many* relationship, the two ends have a multiplicity of 1 and *, respectively. You can see this in Figure 14-2—the lines between entities represent associations, and the multiplicity appears at each end of the line. So an item at the first end can be related to any number of items at the second end; an item at the second end is always related to exactly one item at the first. In C#, the entity at the 1 end would have a navigation property that offers a collection, in order to provide access to the *many* end. The entity at the * end would provide a simpler noncollection property to get back to the one entity it is related to.

A variation on this theme has `0..1` instead of `1` at the first end, and * at the second end as before. This is similar to a one-to-many relationship, except items at the *many* end don't necessarily have to be related to an item at the other end. For example, you might want to represent the relationship between managers and their reports. But if you go far enough up the corporate hierarchy, you will find someone who has no manager—the navigation property would return null. So a simple one-to-many relationship doesn't work here—you would need `0..1` instead of `1` at the *manager* end of the association.

Sometimes *one-to-one* relationships crop up—each item at one end is always related to exactly one item at the other end. This is an unusual kind of relationship because it implies that entities are inextricably and exclusively linked. Relationships that sound like they might be one-to-one are often not. Here's an illustration from popular culture, describing a relationship between a master and an apprentice expressed as: "Always two, there are. No more, no less. A master, and an apprentice."[†] A master always has an apprentice, an apprentice always has a master, so isn't that a one-to-one relationship? In fact, this might need to be a one-to-many relationship because on the death of an apprentice, the master takes a new apprentice. (The apprentice has just one master, as the only career paths are promotion to master or untimely death. So we can at least be sure that this is not a many-to-many relationship.) The constraint expressed here is merely that the master has a one-at-a-time approach to relationships, much like serial monogamy. (For example, both Darth Maul and Darth Vader were apprentices of Darth Sidious.) So if the database needs to reflect the full history rather than just the current state, a one-to-one relationship won't be sufficient. (Although if you only need the database to store the current state, one-to-one might be fine here.) In databases, one-to-one relationships often exist because information about a single entity has been split across multiple tables, perhaps for performance reasons. (The EF lets you map this back to a single entity in the conceptual model, so such relationships are likely to be more common in the store schema than the conceptual schema.)

Variations on one-to-one where one or the other end is optional can be useful.[‡] For example, you might have an entity representing a customer and an entity representing an account. An organization (such as a butcher shop) might choose to have a policy where customers are not required to have accounts, but where accounts are held any single customer can have only one account, and accounts must be held by exactly one customer. (That's not the only imaginable policy, of course.) The relationship between

---

† Yoda discussing Sith terms of employment, from *Star Wars Episode I: The Phantom Menace*.

‡ Opinion is divided on whether this variant can still be called one-to-one. Strictly speaking it's incorrect, but in practice you'll see one-to-zero-or-one relationships widely described informally as one-to-one.

a customer entity and an account entity would have a multiplicity of 1 at the customer end and 0..1 at the account end.

Finally, there are *many-to-many* relationships. For example, you might have an entity type to represent a standard part such as an M3 bolt, and an entity to represent a part manufacturer. Many manufacturers are capable of producing M3 bolts, and most manufacturers produce more than one kind of product. To model the relationship of who produces what in the EDM, you could use an association with a multiplicity of * for both ends of the association. And in code, both entities would have navigation properties offering collections of objects.

However, there's an issue with many-to-many relationships in the EF. In the database, such a relationship is represented as a separate table, where each row contains two foreign keys, one for each end of the relationship. If that's all the table contains, the EF will happily let you map this table to an association in the conceptual model, and the navigation properties will work as described. However, if the table contains other information, you will end up needing to represent it as an entity in its own right. For example, given the product/manufacturer example earlier, it might turn out to be useful to know what product code a particular supplier uses for a particular standard product. There's no place for this information to go if you just have navigation properties on the product and manufacturer that point to one another—you would need an extra entity type to hold this property that is specific to a particular product/manufacturer combination.

This can get slightly awkward when there are columns in the relationship table that your application doesn't particularly care about, but which the EF insists are mapped because they are nonnullable and don't have default values. Your conceptual model would not be able to represent this table as a simple many-to-many association, because that would leave nowhere to map the relationship property. (The underlying issue here is the same one that prevents you from omitting certain database columns from your entities.)

Finally, we'll look at one more feature of the Entity Framework's mapping capabilities: support for inheritance.

Inheritance

Inheritance presents a challenge for an ORM, because the typical object-oriented notions of inheritance don't have any direct parallel in the relational model. Various solutions exist because there isn't one really good way to do this. The Entity Framework supports mappings for a couple of the popular approaches for attempting to bridge this chasm.

While there are several approaches to mapping (which we'll get to shortly), the conceptual model's handling of inheritance works the same way in all cases, and is very similar to inheritance in C#. Any entity type can optionally specify one other entity type as its base type. Entities with a base type inherit all the properties from that base. An entity cannot specify more than one base type, but you are allowed to derive from an entity that derives from another entity (i.e., you can have an inheritance chain). And the corresponding generated entity classes that you use from C# will represent these inheritance relationships with normal class inheritance.

You will need to define mappings for your base entity type in the usual way. All the derived types will inherit these mappings. The question is: how do we map features unique to individual derived types?

The first mapping approach involves mapping all entity types sharing a particular base entity type to a single table in the database. The entity type the EF chooses to represent a particular row is chosen based on a *discriminator* column—in the mapping you simply provide a list that says, for example, if the discriminator column contains 1, the entity type is `Employee`, and if it's 2, the type is `Manager`, while if it's 3, the type is `Director`, and so on. These derived types will presumably have additional properties distinguishing them from one another, and these would map to nullable columns in the table. They will need to be nullable, because these columns will have values only when you're using the derived types that support them—non-nullable database columns need to be mapped to properties in the base entity type if you're using this mapping style.

The second mapping approach uses a separate table for each derived type. Derived types still inherit the base mappings, so in this scenario, derived entity types will be involved with two or more tables: the table unique to the derived type, along with any tables used by the base type. This approach requires all the tables involved to use the same primary key.

None of these mapping features would be much use without some way to retrieve data from the database, so we'll now look at how to execute queries in the Entity Framework.

Queries

We've seen some simple LINQ-based examples for retrieving data from the database with the Entity Framework. Under the covers, the EF turns a LINQ query into a SQL query that the database understands. In fact, there are two ways of getting the EF to query the database for data: LINQ and something called Entity SQL. We've seen some simple LINQ to Entities examples already, but we'll now look at it in more detail.

LINQ to Entities

The LINQ provider for the Entity Framework, LINQ to Entities, supports all of the standard LINQ operators we saw in Chapter 8, but it works a little differently. The idea of *deferred execution* is still present, and it's even more important. The point at which you cause the LINQ query to execute—the instant at which your code first starts trying to use the results—is the point at which the EF will need to send a request to the database. So looking at the code from Example 14-3, the statement shown in Example 14-9 does not get anything from the database.

Example 14-9. Simple LINQ to Entities query expression

```
var orders = from order in dbContext.SalesOrderHeaders
             where order.OrderDate == orderDate
             select order;
```

As always with LINQ, a query expression only *defines* a query—`orders` is an object that knows what it's supposed to return if anything happens to enumerate it. So it's the `foreach` loop in Example 14-3 that kicks off the actual request.

The way the EF processes the request is different from how LINQ to Objects works. LINQ to Objects works by forming a chain of operators that work sequentially—the source collection might pass through the `Where` operator, followed by, say, an `OrderBy` or a `Group` operator. The `Where` operator in LINQ to Objects works by walking through every single item in the source, discarding the ones that don't meet the filter criteria, and the ones that do meet the criteria get passed on to the next item in the chain.

We really don't want data access code to work that way, and as mentioned earlier, the EF lets the database do the filtering, which is far more efficient than fetching an entire table and then filtering the items in code. We'll now verify that it really works this way by using the SQL Profiler tool to examine what the EF does for us.

 SQL Profiler is not part of SQL Server 2008 Express, not even if you install the version with advanced services and Management Studio. You will need a full edition of SQL Server. (The Developer edition will do.) SQL Profiler works just fine with the Express version of the database, but it's distributed and licensed only as part of the fuller editions. As long as you have a suitable license, you can install just the tools from a full edition SQL Server onto a machine that has only the Express version of the database, and it will work just fine. (Unfortunately, if you already installed the Express version of Management Studio, you can't install the full management tools on the same machine.)

A full description of the SQL Profiler is beyond the scope of this book—we're using it to show you exactly what the Entity Framework asked the database to do. However, it's a profoundly useful tool; even if you use it only for the simple task of discovering what SQL queries are being executed. If you plan to do much work with databases, it's well worth learning how to use it.

By single-stepping through the code in Visual Studio while running the SQL Profiler, we can see that nothing appears in the profiler until we start to execute the `foreach` loop, at which point the profiler shows an `Audit Login` message, indicating that our program has opened a connection to the database. This is followed by a

`RPC:Completed` message, indicating that SQL Server processed a request. When we select this message, the profiler shows the SQL that the EF just ran for us:

```
exec sp_executesql N'SELECT
[Extent1].[SalesOrderID] AS [SalesOrderID],
[Extent1].[RevisionNumber] AS [RevisionNumber],
[Extent1].[OrderDate] AS [OrderDate],
[Extent1].[DueDate] AS [DueDate],
[Extent1].[ShipDate] AS [ShipDate],
[Extent1].[Status] AS [Status],
[Extent1].[OnlineOrderFlag] AS [OnlineOrderFlag],
[Extent1].[SalesOrderNumber] AS [SalesOrderNumber],
[Extent1].[PurchaseOrderNumber] AS [PurchaseOrderNumber],
[Extent1].[AccountNumber] AS [AccountNumber],
[Extent1].[CustomerID] AS [CustomerID],
[Extent1].[ShipToAddressID] AS [ShipToAddressID],
[Extent1].[BillToAddressID] AS [BillToAddressID],
[Extent1].[ShipMethod] AS [ShipMethod],
[Extent1].[CreditCardApprovalCode] AS [CreditCardApprovalCode],
[Extent1].[SubTotal] AS [SubTotal],
[Extent1].[TaxAmt] AS [TaxAmt],
[Extent1].[Freight] AS [Freight],
[Extent1].[TotalDue] AS [TotalDue],
[Extent1].[Comment] AS [Comment],
[Extent1].[rowguid] AS [rowguid],
[Extent1].[ModifiedDate] AS [ModifiedDate]
FROM [SalesLT].[SalesOrderHeader] AS [Extent1]
WHERE [Extent1].[OrderDate] = @p__linq__0',
N'@p__linq__0 datetime',@p__linq__0='2004-06-01 00:00:00'
```

It might be quite long, but structurally that's a pretty simple `SELECT` statement. The only reason it's so large is that it explicitly requests every column required by the entity (and it has specified each column in a fairly verbose manner). The interesting part is in the last two lines. The penultimate line is a parameterized `WHERE` clause comparing the OrderDate to a named argument. This is what became of our LINQ query's where clause. And the final line provides a value for that named argument.

Note that you're free to chain operators together in LINQ to Entities just as you can in LINQ to Objects. For example, we could build on the orders query from Example 14-3:

```
var orderedOrders = orders.OrderBy(order => order.OrderDate);
```

Or, if you'd prefer to carry on using LINQ syntax, Example 14-10 is equivalent.

Example 14-10. Chained query

```
var orderedOrders = from order in orders
                    orderby order.OrderDate
                    select order;
```

This doesn't execute the orders query. It just means we have two queries now—the orders query that just filters, and then the orderedOrders query that filters and then sorts. You could think of this chained query as shorthand for Example 14-11, which explicitly combines the clauses from Example 14-9 and Example 14-10 into one query.

Example 14-11. That same query, written out in full

```
var orderedOrders = from order in dbContext.SalesOrderHeaders
                    where order.OrderDate == orderDate
                    orderby order.OrderDate
                    select order;
```

Regardless of the various equivalent ways we would build the second query, the result of executing it (e.g., by iterating over it in a foreach loop) is, as you'd expect, a SQL query that includes an ORDER BY clause as well as a WHERE clause. (And as it happens, that's not hugely useful because in this example database, all the orders have the exact same date. With slightly more realistic data, this would have the expected effect, though.)

So LINQ to Entities queries work in a fundamentally different way from the LINQ to Objects queries we saw previously. In LINQ to Objects, the expression in a where clause is simply a delegate in disguise—it's a method that the Where operator calls for each item in turn to work out whether to include that in the results. But with LINQ to Entities (and LINQ to SQL for that matter) the LINQ query's where clause has been translated into T-SQL and sent to the database—the expression we wrote in C# ends up running in a different language, probably on a different machine. If you want to understand how these kinds of queries are able to work so differently for different providers, see the sidebar on the next page.

This translation is obviously very useful for shifting the work to the database, but it brings some limitations. If you try to add arbitrary method calls into the middle of a LINQ query, it'll fail in LINQ to Entities. For example, suppose we have the following helper:

```
static DateTime NextDay(DateTime dt)
{
    return dt + TimeSpan.FromDays(1);
}
```

We could try to use this in a LINQ query:

```
var orders = from order in dbContext.SalesOrderHeaders
             where order.OrderDate == NextDay(orderDate)
             select order;
```

With LINQ to Objects this would work just fine—it's all just C# code, and you can use any valid Boolean expression in a where clause, including expressions that invoke methods. But with LINQ to Entities, although this will compile, the EF will throw a NotSupportedException at the point at which you try to execute the query. Its error message will read:

```
LINQ to Entities does not recognize the method 'System.DateTime
  NextDay(System.DateTime)' method, and this method cannot be translated into
  a store expression.
```

LINQ to Entities queries are limited to the things that the EF knows how to turn into database queries, and since it doesn't know anything about this NextDay method you've written, it can't work out how to do that. Of course, when you bear in mind that a LINQ to Entities query executes on the database, it's hardly surprising that you can't invoke arbitrary methods in your application from the middle of a query. But the EF integrates some database features into your code so seamlessly that it's sometimes easy to forget where the boundary between your application and the database lies.

Functions Delegates Versus Expressions

Database LINQ providers are able to translate LINQ queries into SQL because their versions of the LINQ operators exploit a feature added to C# 3.0 specifically to support this sort of thing. If you compare the LINQ to Entities declaration of the `Where` operator with its LINQ to Objects counterpart, you'll see a difference. As we saw in Chapter 8, LINQ to Objects is implemented as a set of extension methods for the `IEnumerable<T>` interface defined by the `Enumerable` type in the `System.Linq` namespace. Its `Where` operator is declared like this:

```
public static IEnumerable<TSource> Where<TSource>(
    this IEnumerable<TSource> source,
    Func<TSource, bool> predicate)
```

LINQ to Entities works in a similar fashion, but the extension methods are all for `IQueryable<T>`. Since the various properties the object context provides for accessing tables all implement `IQueryable<T>`, you'll end up using those extension methods instead of the LINQ to Objects ones. They are defined by the `Queryable` type, again in the `System.Linq` namespace. Here's its definition of the `Where` operator:

```
public static IQueryable<TSource> Where<TSource>(
    this IQueryable<TSource> source,
    Expression<Func<TSource, bool>> predicate)
```

Obviously, the first parameter is now an `IQueryable<T>`, but the second parameter's type is also different—rather than accepting a delegate for a predicate function, it now takes an *expression*. The `Expression<T>` type is a special type recognized by the C# compiler (and also the VB.NET compiler). When you call methods that expect an `Expression<Func<T, TResult>>`, you just provide a normal lambda like you can with an ordinary `Func<T,TResult>`, but the compiler builds a data structure that is essentially an abstract syntax tree for the expression—in effect, an object model describing that structure of the code.

So while this version of the `Where` operator looks completely normal when we use it from a LINQ query, it will be passed a description of the expression, rather than a delegate to a method. (An `Expression<T>` isn't compiled into a real method, whereas an ordinary `Func` delegate would be. However, expressions offer a `Compile` method, so you can turn them into code at runtime if necessary.) The database LINQ providers, like the EF and LINQ to SQL, use this description to work out what the database query's `WHERE` clause should look like.

While LINQ to Entities is a very convenient way to build queries, it's just a layer on top of the Entity Framework's underlying query system, which has its own query language.

Entity SQL

The Entity Framework defines a query language for making queries against the conceptual model—rather than running queries against a database, as you do in normal SQL dialects, you can run queries that work directly against the entities in your model, as the name *Entity SQL* (or ESQL) suggests.

 ESQL can be used for queries against the EDM storage model too. So it can also function as a kind of vendor-neutral SQL. But here we're focusing on queries that target the conceptual model.

Why do we need a second way of making queries when we already have LINQ to Entities? Well, from a historical perspective that question has things back to front: during the Entity Framework's development, ESQL was around long before LINQ to Entities. But since LINQ to Entities made it into the first version of the EF, it's still reasonable to ask why we have both, what ESQL is for, and when it might look like a better choice than LINQ.

ESQL's main benefit is that it's sometimes useful to be able to represent a query as text. In fact, the Entity Data Model itself exploits this—there are some advanced scenarios in which ESQL queries can be embedded in the *.edmx* file. LINQ wouldn't be an option here because *.edmx* is just XML; to use LINQ requires a language that supports LINQ.§ If you wanted to store custom queries in a configuration file, you really wouldn't want to have to run the C# compiler at runtime to interpret the queries. And with ESQL you don't need to—you can represent a query as a string and the EF can execute that for you at runtime.

Another feature of a string-based query language is that it's relatively easy to compose queries at runtime. With a LINQ query expression, the structure is fixed at compile time and you only really get to tweak individual arguments, much like a fixed SQL query with a few named arguments. (Technically, it is actually possible to build LINQ queries dynamically. After all, LINQ operators are chained together with simple function calls. However, dynamic composition of `Expression<T>` trees turns out to be surprisingly difficult. It's not a scenario C# attempts to help you with—you end up having to construct the expression trees without the compiler's assistance. This is not for the fainthearted.)

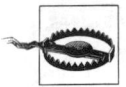 The practice of stitching together strings to form dynamic queries is messy and can be fraught with security issues such as injection attacks. It's occasionally useful if you understand the risks and can mitigate them, but you need to exercise extreme caution.

---

§ And in case you're wondering about LINQ to XML, that doesn't help here. It lets you use LINQ-capable languages like C# or VB.NET to write LINQ queries to look in an XML document. It doesn't let you put LINQ queries in an XML document.

Of course, string-based queries have a massive downside compared to LINQ: the C# compiler cannot offer any help as it doesn't understand ESQL. If your ESQL strings are badly formed, you only get to find that out at runtime. And even if your ESQL is syntactically correct, C# does not understand the relationship between it and your code—whereas with a LINQ to Entities query C# can detect things such as type mismatches, it won't spot when your ESQL gets out of sync with the code that uses the results.

Besides the inherent benefits and disadvantages of a string-based query, there's also the fact that ESQL is, in effect, the native query language for the EF. This means there are a few EF features that can be accessed only through ESQL, although they're all somewhat arcane. For example, an ESQL query can navigate associations between entities even if you've neglected to define navigation properties to represent those associations.

Example 14-12 shows a simple example that illustrates the basic use of ESQL.

Example 14-12. Querying with ESQL

```
using (var dbContext = new AdventureWorksLT2008Entities())
{
    DateTime orderDate = new DateTime(2004, 6, 1);
    var query = dbContext.CreateQuery<SalesOrderHeader>("SELECT VALUE o " +
            "FROM AdventureWorksLT2008Entities.SalesOrderHeaders AS o " +
            "WHERE o.OrderDate = @orderDate",
        new ObjectParameter("orderDate", orderDate));

    foreach (var order in query)
    {
        Console.WriteLine(order.TotalDue);
    }
}
```

This has the same effect as Example 14-3, but using ESQL in place of a LINQ query. While this looks similar to a typical SQL query, the `VALUE` keyword is specific to ESQL. We use this to indicate that we don't want the usual column-like behavior of SQL. You can write a more traditional-looking query in ESQL, such as:

```
SELECT o.TotalDue, o.OrderDate
    FROM AdventureWorksLT2008Entities.SalesOrderHeaders AS o
    WHERE o.OrderDate = @orderDate
```

This asks for specific columns from the entity rather than the whole entity. This is legal ESQL, but it would fail at runtime in the context of Example 14-12. That example creates the query with a call to `CreateQuery<SalesOrderHeader>` on the object context. The generic type argument to `CreateQuery`—`SalesOrderHeader` here—indicates the type of result we're expecting from the query, but this modified query clearly returns something other than a `SalesOrderHeader`. It returns a couple of columns from each matching entity. When you build a query like this, you get back objects that implement `IDataRecord`—a general-purpose interface used across all of ADO.NET to represent a record (such as a table row) whose columns might not be known until runtime. (This is one of the interfaces listed in Table 14-1.) So you'd need to use `CreateQuery<IDataRecord>` to create such a query, and a suitably modified loop to extract the results:

```
var query = dbContext.CreateQuery<IDataRecord>(
    "SELECT o.TotalDue, o.OrderDate " +
        "FROM AdventureWorksLT2008Entities.SalesOrderHeaders AS o " +
        "WHERE o.OrderDate = @orderDate",
    new ObjectParameter("orderDate", orderDate));

foreach (var order in query)
{
    Console.WriteLine(order["TotalDue"]);
}
```

Even if you ask for the whole entity as a single column in the `SELECT` clause, for example:

```
SELECT o
    FROM AdventureWorksLT2008Entities.SalesOrderHeaders AS o
    WHERE o.OrderDate = @orderDate
```

the query will still return `IDataRecord` objects, not entities. Each data record returned by this query would have a single column called `o` that contains a `SalesOrderHeader` entity. To get to the entity you'd need to unwrap it inside your loop:

```
foreach (var row in query)
{
    SalesOrderHeader o = (SalesOrderHeader) row["o"];
    Console.WriteLine(o.TotalDue);
}
```

The `VALUE` keyword is just a shortcut that tells ESQL to omit the `IDataRecord` wrapper, and to return a sequence of unwrapped entities. This enables Example 14-12 to assume that it will get `SalesOrderHeader` entities back from the query.

Mixing ESQL and LINQ

LINQ to Entities and ESQL are not mutually exclusive. You are free to use an ESQL query as the source for a LINQ query. Here's a contrived example:

```
var orders = dbContext.CreateQuery<SalesOrderHeader>("SELECT VALUE o " +
        "FROM AdventureWorksLT2008Entities.SalesOrderHeaders AS o " +
        "WHERE o.OrderDate = @orderDate",
    new ObjectParameter("orderDate", orderDate));

var orderedOrders = from order in orders
                    orderby order.DueDate
                    select order;
```

This might be useful if you wanted to store ESQL queries in some sort of configuration mechanism to allow the exact query to be changed, but to do further processing of the results of that query with LINQ.

The EntityClient ADO.NET Provider

Yet another feature enabled by ESQL is that it lets code built around the v1 ADO.NET mechanisms shown in Example 14-1 work with the EF. The `System.Data.Entity Client` namespace defines concrete types that derive from the abstract base classes listed in Table 14-1: `EntityConnection` derives from `DbConnection`, `EntityCommand` derives from `DbCommand`, and so on. As far as code written to use these abstract base classes is concerned, the Entity Framework ends up looking like just another database with another funky variety of SQL. As long as your ESQL selects only column values and not whole entities, queries will only ever return the same basic data types other providers would, so the behavior will look much like any other ADO.NET v1 provider.

Object Context

As you've seen, the object context provides access to entities. For each entity we define in our EDM, the generated object context class provides a property that we can use as the source for a LINQ query. We've also used its `CreateQuery<T>` method to build ESQL-based queries. The object context provides some other services.

Connection Handling

To execute database queries, it's necessary to connect to a database, so the object context needs connection information. This information typically lives in the *App.config* file—when you first run the EDM wizard, it will add a configuration file if your application does not already have one, and then it adds a connection string. Example 14-13 shows a configuration file containing a typical Entity Framework connection string. (This has been split over multiple lines to fit—normally the `connectionString` attribute is all on one line.)

Example 14-13. Connection string in App.config

```
<configuration>
  <connectionStrings>
    <add name="AdventureWorksLT2008Entities"
        connectionString="metadata=res://*/AdventureWorksModel.csdl|
res://*/AdventureWorksModel.ssdl|res://*/AdventureWorksModel.msl;
provider=System.Data.SqlClient;provider connection string=
&quot;Data Source=.\sqlexpress;Initial Catalog=AdventureWorksLT2008;
Integrated Security=True;MultipleActiveResultSets=True&quot;"
        providerName="System.Data.EntityClient" />
  </connectionStrings>
</configuration>
```

This is a rather more complex connection string than the one we saw back in Example 14-1, because the Entity Framework needs three things in its connection string: information on where to find the EDM definition, the type of underlying database provider to use, and the connection string to pass to that underlying provider. This last part—an ordinary SQL Server connection string, enclosed in " character entities—is highlighted in Example 14-13 in bold.

The three URIs in the metadata section of the `connectionString`—the ones beginning with `res://`—point to the three parts of the EDM: the conceptual schema, the storage schema, and the mappings. Visual Studio extracts these from the *.edmx* file and embeds them as three XML resource streams in the compiled program. Without these, the EF wouldn't know what the conceptual and storage schemas are supposed to look like, or how to map between them.

> It may seem a bit weird for the locations of these EDM resources to be in a connection string. It might seem more natural for the XML to use a separate attribute for each one. However, as you've seen, the `System.Data.EntityClient` namespace conforms to the ADO.NET v1 model so that it's possible for old-style data access code to perform queries against the EDM. Since the ADO.NET v1 model includes an assumption that it's possible to put all the information defining a particular data source into a single connection string, the Entity Framework has to follow suit. And since the EF cannot function without the XML EDM definitions, the connection string has to say where those live.

After the EDM metadata resources, you can see a `provider` property, which in Example 14-13 indicates that the underlying database connection is to be provided by the SQL Server client. The EF passes the `provider connection string` on to that provider.

You don't have to use the *App.config* to configure the connection. The object context offers a constructor overload that accepts a connection string. The configuration file is useful—it's where the object context's no-parameters constructor we've been using in the examples gets its connection information from—but what if you want to let just the underlying database connection string be configurable, while keeping the parts of the connection string identifying the EDM resources fixed? Example 14-14 shows how you could achieve this. It retrieves the configured values for these two pieces and uses the `EntityConnectionStringBuilder` helper to combine this with the EDM resource locations, forming a complete EF connection string.

Example 14-14. Passing an explicit connection string

```
using System.Configuration;
using System.Data.EntityClient;

...


// Retrieve the connection string for the underlying database provider.
ConnectionStringSettings dbConnectionInfo =
    ConfigurationManager.ConnectionStrings["AdventureWorksSql"];

var csb = new EntityConnectionStringBuilder();
```

```
csb.Provider = dbConnectionInfo.ProviderName;
csb.ProviderConnectionString = dbConnectionInfo.ConnectionString;
csb.Metadata = "res://*/AdventureWorksModel.csdl|" +
    "res://*/AdventureWorksModel.ssdl|res://*/AdventureWorksModel.msl";


using (var dbContext = new AdventureWorksLT2008Entities(csb.ConnectionString))
{
    ...
}
```

This code uses the `ConfigurationManager` in the `System.Configuration` namespace, which provides a `ConnectionStrings` property. (This is in a part of the .NET Framework class library that's not referenced by default in a .NET console application, so we need to add a reference to the `System.Configuration` component for this to work.) This provides access to any connection strings in your *App.config* file; it's the same mechanism the EF uses to find its default connection string. Now that Example 14-14 is providing the EDM resources in code, our configuration file only needs the SQL Server part of the connection string, as shown in Example 14-15 (with a long line split across multiple lines to fit). So when the application is deployed, we have the flexibility to configure which database gets used, but we have removed any risk that such a configuration change might accidentally break the references to the EDM resources.

Example 14-15. SQL Server connection string

```
<configuration>
  <connectionStrings>
    <add name="AdventureWorksSql" providerName="System.Data.SqlClient"
        connectionString="Data Source=.\sqlexpress;
                Initial Catalog=AdventureWorksLT2008;
                Integrated Security=True;MultipleActiveResultSets=True"
    />

  </connectionStrings>
</configuration>
```

Besides being able to change the connection information, what else can we do with the connection? We could choose to open the connection manually—we might want to verify that our code can successfully connect to the database. But in practice, we don't usually do that—the EF will connect automatically when we need to. The main reason for connecting manually would be if you wanted to keep the connection open across multiple requests—if the EF opens a connection for you it will close it again. In any case, we need to be prepared for exceptions anytime we access the database—being able to connect successfully is no guarantee that someone won't trip over a network cable at some point between us manually opening the connection and attempting to execute a query. So in practice, the connection string is often the only aspect of the connection we need to take control of.

Creating, Updating, and Deleting

So far, all of our examples have just fetched existing data from the database. Most real applications will also need to be able to add, change, and remove data. So as you'd expect, the Entity Framework supports the full range of so-called CRUD (Create, Read, Update, and Delete) operations. This involves the object context, because it is responsible for tracking changes and coordinating updates.

Updates—modifications to existing records—are pretty straightforward. Entities' properties are modifiable, so you can simply assign new values. However, the EF does not attempt to update the database immediately. You might want to change multiple properties, in which case it would be inefficient to make a request to the database for each property in turn, and that might not even work—integrity constraints in the database may mean that certain changes need to be made in concert. So the EF just remembers what changes you have made, and attempts to apply those changes back to the database only when you call the object context's `SaveChanges` method. Example 14-16 does this. In fact, most of the code here just fetches a specific entity—the most recent order of a particular customer—and only the last couple of statements modify that order.

Example 14-16. Modifying an existing entity

```
using (var dbContext = new AdventureWorksLT2008Entities())
{
    var orderQuery = from customer in dbContext.Customers
                     where customer.CustomerID == 29531
                     from order in customer.SalesOrderHeaders
                     orderby order.OrderDate descending
                     select order;

    SalesOrderHeader latestOrder = orderQuery.First();

    latestOrder.Comment = "Call customer when goods ready to ship";

    dbContext.SaveChanges();
}
```

To add a brand-new entity, you need to create a new entity object of the corresponding class, and then tell the object context you've done so—for each entity type, the context provides a corresponding method for adding entities. In our example, the context has `AddToCustomers`, `AddToSalesOrderHeaders`, and `AddToSalesOrderDetails` methods. You will need to make sure you satisfy the database's constraints, which means that the code in Example 14-17 will *not* be enough.

Example 14-17. Failing to meet constraints on a new entity

```
SalesOrderDetail detail = new SalesOrderDetail();
dbContext.AddToSalesOrderDetails(detail);

// Will throw an exception!
dbContext.SaveChanges();
```

The Entity Framework will throw an `UpdateException` when Example 14-17 calls `SaveChanges` because the entity is missing all sorts of information. The example database's schema includes a number of integrity constraints, and will refuse to allow a new row to be added to the `SalesOrderDetail` table unless it meets all the requirements. Example 14-18 sets the bare minimum number of properties to keep the database happy. (This is probably not good enough for real code, though—we've not specified any price information, and the numeric price fields will have default values of 0; while this doesn't upset the database, it might not please the accountants.)

Example 14-18. Adding a new entity

```
// ...where latestOrder is a SalesOrderHeader fetched with code like
// that in Example 14-16.

SalesOrderDetail detail = new SalesOrderDetail();
detail.SalesOrderHeader = latestOrder;
detail.ModifiedDate = DateTime.Now;
detail.OrderQty = 1;
detail.ProductID = 680;      // HL Road Frame - Black, 58

dbContext.AddToSalesOrderDetails(detail);

dbContext.SaveChanges();
```

Several of the constraints involve relationships. A `SalesOrderDetail` row must be related to a particular row in the `Product` table, because that's how we know what products the customer has ordered. We've not defined an entity type corresponding to the `Product` table, so Example 14-18 just plugs in the relevant foreign key value directly.

The database also requires that each `SalesOrderDetail` row be related to exactly one `SalesOrderHeader` row—remember that this was one of the one-to-many relationships we saw earlier. (The header has a multiplicity of one, and the detail has a multiplicity of many.) The constraint in the database requires the `SalesOrderID` foreign key column in each `SalesOrderDetail` row to correspond to the key for an existing `SalesOrder Header` row. But unlike the `ProductID` column, we don't set the corresponding property directly on the entity. Instead, the second line of Example 14-18 sets the new entity's `SalesOrderHeader` property, which as you may recall is a *navigation property*.

When adding new entities that must be related to other entities, you normally indicate the relationships with the corresponding navigation properties. In this example, you could add the new `SalesOrderDetail` object to a `SalesOrderHeader` object's `SalesOrderDetails` navigation property—since a header may have many related details, the property is a collection and offers an `Add` method. Or you can work with the other end of the relationship as Example 14-18 does. This is the usual way to deal with the relationships of a newly created entity—setting foreign key properties directly as we did for the other relationships here is somewhat unusual. We did that only because our EDM does not include all of the relevant entities—we represent only three of the tables because a complete model for this particular example would have been too big to fit legibly onto a single page. There may also be situations where you know that in your particular application, the key values required will never change, and you might choose to cache those key values to avoid the overhead of involving additional entities.

We've seen how to update existing data and add new data. This leaves deletion. It's pretty straightforward: if you have an entity object, you can pass it to the context's `DeleteObject` method, and the next time you call `SaveChanges`, the EF will attempt to delete the relevant row, as shown in Example 14-19.

Example 14-19. Deleting an entity

```
dbContext.DeleteObject(detail);

dbContext.SaveChanges();
```

As with any kind of change to the database, this will succeed only if it does not violate any of the database's integrity constraints. For example, deleting an entity at the *one* end of a one-to-many relationship may fail if the database contains one or more rows at the *many* end that are related to the item you're trying to delete. (Alternatively, the database might automatically delete all related items—SQL Server allows a constraint to require *cascading deletes*. This takes a different approach to enforcing the constraint—rather than rejecting the attempt to delete the parent item, it deletes all the children automatically.)

Example 14-18 adds new information that relates to information already in the database—it adds a new detail to an existing order. This is a very common thing to do, but it raises a challenge: what if code elsewhere in the system was working on the same data? Perhaps some other computer has deleted the order you were trying to add detail for. The EF supports a couple of common ways of managing this sort of hazard: transactions and optimistic concurrency.

Transactions

Transactions are an extremely useful mechanism for dealing with concurrency hazards efficiently, while keeping data access code reasonably simple. Transactions provide the illusion that each individual database client has exclusive access to the entire database for as long as it needs to do a particular job—it has to be an illusion because if clients really took it in turns, scalability would be severely limited. So transactions perform the neat trick of letting work proceed in parallel except for when that would cause a problem—as long as all the transactions currently in progress are working on independent data they can all proceed simultaneously, and clients have to wait their turn only if they're trying to use data already involved (directly, or indirectly) in some other transaction in progress.‖

The classic example of the kind of problem transactions are designed to avoid is that of updating the balance of a bank account. Consider what needs to happen to your account when you withdraw money from an ATM—the bank will want to make sure that your account is debited with the amount of money withdrawn. This will involve subtracting that amount from the current balance, so there will be at least two operations: discovering the current balance, and then updating it to the new value. (Actually it'll be a whole lot more complex than that—there will be withdrawal limit checks, fraud detection, audit trails, and more. But the simplified example is enough to illustrate how transactions can be useful.) But what happens if some other transaction occurs at the same time? Maybe you happen to be making a withdrawal at the same time as the bank processes an electronic transfer of funds.

If that happens, a problem can arise. Suppose the ATM transaction and the electronic transfer both read the current balance—perhaps they both discover a balance of $1,234. Next, if the transfer is moving $1,000 from your account to somewhere else, it will write back a new balance of $234—the original balance minus the amount just deducted. But there's the ATM transfer—suppose you withdraw $200. It will write back a new balance of $1,034. You just withdrew $200 and paid $1,000 to another account, but your account only has $200 less in it than before rather than $1,200—that's great for you, but your bank will be less happy. (In fact, your bank probably has all sorts of checks and balances to try to minimize opportunities such as this for money to magically come into existence. So they'd probably notice such an error even if they weren't using transactions.) In fact, neither you nor your bank really wants this to happen, not least because it's easy enough to imagine similar examples where you lose money.

This problem of concurrent changes to shared data crops up in all sorts of forms. You don't even need to be modifying data to observe a problem: code that only ever reads can still see weird results. For example, you might want to count your money, in which case looking at the balances of all your accounts would be necessary—that's a read-only operation. But what if some other code was in the middle of transferring money between two of your accounts? Your read-only code could be messed up by other code modifying the data.

‖ In fact, it gets a good deal cleverer than that. Databases go to some lengths to avoid making clients wait for one another unless it's absolutely necessary, and can sometimes manage this even when clients are accessing the same data, particularly if they're only reading the common data. Not all databases do this in the same way, so consult your database documentation for further details.

A simple way to avoid this is to do one thing at a time—as long as each task completes before the next begins, you'll never see this sort of problem. But that turns out to be impractical if you're dealing with a large volume of work. And that's why we have transactions—they are designed to make it look like things are happening one task at a time, but under the covers they allow tasks to proceed concurrently as long as they're working on unrelated information. So with transactions, the fact that some other bank customer is in the process of performing a funds transfer will not stop you from using an ATM. But if a transfer is taking place on one of your accounts at the same time that you are trying to withdraw money, transactions would ensure that these two operations take it in turns.

So code that uses transactions effectively gets exclusive access to whatever data it is working with right now, without slowing down anything it's not using. This means you get the best of both worlds: you can write code as though it's the only code running right now, but you get good throughput.

How do we exploit transactions in C#? Example 14-20 shows the simplest approach: if you create a `TransactionScope` object, the EF will automatically enlist any database operations in the same transaction. The `TransactionScope` class is defined in the `System.Transactions` namespace in the `System.Transactions` DLL (another class library DLL for which we need to add a reference, as it's not in the default set).

Example 14-20. TransactionScope

```
using (var dbContext = new AdventureWorksLT2008Entities())
{
    using (var txScope = new TransactionScope())
    {
        var customersWithOrders = from cust in dbContext.Customers
                                  where cust.SalesOrderHeaders.Count > 0
                                  select cust;

        foreach (var customer in customersWithOrders)
        {
            Console.WriteLine("Customer {0} has {1} orders",
                customer.CustomerID, customer.SalesOrderHeaders.Count);
        }

        txScope.Complete();
    }
}
```

For as long as the `TransactionScope` is active (i.e., until it is disposed at the end of the using block), all the requests to the database this code makes will be part of the same transaction, and so the results should be consistent—any other database client that tries to modify the state we're looking at will be made to wait (or we'll be made to wait for them) in order to guarantee consistency. The call to `Complete` at the end indicates that we have finished all the work in the transaction, and are happy for it to commit—without this, the transaction would be aborted at the end of the scope's using block.

For a transaction that modifies data, failure to call `Complete` will lose any changes. Since the transaction in Example 14-20 only reads data, this might not cause any visible problems, but it's difficult to be certain. If a `TransactionScope` was already active on this thread (e.g., a function farther up the call stack started one) our `Transaction Scope` could join in with the same transaction, at which point failure to call `Complete` on our scope would end up aborting the whole thing, possibly losing data. The documentation recommends calling `Complete` for all transactions except those you want to abort, so it's a good practice always to call it.

Transaction Length

When transactions conflict because multiple clients want to use the same data, the database may have no choice but to make one or more of the clients wait. This means you should keep your transaction lifetimes as short as you possibly can—slow transactions can bog down the system. And once that starts happening, it becomes a bit of a pile-up—the more transactions that are stuck waiting for something else to finish, the more likely it is that new transactions will want to use data that's already under contention. The rosy "best of both worlds" picture painted earlier evaporates.

Worse, conflicts are sometimes irreconcilable—a database doesn't know at the start of a transaction what information will be used, and sometimes it can find itself in a place where it cannot proceed without returning results that will look inconsistent, in which case it'll just fail with an error. (In other words, the clever tricks databases use to minimize how often transactions block sometimes backfire.) It's easy enough to contrive pathological code that does this on purpose, but you hope not to see it in a live system. The shorter you make your transactions the less likely you are to see troublesome conflicts.

You should never start a transaction and then wait for user input before finishing the transaction—users have a habit of going to lunch mid-transaction. Transaction duration should be measured in milliseconds, not minutes.

`TransactionScope` represents an *implicit transaction*—any data access performed inside its `using` block will automatically be enlisted on the transaction. That's why Example 14-20 never appears to use the `TransactionScope` it creates—it's enough for it to exist. (The transaction system keeps track of which threads have active implicit transactions.) You can also work with transactions explicitly—the object context provides a `Connection` property, which in turn offers explicit `BeginTransaction` and `EnlistTran saction` methods. You can use these in advanced scenarios where you might need to control database-specific aspects of the transaction that an implicit transaction cannot reach.

 These transaction models are not specific to the EF. You can use the same techniques with ADO.NET v1-style data access code.

Besides enabling isolation of multiple concurrent operations, transactions provide another very useful property: atomicity. This means that the operations within a single transaction succeed or fail as one: *all* succeed, or *none* of them succeed—a transaction is indivisible in that it cannot complete partially. The database stores updates performed within a transaction provisionally until the transaction completes—if it succeeds, the updates are permanently committed, but if it fails, they are rolled back and it's as though the updates never occurred. The EF uses transactions automatically when you call SaveChanges—if you have not supplied a transaction, it will create one just to write the updates. (If you have supplied one, it'll just use yours.) This means that SaveChanges will always either succeed completely, or have no effect at all, whether or not you provide a transaction.

Transactions are not the only way to solve problems of concurrent access to shared data. They are bad at handling long-running operations. For example, consider a system for booking seats on a plane or in a theater. End users want to see what seats are available, and will then take some time—minutes probably—to decide what to do. It would be a terrible idea to use a transaction to handle this sort of scenario, because you'd effectively have to lock out all other users looking to book into the same flight or show until the current user makes a decision. (It would have this effect because in order to show available seats, the transaction would have had to inspect the state of every seat, and could potentially change the state of any one of those seats. So all those seats are, in effect, owned by that transaction until it's done.)

Let's just think that through. What if every person who flies on a particular flight takes two minutes to make all the necessary decisions to complete his booking? (Hours of queuing in airports and observing fellow passengers lead us to suspect that this is a hopelessly optimistic estimate. If you know of an airline whose passengers are that competent, please let us know—we'd like to spend less time queuing.) The Airbus A380 aircraft has FAA and EASA approval to carry 853 passengers, which suggests that even with our uncommonly decisive passengers, that's still a total of more than 28 hours of decision making for each flight. That sounds like it could be a problem for a daily flight.# So there's no practical way of avoiding having to tell the odd passenger that, sorry, in between showing him the seat map and choosing the seat, someone else got in there first. In other words, we are going to have to accept that sometimes data will

---

#And yes, bookings for daily scheduled flights are filled up gradually over the course of a few months, so 28 hours per day is not necessarily a showstopper. Even so, forcing passengers to wait until nobody else is choosing a seat would be problematic—you'd almost certainly find that your customers didn't neatly space out their usage of the system, and so you'd get times where people wanting to book would be unable to. Airlines would almost certainly lose business the moment they told customers to come back later.

change under our feet, and that we just have to deal with it when it happens. This requires a slightly different approach than transactions.

Optimistic Concurrency

Optimistic concurrency describes an approach to concurrency where instead of enforcing isolation, which is how transactions usually work, we just make the cheerful assumption that nothing's going to go wrong. And then, crucially, we verify that assumption just before making any changes.

 In practice, it's common to use a mixture of optimistic concurrency and transactions. You might use optimistic approaches to handle long-running logic, while using short-lived transactions to manage each individual step of the process.

For example, an airline booking system that shows a map of available seats in an aircraft on a web page would make the optimistic assumption that the seat the user selects will probably not be selected by any other user in between the moment at which the application showed the available seats and the point at which the user picks a seat. The advantage of making this assumption is that there's no need for the system to lock anyone else out—any number of users can all be looking at the seat map at once, and they can all take as long as they like.

Occasionally, multiple users will pick the same seat at around the same time. Most of the time this won't happen, but the occasional clash is inevitable. We just have to make sure we notice. So when the user gets back to us and says that he wants seat 7K, the application then has to go back to the database to see if that seat is in fact still free. If it is, the application's optimism has been vindicated, and the booking can proceed. If not, we just have to apologize to the user (or chastise him for his slowness, depending on the prevailing attitude to customer service in your organization), show him an updated seat map so that he can see which seats have been claimed while he was dithering, and ask him to make a new choice. This will happen only a small fraction of the time, and so it turns out to be a reasonable solution to the problem—certainly better than a system that is incapable of taking enough bookings to fill the plane in the time available.

Sometimes optimistic concurrency is implemented in an application-specific way. The example just described relies on an understanding of what the various entities involved mean, and would require us to write code that explicitly performs the check described. But slightly more general solutions are available—they are typically less efficient, but they can require less code. The EF offers some of these ignorant-but-effective approaches to optimistic concurrency.

The default EF behavior seems, at a first glance, to be ignorant and broken—not only does it optimistically assume that nothing will go wrong, but it doesn't even do anything to check that assumption. We might call this blind optimism—we don't even get to discover when our optimism turned out to be unfounded. While that sounds bad, it's actually the right thing to do if you're using transactions—transactions enforce isolation and so additional checks would be a waste of time. But if you're not using transactions, this default behavior is not good enough for code that wants to change or add data—you'll risk compromising the integrity of your application's state.

To get the EF to check that updates are likely to be sound, you can tell it to check that certain entity properties have not changed since the entity was populated from the database. For example, in the `SalesOrderDetail` entity, if you select the `ModifiedDate` property in the EDM designer, you could go to the Properties panel and set its Concurrency Mode to Fixed (its default being None). This will cause the EF to check that this particular column's value is the same as it was when the entity was fetched whenever you update it. And as long as all the code that modifies this particular table remembers to update the `ModifiedDate`, you'll be able to detect when things have changed.

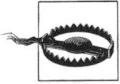

While this example illustrates the concept, it's not entirely robust. Using a date and time to track when a row changes has a couple of problems. First, different computers in the system are likely to have slight differences between their clocks, which can lead to anomalies. And even if only one computer ever accesses the database, its clock may be adjusted from time to time. You'd end up wanting to customize the SQL code used for updates so that everything uses the database server's clock for consistency. Such customizations are possible, but they are beyond the scope of this book. And even that might not be enough—if the row is updated often, it's possible that two updates might have the same timestamp due to insufficient precision. A stricter approach based on GUIDs or sequential row version numbers is more robust. But this is the realm of database design, rather than Entity Framework usage—ultimately you're going to be stuck with whatever your DBA gives you.

If any of the columns with a Concurrency Mode of Fixed change between reading an entity's value and attempting to update it, the EF will detect this when you call `SaveChanges` and will throw an `OptimisticConcurrencyException`, instead of completing the update.

The EF detects changes by making the SQL `UPDATE` conditional—its `WHERE` clause will include checks for all of the `Fixed` columns. It inspects the updated row count that comes back from the database to see whether the update succeeded.

How you deal with an optimistic concurrency failure is up to your application—you might simply be able to retry the work, or you may have to get the user involved. It will depend on the nature of the data you're trying to update.

The object context provides a Refresh method that you can call to bring entities back into sync with the current state of the rows they represent in the database. You could call this after catching an OptimisticConcurrencyException as the first step in your code that recovers from a problem. (You're not actually required to wait until you get a concurrency exception—you're free to call Refresh at any time.) The first argument to Refresh tells it what you'd like to happen if the database and entity are out of sync. Passing RefreshMode.StoreWins tells the EF that you want the entity to reflect what's currently in the database, even if that means discarding updates previously made in memory to the entity. Or you can pass RefreshMode.ClientWins, in which case any changes in the entity remain present in memory. The changes will not be written back to the database until you next call SaveChanges. So the significance of calling Refresh in ClientWins mode is that you have, in effect, acknowledged changes to the underlying database—if changes in the database were previously causing SaveChanges to throw an OptimisticConcurrencyException, calling SaveChanges again after the Refresh will not throw again (unless the database changes again in between the call to Refresh and the second SaveChanges).

Context and Entity Lifetime

If you ask the context object for the same entity twice, it will return you the same object both times—it remembers the identity of the entities it has returned. Even if you use different queries, it will not attempt to load fresh data for any entities already loaded unless you explicitly pass them to the Refresh method.

> Executing the same LINQ query multiple times against the same context will still result in multiple queries being sent to the database. Those queries will typically return all the current data for the relevant entity. But the EF will look at primary keys in the query results, and if they correspond to entities it has already loaded, it just returns those existing entities and won't notice if their values in the database have changed. It looks for changes only when you call either SaveChanges or Refresh.

This raises the question of how long you should keep an object context around. The more entities you ask it for, the more objects it'll hang on to. Even when your code has finished using a particular entity object, the .NET Framework's garbage collector won't be able to reclaim the memory it uses for as long as the object context remains alive, because the object context keeps hold of the entity in case it needs to return it again in a later query.

> The way to get the object context to let go of everything is to call Dispose. This is why all of the examples that show the creation of an object context do so in a using statement.

There are other lifetime issues to bear in mind. In some situations, an object context may hold database connections open. And also, if you have a long-lived object context, you may need to add calls to Refresh to ensure that you have fresh data, which you wouldn't have to do with a newly created object context. So all the signs suggest that you don't want to keep the object context around for too long.

How long is too long? In a web application, if you create an object context while handling a request (e.g., for a particular page) you would normally want to Dispose it before the end of that request—keeping an object context alive across multiple requests is typically a bad idea. In a Windows application (WPF or Windows Forms), it might make sense to keep an object context alive a little longer, because you might want to keep entities around while a form for editing the data in them is open. (If you want to apply updates, you normally use the same object context you used when fetching the entities in the first place, although it's possible to detach an entity from one context and attach it later to a different one.) In general, though, a good rule of thumb is to keep the object context alive for no longer than is necessary.

WCF Data Services

The last data access feature we'll look at is slightly different from the rest. So far, we've seen how to write code that uses data in a program that can connect directly to a database. But WCF Data Services lets you present data over HTTP, making data access possible from code in some scenarios where direct connections are not possible. It defines a URI structure for identifying the data you'd like to access, and the data itself can be represented in either JSON or the XML-based Atom Publishing Protocol (AtomPub).

As the use of URIs, JSON, and XML suggests, WCF Data Services can be useful in web applications. Silverlight cannot access databases directly, but it can consume data via WCF Data Services. And the JSON support means that it's also relatively straightforward for script-based web user interfaces to use.

WCF Data Services is designed to work in conjunction with the Entity Framework. You don't just present an entire database over HTTP—that would be a security liability. Instead, you define an Entity Data Model, and you can then configure which entity types should be accessible over HTTP, and whether they are read-only or support other operations such as updates, inserts, or deletes. And you can add code to implement further restrictions based on authentication and whatever security policy you require. (Of course, this still gives you plenty of scope for creating a security liability. You need to think carefully about exactly what information you want to expose.)

To show WCF Data Services in action, we'll need a web application, because it's an HTTP-based technology. If you create a new project in Visual Studio, you'll see a Visual C#→Web category on the left, and the Empty ASP.NET Web Application template will suit our needs here. We need an Entity Data Model to define what information we'd like to expose—for this example, we'll use the same EDM we've been using all along, so the steps will be the same as they were earlier in the chapter.

To expose this data over HTTP, we add another item to the project—under the Visual C#→Web template category we choose the WCF Data Service template. We'll call the service MyData. Visual Studio will add a *MyData.svc.cs* file to the project, which needs some tweaking before it'll expose any data—it assumes that it shouldn't publish any information that we didn't explicitly tell it to.

The first thing we need to do is modify the base class of the generated MyData class—it derives from a generic class called DataService, but the type argument needs to be filled in—Visual Studio just puts a comment in there telling you what to do. We will plug in the name of the object context class:

```
public class MyData : DataService<AdventureWorksLT2008Entities>
```

This class contains an InitializeService method to which we need to add code for each entity type we'd like to make available via HTTP. Example 14-21 makes all three entity types in the model available for read access.

Example 14-21. Making entities available

```
public static void InitializeService(IDataServiceConfiguration config)
{
    config.SetEntitySetAccessRule("Customers",
                                  EntitySetRights.AllRead);
    config.SetEntitySetAccessRule("SalesOrderHeaders",
                                  EntitySetRights.AllRead);
    config.SetEntitySetAccessRule("SalesOrderDetails",
                                  EntitySetRights.AllRead);
}
```

We can now look at how the data appears. If we press F5, Visual Studio opens a web browser showing the MyData.svc URL for our web application. It shows an XML file describing the available entity types, as Example 14-22 shows. (The exact value you see in the xml:base may be different—it depends on the port number Visual Studio chooses for debugging.)

Example 14-22. Available entities described by the web service

```
<service xml:base="http://localhost:1181/MyData.svc/"
   xmlns:atom="http://www.w3.org/2005/Atom"
   xmlns:app="http://www.w3.org/2007/app"
   xmlns="http://www.w3.org/2007/app">
  <workspace>
    <atom:title>Default</atom:title>
    <collection href="Customers">
      <atom:title>Customers</atom:title>
    </collection>
    <collection href="SalesOrderDetails">
      <atom:title>SalesOrderDetails</atom:title>
    </collection>
    <collection href="SalesOrderHeaders">
```

```
      <atom:title>SalesOrderHeaders</atom:title>
    </collection>
  </workspace>
</service>
```

Notice that each `<collection>` element has an `href` attribute. Typically, `href` attributes denote a link to another resource, the attribute value being a relative URL. So you can just stick an entity name on the end of the URL. The exact URL will depend on the port number Visual Studio picks for the test web server, but something like *http://localhost:1181/MyData.svc/Customers* will return all the customers in the system.

 There are two things to be aware of when looking at entities in the browser with this sort of URL. First, the simplest URLs will return *all* the entities of the specified type, which might take a long time. We'll see how to be more selective in a moment. Second, by default the web browser will notice that the data format being used is a variant of Atom, and will attempt to use the same friendly feed rendering you would get on other Atom- and RSS-based feeds. (Lots of blogs offer an Atom-based feed format.) Unfortunately, the browser's friendly rendering is aimed at the kind of Atom features usually found in blogs, and it doesn't always understand AtomPub feeds, so you might just get an error.

To deal with the second problem, you could just View Source to see the underlying XML, or you can turn off friendly feed rendering. In IE8, you open the Internet Options window and go to the Content tab. Open the Feed and Web Slice Settings window from there, and uncheck the "Turn on feed reading view" checkbox. (If you've already looked at a feed and hit this problem, you might need to close all instances of IE after making this change and try again.)

WCF Data Services lets you request a specific entity by putting its primary key inside parentheses at the end of the URL. For example, *http://localhost:1181/MyData.svc/Customers(29531)* fetches the customer entity whose ID is 29531. If you try this, you'll see a simple XML representation of all the property values for the entity. In that same XML document, you'll also find this element:

```
<link rel="http://schemas.microsoft.com/ado/2007/08/dataservices/related/
SalesOrderHeaders"
 type="application/atom+xml;type=feed"
 title="SalesOrderHeaders"
 href="Customers(29531)/SalesOrderHeaders"
/>
```

This is how associations in the EDM show up—if an entity has related entities available through an association, it will offer a link to the URL on which those associations can be found. So as the `href` in this example shows, you can just stick `SalesOrderHeaders` on the end of the customer instance URL to get all the related orders for customer 29531, as in the following:

```
http://localhost:1181/MyData.svc/Customers(29531)/SalesOrderHeaders
```

So you can see how joins across relationships turn into URLs, and also how simple key-based queries work. In fact, the URL syntax also supports more complex queries based on properties. For example, this returns all customers whose `FirstName` has the value `Cory`:

```
http://localhost:1181/MyData.svc/Customers?$filter=FirstName%20eq%20'Cory'
```

(The `%20` is how URLs represent spaces, so we've really just appended `$filter=First Name eq 'Cory'` to the URL.) The URL syntax also supports ordering and paging. Many standard LINQ operators are not supported, including grouping and joining.

You don't have to work directly with these URLs and XML documents—WCF Data Services includes a client-side component that supports LINQ. So you can run LINQ queries that will be converted into HTTP requests that use the URL structure you see here. We can demonstrate this by adding a new console application to the same solution as our web application. If we right-click on the console application's References item in the Solution Explorer and select Add Service Reference, clicking Discover in the dialog that opens will show the WCF Data Service from the other project. Selecting this and clicking OK generates code to represent each entity type defined by the service. That enables us to write code such as Example 14-23.

Example 14-23. Client-side WCF Data Services code

```
var ctx = new AdventureWorksLT2008Entities(
    new Uri("http://localhost:1181/MyData.svc"));
var customers = from customer in ctx.Customers
                where customer.FirstName == "Cory"
                select customer;

foreach (Customer customer in customers)
{
    Console.WriteLine(customer.CompanyName);
}
```

This looks superficially similar to the Entity Framework code we saw earlier—we still have an object context, for example. Visual Studio generated the `Adventure WorksLT2008Entities` class when we imported the service reference, and it derives from `DataServiceContext`. It's slightly different from the EF context—it's not disposable, for one thing. (That's why there's no `using` statement here—this object context doesn't implement `IDisposable`.) And it's a lot simpler—it doesn't do any change tracking. (That's why it doesn't need to implement `IDisposable`.) It's really just a convenient way to extract the information that an WCF Data Service exposes as objects in C#.

The LINQ query here will generate a suitable URL that encodes the query—filtering by `FirstName` in this case. And as with a database query, it won't actually make the request until we start to enumerate the results—this LINQ provider follows the usual deferred execution pattern.

 The range of query types supported by the WCF Data Services LINQ provider is much more limited than that offered by LINQ to Entities, LINQ to SQL, or most LINQ providers. It can only implement queries that are possible to turn into WCF Data Services URLs, and the URL syntax doesn't cover every possible kind of LINQ query.

WCF Data Services also offers more advanced features than those shown here. For example, you can arrange for entities to be updatable and creatable, and you can provide custom filtering code, to control exactly which entities are returned.

Summary

In this chapter, we saw that the .NET Framework offers a range of data access mechanisms. The original interface-based API supports direct database access. The Entity Framework makes it easier for C# code to work with data from the database, as well as providing some support for controlling the mapping between the database and the object model representing the data. And WCF Data Services is able to take some or all of an Entity Data Model and present it over HTTP, with either AtomPub or JSON, thus making your data available to AJAX and Silverlight clients.

CHAPTER 15

Assemblies

One of C#'s strengths is the ease with which your code can use all sorts of external components. All C# programs use the components that make up the .NET Framework class library, but many cast their net wider—GUI application developers often buy control libraries, for example. And it's also common for software developers to want their own code to be reusable—perhaps you've built up a handy library of utilities that you want to use in all the projects in your organization.

Whether you're producing or consuming components, C# makes it simple to achieve *binary reuse*—the ability to reuse software in its compiled binary form without needing the source code. In this chapter, we'll look at the mechanisms that make this possible.

.NET Components: Assemblies

In .NET, an *assembly* is a single software component. It is usually either an executable program with a file extension of *.exe*, or a library with a *.dll* extension. An assembly can contain compiled code, resources (such as bitmaps or string tables), and *metadata*, which is information about the code such as the names of types and methods, inheritance relationships between types, whether items are `public` or `private`, and so on.

In other words, the compiler takes pretty much all the information in the source files that you added to your project in Visual Studio, and "assembles" it into a single result: an assembly.

We use this same name of "assembly" for both executables and libraries, because there's not much difference between them—whether you're building a program or a shared library, you're going to end up with a file containing your code, resources, and metadata, and so there wouldn't be any sense in having two separate concepts for such similar requirements. The only significant difference is that an executable needs an *entry point*—the piece of code that runs when the program starts, usually the `Main` method in C#. Libraries don't have an equivalent, but otherwise, there's no technical difference between a *.dll* and an *.exe* in .NET.

Of course, libraries normally export functionality. It's less common for executables to do that, but they can if they want to—in .NET it's possible for an *.exe* to define public classes that can be consumed from other components. That might sound odd, but it can be desirable: it enables you to write a separate program to perform automated testing of the code in your main executable.

So, every time you create a new C# project in Visual Studio, you are in effect defining a new assembly.

No assembly can exist in isolation—the whole point is to enable reuse of code, so assemblies need some way to use other assemblies.

References

You can choose to use an external assembly by adding a *reference* to it in your project. Figure 15-1 shows how the Solution Explorer presents these—you can see the set of references you get in any new console application. All project types provide you with a few references to get you started, and while the exact set depends on the sort of project—a WPF application would include several UI-related libraries that you don't need in a console application, for example—the ones shown here are available by default in most projects.

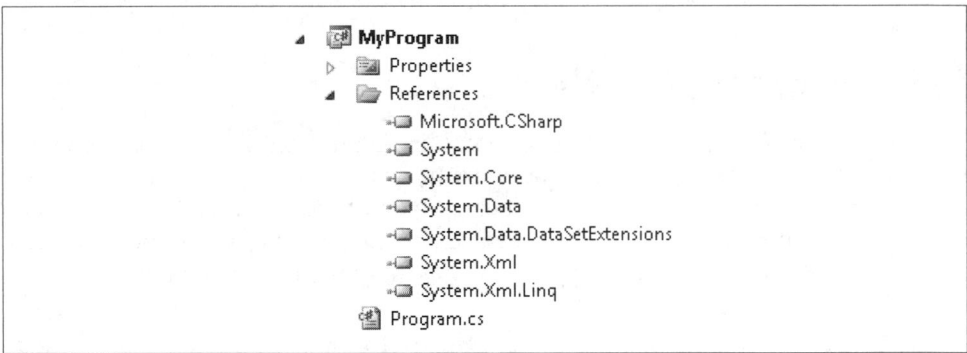

Figure 15-1. Default project references in Visual Studio

C# projects have an implicit reference to mscorlib. This defines critical types such as String and Object, and you will not be able to compile code without these. Since it's mandatory, Visual Studio doesn't show it in the References list.

Once you've got a reference to an assembly, your program is free to use any of the public types it offers. For example, the System.Core library visible in Figure 15-1 defines the types that make up the LINQ to Objects services that Chapter 8 described.

 There's a point that we mentioned in Chapter 2, which is vitally important and often catches people out, so it bears repeating: assemblies and namespaces are not the same thing. There is no `System.Core` namespace. It's easy to get confused because in a lot of cases, there is some apparent similarity—for example, five of the seven assemblies shown in Figure 15-1 have names that correspond to namespaces. But that's just a convention, and a very loose one at that, as we discussed in detail in the sidebar "Namespaces and Libraries" on page 22.

You can add references to additional DLLs by right-clicking the References item in the Solution Explorer and choosing the Add Reference menu item. We've mentioned this in passing a couple of times in earlier chapters, but let's take a closer look. Figure 15-2 shows the dialog that appears. You may find that when you open it, it initially shows the Projects tab, which we'll use later. Here, we've switched to the .NET tab, which shows the various .NET components Visual Studio has found.

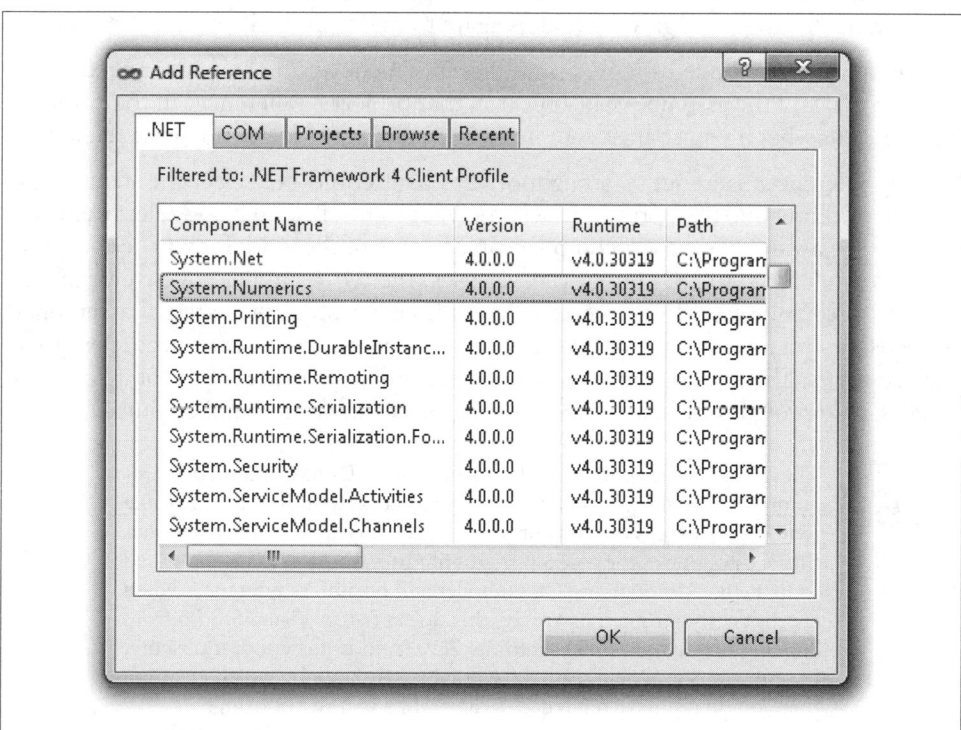

Figure 15-2. The .NET tab of the Add Reference dialog

Visual Studio looks in a few different places on your system when populating this list. All the assemblies in the .NET Framework class library will be here, of course, but you'll often find others. For example, companies that sell controls often provide an SDK which, when installed, advertises its presence to Visual Studio, enabling its assemblies to show up in this list too.

 If you're wondering how you're meant to know that you need a particular assembly, the documentation tells you. If you look in the Visual Studio help, or online in the MSDN documentation, each class definition tells you which namespace and assembly the class is defined in.

You'll notice that Figure 15-2 shows some other tabs. The COM tab contains all the COM components Visual Studio has found on your system. These are not .NET components, but it's possible to use them from C# as we'll see in Chapter 19.

Sometimes you'll need to use a component which, for whatever reason, isn't listed in the .NET tab. That's not a problem—you can just use the Browse tab, which contains a normal file-browsing UI. When you add an assembly with the Browse tab, it gets added to the Recent tab, so if you need to use it again in a different project, this saves you from navigating through your folders again to find it in the Browse tab.

Once you've selected one or more assemblies in whichever tab suits your needs, you can click OK and the assembly will appear in that project's References in the Solution Explorer. But what if you change your mind later, and want to get rid of the reference?

Deleting references is about as straightforward as it could be: select the item in the Solution Explorer and then press the Delete key, or right-click on it and select Remove. However, be aware that the C# compiler can do some of the work for you here. If your code has a reference to a DLL that it never uses, the C# compiler effectively ignores the reference. Your assembly's metadata includes a list of all the external assemblies you're using, but the compiler omits any unused assemblies in your project references. (Consequently, the fact that most programs are unlikely to use all of the references Visual Studio provides by default doesn't waste space in your compiled output.)

 Things are slightly more complex in Silverlight. Unlike other .NET programs, Silverlight projects put the compiled assembly into a ZIP file (with a *.xap* extension). If your project has references to any assemblies that are not one of the core Silverlight libraries, those will also be added to that ZIP. Although the C# compiler still optimizes references when it produces your main assembly, this doesn't stop Visual Studio from copying unused assemblies into the ZIP. (And it has good, if obscure, reasons for doing that.) So, in Silverlight, it is actually worth ensuring that you do not have references to any DLLs you're not using.

Making use of existing libraries is only half the story, of course. What if you want to produce your own library?

Writing Libraries

Visual Studio offers special project types for writing libraries. Some of these are specific to particular kinds of projects—you can write a WPF control library or an activity library for use in a Workflow application, for example. The more specialized library projects provide an appropriate set of references, and offer some templates suitable for the kinds of applications they target, but the basic principles are the same for all libraries. To illustrate the techniques, we'll be using the simplest project: a Class Library project.

But before we do that, we need to think about our Visual Studio solution. Solutions allow us to work with multiple related projects, but most of the examples in this book have needed only a single project, so we've pretty much ignored solutions up to now. But if we want to show a library in action, we'll also need some code that uses that library: we're going to need at least two projects. And since they're connected, we'll want to put them in the same solution. There are various ways you can do that, and depending on exactly how you've configured Visual Studio, it may or may not hide some of the details from you. But if you want to be in complete control, it's often easiest to start by creating an empty solution and then to add projects one at a time—that way, even if you've configured Visual Studio to hide solutions with simple projects, you'll still be able to see what's happening.

To create a new solution, open the New Project dialog in the usual way, and then in the Installed Templates section on the left, expand Other Project Types and select Visual Studio Solutions. This offers a Blank Solution template in the middle of the dialog. In this example, we're going to call our solution `AssemblyExample`. When you click OK, Visual Studio will create a folder called *AssemblyExample*, which will contain an *AssemblyExample.sln* file, but you won't have any projects yet. Right-click on the solution and choose Add→New Project from the context menu. This open the Add New Project dialog, which is almost identical to the New Project dialog, except it adds projects to the solution you have open, rather than creating a new one.

For the examples in this chapter, we're going to add two projects to the solution, both from templates in the Visual C#→Windows section: a Console Application called `MyProgram`, and a Class Library called `MyLibrary`. (Create them in that order—Visual Studio picks the first one you create as the one to debug when you hit F5. You want that to be the program, because you can't run a library. Although if you were to do it in the other order, you could always right-click on MyProgram and choose Set as Startup Project.)

A newly created Class Library project contains a source file, *Class1.cs*, which defines a rather boring class shown in Example 15-1. Notice that Visual Studio has chosen to follow the convention that the namespace matches the assembly name.

Example 15-1. The default class in a new Class Library project

```
using System;
using System.Collections.Generic;
using System.Linq;
using System.Text;

namespace MyLibrary
{
    public class Class1
    {
    }
}
```

We can try to use this class from the *Program.cs* file in the console application. Example 15-2 shows that file, with the necessary additions in bold.

Example 15-2. Using an external class

```
using System;
using System.Collections.Generic;
using System.Linq;
using System.Text;
using MyLibrary;

namespace MyProgram
{
    class Program
    {
        static void Main(string[] args)
        {
            var o = new Class1();
        }
    }
}
```

This won't compile. We get this error:

```
error CS0246: The type or namespace name 'MyLibrary' could not be found (are
  you missing a using directive or an assembly reference?)
```

The compiler appears not to recognize the MyLibrary namespace. Of course it doesn't—that's defined in a completely separate project than the MyProgram project that contains *Program.cs*. As the error helpfully points out, we need to add a reference in MyProgram to MyLibrary. And this time, the Add Reference dialog's default choice of the Projects tab, shown in Figure 15-3, is exactly what we want. MyLibrary is the only project listed because it's the only other project in the solution—we can just select that and click OK.

The code will now build correctly because MyProgram has access to Class1 in MyLibrary. But that's not to say it has access to *everything* in the library. Right-click on MyLibrary in the Solution Explorer, select Add→Class, and create a new class called MyType. Now in *Program.cs*, we can modify the line that creates the object so that it creates an instance of our newly added MyType instead of Class1, as Example 15-3 shows.

Example 15-3. Instantiating MyType

```
var o = new MyType();
```

This fails to compile, but we get a different error:

```
error CS0122: 'MyLibrary.MyType' is inaccessible due to its protection level
```

(Well, actually, we get two errors, but the second one is just a distracting additional symptom, so we won't show it here. It's this first one that describes the problem.) The C# compiler has found the `MyType` class, and is telling us we can't use it because of *protection*.

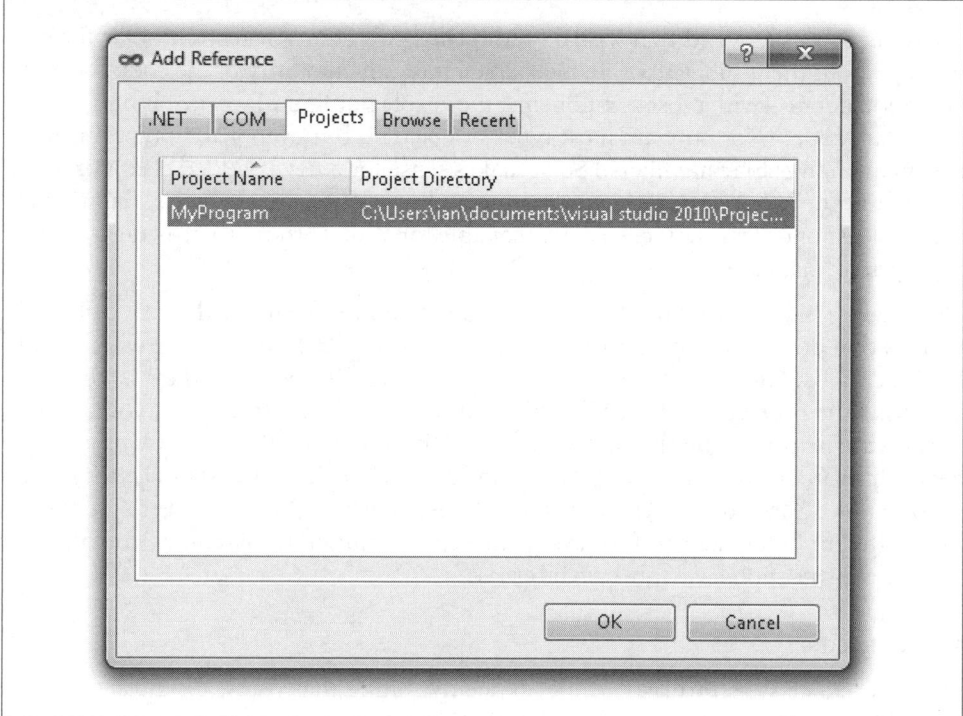

Figure 15-3. The Projects tab of the Add Reference dialog

Protection

In Chapter 3, we saw how you can decide which members of a class are accessible to code outside the class, marking members as `public`, `private`, or `protected`. And if you didn't specify a protection level, members were `private` by default. Well, it's a similar story with members of an assembly—by default, a type is not accessible outside its defining assembly. The only reason `MyProgram` was able to use `Class1` is that the class definition has `public` in front of it, as you can see in Example 15-1. But as Example 15-4 shows, Visual Studio didn't do that for the second class we added.

Example 15-4. Type with the default protection

```
using System;
using System.Collections.Generic;
using System.Linq;
using System.Text;

namespace MyLibrary
{
    class MyType
    {
    }
}
```

It may seem a little weird that Visual Studio chose different protection levels for our two types, but there's logic to it. In most assemblies, the majority of the code is implementation detail—with most components, the visible public surface area is only a fraction of the code. (Not only are most types not `public`, but even `public` types usually have many non-`public` members.) So, it makes sense for a newly added class not to be `public`. On the other hand, if we're writing a library, presumably we're planning to make at least one class `public`, so it's reasonable for Visual Studio to provide us with a single `public` class as our starting point.

Some people like to avoid implicit protection—if you're reading code such as Example 15-4 that doesn't say what protection level it wants, it's difficult to tell whether the developer chose the default deliberately, or simply hasn't bothered to think about it. Specifying the protection level explicitly avoids this problem. However, if you try putting `private` in front of the class in Example 15-4, it won't compile—`private` protection means "private to the containing class" and since `MyType` isn't a nested class, there is no containing class, so `private` would have no meaning here. We're trying to say something different here—we want to say "private to the containing assembly" and there's a different protection level for that: `internal`.

Internal protection

If you mark a class as `internal`, you're explicitly stating that you want the class to be accessible only from within the assembly that defines it. You are, in effect, saying the class is an implementation detail, and not part of the API presented by your assembly. This is the default protection level for a normal class. (For a nested class, the default protection level is `private`.)

You can also apply `internal` to members of a class. For example, we could make the class `public`, but its constructor `internal`, as Example 15-5 shows.

Example 15-5. Public type, internal constructor

```
public class MyType
{
    internal MyType() { }
}
```

This would enable `MyProgram` to declare variables of type `MyType`, which it was not able to do before we made the class `public`. But it's still unable to construct a new `MyType`. So, in Example 15-6, the first line will compile, but we will get an error on the second line because there are no accessible constructors.

Example 15-6. Using the type and using its members

```
MyType o;              // Compiles OK
o = new MyType();      // Error
```

This is more useful than it might seem. This has enabled `MyLibrary` to define a type as part of its public API, but to retain control over how instances of that type are created. This lets it force users of the library to go through a factory method, which can be useful for several reasons:

- Some objects require additional work after construction—perhaps you need to register the existence of an object with some other part of your system.

- If your objects represent specific real entities, you might want to ensure that only code you trust gets to create new objects of a particular type.

- You might sometimes want to create a derived type, choosing the exact class at runtime.

Example 15-7 shows a very simple factory method which does none of the above, but crucially our library has reserved the right to do any or all of these things in the future. We've chosen to expose this factory method from the other type in the library project, `Class1`. This class gets to use the `internal` constructor for `MyType` because it lives in the same assembly.

Example 15-7. Factory method for a public type with an internal constructor

```
public class Class1
{
    public static MyType MakeMeAnInstance()
    {
        return new MyType();
    }
}
```

Our `MyProgram` project can then use this method to get `Class1` to construct an instance of `MyType` on its behalf, as Example 15-8 shows.

Example 15-8. Using a type with an internal constructor from outside

```
MyType o = Class1.MakeMeAnInstance();
```

 Example 15-7 shows another reason it can be useful to have a `public` class with no `public` constructors. `Class1` offers a `public static` method, meaning the class is useful even if we never construct it. In fact, as it stands, there's never any reason to construct a `Class1`, because it contains no instance members. Classes that offer `public static` members but which are never constructed are rather common, and we can make it clear that they're not meant to be constructed by putting the keyword `static` before `class`. This would prevent even code in the `MyLibrary` project from constructing an instance of `Class1`.

Occasionally, it can be useful to make the `internal` features of an assembly accessible to one or more other specific assemblies. If you write a particularly large class library, it might be useful to split it into multiple assemblies much like the .NET Framework class library. But you might want to let these all use one another's internal features, without exposing those features to code that uses your library. Another particularly important reason is unit testing: if you want to write unit tests for an implementation detail of your class, then if you don't want to put the test code in the same project as the class under test, you'll need to grant your test project access to the internals of the code being tested. This can be done by applying an assembly-level attribute, which normally goes in the *AssemblyInfo.cs* file, which you can find by expanding the Properties section of your project in the Solution Explorer. Attributes are discussed in Chapter 17, but for now, just know that you can put the code in Example 15-9 in that file.

Example 15-9. Selectively making internals accessible

```
[assembly: InternalsVisibleTo("MyProgram")]
```

If we put this in the *AssemblyInfo.cs* of `MyLibrary`, `MyProgram` will now be able to use internal features such as the `MyType` constructor directly. But this raises an interesting problem: clearly anyone is free to write an assembly called `MyProgram` and by doing so, will be able to get access to the internals, so if we thought we were only opening up our code to a select few we need to think again. It's possible to get a bit more selective than this, and for that we need to look in more detail at how assemblies are named.

Naming

By default, when you create a new assembly—either a program or a library—its name is based on the filename, but with the file extension stripped. This means that our two example projects in this chapter build assemblies whose filenames are *MyProgram.exe* and *MyLibrary.dll*. But as far as the .NET Framework is concerned, their names are `MyProgram` and `MyLibrary`, respectively, which is why Example 15-9 just specified `MyProgram`, and not `MyProgram.exe`.

Actually, that's not the whole truth. These are the *simple names*, but there's more to assembly names. We can ask the .NET Framework to show us the full name of a type's containing assembly, using the code in Example 15-10.

Example 15-10. Getting a type's containing assembly's name

```
Console.WriteLine(typeof(MyType).Assembly.FullName);
```

Running this produces the following output:

```
MyLibrary, Version=1.0.0.0, Culture=neutral, PublicKeyToken=null
```

As you can see, there are four parts to an assembly name. First there is the simple name, but this is followed by a version number. Assemblies always have a version number. If you don't specify one, the compiler sets it to 0.0.0.0. But Visual Studio puts an assembly-level attribute in the *AssemblyInfo.cs* file setting it to 1.0.0.0, which is why we see that in the output. You would typically change the version each time you formally release your code. Example 15-11 shows the (unsurprising) syntax for the version attribute.

Example 15-11. Setting an assembly's version

```
[assembly: AssemblyVersion("1.2.0.7")]
```

The next part of the name is the culture. This is normally used only on components that contain localized resources for applications that need to support multiple languages. Those kinds of assemblies usually contain no code—they hold nothing but resources. Assemblies that contain code don't normally specify a culture, which is why we see `Culture=neutral` in the name for our `MyLibrary` assembly.

Finally, there's the `PublicKeyToken`. This is `null` in our example, because we're not using it. But this is the part of the name that lets us say we don't just want any old assembly with a simple name of `MyProgram`. We can demand a specific bit of code by requiring the component to be signed.

Signing and Strong Names

Assemblies can be digitally signed. There are two ways to do this—you can use Authenticode signing just as you can for any Windows DLL or EXE, but such signatures don't have any relevance to an assembly's name. However, the other signing mechanism is specific to .NET, and is directly connected to the assembly name.

If you look at any of the assemblies in the .NET Framework class library, you'll see they all have a nonnull `PublicKeyToken`. Running Example 15-10 against `string` instead of `MyType` produces this output:

```
mscorlib, Version=4.0.0.0, Culture=neutral, PublicKeyToken=b77a5c561934e089
```

The version number changes from time to time, of course—it didn't look quite like that in .NET 1.0. However, the important part here is the `PublicKeyToken`. Assemblies with this feature in their name are called *strongly named* assemblies. But what does that mean?

If you add a reference to a strongly named assembly, the C# compiler includes the full name in your program's metadata. This means that when the .NET Framework loads our program, it will see that we have a reference to `mscorlib`, and that we're expecting its strong name to include that public key token. The framework requires strongly named components to be digitally signed (using a signing mechanism specific to .NET assemblies). And it will also require that the public key of the key pair used to generate the signature has a value which, when run through a particular cryptographic hash algorithm, matches the `PublicKeyToken`.

This provides some protection against ending up using the wrong assembly. It also provides some protection against using a copy of what was originally the right assembly, but which has been tampered with, possibly by someone up to no good.

If the .NET Framework attempts to load the wrong assembly, things won't match. Perhaps the assembly it found isn't signed at all, in which case it'll throw an exception, because it knows we're looking for a strongly named assembly. Or perhaps it attempts to load an assembly that is strongly named, but which was signed with a different key pair. Even if it is correctly signed, the different key will mean that the hash of the public key will not match the `PublicKeyToken` we're expecting, and again the component will fail to load.

Alternatively, we might end up with an assembly with the right name, but which has either been tampered with or has become corrupted. In this case, the public key of the key pair used to sign the assembly will match the `PublicKeyToken`, but the signature will not be valid—digital signatures are designed to detect when the thing they've been applied to has changed.

You may be thinking: can't we just generate a new signature, choosing the same key pair that the original assembly used? Well, if you have access to the key pair, then yes, you can—that's how Microsoft is able to build new versions of `mscorlib` with the same `PublicKeyToken` as earlier versions. But if you're not in possession of the key pair—if all you know is the public key—you're not going to be able to generate a new valid signature unless you have some way of cracking the cryptography that underpins the digital signature. (Alternatively, you could also try to create a new key pair which happens to produce the same `PublicKeyToken` as the assembly you're trying to mimic. But again this would require you to defeat the cryptography—hashing algorithms are designed specifically to prevent this sort of thing.) So, as long as the private key has been kept private, only someone with access to the key can generate a new assembly with the same `PublicKeyToken`.

Not all key pairs are kept private. An open source project may want to give a component a strong name just so that it can have a globally unique name, while enabling anyone to build his own version. In these cases the full key pair is made available along with the source code, in which case the strong name brings no assurances as to the integrity of the code. But it still offers identity—it enables you to refer to the library by a distinct name, which can be useful in itself.

We can therefore be reasonably confident that if we add a reference to a strongly named assembly, we're going to get the assembly we are expecting. (The exact level of confidence depends not just on the privacy of the key, but also on the integrity of the machine on which we're running the code. If someone has hacked our copy of the .NET Framework, clearly we can't depend on it to verify strong names. But then we probably have bigger problems at that point.)

You can apply a strong name to your own components. We're not going to show how to do that here, mainly because it opens up key management problems—these are security issues that are beyond the scope of this book. But if you'd like to know more, see *http://msdn.microsoft.com/library/wd40t7ad*.

We've seen how components can refer to one another, and how assemblies are named. But one important question remains: how does the .NET Framework know where to load them from?

Loading

The .NET Framework automatically loads assemblies for us. It does this on demand—it does *not* load every assembly we reference when the program starts, as that could add delays of several seconds. Typically, loading happens at the point at which we first invoke a method that uses a type from the relevant assembly. Be careful, though: this means we can end up loading an assembly that we never use. Consider Example 15-12.

Example 15-12. A rare occurrence

```
public void Foo()
{
    if (DateTime.Now.Year == 1973)
    {
        SomeExternalType.Disco();
    }
}
```

Unless you run this on a computer whose clock is incredibly inaccurate the body of that `if` statement is never going to run. Despite this, when you first call `Foo`, the .NET Framework will ensure that the assembly that contains `SomeExternalType` is loaded, if it hasn't already been. Life is significantly simpler for the JIT compiler (and it can therefore do its job faster) if it loads all the types and assemblies a method might use up front, rather than loading each one on demand. The downside is that assemblies sometimes load slightly earlier than you might expect, but this isn't usually a problem in practice.

 Visual Studio can show you exactly when assemblies load. If you run an application in the debugger, it will display a message to the Output panel for each assembly your program loads. If you don't have the Output panel open, you can show it from the View menu. This can sometimes be useful if you have an application that is taking longer than expected to start up—take a look through the assemblies listed in the Output window, and if you see any you weren't expecting, perhaps you have some code like Example 15-12 that is unnecessarily loading something you're not really using.

We know *when* assemblies are loaded. But from *where* are they loaded? There are many different places they could theoretically come from, but in the vast majority of cases, it'll be one of two locations: either the same folder the application lives in or something called the GAC.

Loading from the Application Folder

When you add a reference from one project to another, Visual Studio copies the DLL being referenced into the consuming application's folder. So, if we look in the *bin\Debug* folder for the `MyProgram` example shown earlier in this chapter, we'll see both *MyProgram.exe* and a copy of *MyLibrary.dll*.

An obvious upshot of this approach is that each application that uses a particular library will have its own copy. This may seem a little wasteful, and may even seem contrary to the spirit of DLLs—traditionally DLLs have offered a performance benefit by allowing disk space and memory to be shared by applications that use common DLLs. And while that's true, sharing can cause a lot of problems—installing a new application could end up breaking old applications, because the new application might bring a new version of a shared DLL that turns out not to work with programs expecting the older version.

To prevent this, .NET encourages isolation between applications—if each application brings its own copy of the libraries it requires, the chances of things breaking when new applications are installed are much lower. And now that disk and memory are much cheaper than they were back in the 1980s when DLLs were introduced, "not breaking everything" seems like a worthwhile return for using a bit more space.

However, .NET does support a shared model, through the GAC.

Loading from the GAC

The *global assembly cache* (GAC) is a machine-wide repository of shared .NET assemblies. All the assemblies that make up the .NET Framework class library live in the GAC, and other components can be added to it.

To live in the GAC, an assembly *must* be strongly named. This is to avoid naming collisions—if multiple applications all decide to provide their own shared component called *Utils.dll*, we need some way of distinguishing between them if they're going to live in a shared repository. Strong names give us this—signing key pairs are unique.

The GAC tries to avoid the problem of one application's new DLLs breaking an existing application that was relying on older DLLs. The GAC is therefore able to hold multiple versions of the same DLL. For example, if you install one of the "Team" editions of Visual Studio 2008 and Visual Studio 2010 on a single machine, you'll find various assemblies in the GAC whose names begin with `Microsoft.TeamFoundation`, and there will be two versions of each, one with version 9.0.0.0 and one with 10.0.0.0. So, even when using this shared model, you'll get the version of the DLL you were expecting even if other versions have been installed since.

Loading from a Silverlight .xap File

Silverlight adds a complication: applications are downloaded from the Web, so it doesn't really make sense to talk about an "application folder." However, in practice, the rules are pretty similar as for the full .NET Framework. When you build a Silverlight application, Visual Studio creates a ZIP file (with a *.xap* extension) that contains your program's main assembly. If you add a reference to any assemblies that are not part of the core set of assemblies offered by Silverlight, Visual Studio will add those assemblies to the ZIP too. This is conceptually equivalent to putting those DLLs in the application folder with a full .NET application.

Silverlight doesn't have a GAC. It does have a core set of assemblies stored centrally, which are available to all applications, but you can't add additional assemblies to this, unlike with the GAC. The shared assemblies are the ones that are built into the Silverlight plug-in itself, and they are the main libraries in its version of the .NET Framework class library.

 A lot of the libraries in the Silverlight SDK are not part of the core set built into the plug-in. This is because Microsoft wanted to ensure that Silverlight was a small download—if it was too hefty, that might put people off installing it. The downside is that some library features require you to include a copy of the library in your *.xap* file.

Explicit Loading

You can ask the .NET Framework to load an assembly explicitly. This makes it possible to decide to load additional components at runtime, making it possible to create applications whose behavior can be extended at runtime.

The `Assembly` class in the `System.Reflection` namespace offers a static `LoadFile` method, and you can pass the path to the assembly's location on disk. If you don't know where the assembly is but you know its fully qualified name (i.e., a four-part name, like the one printed out by Example 15-10) you can call `Assembly.Load`. And if you have only part of the name—just the simple name, for example—you can call `Assembly.LoadWith PartialName`.

Things are slightly different in Silverlight. You have to download the assembly yourself, which you can do with the `WebClient` class, described in Chapter 13. You'll need to get the assembly itself (and not a *.xap* containing the assembly), and then you can simply construct an `AssemblyPart`, passing the `Stream` containing the downloaded DLL to its `Load` method, and it will load the assembly. (If the assembly you want to use is in a *.xap*, it's still possible to load dynamically, it's just rather more complicated—you need to use the `Application.GetResourceStream` method to extract the assembly from the *.xap* before passing it to an `AssemblyPart`.)

All of these various techniques for loading assemblies will leave you with an `Assembly` object, which you can use to discover what types the assembly offers, and instantiate them at runtime. Chapter 17 shows how to use the `Assembly` class.

If you're considering using any of these techniques, you should look at the *Managed Extensibility Framework* (MEF), a part of the .NET Framework class library designed specifically to support dynamic extensibility. It can handle a lot of the detailed issues of loading assemblies and locating types for you. This lets you focus on the types you want to use, rather than the mechanisms necessary to load them. You can find information about MEF at *http://msdn.microsoft.com/library/dd460648* and you can even get hold of the source code for it from *http://code.msdn.microsoft.com/mef*.

The advantage of loading assemblies explicitly is that you don't need to put a reference into your project at compile time. You can decide at runtime which assemblies to load. This can be useful for plug-in systems, where you want to load assemblies dynamically to extend your application's functionality. You might allow third-party assemblies, so other people or companies can extend your application. However, if you decide to support plug-ins, there's one thing you need to be aware of: unloading can be problematic.

Unloading

Once you've loaded an assembly, unloading it is tricky. The .NET Framework commits various resources to the assembly for the lifetime of the application, and there's no method you can call to unload an assembly. This makes it easy to find yourself in a situation where you want to delete a DLL, but you can't because your .NET application is holding onto it. (The .NET Framework locks the file to prevent deletion or modification for as long as the assembly is loaded.)

There is a way around this. Strictly speaking, the assembly is loaded for the lifetime of the *appdomain*. An appdomain is a similar sort of idea to an operating system process—it's an environment that can load and run code, and which is isolated from other app-domains. The difference is that you can have multiple appdomains in a single process. If you really need to be able to unload DLLs after loading them, the way to do it is to create a separate appdomain. Once you're done, you can destroy the appdomain, at which point it will unload any DLLs it had loaded.

Appdomain programming is an advanced topic that is beyond the scope of this book—we mention it mainly because it's important to be aware that there's a potential problem if you start loading assemblies dynamically, and it's useful to know that a solution exists. More information about appdomains can be found at *http://msdn.microsoft.com/library/2bh4z9hs* and *http://blogs.msdn.com/cbrumme/archive/2003/06/01/51466.aspx* (which despite being an obviously rather old URL, continues to be one of the most comprehensive descriptions around).

Summary

An assembly is a .NET component, and can be either an executable program or a library. C# code is always packaged into an assembly, along with the metadata necessary to describe that code, and assemblies can optionally include resources such as bitmaps or other binary streams. Assemblies offer an additional protection boundary beyond those we saw with classes in Chapter 3—you can make types and members available only within the defining assembly. And we saw how components can be installed in the same directory as the application that uses them, stored centrally in the GAC, or loaded dynamically at runtime.

CHAPTER 16

Threads and Asynchronous Code

A quotation variously ascribed to A.J.P. Taylor, Arnold Toybnee, and Winston Churchill describes history as "just one thing after another." C# code is much the same—we write sequences of statements that will be executed one after another. Loops and conditional statements spice things up a little by changing the order, but there is always an order. While individual bits of C# code behave this way, programs as a whole do not have to.

For example, web servers are able to handle multiple requests simultaneously. The user interface for a program working on a slow operation should be able to respond if the user clicks a Cancel button before that slow work is complete. And more or less any computer bought recently will have a multicore processor capable of executing multiple pieces of code simultaneously.

C# can handle this kind of concurrent work thanks to the .NET Framework's support for multithreading and asynchronous programming. We have a wide array of concurrency tools and there are many ways to use them—each example in the previous paragraph would use a different combination of threading mechanisms. Since there are many ways to approach concurrency problems, it's worth drawing a clear distinction between the most common reasons for using the techniques and features this chapter describes.

Perhaps the most easily understood goal is *parallel execution*. A computer with a multicore processor (or maybe even multiple separate processor chips) has the capacity to run multiple bits of code simultaneously. If your program performs processor-intensive tasks, it might be able to work faster by using several cores at once. For example, video encoding is a slow, computationally complex process, and if you have, say, a quad-core computer, you might hope that by using all four cores simultaneously you'd be able to encode a video four times faster than you could with a conventional one-thing-after-another approach. As we'll see, things never work out quite that well in practice—video encoding on four cores might turn out to run only three times as fast as it does on one core, for example. But even though results often fall short of naive expectations, the ability to perform multiple calculations at the same time—in parallel, as it were—can often provide a worthwhile speed boost. You'll need to use some of the programming techniques in this chapter to achieve this in C#.

A less obvious (but, it turns out, more widespread) use of multithreading is *multiplexing*—sharing a single resource across multiple simultaneous operations. This is more or less the inverse of the previous idea—rather than taking one task and spreading it across multiple processor cores, we are trying to run more tasks than there are processor cores. Web servers do this. Interesting websites usually rely on databases, so the typical processing sequence for a web page looks like this: inspect the request, look up the necessary information in the database, sit around and wait for the database to respond, and then generate the response. If a web server were to handle requests one at a time, that "sit around and wait" part would mean servers spent large amounts of time sitting idle. So even on a computer with just one processor core, handling one request at a time would be inefficient—the CPU could be getting on with processing other requests instead of idly waiting for a response from a database. Multithreading and asynchronous programming make it possible for servers to keep multiple requests on the go simultaneously in order to make full use of the available CPU resources.

A third reason for using multithreading techniques is to ensure the *responsiveness* of a user interface. A typical desktop application usually has different motives for multithreading than a server application—since the program is being used by just one person, it's probably not helpful to build an application that can work on large numbers of requests simultaneously to maximize the use of the CPU. However, even though an individual user will mostly want to do one thing at a time, it's important that the application is still able to respond to input if the one thing being done happens to be going slowly—otherwise, the user may suspect that the application has crashed. So rather than being able to do numerous things at once we have less ambitious aims: work in progress shouldn't stop us from being able to do something else as soon as the user asks. This involves some similar techniques to those required in multiplexing, although the need for cancellation and coordination can make user interface code more complex than server code, despite having fewer things in progress at any one time.

A related reason for employing concurrency is *speculation*. It may be possible to improve the responsiveness to user input by anticipating future actions, starting on the work before the user asks for it. For example, a map application might start to fetch parts of the map that haven't scrolled into view yet so that they are ready by the time the user wants to look at them. Obviously, speculative work is sometimes wasted, but if the user has CPU resources that would otherwise be sitting idle, the benefits can outweigh the effective cost.

Although parallel execution, multiplexing, and responsiveness are distinct goals, there's considerable overlap in the tools and techniques used to achieve them. So the ideas and features shown in this chapter are applicable to all of these goals. We'll begin by looking at threads.

Threads

Threads execute code. They keep track of which statement to execute next, they store the values of local variables, and they remember how we got to the current method so that execution can continue back in the calling method when the current one returns. All programs require these basic services in order to get anything done, so operating systems clearly need to be able to provide at least one thread per program. Multithreading just takes that a step further, allowing several different flows of execution—several *threads*—to be in progress at once even within a single program.

Example 16-1 executes code on three threads. All programs have at least one thread—the .NET Framework creates a thread on which to call your `Main` method[*]—but this example creates two more by using the `Thread` class in the `System.Threading` namespace. The `Thread` constructor takes a delegate to a method that it will invoke on the newly created thread when you call `Start`.

Example 16-1. Creating threads explicitly

```
using System;
using System.Threading;

class Program
{
    static void Main(string[] args)
    {
        Thread t1 = new Thread(One);
        Thread t2 = new Thread(Two);

        t1.Start();
        t2.Start();

        for (int i = 0; i < 100; ++i)
        {
            Console.WriteLine("Main: " + i);
        }

    }

    static void One()
    {
        for (int i = 0; i < 100; ++i)
        {
            Console.WriteLine("One: " + i);
        }
    }

    static void Two()
    {
```

---

[*] In fact, the CLR creates some utility threads for various purposes, so if you inspect the process's thread count, you'll see more than one.

```
        for (int i = 0; i < 100; ++i)
        {
            Console.WriteLine("Two: " + i);
        }
    }
}
```

All three threads do the same thing here—they loop around 100 times, printing out a message to show how far they've gotten. Here are the first few lines of output I get on my system:

```
Main: 0
Main: 1
Main: 2
Main: 3
Main: 4
Main: 5
Main: 6
Main: 7
Two: 0
One: 0
One: 1
One: 2
One: 3
One: 4
One: 5
One: 6
One: 7
Main: 8
Main: 9
Main: 10
Main: 11
...
```

You can see that the main thread managed to count up to 7 before the others got going—this is normal, because it takes a little while for a new thread to get up to speed, and it's often possible for the thread that called Start to make considerable progress before the threads it created do any visible work. And once they're underway, you can see that all three loops are making progress, although the interleaving is a little surprising.

This illustrates an important feature of multithreaded code—it tends to be somewhat unpredictable. This particular program can print something different each time. We don't want to fill the book with page after page of this kind of output, so here's a quick summary of how a different run on the same machine started out: Main got up to 7 as before, then One printed the number 0, and after that, Two printed numbers from 0 all the way up to 27 before either of the other threads managed to get any more numbers out. And just for fun, here's what we saw when running on a virtual machine hosted on the same hardware, but with just two virtual cores available in the VM: One manages to get all the way to 25 before Main gets a look in, and Two doesn't print out its first line until One has gotten to 41 and Main has gotten to 31. The specifics here are not all that interesting; the main point is the variability.

The behavior depends on things such as how many CPU cores the computer has and what else the machine was doing at the time. The fact that this particular example ends up with each individual thread managing to print out relatively long sequences before other threads interrupt is a surprising quirk—we got this output by running on a quad-core machine, so you'd think that all three threads would be able to run more or less independently. But this example is complicated by the fact that all the threads are trying to print out messages to a single console window. This is an example of *contention*—multiple threads fighting over a single resource. In general, it would be our responsibility to coordinate access, but the .NET Framework happens to resolve it for us in the specific case of `Console` output by making threads wait if they try to use the console while another thread is using it. So these threads are spending most of their time waiting for their turn to print a message. Once threads start waiting for things to happen, strange behaviors can emerge because of how they interact with the OS scheduler.

Threads and the OS Scheduler

Threads don't correspond directly to any physical feature of your computer—a program with four threads running on a quad-core computer *might* end up running one thread on each core, but it doesn't usually happen that way. For one thing, your program shares the computer with other processes, so it can't have all the cores to itself. Moreover, one of the main ideas behind threads is to provide an abstraction that's mostly independent of the real number of processor cores. You are free to have far more threads than cores. It's the job of the operating system scheduler to decide which thread gets to run on any particular processor core at any one time. (Or, more accurately, which thread gets to run on any particular *logical processor*—see the sidebar on the next page.)

A machine will usually have lots of threads—a quick glance at the Windows Task Manager's Performance pane indicates that this machine currently has 1,340 threads. Who'd have thought that writing a book would be such a complex activity? The extent to which this outnumbers the machine's four CPU cores highlights the fact that threads are an abstraction. They offer the illusion that the computer has an almost endless capacity for executing concurrent tasks.

Threads are able to outnumber logical processors by this margin because most threads spend the majority of their time waiting for something to happen. Most of those 1,340 threads have called operating system APIs that have *blocked*—they won't return until they have some information to provide. For example, desktop applications spend most of their time inside a Windows API call that returns messages describing mouse and keyboard input and the occasional system message (such as color scheme change notifications). If the user doesn't click on or type into an application, and if there are no system messages, these applications sit idle—their main thread remains blocked inside the API call until there's a message to return. This explains how a quad-core machine can support 1,340 threads while the CPU usage registers as just 1 percent.

Logical Processor, Cores, and Simultaneous Multithreading

Unlike the software threads created in Example 16-1, a *logical processor* is a real, physical thing. It's a part of a CPU capable of running one piece of code at a time. In the pictures that CPU vendors sometimes produce showing the innards of a processor, it's possible to identify the discrete areas of the chip that correspond to each logical processor. For this reason, a logical processor is also sometimes called a *hardware thread*. You can see how many logical processors a machine has in the Windows Task Manager—its Performance tab shows a CPU usage graph for each logical processor.

There are several different approaches to providing multiple hardware threads. A few years ago it was simple—a single CPU could do only one thing at a time, so you had exactly as many logical processors as you had CPU chips in your computer. But there are now a couple of ways to have multiple logical processors on a single chip.

A multicore CPU is conceptually fairly straightforward: roughly speaking, it's a single chip that happens to have multiple processors on it. But there's another technology known as *simultaneous multithreading* or SMT (or *hyperthreading*, in Intel's marketing terminology) in which a single core is able to execute multiple pieces of code simultaneously.

SMT requires less hardware than full multicore—in SMT some of the processing resources are shared. For example, a core might have only one piece of hardware capable of performing floating-point division operations, and there might also be just one piece of hardware dedicated to floating-point multiplication. If one hardware thread wants to multiply at the same time another hardware thread running on the same core wants to divide, those operations would be able to proceed in parallel, but if both want to perform division at the same time, one will have to wait until the other finishes. SMT processors have multiple sets of some resources—each hardware thread has its own set of registers, for example, and may have its own local hardware for certain frequently used arithmetic operations. So by duplicating only some of the hardware, SMT aims to cram multiple hardware threads into less silicon than a full multicore approach can, at the cost of less parallelism when threads end up competing for shared resources within the CPU.

Some CPUs use both techniques. For example, in some quad-core CPUs each core uses SMT to support two logical processors, so the CPU offers a total of eight logical processors. And of course, a computer might contain more than one processor chip—high-end motherboards offer multiple CPU slots. A machine with two quad-core processors with two SMT hardware threads per core would offer 16 logical processors, for example.

When a blocking API is finally ready to return, the thread becomes *runnable*. The operating system's *scheduler* is responsible for deciding which runnable threads get to use which logical processors. In an ideal world, you'll have exactly enough runnable threads to make full and perfect use of the CPU cycles you've paid for. In practice, there's usually a mismatch, so either one or more logical processors will be idle, or there will be contention for processing resources.

In the latter case—where there are more runnable threads than logical processors—the scheduler has to decide which threads currently most deserve to run. If a thread runs without blocking for a while (typically a few milliseconds) and there are other runnable threads, the OS scheduler may *preempt* that thread—it interrupts its execution, stores information about what it was doing at the point at which it was preempted, and gives a different thread some CPU time. If a logical processor becomes available later (either because enough threads block or because some other thread was preempted) the OS will put things back to how they were before preemption, and allow it to carry on. The time for which a thread will be allowed to run before preemption is known as a *quantum*.

The upshot of this is that even if you have more threads than logical processors, and all of the threads are trying to execute code simultaneously, the OS scheduler arranges for all of them to make progress, despite outnumbering the logical processors. This illusion has a price: preempting a thread and scheduling a different thread to use the CPU slows things down, and you'll often want to use the techniques we'll see later that try to avoid forcing the scheduler to do this.

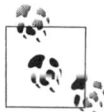 .NET's threading system is designed so that threads do not have to correspond directly to OS threads, but in practice they always do. At one point, Microsoft thought that .NET threads would need to be able to correspond to OS *fibers*, an alternative to threads where the application takes a more active part in scheduling decisions. This requirement came from a SQL Server 2005 feature that was cut shortly before the final release, so the distinction between OS threads and .NET threads is now essentially academic (although the feature could conceivably reemerge in a future version). It's useful to be aware of this because a handful of API features are designed to accommodate this feature, and also because there are plenty of articles you may run into on the Internet written either before the feature was cut or by people who haven't realized it was cut.

The Stack

Each thread has its own call stack, which means that items that live on the stack—function arguments and local variables—are local to the thread. We can exploit this to simplify Example 16-1, which contains three almost identical loops. Example 16-2 has just one copy of the loop which is shared by all three threads.

Example 16-2. Per-thread state on the stack

```
using System;
using System.Threading;

class Program
{
    static void Main(string[] args)
    {
        Thread t1 = new Thread(Go);
        Thread t2 = new Thread(Go);
```

```
        t1.Start("One");
        t2.Start("Two");

        Go("Main");
    }

    static void Go(object name)
    {
        for (int i = 0; i < 100; ++i)
        {
            Console.WriteLine("{0}: {1}", name, i);
        }
    }
}
```

The Go method here contains the common loop—it has been modified slightly to take an argument so that each thread can print out either One, Two, or Main as before. Running this produces similar output to the previous example. (It's not identical, of course, because these examples produce slightly different output every time they run.)

 We used a different overload of the Start method—we're now passing an argument. And less obviously, we're using a different constructor overload for Thread too—Example 16-1 used a constructor that accepts a delegate to a method taking zero arguments, but Example 16-2 uses an overload that accepts a delegate to a method that takes a single object argument. This overload provides one way of passing information into a thread when you start it—the argument we pass to Start is passed on to the Go method here.

This example illustrates an important point: multiple threads can be inside the same function at any time. All three threads in Example 16-2 spend most of their time inside the Go method. But since each thread gets its own stack, the values of the name argument and the loop variable (i) can be different for each thread.

Information that lives elsewhere is not intrinsically private to one thread. Example 16-3 shows another variation on our example. As with Example 16-2, it uses a common Go method to run a loop on all three threads, but the loop variable (i) is now a static field of the Program class—all three threads share the same variable.

Example 16-3. Erroneous sharing of state between threads

```
using System;
using System.Threading;

class Program
{
    // Visible to all threads. (Bad, in this example.)
    static int i;
```

```
static void Main(string[] args)
{
    i = 0;
    Thread t1 = new Thread(Go);
    Thread t2 = new Thread(Go);

    t1.Start("One");
    t2.Start("Two");

    Go("Main");
}

static void Go(object name)
{
    // Modifying shared state without suitable protection - bad!
    for ( ; i < 100; ++i)
    {
        Console.WriteLine("{0}: {1}", name, i);
    }
}
}
```

This example has a problem: all three threads will try to read and write the shared field, and things often go wrong when you do this. You might think that with three threads all sharing a single common counter, with each thread incrementing that counter every time they loop and each thread running until the counter hits 100, we'd just see all the numbers from 0 to 99 once. But it's not quite that simple. For one thing, you might see all three threads print out 0, because they may all get to the point where they're trying to print out the first value before any of them has gotten as far as trying to increment the counter. (Remember, a for loop executes its iterator clause—the ++i in this example—at the *end* of each iteration.) Then again you might not see that—it all really depends on when the OS scheduler lets the threads run. But there's a subtler problem: if two threads both attempt to execute the ++i at the same time, we may see anomalous results—the value of i may end up being lower than the number of times it has been incremented, for example. If you want to share state between threads, you'll need to use some of the synchronization mechanisms discussed later in this chapter.

Be aware that using local variables is not necessarily a guarantee that the state you're working with lives on the stack. For example, when using reference types (and most types are reference types) you need to keep in mind the distinction between the variable that contains the reference and the object to which that reference refers. Example 16-4 uses nothing but local variables, but ends up using the same StringBuilder object from all three threads—each thread might have its own local variable to refer to that object, but all three variables refer to the same object.

Example 16-4 does something slightly unusual with the `Thread` constructor. Our `Go` method now requires two arguments—the `StringBuilder` and the name—but `Thread` doesn't provide a way to pass in more than one argument; we get to choose an argument count of either zero or one. So we're using a lambda here to provide a zero-argument method for `Thread`, and that lambda passes the two arguments into `Go`, including the new `StringBuilder` argument. It has also enabled us to declare that the `Go` method is expecting the name to be a `string`, rather than the less specific `object` type used in the previous example. This technique doesn't have anything to do with threading; it's just a useful trick when you find yourself confronted with an API that takes a delegate that doesn't have enough arguments. (And it's not the cause of the problem here. Less concise ways of passing the object in would have had the same problem, and so would the use of multiple methods, which Example 16-1 illustrated.)

Example 16-4. Local variables, but shared state

```
using System;
using System.Threading;
using System.Text;

class Program
{
    static void Main(string[] args)
    {
        StringBuilder result = new StringBuilder();

        // Sharing the StringBuilder between threads. BAD!
        Thread t1 = new Thread(() => Go(result, "One"));
        Thread t2 = new Thread(() => Go(result, "Two"));

        t1.Start();
        t2.Start();

        Go(result, "Main");

        t1.Join();
        t2.Join();

        Console.WriteLine(result);
    }

    static void Go(StringBuilder sb, string name)
    {
```

```
        for (int i = 0; i < 100; ++i)
        {
            // All threads using the same StringBuilder - BAD!
            sb.AppendFormat("{0}: {1}", name, i);
            sb.AppendLine();
        }
    }
}
```

By the way, you'll have noticed that this code calls Join on both Thread objects. The Join method blocks until the thread has finished—this code needs to do that because it prints the output only once the threads are done. This is a simple example of coordinating operations across multiple threads. However, it's not sufficient to avoid problems here. Looking at the output, it's clear that all is not well. Here are the first few lines, running on a quad-core system:

```
Main: One: Two: 00
Main:
1

2
MainTwo: 3
Main: 1
2
2
Two: 3One: Two: 4
Two: One: 6Two: One: 7
One: 8
: One: 9
```

That's a whole lot more chaotic than the previous examples, which merely scrambled the order of the lines, and lost the odd increment. The reason this has gone more obviously wrong is that with the earlier examples, our attempt to observe the system profoundly changed its behavior. (That happens a lot with multithreaded code.) The calls to Console.WriteLine were imposing some order on the system, because the .NET Framework was forcing the threads to take it in turns when printing their output—that's why we don't get lines mixed up with one another. But Example 16-4 does all of its work in memory using a StringBuilder, and since it calls Console.WriteLine just once when it's done, to print the results, nothing is forcing things to happen in any particular order, and so we can see the chaos in full effect.

 There's another reason `Console.WriteLine` is likely to have a significant effect on behavior: it's relatively slow. The actual work being done by the examples so far is trivial—incrementing counters takes very little time, and concatenating strings is more complex but still pretty fast. Writing messages out to the screen is orders of magnitude slower. (The same would apply if you were writing messages to a logfile or the debugger.) So our previous examples were spending almost all of their time inside the code added to observe the code's behavior, and almost no time executing the behavior we were hoping to observe.

This sort of problem makes multithreaded code remarkably resistant to debugging—it is far more sensitive to the observer's paradox than other kinds of code. Generally speaking, as soon as you try to examine a threading bug, the bug goes away. (It comes back as soon as you stop looking, of course. Plenty of systems have gone live with debugging code compiled in because the debugging code made certain problems "go away." Don't rely on that—threading problems that appear to go away when you haven't really fixed them are really just hiding.)

Just to be clear, the reason for the chaos is that even though each thread has its own local `sb` variable held privately on that thread's stack, they all refer to the same `String Builder` object—we have three references to the same object. All three threads are trying to add output to the same `StringBuilder` at the same time, and the result is a mess.

You need to be absolutely clear in your head on where the information you're working with lives, where it came from, and whether other threads might be able to see it. Objects created by a particular thread are OK as long as you never make them visible to other threads—Example 16-4 hit problems because the main thread created a `StringBuilder` and then arranged for it to be accessible from the other two threads.

This means you need to be especially careful when using nested methods—either anonymous delegates or lambdas—because these provide a way to share local variables between threads. Example 16-5 shows how the problem in Example 16-3 can happen even with value type local variables. It has just one loop count variable (`i`) shared between all the threads, but it does this without making it a field—it's a local variable.

Example 16-5. Local value type variables as shared state

```
using System;
using System.Threading;

class Program
{
    static void Main(string[] args)
    {
        // Visible to all threads, thanks to use of
        // anonymous method. (Bad, in this example.)
        int i = 0;

        ParameterizedThreadStart go = delegate(object name)
```

```
        {
            // Modifying shared state without suitable protection - bad!
            for (; i < 100; ++i)
            {
                Console.WriteLine("{0}: {1}", name, i);
            }
        };


        Thread t1 = new Thread(go);
        Thread t2 = new Thread(go);

        t1.Start("One");
        t2.Start("Two");

        go("Main");
    }
}
```

This example demonstrates that while it may be convenient to think of value type local variables as living on the stack, it's not always true. Example 16-5 contains an anonymous method that makes use of the local i variable declared by the containing method (Main), so the C# compiler has been obliged to convert that variable into a field inside a generated class, in order to make it possible for that one variable to be used from multiple methods.

To summarize: information that really does live on the stack is private to a particular thread. Unfortunately, using local variables doesn't necessarily guarantee that the state you're working with is on the stack. Be wary of reference types—no matter where the reference lives, the thing it refers to will not be on the stack, so you need to understand what other code might have a reference to the object you're using. Be wary of value types whose implementation you do not control—value types are allowed to contain fields of reference types, so you're not guaranteed to be safe just because you're using a value type. And be wary of lambdas and anonymous methods—they can move information off the stack and into a place where it's accessible to multiple threads at once. We'll see later what to do if you really have to share information across threads.

The examples we've seen so far create threads explicitly in order to illustrate the operation of multiple threads. But .NET often creates threads automatically without you having created Thread objects. The most obvious example is the thread that the .NET Framework calls your Main method on, but there are others—some of the asynchronous communication mechanisms we saw in Chapter 13 call back into your code on different threads than the one you started work on. We'll be seeing more examples of this later in the chapter when we examine .NET's Asynchronous Programming Model.

In fact, it's relatively unusual to create new threads explicitly. If you need concurrent execution and you're not using some part of the .NET Framework that supplies you with threads when you need them, it's often better to use the thread pool or the Task Parallel Library, both of which we'll see later.

One problem with explicit thread creation is in knowing how many to create. Threads are relatively expensive—each one consumes system resources, and there are also factors that can limit the number of threads in a single process. There's also a cost in switching between threads—the *context switch* that occurs when the OS scheduler moves a thread from one logical processor to another. If you have many more runnable threads than logical processors, you'll pay this cost on a very regular basis, and it can start to have a significant effect on throughput. In an ideal world you would have no more threads than logical processors, avoiding any context switch overhead. However, most threads block from time to time, so in reality you tend to need more threads than logical processors if you want to fully use your CPU cycles. In general, you should try to keep the thread count as low as is practical—a single program that creates more than a handful per logical processor is likely to have problems.

 Never build a service that creates a new thread for each incoming request. This is a classic rookie mistake, as it seems like an obvious thing to do. It appears to work for light workloads, but it runs straight into two of the biggest performance problems you can hit with threads. First, creating threads is expensive, so if each thread exists only for as long as it takes to handle a single request, you risk spending more CPU time on setting up and destroying threads than on useful work. Second, this approach doesn't limit the number of threads, so as the system gets busy, its performance will get disproportionately worse thanks to context switching overhead and the memory footprint of the resources associated with each thread. You can avoid these problems by using either the asynchronous patterns or the thread pool techniques described later in this chapter.

Creating just enough threads is often hard, because getting the balance right depends on things such as your application's current workload, other work in progress on the machine, and characteristics of the machine itself. Fortunately, .NET provides the thread pool to make this sort of thing easier.

The Thread Pool

The .NET Framework provides a *thread pool*, which is a collection of worker threads available to perform short pieces of work. The thread pool continuously adjusts the number of threads that are allowed to process work items simultaneously in an attempt to optimize throughput.

The exact algorithm used to adjust the thread count is not documented, but as a general rule, if the system is not busy, work will typically be serviced very quickly after you queue it up. But as the computer becomes busier, items will sit in the queue for longer—the thread pool tries to avoid the overheads of preemption, thread switching, and resource contention by not running too much concurrent work. When a system is already busy, trying to process more work items would probably slow it down further, and so keeping items queued up and processing fewer at a time is likely to result in better overall performance.

The simplest way to use the thread pool is through its `QueueUserWorkItem` method. Example 16-6 shows a modification to the previous examples—rather than creating threads, it uses the thread pool. `QueueUserWorkItem` takes a delegate to any method that accepts a single object as its argument, so it's happy with the same `Go` method as Example 16-2. (Unlike the `Thread` constructor, there's no overload that accepts a method without an argument—the thread pool insists on there being an argument whether you have a use for one or not.)

Example 16-6. Queuing work items for the thread pool

```
static void Main(string[] args)
{
    ThreadPool.QueueUserWorkItem(Go, "One");
    ThreadPool.QueueUserWorkItem(Go, "Two");

    Go("Main");
    // Problem: not waiting for work items to complete!
}
```

This example has a problem: if the main thread finishes first, the program may exit before the thread pool work items complete. So this only illustrates how to *start* work on the thread pool. This might not be a problem in practice—it depends on your application's typical life cycle, but you may need to add additional code to coordinate completion. Running on a quad-core machine, this particular example behaves in much the same way as the previous ones, because the thread pool ends up creating a thread for both work items. On a single-core machine, you might see a difference—it could decide to let the first item run to completion and then run the second afterward.

The thread pool is designed for fairly short pieces of work. One of the most important jobs it was originally introduced for was to handle web requests in ASP.NET web applications, so if you're wondering how much work constitutes "fairly short," a reasonable answer is "about as much work as it takes to generate a web page."

.NET 4 introduces a new way to use the thread pool, the Task Parallel Library, which offers a couple of advantages. First, it handles certain common scenarios more efficiently than `QueueUserWorkItem`. Second, it offers more functionality. For example, tasks have much more comprehensive support for handling errors and completion, issues Example 16-6 utterly fails to address. If the main thread finishes before either of the work items is complete, that example will simply exit without waiting for them! And if you want the main thread to discover exceptions that occurred on the thread pool threads, there's no easy way to do that. If any of these things is important to you, the Task Parallel Library is a better way to use the thread pool. There's a whole section on that later in this chapter. For now, we'll continue looking at some aspects of threading that you need to know, no matter what multithreading mechanisms you may be using.

Thread Affinity and Context

Not all threads are equal. Some work can be done on only certain threads. For example, WPF and Windows Forms both impose a similar requirement: an object representing something in the user interface must be used only on the thread that created that object in the first place. These objects have *thread affinity*, meaning that they belong to one particular thread.

 Not all things with thread affinity are quite as obstinate as user interface elements. For example, while some COM objects have thread affinity issues, they are usually more flexible. (COM, the Component Object Model, is the basis of various Windows technologies including ActiveX controls. It predates .NET, and we'll see how to use it from .NET in Chapter 19.) .NET handles some of the COM thread affinity work for you, making it possible to use a COM object from any thread. The main ways in which COM's thread affinity will affect you are that certain objects will have different performance characteristics depending on which thread you call them on, and there may be additional complications if your COM objects use callbacks.

So thread affinity just means that the thread you're calling on makes a difference. It doesn't always mean that using the wrong thread is guaranteed to fail—it depends on what you're using.

If you never write multithreaded code, you never have to worry about thread affinity— if you do everything on one thread, it will always be the right one. But as soon as multiple threads get involved—either explicitly or implicitly[†]—you may need to add code to get things back on the right thread.

ASP.NET has a similar problem. It makes contextual information about the current request available to the thread handling the request, so if you use multiple threads to handle a single request, those other threads will not have access to that contextual information. Strictly speaking, this isn't a thread affinity issue—ASP.NET can use different threads at different stages of handling a single request—but it presents the same challenge to the developer: if you start trying to use ASP.NET objects from some random thread, you will have problems.

The .NET Framework defines a solution that's common to WPF, Windows Forms, and ASP.NET. The `SynchronizationContext` class can help you out if you find yourself on the wrong thread when using any of these frameworks. Example 16-7 shows how you can use this in an event handler for a GUI application—the click handler for a button, perhaps.

[†] Always remember that even if you have not created any threads explicitly, that doesn't mean you're necessarily writing single-threaded code. Some .NET Framework classes will bring extra threads into play implicitly. For example, the CLR's garbage collector runs finalizers on a distinct thread.

Example 16-7. Handling thread affinity with SynchronizationContext

```
SynchronizationContext originalContext = SynchronizationContext.Current;

ThreadPool.QueueUserWorkItem(delegate
    {
        string text = File.ReadAllText(@"c:\temp\log.txt");

        originalContext.Post(delegate
        {
            myTextBox.Text = text;
        }, null);
    });
```

The code reads all the text in from a file, and that's something that might take awhile. Event handlers in WPF and Windows Forms are called on the thread that the event source belongs to—a UI thread. (Or *the* UI thread if, like most desktop applications, you have only one UI thread.) You should never do slow work on a UI thread—thread affinity means that if your code is busy using that thread, none of the UI elements belonging to that thread will be able to do anything until you're finished. The user interface will be unresponsive for as long as you keep the thread busy. So Example 16-7 uses the thread pool to do the work, keeping the UI thread free.

But the code wants to update the UI when it has finished—it's going to put the text it has retrieved from the file into a text box. Since a text box is a UI element, it has thread affinity—we can update it only if we're on the UI thread. This is where `Synchroniza tionContext` comes to the rescue.

Before starting the slow work, Example 16-7 reads the `SynchronizationContext` class's `Current` property. This static property returns an object that represents the context you're in when you read it—precisely what that means will depend on what UI framework you're using. (The object you get back works differently depending on whether your application uses WPF, Windows Forms, or ASP.NET.) But the exact implementation doesn't matter—you just need to hold on to it until you need to get back to that context. Having grabbed the context while we were in the click handler, we then kick off the work in the thread pool. And once that work is complete, it calls the stored `SynchronizationContext` object's `Post` method. `Post` takes a delegate, and it'll invoke that delegate back in whatever context you were in when you grabbed the context. So in this case, it'll invoke our delegate on the UI thread that the button belongs to. Since we're back on our application's UI thread, we're now able to update the text box.

Common Thread Misconceptions

There are some persistent myths surrounding threads, which sometimes lead to their overuse. As the current trend seems to be for the number of logical processors in typical machines to edge ever upward, developers sometimes feel practically obliged to write multithreaded code. Since using threads correctly is difficult and error-prone, it's worth tackling some of these myths, in case you're in a situation where a single-threaded solution might actually be better.

Myth: Threads are necessary to get work done

You need a thread to run code, but that's not the only kind of work computers do. In fact, it's a fairly unusual program that spends most of the time executing code; CPU usage of 100 percent is often a sign that a program has hung. Computers contain various kinds of specialized hardware capable of getting on with work while the CPU is either idle or off doing something else—messages can be sent and received over the network, data can be read from and written to disk, graphics can be rendered, sound can be played. Code needs to run to *coordinate* these activities, but that typically needs to happen at the start, when kicking off some work, and then again at the end once the work completes. In between, all the interesting work is being done by specialized hardware. The CPU has no role to play, and may well enter a low-power idle state where it's not doing any work at all.

 That's why the fans on some computers spin up into high speed when the machine gets busy—most of the time the CPU is asleep and consuming relatively little power. The cooling system's full capacity is needed only when the CPU is executing code for sustained periods.

Nontrivial code in real programs tends to involve multifaceted work, so the CPU might have work to do at various stages besides the start and finish, but even then, you tend to see long periods of waiting for things to happen punctuated by short bursts of CPU activity, particularly when multiple machines are involved (such as a web server and a database server). Even fast computer networks can take hundreds of microseconds to send a message, and while that may appear instantaneous to human eyes, modern CPUs are able to execute hundreds of thousands of instructions in that time. Measured against how fast CPUs run, network communications always appear glacially slow. And it's a similar story with most I/O.

The nature of I/O is often not obvious from the way APIs are structured. For example, look at the call to `File.ReadAllText` in Example 16-7—the obvious way to think of that is as a method that reads all the contents of a file off disk and returns the contents as text once it's finished. It seems like the thread we use to call that method is busy doing work for as long as it takes. But in fact, most of the time the thread is inside that method, it will almost certainly be blocked—it won't be in a runnable state, because it's waiting for the disk controller in the computer to fetch the file's content off disk. And unless the disk in question is a solid state drive, it could take milliseconds to get the information into memory—that part of the process will take orders of magnitude longer than the code inside `ReadAllText` that converts those bytes back into a .NET string object.

 Solid state drives change things only a little. You don't need to wait for bits of metal to lumber into position, but the fact that they are physically separate components slows things down—it will take time for the disk controller hardware to send suitable messages to the drive, and for the drive to send a response. The difference between the time spent retrieving data and processing that data will not be as dramatic, but the code will still account for a small proportion.

The one situation in which this particular example might be dominated by CPU usage rather than time spent waiting for I/O is if the file in question is already in the operating system's filesystem cache—when the OS reads data off disk it tends to keep a copy in memory for a while just in case you need it again. In that case, the disk doesn't need to be involved at all, and it really is all CPU time. You need to be wary of this when testing performance—the first time a particular file is read will be much slower than all the rest. If you run a test hundreds of times to get a good average measurement, you'll be ignoring the "first" and testing the "all the rest" case, but in a desktop application the one most users will notice is often the first case. For interactive code, the worst case can matter far more than the average.

An upshot of this is that using asynchronous APIs is sometimes much more effective than creating lots of threads. On the server, this can yield better throughput because you avoid the overheads associated with having more threads than you need. And on the client, it can sometimes simplify code considerably, as some asynchronous APIs let you work with a single-threaded model with no loss of responsiveness.

Myth: Multiple logical processors will necessarily make things faster

For years, processors managed to double CPU performance on a regular basis—a new processor would do everything that the one you bought a couple of years ago could do, but twice as fast. We were in the luxurious position where our code just got faster and faster without having to do anything, and because the growth was exponential—doubling up again and again   the cumulative effects were astounding. Computers are tens of millions of times faster than they were a few decades ago.

Sadly, that all stopped a few years ago because we started running into some harsh realities of physics. In response to this, CPU vendors have switched to providing more and more logical processors as a means of continuing to deliver processors that are, in some sense, twice as fast as the ones from a couple of years ago. They can do this because even though clock speeds have stopped doubling up, Moore's law—that the number of transistors per chip doubles roughly every two years—is still in action for the time being.

Unfortunately, the doubling in speed between a single-core and dual-core system is hypothetical. Technically, the dual-core system might be able to perform twice as many calculations as the single-core one in any given length of time, but this is an improvement only if it's possible to divide the work the user needs to do in a way that keeps both cores busy, and even if that's possible, it's effective only if other resources in the system such as memory and disk are able to provide input to the calculations fast enough for this double-speed processing.

Work often cannot progress in parallel. The second step of a calculation might depend on the results of the first step, in which case you can't usefully run the two steps on different cores—the core running the second step would just have to sit around and wait for the result from the first step. It would probably be faster to run both steps on a single core, because that avoids the overheads of getting the results of the first step out of the first core and into the second core. Where the calculations are sequential, multiple cores don't help.

So the nature of the work matters. Certain jobs are relatively easy to parallelize. For example, some kinds of image processing can be spread over multiple logical processors—if the processing is localized (e.g., applying a blur effect by smearing nearby pixels into one another), it's possible for different logical processors to be working on different parts of the image. Even here you won't get a 4x speedup on a four-core system, because some coordination might be necessary at the boundaries, and other parts of the system such as memory bandwidth may become a bottleneck, but these sorts of tasks typically see a useful improvement. However, these so-called *embarrassingly parallel* tasks are the exception rather than the rule—a lot of computation is sequential in practice. And of course, many problems live in a middle ground, where they can exploit parallelism up to a certain point, and no further. So there's usually a limit to how far multithreading can help programs execute faster.

That doesn't stop some people from trying to use as many multiple logical processors as possible, or from realizing when doing so has failed to make things better. It's easy to be distracted by achieving high CPU usage, when the thing you really want to measure is how quickly you can get useful work done.

Myth: Maxing the CPU must mean we're going really fast

It's possible to construct parallel solutions to problems that manage to use all the available CPU time on all logical processors, and yet which proceed more slowly than single-threaded code that does the same job on one logical processor. Figure 16-1 shows the CPU load reported by the Windows Task Manager for two different solutions to the same task.

The image on the left might make you feel that you're making better use of your multicore system than the one on right. The righthand side is using far less than half the available CPU capacity. But measuring the elapsed time to complete the task, the code that produced the lefthand image took about 15 times longer to complete than the code that produced the righthand one!

The job in hand was trivial—both examples just increment a field 400 million times. Example 16-8 shows both main loops. The Go function is the one that gets invoked concurrently on four threads. GoSingle just runs multiple times in succession to perform the iterations sequentially.

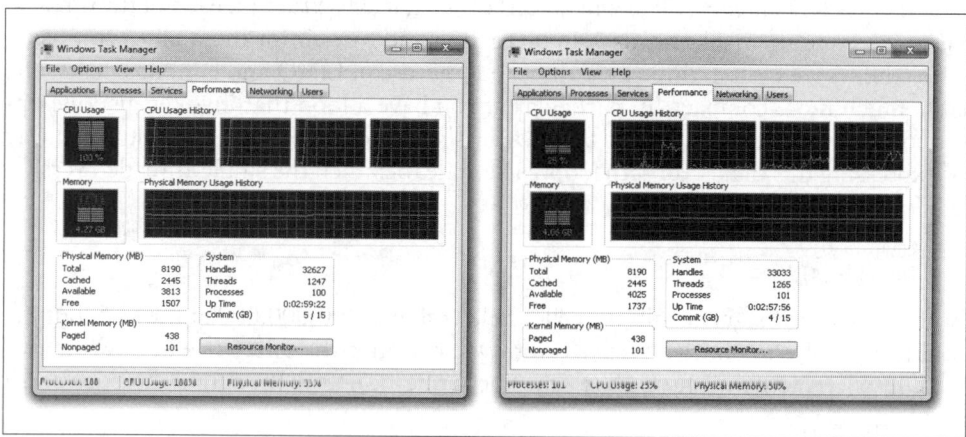

Figure 16-1. Using all logical processors (left) versus just one (right)

Example 16-8. Multithreaded versus single-threaded

```csharp
class Program
{
    static int Count;
    const int Iterations = 100000000;

    static void Go()
    {
        for (int i = 0; i < Iterations; ++i)
        {
            Interlocked.Increment(ref Count);
        }
    }

    static void GoSingle(int repeat)
    {
        for (int outer = 0; outer < repeat; ++outer)
        {
            for (int i = 0; i < Iterations; ++i)
            {
                Count += 1;
            }
        }
    }

    ...
```

Here's the code that launches `Go` concurrently:

```
Count = 0;
List<Thread> threads = (from i in Enumerable.Range(0, 4)
                            select new Thread(Go)).ToList();

threads.ForEach(t => t.Start());
threads.ForEach(t => t.Join());
```

This creates four threads, all of which call `Go`. Next, it calls `Start` on each of the threads. Having started them all, it calls `Join` on each thread to wait for them all to complete. (We could have written three loops here, but our use of LINQ and lambdas makes the code much more compact. In particular, if you have a loop that invokes just one operation on every item in a list the `List<T>` class's `ForEach` method is a less cluttered way of expressing this than a `foreach` loop.) The code to launch the single-threaded version is a lot simpler:

```
Count = 0;
GoSingle(4);
```

Both produce the same result: the `Count` field contains 400,000,000 at the end. But the multithreaded version was much slower. One reason is the difference in how the two versions increment the `Count`. Here's the line in question from the single-threaded code:

```
Count += 1;
```

But if we try that in the multithreaded version, it doesn't work. It certainly makes it run nice and quickly—about three times faster than the single-threaded version—but trying it a few times, `Count` comes to 110,460,151, then 133,533,503, then 133,888,803... The majority of increments are getting lost—that's the sort of thing that happens when you don't use suitable protection for accessing shared state. That's why the multithreaded version needs to do this:

```
Interlocked.Increment(ref Count);
```

The `Interlocked` class in the `System.Threading` namespace provides methods that perform certain simple operations in ways that work even if multiple threads try to use them on the same data at the same time. As the name suggests, `Increment` increments the count, and it does this in a way that locks out any other logical processors attempting to do the same thing at the same time. It forces the logical processors to take it in turns.

It works—the `Count` total is correct with this code in place—but at some cost. On a quad-core system, with all four cores burning away at 100 percent, this takes 15 times longer than the simple single-threaded solution.

In fact, the cost of `Interlocked.Increment` does not fully explain the difference. Modifying the single-threaded version to work the same way makes it run about five times slower, but that's still three times faster than the multithreaded code. So a considerable amount of the slowdown is down to the communication costs between the processors.

Don't take these numbers too seriously. This is clearly a contrived example. (If we wanted it to run really fast we could just have initialized Count to 400,000,000 to start with, and removed the loop.) But while the details are spurious the basic principle applies broadly: the cost of contention between logical processors that are supposed to be cooperating can work against you. Sometimes they merely erode the benefit—you might see a 2.5x speedup on a quad-core system, for example. But sometimes they really do negate the benefit—contrived though this example may be, much worse examples have cropped up in real systems.

> Some implementations may come out worse on some systems and better on others. For example, some parallel algorithms take a considerable hit relative to their sequential counterparts in order to be able to scale well on more processors. Such an algorithm might make sense only on systems where you have a large number of processors—it might be slower than the single-threaded version on a dual-core system, but very worthwhile on a system with 16 logical processors, for example.

The bottom line is that if you want to understand whether a parallel solution is effective, you need to compare it against a single-threaded solution on the same hardware. Just because your CPU loads indicate that you're being extremely parallel, that's not necessarily the same as being really fast. And unless your code will only ever run on a single hardware configuration, you need to perform the same comparison on lots of different machines to get a good idea of how often a parallel solution might be the best choice.

Multithreaded Coding Is Hard

Even when multithreaded code provides a demonstrable performance benefit, it's very hard to get right. We've already seen a few bizarre behaviors in some extremely simple examples. Achieving correct behavior in a real concurrent system can be very challenging. So we'll look at two of the most common classes of pitfalls before examining some strategies for avoiding them.

Race conditions

The anomalies we've seen so far have all been examples of a kind of concurrency hazard known as a *race*, so called because the outcome is determined by which participant gets to a particular place first. Example 16-1 displays different output each time it runs, because there are three threads all trying to print to the same console window, and the only thing that determines which one gets to print the next line is whichever happens to be the next to call Console.WriteLine.[‡] There is no coordination between the threads, and so they all pile in at once. It's a relatively complicated example in some ways,

---

[‡] More accurately, it's whichever thread acquires the lock Console.WriteLine uses internally to serialize access to the console.

because most of the race happens where we can't see it—that example spends almost all of its time inside `Console.WriteLine`. It's easier to understand races when you can see all of the code.

So consider the broken variation of Example 16-8 where the concurrently executing `Go` method used a simple `Count += 1` instead of `Interlocked.Increment`. We saw that using the `+=` operator resulted in lost increments, but why? The `+=` operator has to do three things: first it must read the current value of `Count`, then it has to add 1 to that value, and finally it has to store the result back into the variable. The RAM chips in your computer don't have the ability to perform calculations, so there's no getting away from the fact that the value has to go into the CPU so that it can calculate the new value, and then it has to be written back out again so that the new value is not forgotten. There will always be a read and then a write.

Consider what happens when two threads try to increment the same `Count` field. Let's call them Thread A and Thread B. Table 16-1 shows one possible sequence of events. In this case it works out fine: `Count` starts at 0, is incremented twice, and ends up at 2.

Table 16-1. Two increments, one after the other

Count	Thread A	Thread B
0	Read Count (0)	
0	Add 1 (0 + 1 = 1)	
1	Write Count (1)	
1		Read Count (1)
1		Add 1 (1 + 1 = 2)
2		Write Count (2)

But it might not work so well. Table 16-2 shows what happens if the work overlaps, as could easily happen with multiple logical processors. Thread B reads the current `Count` while Thread A was already part of the way through the job of incrementing it. When Thread B comes to write back its update, it has no way of knowing that Thread A has updated the value since B did its read, so it effectively loses A's increment.

Table 16-2. Lost increment due to overlap

Count	Thread A	Thread B
0	Read Count (0)	
0	Add 1 (0 + 1 = 1)	Read Count (0)
1	Write Count (1)	Add 1 (0 + 1 = 1)
1		Write Count

There are lots of variations on the order, some of which work fine and some of which fail. If your code makes possible an ordering that produces wrong results, sooner or later you'll run into it.

 Don't fall into the trap of believing that a highly improbable outcome is effectively impossible. You'll be fooling yourself—sooner or later the problem will bite. The only difference with the highly improbable problems is that they're extremely hard to diagnose and debug.

The example shown here is about as simple as a race gets. With real code things tend to be a lot more complex, as you will probably be dealing with data structures more intricate than a single integer. But in general, if you have information which is visible to multiple threads and at least one of those threads is changing that information in any way, race conditions are likely to emerge if you don't take steps to prevent them.

The solution to races is, on the face of it, obvious: the threads need to take it in turns. If threads A and B simply coordinated their operations so that either would wait until the other was done when an update is in progress, we could avoid the problem. `Inter` `locked.Increment` does exactly that, although it's rather specialized. For the occasions when you're doing something more complex than incrementing a field, .NET provides a set of synchronization mechanisms that let you force threads to take it in turns. We'll get to these shortly. However, this solution introduces another class of problem.

Deadlocks and livelocks

When code waits in order to avoid stepping on other threads' toes, it's possible for the application to lock up, because all the threads can end up waiting for each other to finish. This tends not to happen with simple, short operations involving just a single piece of data. Lockups typically occur when a thread that already has exclusive access to some data starts waiting for something else.

The standard example involves transferring money between two bank accounts; let's call them X and Y. Suppose two threads, A and B, are both attempting to transfer money between these two accounts; A transfers money from X to Y while B transfers from Y to X. Both threads will need to use some sort of synchronization mechanism to get exclusive access to the accounts in order to avoid race conditions of the kind previously discussed. But imagine that the following happens:

1. Initially, no threads are attempting to do anything to either account.
2. Thread A gets exclusive access to Account X.
3. Thread B gets exclusive access to Account Y.
4. Thread A attempts to get exclusive access to Account Y—it can't because B has access, so A waits for B to relinquish Account Y.
5. Thread B attempts to get exclusive access to Account X—it can't because A has access, so B waits for A to relinquish Account X.

The exact mechanism used to manage exclusive access is irrelevant because the outcome is the same: A has come to a halt waiting for B to let go of Y. But B isn't going to let go of Y until it has managed to acquire X, and unfortunately it won't be able to—A is in possession of X and has just come to a halt. Neither side can proceed because each is waiting for the other to let go. This is sometimes known as a *deadly embrace*.

This condition can cause both *deadlocks* and *livelocks*, and the distinction has to do with the mechanism used to manage exclusive access. If threads go into a blocked state while waiting for access, neither thread is runnable once we hit the deadly embrace, and that's typically described as a deadlock—the symptom is a system that has gone idle, despite having work to be getting on with. A livelock is similar, but tends to involve synchronization mechanisms that use CPU cycles while waiting—some synchronization primitives actively poll for availability rather than blocking. Active polling is just as subject to a deadly embrace as a blocking approach, it just has different symptoms—livelocks hang with high CPU usage.

 The two concurrency hazards just described—races and deadly embraces—are not the only kinds of multithreading problems. There are endless ways in which you can get into trouble in concurrent systems, so we can really only scratch the surface. For example, besides issues that can compromise the correct behavior of your code, a whole host of concurrency issues can cause performance problems. For a deep discussion of the issues and what to do about them, we recommend *Concurrent Programming on Windows* by Joe Duffy (Addison-Wesley).

What can we do to avoid the numerous pitfalls of multithreaded code?

Multithreading Survival Strategies

There are several approaches for mitigating the difficulties of multithreading, each with a different trade-off between difficulty and flexibility.

Abstinence

Obviously, the simplest way to avoid the risks inherent in multithreading is not to do it at all. This doesn't necessarily mean abandoning everything in this chapter, however. One of the asynchronous patterns can enable certain kinds of applications to get some of the benefits of asynchrony while sticking with a single-threaded programming model.

Isolation

If you're going to have multiple threads, a good way to keep things simple is to avoid sharing information between them. ASP.NET encourages this model—it uses the thread pool to handle multiple requests simultaneously, but by default each individual request runs your code on just one thread. (You can opt into an explicitly asynchronous model if you want to use multiple threads per request, but for straightforward scenarios the single-threaded style is best.) So although the web application as a whole is able to run multiple concurrent threads, those threads don't interact.

This approach requires some discipline. There's nothing in .NET that enforces isolation[§]—you simply have to choose not to share data between threads. In a web application, that's relatively easy because HTTP naturally discourages stateful communications, although if you start using caching techniques to improve performance, you lose some isolation because all your requests will end up using shared objects in your cache. And any information in a static field (or any object reachable directly or indirectly from a static field) is potentially shared.

Chances are good that most multithreaded applications will have at least some information that needs to be accessed by several threads, so complete isolation may not be realistic. But maximizing isolation is a good idea—keeping as much information as possible local to individual threads means not having to worry about concurrency hazards for any of that information.

Immutability

When you really have to share data, you can often avoid many concurrency hazards by sharing only *immutable* data, that is, data that cannot be altered. Fields marked with `readonly` cannot be modified after construction—the C# compiler enforces this—so you don't have to worry about whether those fields are being changed by other threads as you try to use them. You need to be careful, though—`readonly` applies only to the field itself, and not the object the field refers to if it's a reference type. (And even if the field is a value type, if that value itself contains fields of reference types, the objects being referred to are not affected by `readonly`.) So as with isolation, this is an option that requires some discipline.

Synchronization

If you're writing multithreaded code, sooner or later you will probably need to have at least some information that is accessible to multiple threads, and which occasionally needs to be changed—isolation and immutability are sometimes simply not options. In this case, you'll need to synchronize access to the data—for example, anytime shared information is being modified, you'll need to make sure no other threads are trying to read or write that information. This requires the most discipline of any of the solutions described here, and is likely to be the most complex, but it offers the most flexibility.

The .NET Framework provides a wide range of features to help you synchronize the way your threads access shared information, and these are the topic of the next section.

[§] .NET does have an isolation mechanism: you can divide code into so-called *appdomains*. But this adds its own complications and is designed for slightly more coarse-grained divisions, and it's really not well suited to this problem. ASP.NET can use this to isolate multiple web applications sharing a process, but does not use it to isolate individual requests.

Synchronization Primitives

There are two important ways in which the operations of multiple threads may need to be coordinated. When you have shared modifiable data, it needs to be possible to make threads take it in turns to access that data. But it's also often important for threads to be able to discover when something has happened—a thread might want to enter a blocking state until such time as it has useful work to do, for example. So some synchronization primitives provide notification rather than exclusive access. Some offer a combination of the two.

Monitor

The most widely used synchronization primitive in .NET is the monitor. It is supported directly by the .NET Framework—any object can be used with this facility—and also by C#, which provides a special keyword for working with monitors. Monitors offer both mutual exclusion and notification.

The simplest use of a monitor is to ensure that threads take it in turns to access shared state. Example 16-9 shows some code that would need the kind of protection a monitor can provide before we could use it from multiple threads. It is designed for handling lists of recently used strings—you might use this sort of code to provide a recently used file list on an application's File menu. This code makes no attempt to protect itself in the face of multithreading.

Example 16-9. Code unsuitable for multithreading

```
class MostRecentlyUsed
{
    private List<string> items = new List<string>();
    private int maxItems;

    public MostRecentlyUsed(int maximumItemCount)
    {
        maxItems = maximumItemCount;
    }

    public void UseItem(string item)
    {
        // If the item was already in the list, and isn't the first
        // item, remove it from its current position, since we're
        // about to make it this first item.
        int itemIndex = items.IndexOf(item);
        if (itemIndex > 0)
        {
            items.RemoveAt(itemIndex);
        }

        // If the item's already the first, we don't need to do anything.
        if (itemIndex != 0)
        {
```

```
        items.Insert(0, item);

        // Ensure we have no more than the maximum specified
        // number of items.
        if (items.Count > maxItems)
        {
            items.RemoveAt(items.Count - 1);
        }
    }
}

public IEnumerable<string> GetItems()
{
    return items.ToArray();
}
}
```

Example 16-10 is some test code to exercise the class.

Example 16-10. Testing the MostRecentlyUsed class

```
const int Iterations = 10000;

static void TestMru(MostRecentlyUsed mru)
{
    // Initializing random number generator with thread ID ensures
    // each thread provides different data. (Although it also makes
    // each test run different, which may not be ideal.)
    Random r = new Random(Thread.CurrentThread.ManagedThreadId);
    string[] items = { "One", "Two", "Three", "Four", "Five",
                       "Six", "Seven", "Eight" };
    for (int i = 0; i < Iterations; ++i)
    {
        mru.UseItem(items[r.Next(items.Length)]);
    }
}
```

Example 16-10 just feeds in strings from a fixed set of items at random. Calling this test function from just one thread produces the expected results: at the end, the Mos tRecentlyUsed object just returns the most recent items put into it by this test. However, the multithreaded test in Example 16-11 causes something quite different to happen.

Example 16-11. Executing a multithreaded test

```
MostRecentlyUsed mru = new MostRecentlyUsed(4);

const int TestThreadCount = 2;
List<Thread> threads = (from i in Enumerable.Range(0, TestThreadCount)
                        select new Thread(() => TestMru(mru))).ToList();

threads.ForEach(t => t.Start());
threads.ForEach(t => t.Join());

foreach (string item in mru.GetItems())
{
```

```
        Console.WriteLine(item);
}
```

This example crashes on a multicore machine—after awhile, it throws an `ArgumentOu`
`tOfRangeException`. It doesn't crash at the same place on every run; it crashes inside
either of the two calls to the `List<T>` class's `RemoveAt` method.

The exceptions occur due to races. For instance, consider this line of code from Example 16-9:

```
        items.RemoveAt(items.Count - 1);
```

This reads the value of the `Count` property, then subtracts 1 to get the index of the last
item in the list, and then removes that last item. The race here is that some other thread
may manage to remove an item from the list in between this thread reading the `Count`
property and calling `RemoveAt`. This causes the method to throw an `ArgumentOutOfRan`
`geException`, because we end up asking it to remove an item at an index that's after the
final item.

In fact, we're lucky we got an exception at all. The `List<T>` class makes no guarantees
when we use it from multiple threads. Here's what the documentation for the class says
in the Thread Safety section:

> Public static members of this type are thread safe. Any instance members are not guar-
> anteed to be thread safe.

This means that it's our problem to make sure we never try to use a `List<T>` instance
from more than one thread at a time. It could fail in subtler ways than crashing—it
could corrupt data, for example.

 `List<T>` is not unusual. Most types in the .NET Framework class library
make no guarantees of thread safety for instance members.

We could add similar documentation to our `MostRecentlyUsed` class, declaring that it
does not make any guarantees either. In fact, that might well be the best option—it's
very difficult for an individual class to guarantee to work correctly in all possible multithreading scenarios. Only the application that uses the class really knows what constitutes correct behavior. For example, it might be necessary for a `MostRecentlyUsed`
object to be kept in sync with some other object, in which case the application is going
to have to manage all synchronization itself, and there's nothing useful that our class
could do on its own. This is one reason why the lack of thread safety guarantees is so
widespread in the class libraries—there isn't a good general-purpose definition of
thread-safe for individual types.

If we decide to make it the application's problem, how would that look? We don't have
a real application here, only a test, so our test code would need to synchronize its calls
into our object. Example 16-12 shows a suitably modified version of the test method

from Example 16-10. (Note that Example 16-11 adds code that also uses the same object, so you might think we need to make a similar modification there. However, it waits until all the test threads have finished before touching the object, so its reads won't overlap with their writes, making locking superfluous. Therefore, Example 16-12 is sufficient in this case.)

Example 16-12. Synchronization in the calling code

```
static void TestMru(MostRecentlyUsed mru)
{
    Random r = new Random(Thread.CurrentThread.ManagedThreadId);
    string[] items = { "One", "Two", "Three", "Four", "Five",
                       "Six", "Seven", "Eight" };
    for (int i = 0; i < Iterations; ++i)
    {
        lock (mru)
        {
            mru.UseItem(items[r.Next(items.Length)]);
        }
    }
}
```

The only modification here is to wrap the call to the `MostRecentlyUsed` type's `UseItem` method with a `lock` block. The C# `lock` syntax generates some code that uses the `Monitor` class, along with some exception handling. Here's what the `lock` block in Example 16-12 is equivalent to:

```
MostRecentlyUsed referenceToLock = mru);
bool lockAcquired = false;
try
{
    Monitor.Enter(referenceToLock, ref lockAcquired);
    mru.UseItem(items[r.Next(items.Length)]);
}
finally
{
    if (lockAcquired)
    {
        Monitor.Exit(referenceToLock);
    }
}
```

(This is what C# 4.0 generates. Older versions do something slightly simpler that mishandles an obscure and unusual failure mode. But the basic idea is the same in either case. The generated code copies the `mru` reference into a separate variable to ensure correct operation even if the code inside the lock block were to change `mru`.)

The documentation says that `Monitor.Enter` acquires an exclusive lock on the object passed as the first argument, but what exactly does that mean? Well, the first thread to do this will find that `Monitor.Enter` returns immediately. Any other threads that try to make the same call on the same object will be made to wait—`Monitor.Enter` on those other threads will not return until the thread that currently owns the lock releases it by calling `Monitor.Exit`. Only one thread can hold the lock at any time, so if multiple other threads are waiting for the same object's lock in `Monitor.Enter`, the .NET Framework will pick just one as the next owner of the lock, and the other threads will continue to be blocked.

 Holding a lock on an object has only one effect: it prevents any other thread from acquiring a lock on that object. It does nothing else. In particular, it does *not* prevent other threads from using that object. So it would be a mistake to think that acquiring the lock on an object means you have locked the object. That may sound like splitting hairs, but it's the difference between working and broken code.

Use of monitors is entirely a matter of convention—it is up to you to decide which objects' locks you use to protect which information. Example 16-12 happens to acquire a lock on the very object whose state is being protected, but in fact, it's quite common— preferable, even—to create separate objects whose only job is to be the thing on which you acquire a lock. There are a couple of reasons for this. First, you'll often want multiple pieces of data to fall under the protection of a single lock—perhaps updates to our `MostRecentlyUsed` object need to be done in conjunction with changes to other state within the application, such as a history-tracking service. When multiple objects are involved, arbitrarily choosing one of those objects to act as the lock target is likely to make your code harder to follow, because it may not be clear to someone reading your code that you're using that object's lock to protect multiple objects rather than just the one whose lock you're acquiring. If you create a special object whose only purpose is locking, this makes it clear to anyone reading your code that she needs to think about what state that lock protects.

The other reason to avoid acquiring a lock on the object you want to synchronize access to is that you can't always be sure that the object doesn't acquire a lock on itself—some developers write `lock(this)` inside instance methods when trying to make thread-safe objects (for whatever definition of thread-safe they have chosen). It is a bad practice to acquire a lock on your `this` reference, of course, because you can't necessarily know whether someone using your object will decide to try to acquire a lock on it for his own purposes—internal locking is an implementation detail, but your `this` reference is public, and you don't usually want implementation details to be public.

So in short, you shouldn't try to acquire a lock on any object you are trying to synchronize access to.

Bearing all that in mind, what should we do if we want to try to make our `MostRecentlyUsed` class more robust in multithreaded environments? First, we need to decide what multithreading scenarios we want to support. Simply declaring that we want the type to be thread-safe is meaningless.

So let's say that we want to allow multiple threads to call UseItem and GetItems simultaneously without causing exceptions. That's a pretty weak guarantee—notice we've said nothing about what state the object will be in afterward, merely that it won't actually blow up. Surely it would be better to guarantee to handle the calls in the order in which they were made. Unfortunately, we can't do this if the locking logic lives entirely inside the class. The OS scheduler might decide to preempt a thread moments after it called UseItem, and before it has had a chance to get to any of our synchronization code.

For example, consider what could happen if Thread A calls UseItem, and then before that call returns, Thread B also calls UseItem, and before either returns, Thread C calls GetItems. It's fairly easy to think of at least five reasonable outcomes. GetItems might return neither of the items passed in by A and B. It might return both, and there are two ways it could do this—GetItems returns an ordered list and either A or B might come first. Or it could return just one—either the one passed by A or just the one passed by B. If you need coordination *across* multiple calls like this it's not going to be possible to do that *inside* MostRecentlyUsed, because you only have the opportunity to start synchronization work once calls are already underway. This is another reason why synchronization code usually belongs at the application level and not in the individual objects. So about the best we can hope to achieve within this class is to prevent the exceptions from occurring when it's used from multiple threads. Example 16-13 does this.

Example 16-13. Adding locking to a class

```
class MostRecentlyUsed
{
    private List<string> items = new List<string>();
    private int maxItems;
    private object lockObject = new object();

    public MostRecentlyUsed(int maximumItemCount)
    {
        maxItems = maximumItemCount;
    }

    public void UseItem(string item)
    {
        lock (lockObject)
        {
            // If the item was already in the list, and isn't the first item,
            // remove it from its current position, since we're about to make
            // it this first item.
            int itemIndex = items.IndexOf(item);
            if (itemIndex > 0)
            {
                items.RemoveAt(itemIndex);
            }

            // If the item's already the first, we don't need to do anything.
```

```
        if (itemIndex != 0)
        {
            items.Insert(0, item);

            // Ensure we have no more than the maximum specified
            // number of items.
            if (items.Count > maxItems)
            {
                items.RemoveAt(items.Count - 1);
            }
        }
    }
}

public IEnumerable<string> GetItems()
{
    lock (lockObject)
    {
        return items.ToArray();
    }
}
}
```

Notice that we added a new field, `lockObject`, which holds a reference to an object whose only job is to be the thing on which we acquire a lock. And we simply acquire this lock inside the methods that work with the list of items. We have to hold the lock for the whole of the `UseItem` method, because the code looks at the state of the items list right at the start, and then the rest of its operation is guided by what it found. The code simply won't work if the items list changes halfway through, and so we hold on to the lock for the duration.

In this particular case, holding the lock for the whole method is unlikely to cause problems because this method won't take long to run. But as a general rule, you want to avoid holding locks for any longer than necessary. The longer you hold a lock, the greater the chances of some other thread wanting to acquire the same lock, and being forced to wait. It's a particularly bad idea to call code that might make a request over a network and wait for a response while you're holding a lock (e.g., holding a lock while making a request to a database).

 Be particularly wary of acquiring multiple locks—holding on to a lock while attempting to acquire another is a good recipe for deadlock. Sometimes it's inevitable, though, in which case you need to devise a strategy to avoid deadlocks. That's beyond the scope of this book, but if you find yourself in this situation *lock leveling* is a suitable solution to this problem—searching the Web for "lock leveling for multithreading" would be a good place to start.

As we mentioned several pages ago, the `Monitor` class isn't just about locking. It also provides a form of notification.

Notification

Suppose we want to write some code that tests our `MostRecentlyUsed` class in multi-threaded scenarios. Even relatively simple tests pose a challenge: for example, what if we want to verify that after a call to `UseItem` has returned on one thread, the item it passed in becomes visible as the first item returned if some different thread calls `GetItems`? We're not testing concurrent use—we're just testing sequential operations, where one thing happens on one thread and then something else happens on another. How would we write a test that coordinated these steps across threads? We need one thread to wait until the other has done something. We could just use the `Thread` class's `Join` method again, waiting for the first thread to exit. But what if we don't want to let it exit? We might want to perform a sequence of operations, with each thread taking it in turns.

Monitors can help with this—as well as protecting shared state, they also provide a way to discover when that state may have changed. The `Monitor` class provides a `Wait` method that operates in conjunction with either a method called `Pulse` or the related `PulseAll`. A thread that is waiting for something to change can call `Wait`, which will block until some other thread calls `Pulse` or `PulseAll`. You must already hold the lock on the object you pass as an argument to `Wait`, `Pulse`, or `PulseAll`. Calling them without possessing the lock will result in an exception.

Example 16-14 uses this mechanism to provide the ability for one thread to wait for a second thread to do something. The class's only interesting state is a single `bool` field, `canGo`, which is initially `false` but will be set to `true` when the second thread does whatever we're waiting for—that thread will call `GoNow` to indicate this. Since this field is going to be used from multiple threads, we need synchronization, so `WaitForIt` also has a `lockObject` field which refers to an object whose only job is to be the object for which we acquire a lock in order to protect access to `canGo`.

You should never attempt to acquire a lock directly on a `bool`, or on any other value type. You can acquire a lock only on a reference type, so if you attempt to pass a `bool` to `Monitor.Enter`, the C# compiler will do what it always does when you pass a value to a method that expects an object: it will create code that generates a box for the `bool`, as we saw in Chapter 4. You would be acquiring a lock on that box, not on the `bool` itself. That's a problem, because you get a new box every time, and so your locking would do nothing useful.

The `lock` keyword in C# prevents you from trying to acquire a lock on a value—you'll get a compiler error if you try. But if you call the `Monitor` class's methods directly, C# will not prevent you from making this mistake. So this is another good reason to get into the habit of creating an object that is separate from the state it protects, and acquiring locks on that object.

Example 16-14. Coordinating threads with Monitor

```
class WaitForIt
{
    private bool canGo;
    private object lockObject = new object();

    public void WaitUntilReady()
    {
        lock (lockObject)
        {
            while (!canGo)
            {
                Monitor.Wait(lockObject);
            }
        }
    }

    public void GoNow()
    {
        lock (lockObject)
        {
            canGo = true;
            // Wake me up, before you go go.
            Monitor.PulseAll(lockObject);
        }
    }
}
```

Both methods in this example acquire the lock before doing anything, because both inspect the `canGo` field, and we expect these to be called on different threads. `WaitUntilReady` then sits in a loop until that field is `true`. Each time it goes around the loop, it calls `Monitor.Wait`. This has three effects: first, it relinquishes the lock—that's important, because otherwise, the thread that called `GoNow` would never get as far as setting the `canGo` field; second, it makes the thread calling `WaitUntilReady` block until some other thread calls either `Pulse` or `PulseAll` for `lockObject`; third, when `Wait` returns, it reacquires the lock.

Why use a loop here? Wouldn't an `if` statement followed by a single call to `Wait` work? In this case it would, but in general it's surprisingly easy to end up generating spurious notifications. Suppose we modified this example so that as well as offering a `GoNow`, we had a third method called `OhHangOnAMinute` which put the `canGo` field back to `false`—the class becomes a gate which can open and close. It would be possible that by the time `WaitUntilReady` is woken up after a call to `GoNow`, the field had already transitioned back to `false` because of a call to `OhHangOnAMinute`.

And while that can't happen with this simpler example, in general it's good to get in the habit of checking to see if the condition you were waiting for really holds when you come out of a wait, and be prepared to wait again if it doesn't.

The `GoNow` method acquires the lock to make sure it's safe to modify the `canGo` field, which it sets to `true`. Then it calls `PulseAll`—this tells the .NET Framework to wake up *all* threads currently waiting on `lockObject` as soon as we release the lock. (`Pulse` would just release a single thread, but since our `WaitForIt` class just has two states— not ready and ready—it needs to release all waiting threads when it becomes ready.) `GoNow` then returns, releasing the lock as the flow of execution leaves the `lock` block, which means that any threads waiting inside `WaitUntilReady` are now no longer blocked waiting for the pulse.

However, if multiple threads are waiting, they won't all start running at once, because `Monitor.Wait` reacquires the lock before returning. It relinquishes the lock only temporarily while it waits—it insists that we hold the lock before calling it, and we will be holding the lock again when it returns. Consequently, if `PulseAll` happened to release multiple threads, they still have to take it in turns as they come out of `Wait`.

When `WaitUntilReady` gets to proceed, the loop will check `canGo` again, and this time it will be `true` and the loop will finish. The code will then leave the `lock` block, releasing the lock on `lockObject`, enabling the next waiting thread (if there are any) to do the same thing—and so all waiting threads will become unblocked one after another.

 The monitor's close integration between locking and notification may seem a little odd—it's even getting in our way here. This example would work perfectly well if all waiting threads were released simultaneously, instead of having to wait while they acquire the lock in turn. But in fact, the combined locking and notification is critical to most uses of Pulse and Wait. Notifications concern a change to shared state, so it's vital that code that raises notifications be in possession of the lock, and also that when code discovers a notification, it is in possession of the lock so that it can look at the modified state immediately. Without this, all sorts of subtle races can occur in the gap between notification and lock acquisition or the gap between releasing a lock and waiting for notification.

Example 16-15 shows a simple program that uses the WaitForIt class from Example 16-14. It creates a thread that waits for a while and then calls the GoNow method. The main thread waits for that to happen by calling the WaitUntilReady method after starting the thread.

Example 16-15. Using WaitForIt

```
class Program
{
    static void Main(string[] args)
    {
        WaitForIt waiter = new WaitForIt();

        ThreadStart twork = delegate
        {
            Console.WriteLine("Thread running...");
            Thread.Sleep(1000);
            Console.WriteLine("Notifying");
            waiter.GoNow();
            Console.WriteLine("Notified");
            Thread.Sleep(1000);
            Console.WriteLine("Thread exiting...");
        };

        Thread t = new Thread(twork);
        Console.WriteLine("Starting new thread");
        t.Start();
        Console.WriteLine("Waiting for thread to get going");
        waiter.WaitUntilReady();
        Console.WriteLine("Wait over");

    }
}
```

The output shows why this sort of coordination is often necessary:

```
Starting new thread
Waiting for thread to get going
Thread running...
```

```
Notifying
Notified
Wait over
Thread exiting...
```

Notice that the new thread didn't start up immediately—the main thread prints its "Waiting for thread to get going" message after calling `Start` to run the thread, but this message appears before the new thread prints "Thread running..." which is the very first thing that thread does. In other words, just because the `Thread` class's `Start` method has returned, you have no guarantee that the newly created thread has actually done anything yet. Only through the use of coordination mechanisms such as `Wait` and `Pulse` can we impose some kind of order across multiple threads.

 Never use `Thread.Sleep` to try to solve ordering problems in production code—it's not a dependable or efficient technique. Example 16-15 uses it to make the coordination problems more visible, but while it can be used to amplify or explore problems in examples, you cannot rely on it, because it makes no guarantees—making one thread sleep for a while to give another thread a chance to catch up does not guarantee that the other thread *will* catch up, particularly on systems that experience heavy load.

The main thread happens not to get to run immediately after the other thread calls `GoNow`. (Or at least, if it did run, it didn't run for long enough to print out its "Wait over" message—the other thread got in there first with its "Notified" message.) You might see slightly different results each time you run. Even though we can impose a little bit of order there's still going to be quite a lot of unpredictability in the exact order of events. As you design multithreaded code, it's important to be very clear about how much order you are imposing with locking and notifications—in this case, we are guaranteeing that our main thread cannot possibly get to the line that prints out "Wait over" before the second thread has reached the line that calls `GoNow`, but that's the only constraint—the progress of the two threads could still be interleaved in numerous different ways. You should never assume that the detailed order of events you observe in practice will necessarily always happen.

While the `Monitor` class and the C# `lock` keyword are the most widely used synchronization mechanisms, there are some alternatives.

Other Lock Types

Monitors are very useful and are typically a good first choice for locking, but there are some scenarios in which more specialized alternatives might offer slightly better performance or greater flexibility. Since it's relatively unusual to use these alternatives, we won't illustrate them in detail—this section will just describe what's there and when it might be useful to you.

To understand why the alternatives exist, it's useful to know something more about the capabilities and limitations of monitors. Monitors are designed for use within a single appdomain—you cannot use them to synchronize operations between processes, nor between appdomains sharing a process. Cross-process coordination is possible in Windows, but you need to use other mechanisms to do that. One reason for this is that monitors try to avoid getting the OS scheduler involved in locking where possible.

If your code hits a `lock` statement (or calls `Monitor.Enter` directly) for an object on which no other thread currently has a lock, the .NET Framework is able to handle this situation efficiently. It does not need to make calls into the operating system. Monitors can do this because they're appdomain-local; to ensure cross-appdomain synchronization typically means getting help from the OS, and once you need to call into the OS, lock acquisition becomes many times more expensive. So when there's no contention, monitors work really well. But once blocking occurs—either due to contention or because of an explicit call to `Wait`—the OS scheduler has to get involved because it's the only thing that can move a thread between runnable and blocked states. This is usually a good thing, because it means the thread can wait efficiently; once a thread becomes blocked it doesn't consume CPU cycles, and the CPU is free to get on with other useful work, or it may be able to go into its power-efficient idle state when no threads need to run, which is particularly important for laptops running on battery power. However, there are some situations where the cost of getting the OS involved outweighs the benefits. This brings us to the first of the specialized lock types.

SpinLock

`SpinLock`, which is new in .NET 4, provides similar locking functionality to monitors, but when contention occurs it will just sit in a loop checking and checking and checking again to see if the lock has become free yet—the thread will consume CPU cycles while it does this. The "spin" in `SpinLock` refers to the code spinning around in this loop waiting for the lock.

That might sound like an awful idea compared to the nice power-efficient wait state that a thread can enter into when blocking on a monitor. And often, it's exactly as bad an idea as it sounds. The majority of the time you won't want to use `SpinLock`. But it offers one possible advantage: because it never falls back onto the OS scheduler, it's a more lightweight construct than a monitor, and so *if* you very rarely encounter contention for a particular lock, it might be cheaper. (And if the contention does occur but is extremely short-lived, it's possible that on a multicore system the cost of spinning very briefly might actually be lower than the cost of getting the scheduler involved. In general, spinlock contention on a single-processor system is bad, although the

`SpinLock` implementation mitigates this a little by yielding[||] when it fails to acquire the lock on a single-processor machine.)

 `SpinLock` is a value type—a struct. This contributes to its lightweight nature, as it can live inside other objects, rather than needing its own space on the heap. Of course, this also means you need to be careful not to assign a `SpinLock` into a local variable, because you'd end up making a copy, and locking that copy would not be useful.

Never use `SpinLock` without comparative performance tests: test all the performance metrics you care about using ordinary monitors and compare that against how the same test suite works when you replace a particular lock with a `SpinLock`, and consider switching only if the tests demonstrate a clear benefit. If you don't have a test infrastructure capable of verifying that you meet all of your performance requirements, or if you don't have quantitative, clearly specified performance requirements, your project is not ready for `SpinLock`.

 For some reason, a lot of developers just love to be armchair performance tuners. An astounding amount of time and effort is wasted on mailing lists, on web forums, and in internal company meetings on heated debates over which constructs are theoretically faster than others. Sadly, empirical testing of any kind rarely enters into the equation in such discussions.

If someone tries to claim by logical argument alone that a particular technique is faster, be highly suspicious of her claims. Exotic and specialized synchronization primitives such as `SpinLock` seem to bring out the worst in these people. (And that's the main reason we're even mentioning it—sooner or later you'll have to deal with someone who has become obsessed with finding a way to use `SpinLock`.) Testing and measurement is the only reliable path to performance.

Reader/writer locks

Earlier in this chapter, we suggested immutability as a way to avoid having to synchronize access to your data—in the .NET Framework, it's safe for any number of threads to read the same data simultaneously as long as no threads are trying to modify that data at the same time. Sometimes you may find yourself in the frustrating situation of having data that is *almost* read-only—perhaps a website contains a message of the day which, presumably, changes only once a day, but which you may need to incorporate into each of the hundreds of web pages your busy website serves up every second of the day.

[||] *Yielding* is when a thread tells the OS scheduler that it wants to give other threads a turn using the CPU now, rather than waiting to be preempted. If there are no other runnable threads, yielding does nothing, and the thread will continue to run.

The monitor's mutually exclusive locking—where only one thread at a time gets to acquire a lock—seems ill-suited to this scenario. You could find that this shared data becomes a bottleneck—all threads are taking it in turns to access it, even though that really needs to happen only once a day. This is where reader/writer locks come in.

The idea behind a reader/writer lock is that when you acquire the lock, you declare whether you need to modify the data or just read it. The lock will allow any number of threads to get a read lock simultaneously, but if a thread tries to get a write lock, it'll have to wait until all the current readers are done, and then, once a thread has a write lock, other threads attempting to get a lock of any kind will be made to wait until the write lock has been released. In other words, this kind of lock supports any number of simultaneous readers, but writers get exclusive access. (The precise details are, as ever, a little more complex, as a lock of this kind has to avoid the scenario where a never-ending stream of readers causes a writer to wait forever. New readers may be made to wait even when other readers are currently active simply to clear the decks for a waiting writer.)

While this sounds good in theory, the practical benefits can sometimes fall short of what theory might suggest. You shouldn't even contemplate using a reader/writer lock unless you are seeing performance problems with a simpler monitor-based solution. This kind of lock is more complex, and so it's quite possible you'll end up making things slower, particularly in cases where you weren't seeing much contention. (The example we gave of a website with a message of the day is quite likely to fall into that category. If the message is just a string, how long does it take to get hold of a reference to a string, really? Even with hundreds of requests per second, the chances of contention are probably pretty small.)

It doesn't help that the first implementation offered by the .NET Framework—the ReaderWriterLock—was, frankly, not very good. Your monitor-based solution had to be in a world of pain before ReaderWriterLock looked preferable. Unfortunately, some of the problems of this lock couldn't be fixed without risking breaking existing code, so .NET 3.5 introduced a much better replacement, ReaderWriterLockSlim. If you need reader/writer locking, you should use this newer variant unless you absolutely have to support older versions of .NET. Be aware that unlike ReaderWriterLock, ReaderWriter LockSlim implements IDisposable, so you need to arrange for it to be disposed at the right time. This means that if you use it as an implementation detail of a class, your class will probably need to implement IDisposable too.

Mutexes

The Mutex class provides a similar style of locking to monitor. The name is short for *mutually exclusive* indicating that only one thread can acquire the lock at any time. A mutex is significantly more expensive than a monitor because it always gets the OS scheduler involved. And it does that because mutexes work across process boundaries—you can create a Mutex object with a name, and if another process in the same Windows login session creates another Mutex object with the same name, that object refers to the same underlying Windows synchronization object. So to acquire a `Mutex`, you don't merely have to be the only thread in your application in possession of the lock; you will be the only thread on the whole login session in possession of the lock. (You can even make a global mutex that spans all login sessions, meaning that yours will be the only thread on the entire machine in possession of the lock.)

If you create a mutex without a name, it will be local to the process, but it still relies on the OS because a `Mutex` is essentially a wrapper around a mutex object provided by the Windows kernel.

Other Coordination Mechanisms

Monitors are not just for locking, of course—they offer coordination facilities through pulsing and waiting. And the .NET Framework offers some slightly more specialized types for coordination too.

Events

Events provide a very similar service to the `WaitForIt` class we built in Example 16-14—an event is effectively a Boolean variable you can wait on. And rather than being a simple one-shot mechanism as in Example 16-14, an event can go back and forth between its two states.

.NET offers `ManualResetEvent` and `AutoResetEvent` classes. The latter automatically reverts to its default state when letting waiting threads go, whereas the manual one remains in its so-called *signaled* state until you explicitly reset it.

> `AutoResetEvent` can be problematic. There isn't necessarily any correspondence between the number of times you signal it and the number of times it releases threads. If you signal it twice in a row when no threads are waiting, it doesn't keep count—it's just as signaled after the second signal as it was after the first one. This can lead to bugs where you occasionally miss signals, and your code can grind to a halt. Approach with caution.

These types are wrappers around the underlying Windows event synchronization primitive, so as with `Mutex`, you can use events for cross-process coordination. And of course, this also means that you incur the cost of getting the OS scheduler involved.

.NET 4 introduces an alternative called `ManualResetEventSlim`. This will use busy-waiting techniques similar to a spinlock for short waits. So just like the `Monitor`, it gets the scheduler involved only when a wait is necessary. Therefore, unless you really need the extra features available from the nonslim version (e.g., you need cross-process synchronization) the `ManualResetEventSlim` class is a better choice than `ManualResetEvent` if you're using .NET 4 or later.

Countdown

.NET 4 introduces the `CountdownEvent` class, which provides a handy solution to a fairly common problem: knowing when you're done. Remember back in Example 16-6, we ran into an issue with the thread pool. We queued up a couple of pieces of work, but we had no way of knowing when they were done. One solution to that would be to use the Task Parallel Library, which we'll get to shortly, but an alternative would have been to use the `CountdownEvent` class.

`CountdownEvent` is very simple. For each piece of work you start, you call `AddCount` (or if you know how many pieces of work there will be up front, you can pass that number into the constructor). For each piece of work that completes you call `Signal`. And if you need to wait for all outstanding work to complete (e.g., before your program exits), just call `Wait`.

BlockingCollection

The `System.Collections.Concurrent` namespace provides various collection classes that are designed to be used in multithreaded environments. They look a little different from the normal collection classes because they are designed to be used without needing any locking, which means they can't offer features that rely on things staying consistent from one moment to the next. Numerical indexing is out, for example, because the number of items in the collection may change, as we saw when trying to use `List<T>` in a multithreaded fashion in Example 16-11. So these are not thread-safe versions of normal collection classes—they are collections whose APIs are designed to support multithreaded use without the caller needing to use locks.

`BlockingCollection` is not just a multithreaded collection; it also offers associated co-ordination. It provides a way for threads to sit and wait for items to become available in the collection. Its `Take` method will block if the collection is empty. Once data becomes available, `Take` will return one item. Any number of threads may be waiting inside `Take` at any time, and other threads are free to call `Add`. If you `Add` enough items that all the threads waiting to `Take` are satisfied, and then you keep calling `Add`, that's when items start to get added to the collection. And if the collection is nonempty, calls to `Take` will return immediately.

This allows you to have one or more threads dedicated to processing work items generated by other threads. The `BlockingCollection` acts as a kind of buffer—if you generate items faster than you process them, they will queue up in the `BlockingCollec tion`, and if the processing threads catch up, they will block efficiently until more items come along.

You could use this in a WPF application that needs to do slow work in the background—the UI thread could add work into a blocking collection, and then one or more worker threads could take items from the collection and process them. This is not hugely different from using the thread pool, but it gives you the opportunity to limit the number of worker threads—if you had just a single thread that performs background work, you might be able to get away with much simpler synchronization code, because all your background work is always done by the same thread.

We've looked at how to create threads explicitly and at the tools available for ensuring that our programs function correctly in a multithreaded world. Next we're going to look at asynchronous programming models, where we don't explicitly create new threads. We will need the locking and synchronization techniques we just explored because we are still working in a concurrent world; it's just a slightly different programming style.

Asynchronous Programming

Some things are intrinsically slow. Reading all of the audio data off a CD, downloading a large file from a server at the end of a low-bandwidth connection on the opposite side of the world, or playing a sound—all of these processes have constraints that mean they'll take a long time to complete, maybe seconds, minutes, or even hours. How should these sorts of operations look to the programmer?

One simple answer is that they don't have to look different than faster operations. Our code consists of a sequence of statements—one thing after another—and some statements take longer than others. This has the useful property of being easy to understand. For example, if our code calls the `WebClient` class's `DownloadString` method, our program doesn't move on to the next step until the download is complete, and so we can know not just what our code does, but also the order in which it does it.

This style of API is sometimes described as *synchronous*—the time at which the API returns is determined by the time at which the operation finishes; execution progresses through the code in sync with the work being done. These are also sometimes known as *blocking* APIs, because they block the calling thread from further progress until work is complete.

Blocking APIs are problematic for user interfaces because the blocked thread can't do anything else while slow work is in progress. Thread affinity means that code which responds to user input has to run on the UI thread, so if you're keeping that thread busy, the UI will become unresponsive. It's really annoying to use programs that stop responding to user input when they're working—these applications seem to freeze anytime something takes too long, making them very frustrating to use. Failing to respond to user input within 100 ms is enough to disrupt the user's concentration. (And it gets worse if your program's user interface uses animation—the occasional glitch of just 15 ms is enough to make a smooth animation turn into something disappointingly choppy.)

Threads offer one solution to this: if you do all your potentially slow work on threads that aren't responsible for handling user input, your application can remain responsive. However, this can sometimes seem like an overcomplicated solution—in a lot of cases, slow operations don't work synchronously under the covers. Take fundamental operations such as reading and writing data from and to devices such as network cards or disks, for example. The kernel-mode device drivers that manage disk and network I/O are instructed by the operating system to start doing some work, and the OS expects the driver to configure the hardware to perform the necessary work and then return control to the operating system almost immediately—on the inside, Windows is built around the assumption that most slow work proceeds *asynchronously*, that there's no need for code to progress strictly in sync with the work.

This asynchronous model is not limited to the internals of Windows—there are asynchronous public APIs. These typically return very quickly, long before the work in question is complete, and you then use either a notification mechanism or polling to discover when the work is finished. The exact details vary from one API to another, but these basic principles are universal. Many synchronous APIs really are just some code that starts an asynchronous operation and then makes the thread sleep until the operation completes.

An asynchronous API sounds like a pretty good fit for what we need to build responsive interactive applications.# So it seems somewhat ludicrous to create multiple threads in order to use synchronous APIs without losing responsiveness, when those synchronous APIs are just wrappers on top of intrinsically asynchronous underpinnings. Rather than creating new threads, we may as well just use asynchronous APIs directly where they are available, cutting out the middle man.

.NET defines two common patterns for asynchronous operations. There's a low-level pattern which is powerful and corresponds efficiently to how Windows does things under the covers. And then there's a slightly higher-level pattern which is less flexible but considerably simpler to use in GUI code.

The Asynchronous Programming Model

The Asynchronous Programming Model (APM) is a pattern that many asynchronous APIs in the .NET Framework conform to. It defines common mechanisms for discovering when work is complete, for collecting the results of completed work, and for reporting errors that occurred during the asynchronous operation.

APIs that use the APM offer pairs of methods, starting with `Begin` and `End`. For example, the `Socket` class in the `System.Net.Sockets` namespace offers numerous instances of this pattern: `BeginAccept` and `EndAccept`, `BeginSend` and `EndSend`, `BeginConnect` and `EndConnect`, and so on.

#Asynchronous APIs tend to be used slightly differently in server-side code in web applications. There, they are most useful for when an application needs to communicate with multiple different external services to handle a single request.

The exact signature of the Begin method depends on what it does. For example, a socket's BeginConnect needs the address to which you'd like to connect, whereas BeginReceive needs to know where you'd like to put the data and how much you're ready to receive. But the APM requires all Begin methods to have the same final two parameters: the method must take an AsyncCallback delegate and an object. And it also requires the method to return an implementation of the IAsyncResult interface. Here's an example from the Dns class in System.Net:

```
public static IAsyncResult BeginGetHostEntry(
    string hostNameOrAddress,
    AsyncCallback requestCallback,
    object stateObject
)
```

Callers may pass a null AsyncCallback. But if they pass a non-null reference, the type implementing the APM is required to invoke the callback once the operation is complete. The AsyncCallback delegate signature requires the callback method to accept an IAsyncResult argument—the APM implementation will pass in the same IAsyncResult to this completion callback as it returns from the Begin method. This object represents an asynchronous operation in progress—many classes can have multiple operations in progress simultaneously, and the IAsyncResult distinguishes between them.

Example 16-16 shows one way to use this pattern. It calls the asynchronous BeginGetHostEntry method provided by the Dns class. This looks up the IP address for a computer, so it takes a string—the name of the computer to find. And then it takes the two standard final APM arguments—a delegate and an object. We can pass anything we like as the object—the function we call doesn't actually use it, it just hands it back to us later. We could pass null because our example doesn't need the argument, but we're passing a number just to demonstrate where it comes out. The reason the APM offers this argument is so that if you have multiple simultaneous asynchronous operations in progress at once, you have a convenient way to associate information with each operation. (This mattered much more in older versions of C#, which didn't offer anonymous methods or lambdas—back then this argument was the easiest way to pass data into the callback.)

Example 16-16. Using the Asynchronous Programming Model

```
class Program
{
    static void Main(string[] args)
    {
        Dns.BeginGetHostEntry("oreilly.com", OnGetHostEntryComplete, 42);

        Console.ReadKey();
    }

    static void OnGetHostEntryComplete(IAsyncResult iar)
    {
        IPHostEntry result = Dns.EndGetHostEntry(iar);
        Console.WriteLine(result.AddressList[0]);
```

```
        Console.WriteLine(iar.AsyncState);
    }
}
```

The `Main` method waits until a key is pressed—much like with work items in the thread pool, having active asynchronous requests will not keep the process alive, so the program would exit before finishing its work without that `ReadKey`. (A more robust approach for a real program that needed to wait for work to complete would be to use the `CountdownEvent` described earlier.)

The `Dns` class will call the `OnGetHostEntryComplete` method once it has finished its lookup. Notice that the first thing we do is call the `EndGetHostEntry` method—the other half of the APM. The `End` method always takes the `IAsyncResult` object corresponding to the call—recall that this identifies the call in progress, so this is how `EndGetHostEn try` knows which particular lookup operation we want to get the results for.

 The APM says nothing about which thread your callback will be called on. In practice, it's often a thread pool thread, but not always. Some individual implementations might make guarantees about what sort of thread you'll be called on, but most don't. And since you don't usually know what thread the callback occurred on, you will need to take the same precautions you would when writing multithreaded code where you explicitly create new threads. For example, in a WPF or Windows Forms application, you'd need to use the `SynchronizationContext` class or an equivalent mechanism to get back to a UI thread if you wanted to make updates to the UI when an asynchronous operation completes.

The `End` method in the APM returns any data that comes out of the operation. In this case, there's a single return value of `IPHostEntry`, but some implementations may return more by having `out` or `ref` arguments. Example 16-16 then prints the results, and finally prints the `AsyncState` property of the `IAsyncResult`, which will be 42—this is where the value we passed as the final argument to `BeginGetHostEntry` pops out.

This is not the only way to use the Asynchronous Programming Model—you are allowed to pass `null` as the delegate argument. You have three other options, all revolving around the `IAsyncResult` object returned by the `Begin` call. You can poll the `IsCompleted` property to test for completion. You can call the `End` method at any time—if the work is not finished this will block until it completes.* Or you can use the `Asyn cWaitHandle` property—this returns an object that is a wrapper around a Win32 synchronization handle that will become signaled when the work is complete. (That last one is rarely used, and has some complications regarding ownership and lifetime of the handle, which are described in the MSDN documentation. We mention this technique only out of a pedantic sense of duty to completeness.)

---

* This isn't always supported. For example, if you attempt such an early call on an `End` method for a networking operation on the UI thread in a Silverlight application, you'll get an exception.

 You are *required* to call the End method at some point, no matter how you choose to wait for completion. Even if you don't care about the outcome of the operation you must still call the End method. If you don't, the operation might leak resources.

Asynchronous operations can throw exceptions. If the exception is the result of bad input, such as a null reference where an object is required, the Begin method will throw an exception. But it's possible that something failed while the operation was in progress—perhaps we lost network connectivity partway through some work. In this case, the End method will throw an exception.

The Asynchronous Programming Model is widely used in the .NET Framework class library, and while it is an efficient and flexible way to support asynchronous operations, it's slightly awkward to use in user interfaces. The completion callback typically happens on some random thread, so you can't update the UI in that callback. And the support for multiple simultaneous operations, possible because each operation is represented by a distinct IAsyncResult object, may be useful in server environments, but it's often just an unnecessary complication for client-side code. So there's an alternative pattern better suited to the UI.

The Event-Based Asynchronous Pattern

Some classes offer an alternative pattern for asynchronous programming. You start an operation by calling a method whose name typically ends in *Async*; for example, the WebClient class's DownloadDataAsync method. And unlike the APM, you do not pass a delegate to the method. Completion is indicated through an event, such as the DownloadDataCompleted event. Classes that implement this pattern are required to use the SynchronizationContext class (or the related AsyncOperationManager) to ensure that the event is raised in the same context in which the operation was started. So in a user interface, this means that completion events are raised on the UI thread.

This is, in effect, a single-threaded asynchronous model. You have the responsiveness benefits of asynchronous handling of slow operations, with fewer complications than multithreaded code. So in scenarios where this pattern is an option, it's usually the best choice, as it is far simpler than the alternatives. It's not always available, because some classes offer only the APM. (And some don't offer any kind of asynchronous API, in which case you'd need to use one of the other multithreading mechanisms in this chapter to maintain a responsive UI.)

 Single-threaded asynchronous code is more complex than sequential code, of course, so there's still scope for trouble. For example, you need to be careful that you don't attempt to set multiple asynchronous operations in flight simultaneously that might conflict. Also, components that implement this pattern call you back on the right thread only if you use them from the right thread in the first place—if you use a mixture of this pattern and other multithreading mechanisms, be aware that operations you kick off from worker threads will not complete on the UI thread.

There are two optional features of the event-based asynchronous model. Some classes also offer progress change notification events, such as the WebClient class's Download ProgressChanged event. (Such events are also raised on the original thread.) And there may be cancellation support. For example, WebClient offers a CancelAsync method.

Ad Hoc Asynchrony

There's no fundamental need for code to use either the APM or the event-based asynchronous pattern. These are just conventions. You will occasionally come across code that uses its own unusual solution for asynchronous operation. This can happen when the design of the code in question is constrained by external influences—for example, the System.Threading namespace defines an Overlapped class that provides a managed representation of a Win32 asynchronous mechanism. Win32 does not have any direct equivalent to either of the .NET asynchronous patterns, and just tends to use function pointers for callbacks. .NET's Overlapped class mimics this by accepting a delegate as an argument to a method. Conceptually, this isn't very different from the APM, it just happens not to conform exactly to the pattern.

The standard asynchronous patterns are useful, but they are somewhat low-level. If you need to coordinate multiple operations, they leave you with a lot of work to do, particularly when it comes to robust error handling or cancellation. The Task Parallel Library provides a more comprehensive scheme for working with multiple concurrent operations.

The Task Parallel Library

.NET 4 introduces the Task Parallel Library (TPL), a set of classes in the System.Thread ing.Tasks namespace that help coordinate concurrent work. In some respects, the TPL superficially resembles the thread pool, in that you submit small work items (or *tasks*) and the TPL will take care of working out how many threads to use at once in order to run your work. But the TPL provides various services not available through direct use of the thread pool, especially in the areas of error handling, cancellation, and managing relationships between tasks.

You can associate tasks with one another—for example, tasks can have a parent-child relationship, which provides a way to wait until all of the tasks related to some higher-level operation are complete. You can also arrange for the completion of one task to kick off another related task.

Error handling gets tricky with asynchronous and concurrent code—what do you do if you've built an operation out of 20 related concurrent tasks, and just one of them fails while the rest are either in progress, already complete, or not yet started? The TPL provides a system for bringing work to an orderly halt, and collecting in a single place all of the errors that occurred.

The mechanisms required to halt work in the event of an error are also useful if you want to be able to stop work in progress for some other reason, such as when the user clicks a Cancel button.

We'll start by looking at the most important concept in the TPL, which is, unsurprisingly, the task.

Tasks

A *task* is some work your program needs to do. It is represented by an instance of the Task class, defined in the System.Threading.Tasks namespace. This does not define exactly how the work will be done. The work for a task might be a method to be executed, but a task could also involve asynchronous work that executes without needing to tie up a thread—the TPL has support for creating task objects that work with APM implementations, for instance. Example 16-17 shows how to create new tasks that execute code.

Example 16-17. Executing code with tasks

```
using System;
using System.Threading.Tasks;

namespace TplExamples
{
    class Program
    {
        static void Main(string[] args)
        {
            Task.Factory.StartNew(Go, "One");
            Task.Factory.StartNew(Go, "Two");

            Console.ReadKey();
        }

        static void Go(object name)
        {
            for (int i = 0; i < 100; ++i)
            {
                Console.WriteLine("{0}: {1}", name, i);
            }
```

```
        }
    }
}
```

The Task class provides a static Factory property that returns a TaskFactory object, which can be used to create new tasks. The TPL defines the TaskFactory abstraction so that it's possible to plug in different task creation strategies. The default factory returned by Task.Factory creates new tasks that execute code on the thread pool, but it's possible to create factories that do something else. For example, you could make a task factory that creates tasks that will run on a UI thread.

A factory's StartNew method creates a code-based task. You pass it a delegate—it'll accept either a method with no arguments or a method that takes a single object as an argument. If you want to pass more arguments, you can use the same lambda-based trick we saw in Example 16-4. Example 16-18 uses this to pass two arguments to Go, while using the overload of StartNew that takes a zero-argument method. (The empty () tells C# to build a zero-argument lambda, which becomes the method StartNew invokes.)

Example 16-18. Passing more arguments with lambdas

```
static void Main(string[] args)
{
    Task.Factory.StartNew(() => Go("One", 100));
    Task.Factory.StartNew(() => Go("Two", 500));

    Console.ReadKey();
}

static void Go(string name, int iterations)
{
    for (int i = 0; i < iterations; ++i)
    {
        Console.WriteLine("{0}: {1}", name, i);
    }
}
```

These last two examples look pretty similar to the thread pool examples from earlier, and they suffer from the same problem: they don't know when the work is complete, so we've used the dubious solution of waiting for the user to press a key so that the program doesn't exit until the work is done. Fortunately, tasks provide a much better solution to this: we can wait until they are finished. Task provides a Wait method that blocks until the task is complete. This is an instance method, so we'd call it once for each task. There's also a static WaitAll method that takes an array of Task objects and blocks until they are all complete, illustrated in Example 16-19. (This method uses the params modifier on its one argument, so we can just pass each task as though it were a separate argument. The C# compiler will take the two tasks Example 16-19 passes to WaitAll and wrap them in an array for us.)

Example 16-19. Task.WaitAll

```
static void Main(string[] args)
{
    Task t1 = Task.Factory.StartNew(() => Go("One", 100));
    Task t2 = Task.Factory.StartNew(() => Go("Two", 500));

    Task.WaitAll(t1, t2);
}
```

Alternatively, we could create a parent task that contains both of these tasks as children.

Parent-child relationships

If you write a code-based task that creates new tasks from within an existing task, you can make those new tasks children of the task in progress. Example 16-20 creates the same two tasks as the previous examples, but does so inside another task, passing in the `AttachedToParent` member of the `TaskCreateOptions` enumeration to establish the parent-child relationship.

Example 16-20. Task with children

```
static void Main(string[] args)
{
    Task t = Task.Factory.StartNew(() =>
    {
        Task.Factory.StartNew(() => Go("One", 100),
                        TaskCreationOptions.AttachedToParent);
        Task.Factory.StartNew(() => Go("Two", 500),
                        TaskCreationOptions.AttachedToParent);
    });

    t.Wait();
}
```

Notice that this example calls `Wait` only on the parent task. For a task to be considered complete, not only must it have finished running, but so must all of its children. (And that means that if the children have children of their own, those all have to complete too.) So there's no need to list all the tasks and pass them to `WaitAll` if there's a single top-level task that all the rest descend from.

Fine-grained concurrency

Although code-based tasks are superficially similar to thread pool work items, the TPL is designed to let you use much smaller tasks than would work efficiently when using the thread pool directly. The TPL encourages *fine-grained concurrency*—the idea is that you provide it with a large number of small work items, which gives it plenty of freedom to work out how to allocate that work across logical processors. This is sometimes described as *overexpression* of concurrency. The theory is that as newer computers come out with more and more logical processors, code that overexpresses its concurrency will be able to take advantage of the higher logical processor count.

The TPL uses the CLR thread pool internally, so it might seem surprising that the TPL is able to handle small work items more efficiently, but the TPL provides access to some features added to the thread pool in .NET 4, which you can't use with the `ThreadPool` class. The `ThreadPool` class typically starts work in the order you queued it up, so it's a *FIFO* (first in, first out) queue. (This is absolutely not guaranteed by the documentation, but the fact that the `ThreadPool` has behaved this way for years means that changing this behavior would doubtless break lots of code.) But when you set up work as `Task` objects the thread pool works differently. Each logical processor gets its own separate queue, and typically processes tasks in its queue in *LIFO* (last in, first out) order. This turns out to be far more efficient in a lot of scenarios, particularly when the work items are small. This ordering is not strict, by the way; if one logical processor manages to empty its work queue while others still have plenty to do, the idle processor may *steal* work from another processors, and will do so from the back end of its queue. (If you're wondering about the rationale behind how the thread pool orders tasks, see the sidebar below.)

LIFO Queues and Work Stealing

Three of the thread pool's features—per-logical-processor queues, LIFO ordering, and stealing from the end of the queue—share a single goal: working efficiently with CPU caches.

When possible, you want a task to be executed on the same logical processor that generated the work because that logical processor's cache probably already contains a lot of the information relating to the task. Handling the task on a different logical processor would mean shuffling data out of the originating logical processor and into the one running the task. That's why each logical processor has its own queue, and new tasks are allocated to the queue of the logical processor that creates them.

The rationale behind LIFO ordering is that the most recently created tasks are the ones most likely to have associated data still in the cache, so the average throughput will be better if we handle those first.

One reason work stealing between CPUs happens from the back end of the queue is that when stealing work from another logical processor you want to pick the item that is *least* likely to still have data sitting in the other logical processor's cache, to minimize the amount of data that may need to be moved. So in that case, the oldest item is the best bet. Another benefit of this is that it can reduce contention—queues can be constructed in such a way that different CPUs can access opposite ends of the queue simultaneously.

The examples we've seen so far simply perform work and return no results. But a task can produce a result.

Tasks with results

The Task<TResult> class derives from Task and adds a Result property which, once the task is complete, contains the result produced by the task. Task<TResult> represents a concept known in some concurrent programming literature as a *future*—it represents some work that will produce a result at some point.

The TaskFactory.StartNew method we've already used can create either kind of task—it has overloads that accept methods that return a result. (So you can pass a Func<TResult> or Func<object, TResult>, instead of the Action or Action<object> passed in the previous examples.) These overloads return a Task<TResult>. (Alternatively, you can call StartNew on the Task<TResult>.Factory static property.)

You can start a Task<TResult> and then call Wait to wait for the result, or you can read the Result property, which will call Wait for you if the result is not yet available. But blocking until the task is complete may not be especially useful—it's just a very roundabout way of invoking the code synchronously. In fact, you might sometimes want to do this—you might create multiple child tasks and then wait for all of them to complete, and you'd be able to take advantage of the TPL's common exception-handling framework to manage any errors. However, it's often useful to be able to provide some sort of callback method to be invoked once the task completes, rather than blocking. You can do this with a continuation.

Continuations

A continuation is a task that gets invoked when another tasks completes.[†] The Task class provides a ContinueWith method that lets you provide the code for that continuation task. It requires a delegate that takes as its single argument the task that just completed. ContinueWith offers overloads that allow the delegate to return a value (in which case the continuation task will be another Task<TResult>), or not to return a value (in which case the continuation task will just be a Task). ContinueWith returns the Task object that represents the continuation. So you can string these things together:

```
static void Main(string[] args)
{
    Task t = Task.Factory.StartNew(() => Go("One", 100))
                    .ContinueWith(t1 => Go("Two", 500))
                    .ContinueWith(t2 => Go("Three", 200));
    t.Wait();
}
```

This will execute the three tasks one after another. Notice that the t variable here refers to the third task—the final continuation. So t.Wait() will wait until all the tasks are complete—it doesn't need to wait for the first two because the final task can't even

---

† In case you've come across continuations in the sense meant by languages such as Scheme that offer *call with current continuation*, be aware that this is not the same idea. There's a tenuous connection in the sense that both represent the ability to continue some work sometime later, but they're really quite different.

start until the others are finished; waiting for the last task implicitly means waiting for all three here.

Continuations are slightly more interesting when the initial task produces a result—the continuation can then do something with the output. For example, you might have a task that fetches some data from a server and then have a continuation that puts the result into the user interface. Of course, we need to be on the correct thread to update the UI, but the TPL can help us with this.

Schedulers

The TaskScheduler class is responsible for working out when and how to execute tasks. If you don't specify a scheduler, you'll end up with the default one, which uses the thread pool. But you can provide other schedulers when creating tasks—both StartNew and ContinueWith offer overloads that accept a scheduler. The TPL offers a scheduler that uses the SynchronizationContext, which can run tasks on the UI thread. Example 16-21 shows how to use this in an event handler in a WPF application.

Example 16-21. Continuation on a UI thread

```
void OnButtonClick(object sender, RoutedEventArgs e)
{
    TaskScheduler uiScheduler =
        TaskScheduler.FromCurrentSynchronizationContext();
    Task<string>.Factory.StartNew(GetData)
                .ContinueWith((task) => UpdateUi(task.Result),
                              uiScheduler);
}

string GetData()
{
    WebClient w = new WebClient();
    return w.DownloadString("http://oreilly.com/");
}

void UpdateUi(string info)
{
    myTextBox.Text = info;
}
```

This example creates a task that returns a string, using the default scheduler. This task will invoke the GetData function on a thread pool thread. But it also sets up a continuation using a TaskScheduler that was obtained by calling FromCurrentSynchronization Context. This grabs the SynchronizationContext class's Current property and returns a scheduler that uses that context to run all tasks. Since the continuation specifies that it wants to use this scheduler, it will run the UpdateUi method on the UI thread.

The upshot is that GetData runs on a thread pool thread, and then its return value is passed into UpdateUi on the UI thread.

We could use a similar trick to work with APM implementations, because task factories provide methods for creating APM-based tasks.

Tasks and the Asynchronous Programming Model

`TaskFactory` and `TaskFactory<TResult>` provide various overloads of a `FromAsync` method. You can pass this the `Begin` and `End` methods from an APM implementation, along with the arguments you'd like to pass, and it will return a `Task` or `Task<TResult>` that executes the asynchronous operation, instead of one that invokes a delegate. Example 16-22 uses this to wrap the asynchronous methods we used from the `Dns` class in earlier examples in a task.

Example 16-22. Creating a task from an APM implementation

```
TaskScheduler uiScheduler = TaskScheduler.FromCurrentSynchronizationContext();
Task<IPHostEntry>.Factory.FromAsync(
                Dns.BeginGetHostEntry, Dns.EndGetHostEntry,
                "oreilly.com", null)
    .ContinueWith((task) => UpdateUi(task.Result.AddressList[0].ToString()),
                uiScheduler);
```

`FromAsync` offers overloads for versions of the APM that take zero, one, two, or three arguments, which covers the vast majority of APM implementations. As well as passing the `Begin` and `End` methods, we also pass the arguments, and the additional object argument that all APM `Begin` methods accept. (For the minority of APM implementations that either require more arguments or have `out` or `ref` parameters, there's an overload of `FromAsync` that accepts an `IAsyncResult` instead. This requires slightly more code, but enables you to wrap any APM implementation as a task.)

We've seen the main ways to create tasks, and to set up associations between them either with parent-child relationships or through continuations. But what happens if you want to stop some work after you've started it? Neither the thread pool nor the APM supports cancellation, but the TPL does.

Cancellation

Cancellation of asynchronous operations is surprisingly tricky. There are lots of awkward race conditions to contend with. The operation you're trying to cancel might already have finished by the time you try to cancel it. Or if it hasn't it might have gotten beyond the point where it is able to stop, in which case cancellation is doomed to fail. Or work might have failed, or be about to fail when you cancel it. And even when cancellation is possible, it might take awhile to do. Handling and testing every possible combination is difficult enough when you have just one operation, but if you have multiple related tasks, it gets a whole lot harder.

Fortunately, .NET 4 introduces a new cancellation model that provides a well thought out and thoroughly tested solution to the common cancellation problems. This cancellation model is not limited to the TPL—you are free to use it on its own, and it also crops up in other parts of the .NET Framework. (The data parallelism classes we'll be looking at later can use it, for example.)

If you want to be able to cancel an operation, you must pass it a `CancellationToken`. A cancellation token allows the operation to discover whether the operation has been canceled—it provides an `IsCancellationRequested` property—and it's also possible to pass a delegate to its `Register` method in order to be called back if cancellation happens.

`CancellationToken` only provides facilities for discovering that cancellation has been requested. It does not provide the ability to initiate cancellation. That is provided by a separate class called `CancellationTokenSource`. The reason for splitting the discovery and control of cancellation across two types is that it would otherwise be impossible to provide a task with cancellation notifications without also granting that task the capability of initiating cancellation. `CancellationTokenSource` is a factory of cancellation tokens—you ask it for a token and then pass that into the operation you want to be able to cancel. Example 16-23 is similar to Example 16-21, but it passes a cancellation token to `StartNew`, and then uses the source to cancel the operation if the user clicks a Cancel button.

Example 16-23. Ineffectual cancellation

```
private CancellationTokenSource cancelSource;

void OnButtonClick(object sender, RoutedEventArgs e)
{
    cancelSource = new CancellationTokenSource();

    TaskScheduler uiScheduler =
        TaskScheduler.FromCurrentSynchronizationContext();
    Task<string>.Factory.StartNew(GetData, cancelSource.Token)
                .ContinueWith((task) => UpdateUi(task.Result),
                                uiScheduler);
}

void OnCancelClick(object sender, RoutedEventArgs e)
{
    if (cancelSource != null)
    {
        cancelSource.Cancel();
    }
}


string GetData()
{
    WebClient w = new WebClient();
    return w.DownloadString("http://oreilly.com/");
}
```

```
void UpdateUi(string info)
{
    cancelSource = null;
    myTextBox.Text = info;
}
```

In fact, cancellation isn't very effective in this example because this particular task consists of code that makes a single blocking method call. Cancellation will usually do nothing here in practice—the only situation in which it would have an effect is if the user managed to click Cancel before the task had even begun to execute. This illustrates an important issue: cancellation is never forced—it uses a cooperative approach, because the only alternative is killing the thread executing the work. And while that would be possible, forcibly terminating threads tends to leave the process in an uncertain state—it's usually impossible to know whether the thread you just zapped happened to be in the middle of modifying some shared state. Since this leaves your program's integrity in doubt, the only thing you can safely do next is kill the whole program, which is a bit drastic. So the cancellation model requires cooperation on the part of the task in question. The only situation in which cancellation would have any effect in this particular example is if the user managed to click the Cancel button before the task had even begun.

If you have divided your work into numerous relatively short tasks, cancellation is more useful—if you cancel tasks that have been queued up but not yet started, they will never run at all. Tasks already in progress will continue to run, but if all your tasks are short, you won't have to wait long. If you have long-running tasks, however, you will need to be able to detect cancellation and act on it if you want to handle cancellation swiftly. This means you will have to arrange for the code you run as part of the tasks to have access to the cancellation token, and they must test the IsCancellationRequested property from time to time.

Cancellation isn't the only reason a task or set of tasks might stop before finishing—things might be brought to a halt by exceptions.

Error Handling

A task can complete in one of three ways: it can run to completion, it can be canceled, or it can *fault*. The Task object's TaskStatus property reflects this through RanToComple tion, Canceled, and Faulted values, respectively, and if the task enters the Faulted state, its IsFaulted property also becomes true. A code-based task will enter the Faulted state if its method throws an exception. You can retrieve the exception information from the task's Exception property. This returns an AggregateException, which contains a list of exceptions in its InnerExceptions property. It's a list because certain task usage patterns can end up hitting multiple exceptions; for example, you might have multiple failing child tasks.

If you don't check the `IsFaulted` property and instead just attempt to proceed, either by calling `Wait` or by attempting to fetch the `Result` of a `Task<TResult>`, the `Aggrega teException` will be thrown back into your code.

It's possible to write code that never looks for the exception. Example 16-17 starts two tasks, and since it ignores the `Task` objects returned by `StartNew`, it clearly never does anything more with the tasks. If they were children of another task that wouldn't matter—if you ignore exceptions in child tasks they end up causing the parent task to fault. But these are not child tasks, so if exceptions occur during their execution, the program won't notice. However, the TPL tries hard to make sure you don't ignore such exceptions—it uses a feature of the garbage collector called *finalization* to discover when a `Task` that faulted is about to be collected without your program ever having noticed the exception. When it detects this, it throws the `AggregateException`, which will cause your program to crash unless you've configured your process to deal with unhandled exceptions. (The .NET Framework runs all finalizers on a dedicated thread, and it's this thread that the TPL throws the exception on.) The `TaskScheduler` class offers an `UnobservedTaskException` event that lets you customize the way these unhandled exceptions are dealt with.

The upshot is that you should write error handling for any nonchild tasks that could throw. One way to do this is to provide a continuation specifically for error handling. The `ContinueWith` method takes an optional argument whose type is the `TaskContinua tionOptions` enumeration, which has an `OnlyOnFaulted` value—you could use this to build a continuation that will run only when an unanticipated exception occurs. (Of course, unanticipated exceptions are always bad news because, by definition, you weren't expecting them and therefore have no idea what state your program is in. So you probably need to terminate the program, which is what would have happened anyway if you hadn't written any error handling. However, you do get to write errors to your logs, and perhaps make an emergency attempt to write out unsaved data somewhere in the hope of recovering it when the program restarts.) But in general, it's preferable to handle errors by putting normal `try...catch` blocks inside your code so that the exceptions never make it out into the TPL in the first place.

Data Parallelism

The final concurrency feature we're going to look at is data parallelism. This is where concurrency is driven by having lots of data items, rather than by explicitly creating numerous tasks or threads. It can be a simple approach to parallelism because you don't have to tell the .NET Framework anything about how you want it to split up the work.

With tasks, the .NET Framework has no idea how many tasks you plan to create when you create the first one, but with data parallelism, it has the opportunity to see more of the problem before deciding how to spread the load across the available logical processors. So in some scenarios, it may be able to make more efficient use of the available resources.

Parallel For and ForEach

The `Parallel` class provides a couple of methods for performing data-driven parallel execution. Its `For` and `ForEach` methods are similar in concept to C# `for` and `foreach` loops, but rather than iterating through collections one item at a time, on a system with multiple logical processors available it will process multiple items simultaneously.

Example 16-24 uses `Parallel.For`. This code calculates pixel values for a fractal known as the Mandelbrot set, a popular parallelism demonstration because each pixel value can be calculated entirely independently of all the others, so the scope for parallel execution is effectively endless (unless machines with more logical processors than pixels become available). And since it's a relatively expensive computation, the benefits of parallel execution are easy to see. Normally, this sort of code would contain two nested `for` loops, one to iterate over the rows of pixels and one to iterate over the columns in each row. In this example, the outer loop has been replaced with a `Parallel.For`. (So this particular code cannot exploit more processors than it calculates lines of pixels—therefore, we don't quite have scope for per-pixel parallelism, but since you would typically generate an image a few hundred pixels tall, there is still a reasonable amount of scope for concurrency here.)

Example 16-24. Parallel.For

```
static int[,] CalculateMandelbrotValues(int pixelWidth, int pixelHeight,
    double left, double top, double width, double height, int maxIterations)
{
    int[,] results = new int[pixelWidth, pixelHeight];

    // Non-parallel version of following line would have looked like this:
    // for(int pixelY = 0; pixelY < pixelHeight; ++pixelY)
    Parallel.For(0, pixelHeight, pixelY =>
    {
        double y = top + (pixelY * height) / (double) pixelHeight;
        for (int pixelX = 0; pixelX < pixelWidth; ++pixelX)
        {
            double x = left + (pixelX * width) / (double) pixelWidth;

            // Note: this lives in the System.Numerics namespace in the
            // System.Numerics assembly.
            Complex c = new Complex(x, y);
            Complex z = new Complex();

            int iter;
            for (iter = 1; z.Magnitude < 2 && iter < maxIterations; ++iter)
            {
                z = z * z + c;
            }
            if (iter == maxIterations) { iter = 0; }
            results[pixelX, pixelY] = iter;
        }
    });
```

```
    return results;
}
```

This structure, seen in the preceding code:

```
Parallel.For(0, pixelHeight, pixelY =>
{
    ...
});
```

iterates over the same range as this:

```
for(int pixelY = 0, pixelY < pixelHeight; ++pixelY)
{
    ...
}
```

The syntax isn't identical because `Parallel.For` is just a method, not a language feature. The first two arguments indicate the range—the start value is inclusive (i.e., it will start from the specified value), but the end value is exclusive (it stops one short of the end value). The final argument to `Parallel.For` is a delegate that takes the iteration variable as its argument. Example 16-24 uses a lambda, whose minimal syntax introduces the least possible extra clutter over a normal `for` loop.

`Parallel.For` will attempt to execute the delegate on multiple logical processors simultaneously, using the thread pool to attempt to make full, efficient use of the available processors. The way it distributes the iterations across logical processors may come as a surprise, though. It doesn't simply give the first row to the first logical processor, the second row to the second logical processor, and so on. It carves the available rows into chunks, and so the second logical processor will find itself starting several rows ahead of the first. And it may decide to subdivide further depending on the progress your code makes. So you must not rely on the iteration being done in any particular order. It does this chunking to avoid subdividing the work into pieces that are too small to handle efficiently. Ideally, each CPU should be given work in lumps that are large enough to minimize context switching and synchronization overheads, but small enough that each CPU can be kept busy while there's work to be done. This chunking is one reason why data parallelism can sometimes be more efficient than using tasks directly—the parallelism gets to be exactly as fine-grained as necessary and no more so, minimizing overheads.

Arguably, calling Example 16-24 *data parallelism* is stretching a point—the "data" here is just the numbers being fed into the calculations. `Parallel.For` is no more or less data-oriented than a typical `for` loop with an `int` loop counter—it just iterates a numeric variable over a particular range in a list. However, you could use exactly the same construct to iterate over a range of data instead of a range of numbers. Alternatively, there's `Parallel.ForEach`, which is very similar in use to `Parallel.For`, except, as you'd expect, it iterates over any `IEnumerable<T>` like a C# `foreach` loop, instead of using a range of integers. It reads ahead into the enumeration to perform chunking. (And if you provide it with an `IList<T>` it will use the list's indexer to implement a more efficient partitioning strategy.)

There's another way to perform parallel iteration over enumerable data: PLINQ.

PLINQ: Parallel LINQ

Parallel LINQ (PLINQ) is a LINQ provider that enables any `IEnumerable<T>` to be processed using normal LINQ query syntax, but in a way that works in parallel. On the face of it, it's deceptively simple. This:

```
var pq = from x in someList
         where x.SomeProperty > 42
         select x.Frob(x.Bar);
```

will use LINQ to Objects, assuming that `someList` implements `IEnumerable<T>`. Here's the PLINQ version:

```
var pq = from x in someList.AsParallel()
         where x.SomeProperty > 42
         select x.Frob(x.Bar);
```

The only difference here is the addition of a call to `AsParallel`, an extension method that the `ParallelEnumerable` class makes available on all `IEnumerable<T>` implementations. It's available to any code that has brought the `System.Linq` namespace into scope with a suitable `using` declaration. `AsParallel` returns a `ParallelQuery<T>`, which means that the normal LINQ to Objects implementation of the standard LINQ operators no longer applies. All the same operators are available, but now they're supplied by `ParallelEnumerable`, which is able to execute certain operators in parallel.

> Not all queries will execute in parallel. Some LINQ operators essentially force things to be done in a certain order, so PLINQ will inspect the structure of your query to decide which parts, if any, it can usefully run in parallel.

Iterating over the results with `foreach` can restrict the extent to which the query can execute in parallel, because `foreach` asks for items one at a time—upstream parts of the query may still be able to execute concurrently, but the final results will be sequential. If you'd like to execute code for each item and to allow work to proceed in parallel even for this final processing step, PLINQ offers a `ForAll` operator:

```
pq.ForAll(x => x.DoSomething());
```

This will execute the delegate once for each item the query returns, and can do so in parallel—it will use as many logical processors concurrently as possible to evaluate the query and to call the delegate you provide.

This means that all the usual multithreading caveats apply for the code you run from `ForAll`. In fact, PLINQ can be a little dangerous as it's not that obvious that your code is going to run on multiple threads—it manages to make parallel code look just a bit too normal. This is not always a problem—LINQ tends to encourage a functional style of programming in its queries, meaning that most of the data involved will be used in a read-only fashion, which makes dealing with threading much simpler. But code executed by `ForAll` is useful only if it has no side effects, so you need to be careful with whatever you put in there.

Summary

To exploit the potential of multicore CPUs, you'll need to run code on multiple threads. Threads can also be useful for keeping user interfaces responsive in the face of slow operations, although asynchronous programming techniques can be a better choice than creating threads explicitly. While you can create threads explicitly, the thread pool—used either directly or through the Task Parallel Library—is often preferable because it makes it easier for your code to adapt to the available CPU resources on the target machine. For code that needs to process large collections of data or perform uniform calculations across large ranges of numbers, data parallelism can help parallelize your execution without adding too much complication to your code.

No matter what multithreading mechanisms you use, you are likely to need the synchronization and locking primitives to ensure that your code avoids concurrency hazards such as races. The monitor facility built into every .NET object, and exposed through the `Monitor` class and C# `lock` keyword, is usually the best mechanism to use, but some more specialized primitives are available that can work better if you happen to find yourself in one of the scenarios for which they are designed.

CHAPTER 17

Attributes and Reflection

As well as containing code and data, a .NET program can also contain *metadata*. Metadata is information about the data—that is, information about the types, code, fields, and so on—stored along with your program. This chapter explores how some of that metadata is created and used.

A lot of the metadata is information that .NET needs in order to understand how your code should be used—for example, metadata defines whether a particular method is `public` or `private`. But you can also add custom metadata, using *attributes*.

Reflection is the process by which a program can read its own metadata, or metadata from another program. A program is said to reflect on itself or on another program, extracting metadata from the reflected assembly and using that metadata either to inform the user or to modify the program's behavior.

Attributes

An *attribute* is an object that represents data you want to associate with an element in your program. The element to which you attach an attribute is referred to as the *target* of that attribute. For example, in Chapter 12 we saw the `XmlIgnore` attribute applied to a property:

```
[XmlIgnore]
public string LastName { get; set; }
```

This tells the XML serialization system that we want it to ignore this particular property when converting between XML and objects of this kind. This illustrates an important feature of attributes: they don't do anything on their own. The `XmlIgnore` attribute contains no code, nor does it cause anything to happen when the relevant property is read or modified. It only has any effect when we use XML serialization, and the only reason it does anything then is because the XML serialization system goes looking for it.

Attributes are passive. They are essentially just annotations. For them to be useful, something somewhere needs to look for them.

Types of Attributes

Some attributes are supplied as part of the CLR, some by the . NET Framework class libraries, and some by other libraries. In addition, you are free to define custom attributes for your own purposes.

Most programmers will use only the attributes provided by existing libraries, though creating your own custom attributes can be a powerful tool when combined with reflection, as described later in this chapter.

Attribute targets

If you search through the .NET Framework class libraries, you'll find a great many attributes. Some attributes can be applied to an assembly, others to a class or interface, and some, such as [XmlIgnore], are applied to properties and fields. Most attributes make sense only when applied to certain things—the XmlIgnore attribute cannot usefully be applied to a method, for example, because methods cannot be serialized to XML. So each attribute type declares its *attribute targets* using the AttributeTargets enumeration. Most of the entries in this enumeration are self-explanatory, but since a few are not entirely obvious, Table 17-1 shows a complete list.

Table 17-1. Possible attribute targets

Member name	Attribute may be applied to
All	Any of the following elements: assembly, class, constructor, delegate, enum, event, field, interface, method, module, parameter, property, return value, or struct
Assembly	An assembly
Class	A class
Constructor	A constructor
Delegate	A delegate
Enum	An enumeration
Event	An event
Field	A field
GenericParameter	A type parameter for a generic class or method
Interface	An interface
Method	A method
Module	A module
Parameter	A parameter of a method
Property	A property (both get and set, if implemented)
ReturnValue	A return value
Struct	A struct

Applying attributes

You apply most attributes to their targets by placing them in square brackets immediately before the target item. A couple of the target types don't correspond directly to any single source code feature, and so these are handled differently. For example, an assembly is a single compiled .NET executable or library—it's everything in a single project—so there's no one feature in the source code to which to apply the attribute. Therefore, you can apply assembly attributes at the top of any file. The module attribute target type works the same way.*

 You must place assembly or module attributes after all using directives and before any code.

You can apply multiple attributes, one after another:

```
[assembly: AssemblyDelaySign(false)]
[assembly: AssemblyKeyFile(".\\keyFile.snk")]
```

Alternatively, you can put them all inside a single pair of square brackets, separating the attributes with commas:

```
[assembly: AssemblyDelaySign(false),
 assembly: AssemblyKeyFile(".\\keyFile.snk")]
```

The System.Reflection namespace offers a number of attributes, including attributes for assemblies (such as the AssemblyKeyFileAttribute), for configuration, and for version attributes. Some of these are recognized by the compiler—the key file attribute gets used if the compiler generates a digital signature for your component, for example.

Custom Attributes

You are free to create your own custom attributes and use them at runtime as you see fit. Suppose, for example, that your development organization wants to keep track of bug fixes. You already keep a database of all your bugs, but you'd like to tie your bug reports to specific fixes in the code.

You might add comments to your code along the lines of:

```
// Bug 323 fixed by Jesse Liberty 1/1/2010.
```

This would make it easy to see in your source code, but since comments get stripped out at compile time this information won't make it into the compiled code. If we wanted

---

* Modules are the individual files that constitute an assembly. The vast majority of assemblies consist of just one file, so it's very rare to encounter situations in which you need to deal with an individual module as opposed to the whole assembly. They are mentioned here for completeness.

to change that, we could use a custom attribute. We would replace the comment with something like this:

```
[BugFixAttribute(323, "Jesse Liberty", "1/1/2010",
                 Comment="Off by one error")]
```

You could then write a program to read through the metadata to find these bug-fix annotations, and perhaps it might go on to update a bug database. The attribute would serve the purposes of a comment, but would also allow you to retrieve the information programmatically through tools you'd create.

 This may be a somewhat artificial example, however, because you might not really want this information to be compiled into the shipping code.

Defining a custom attribute

Attributes, like most things in C#, are embodied in classes. To create a custom attribute, derive a class from `System.Attribute`:

```
public class BugFixAttribute : System.Attribute
```

You need to tell the compiler which kinds of elements this attribute can be used with (the attribute target). We specify this with (what else?) an attribute:

```
[AttributeUsage(AttributeTargets.Class |
    AttributeTargets.Constructor |
    AttributeTargets.Field |
    AttributeTargets.Method |
    AttributeTargets.Property,
    AllowMultiple = true)]
```

`AttributeUsage` is an attribute applied to an attribute class. It provides data about the metadata: a *meta-attribute*, if you will.

We have provided the `AttributeUsage` attribute constructor with two arguments. The first is a set of flags that indicate the target—in this case, the class and its constructor, fields, methods, and properties. The second argument is a flag that indicates whether a given element might receive more than one such attribute. In this example, `AllowMultiple` is set to `true`, indicating that class members can have more than one `BugFixAttribute` assigned.

Naming an attribute

The new custom attribute in this example is named `BugFixAttribute`. The convention is to append the word *Attribute* to your attribute name. The compiler recognizes this convention, by allowing you to use a shorter version of the name when you apply the attribute. Thus, you can write:

```
[BugFix(123, "Jesse Liberty", "01/01/08", Comment="Off by one")]
```

The compiler will first look for an attribute class named `BugFix` and, if it doesn't find that, will then look for `BugFixAttribute`.

Constructing an attribute

Although attributes have constructors, the syntax we use when applying an attribute is not quite the same as that for a normal constructor. We can provide two types of argument: *positional* and *named*. In the `BugFix` example, the programmer's name, the bug ID, and the date are positional parameters, and `comment` is a named parameter. Positional parameters are passed in through the constructor, and must be passed in the order declared in the constructor:

```
public BugFixAttribute(int bugID, string programmer,
string date)
{
    this.BugID = bugID;
    this.Programmer = programmer;
    this.Date = date;
}
```

Named parameters are implemented as fields or as properties:

```
public string Comment    { get; set; }
```

You may be wondering why attributes use a different syntax for named arguments than we use in normal method and constructor invocation, where named arguments take the form `Comment: "Off by one"`, using a colon instead of an equals sign. The inconsistency is for historical reasons. Attributes have always supported positional and named arguments, but methods and normal constructor calls only got them in C# 4.0. The mechanisms work quite differently—the C# 4.0 named argument syntax is mainly there to support optional arguments, and it only deals with real method arguments, whereas with attributes, named arguments are not arguments at all—they are really properties in disguise.

It is common to create read-only properties for the positional parameters:

```
public int BugID    { get; private set; }
```

Using an attribute

Once you have defined an attribute, you can put it to work by placing it immediately before its target. To test the `BugFixAttribute` of the preceding example, the following program creates a simple class named `MyMath` and gives it two functions. Assign `BugFixAttribute`s to the class to record its code-maintenance history:

```
[BugFixAttribute(121,"Jesse Liberty","01/03/08")]
[BugFixAttribute(107,"Jesse Liberty","01/04/08",
                Comment="Fixed off by one errors")]
public class MyMath
```

These attributes are stored with the metadata. Example 17-1 shows the complete program.

Example 17-1. Working with custom attributes

```
using System;

namespace CustomAttributes
{
    // create custom attribute to be assigned to class members
    [AttributeUsage(AttributeTargets.Class |
                    AttributeTargets.Constructor |
                    AttributeTargets.Field |
                    AttributeTargets.Method |
                    AttributeTargets.Property,
                    AllowMultiple = true)]
    public class BugFixAttribute : System.Attribute
    {
        // attribute constructor for positional parameters
        public BugFixAttribute
        (
            int bugID,
            string programmer,
            string date
        )
        {
            this.BugID = bugID;
            this.Programmer = programmer;
            this.Date = date;
        }

        // accessors
        public int BugID { get; private set; }
        public string Date { get; private set; }
        public string Programmer { get; private set; }

        // property for named parameter
        public string Comment { get; set; }
    }

    // ********* assign the attributes to the class ********

    [BugFixAttribute(121, "Jesse Liberty", "01/03/08")]
    [BugFixAttribute(107, "Jesse Liberty", "01/04/08",
                     Comment = "Fixed off by one errors")]
    public class MyMath
    {
        public double DoFunc1(double param1)
        {
            return param1 + DoFunc2(param1);
        }

        public double DoFunc2(double param1)
        {
            return param1 / 3;
```

```
        }
    }

    public class Tester
    {
        static void Main(string[] args)
        {
            MyMath mm = new MyMath();
            Console.WriteLine("Calling DoFunc(7). Result: {0}",
            mm.DoFunc1(7));
        }
    }
}
```

```
Output:
Calling DoFunc(7). Result: 9.3333333333333333
```

As you can see, the attributes had absolutely no impact on the output. This is not surprising because, as we said earlier, attributes are passive—they only affect things that go looking for them, and we've not yet written anything that does that. In fact, for the moment, you have only our word that the attributes exist at all. We'll see how to get at this metadata and use it in a program in the next section.

Reflection

For the attributes in the metadata to be useful, you need a way to access them at runtime. The classes in the Reflection namespace, along with the System.Type class, provide support for examining and interacting with the metadata.

Reflection is generally used for any of four tasks:

Inspecting metadata
> This might be used by tools and utilities that wish to display metadata, or by class library features that modify their behavior based on metadata.

Performing type discovery
> Your code can examine the types in an assembly and interact with or instantiate those types. An application that supports plug-ins might use this to discover what features a plug-in DLL offers.

Late binding to methods and properties
> This allows the programmer to invoke properties and methods on objects dynamically instantiated, based on type discovery. This is also known as *dynamic invocation*. (As we'll see in Chapter 18, C# 4.0 has introduced an easier way to do this than using reflection.)

Creating types at runtime
> You can generate new types at runtime. You might do this when a custom class containing code generated at runtime, specialized for a particular task, will run

significantly faster than a more general-purpose solution. This is an advanced technique that is beyond the scope of this book.

Inspecting Metadata

In this section, we will use the C# reflection support to read the metadata in the MyMath class.

The reflection system defines numerous classes, each designed to provide information about a particular kind of metadata. For example, the ConstructorInfo provides access to all the metadata for a constructor, while PropertyInfo gives us the metadata for a property. Our custom attribute in Example 17-1 can be applied to a wide range of targets, so we're going to encounter several different metadata types. However, all of our supported targets have something in common—they are all things that can be members of classes. (That's plainly true for properties, methods, fields, and constructors. Our attribute can also be applied to classes, which seems like an exception because they're often not members of other types, but the point is that they can be.) And so, the metadata types for all our supported target types derive from a common base class, MemberInfo.

MemberInfo is defined in the System.Reflection namespace. We can use it to discover the attributes of a member and to provide access to the metadata. We'll start by getting hold of the metadata for a particular type:

```
System.Reflection.MemberInfo inf = typeof(MyMath);
```

We're using the typeof operator on the MyMath type, which returns an object of type Type, which derives from MemberInfo.

 The Type class is the heart of the reflection classes. Type encapsulates a representation of the type of an object. The Type class is the primary way to access metadata—we can use it to get hold of information about the other members of a class (e.g., methods, properties, fields, events, etc.).

The next step is to call GetCustomAttributes on this MemberInfo object, passing in the type of the attribute we want to find. It returns an array of objects, each of type BugFixAttribute:

```
object[] attributes;
attributes =
    inf.GetCustomAttributes(typeof(BugFixAttribute),false);
```

You can now iterate through this array, printing out the properties of the BugFixAttribute object. Example 17-2 replaces the Main method in the Tester class from Example 17-1.

Example 17-2. Using reflection

```
public static void Main(string[] args)
{
    MyMath mm = new MyMath();
    Console.WriteLine("Calling DoFunc(7). Result: {0}",
                        mm.DoFunc1(7));

    // get the member information and use it to
    // retrieve the custom attributes
    System.Reflection.MemberInfo inf = typeof(MyMath);
    object[] attributes;
    attributes = inf.GetCustomAttributes(
                        typeof(BugFixAttribute), false);

    // iterate through the attributes, retrieving the
    // properties
    foreach (Object attribute in attributes)
    {
        BugFixAttribute bfa = (BugFixAttribute)attribute;
        Console.WriteLine("\nBugID: {0}", bfa.BugID);
        Console.WriteLine("Programmer: {0}", bfa.Programmer);
        Console.WriteLine("Date: {0}", bfa.Date);
        Console.WriteLine("Comment: {0}", bfa.Comment);
    }
}
```

```
Output:
Calling DoFunc(7). Result: 9.3333333333333333

BugID: 121
Programmer: Jesse Liberty
Date: 01/03/08
Comment:

BugID: 107
Programmer: Jesse Liberty
Date: 01/04/08
Comment: Fixed off by one errors
```

When you put this replacement code into Example 17-1 and run it, you can see the metadata printed as you'd expect.

Type Discovery

You can use reflection to explore and examine the contents of an assembly. You can find the types it contains. You can discover the methods, fields, properties, and events associated with a type, as well as the signatures of each of the type's methods. You can also discover the interfaces supported by the type, and the type's base class.

If we were using this to support a plug-in system for extending our application, we'd need to load at runtime assemblies we didn't know about when we wrote our application. We can load an assembly dynamically with the `Assembly.Load()` static method.

The `Assembly` class encapsulates the actual assembly itself, for purposes of reflection. One signature for the `Load` method is:

```
public static Assembly Load(string assemblyName)
```

For example, *Mscorlib.dll* has the core classes of the .NET Framework, so we can pass that to the `Load()` method:

```
Assembly a = Assembly.Load("Mscorlib");
```

(In fact *Mscorlib.dll* will already be loaded, but this method doesn't mind—it returns the assembly we asked for, loading it first if necessary.) There's also a `LoadFrom` method that takes a file path. Once the assembly is loaded, we can call `GetTypes()` to return an array of `Type` objects. A `Type` object represents a specific type declaration, such as a class, interface, array, struct, delegate, or enumeration:

```
Type[] types = a.GetTypes();
```

The assembly returns an array of types that we can display in a `foreach` loop, as shown in Example 17-3. Because this example uses the `Type` class, you will want to add a `using` directive for the `System.Reflection` namespace.

Example 17-3. Reflecting on an assembly

```csharp
using System;
using System.Reflection;

namespace ReflectingAnAssembly
{
    public class Tester
    {
        public static void Main()
        {
            // what is in the assembly
            Assembly a = Assembly.Load("Mscorlib");
            Type[] types = a.GetTypes();
            foreach (Type t in types)
            {
                Console.WriteLine("Type is {0}", t);
            }
            Console.WriteLine(
                "{0} types found", types.Length);
        }
    }
}
```

The output from this would fill many pages. Here is a short excerpt:

```
Type is System.Object
Type is ThisAssembly
Type is AssemblyRef
Type is System.ICloneable
Type is System.Collections.IEnumerable
Type is System.Collections.ICollection
```

```
Type is System.Collections.IList
Type is System.Array
```

This example obtained an array filled with the types from the core library and printed them one by one. The array contained 2,779 entries when run against .NET version 4.0.

Reflecting on a Specific Type

Instead of iterating through all the types, you can ask the reflection system for a single specific one. This may seem odd—if you already know what type you want, why would you need to use reflection to find things out about it at runtime? In fact, this can be useful for several reasons—some applications let users put the name of a type in a configuration file, so the program only discovers the name of the type it requires at runtime, and wants to look up just that one type. To do so, you extract a type from the assembly with the GetType() method, as shown in Example 17-4.

Example 17-4. Reflecting on a type

```
using System;
using System.Reflection;

namespace ReflectingOnAType
{
    public class Tester
    {
        public static void Main()
        {
            // examine a single type
            Assembly a = Assembly.Load("Mscorlib");
            Type theType = a.GetType("System.Reflection.Assembly");
            Console.WriteLine("\nSingle Type is {0}\n", theType);
        }
    }
}
```

```
Output:
Single Type is System.Reflection.Assembly
```

It can sometimes be useful to get hold of the Type object for a specific type known to you at compile time. This may seem odd, for the reasons described earlier, but the usual reason for doing this is not so that you can learn more about the type. You may need to do it to compare one type object with another. For example, if we wanted to find all of the types in *mscorlib* that derive from the MemberInfo class, we would need to get hold of the Type object for MemberInfo. Example 17-5 does this.

Example 17-5. Using a specific type object for comparison purposes

```
using System;
using System.Linq;
using System.Reflection;

namespace UsingASpecificType
```

```
{
    public class Tester
    {
        public static void Main()
        {
            // examine a single type
            Assembly a = Assembly.Load("Mscorlib");

            var matchingTypes = from t in a.GetTypes()
                                where typeof(MemberInfo).IsAssignableFrom(t)
                                select t;

            foreach (Type t in matchingTypes)
            {
                Console.WriteLine(t);
            }
        }
    }
}
```

This uses a LINQ query to find the matching types. It illustrates one of the things you
can do with a Type object—its IsAssignableFrom method tells you whether it's possible
to assign an instance of one type into a field or variable of another type. So this code
looks at every type, and asks whether it can be assigned into a variable of type
MemberInfo. (This casts the net slightly wider than merely looking at the base class—
this query will find all types that derive either directly or indirectly from MemberInfo.)
Since we know exactly what target type we're interested in, we use the C# typeof
operator to get the Type object for that exact type.

Finding all type members

You can ask a Type object for all its members using the GetMembers() method of the
Type class, which lists all the methods, properties, and fields, as shown in Example 17-6.

Example 17-6. Reflecting on the members of a type

```
using System;
using System.Reflection;

namespace ReflectingOnMembersOfAType
{
    public class Tester
    {
        public static void Main()
        {
            // examine a single type
            Assembly a = Assembly.Load("Mscorlib");
            Type theType = a.GetType("System.Reflection.Assembly");
            Console.WriteLine("\nSingle Type is {0}\n", theType);

            // get all the members
            MemberInfo[] mbrInfoArray = theType.GetMembers();
            foreach (MemberInfo mbrInfo in mbrInfoArray)
```

```
        {
            Console.WriteLine("{0} is a {1}",
                    mbrInfo, mbrInfo.MemberType);
        }
    }
  }
}
```

Once again, the output is quite lengthy, but within the output you see fields, methods, constructors, and properties, as shown in this excerpt:

```
System.Type GetType(System.String, Boolean, Boolean) is a Method
System.Type[] GetExportedTypes() is a Method
System.Reflection.Module GetModule(System.String) is a Method
System.String get_FullName() is a Method
```

Finding type methods

You might want to focus on methods only, excluding the fields, properties, and so forth. To do so, find the call to `GetMembers()`:

```
MemberInfo[] mbrInfoArray =
    theType.GetMembers();
```

and replace it with a call to `GetMethods()`:

```
mbrInfoArray = theType.GetMethods();
```

The output now contains nothing but the methods:

```
Output (excerpt):
Boolean Equals(System.Object) is a Method
System.String ToString() is a Method
System.String CreateQualifiedName(
System.String, System.String) is a Method
Boolean get_GlobalAssemblyCache() is a Method
```

Late Binding

Once you find a method, you can invoke it using reflection. For example, you might like to invoke the `Cos()` method of `System.Math`, which returns the cosine of an angle.

You can, of course, call `Cos()` in the normal course of your code, but reflection allows you to bind to that method at runtime. This is called *late binding*, and offers the flexibility of choosing at runtime which object to bind to and invoking it programmatically. The `dynamic` keyword added in C# 4.0, discussed in Chapter 18, can do this for you, but you may sometimes want to control the underlying mechanisms for late binding yourself. This can be useful when creating a custom script to be run by the user or when working with objects that might not be available at compile time.

To invoke `Cos()`, first get the `Type` information for the `System.Math` class:

```
Type theMathType = typeof(System.Math);
```

Once we have type information, we could dynamically create an instance of the type using a static method of the `Activator` class. However, we don't need to here because `Cos()` is static. In fact, all members of `System.Math` are static, and even if you wanted to create an instance, you can't because `System.Math` has no public constructor. However, since you will come across types that need to be instantiated so that you can call their nonstatic members, it's important to know how to create new objects with reflection.

The `Activator` class contains three methods, all static, which you can use to create objects. The methods are as follows:

`CreateComInstanceFrom`
> Creates instances of COM objects.

`CreateInstanceFrom`
> Creates a reference to an object from a particular assembly and type name.

`CreateInstance`
> Creates an instance of a particular type from a `Type` object. For example:

```
Object theObj = Activator.CreateInstance(someType);
```

Back to the `Cos()` example. Our `theMathType` variable now refers to a `Type` object which we obtained by calling `GetType`.

Before we can invoke a method on the type, we must get the method we need from the `Type` object. To do so, we call `GetMethod()`, passing the method name:

```
MethodInfo cosineInfo =
  theMathType.GetMethod("Cos");
```

 There's obviously a problem here if you need to deal with overloaded methods. That's not an issue for this particular example—there's only one `Cos` method. But if you need to deal with multiple methods of the same name, you can use an alternative overload of `GetMethod` that takes two arguments. After the method name you can pass an array of the argument types, which allows you to uniquely identify the overload you require. We could use that here if we wanted even though it's not necessary—we could create a `Type[]` array containing one entry: the `typeof(double)`. This would tell `GetMethod` that we are looking specifically for a method called `Cos` that takes a single argument of type `double`.

You now have an object of type `MethodInfo` which provides an `Invoke` method that calls the method this `MethodInfo` represents. Normally, the first argument to `Invoke` would be the object on which we want to invoke the method. However, because this is a static method, there is no object, so we just pass `null`. And then we pass the arguments for the function. `Invoke` is capable of calling any method, regardless of how many arguments it has, so it expects the arguments to be wrapped in an array, even if there's only one:

```
Object[] parameters = new Object[1];
parameters[0] = 45 * (Math.PI/180); // 45 degrees in radians
Object returnVal = cosineInfo.Invoke(null, parameters);
```

Example 17-7 shows all the steps required to call the `Cos()` method dynamically.

Example 17-7. Dynamically invoking a method

```
using System;
using System.Reflection;

namespace DynamicallyInvokingAMethod
{
    public class Tester
    {
        public static void Main()
        {
            Type theMathType = Type.GetType("System.Math");
            // Since System.Math has no public constructor, this
            // would throw an exception.
            // Object theObj =
            //     Activator.CreateInstance(theMathType);

            // array with one member
            Type[] paramTypes = new Type[1];
            paramTypes[0] = Type.GetType("System.Double");

            // Get method info for Cos()
            MethodInfo CosineInfo =
                theMathType.GetMethod("Cos", paramTypes);

            // fill an array with the actual parameters
            Object[] parameters = new Object[1];
            parameters[0] = 45 * (Math.PI / 180); // 45 degrees in radians
            Object returnVal =
                CosineInfo.Invoke(theMathType, parameters);
            Console.WriteLine(
                "The cosine of a 45 degree angle {0}",
                returnVal);
        }
    }
}
```

```
Output:
The cosine of a 45 degree angle 0.707106781186548
```

That was a lot of work just to invoke a single method. The power, however, is that you can use reflection to discover an assembly on the user's machine, to query what methods are available, and to invoke one of those members dynamically. Chapter 18 will show how you can use the **dynamic** keyword to automate this for certain scenarios.

Summary

All .NET components contain metadata. Some of this is essential information about the structure of our code—the metadata includes the list of types, their names, the members they define, the arguments accepted by the methods, and so on. But the metadata system is also extensible—attributes can be embedded alongside the core metadata, and these can then be discovered at runtime. Finally, we saw that some metadata features can make use of the items they represent—we can use method information to invoke a method we discovered dynamically, for example.

CHAPTER 18

Dynamic

Older versions of C# had trouble interacting with certain kinds of programs, especially those in the Microsoft Office family. You could get the job done, but before C# 4.0, it needed a lot of effort, and the results were ugly. The problem came down to a clash of philosophies: Office embraces a *dynamic* style, while C# used to lean heavily toward the *static* style. C# 4.0 now provides better support for the dynamic style, making it much easier to program Microsoft Office and similar systems from C#.

Static Versus Dynamic

What exactly is the difference between static and dynamic? The terminology is slightly confusing because C# has a keyword called `static` which is unrelated, so you'll need to put your knowledge of that `static` to one side for now. When it comes to the dynamic/static distinction, something is dynamic if it is decided at runtime, whereas a static feature is determined at compile type. If that sounds rather abstract, it's because the distinction can apply to lots of different things, including the choice of which method to call, the type of a variable or an expression, or the meaning of an operator.

Let's look at some concrete examples. The compiler is able to work out quite a lot of things about code during compilation, even code as simple as Example 18-1.

Example 18-1. Simple code with various static features

```
var myString = Console.ReadLine();
var modifiedString = myString.Replace("color", "colour");
```

We've used the `var` keyword here, so we've not told the compiler what type these variables have, but it can work that out for us. The `Console.ReadLine()` method has a return type of `string`, meaning that `myString` must be of type `string`—the variable's type can never be anything else, and so we say that it has a static type. (And obviously, the same would be true for any variable declared with an explicit type—declaring `myString` explicitly as a `string` would have changed nothing.) Likewise, the compiler is able to work out that `modifiedString` is also a `string`. Any variable declared with `var` will have a static type.

The compiler determines other aspects of code statically besides the types of variables. For example, there are method calls. The `Console.ReadLine()` call is straightforward. `Console` is a class name, so our code has been explicit about where to find the method. Since there's no scope for ambiguity over which method we mean, this is a static method invocation—we know at compile time exactly which method will be called at runtime.

The `myString.Replace` method is slightly more interesting: `myString` refers to a variable, not a class, so to understand which method will be invoked, we need to know what type `myString` is. But as we already saw, in this example, its type is known statically to be `string`. As it happens, there are two overloads of `Replace`, one that takes two `string` arguments and one that takes two `char` arguments. In this code, we are passing to `string` literals, so the argument types are also known statically. This means that the compiler can work out which overload we require, and bakes that choice into the compiler output—once compilation completes, the exact method that Example 18-1 invokes is fixed. All the decisions are made at compile time here, and nothing can change the decision at runtime, and this is the nature of the static style.

Dynamic features defer decisions until runtime. For example, in a language that supports dynamic method invocation, the business of working out exactly which method to run doesn't happen until the program gets to the point where it tries to invoke the method. This means that dynamic code doesn't necessarily do the same thing every time it runs—a particular piece of code might end up invoking different methods from time to time.

You might be thinking that we've seen C# features in earlier chapters that enable this. And you'd be right: virtual methods, interfaces, and delegates all provide us with ways of writing code which picks the exact method to run at runtime. Static/dynamic is more of a continuum than a binary distinction. Virtual methods are more dynamic than nonvirtual methods, because they allow runtime selection of the method. Interfaces are more dynamic than virtual methods, because an object does not have to derive from any particular base class to implement a particular interface. Delegates are more dynamic than interfaces because they remove the requirement for the target to be compatible with any particular type, or even to be an object—whereas virtual methods and interfaces require instance methods, delegates also support those marked with the `static` keyword. (Again, try not to get distracted by the overlap in terminology here.) As you move through each of these mechanisms, the calling code knows slightly less about called code—there's more and more freedom for things to change at runtime.

However, these mechanisms all offer relatively narrow forms of dynamism. The distinctions just listed seem rather petty next to a language that wholeheartedly embraces a dynamic style. JavaScript, for example, doesn't even require the caller to know exactly how many arguments the method is expecting to receive.* And in Ruby, it's possible for an object to decide dynamically whether it feels like implementing a particular method at all, meaning it can decide at runtime to implement methods its author hadn't thought to include when originally writing the code!

The Dynamic Style and COM Automation

Microsoft Office is programmable through a system called COM automation, which has an adaptable approach to argument counts. Office uses this to good effect. It offers methods which are remarkably flexible because they take an astonishing number of arguments, enabling you to control every conceivable aspect of the operation. The Office APIs are designed to be used from the *Visual Basic for Applications* (VBA) language, which uses a dynamic idiom, so it doesn't matter if you leave out arguments you're not interested in. Its dynamic method invocation can supply reasonable defaults for any missing values. But this leaves more statically inclined languages with a problem. C# 3.0 requires the number and type of arguments to be known at compile time (even with delegate invocation, the most dynamic form of method invocation available in that language). This means that you don't get to leave out the parts you don't care about—you are forced to provide values for every single argument.

So although the designers of Microsoft Word intended for you to be able to write code roughly like that shown in Example 18-2:

Example 18-2. Word automation as Microsoft intended

```
var doc = wordApp.Documents.Open("WordFile.docx", ReadOnly:true);
```

in C# 3.0 you would have been forced to write the considerably less attractive code shown in Example 18-3.

Example 18-3. Word automation before C# 4.0

```
    object fileName = @"WordFile.docx";
    object missing = System.Reflection.Missing.Value;
    object readOnly = true;
    var doc = wordApp.Documents.Open(ref fileName, ref missing, ref readOnly,
        ref missing, ref missing, ref missing, ref missing, ref missing,
        ref missing, ref missing, ref missing, ref missing, ref missing,
        ref missing, ref missing, ref missing);
```

---

* Yes, so C# supports variable-length argument lists, but it fakes it. Such methods really have a fixed number of arguments, the last of which happens to be an array. There is only one variable-length `Console.WriteLine` method, and the compiler is able to determine statically when you use it.

Not only has C# 3.0 insisted that we supply a value for every argument (using a special "this argument intentionally left blank" value to signify our intent to provide no particular value), but it has also insisted that we stick precisely to the rules of the type system. Word has chosen about the most general-purpose representation available to ensure maximum flexibility, which is why we see `ref` in front of every argument—it's keeping open the possibility of passing data back out through any of these arguments. It doesn't care that this gives the methods an unusually complex signature, because it just assumes that we'll be using a language whose dynamic method invocation mechanism will automatically perform any necessary conversions at runtime. But if you're using a language with no such mechanism, such as C# 3.0, it's all rather unpleasant.

In fact, the way COM automation works is that the target object is ultimately responsible for dealing with defaults, coercion, and so on. The real problem is that C# 3.0 doesn't have any syntax for exploiting this—if you want to defer to the COM object, you have to use the dynamic method invocation services provided by reflection, which were described in Chapter 17. Unfortunately, doing that from C# 3.0 looks even more unpleasant than Example 18-3.

Fortunately, C# 4.0 adds new dynamic features to the language that let us write code like Example 18-2, just as Word intended.

The dynamic Type

C# 4.0 introduces a new type called `dynamic`. In some ways it looks just like any other type such as `int`, `string`, or `FileStream`: you can use it in variable declarations, or function arguments and return types, as Example 18-4 shows. (The method reads a little oddly—it's a `static` method in the sense that it does not relate to any particular object instance. But it's dynamic in the sense that it uses the `dynamic` type for its parameters and return value.)

Example 18-4. Using dynamic

```
static dynamic AddAnything(dynamic a, dynamic b)
{
    dynamic result = a + b;
    Console.WriteLine(result);
    return result;
}
```

While you can use `dynamic` almost anywhere you could use any other type name, it has some slightly unusual characteristics, because when you use `dynamic`, you are really saying "I have no idea what sort of thing this is." That means there are some situations where you can't use it—you can't derive a class from `dynamic`, for example, and `typeof(dynamic)` will not compile. But aside from the places where it would be meaningless, you can use it as you'd use any other type.

To see the dynamic behavior in action, we can try passing in a few different things to the `AddAnything` method from Example 18-4, as Example 18-5 shows.

Example 18-5. Passing different types

```
Console.WriteLine(AddAnything("Hello", "world").GetType().Name);
Console.WriteLine(AddAnything(31, 11).GetType().Name);
Console.WriteLine(AddAnything("31", 11).GetType().Name);
Console.WriteLine(AddAnything(31, 11.5).GetType().Name);
```

`AddAnything` prints the value it calculates, and Example 18-5 then goes on to print the type of the returned value. This produces the following output:

```
Helloworld
String
42
Int32
3111
String
42.5
Double
```

The + operator in `AddAnything` has behaved differently (dynamically, as it were) depending on the type of data we provided it with. Given two strings, it appended them, producing a string result. Given two integers, it added them, returning an integer as the result. Given some text and a number, it converted the number to a string, and then appended that to the first string. And given an integer and a double, it converted the integer to a double and then added it to the other double.

If we weren't using `dynamic`, every one of these would have required C# to generate quite different code. If you use the + operator in a situation where the compiler knows both types are strings, it generates code that calls the `String.Concat` method. If it knows both types are integers, it will instead generate code that performs arithmetic addition. Given an integer and a double, it will generate code that converts the integer to a double, followed by code to perform arithmetic addition. In all of these cases, it would uses the static information it has about the types to work out what code to generate to represent the expression `a + b`.

Clearly C# has done something quite different with Example 18-4. There's only one method, meaning it had to produce a single piece of code that is somehow able to execute any of these different meanings for the + operator. The compiler does this by generating code that builds a special kind of object that represents an addition operation, and this object then applies similar rules at runtime to those the compiler would have used at compile time if it knew what the types were. (This makes `dynamic` very different from `var`—see the sidebar on the next page.)

dynamic Versus var

At first glance, the difference between dynamic and var may not be entirely obvious. With either, you do not have to tell the compiler explicitly what type of data you're working with—the compiler ultimately ensures that the right thing happens. For example, whether using dynamic or var, the + operator has the same effect that it would have if you had used it with explicitly typed variables. So why do we need both?

The difference is timing: var does things much earlier. The C# compiler insists on being able to work out what type of data is in a var variable at compile time. But with dynamic, it works it out at runtime. This means there are some things you can do with dynamic that you cannot do with var. As Example 18-4 showed, you can use dynamic for the arguments of a function declaration, and also for its return type. But this would be illegal with var:

```
static var WillNotCompile(var a, var b) // Error
{
    return a + b;
}
```

The compiler has insufficient information to work out at compile time what the argument and return types are here. But with dynamic, that doesn't matter—the compiler doesn't need to know at compile type what type of data we're using because it will generate code that works out what to do at runtime.

Here's another thing that dynamic can do that var cannot:

```
dynamic differentTypes = "Text";
differentTypes = 42;
differentTypes = new object();
```

The value in differentTypes changed from one line to the next. If we had used var, this would have been illegal—a var variable's type is determined by the expression used to initialize it, so in this case, it would have been a string, meaning the second line would have failed to compile.

So dynamic and var perfectly represent the distinction between dynamic and static: a dynamic variable's type (and consequently the behavior of any operations using that variable) is determined at runtime; a var variable's type is static—it is determined at compile time and cannot change.

So the behavior is consistent with what we're used to with C#. The + operator continues to mean all the same things it can normally mean, it just picks the specific meaning at runtime—it decides dynamically. The + operator is not the only language feature capable of dynamic operation. As you'd expect, when using numeric types, all the mathematical operators work. In fact, most of the language elements you can use in a normal C# expression work as you'd expect. However, not all operations make sense in all scenarios. For example, if you tried to add a COM object to a number, you'd get an exception. (Specifically, a RuntimeBinderException, with a message complaining that the + operator cannot be applied to your chosen combination of types.) A COM object such as one representing an Excel spreadsheet is a rather different sort of thing from a .NET object. This raises a question: what sorts of objects can we use with dynamic?

Object Types and dynamic

Not all objects behave in the same way when you use them through the dynamic keyword. C# distinguishes between three kinds of objects for dynamic purposes: COM objects, objects that choose to customize their dynamic behavior, and ordinary .NET objects. We'll see several examples of that second category, but we'll start by looking at the most important dynamic scenario: interop with COM objects.

COM objects

COM objects such as those offered by Microsoft Word or Excel get special handling from dynamic. It looks for COM automation support (i.e., an implementation of the IDispatch COM interface) and uses this to access methods and properties. Automation is designed to support runtime discovery of members, and it provides mechanisms for dealing with optional arguments, coercing argument types where necessary. The dynamic keyword defers to these services for all member access. Example 18-6 relies on this.

Example 18-6. COM automation and dynamic

```
static void Main(string[] args)
{
    Type appType = Type.GetTypeFromProgID("Word.Application");
    dynamic wordApp = Activator.CreateInstance(appType);

    dynamic doc = wordApp.Documents.Open("WordDoc.docx", ReadOnly:true);
    dynamic docProperties = doc.BuiltInDocumentProperties;
    string authorName = docProperties["Author"].Value;
    doc.Close(SaveChanges:false);
    Console.WriteLine(authorName);
}
```

The first two lines in this method just create an instance of Word's application COM class. The line that calls wordApp.Documents.Open will end up using COM automation to retrieve the Document property from the application object, and then invoke the Open method on the document object. That method has 16 arguments, but dynamic uses the mechanisms provided by COM automation to offer only the two arguments the code has provided, letting Word provide defaults for all the rest.

Although dynamic is doing some very COM-specific work here, the syntax looks like normal C#. That's because the compiler has no idea what's going on here—it never does with dynamic. So the syntax looks the same regardless of what happens at runtime.

If you are familiar with COM you will be aware that not all COM objects support automation. COM also supports *custom interfaces*, which do not support dynamic semantics—they rely on compile-time knowledge to work at all. Since there is no general runtime mechanism for discovering what members a custom interface offers, dynamic is unsuitable for dealing with these kinds of COM interfaces. However, custom interfaces are well suited to the COM interop services described in Chapter 19. dynamic was added to C# mainly because of the problems specific to automation, so trying to use it with custom COM interfaces would be a case of the wrong tool for the job. dynamic is most likely to be useful for Windows applications that provide some sort of scripting feature because these normally use COM automation, particularly those that provide VBA as their default scripting language.

Silverlight script objects

Silverlight applications can run in the web browser, which adds an important interop scenario: interoperability between C# code and browser objects. Those might be objects from the DOM, or from script. In either case, these objects have characteristics that fit much better with dynamic than with normal C# syntax, because these objects decide which properties are available at runtime.

Silverlight 3 used C# 3.0, so dynamic was not available. It was still possible to use objects from the browser scripting world, but the syntax was not quite as natural. For example, you might have defined a JavaScript function on a web page, such as the one shown in Example 18-7.

Example 18-7. JavaScript code on a web page

```
<script type="text/javascript">
    function showMessage(msg)
    {
        var msgDiv = document.getElementById("messagePlaceholder");
        msgDiv.innerText = msg;
    }
</script>
```

Before C# 4.0, you could invoke this in a couple of ways, both of which are illustrated in Example 18-8.

Example 18-8. Accessing JavaScript in C# 3.0

```
ScriptObject showMessage = (ScriptObject)
    HtmlPage.Window.GetProperty("showMessage");
showMessage.InvokeSelf("Hello, world");

// Or...

ScriptObject window = HtmlPage.Window;
window.Invoke("showMessage", "Hello, world");
```

While these techniques are significantly less horrid than the C# 3.0 code for COM automation, they are both a little cumbersome. We have to use helper methods—`GetProperty`, `InvokeSelf`, or `Invoke` to retrieve properties and invoke functions. But Silverlight 4 supports C# 4.0, and all script objects can now be used through the `dynamic` keyword, as Example 18-9 shows.

Example 18-9. Accessing JavaScript in C# 4.0

```
dynamic window = HtmlPage.Window;
window.showMessage("Hello, world");
```

This is a far more natural syntax, so much so that the second line of code happens to be valid JavaScript as well as being valid C#. (It's idiomatically unusual—in a web page, the `window` object is the global object, and so you'd normally leave it out, but you're certainly allowed to refer to it explicitly, so if you were to paste that last line into script in a web page, it would do the same thing as it does in C#.) So `dynamic` has given us the ability to use JavaScript objects in C# with a very similar syntax to what we'd use in JavaScript itself—it doesn't get much more straightforward than that.

> The Visual Studio tools for Silverlight do not automatically add a reference to the support library that enables `dynamic` to work. So when you first add a `dynamic` variable to a Silverlight application, you'll get a compiler error. You need to add a reference to the `Microsoft.CSharp` library in your Silverlight project. This applies only to Silverlight projects—other C# projects automatically have a reference to this library.

Ordinary .NET objects

Although the `dynamic` keyword was added mainly to support interop scenarios, it is quite capable of working with normal .NET objects. For example, if you define a class in your project in the normal way, and create an instance of that class, you can use it via a `dynamic` variable. In this case, C# uses .NET's reflection APIs to work out which methods to invoke at runtime. We'll explore this with a simple class, defined in Example 18-10.

Example 18-10. A simple class

```
class MyType
{
    public string Text { get; set; }
    public int Number { get; set; }

    public override string ToString()
    {
        return Text + ", " + Number;
    }

    public void SetBoth(string t, int n)
    {
```

```
            Text = t;
            Number = n;
        }

        public static MyType operator + (MyType left, MyType right)
        {
            return new MyType
            {
                Text = left.Text + right.Text,
                Number = left.Number + right.Number
            };
        }
    }
}
```

We can use objects of this through a **dynamic** variable, as Example 18-11 shows.

Example 18-11. Using a simple object with dynamic

```
dynamic a = new MyType { Text = "One", Number = 123 };
Console.WriteLine(a.Text);
Console.WriteLine(a.Number);
Console.WriteLine(a.Problem);
```

The lines that call **Console.WriteLine** all use the dynamic variable **a** with normal C#
property syntax. The first two do exactly what you'd expect if the variable had been
declared as **MyType** or **var** instead of **dynamic**: they just print out the values of the **Text**
and **Number** properties. The third one is more interesting—it tries to use a property that
does not exist. If the variable had been declared as either **MyType** or **var**, this would not
have compiled—the compiler would have complained at our attempt to read a property
that it knows is not there. But because we've used **dynamic**, the compiler does not even
attempt to check this sort of thing at compile time. So it compiles, and instead it fails
at runtime—that third line throws a **RuntimeBinderException**, with a message complaining that the target type does not define the **Problem** member we're looking for.

This is one of the prices we pay for the flexibility of dynamic behavior: the compiler is
less vigilant. Certain programming errors that would be caught at compile time when
using the static style do not get detected until runtime. And there's a related price:
IntelliSense relies on the same compile-time type information that would have noticed
this error. If we were to change the variable in Example 18-11's type to either **MyType**
or **var**, we would see IntelliSense pop ups such as those shown in Figure 18-1 while
writing the code.

Visual Studio is able to show the list of available methods because the variable is statically typed—it will always refer to a **MyType** object. But with **dynamic**, we get much less
help. As Figure 18-2 shows, Visual Studio simply tells us that it has no idea what's
available. In this simple example, you could argue that it should be able to work it
out—although we've declared the variable to be **dynamic**, it can only ever be a **MyType**
at this point in the program. But Visual Studio does not attempt to perform this sort of
analysis for a couple of reasons. First, it would work for only relatively trivial scenarios
such as these, and would fail to work anywhere you were truly exploiting the dynamic

nature of dynamic—and if you don't really need the dynamism, why not just stick with statically typed variables? Second, as we'll see later, it's possible for a type to customize its dynamic behavior, so even if Visual Studio knows that a dynamic variable always refers to a MyType object, that doesn't necessarily mean that it knows what members will be available at runtime. Another upshot is that with dynamic variables, IntelliSense provides the rather less helpful pop up shown in Figure 18-2.

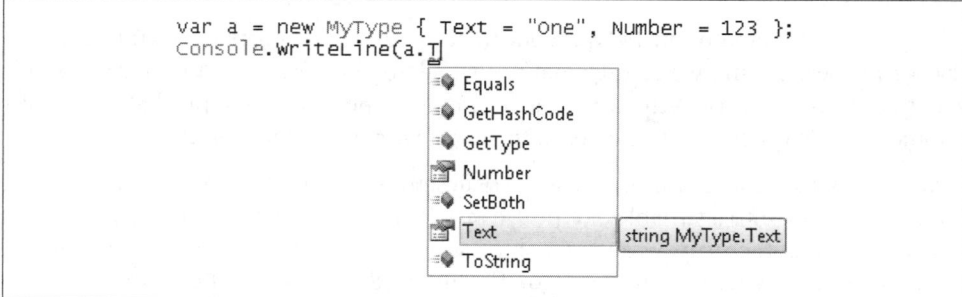

Figure 18-1. IntelliSense with a statically typed variable

```
dynamic a = new MyType { Text = "one", Number = 123 };
Console.writeLine(a.T
                        (dynamic expression)
                        This operation will be resolved at runtime.
```

Figure 18-2. IntelliSense with a dynamically typed variable

Example 18-11 just reads the properties, but as you'd expect, we can set them, too. And we can also invoke methods with the usual syntax. Example 18-12 illustrates both features, and contains no surprises.

Example 18-12. Setting properties and calling methods with dynamic

```
dynamic a = new MyType();
a.Number = 42;
a.Text = "Foo";
Console.WriteLine(a);
dynamic b = new MyType();
b.SetBoth("Bar", 99);
Console.WriteLine(b);
```

Our MyType example also overloads the + operator—it defines what should occur when we attempt to add two of these objects together. This means we can take the two objects from Example 18-12 and pass them to the AddAnything method from Example 18-4, as Example 18-13 shows.

Example 18-13. Using an overloaded + operator

```
MyType c = AddAnything(a, b);
Console.WriteLine(c);
```

Recall that Example 18-4 just uses the normal C# syntax for adding two things together. We wrote that code before even writing the MyType class, but despite this, it works just fine—it prints out:

```
    FooBar, 141
```

The custom + operator in MyType concatenates the Text properties and adds the Number properties, and we can see that's what's happened here. Again, this shouldn't really come as a surprise—this is another example of the basic principle that operations should work the same way when used through dynamic as they would statically.

Example 18-13 illustrates another feature of dynamic—assignment. You can, of course, assign any value into a variable of type dynamic, but what's more surprising is that you can also go the other way—you are free to assign an expression of dynamic type into a variable of any type. The first line of Example 18-13 assigns the return value of AddAnything into a variable of type MyType. Recall that AddAnything has a return type of dynamic, so you might have thought we'd need to cast the result back to MyType here, but we don't. As with all dynamic operations, C# lets you try whatever you want at compile time and then tries to do what you asked at runtime. In this case, the assignment succeeds because AddAnything ended up adding two MyType objects together to return a reference to a new MyType object. Since you can always assign a reference to a MyType object into a MyType variable, the assignment succeeds. If there's a type mismatch, you get an exception at runtime. This is just another example of the same basic principle; it's just a bit subtler because assignment is usually a trivial operation in C#, so it's not immediately obvious that it might fail at runtime.

While most operations are available dynamically, there are a couple of exceptions. You cannot invoke methods declared with the static keyword via dynamic. In some ways, this is unfortunate—it could be useful to be able to select a particular static (i.e., noninstance) method dynamically, based on the type of object you have. But that would be inconsistent with how C# works normally—you are not allowed to invoke static methods through a statically typed variable. You always need to call them via their defining type (e.g., Console.WriteLine). The dynamic keyword does not change anything here.

Extension methods are also not available through dynamic variables. On the one hand, this makes sense because extension methods are really just static methods disguised behind a convenient syntax. On the other hand, that convenient syntax is designed to make it look like these are really instance methods, as Example 18-14 shows.

Example 18-14. Extension methods with statically typed variables

```
using System.Collections.Generic;
using System.Linq;

class Program
{
    static void Main()
    {
        IEnumerable<int> numbers = Enumerable.Range(1, 10);
        int total = numbers.Sum();
    }
}
```

The call to `numbers.Sum()` makes it look like `IEnumerable<int>` defines a method called Sum. In fact there is no such method, so the compiler goes looking for extension methods—it searches all of the types in all of the namespaces for which we have provided `using` directives. (That's why we've included the whole program here rather than just a snippet—you need the whole context including the `using System.Linq;` directive for that method call to make sense.) And it finds that the `Enumerable` type (in the `System.Linq` namespace) offers a suitable `Sum` extension method.

If we change the first line in the Main method to the code shown in Example 18-15, things go wrong.

Example 18-15. Replacing IEnumerable<int> with dynamic

```
dynamic numbers = Enumerable.Range(1, 10);
```

The code still compiles, but at runtime, when we reach the call to `Sum`, it throws a `RuntimeBinderException` complaining that the target object does not define a method called `Sum`.

So, in this case, C# has abandoned the usual rule of ensuring that the runtime behavior with `dynamic` matches what statically typed variables would have delivered. The reason is that the code C# generates for a dynamic call does not contain enough context. To resolve an extension method, it's necessary to know which `using` directives are present. In theory, it would have been possible to make this context available, but it would significantly increase the amount of information the C# compiler would need to embed—anytime you did anything to a `dynamic` variable, the compiler would need to ensure that a list of all the relevant namespaces was available. And even that wouldn't be sufficient—at compile time, C# only searches for extension methods in the assemblies your project references, so to deliver the same method resolution semantics at runtime that you get statically would require that information to be made available too.

Worse, this would prevent the C# compiler from being able to optimize your project references. Normally, C# detects when your project has a reference to an assembly that your code never uses, and it removes any such references at compile time.[†] But if your program made any dynamic method calls, it would need to keep references to apparently unused assemblies, just in case they turn out to be necessary to resolve an extension method call at runtime.

So while it would have been possible for Microsoft to make this work, there would be a significant price to pay. And it would probably have provided only marginal value, because it wouldn't even be useful for the most widely used extension methods. The biggest user of extension methods in the .NET Framework class library is LINQ—that Sum method is a standard LINQ operator, for example. It's one of the simpler ones. Most of the operators take arguments, many of which expect lambdas. For those to compile, the C# compiler depends on static type information to create a suitable delegate. For example, there's an overload of the Sum operator that takes a lambda, enabling you to compute the sum of a value calculated from the underlying data, rather than merely summing the underlying data itself. Example 18-16 uses this overload to calculate the sum of the squares of the numbers in the list.

Example 18-16. Lambdas and types

```
int total = numbers.Sum(x => x * x);
```

When the numbers variable has a static type (IEnumerable<int> in our case) this works just fine. But if numbers is dynamic, the compiler simply doesn't have enough information to know what code it needs to generate for that lambda. Given sufficiently heroic efforts from the compiler, it could embed enough information to be able to generate all the necessary code at runtime, but for what benefit? LINQ is designed for a statically typed world, and dynamic is designed mainly for interop. So Microsoft decided not to support these kinds of scenarios with dynamic—stick with static typing when using LINQ.

Objects from other dynamic languages

The dynamic keyword uses an underlying mechanism that is not unique to C#. It depends on a set of libraries and conventions known as the DLR—the Dynamic Language Runtime. The libraries are built into the .NET Framework, so these services are available anywhere .NET 4 or later is available. This enables C# to work with dynamic objects from other languages.

Earlier in this chapter, we mentioned that in the Ruby programming language, it's possible to write code that decides at runtime what methods a particular object is going to offer. If you're using an implementation of Ruby that uses the DLR (such as Iron-Ruby), you can use these kinds of objects from C#. The DLR website provides open

---

† This optimization doesn't occur for Silverlight projects, by the way. The way Silverlight uses control libraries from Xaml means Visual Studio has to be conservative about project references.

source implementations of two languages that use the DLR: IronPython and IronRuby (see *http://dlr.codeplex.com/*).

ExpandoObject

The .NET Framework class library includes a class called `ExpandoObject`, which is designed to be used through `dynamic` variables. It chooses to customize its dynamic behavior. (It does this by implementing a special interface called `IDynamicMetaObject Provider`. This is defined by the DLR, and it's also the way that objects from other languages are able to make their language-specific dynamic behavior available to C#.) If you're familiar with JavaScript, the idea behind `ExpandoObject` will be familiar: you can set properties without needing to declare them first, as Example 18-17 shows.

Example 18-17. Setting dynamic properties

```
dynamic dx = new ExpandoObject();

dx.MyProperty = true;
dx.AnotherProperty = 42;
```

If you set a property that the `ExpandoObject` didn't previously have, it just grows that as a new property, and you can retrieve the property later on. This behavior is conceptually equivalent to a `Dictionary<string, object>`, the only difference being that you get and set values in the dictionary using C# property accessor syntax, rather than an indexer. You can even iterate over the values in an `ExpandoObject` just as you would with a dictionary, as Example 18-18 shows.

Example 18-18. Iterating through dynamic properties

```
foreach (KeyValuePair<string, object> prop in dx)
{
    Console.WriteLine(prop.Key + ": " + prop.Value);
}
```

If you are writing C# code that needs to interoperate with another language that uses the DLR, this class can be convenient—languages that fully embrace the dynamic style often use this sort of dynamically populated object in places where a more statically inclined language would normally use a dictionary, so `ExpandoObject` can provide a convenient way to bridge the gap. `ExpandoObject` implements `IDictionary<string, object>`, so it speaks both languages. As Example 18-19 shows, you add properties to an `ExpandoObject` through its dictionary API and then go on to access those as dynamic properties.

Example 18-19. ExpandoObject as both dictionary and dynamic object

```
ExpandoObject xo = new ExpandoObject();

IDictionary<string, object> dictionary = xo;
dictionary["Foo"] = "Bar";
```

```
dynamic dyn = xo;
Console.WriteLine(dyn.Foo);
```

This trick of implementing custom dynamic behavior is not unique to `ExpandoObject`—
we are free to write our own objects that do the same thing.

Custom dynamic objects

The DLR defines an interface called `IDynamicMetaObjectProvider`, and objects that implement this get to define how they behave when used dynamically. It is designed to
enable high performance with maximum flexibility, which is great for anyone using
your type, but it's a lot of work to implement. Describing how to implement this interface would require a fairly deep discussion of the workings of the DLR, and is beyond
the scope of this book. Fortunately, a more straightforward option exists.

The `System.Dynamic` namespace defines a class called `DynamicObject`. This implements
`IDynamicMetaObjectProvider` for you, and all you need to do is override methods representing whichever operations you want your dynamic object to support. If you want
to support dynamic properties, but you don't care about any other dynamic features,
the only thing you need to do is override a single method, `TryGetMember`, as Example 18-20 shows.

Example 18-20. Custom dynamic object

```
using System;
using System.Dynamic;

public class CustomDynamic : DynamicObject
{
    private static DateTime FirstSighting = new DateTime(1947, 3, 13);

    public override bool TryGetMember(GetMemberBinder binder,
                                      out object result)
    {
        var compare = binder.IgnoreCase ?
            StringComparer.InvariantCultureIgnoreCase :
            StringComparer.InvariantCulture;
        if (compare.Compare(binder.Name, "Brigadoon") == 0)
        {
            // Brigadoon famous for appearing only once every hundred years.
            DateTime today = DateTime.Now.Date;
            if (today.DayOfYear == FirstSighting.DayOfYear)
            {
                // Right day, what about the year?
                int yearsSinceFirstSighting = today.Year - FirstSighting.Year;
                if (yearsSinceFirstSighting % 100 == 0)
                {
                    result = "Welcome to Brigadoon. Please drive carefully.";
                    return true;
                }
            }
        }
    }
}
```

```
        return base.TryGetMember(binder, out result);
    }
}
```

This object chooses to define just a single property, called `Brigadoon`.‡ Our `TryGetMember` will be called anytime some code attempts to read a property from our object. The `GetMemberBinder` argument provides the name of the property the caller is looking for, so we compare it against our one and only supported property name. The binder also tells us whether the caller prefers a case-sensitive comparison—in C# `IgnoreCase` will be `false`, but some languages (such as VB.NET) prefer case-insensitive comparisons. If the name matches, we then decide at runtime whether the property should be present or not—this particular property is available for only a day at a time once every 100 years. This may not be hugely useful, but it illustrates that objects may choose whatever rules they like for deciding what properties to offer.

 If you're wondering what you would get in exchange for the additional complexity of `IDynamicMetaObjectProvider`, it makes it possible to use caching and runtime code generation techniques to provide high-performance dynamic operation. This is a lot more complicated than the simple model offered by `DynamicObject`, but has a significant impact on the performance of languages in which the dynamic model is the norm.

dynamic in Noninterop Scenarios?

The main motivation behind `dynamic`'s introduction was to make it possible to use Office without writing horrible code. It also has uses in other interop scenarios such as dealing with browser script in Silverlight, and working with dynamic languages. But would you ever use it in a pure C# scenario? The dynamic style has become increasingly fashionable in recent years—some popular JavaScript libraries designed for client-side web code make cunning use of dynamic idioms, as do certain web frameworks. Some developers even go as far as to claim that a dynamic style is inherently superior to a static style. If that's the way the wind is blowing, should C# developers follow this trend?

Tantalizingly, for those keen on dynamic languages, `dynamic` has brought some dynamic language features to C#. However, the key word here is *some*. C# 4.0 added `dynamic` to improve certain interop scenarios, not to support whole new programming idioms. It is therefore not helpful to think of `dynamic` in terms of "dynamic extensions for C#."

If you attempt to use C# as though it were a fully fledged dynamic language, you'll be stepping outside the language's core strength, so you will inevitably run into problems. We've already seen a LINQ example that did not mix well with `dynamic`, and that failure

---

‡ According to popular legend, Brigadoon is a Scottish village which appears for only one day every 100 years.

was a symptom of a broader problem. The underlying issue is that delegates are not as flexible as you might expect when it comes to dynamic behavior. Consider the method shown in Example 18-21.

Example 18-21. A simple filter

```
static bool Test(int x)
{
    return x < 100;
}
```

We can use this in conjunction with the LINQ `Where` operator, as Example 18-22 shows.

Example 18-22. Filtering with LINQ

```
var nums = Enumerable.Range(1, 200);
var filteredNumbers = nums.Where(Test);
```

What if we wanted to make this more general-purpose? We could modify `Test` so that instead of working only with `int`, it works with any built-in numeric type, or indeed any type that offers a version of the `<` operator that can be used with `int`. We could do that by changing the argument to `dynamic`, as Example 18-23 shows.

Example 18-23. A dynamic filter

```
static bool Test(dynamic x)
{
    return x < 100;
}
```

Unfortunately, this change would cause the code in Example 18-22 to fail with a compiler error. It complains that there are no overloads that match delegate `System.Func<int,bool>`, which is the function type the `Where` method expects here. This is frustrating because our `Test` method is certainly capable of accepting an `int` and returning a `bool`, but despite this, we need to add our own wrapper. Example 18-24 does the job.

Example 18-24. Making a dynamic filter palatable for LINQ

```
var filteredNumbers = nums.Where(x => Test(x));
```

This is a little weird because it seems like it should mean exactly the same as the equivalent line in Example 18-22. We've had to add some extra code just to keep the C# type system happy, and normally that's exactly the sort of thing the dynamic style is supposed to let you avoid. Part of the problem here is that we're trying to use LINQ, a thoroughly static-oriented API. But it turns out that there's a deeper problem here, which we can illustrate by trying to write our own `dynamic`-friendly version of `Where`. Example 18-25 will accept anything as its `test` argument. This `DynamicWhere` method will be happy as long as `test` can be invoked as a method that returns a `bool` (or something implicitly convertible to `bool`).

Example 18-25. A dynamic-friendly Where implementation

```
static IEnumerable<T> DynamicWhere<T>(IEnumerable<T> input, dynamic test)
{
    foreach (T item in input)
    {
        if (test(item))
        {
            yield return item;
        }
    }
}
```

This compiles, and will behave as intended if you can manage to invoke it, but unfortunately it doesn't help. Example 18-26 tries to use this, and it will not compile.

Example 18-26. Attempting (and failing) to call DynamicWhere

```
var filteredNumbers = DynamicWhere(nums, Test);  // Compiler error
```

The C# compiler complains:

```
Argument 2: cannot convert from 'method group' to 'dynamic'
```

The problem is that we've given it too much latitude. Example 18-25 will work with a wide range of delegate types. It would be happy with `Predicate<object>`, `Predicate<dynamic>`, `Predicate<int>`, `Func<object, bool>`, `Func<dynamic, bool>`, or `Func<int, bool>`. Or you could define a custom delegate type of your own that was equivalent to any of these. The only thing the C# compiler can see is that `DynamicWhere` expects a `dynamic` argument, so for all it knows, it could pass any type at all. All it would have to do is pick one that fits the `Test` method's signature—any delegate type with a single argument and a return type of `bool` would do. But it doesn't have any rule to say which particular delegate type to use by default here.

In Example 18-22, the compiler knew what to do because the `Where` method expected a specific delegate type: `Func<int, bool>`. Since there was only one possible option, the C# compiler was able to create a delegate of the right kind. But now that it has too much choice, we need to narrow things down again so that it knows what to do. Example 18-27 shows one way to do this, although you could cast to any of the delegate types mentioned earlier.

Example 18-27. Giving DynamicWhere a clue

```
var filteredNumbers = DynamicWhere(nums, (Predicate<dynamic>) Test);
```

Again, we've ended up doing extra work just to satisfy the C# type system, which is the opposite of what you'd usually expect in the dynamic idiom—types are supposed to matter less.

This is exactly the sort of problem you'll run into if you attempt to treat C# as a dynamic programming language—the underlying issue here is that `dynamic` was designed to solve specific interop problems. It does that job very well, but C# as a whole is not really at home in the dynamic style. So it's not a good idea to attempt to make heavy use of that style in your C# code.

Summary

C# 4.0's new `dynamic` keyword makes it much easier to use objects that were designed to be used from dynamic programming languages. In particular, COM automation APIs such as those offered by the Microsoft Office suite are far more natural to use than they have been in previous versions of the language. Interoperating with browser script objects in Silverlight is also easier than before.

CHAPTER 19

Interop with COM and Win32

Programmers love a clean slate. The thought of throwing away all the code we've ever written and starting over can seem alluring, but this typically isn't a viable option for most companies. Many development organizations have made a substantial investment in developing and purchasing COM components and ActiveX controls. Microsoft has made a commitment to ensure that these legacy components are usable from within .NET applications, and (perhaps less important) that .NET components are easily callable from COM. The ability to mix managed .NET code with unmanaged code from the older worlds of Win32 and COM is called *interoperability*, or as it's usually abbreviated, *interop*.

This chapter describes the support .NET provides for using ActiveX controls and COM components into your application, exposing .NET classes to COM-based applications, and making direct calls to Win32 APIs. You'll also learn about C# pointers and keywords for accessing memory directly, which can be necessary for using some unmanaged APIs.

Importing ActiveX Controls

ActiveX controls are COM components designed to be dropped into a form. They usually have a user interface, although you may come across nonvisual controls. When Microsoft developed the OCX standard, which allowed developers to build ActiveX controls in C++ and use them with VB (and vice versa), the ActiveX control revolution began. That was way back in 1994, and since then thousands of such controls have been developed, sold, and used. They are small, usually easy to work with, and are an effective example of binary reuse. That ActiveX controls are still popular more than a decade and a half after their invention demonstrates just how useful a lot of developers find them.

COM objects are quite different from .NET objects under the covers. But Microsoft was well aware of how popular ActiveX controls had become by the time .NET was launched, and so it made sure that the .NET Framework and Visual Studio work hard to bridge the gap between the COM and .NET worlds. Visual Studio is able to import COM components into any .NET project, and makes it particularly easy to use ActiveX controls from Windows Forms.

Importing a Control in .NET

For our first example, we're going to use a fairly common ActiveX control that happens to be installed on most of the authors' systems: the Adobe PDF Reader control. If you've installed either Adobe's PDF reader or its Acrobat software, you'll have this control too. It allows any application to show a PDF file.

To get started, create a C# Windows Forms application in Visual Studio 2010. Ensure that the Toolbox is visible—if it's not, there's an item on the View menu to show it. Right-click on the Toolbox and select Add Tab, and then create a new tab called ActiveX, to make it easy to find the ActiveX controls among all the others available. Inside this new tab, right-click again, and select the Choose Items option. This will bring up the Choose Toolbox Items dialog box. Select the COM Components tab, as shown in Figure 19-1. You can select any number of controls—here we're just selecting the Adobe PDF Reader.

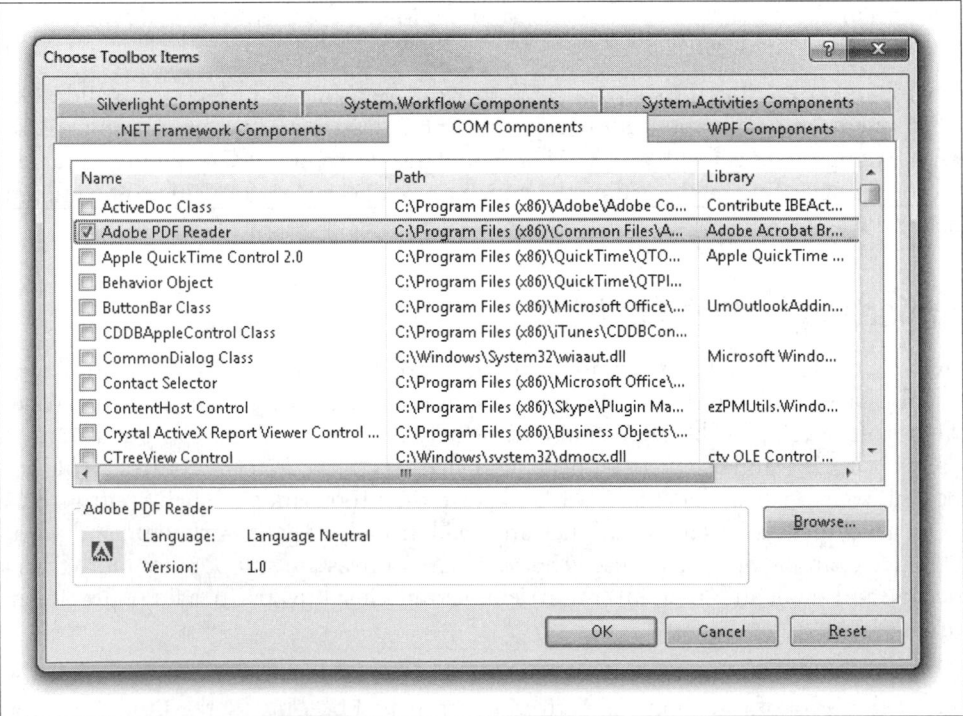

Figure 19-1. Adding a COM component

When you click OK, you should see the component in the new tab in the Toolbox, as Figure 19-2 shows.

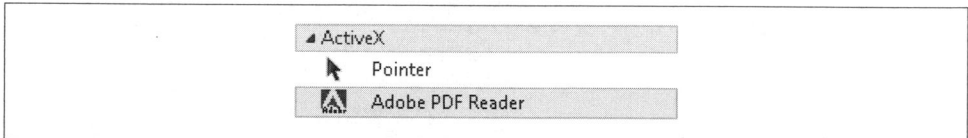

Figure 19-2. ActiveX control in the toolbox

Now you can drag this control onto your form. Figure 19-3 shows how the control looks on a form in the designer. You can set its size and position just like you would any normal control. Windows Forms layout concepts like anchoring work too—we could anchor the control to all four sides of the window to make it resize as the window resizes.

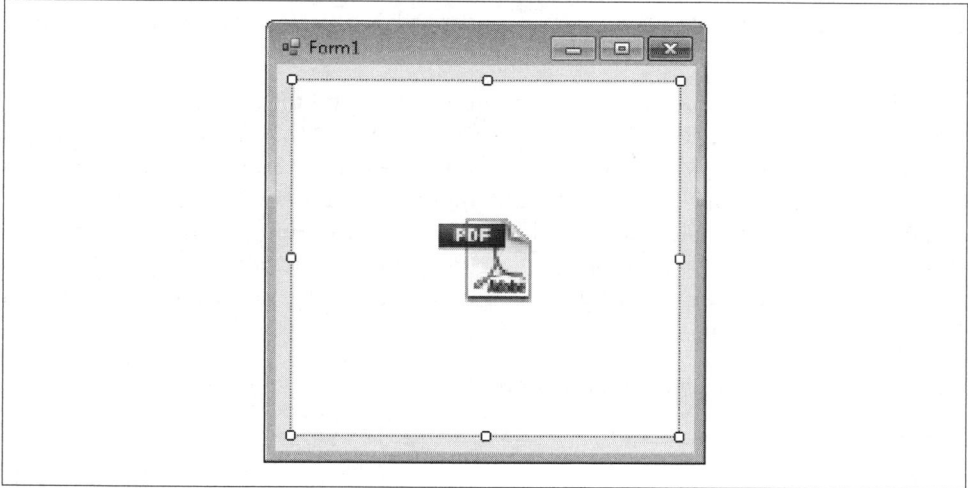

Figure 19-3. Form with PDF ActiveX control

Left to its own devices, this particular control won't do anything—we have to give it a PDF file to load before it will even show a UI, and that means using the control's API. Fortunately, one of the things Visual Studio did for us when we dragged the control onto the form was to import the component's *type library*. A COM type library contains metadata—it lists the available classes, and describes their methods, properties, and events. This is similar in concept to the .NET metadata we explored in Chapter 17, but the details are all very different. Fortunately, the differences are not a problem, because when Visual Studio imported the type library, it generated a DLL containing the same information but as a .NET component. This makes it possible to use the PDF component from C#. You can see this generated library by expanding the References section of the Solution Explorer, as Figure 19-4 shows.

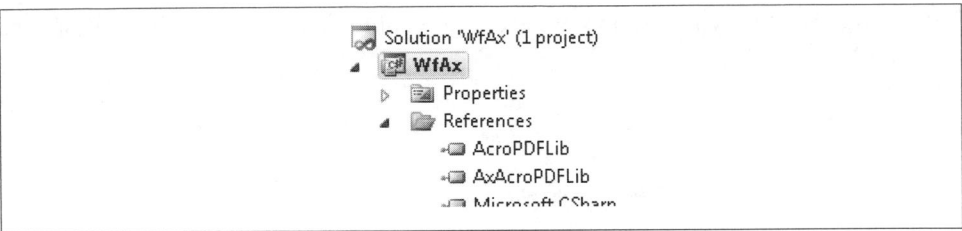

Figure 19-4. Imported type library and ActiveX wrapper

`AcroPDFLib` is the imported type library. You'll see a DLL like this when you import any kind of COM component into a .NET project. But there's a second item there, `AxAcroPDFLib`, and it is specific to ActiveX controls. (Not all COM components are designed for UI use.) This ActiveX-specific generated DLL contains a class that derives from a special base class called `AxHost`, which is a Windows Forms control that can host an ActiveX control. Visual Studio generates a class called `AxAcroPDF` that derives from `AxHost`, and puts it in that `AxAcroPDFLib`. It's this `AxAcroPDF` class that has ended up on our form. This ActiveX wrapper provides .NET-callable versions of all the methods the control makes available to COM programs.

So the upshot is that we can write C# in our code behind that invokes methods, sets properties, and handles events from this ActiveX control. In other words, it makes it feel just like a normal control, and that's the point—Visual Studio has neatly hidden the fact that COM and .NET work very differently under the covers by generating these interop libraries for us. Example 19-1 shows a how we can program the control—it shows the form's constructor in the code behind, and after the usual call to `InitializeComponent`, we're setting the control's `src` property, to tell it from where we'd like it to fetch a PDF file.

Example 19-1. Setting a property on the control

```csharp
public Form1()
{
    InitializeComponent();

    string pdf = "http://www.interact-sw.co.uk/downloads/ExamplePdf.pdf";
    pdfAxCtl.src = pdf;
}
```

If we run the program, it loads the PDF document. As you can see from Figure 19-5, the control includes its own UI elements for interacting with the document. If you use Adobe's reader, this will probably look familiar to you—the same ActiveX control typically gets used when you view PDF files in a web browser.

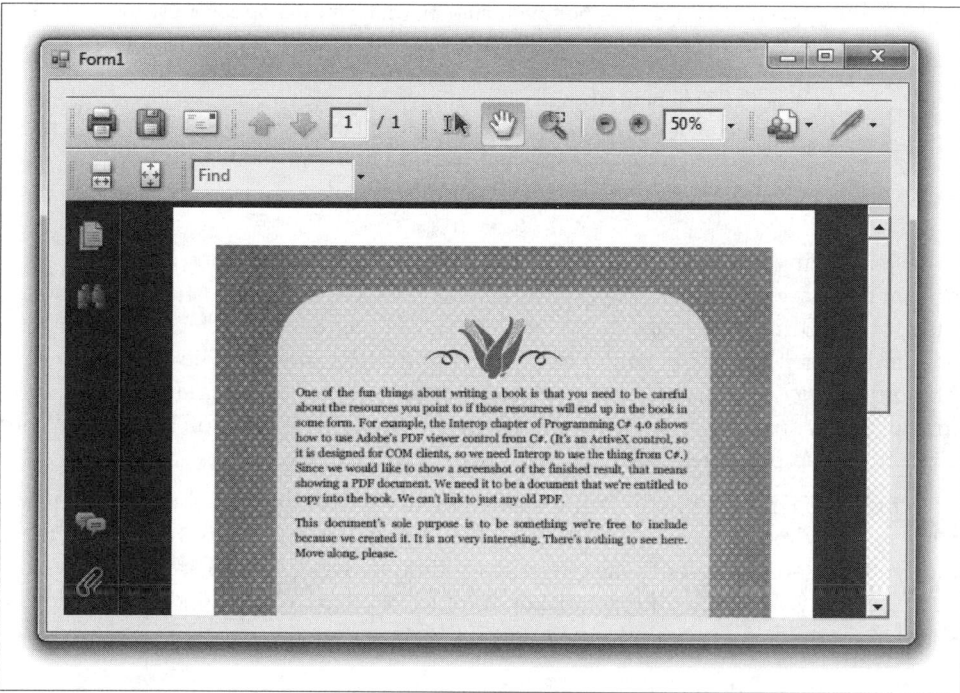

Figure 19-5. ActiveX control in a Windows Forms application

Interop Assemblies

As we saw in the preceding section, Visual Studio can generate assemblies containing .NET representations of type information from COM type libraries. These assemblies are called *interop assemblies*.

There's a potential problem here: what happens if multiple developers all generate interop assemblies for the same COM component? Most of the time this will be OK, because these duplicates will be in separate applications. However, what if you have two .NET libraries that both use the same COM component?

For example, suppose you are building a document processing system that uses Microsoft Word's COM API. If your system includes two libraries, both of which need to use Word, the developers of those libraries would add COM references, and you'd end up with two interop assemblies for Word. But if a single application uses both of those libraries, you would end up with two different interop assemblies for the same COM types *in the same process*. This is a problem, because there would be two different representations for what is supposed to be the same type.

Word's COM API supports automation, which means we could use the `dynamic` keyword shown in Chapter 18. This removes the need for interop assemblies, sidestepping the problem. However, some parts of Word's API fit perfectly well with static typing, which means developers may choose not to use `dynamic`, letting them take advantage of Intelli-Sense and additional compile-time checks. Or the code may have been written before `dynamic` was introduced in C# 4.0.

To avoid having multiple .NET types for one COM type, the author of a COM component can provide a *primary interop assembly* (PIA). For example, Microsoft provides PIAs for the Office suite—if you look in the .NET tab of the Add Reference dialog, you will find assemblies whose names begin *Microsoft.Office.Interop*. The PIA for Word is *Microsoft.Office.Interop.Word*. If you have multiple components in a single application that all use Word, then as long as they use the PIA, they'll all agree on how each Word COM type is represented in .NET.

The one problem with PIAs is that installing them on the target machine can be problematic. They're fairly big—the Office 2007 PIA installer is 6.3 MB. Integrating them into your installation process also requires additional work. These are not showstoppers, but they certainly add significant complexity. This is why C# 4.0 provides a simpler alternative, known informally as *no PIA*.

No PIA

.NET 4 adds a new feature to the type system, *type equivalence*, which makes it possible for two different type definitions to be treated as though they are the same type. This makes it possible to do without PIAs at runtime—if all interop assemblies are equal, there's no need for a primary one.

Although type equivalence makes this possible, it's an opt-in feature. For two types to be equivalent, they must have the same structure, and they must be marked with the `TypeIdentifier` custom attribute. (Attributes are discussed in Chapter 17.) So this new feature does not change the behavior of existing code.

C# 4.0's no-PIA feature exploits type equivalence: you can embed interop type information in your assembly, avoiding the need for a separate interop assembly of any kind. When your project has a reference to a PIA such as *Microsoft.Office.Interop.Word*, Visual Studio works out which types your code really uses, and copies them into the compiled output, adding the necessary annotations to enable type equivalence. Even though the project has a reference to the PIA, your compiled assembly does not—it contains all the information it needs.

This has two benefits. First, you don't need to install the PIAs on the target machine. Second, it typically makes things smaller. That may sound surprising—if every assembly has its own copy of the interop type definitions, you'd think things would get larger. However, in practice, most assemblies tend to use only a fraction of the types defined by the COM components they use. If each assembly contains just a handful of type definitions, that's likely to take less space than the 6.3 MB required by the full Office PIAs, for example.

 You cannot use interop type embedding with ActiveX control wrappers, because the generated wrapper does not just contain COM type information. It also contains generated code.

You might not always want to embed interop information. It might be that in your deployment scenario, you can always rely on the PIAs being present—perhaps your application will only ever run on machines on which you have preinstalled the relevant components. In this case, installation of PIAs is a nonissue for your application, and the additional space required by embedding becomes pure overhead. So you can turn the feature off. Interop type embedding is controlled per-reference, and is on by default for a newly created reference. If you select an interop assembly in your project's References in the Solution Explorer, the Properties panel will offer an Embed Interop Types setting. Changing this to False reverts to the old behavior of relying on the PIA.

64-bit Versus 32-bit

Interop with unmanaged code raises a challenge on 64-bit systems. Whether you're using COM components such as ActiveX controls, or plain old unmanaged DLLs, you need to be aware of whether the code you wish to use is 32-bit or 64-bit; you need to know its *bitness*, as it's sometimes called. If you ignore this issue, there's a risk that your code will not work on 64-bit versions of Windows.

In general, it's not possible for a single piece of machine code to execute successfully in both 32-bit and 64-bit environments—you need different binary code. The 64-bit Intel Itanium has a CPU architecture that is a radical departure from the x86 system used in 32-bit Windows—the machine understands an entirely different set of instructions in 64-bit mode. The more popular x64 architecture you'll find in most 64-bit PCs has a lot more in common with its x86 predecessor, but even so, you need different binary in 32-bit and 64-bit modes. The only reason existing 32-bit applications can run at all on 64-bit versions of Windows is that 64-bit Windows can host 32-bit processes. (You can see which these are in the Windows Task Manager's Processes tab—the 32-bit processes all have *32 in the Image Name column. Obviously, you'll see this only if you're running 64-bit Windows, as the information would be redundant on a 32-bit system.) Windows puts the CPU into a different mode for these processes—its 64-bit features are hidden, enabling legacy 32-bit code to run.

Despite this, .NET programs often don't need to care about bitness. C# compiles into a CPU-independent intermediate language which is compiled just in time (JIT) into executable code when the program runs. If you run your code on a 32-bit version of Windows (or in a 32-bit process on 64-bit Windows), the CLR will JIT-compile your program into 32-bit code. If you're running in a 64-bit process, it will JIT-compile into 64-bit code instead. This means you don't have to commit to a particular bitness when you write the code.

Unmanaged code doesn't have this luxury, because the executable binary code gets created at compile time—the developer has to tell the C++ compiler whether to produce 32-bit or 64-bit code. So if you're using an unmanaged DLL or a COM component, it will be capable of running in only one bitness. A process in Windows cannot contain a mixture of 32-bit and 64-bit code—bitness is fixed per-process. If you attempt to load an unmanaged 32-bit component into a 64-bit process, Windows will refuse. If it's a COM component (e.g., an ActiveX control) you'll get a `COMException`, with this error text:

```
Class not registered (Exception from HRESULT: 0x80040154 (REGDB_E_CLASSNOTREG))
```

This can be perplexing if the component you require appears to be installed. But what's happened here is that .NET went looking for a 64-bit version of the component, and it didn't find one, so it complains that the COM class you were looking for does not seem to be installed.

 It's possible to install both 32-bit and 64-bit versions of COM components, in which case you wouldn't get this error. However, that's relatively uncommon. Most ActiveX controls are 32-bit.

It would be nice if either COM or .NET were to produce a more informative error, such as "The component you require is available only in 32-bit form, but you're running as a 64-bit process." This would involve performing extra work on an operation that's already doomed, just to tell you something you can work out for yourself. This would be a waste of CPU cycles, which is presumably why .NET doesn't do this.

With normal DLLs, the same issue exists, although you'll get a slightly different exception: `BadImageFormatException`. (The word *image* is sometimes used to refer to a compiled binary component designed to be loaded into a process and executed.) This can be rather alarming, because if you read the error message in the exception, or you take a glance at the exception's documentation, it's easy to get the impression that the DLL you are trying to load is corrupt. But what's really going on here is that it's simply in a format that cannot be loaded into your process—you're in a 64-bit process and you're trying to load a 32-bit DLL.

To avoid these problems, Visual Studio automatically configures WPF and Windows Forms projects to run in 32-bit mode. If you open the project properties and go to the Build tab, you'll see a "Platform target:" setting, and for GUI projects, this defaults to x86, as Figure 19-6 shows. This makes the application always run as a 32-bit process, even on 64-bit Windows. This is unlikely to cause problems for most user interfaces—it's pretty unusual for a GUI to process such large volumes of data that 64-bit processing becomes a necessity. GUI programs are more likely to use ActiveX controls than to have massive memory requirements, so this conservative default makes sense. (And if you're writing an unusual application that really does need a multigigabyte address space, you can always change this project setting.)

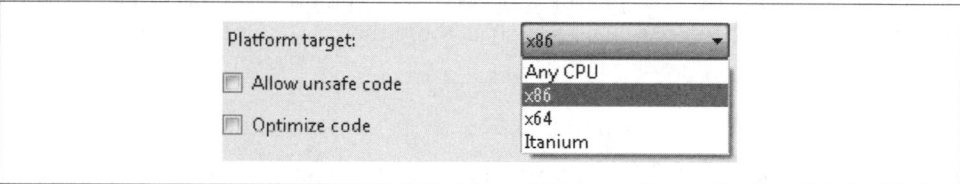

Figure 19-6. Project bitness

Things can get slightly trickier with class libraries. Visual Studio sets the platform target to Any CPU for library projects. The platform target setting has a slightly different significance for libraries, because a library doesn't get to decide the bitness of its process. The 32/64 decision is made when the process starts up, so it's the platform target of the *.exe* file that matters; by the time a library loads, it's too late to change. So Any CPU makes more sense—libraries tend to need to be more flexible. However, if you write a library that uses interop, you may want to change this setting. If your library depends on unmanaged code that is available only in 32-bit form, it will not be able to run usefully in a 64-bit process, and you should advertise that fact by changing the library's platform target to x86. Your DLL will then refuse to load in a 64-bit process, which may seem annoying, but it would be much more annoying if it loaded happily, only to fail later on at runtime. Better for the component to make it perfectly clear up front that it needs a 32-bit process.

There's often nothing stopping unmanaged component authors producing both 32-bit and 64-bit versions of their code, by the way. It makes building, deploying, testing, and supporting the component more complicated, but it's absolutely possible. Bitness is an issue for .NET only because in practice, most unmanaged components that are out there today are 32-bit only. (So while component authors could have provided 64-bit versions, they mostly haven't.) If the unmanaged code you depend on is available in all forms, you're free to set your platform target to Any CPU.

You may well find that some components are available in 64-bit mode for x64 systems, but not Itanium systems. So your platform target would, in effect, be "x86 or x64, but not Itanium." Unfortunately, there's no such setting, so in practice, you'd probably choose Any CPU so that it works on x86 and x64. Itanium systems will see a runtime error, but system administrators can force a process to run as 32-bit to work around this. In April 2010, Microsoft announced that future versions of Windows and Visual Studio will not support the Itanium, so this particular interop issue looks likely to go away in the long run.

If the DLLs you're using through interop are part of the Win32 API, you will usually be free to run in either 32-bit or 64-bit mode, because Windows presents its API in both flavors. So let's see how to use DLLs such as those that make up the Win32 API.

P/Invoke

COM components aren't the only kind of unmanaged code you might need to work with. For example, you may sometimes want to call a Win32 API. With each new version of .NET, there has been less need to do this, because the framework class libraries provide .NET-friendly wrappers for more and more of the underlying services, but there are still a few places where it's useful to use a Win32 API directly. We do this in C# using a feature called *P/Invoke*.

The *P* is short for *Platform*, because this facility was originally intended only to provide access to the underlying platform API. In fact, you can use it to call functions in *any* DLL—it's not limited to DLLs that are part of the Win32 API.

To see how this works, let's look at a method offered by the Windows *kernel32.dll* library called `MoveFile`.[*] Unlike COM components, ordinary Win32 DLLs do not include enough metadata to describe fully the methods they offer—they're designed to be called from C or C++, and the full descriptions live in header files provided as part of the Windows SDK. But the C# compiler doesn't know how to read C header files, so we need to provide a complete description of the signature of the method we plan to use. We do this by declaring the method as a `static extern` and use the `DllImport` attribute:

```
[DllImport("kernel32.dll", EntryPoint="MoveFile",
  ExactSpelling=false, CharSet=CharSet.Unicode,
  SetLastError=true)]
```

---

[*] This example is for illustrative purposes—in a real program, you'd just use the `FileInfo` class's `MoveTo` method because it's more convenient. `FileInfo` uses P/Invoke internally—it calls the Win32 `MoveFile` for you when you call `MoveTo`.

```
static extern bool MoveFile(
  string sourceFile, string destinationFile);
```

The `DllImport` attribute class is used to indicate that an unmanaged method will be invoked through P/Invoke. The parameters are as follows:

DLL name
  This is the name of the DLL that contains the method you are invoking.

`EntryPoint`
  This indicates the name of the DLL entry point (the method) to call.

`ExactSpelling`
  The CLR understands certain DLL method naming conventions. For example, there is in fact no `MoveFile` method—there are two methods, `MoveFileA` and `MoveFileW`, designed for the ANSI and Unicode string representations, respectively. Setting `ExactSpelling` to `false` lets the CLR select a method based on these rules.

`CharSet`
  This indicates how the string arguments to the method should be marshaled.

`SetLastError`
  Setting this to `true` allows you to call `Marshal.GetLastWin32Error`, and check whether an error occurred when invoking this method.

In fact, all of these are optional except for the DLL name. If you leave out `EntryPoint`, .NET uses the method name as the entry point name. `ExactSpelling` is `false` by default—you set this to `true` only if you want to disable the use of normal naming conventions. And if you leave out `CharSet`, the CLR will use Unicode if it's available. `SetLastError` is off by default, so although it's optional, it's usually a good idea to set it. Therefore, in practice, we would probably just write this:

```
[DllImport("kernel32.dll", SetLastError=true)]
static extern bool MoveFile(
  string sourceFile, string destinationFile);
```

The main reason P/Invoke offers all these optional settings is that some DLLs don't follow the usual conventions. Most of the time the defaults do the right thing, but just occasionally you need to override them.

With this declaration in place, we can now call `MoveFile()` like any other static method. So if that declaration were inside a class called `Tester`, we could write:

```
Tester.MoveFile(file.FullName, file.FullName + ".bak");
```

We pass in the original filename and the new name, and Windows moves the file for us. In this example, there is no advantage—and actually a considerable disadvantage—to using P/Invoke. (Situations where you truly need P/Invoke are increasingly rare and obscure. To illustrate the mechanisms, we've picked an example that's simple enough not to obscure the details of how P/Invoke works, but this means it's not a scenario in which you'd use P/Invoke in practice.) You have left the world of managed code, and the result is that you've abandoned type safety and your code will no longer run in

"partial-trust" scenarios. Example 19-2 shows the complete source code for using P/
Invoke to move the files.

Example 19-2. Using P/Invoke to call a Win32 API method

```
using System;
using System.IO;
using System.Runtime.InteropServices;

namespace UsingPInvoke
{
    class Tester
    {

        // declare the WinAPI method you wish to P/Invoke
        [DllImport("kernel32.dll", EntryPoint = "MoveFile",
        ExactSpelling = false, CharSet = CharSet.Unicode,
        SetLastError = true)]
        static extern bool MoveFile(
        string sourceFile, string destinationFile);

        public static void Main()
        {
            // make an instance and run it
            Tester t = new Tester();
            string theDirectory = @"c:\test\media";
            DirectoryInfo dir =
            new DirectoryInfo(theDirectory);
            t.ExploreDirectory(dir);
        }

        // Set it running with a directory name
        private void ExploreDirectory(DirectoryInfo dir)
        {

            // make a new subdirectory
            string newDirectory = "newTest";
            DirectoryInfo newSubDir =
            dir.CreateSubdirectory(newDirectory);

            // get all the files in the directory and
            // copy them to the new directory
            FileInfo[] filesInDir = dir.GetFiles();
            foreach (FileInfo file in filesInDir)
            {
                string fullName = newSubDir.FullName +
                "\\" + file.Name;
                file.CopyTo(fullName);
                Console.WriteLine("{0} copied to newTest",
                file.FullName);
            }

            // get a collection of the files copied in
            filesInDir = newSubDir.GetFiles();
```

```
        // delete some and rename others
        int counter = 0;
        foreach (FileInfo file in filesInDir)
        {
            string fullName = file.FullName;

            if (counter++ % 2 == 0)
            {
                // P/Invoke the Win API
                Tester.MoveFile(fullName, fullName + ".bak");

                Console.WriteLine("{0} renamed to {1}",
                fullName, file.FullName);
            }
            else
            {
                file.Delete();
                Console.WriteLine("{0} deleted.",
                fullName);
            }
        }
        // delete the subdirectory
        newSubDir.Delete(true);
    }
}
}
```

Output:

```
c:\test\media\chimes.wav copied to newTest
c:\test\media\chord.wav copied to newTest
c:\test\media\desktop.ini copied to newTest
c:\test\media\ding.wav copied to newTest
c:\test\media\dts.wav copied to newTest
c:\test\media\flourish.mid copied to newTest
c:\test\media\ir_begin.wav copied to newTest
c:\test\media\ir_end.wav copied to newTest
c:\test\media\ir_inter.wav copied to newTest
c:\test\media\notify.wav copied to newTest
c:\test\media\onestop.mid copied to newTest
c:\test\media\recycle.wav copied to newTest
c:\test\media\ringout.wav copied to newTest
c:\test\media\Speech Disambiguation.wav copied to newTest
c:\test\media\Speech Misrecognition.wav copied to newTest
c:\test\media\newTest\chimes.wav renamed to c:\test\media\newTest\chimes.wav
c:\test\media\newTest\chord.wav deleted.
c:\test\media\newTest\desktop.ini renamed to c:\test\media\newTest\desktop.ini
c:\test\media\newTest\ding.wav deleted.
c:\test\media\newTest\dts.wav renamed to c:\test\media\newTest\dts.wav
c:\test\media\newTest\flourish.mid deleted.
c:\test\media\newTest\ir_begin.wav renamed to c:\test\media\newTest\ir_begin.wav
c:\test\media\newTest\ir_end.wav deleted.
c:\test\media\newTest\ir_inter.wav renamed to c:\test\media\newTest\ir_inter.wav
c:\test\media\newTest\notify.wav deleted.
c:\test\media\newTest\onestop.mid renamed to c:\test\media\newTest\onestop.mid
```

```
c:\test\media\newTest\recycle.wav deleted.
c:\test\media\newTest\ringout.wav renamed to c:\test\media\newTest\ringout.wav
c:\test\media\newTest\Speech Disambiguation.wav deleted.
```

Pointers

Until now, you've seen no code using C/C++-style pointers. Pointers are central to the C family of languages, but in C#, pointers are relegated to unusual and advanced programming; typically, they are used only with P/Invoke, and occasionally with COM. C# supports the usual C pointer operators, listed in Table 19-1.

Table 19-1. C# pointer operators

Operator	Meaning
&	The address-of operator returns a pointer to the address of a value.
*	The dereference operator returns the value at the address of a pointer.
->	The member access operator is used to access the members of a type via a pointer.

In theory, you can use pointers anywhere in C#, but in practice, they are almost never required outside of interop scenarios, and their use is nearly always discouraged. When you do use pointers, you must mark your code with the C# unsafe modifier. The code is marked as unsafe because pointers let you manipulate memory locations directly, defeating the usual type safety rules. In unsafe code, you can directly access memory, perform conversions between pointers and integral types, take the address of variables, perform pointer arithmetic, and so forth. In exchange, you give up garbage collection and protection against uninitialized variables, dangling pointers, and accessing memory beyond the bounds of an array. In essence, the unsafe keyword creates an island of code within your otherwise safe C# application that is subject to all the pointer-related bugs C++ programs tend to suffer from. Moreover, your code will not work in partial-trust scenarios.

 Silverlight does not support unsafe code at all, because it only supports partial trust. Silverlight code running in a web browser is always constrained, because code downloaded from the Internet is not typically considered trustworthy. Even Silverlight code that runs out of the browser is constrained—the "elevated" permissions such code can request still don't grant full trust. Silverlight depends on the type safety rules to enforce security, which is why unsafe code is not allowed.

As an example of when this might be useful, read a file to the console by invoking two Win32 API calls: CreateFile and ReadFile. ReadFile takes, as its second parameter, a pointer to a buffer. The declaration of the two imported methods is straightforward:

```
[DllImport("kernel32", SetLastError=true)]
static extern unsafe int CreateFile(
```

```
        string filename,
        uint desiredAccess,
        uint shareMode,
        uint attributes,
        uint creationDisposition,
        uint flagsAndAttributes,
        uint templateFile);

    [DllImport("kernel32", SetLastError=true)]
    static extern unsafe bool ReadFile(
        int hFile,
        void* lpBuffer,
        int nBytesToRead,
        int* nBytesRead,
        int overlapped);
```

You will create a new class, `APIFileReader`, whose constructor will invoke the `CreateFile()` method. The constructor takes a filename as a parameter, and passes that filename to the `CreateFile()` method:

```
public APIFileReader(string filename)
{
    fileHandle = CreateFile(
        filename, // filename
        GenericRead, // desiredAccess
        UseDefault, // shareMode
        UseDefault, // attributes
        OpenExisting, // creationDisposition
        UseDefault, // flagsAndAttributes
        UseDefault); // templateFile
}
```

The `APIFileReader` class implements only one other method, `Read()`, which invokes `ReadFile()`. It passes in the file handle created in the class constructor, along with a pointer into a buffer, a count of bytes to retrieve, and a reference to a variable that will hold the number of bytes read. It is the pointer to the buffer that is of interest to us here. To invoke this API call, you must use a pointer.

Because you will access it with a pointer, the buffer needs to be *pinned* in memory; we've given `ReadFile` a pointer to our buffer, so we can't allow the .NET Framework to move that buffer during garbage collection until `ReadFile` is finished. (Normally, the garbage collector is forever moving items around to make more efficient use of memory.) To accomplish this, we use the C# `fixed` keyword. `fixed` allows you to get a pointer to the memory used by the buffer, and to mark that instance so that the garbage collector won't move it.

Pinning reduces the efficiency of the garbage collector. If an interop scenario forces you to use pointers, you should try to minimize the duration for which you need to keep anything pinned. This is another reason to avoid using pointers for anything other than places where you have no choice.

The block of statements following the `fixed` keyword creates a scope, within which the memory will be pinned. At the end of the `fixed` block, the instance will be unpinned, and the garbage collector will once again be free to move it. This is known as *declarative pinning*:

```
public unsafe int Read(byte[] buffer, int index, int count)
{
    int bytesRead = 0;
    fixed (byte* bytePointer = buffer)
    {
        ReadFile(
            fileHandle,
            bytePointer + index,
            count,
            &bytesRead, 0);
    }
    return bytesRead;
}
```

You may be wondering why we didn't also need to pin `bytesRead`—the `ReadFile` method expects a pointer to that too. It was unnecessary because `bytesRead` lives on the stack here, not the heap, and so the garbage collector would never attempt to move it. C# knows this, so it lets us use the `&` operator to get the address without having to use `fixed`. If we had applied that operator to an `int` that was stored as a field in an object, it would have refused to compile, telling us that we need to use `fixed`.

 You need to make absolutely sure that you don't unpin the memory too early. Some APIs will keep hold of pointers you give them, continuing to use them even after returning. For example, the `ReadFileEx` Win32 API can be used asynchronously—you can ask it to return before it has fetched the data. In that case you would need to keep the buffer pinned until the operation completes, rather than merely keeping it pinned for the duration of the method call.

Notice that the method must be marked with the `unsafe` keyword. This creates an unsafe context which allows you to create pointers—the compiler will not let you use pointers or `fixed` without this. In fact, it's so keen to discourage the use of unsafe code that you have to ask twice: the `unsafe` keyword produces compiler errors unless you also set the `/unsafe` compiler option. In Visual Studio, you can find this by opening the project properties and clicking the Build tab, which contains the "Allow unsafe code" checkbox shown in Figure 19-7.

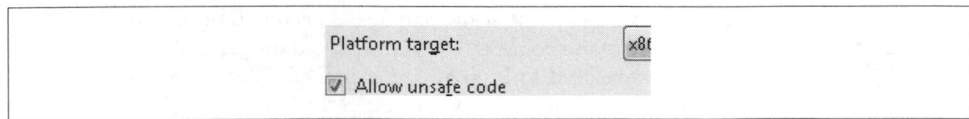

Figure 19-7. Enabling the use of unsafe code

The test program in Example 19-3 instantiates the APIFileReader and an ASCIIEncod
ing object. It passes the filename (*8Swnn10.txt*) to the constructor of the APIFileR
eader and then creates a loop to repeatedly fill its buffer by calling the Read() method,
which invokes the ReadFile API call. An array of bytes is returned, which is converted
to a string using the ASCIIEncoding object's GetString() method. That string is passed
to the Console.Write() method, to be displayed on the console. (As with the
MoveFile example, this is obviously a scenario where in practice, you'd just use the
relevant managed APIs provided by the .NET Framework in the System.IO namespace.
This example just illustrates the programming techniques for pointers.)

 The text that it will read is a short excerpt of *Swann's Way* (by Marcel
Proust), currently in the public domain and available for download as
text from Project Gutenberg (*http://www.gutenberg.org/wiki/Main
_Page*).

Example 19-3. Using pointers in a C# program

```
using System;
using System.Runtime.InteropServices;
using System.Text;

namespace UsingPointers
{
    class APIFileReader
    {
        const uint GenericRead = 0x80000000;
        const uint OpenExisting = 3;
        const uint UseDefault = 0;
        int fileHandle;

        [DllImport("kernel32", SetLastError = true)]
        static extern unsafe int CreateFile(
        string filename,
        uint desiredAccess,
        uint shareMode,
        uint attributes,
        uint creationDisposition,
        uint flagsAndAttributes,
        uint templateFile);

        [DllImport("kernel32", SetLastError = true)]
        static extern unsafe bool ReadFile(
        int hFile,
        void* lpBuffer,
        int nBytesToRead,
        int* nBytesRead,
        int overlapped);

        // constructor opens an existing file
        // and sets the file handle member
        public APIFileReader(string filename)
```

```
    {
        fileHandle = CreateFile(
        filename, // filename
        GenericRead, // desiredAccess
        UseDefault, // shareMode
        UseDefault, // attributes
        OpenExisting, // creationDisposition
        UseDefault, // flagsAndAttributes
        UseDefault); // templateFile
    }

    public unsafe int Read(byte[] buffer, int index, int count)
    {
        int bytesRead = 0;
        fixed (byte* bytePointer = buffer)
        {
            ReadFile(
            fileHandle, // hfile
            bytePointer + index, // lpBuffer
            count, // nBytesToRead
            &bytesRead, // nBytesRead
            0); // overlapped
        }
        return bytesRead;
    }
}

class Test
{
    public static void Main()
    {
        // create an instance of the APIFileReader,
        // pass in the name of an existing file
        APIFileReader fileReader = new APIFileReader("8Swnn10.txt");

        // create a buffer and an ASCII coder
        const int BuffSize = 128;
        byte[] buffer = new byte[BuffSize];
        ASCIIEncoding asciiEncoder = new ASCIIEncoding();

        // read the file into the buffer and display to console
        while (fileReader.Read(buffer, 0, BuffSize) != 0)
        {
            Console.Write("{0}", asciiEncoder.GetString(buffer));
        }
    }
}
}
```

The key section of code where you create a pointer to the buffer and fix that buffer in memory using the fixed keyword is shown in bold.

This produces more than a page full of output, so we've truncated it here, but it begins:

```
Altogether, my aunt used to treat him with scant ceremony. Since she was of
the opinion that he ought to feel flattered by our invitations, she thought
it only right and proper that he should never come to see us in summer without
a basket of peaches or raspberries from his garden, and that from each of his
visits to Italy he should bring back some photographs of old masters for me.
...
```

C# 4.0 Interop Syntax Enhancements

Earlier in this chapter we saw C# 4.0's support for embedding interop type information, which can remove the need for primary interop assemblies. That feature has no visible impact on syntax—it just makes life easier during installation. However, C# 4.0 has added a couple of features that offer better syntax for certain interop tasks.

Indexed Properties

Suppose you were to write the following C#:

```
someObject.MyProperty["foo"] = 42;
```

Before C# 4.0, there was only one way to interpret this: this code gets `MyProperty`, and then uses the returned object's indexer to set a value of 42 using an indexer argument of `"foo"`. Remember that properties are just method calls in disguise, so the code is equivalent to:

```
someObject.get_MyProperty().set_Item("foo", 42);
```

 When you write an indexer in C#, its getter and setter turn into methods called get_Item and set_Item.

Unfortunately, some COM components have properties that work in a slightly different way, and these are called *indexed properties*. Whereas in C#, indexers are a type-level feature, in COM, any individual property may define an indexer. COM properties are really just method calls just like in C#, but with an indexed property, the explicit code would look more like this:

```
someObject.set_MyProperty("foo", 42);
```

Indexed properties require fewer objects. The traditional C# interpretation requires `MyProperty` to return a distinct object whose job is to provide the indexer, through which we access the values of interest. But with indexed properties, no intermediate object is required—`someObject` provides accessors that give us direct access.

Before C# 4.0, the only way to use indexed properties was via the method call syntax. But now you can use the indexer syntax, which will tend to make the code look more natural, since that's how the author of the COM component would have expected the property to be used.

 C# 4.0 adds the ability to consume indexed properties, but you cannot write your own. The C# designers do not want to add confusion by providing two different idioms—there's only one way to write a property that provides this syntax, which is one less decision developers have to make. Support for indexed properties is only present to make interop easier.

Optional ref

As we saw in Chapter 18, some COM components have methods where optional arguments are declared as `ref object`, meaning that the argument is a reference to an object reference. This led to some rather ugly code, such as that shown in Example 19-4.

Example 19-4. Ugliness by reference

```
object fileName = @"WordFile.docx";
object missing = System.Reflection.Missing.Value;
object readOnly = true;
var doc = wordApp.Documents.Open(ref fileName, ref missing, ref readOnly,
    ref missing, ref missing, ref missing, ref missing, ref missing,
    ref missing, ref missing, ref missing, ref missing, ref missing,
    ref missing, ref missing, ref missing);
```

The `ref missing` means: pass the object reference that's in the variable called `missing`, and give the method the option to modify the `missing` variable so that it refers to some other object, or `null` on return, if it wants.

This is a common pattern with some COM libraries, because it provides a lot of flexibility. But it makes for unpleasant-looking calling code in C# 3.0. However, C# 4.0 makes `ref` optional when you're using an interop type, which means we can modify the last line of Example 19-4 as shown in Example 19-5.

Example 19-5. Omitting ref

```
var doc = wordApp.Documents.Open(fileName, missing, readOnly,
    missing, missing, missing, missing, missing,
    missing, missing, missing, missing, missing,
    missing, missing, missing);
```

That's a lot better, but we can go further. C# 4.0 adds support for optional arguments—methods can specify the default value to be supplied when the caller omits an argument. On its own, that wouldn't help here, because in general, C# does not allow `ref` arguments to be optional. However, if it has decided to make the `ref` optional, as it does in interop scenarios, then it also allows the argument itself to be optional as long as a default value is available. And since the Word PIA provides default values for all the arguments in the method we're using here, we can reduce the call to just the code in Example 19-6.

Example 19-6. Optional arguments

```
var doc = wordApp.Documents.Open(FileName: fileName, ReadOnly: readOnly);
```

We've used named arguments here because the arguments are no longer consecutive—we only want to supply the first and third, so we name them to make it clear. Named arguments were discussed in Chapter 3.

 As Example 19-6 shows, the support for optional `ref` arguments fixes many of the problems that motivated the use of `dynamic` in Chapter 18. C# now offers multiple ways to solve some interop problems, but how should you choose? Well, `dynamic` becomes particularly important when type information lets you down—sometimes COM automation APIs don't provide enough type information at compile time, leaving you with properties whose type is nothing more informative than `object`, at which point, `dynamic` is usually the best bet. But static typing provides IntelliSense, and can offer better compile-time checks. So it's probably best to stick with static typing until you hit a point where that stops working.

Summary

Sometimes you'll need to use components or APIs that were not designed with .NET in mind. You can use COM components and Win32 DLLs from C# thanks to the .NET Framework's interop services. Visual Studio provides additional support specific to ActiveX controls, making it easy to incorporate these into Windows Forms applications. The world of unmanaged code sometimes requires us to work directly with raw memory in an unsafe fashion, and to enable this, C# offers C-style pointers. We strongly discourage you from using them for anything other than interop.

CHAPTER 20

WPF and Silverlight

WPF and Silverlight are related technologies for building user interfaces in .NET. Although they are aimed at two significantly different scenarios, they share so many concepts and features that it makes sense to discuss both of them at the same time—almost everything in this chapter applies to both WPF and Silverlight.

As its name suggests, the Windows Presentation Foundation (WPF) is for building interactive applications that run on Windows. WPF applications typically run as stand-alone applications, requiring an installation step to get them onto the target machine, as they may need prerequisites to be installed first. (WPF is .NET-based, so it requires the .NET Framework to be installed.) This means they are deployed like old-school Windows desktop applications. However, WPF makes it easy for applications to exploit the graphical potential of modern computers in a way that is extremely hard to achieve with more traditional Windows UI technologies. WPF applications don't have to *look* old-school.

Silverlight is for web applications, or more specifically, so-called Rich Internet Applications (RIAs). It does not depend on the full .NET Framework—it is a browser plug-in that provides a self-contained, lightweight, cross-platform version of the framework. The whole Silverlight runtime is around a 5 MB download, whereas the full .NET Framework is far more than 200 MB*—and Silverlight installs in seconds rather than minutes. Once the plug-in is installed, Silverlight content downloads as part of a web page, just like AJAX and Flash content, with no installation step for new applications. (Like with Flash-based Adobe AIR applications, it's also possible for a Silverlight application to run out-of-browser once it has been downloaded, if the user consents.) But because Silverlight contains a form of the .NET Framework, you get to write client-side code in C#, which can run in all of the popular web browsers, on both Windows and Mac OS X.

---

* It's not usually necessary to download the entire .NET Framework—an online installer can determine which bits are required for the target machine. Even so, a full Silverlight download ends up being about one-fifth the size of the smallest possible download required for the full framework.

At the time of this writing, Microsoft does not produce a Silverlight plug-in for Linux. However, an open source project called Moonlight offers a Linux-compatible version of Silverlight. This is based on the Mono project, an open source version of C# and the .NET Framework that can run on various non-Microsoft systems, including Linux.

Microsoft has provided some assistance to the Moonlight project to help its developers achieve compatibility with the Microsoft Silverlight plug-in. However, be aware that the Moonlight plug-in has historically lagged behind Microsoft's—as we write this, Moonlight's current official release is two major version numbers behind Microsoft's. If you need to support Linux desktop machines with a Silverlight-based web application, this lag will limit the features you can use.

Despite the very different environments in which WPF and Silverlight applications run, they have a great deal in common. Both use a markup language called Xaml to define the layout and structure of user interfaces. Their APIs are sufficiently similar that it is possible to write a single codebase that can be compiled for either WPF or Silverlight. There are critical concepts, such as data binding and templating, which you need to understand to be productive in either system.

It's not accurate to say that Silverlight is a subset of WPF. However, this doesn't stop people from saying it; even Microsoft sometimes makes this claim. It's strictly untrue: WPF has many features that Silverlight does not and Silverlight has a few features that WPF does not, so neither is a subset of the other. But even if you allow a slightly woolly interpretation of the word *subset*, it's a misleading way to describe it. Even where both Silverlight and WPF offer equivalent features they don't always work in the same way. A few minutes with a decompilation tool such as Reflector or ILDASM makes it abundantly clear that WPF and Silverlight are quite different beasts on the inside. So if you are contemplating building a single application that works both in the browser as a Silverlight application and on the desktop as a WPF application, it's important to understand the point in the following warning.

While it is *possible* to write a single codebase that can run as both WPF and Silverlight code, this doesn't happen automatically. Silverlight code is likely to need some modification before it will run correctly in WPF. If you have existing WPF code, significant chunks of it may need rewriting before it will run in Silverlight.

Codebases that run on both WPF and Silverlight tend to use conditional compilation—they use the C# preprocessor's `#if`, `#else`, and `#endif` directives to incorporate two different versions of the code in a single source file in the places where differences are required. Consequently, development and testing must be performed on Silverlight and WPF side by side throughout the development process.

In practice, it's not common to need to write a single body of code that runs in both environments. It might be useful if you're writing a reusable user interface component that you plan to use in multiple different applications, but any single application is likely to pick just one platform—either WPF or Silverlight—depending on how and where you need to deploy it.

In this chapter, the examples will use Silverlight, but WPF equivalents would be very similar. We will call out areas in which a WPF version would look different. We will start by looking at one of the most important features, which is common to both WPF and Silverlight.

Xaml and Code Behind

Xaml is an XML-based markup language that can be used to construct a user interface. Xaml is a former acronym—it used to be short for eXtensible Application Markup Language, but as so often happens, for obscure marketing reasons it officially no longer stands for anything. And to be fair, most acronyms are reverse-engineered—the usual process is to look through the list of unused and pronounceable (it's pronounced "Zammel," by the way) three- and four-letter combinations, trying to think of things that the available letters might plausibly stand for.

Since etymology can't tell us anything useful about what Xaml is, let's look at an example. As always, following the examples yourself in Visual Studio is highly encouraged. To do that, you'll need to create a new Silverlight project. There's a separate section under Visual C# in the New Project dialog for Silverlight projects, and you should choose the Silverlight Application template. (Or if you prefer, you can find the WPF Application template in the Windows section underneath Visual C#, although if you choose that, the details will look slightly different from the examples in this chapter.)

When you create a new Silverlight project, Visual Studio will ask you if you'd like it to create a new web project to host the Silverlight application. (If you add a Silverlight project to a solution that already contains a web project, it will also offer to associate the Silverlight application with that web project.) Silverlight applications run from the web browser (initially, at least), so you'll need a web page simply to run your code. It's not strictly necessary to create a whole web application, because if you choose not to, Visual Studio will just generate a web page automatically when you debug or run the project, but in general, Silverlight projects are an element of a web application, so you'd normally want both kinds of projects in your solution. Let it create one for now.

 If you were building a WPF application, you wouldn't have an associated web project, because WPF is for standalone Windows desktop applications.

Once Visual Studio has created the project, it shows a file called *MainPage.xaml*. This is a Xaml file defining the appearance and layout of your user interface. Initially, it contains just a couple of elements: a `<UserControl>` at the root (or a `<Window>` in a WPF project), and a `<Grid>` inside this. We'll add a couple of elements to the user interface so that there's something to interact with. Example 20-1 shows the Xaml you get by default with a new Silverlight project, along with two new elements: a `Button` and a `TextBlock`; the additional content is shown in bold.

Example 20-1. Creating a UI with Xaml

```
<UserControl
    x:Class="SimpleSilverlight.MainPage"
    xmlns="http://schemas.microsoft.com/winfx/2006/xaml/presentation"
    xmlns:x="http://schemas.microsoft.com/winfx/2006/xaml"
    xmlns:d="http://schemas.microsoft.com/expression/blend/2008"
    xmlns:mc="http://schemas.openxmlformats.org/markup-compatibility/2006"
    mc:Ignorable="d" d:DesignWidth="640" d:DesignHeight="480"
    d:DesignHeight="300" d:DesignWidth="400">

    >

    <Grid x:Name="LayoutRoot" Background="White">

        <Button
            x:Name="myButton"
            HorizontalAlignment="Center" VerticalAlignment="Top"
            FontSize="20"
            Content="Click me!"
            />

        <TextBlock
            x:Name="messageText"
            Text="Message will appear here"
            TextWrapping="Wrap"
            TextAlignment="Center"
            FontSize="30" FontWeight="Bold"
            HorizontalAlignment="Center"
            VerticalAlignment="Center"
            />

    </Grid>
</UserControl>
```

 Visual Studio presents Xaml in a split view. At the top it shows how it looks, and at the bottom it shows the Xaml source. You can either edit the source directly or drag items around on the design view at the top, adding new items from the Toolbox. As you make changes in one view the other view updates automatically.

If you run the application by pressing F5, Visual Studio will show the Silverlight application in a web page, as you can see in Figure 20-1.

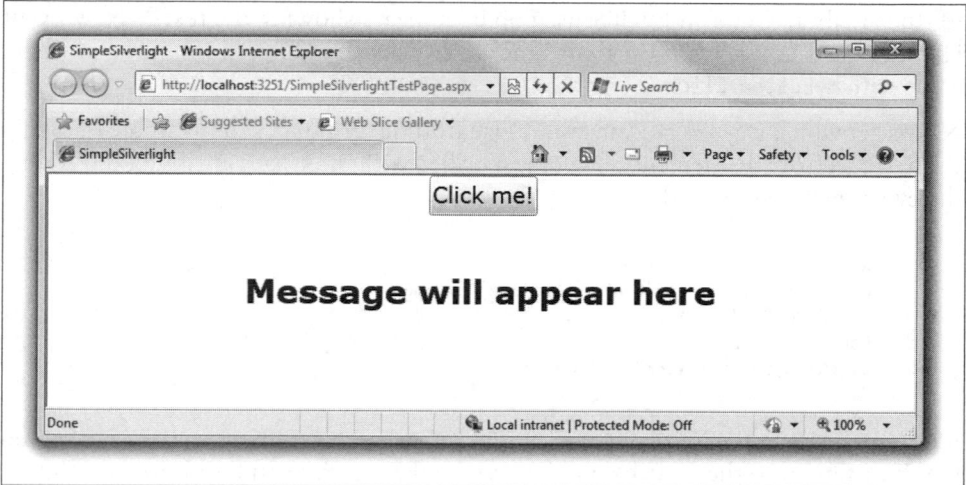

Figure 20-1. Silverlight application in a web browser

 You will see the Silverlight application only if you run the correct page from the web application. Visual Studio will usually launch the right one if you create a brand-new web application at the same time as your Silverlight application. But be aware that if you add other pages to your web application, Visual Studio might pick one of those when you debug and you might not see your Silverlight UI. You can tell Visual Studio to always use the same file in the web project by right-clicking on it in the Solution Explorer and selecting Set as Start Page. (Visual Studio creates two test pages for your Silverlight code—an *.aspx* and an *.html* file, both of which will be named by appending *TestPage* to your Silverlight project's name. Either works; it offers both so that you can choose between a dynamic ASP.NET page and static HTML to host your Silverlight UI.)

This simple Silverlight example contains a button, but if you click it, nothing will happen because we have not defined any behavior. Xaml files in WPF and Silverlight are usually paired with a so-called *code behind* file, a C# (or VB.NET, or whatever language you're using) file that contains code associated with the Xaml file, and we can use this to make the button do something.

The easiest way to add a click handler for the button to your code behind is from the Xaml file. You can just double-click the button on the design view and it will add a click handler. In fact, most user interface elements offer a wide range of events, so you might want a bit more control. You could select the item on the design surface and then go to the Properties panel—it has an Events tab that lists all the available events, and you can double-click on any of these to add a handler. Or if you prefer typing, you can add a handler from the Xaml source editor view. If you go to the `Button` element and start adding a new `Click` attribute, you'll find that when you type the opening quote for the attribute value an IntelliSense pop up appears showing the text "<New Event Handler>". If you press the Tab or Enter key, Visual Studio will fill in the attribute value with myButton_Click.

No matter which way you add an event, Visual Studio populates the attribute by taking the first part from the element's name, as specified with the x:Name attribute, and adding the event name on the end:

```
<Button
    x:Name="myButton"
    HorizontalAlignment="Center" VerticalAlignment="Top"
    FontSize="20"
    Content="Click me!"
    Click="myButton_Click"
    />
```

It doesn't just edit the Xaml—it also adds a method with this name to the code behind file. You can go to the code behind by pressing F7, or you can find it in the Solution Explorer—if you expand a Xaml file node, you'll see a *.xaml.cs* file inside it, and that's the code behind. Example 20-2 shows the click handler, along with some additional code in bold. (You're not obligated to use this naming convention for handlers, by the way. You could rename it after Visual Studio creates the handler, as long as you change both the Xaml and the code behind.)

Example 20-2. Click handler in the code behind

```
private void myButton_Click(object sender, RoutedEventArgs e)
{
    messageText.Text = "Hello, world!";
}
```

Because the Xaml refers to this handler method in the Button element's Click attribute, the method will run anytime the button is clicked. The one line of code we added here refers to the TextBlock element. If you look at the Xaml, you'll see that the element's x:Name attribute has a value of messageText, and this lets us use this name in the code behind to refer to that element. Example 20-2 sets the Text property, which, as you've no doubt guessed, causes the TextBlock to show the specified text when the button is clicked.

 Just to be clear, this is happening on the client side. The Silverlight plug-in downloads your application and then renders the UI as defined by your Xaml. It hosts your code behind (and any other code in your Silverlight project) inside the web browser process, and calls the specified event handlers without needing to communicate any further with the web server. Silverlight applications *can* communicate back with the web server after being loaded, but this click-handling interaction does not involve the server at all, unlike clicking a button on a normal web form.

The Xaml in Example 20-1 and the C# in Example 20-2 both set the Text of the TextBlock. The Xaml does this using standard XML's attribute syntax, while the C# code does it using normal C# property syntax. This highlights an important feature of Xaml: elements typically correspond to objects, and attributes correspond either to properties or to events.

Xaml and Objects

Although Xaml is the usual mechanism for defining the user interface of WPF and Silverlight applications, it's not strictly necessary. You could remove the bold code in Example 20-1 that adds the Button and TextBlock to the Xaml, and instead modify the class definition and constructor in the code behind, as Example 20-3 shows.

Example 20-3. Creating UI elements in code

```
public partial class MainPage : UserControl
{
    private Button myButton;
    private TextBlock messageText;

    public MainPage()
    {
        InitializeComponent();

        myButton = new Button
        {
            HorizontalAlignment = HorizontalAlignment.Center,
            VerticalAlignment = VerticalAlignment.Top,
            FontSize = 20,
            Content = "Click me!"
        };
        myButton.Click += myButton_Click;

        messageText = new TextBlock
        {
            Text = "Message will appear here",
            TextWrapping = TextWrapping.Wrap,
            TextAlignment = TextAlignment.Center,
            FontSize = 30,
            FontWeight = FontWeights.Bold,
            HorizontalAlignment = HorizontalAlignment.Center,
            VerticalAlignment = VerticalAlignment.Center
        };

        LayoutRoot.Children.Add(myButton);
        LayoutRoot.Children.Add(messageText);
    }
    ...
```

Each element that had an `x:Name` attribute has been replaced here with a field in the class, and we initialize that field in the constructor. This example uses the C# object initializer syntax to set the property values to emphasize the structural similarity between this code and the Xaml it replaces, but normal property setter syntax works too, of course.

XML attribute values are just text, whereas in C# we have to provide values of the correct type—enumeration entries, numbers, or strings as appropriate. The Xaml compiler works out how to turn text into something of the appropriate type. (It uses the .NET Framework class library's `TypeConverter` system to do this.) Also, as you will recall C# uses a different syntax to attach event handlers than the one for setting properties—we've used the `+=` syntax here—whereas Xaml uses attribute syntax for both properties and event handlers.

This code has the same effect as Xaml. Xaml is really just a language for creating objects, setting their properties, and attaching event handlers, so for the most part it doesn't really matter whether you use C# or Xaml to create your user interface. This raises the question of why we have Xaml at all, when C# seems to work perfectly well. The main reason Xaml exists is to make it possible to create user interfaces in tools other than a text editor. For example, Microsoft offers a program called Expression Blend, part of its Expression family of design-oriented programs. Blend is a tool for creating WPF and Silverlight user interfaces, and it works mostly in Xaml.

This separation is more than just a convenience for people wanting to write design tools. It's useful to both developers and designers. It enforces some separation, making it possible for designers to work on the visual design of an application, without needing tools that can edit C# source files. In fact, successful collaboration between developers and designers takes a bit more than this—the separation of Xaml and code behind is not in itself sufficient, because it's still fairly easy for designers and developers to trip over one another. If a developer writes code behind that relies on certain elements with particular `x:Name` attributes being present in the Xaml, but the designer decides to delete those elements because they're ugly and then creates new replacements but forgets to give them the same names, we're obviously going to see problems. In practice, a smooth developer/designer workflow goes a bit deeper than this, and relies on other WPF and Silverlight features, most notably templates, which we'll be getting to later. But Xaml is an important part of the solution.

 The `x:Name` attribute is optional. In fact, most Xaml elements tend not to be named—you only name the elements that you need to be able to access from the code behind. This makes the Xaml less cluttered, and if you are working with designers, it makes it easier for them to know which elements are structurally important, and which ones they can rework for design purposes.

The equivalence between elements and objects suggests that Xaml doesn't necessarily have to be used just for the user interface. The Xaml syntax can be used to create .NET objects of almost any kind. As long as a type has a default constructor and can be configured through its properties with suitable type converters, it's possible to use it from Xaml—it's technically possible to create a Windows Forms UI in Xaml, for example. However, Xaml tends to be cumbersome if you use it for types that weren't designed with Xaml in mind, so in practice, it's a much better fit for WPF, Silverlight, and also the Workflow Foundation, all of which are meant to be used from Xaml, than it is for other parts of the .NET Framework.

Xaml and JavaScript

Version 1.0 of Silverlight didn't support .NET at all. It offered Xaml support, but if you wanted anything other than static, noninteractive content, you needed to define the behavior using browser-hosted script. In this situation, Xaml elements clearly don't correspond to .NET objects. However, they still correspond to objects—the JavaScript code can get hold of an object representing any element in the Xaml.

This is still supported in current versions of Silverlight—you can use objects created in Xaml from C#, JavaScript, or both. (JavaScript support can be useful for making interactive splash screens that display while waiting for your main C#-based UI to download.) But JavaScript objects are not the same thing as .NET objects. This raises a question: what sort of objects does Xaml *really* create? Are they .NET objects with JavaScript wrappers? Or are they JavaScript objects with .NET wrappers? The answer is: it depends. They're not ordinary native JavaScript objects, but they're not always .NET objects either. For primitive elements with no interactive behavior, such as graphical shapes or text blocks, both the .NET and the JavaScript objects appear to be wrappers around some internal object that lives inside the plug-in. For more complex objects such as buttons or listboxes, the .NET objects seem to be the real thing, because their behavior is implemented as .NET code.

Given that you have a choice between Xaml and C#, which should you use? Xaml is often easier because you can use tools such as Visual Studio's Xaml designer (or even Expression Blend) to edit the appearance and layout—this can take much less effort than tweaking code repeatedly until the outcome looks the way you want. Obviously, if developers and designers are involved, Xaml is preferable by far, because it enables designers to tweak and refine the appearance without needing to involve developers for every change. But even for a UI being created entirely by developers, an interactive design surface is a much more efficient way to create a layout than code. This doesn't mean you should go out of your way to avoid creating elements in code, however, particularly if code looks like the most straightforward solution to a problem. Use whichever approach is more convenient for the task at hand.

Now that we've seen that Xaml is really just a way of creating objects, what types of objects do Silverlight and WPF offer?

Elements and Controls

Some of the types used to construct a user interface are interactive elements with a distinctive behavior of their own, such as buttons, checkboxes, and listboxes. Although you need code to connect these elements to your application, they have some built-in interactive behavior: buttons light up when the mouse cursor moves over them and look pushed in when clicked; listboxes allow items to be selected; and so on. Other elements are more primitive. There are graphical shape elements and text elements, which are visible to the user but which don't have an intrinsic behavior—if you want them to do more than simply be visible you need to write code to make that happen. And some elements don't even appear directly; for example, there are layout elements that are often not visible themselves, as their job is to decide where other elements go.

You can tell what type of element you're dealing with by looking at the corresponding .NET type's base class. Most UI elements ultimately derive from `FrameworkElement`, but this class has some more specialized subtypes. `Panel` is the base class of layout elements. `Shape` is the base class of elements involving 2D graphical shapes. `Control` is the base class of elements that have some intrinsic interactive behavior of their own.

 This means that not all UI elements are controls. In fact, the majority of UI elements are not controls. Having said that, the term *control* is often used loosely—many authors, and even some parts of Microsoft's documentation, use the term *control* to describe any UI element, including ones that don't in fact derive from `Control`. To further confuse the issue there's a `System.Windows.Controls` namespace, in which not all of the types derive from `Control`.

We believe this is confusing, so in this book, we will use the term *control* only when talking about types that derive from `Control`. When we're discussing features that apply to all UI objects that derive from `FrameworkElement` (which includes all controls) we will use the more general term *element*. But be aware that you will come across other, more confusing conventions on the Web and in other books.

Before we get to the controls, we'll look at how elements are positioned and sized—interactive elements are not much use if you can't choose where they appear.

Layout Panels

Panel is the abstract base class of user interface elements that control the layout of other elements. You choose a particular concrete derived type to determine which layout mechanism to use. Silverlight version 3 offers three[†] panel types: Grid, StackPanel, and Canvas. WPF provides these and a few more, as we'll see shortly.

Grid is the most powerful panel, which is why Visual Studio provides you with one by default in a new UI. As the name suggests, it carves up the available space into rows and columns, and then positions child elements into the resultant grid cells. By default, a Grid has a single row and a single column, making just one big cell, but you can add more. Example 20-4 shows how to do this.

 This example uses a Xaml feature called a *property element*—the <Grid.ColumnDefinitions> element does not represent a child object to be added to the grid, but instead indicates that we want to set the Grid object's ColumnDefinitions property. The <ColumnDefinition> elements it contains are added to the collection in that property, whereas the <Button> elements are added to the collection in the Children property of the Grid.

Example 20-4. Grid with rows and columns

```
<Grid>
    <Grid.ColumnDefinitions>
        <ColumnDefinition Width="Auto" />
        <ColumnDefinition />
        <ColumnDefinition />
    </Grid.ColumnDefinitions>

    <Grid.RowDefinitions>
        <RowDefinition Height="30" />
        <RowDefinition Height="2*" />
        <RowDefinition />
        <RowDefinition Height="Auto" />
    </Grid.RowDefinitions>

    <Button Grid.Column="0" Grid.Row="0"
        Content="(0, 0)" />
    <Button Grid.Column="1" Grid.Row="0"
        Content="(1, 0)" />
    <Button Grid.Column="2" Grid.Row="0"
        Content="(2, 0)" />

    <Button Grid.Column="0" Grid.Row="1"
        Grid.ColumnSpan="3"
```

---

† If you look in the documentation you'll see that more than three types derive from Panel. However, the others are in the System.Windows.Controls.Primitives namespace, signifying that they are not meant for general use. These are specialized panels designed only to be used inside specific controls.

```
        Content="Row 1, 3 columns wide" />

    <Button Grid.Column="0" Grid.Row="2"
        Grid.ColumnSpan="3"
        Content="Row 2, 3 columns wide" />

    <Button Grid.Column="1" Grid.Row="3"
        FontSize="50"
        Content="(3, 1)" />

</Grid>
```

Figure 20-2 shows how this looks. The four rows are fairly clear—each button belongs to just one row. The columns are less obvious—you can see all three clearly in the first row, because there's one button in each, but the next two rows contain just one button each, spanning all three rows. And the final row contains a single button in the second column.

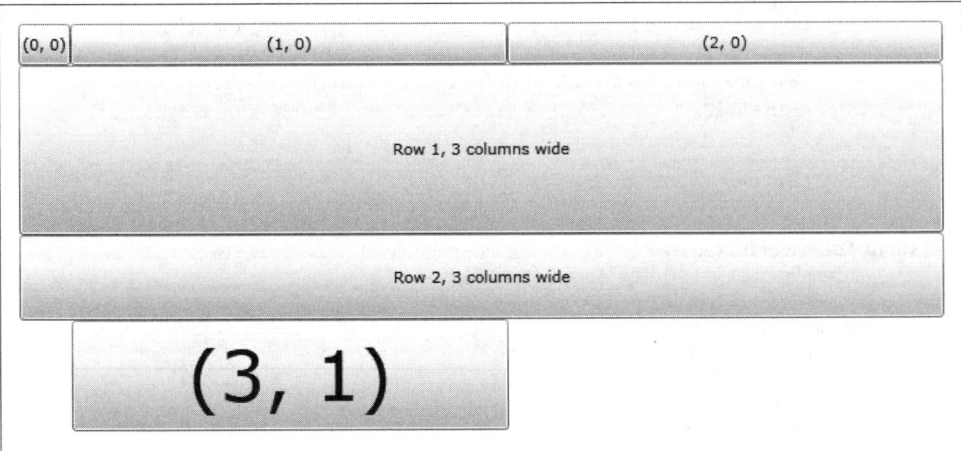

Figure 20-2. Grid children

The Grid knows which columns and rows elements belong to, and how many they span, because each button in Example 20-4 has properties that control this. The Grid.Column and Grid.Row properties do what their names suggest, while the Grid.ColumnSpan and Grid.RowSpan properties determine how many grid cells the element occupies. The column and row default to 0, while the spans default to 1.

 These properties use another special Xaml feature called *attached properties*. An attached property is one defined by a different type (e.g., Grid) than the object it is applied to (e.g., Button). The attached properties in Example 20-4 are attributes, but you can also set attached properties with the property element syntax shown earlier—for example, if a <Grid> element could contain a <ToolTipService.Tool Tip> element, to set the attachable ToolTip property defined by the ToolTipService class.

While Silverlight, WPF, and Xaml support the idea that properties don't necessarily have to be defined by the object on which they are set, C# has no syntax for this. So classes that define attachable properties also define get and set methods to enable those properties to be used from code. For example, the Grid class offers SetColumn, SetRow, and so on.

The rows and columns in Figure 20-2 are different sizes. This is because of the settings on the <RowDefinition> and <ColumnDefinition> elements. The first column's Width has been set to Auto, so it takes its size from the widest child in that column. In this case, only one child belongs exclusively to that column, so the column is exactly wide enough to hold it. The other two columns are at their default width, the value 1*, which causes them to share the remaining space equally. The rows use similar features, except the first row has a fixed height of 30, so it ignores the size of the content and makes every element 30 pixels high. The final row is Auto sized, and since its content has a large font size, it ends up being fairly tall. And the middle two rows use so-called star sizing, so as with the second and third columns, they end up sharing the space left over. However, since they have different star size values—1* and 2*—they get different amounts of space. The 2* row gets to be twice the height of the 1* row. Note that the ratios are all that matter with star sizing—changing 1* and 2* to 10* and 20* would not change the outcome in this example, because 20* is still twice as large as 10*.

So as you can see, a grid can use fixed sizes, it can base sizes on the content at hand, or it can divide the available space proportionally. This makes it a pretty flexible layout mechanism. You can build dock-style layouts where elements are aligned to the top, bottom, left, or right of the available space through the use of Auto sized rows and columns, and by making elements span all the available rows when docking to the left or right, or all the columns when docking to the top or the bottom. You can also stack elements horizontally or vertically by using multiple rows or columns with Auto sizes. And as we'll see, it's even possible to exercise precise control over the size and position of elements within the grid. One slight problem is that your Xaml can get a little verbose when using grids. So there are some simpler panel types.

StackPanel arranges children in a vertical or horizontal stack. Example 20-5 shows a StackPanel with its Orientation set explicitly to Vertical. You can doubtless guess how to make a horizontal stack. (In fact, vertical stacks are the default, so you could leave the orientation out from Example 20-5 without changing its behavior.)

Example 20-5. Vertical StackPanel

```
<StackPanel Orientation="Vertical">
    <Button Content="Buttons" FontSize="30" />
    <Button Content="in" />
    <Button Content="a" />
    <Button Content="stack" />
</StackPanel>
```

Figure 20-3 shows the result. Notice that in the direction of stacking—vertical in this example—the behavior is similar to the `Auto` height grid rows, in that each row has been made tall enough to accommodate the content. In the other direction, the elements have been stretched to fill the available space, although as we'll see shortly, you can change that.

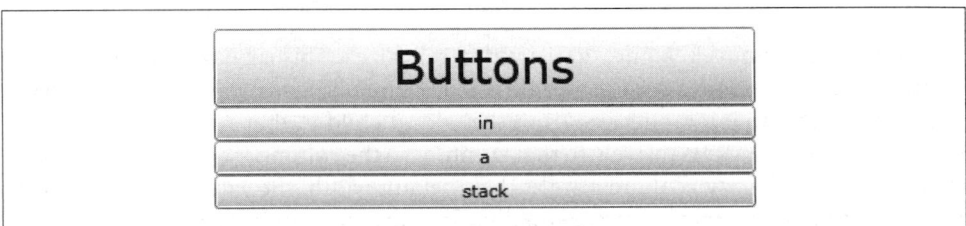

Figure 20-3. Vertical StackPanel

The `Canvas` panel takes an even simpler approach: it doesn't have a layout strategy, and it simply puts elements where you tell it to. As Example 20-6 shows, just as `Grid` offers attachable properties to specify which grid cells elements occupy, `Canvas` defines attachable `Left` and `Top` properties that specify where the elements should appear.

Example 20-6. Explicit positioning with Canvas

```
<Canvas>
    <Button Content="Buttons" FontSize="30" />
    <Button Canvas.Left="20" Canvas.Top="40"
            Content="on" />
    <Button Canvas.Left="80" Canvas.Top="40"
            Content="a" />
    <Button Canvas.Left="60" Canvas.Top="100"
            Content="Canvas" />
</Canvas>
```

As Figure 20-4 shows, the exact positioning possible with a `Canvas` has let us position elements so that they overlap. (This figure includes some of the browser chrome to illustrate that positions are relative to the top-left corner of the `Canvas`.) Notice that the `Canvas` sizes children based on how much space they require—similar to the `Auto` rows and columns, but in this case the buttons are sized to content in both dimensions. Unless you specify explicit widths and heights, a `Canvas` will attempt to give each child exactly as much space as it requires.

Figure 20-4. Buttons on a Canvas

Silverlight and WPF have extensible layout systems, so you can derive your own types from Panel or use libraries that offer other panels. For example, Microsoft offers the Silverlight Toolkit, a free library you can download in source or binary form from *http://silverlight.codeplex.com/*, which defines various controls, panels, and other useful components. This includes two panels, both based on panels that are built into WPF. There's WrapPanel, which lays out its children in much the same way that text is *word-wrapped* in web browsers and word processors—items are arranged from left to right until all the space is used up, at which point the panel starts on a new line. And there's also DockPanel, which lets you arrange elements by stacking them up against the left, right, top, or bottom of the panel. (DockPanel doesn't do anything Grid can't do, but it can be slightly simpler to use.)

Layout in WPF and Silverlight is not just about panels. Panels define the strategy by which elements are allocated a *layout slot*—the area on-screen in which they must fit themselves. But properties are available on all elements—regardless of the panel in use—that can influence both how big the layout slot is and what the element does with the space it is offered.

General-purpose layout properties

All elements have common properties that influence layout. There are Width and Height properties that let you specify an explicit size, rather than basing the size on the content or the available space. This is important for elements that don't otherwise have an intrinsic size. Textual content has a natural size, but some graphical elements such as Ellipse and Rectangle don't. If you were to create an Ellipse without setting the height and put it in a vertical StackPanel it would vanish, because the StackPanel asks it to calculate the minimum amount of space it requires, and if you have not specified any constraints, that'll be zero. So elements with no intrinsic size usually have an explicit Width and Height, or you might use MinWidth and MinHeight to ensure that they never vanish entirely, but are able to expand to fill whatever space is available—some layouts will end up with more space than needed if the user resizes a window, so it can be useful to have a layout that adapts. MaxWidth and MaxHeight let you specify upper limits on just how far elements will expand.

The various width and height properties are useful when an element is being asked to determine its own size, such as in `Auto` sized grid cells. But sometimes an element's layout slot size is imposed on it—for example, if your Silverlight user interface is configured to fill the entire browser window, the user is in charge of how big it is. This is sometimes referred to as *constrained layout*—this describes situations where the layout system has to make things fit a predetermined space, rather than trying to work out how much space is required. Most user interfaces contain a mixture of constrained and unconstrained layout—the top level of the UI is usually constrained by window size, but you might have individual elements such as text blocks or buttons that have to be large enough to display their content.

 When elements that have no intrinsic size are put in a constrained layout, they will fill the space available if you don't set the width and height. For example, if you put an `Ellipse` as the only element of the root `Grid` layout element, and you don't set any of the width or height properties, it will fill the whole Silverlight application UI.

You can even get a mixture of constrained and unconstrained layouts on one element. In Figure 20-3, we saw a vertical stack of elements, and vertically, each one's size was based on its content—since the elements are free to size themselves it means we have unconstrained layout vertically. But the elements are all the same width regardless of content, indicating that constrained layout was in use horizontally. Stack panels always work this way—children are unconstrained in the direction of stacking, but are constrained to have the same sized layout slots in the other direction.

When an element has more space than it needs due to constrained layout, additional properties that determine what the element does with the excess space come into play. The `HorizontalAlignment` attribute lets you position the element within its slot. Example 20-7 shows a modified version of Example 20-5, specifying each of the four `HorizontalAlignment` options.

Example 20-7. Horizontal alignment

```
<StackPanel Orientation="Vertical">
    <Button Content="Buttons" FontSize="30"
            HorizontalAlignment="Left" />
    <Button Content="in"
            HorizontalAlignment="Right" />
    <Button Content="a"
            HorizontalAlignment="Stretch" />
    <Button Content="stack"
            HorizontalAlignment="Center" />
</StackPanel>
```

Figure 20-5 shows the results. As before, each child has been given a layout slot that fills the whole width of the StackPanel, but all except the third row have been sized to content, and have then positioned themselves within their slot based on the HorizontalAlignment property. The third button still fills the whole of its row because its alignment is Stretch. That's the default, which is why elements fill their whole layout slot unless you specify an alignment. VerticalAlignment works in much the same way, offering Top, Bottom, Center, and Stretch.

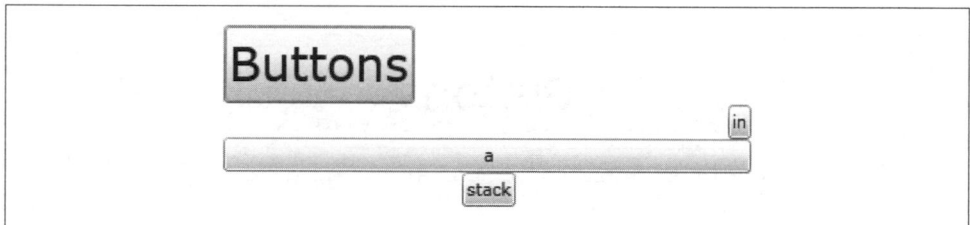

Figure 20-5. Horizontal alignment

 The alignment properties do something only when the layout slot is larger than the element requires. When an element has been given a slot exactly as large as it asked for in either the horizontal or vertical dimension, the corresponding alignment property does nothing. So setting VerticalAlignment on the child of a vertical StackPanel does nothing— the layout slot is already exactly as tall as the element requires, so the element is simultaneously at the top, the bottom, and the center of the slot.

Another very important ubiquitous layout property is Margin—this lets you specify the amount of space you'd like between the edge of an element and the boundary of its layout slot. In unconstrained layout, a margin will cause an element to be given a larger slot than it would otherwise have had, while in constrained layout, it causes an element to fill less of the slot than it otherwise would have. Example 20-8 illustrates this within a vertical StackPanel—since this uses constrained horizontal layout and unconstrained vertical layout for its children, we'll see both effects.

Example 20-8. Buttons with Margin properties

```
<StackPanel Orientation="Vertical">
    <Button Content="Buttons" FontSize="30" />
    <Button Content="in" Margin="10" />
    <Button Content="a" Margin="20" />
    <Button Content="stack" Margin="30" />
</StackPanel>
```

In Figure 20-6, the first button fills the entire width because it has no margin. But each successive button gets narrower, because each has a larger margin than the last. Since the width is constrained, the layout system needs to make the buttons narrower to provide the specified margin between the element's edges and its layout slot. But since the children here are unconstrained vertically, the margin has no effect on their vertical size, and instead ends up adding increasing amounts of space between each element—in the unconstrained case, `Margin` makes the slot larger.

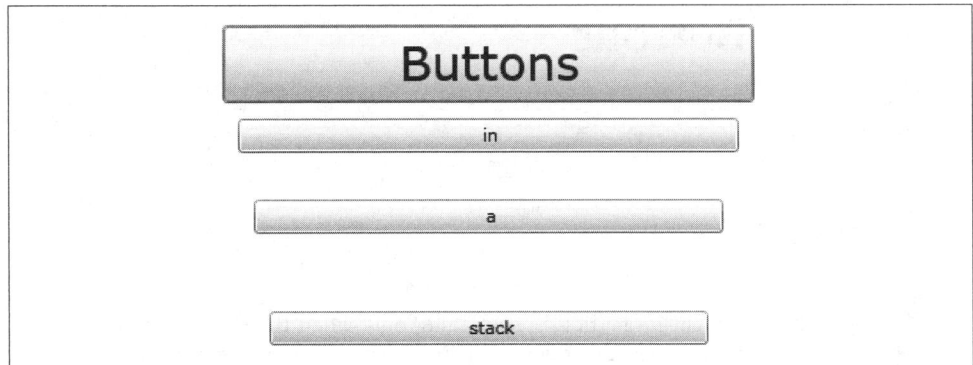

Figure 20-6. Buttons with margins

Example 20-8 specifies the margins as single numbers, denoting a uniform margin on all four sides, but you can be more precise. You can provide two numbers, setting the horizontal and vertical margins. Or you can provide four numbers, indicating the left, top, right, and bottom‡ margins independently. This enables precise positioning of elements within a `Grid`—it turns out that you don't have to use a `Canvas` to specify the position of an element. If you align an element to the left and the top, the first two numbers in a margin effectively determine its position within the containing grid cell, just as the attachable `Canvas.Left` and `Canvas.Top` properties work for children of a `Canvas`. The interactive design surfaces in Visual Studio and Blend use this to let you drag elements around on a grid and place them exactly where you want. It appears to be a completely free form of layout, but if you inspect what these programs do to the Xaml as you move elements around, they simply set the alignment properties appropriately and adjust the margins.

All of the layout features we've looked at so far take a rigidly rectangular approach—everything is either strictly horizontal or strictly vertical. In fact, WPF and Silverlight are a bit more flexible than that, thanks to their support for transforms.

---

‡ Yes, that is a different order than CSS. Silverlight and WPF follow the coordinate geometry convention of specifying pairs of coordinates as horizontal and then vertical measures—x before y. Hence left, then top, followed likewise by right, then bottom.

Transforms

You can apply a transform to any element, modifying its size, position, and orientation, or even skewing it. (If you're familiar with the coordinate geometry features found in most modern graphics system, you'll recognize these as being the usual two-dimensional *affine transformations* possible with a 2×3 matrix.§) Example 20-9 shows another variation on our StackPanel example, with transforms applied to the children.

Example 20-9. Transforms

```
<StackPanel Orientation="Vertical">
    <Button Content="Buttons" FontSize="30">
        <Button.RenderTransform>
            <ScaleTransform ScaleX="1.5" ScaleY="0.5" />
        </Button.RenderTransform>
    </Button>
    <Button Content="in">
        <Button.RenderTransform>
            <RotateTransform Angle="30" />
        </Button.RenderTransform>
    </Button>
    <Button Content="a">
        <Button.RenderTransform>
            <SkewTransform AngleX="30" />
        </Button.RenderTransform>
    </Button>
    <Button Content="stack">
        <Button.RenderTransform>
            <TranslateTransform Y="-50" />
        </Button.RenderTransform>
    </Button>
</StackPanel>
```

As Figure 20-7 shows, the RenderTransform property Example 20-9 uses can mess up the layout. The transform is applied after the layout calculations are complete, so the ScaleTransform on the first button has had the effect of making it too large to fit—the default HorizontalAlignment of Stretch is in effect here, so the button has been made exactly as wide as the containing StackPanel, and then has been scaled to be 1.5 times wider and 0.5 times higher, causing it to be cropped horizontally. Likewise, the elements that have been rotated and skewed have had corners cut off. WPF offers a LayoutTransform property that takes the transform into account before performing layout, which can avoid these problems, but Silverlight does not—you would need to tweak the layout to get things to fit.

 A transform applies not just to the target element, but also to all that element's children. For example, if you apply a RotateTransform to a panel, the panel's contents will rotate.

§ Strictly speaking, it's a 3×3 matrix, but the final column is fixed to contain (0, 0, 1).

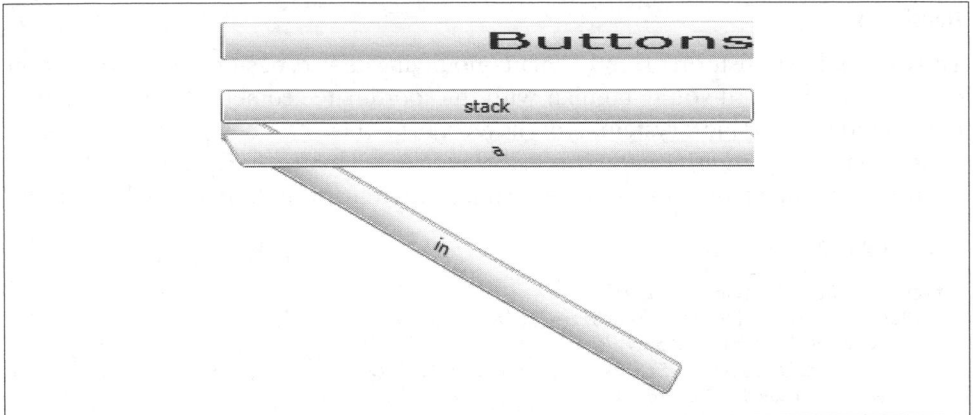

Figure 20-7. Transformed buttons

This support for rotation, scaling, and shearing reveals that WPF and Silverlight are designed to support more graphically interesting user interface styles than traditional, rigidly rectilinear Windows user interfaces. So this seems like a good time to look at some of the graphical elements.

Graphical Elements

WPF and Silverlight support several kinds of graphical elements. The *shape* elements provide scalable vector-oriented two-dimensional shapes. There are also various ways to incorporate bitmap images. Video is supported through the media element. And WPF and Silverlight both provide some support for 3D graphics, although they take rather different approaches.

Shapes

Shape is the base class of various two-dimensional shapes. It's an abstract class, and it defines common properties such as Fill and Stroke to control how the interior and outline of shapes are painted. Some of the derived classes are self-explanatory—it doesn't take much imagination to work out what Ellipse, Rectangle, and Line do. Polyline, Polygon, and Path require a little more explanation.

Polyline lets you define a shape as a series of straight lines—you simply provide a list of coordinate pairs defining each point the shape's outline passes through. Polygon does the same thing, but closes off the shape—it automatically joins the final point with the first one. However, you rarely use either of these, because Path lets you do all this and more. (Expression Blend never creates Polyline or Polygon elements—even if you create a shape whose outline is made up entirely of straight edges, it still makes a Path. And most Xaml export tools from programs such as Adobe Illustrator do the same. So in practice, Path is the one you'll come across. The other two exist because they are slightly simpler to work with from code.)

`Path` lets you define a shape with any mixture of straight and curved segments in its outline. Example 20-10 shows a `Path` made up entirely of straight edges.

Example 20-10. Path with straight edges

```
<Path Fill="Red" Stroke="Black"
    StrokeThickness="5"
    Data="M50,0 L100,50 50,100 0,50 z"
    />
```

The `Data` property defines the shape. It consists of a series of commands and coordinates. The letters indicate the command—the initial `M` means Move to the specified position, (50, 0) in this case. The `L` means draw a Line to the next coordinate. And since this example has three coordinate pairs after the `L`, even though `L` requires only one, that means we repeat the command—so that's three straight line segments passing through the coordinates (100, 50), (50, 100), and (0, 50). Each segment starts where the previous one left off. Finally, the `z` indicates that we'd like to make this a closed shape, so it will join that final point back up with the first one to form the diamond shape you see in Figure 20-8. This shape is filled in and given a thick outline, thanks to the `Fill`, `Stroke`, and `StrokeThickness` properties, which are available on any shape element.

 The shape defined by the `Data` describes the center of the line drawn for the outline. This means that making the `StrokeThickness` larger effectively increases the size of the shape—a thicker outline will encroach into the interior of the shape, but will also expand outward by the same amount. That means that the `Path` in Example 20-10 has a bounding box slightly larger than that implied by the coordinates in the `Data`. The first line segment starts at (50, 0), which is at the very top of the shape, but the stroke thickness means that the peak of the shape actually appears a bit higher. (The peak is at approximately (50, –3.54). The angle of this particular stroke means that the top corner is above the specified point by half the stroke thickness multiplied by $\sqrt{2}$.) So if you put this path at the very top left of the UI its top and left corners will be slightly cropped.

Figure 20-8. Path with straight edges

Path offers more complex commands for drawing curved shapes. Example 20-11 shows a shape with straight line segments and a single cubic Bezier curve segment, indicated with the C command.

Example 20-11. Path with Bezier curve and straight edges

```
<Path Fill="Red" Stroke="Black"
    StrokeThickness="5"
    Data="M50,0 L100,50 C125,74 75,125 50,100 L0,50 z"
    />
```

Cubic Bezier curves require four points to define them. So the C command demands three pairs of coordinates. (The first point is wherever the previous command finished, so it requires three more to bring the total to four.) Therefore, in this case, the three pairs of numbers that follow the C do not constitute three repeated commands as they did with L. You can repeat the C command; you just need to add three pairs for each segment. Figure 20-9 shows the shape defined by Example 20-11.

Figure 20-9. Path with a mixture of straight and curved edges

These examples have used simple named colors for the Fill and Stroke, but you can get more advanced. You can specify hexadecimal RGB colors using a #, as you would with HTML—for example, Fill="#FF8800" indicates a shade of orange, by mixing full-strength red (FF) with slightly more than half-strength green (88) and no blue (00). You can extend this to eight digits to define partially transparent colors—for example, Fill="8000FFFF" specifies an *alpha* (transparency) of 80 (semitransparent), 0 red, and full-strength green and blue, to define a semitransparent shade of turquoise.

You can also create more complex brushes. Linear and radial gradient brushes are available. Example 20-12 sets the fill of a shape to a radial gradient brush, and sets its stroke to be a linear gradient brush.

Example 20-12. Gradient brushes for fill and stroke

```
<Path StrokeThickness="10"
    Data="M50,0 L100,50 C125,74 75,125 50,100 L0,50 z"
    >
  <Path.Fill>
    <RadialGradientBrush>
      <GradientStop Offset="0" Color="Blue" />
      <GradientStop Offset="1" Color="White" />
    </RadialGradientBrush>
```

```
    </Path.Fill>

  <Path.Stroke>
    <LinearGradientBrush StartPoint="0,0"
                          EndPoint="0,1">
      <GradientStop Offset="0" Color="Black" />
      <GradientStop Offset="0.5" Color="White" />
      <GradientStop Offset="1" Color="Black" />
    </LinearGradientBrush>

  </Path.Stroke>
</Path>
```

As you can see in Figure 20-10, these brushes change color across the shape. The radial brush starts from a point in the middle (or some other point—there are properties to control the exact settings) and spreads out to an elliptical boundary. The linear gradient brush simply changes colors between the specified start and end points. Notice that you can run through as many different colors as you like with the `GradientStop` elements.

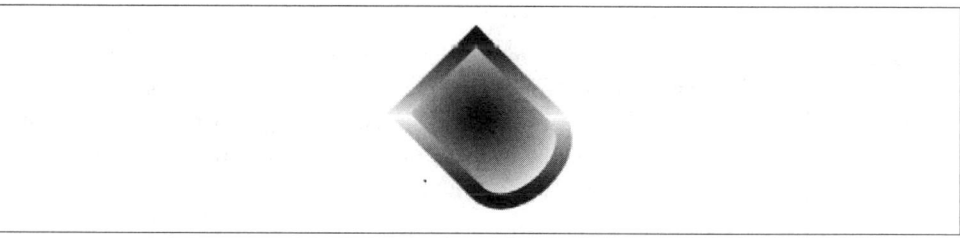

Figure 20-10. Gradient brushes

You can even create a bitmap-based brush with which to paint shapes, so let's look at bitmap handling next.

Images

The shape elements are great for graphics that can be built out of geometric elements. Skilled designers can produce remarkably realistic-looking imagery with these sorts of primitives using tools such as Adobe Illustrator. However, some kinds of pictures do not lend themselves to this sort of construction—photographs, for example. You might be able to draw a stylized rendition of a photograph, but if you just want to incorporate a photographic image directly into an application, bitmaps are the way to go.

Bitmaps are pixel-oriented rather than vector-based. (From a tool perspective, it's like the distinction between Adobe Photoshop and Adobe Illustrator.) Bitmaps do not scale as well—if you enlarge a bitmap, eventually you just see the individual pixels, leading to an appearance that is either jagged or fuzzy, depending on the way in which the bitmap is enlarged. Shapes don't have that problem; because shapes are geometrically defined, WPF or Silverlight can render them perfectly crisply no matter how large you make them. So there's a trade-off here—bitmaps can offer a much more photorealistic impression than vector art, but they don't adapt so well to changes in size. That's why graphics systems need to support both.

The simplest way to use a bitmap is with the `<Image>` element. You can point its `Source` property at any URL that contains a bitmap. Example 20-13 uses a miscellaneous image from one of the authors' blogs. WPF or Silverlight will download and display the image at runtime. (The image may not appear in the design view, though.)

Example 20-13. Image element with HTTP URL

```
<Image Source="http://www.interact-sw.co.uk/images/WpfMidpointGradient.png"
       Stretch="None" />
```

The `Stretch` property indicates how to size the image. The value `None` says that we want the image to be rendered at its natural size. The `Image` element's default behavior is to resize the bitmap so that it fills the layout slot, but that's not always appropriate. This particular image happens to be a screenshot, and those tend to go a bit blurry if you resize them, so disabling stretching is a good idea here. Resizing is less problematic for photographs, though, so the default behavior of stretching to fit is useful there.

The `Image` class is a user interface element, deriving from `FrameworkElement` like any other. But there's also `ImageBrush`—this derives from a different class, `Brush`, in common with the gradient brushes we saw earlier. You can use an `ImageBrush` to paint a shape. Example 20-14 uses the same image to provide the `Fill` of a `Path`. (Again, you may find that the image appears only at runtime, not at design time.)

Example 20-14. Painting a shape with an ImageBrush

```
<Path StrokeThickness="3" Stroke="Black"
      Data="M50,0 L100,50 C125,74 75,125 50,100 L0,50 z"
      >
  <Path.Fill>
    <ImageBrush
      ImageSource="http://www.interact-sw.co.uk/images/WpfMidpointGradient.png"
      />
  </Path.Fill>

</Path>
```

You don't have to download images with HTTP. You can compile an image into a WPF or Silverlight application as a resource—simply adding a JPEG or PNG to the project in Visual Studio will do that. Or with WPF you can point an `Image` or `ImageBrush` at a file on disk.

 Silverlight supports only JPEG and PNG bitmaps—to keep the Silverlight plug-in download small, Microsoft chose a minimal set of formats, and these two cover most bases. JPEG provides efficient compression for photographic and photorealistic images, but does a bad job with screenshots and doesn't support transparency. Conversely, PNG can reproduce screenshots perfectly and supports transparency, but compresses photographic images inefficiently.

WPF supports a much wider range of image types, including TIFF, BMP, and GIF. Moreover, it's built on top of the extensible Windows Imaging Components (WIC) mechanism, so the set of supported formats is not closed. Some digital camera vendors provide WIC drivers for their native raw image formats, so if you have those installed, WPF can display those images directly.

Still images may not be enough for your application. You might want to incorporate movies.

Media

WPF and Silverlight offer the `MediaElement`, which can render videos. It can also be used to play audio files. In use, it's almost identical to the `Image` element; you just point it at a video file rather than a bitmap.

Silverlight offers a `VideoBrush` that lets you create a brush from a video, in the same way that `ImageBrush` lets you create a brush from a bitmap. Slightly surprisingly, WPF does not offer this type—this is a good example of how Silverlight is not a subset of WPF. It's possible to paint things with video in WPF, though; you just do it using something called a `VisualBrush`. `VisualBrush` is far more powerful than `VideoBrush`—it lets you take any UI element (even one that has children, like a panel) and turn it into a brush. So you can wrap a `MediaElement` in a `VisualBrush` to create the same effect; Silverlight doesn't have `VisualBrush`, which is why it provides the more specialized `VideoBrush`.

Speaking of moving images, you can also apply movement to other elements in a user interface.

Animation

WPF and Silverlight allow any element to be animated—most properties that have an impact on the appearance of the UI can be modified over time. Of course, you could achieve that yourself by setting up a timer, and modifying properties of UI elements each time the timer fires. But you can let the animation system do that work for you. A complete description of animation would fill a chapter, but Example 20-15 shows a typical example.

Example 20-15. An animation

```
<UserControl.Resources>
    <Storyboard x:Key="ellipseAnimation">
        <DoubleAnimation
                    From="50" To="100"
                    AutoReverse="True" RepeatBehavior="Forever"
                    Storyboard.TargetName="animatedEllipse"
                    Storyboard.TargetProperty="Width" />
    </Storyboard>
</UserControl.Resources>
```

Animations are separate objects from the things they animate, and typically live in a `Resources` section—all elements have a `Resources` property which is a handy place to put useful objects. It's just a dictionary—a name/value collection—a specialized dictionary similar to those of the kind described in Chapter 9. This particular example would appear as a child of the `UserControl` at the root of the user interface.

While this is a simple example, it illustrates all the important points. The whole thing is contained in a `Storyboard`—this is a collection of animations. Animations are always defined in storyboards, as this enables you to target multiple properties, or perhaps orchestrate a sequence of different animations over time. This example is simple and contains just a single animation, but we're still required to put it in a `Storyboard`.

The animation itself has a `From` and a `To` value specifying the range of values the property will span during the animation—these are numbers because this is a `DoubleAnimation` (as in the `System.Double` floating-point type); if this were a `ColorAnimation` you'd see color values in there instead. The `AutoReverse` and `RepeatBehavior` properties here indicate that this animation runs back and forth indefinitely. And the final two properties indicate the element and property to be animated. So somewhere in the Xaml we'd expect to find an element with the name indicated, for example:

```
<Ellipse x:Name="animatedEllipse"
        Fill="Blue" />
```

Something needs to kick the animation off. In the code behind, you'd extract the animation from the resources and start it like this:

```
Storyboard anim = (Storyboard) Resources["ellipseAnimation"];
anim.Begin();
```

There are other ways to start animations. WPF supports *triggers*, which let you place instructions in Xaml that certain animations should be run when specific things happen. So you could tie an animation to the raising of a `MouseEnter` event, for example, or run an animation when the value of a property changes. You can do something similar in Silverlight using *behaviors*, which make it easy to define a variety of UI responses (such as running animations) with Expression Blend. Both WPF and Silverlight also support automatic running of animations in control templates, as we'll see later.

3D graphics

WPF has basic support for 3D graphics, but that's a topic that would take a whole chapter to cover in itself, so we won't be getting into that in this book. Silverlight doesn't have WPF's 3D features, but it does have some very limited support for 3D in the form of special transforms. Besides the `RenderTransform` we saw earlier, you can set an element's `Projection` property to make it look like it has been rotated in 3D, including perspective effects you can't get with a 2D affine transform. This falls short of the full 3D models you can create in WPF, but provides the bare bones required to build up 3D aspects to the user interface.

Layout and graphical services are necessary to render things on-screen, but most applications require something a little more high-level—standard elements the user can interact with. So WPF and Silverlight provide controls.

Controls

Silverlight and WPF offer a range of controls, similar to many of the common controls you find in typical Windows applications. For example, there are buttons—`CheckBox` and `RadioButton` for selection, `Button` for a basic pushbutton, and `HyperlinkButton` for when you want to make your button look like a hyperlink. There's also `RepeatButton`, which looks like a normal button but repeatedly raises click events for as long as you hold the button down.

For the most part, these work in a very straightforward fashion—you already saw how to handle the `Click` event, in Example 20-2 and Example 20-3. And as you'd expect, the two selection buttons offer events called `Checked` and `Unchecked` to notify you when they're toggled, and an `IsChecked` property to represent the state. However, there is one potentially surprising feature that buttons inherit from their `ContentControl` base class.

Content controls

Many controls have some sort of caption—buttons usually contain text; tab pages have a header label. You might expect these controls to offer a property of type `string` to hold that caption, but if you look at the `Content` property of a `Button` or the `Header` of a `TabItem`, you'll see that these properties are of type `object`. You can put text in there, but you don't have to. Example 20-16 shows an alternative.

Example 20-16. Button with Ellipse as content

```
<Button>
  <Button.Content>
    <Ellipse Fill="Green" Width="100" Height="50" />
  </Button.Content>
</Button>
```

In fact, you don't need to write that `<Button.Content>` property element—the base `ContentControl` class is marked with a `[ContentProperty("Content")]` attribute, which tells the Xaml compiler to treat elements that appear inside the element as the value of the `Content` property. So Example 20-16 is equivalent to this:

```
<Button>
  <Ellipse Fill="Green" Width="100" Height="50" />
</Button>
```

This creates a button with a green ellipse as its content. Or you can get more ambitious and put a panel in there:

```
<Button>
  <StackPanel Orientation="Horizontal">
    <Ellipse Fill="Green" Width="100" Height="50" />
    <TextBlock Text="Click me!" FontSize="45" />
    <Ellipse Fill="Green" Width="100" Height="50" />
  </StackPanel>
</Button>
```

Figure 20-11 shows the results. Content controls let you go completely crazy—there's nothing stopping you from putting buttons inside buttons inside tab controls inside listbox items inside more buttons. Just because you can doesn't mean you should, of course—this would be a terrible design for a user interface. The point is that you're free to put any kind of content in a content control.

Figure 20-11. Button with mixed content

Some controls can contain multiple pieces of content. For example, a `TabItem` has a `Content` property which holds the main body of the tab page, and also a `Header` property for the tab caption. Both properties accept any kind of content. And then the items controls take this a step further.

Items controls

`ItemsControl` is the base class of controls that display multiple items, such as `ListBox`, `ComboBox`, and `TreeView`. If you add children to these controls, each child can be an arbitrary piece of content, much like a button's content but with as many children as you like. Example 20-17 adds various elements to a `ListBox`.

Example 20-17. ListBox with mixed content

```
<ListBox>

    <StackPanel Orientation="Horizontal">
```

```
            <Ellipse Fill="Green" Width="100" Height="50" />
            <TextBlock Text="Text and graphics" FontSize="45" />
            <Ellipse Fill="Green" Width="100" Height="50" />
        </StackPanel>

        <Button Content="Button" />

        <TextBox Text="Editable" />

</ListBox>
```

Figure 20-12 shows the results. As well as showing the content we provided, the ListBox provides the usual visual responses to mouse input—the item underneath the mouse has a slightly darker background than the item below to indicate that it can be selected. The item at the bottom is darker still because it is currently selected. These highlights come from the *item container*—all items controls generate an item container for each child. A ListBox will generate ListBoxItem containers; TreeView generates TreeViewItem objects, and so on.

Figure 20-12. ListBox with mixed content

Sometimes it's useful to bring your own container, because you may need to do more than populate it with a single piece of content. For example, when building a tree view, you don't just need to set the node caption; you may also want to add child nodes. Example 20-18 explicitly creates TreeViewItem containers to define a tree structure.

Example 20-18. Explicit TreeViewItem containers

```
<ctl:TreeView>
    <ctl:TreeViewItem>
        <ctl:TreeViewItem.Header>
            <StackPanel Orientation="Horizontal">
                <Ellipse Fill="Green" Width="100" Height="50" />
                <TextBlock Text="Content" FontSize="45" />
                <Ellipse Fill="Green" Width="100" Height="50" />
            </StackPanel>
        </ctl:TreeViewItem.Header>

        <ctl:TreeViewItem Header="Child A" />
        <ctl:TreeViewItem Header="Child B" />
    </ctl:TreeViewItem>
```

```
<ctl:TreeViewItem>
    <ctl:TreeViewItem.Header>
        <Button Content="Button" />
    </ctl:TreeViewItem.Header>

    <ctl:TreeViewItem Header="Child 1" />
    <ctl:TreeViewItem Header="Child 2" />
    <ctl:TreeViewItem>
        <ctl:TreeViewItem.Header>
            <Button Content="Child 3" />
        </ctl:TreeViewItem.Header>
    </ctl:TreeViewItem>
</ctl:TreeViewItem>

<ctl:TreeViewItem>
    <ctl:TreeViewItem.Header>
        <TextBox Text="Editable" />
    </ctl:TreeViewItem.Header>
</ctl:TreeViewItem>

</ctl:TreeView>
```

Notice the unusual `ctl:` prefix—see the sidebar on the next page for an explanation.

As you can see from Figure 20-13, each `Header` property value has ended up as the label for a single node in the tree. The parent-child relationship of the nodes is determined by the nesting of the `TreeViewItem` elements in the Xaml.

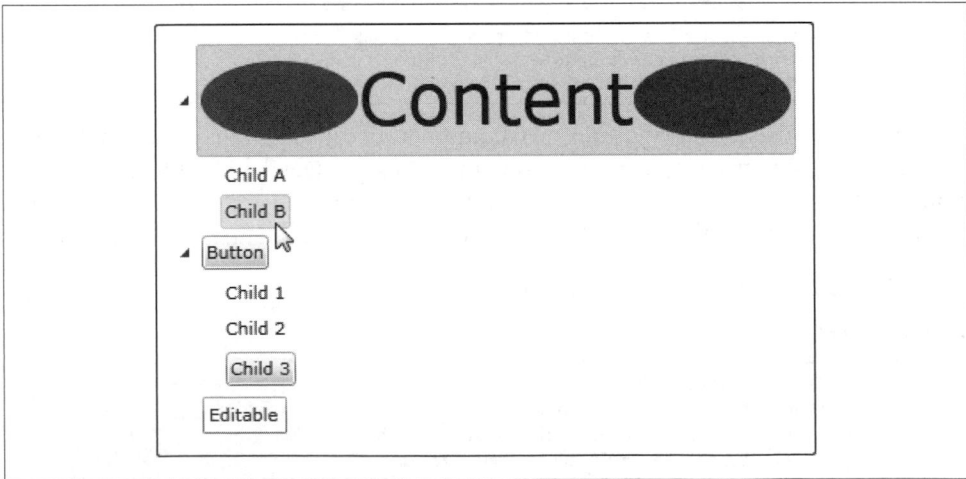

Figure 20-13. TreeView with content

Control Libraries and Xaml

Example 20-18 uses the `TreeView` control and its associated `TreeViewItem` container. These are not built into the main Silverlight plug-in. They are provided as part of the Silverlight SDK in a separate DLL called `System.Windows.Controls`, which ends up getting built into your Silverlight application. Unlike normal .NET applications, Silverlight applications are packaged into a ZIP file (usually given a file extension of *.xap*, which is pronounced "zap") so that multiple components and resources can be bundled into a single application. This file must include any control libraries—either those provided by Microsoft or third parties, or ones you've written.

To build a DLL into your Silverlight application package, you just add a reference to the DLL in Visual Studio in the usual way.

When using controls from libraries, you need to let the Xaml compiler know where it's supposed to find the control. So for Example 20-18 to work, something extra needs to go in the Xaml. The root element would contain an extra XML namespace declaration:

```
xmlns:ctl="clr-namespace:System.Windows.Controls;
assembly=System.Windows.Controls"
```

(That would normally be on one long line with no spaces—it has been split to fit on the page.)

This means that anytime we use an element whose name starts with the `ctl:` prefix, we're using a type defined in the `System.Windows.Controls` namespace, in the `System.Windows.Controls` DLL (or *assembly*, as .NET calls DLLs and EXEs).

While WPF uses the same XML namespace mechanism for control libraries, the `TreeView` is built into the main .NET Framework. So you can use it like any other element, and you don't need to add extra DLLs or XML namespace prefixes.

Microsoft provides a suite of extra controls for Silverlight in the Silverlight Toolkit, available from *http://www.codeplex.com/Silverlight*; at *http://www.codeplex.com/wpf* you'll find the WPF Toolkit, which offers some additional controls for WPF.

While you can add elements directly to items controls like this, it's often easier and more flexible to use data binding, so we'll be coming back to items controls later.

Because this chapter is just an introduction to Silverlight and WPF, we won't go through all the available controls in detail. There are simple data entry controls such as `TextBox`, `AutoCompleteBox`, `Slider`, and `DatePicker`. There are more comprehensive data-oriented controls such as `DataGrid` and `DataPager`. There are also utility controls such as the draggable `Thumb` and `GridSplitter`. But there's one more kind of control we need to look at: user controls.

User Controls

A *user control* is, as the name suggests, a user-defined control. In Silverlight, you'll have at least one of these—your whole user interface is one big user control, as you can see from the `<UserControl>` element at the root of your main page's Xaml. But you can create more. User controls are a useful way to manage complexity.

A problem that crops up a lot in big WPF and Silverlight projects—particularly the first such project any team works on—is the 10,000-line Xaml file. Visual Studio creates one Xaml file for your user interface, and the path of least resistance is to put everything in there. As you add graphical resources, templates, data sources, animations, styles, and all the other things you can put in Xaml, it can grow very large surprisingly quickly. And there's a related problem of having the entire application's functionality in the one code behind file. Such programs are not maintainable, so you need to split things up.

Instead of creating one big Xaml file, it's usually best to try to have as little as possible in your main page. It should typically do nothing more than define the overall layout, saying where each piece of the UI belongs. And then each part can go into its own user control. A user control is simply a Xaml file with some code behind. And since Xaml files with code behind always compile into classes, you can use them from other Xaml files—remember that Xaml is just a way to create objects. Example 20-19 shows the Xaml for an application's main UI that uses this approach.

Example 20-19. Main UI containing nothing but user controls

```
<UserControl
    x:Class="SlUcExample.MainPage"
    xmlns="http://schemas.microsoft.com/winfx/2006/xaml/presentation"
    xmlns:x="http://schemas.microsoft.com/winfx/2006/xaml"
    xmlns:app="clr-namespace:SlUcExample"
    xmlns:d="http://schemas.microsoft.com/expression/blend/2008"
    xmlns:mc="http://schemas.openxmlformats.org/markup-compatibility/2006"
    mc:Ignorable="d" d:DesignWidth="640" d:DesignHeight="480">

    <Grid x:Name="LayoutRoot">
        <Grid.RowDefinitions>
            <RowDefinition Height="Auto" />
            <RowDefinition />
        </Grid.RowDefinitions>

        <Grid.ColumnDefinitions>
            <ColumnDefinition />
            <ColumnDefinition />
        </Grid.ColumnDefinitions>

        <app:SearchBarView      Grid.Column="0" Grid.ColumnSpan="2" />
        <app:ProductListView    Grid.Column="0" Grid.Row="1" />
        <app:ProductDetailsView Grid.Column="1" Grid.Row="1" />

    </Grid>
</UserControl>
```

Notice that this example defines an XML namespace prefix, app, and tells the Xaml compiler that this refers to types in the SlUcExample namespace—the default project namespace for this particular example. This time we don't need the assembly= part because the user controls are defined as part of this project, not in a separate DLL. This prefix then refers to three user controls which would be defined elsewhere in the project.

Defining the user controls themselves is simple. You can add them as new items to your project in Visual Studio, and it will create a Xaml file with a corresponding code behind file, which you edit in exactly the same way as the main UI.

 As you can see in Example 20-19, we chose names that end in *View* for all the user controls. This is not mandatory, but it helps distinguish user control classes, which define appearance and superficial interactive behavior, from the other types that define the core behavior of your application. This distinction isn't useful if you plan to put everything into the code behind, of course, but we presume you have more refined software design sensibilities than that, and will want to ensure that each class in your application has a single, well-defined, reasonably narrow responsibility.

User controls can contain any other controls and elements, so you can use elements built into Silverlight as well as any control libraries you may have acquired. So user controls have a lot of flexibility. However, you don't necessarily have to build a user control anytime you want some custom UI—the scope for customization of built-in controls is greater than you might think, thanks to control templates.

Control Templates

As you already saw, controls are elements that have interactive behavior of some kind—buttons are clickable; you can type into text boxes; you can scroll through the items in a listbox and select them. What may not be obvious is that most controls *only* provide behavior. Controls do not define their own appearance.

This may appear to be a ludicrous claim. After all, if you add a Button to your user interface, you can see it. In fact, the appearance comes from a separate entity called a *template*. Controls have a default template, which is why something appears when you create a control, but this separation of appearance from behavior is important because you are free to replace the default template with your own. This lets you change the appearance of a control completely, without losing any of the behavior.

The behavior of controls is often surprisingly subtle and complex. You might think that a button is a pretty simple sort of thing, and that you could create your own equivalent by handling the MouseLeftButtonDown event on a shape. And while that would give you a clickable element, there's a lot missing. For example, there's the way buttons push down and pop back up. They should respond to keyboard input as well as mouse input.

They should be visible to accessibility tools so that users with visual or coordination issues can use your application. And a button is about as simple as it gets. If you've ever used a Flash application with, say, a scroll bar that just didn't feel like it was working properly you're already familiar with the hazards of trying to recreate basic controls from scratch. Fortunately, control templates mean you don't have to.

 Only controls have templates. So while types such as `Button` and `TextBox` have them, more primitive types such as shapes and `TextBlock` —UI elements that don't have any intrinsic behavior—don't. This shouldn't be too surprising; an `Ellipse` element's only job is to look like an `Ellipse`, so what would it mean for it to have a template? (And what element would you use inside the template to define the appearance? Another `Ellipse`? Where would it get its appearance from?)

The `Control` base class defines a `Template` property. To customize the appearance of a control, you simply set this property. As Example 20-20 shows, the property expects a `ControlTemplate` object, and then inside this, you can put any element you like to define the appearance. (You could, of course, use a panel if you wanted to build up a complex appearance with multiple elements.)

Example 20-20. Button with custom template

```
<Button Content="OK" FontSize="20">
    <Button.Template>
        <ControlTemplate TargetType="Button">
            <Border
                Background="LightBlue"
                BorderThickness="3"
                BorderBrush="Black"
                CornerRadius="10">

                <ContentPresenter
                    Margin="20"
                    Content="{TemplateBinding Content}"
                    HorizontalAlignment="Center"
                    VerticalAlignment="Center"
                    />

            </Border>
        </ControlTemplate>
    </Button.Template>
</Button>
```

Figure 20-14 shows the results. It's rather static—it doesn't offer a visual response to mouse activity yet, but we'll fix that later. But it will still raise the `Click` event when clicked, so it's functional, if rather dull. Notice that we've set the `Content` property of the button, and this content—the text "OK"—has appeared as you'd hope. That doesn't happen automatically; our template needs to say where the content should appear, and that's the purpose of the `ContentPresenter` in Example 20-20. Templates for content controls need one of these placeholders for the Content property to do anything. And if you're defining a template for a control that can hold multiple pieces of content—the Content and Header of a TabItem, for example—you need to provide a ContentPresenter for each.

Figure 20-14. Button with custom template

How does Silverlight (or WPF) know which placeholder corresponds to which property? Look at the Content property of the ContentPresenter in Example 20-20—its value has an unusual syntax. The attribute value is enclosed in braces, which indicates that we're not setting a literal value—in this case the TemplateBinding text signifies that we want to connect this particular property in this element in the template to a corresponding property of this template's control. So {TemplateBinding Content} connects this ContentPresenter to our Button element's Content property, while {TemplateBinding Header} would connect it to the Header property in a control that had such a property.

In fact, it's common to use many template bindings. Example 20-20 hardcodes a lot of features of the appearance into the template, but it's possible to reuse templates on several different controls, at which point you might want to retain the flexibility to change things such as the background color, border thickness, and so on, without needing to define a new template every time. Example 20-21 looks the same as Figure 20-14, but instead of hardcoding everything into the template it picks up more of the control's properties using template bindings.

Example 20-21. Template with less hardcoding

```
<Button Content="OK" Background="LightBlue">
  <Button.Template>
    <ControlTemplate TargetType="Button">
      <Border
          Background="{TemplateBinding Background}"
          BorderThickness="{TemplateBinding BorderThickness}"
          BorderBrush="{TemplateBinding BorderBrush}"
          CornerRadius="10">

        <ContentPresenter
            Margin="{TemplateBinding Padding}"
            Content="{TemplateBinding Content}"
            ContentTemplate="{TemplateBinding ContentTemplate}"
            HorizontalAlignment="{TemplateBinding HorizontalContentAlignment}"
            VerticalAlignment="{TemplateBinding HorizontalContentAlignment}"
            />
```

```
        </Border>
      </ControlTemplate>
    </Button.Template>
</Button>
```

This template is now looking like a candidate for reuse—we might want to apply this to lots of different buttons. The usual way to do this is to wrap it in a style.

Styles

A *style* is an object that defines a set of property values for a particular type of element. Since elements' appearances are defined entirely by their properties—`Template` is a property, remember—this means a style can define as much of a control's appearance as you like. It could be as simple as just setting some basic properties such as `FontFamily` and `Background`, or it could go as far as defining a template along with property values for every property that affects appearance. Example 20-22 sits between these two extremes—it puts the template from Example 20-21 into a style, along with settings for a few other properties.

Example 20-22. Button style

```
<UserControl.Resources>
  <Style x:Key="buttonStyle" TargetType="Button">
    <Setter Property="Background" Value="LightBlue" />
    <Setter Property="BorderBrush" Value="DarkBlue" />
    <Setter Property="BorderThickness" Value="3" />
    <Setter Property="FontSize" Value="20" />

    <Setter Property="Template">
      <Setter.Value>
        <ControlTemplate TargetType="Button">
          <Border
           Background="{TemplateBinding Background}"
           BorderThickness="{TemplateBinding BorderThickness}"
           BorderBrush="{TemplateBinding BorderBrush}"
           CornerRadius="10">

            <ContentPresenter
             Margin="{TemplateBinding Padding}"
             Content="{TemplateBinding Content}"
             ContentTemplate="{TemplateBinding ContentTemplate}"
             HorizontalAlignment="{TemplateBinding HorizontalContentAlignment}"
             VerticalAlignment="{TemplateBinding HorizontalContentAlignment}"
             />

          </Border>
        </ControlTemplate>
      </Setter.Value>
    </Setter>
```

```
        </Style>
    </UserControl.Resources>
```

Notice that the style is inside a **Resources** section—remember that all elements have a **Resources** property, which is a dictionary that can hold useful objects such as styles. We can then apply the style to an element like so:

```
<Button Content="OK" Style="{StaticResource buttonStyle}" />
```

This will pick up all the properties from the style. Again notice the use of braces in the attribute value—this signifies that we're using a *markup extension*, which is a type that works out at runtime how to set the property's real value. We already saw the **TemplateBinding** markup extension, and now we're using **StaticResource**, which looks up an entry in a resource dictionary.

 Unlike the **Template** property, which is available only on controls, the **Style** property is defined by **FrameworkElement**, so it's available on all kinds of elements.

By the way, an element that uses a style is free to override any of the properties the style sets, as shown in Example 20-23.

Example 20-23. Overriding a style property

```
<Button Content="OK" Style="{StaticResource buttonStyle}"
        Background="Yellow" />
```

Properties set directly on the element override properties from the style. This is why it's important to use **TemplateBinding** in templates. The style in Example 20-22 sets a default **Background** color of **LightBlue**, and the template then picks that up with a **TemplateBinding**, which means that when Example 20-23 sets the background to yellow, the control template picks up the new color—that wouldn't have happened if the light blue background had been baked directly into the template. So the combination of styles, templates, and template bindings makes it possible to create a complete look for a control while retaining the flexibility to change individual aspects of that look on a control-by-control basis.

There's one problem with our button style: it's rather static. It doesn't offer any visible response to mouse input. Most controls light up when the mouse cursor moves over them if they are able to respond to input, and the fact that our control doesn't is likely to make users think either that the application has crashed or that the button is merely decorative. We need to fix this.

The Visual State Manager

A control template can include a set of instructions describing how its appearance should change as the control changes its state. These are added with an attachable property called VisualStateGroups, defined by the VisualStateManager class.[‖] Example 20-24 shows a modified version of the template that adds this attachable property.

Example 20-24. Control template with visual state transitions

```
<ControlTemplate TargetType="Button">
    <Border x:Name="background"
      Background="{TemplateBinding Background}"
      BorderThickness="{TemplateBinding BorderThickness}"
      BorderBrush="{TemplateBinding BorderBrush}"
      CornerRadius="10">

        <VisualStateManager.VisualStateGroups>
            <VisualStateGroup x:Name="CommonStates">
                <VisualState x:Name="MouseOver">
                    <Storyboard>
                        <ColorAnimation Storyboard.TargetName="background"
                            Storyboard.TargetProperty="(Border.Background).
                                                      (SolidColorBrush.Color)"
                            To="Red" Duration="0:0:0.5" />
                    </Storyboard>
                </VisualState>
                <VisualState x:Name="Normal">
                    <Storyboard>
                        <ColorAnimation Storyboard.TargetName="background"
                            Storyboard.TargetProperty="(Border.Background).
                                                      (SolidColorBrush.Color)"
                            Duration="0:0:0.5" />
                    </Storyboard>
                </VisualState>
            </VisualStateGroup>

        </VisualStateManager.VisualStateGroups>

        <ContentPresenter
            Margin="{TemplateBinding Padding}"
            Content="{TemplateBinding Content}"
            ContentTemplate="{TemplateBinding ContentTemplate}"
            HorizontalAlignment="{TemplateBinding HorizontalContentAlignment}"
            VerticalAlignment="{TemplateBinding HorizontalContentAlignment}"
            />

    </Border>
</ControlTemplate>
```

‖ This class was originally unique to Silverlight. It was added later to WPF in .NET 4. WPF has an older mechanism called *triggers* that can also be used to get the same results. Triggers are more complex, but are also more powerful. Silverlight does not currently offer them.

The `VisualStateGroups` property contains one or more `VisualStateGroup` elements—the groups you can add in here are determined by the control. `Button` defines two groups: `CommonStates` and `FocusStates`. Each group defines some aspect of the control's state that can vary independently of the other groups. For example, `FocusStates` defines a `Focused` and an `Unfocused` state based on whether the button has the keyboard focus. The `CommonStates` group defines `Normal`, `MouseOver`, `Pressed`, and `Disabled` states—the control can be in only one of those four states at any time, but whether it's focused is independent of whether the mouse cursor is over it, hence the use of different groups. (The groups aren't wholly independent—a disabled button cannot acquire the focus, for example. But you see multiple state groups anytime there's at least some degree of independence.)

Example 20-24 defines behaviors for when the button enters the `MouseOver` state and the `Normal` state, with a `VisualState` for each. These define the animations to run when the state is entered. In this example, both animations target the `Border` element's `Background`. The first animation fades the background to red when the mouse enters, and the second animates it back to its original color when the state returns to normal. (The absence of a `To` property on the second animation causes the property to animate back to its base value.)

 Visual state transitions typically end up being very verbose—the only way to modify properties is with animations, even if you want the changes to happen instantaneously, so even a simple change requires a lot of markup. And you will typically want to provide transitions for all of the states. In practice, you would normally create them interactively in Expression Blend, which will add all the necessary Xaml for you.

So far, everything we've looked at has been strictly about the visible bits, but any real application needs to connect the frontend up to real data. To help with this, WPF and Silverlight offer data binding.

Data Binding

Data binding lets you connect properties of any .NET object to properties of user interface elements. The syntax looks pretty similar to template binding. Example 20-25 shows a simple form with a couple of text entry fields, both using data binding to hook up to a source object.

Example 20-25. Data entry with data binding

```
<Grid>
    <Grid.ColumnDefinitions>
        <ColumnDefinition Width="Auto" />
        <ColumnDefinition />
    </Grid.ColumnDefinitions>
```

```
<Grid.RowDefinitions>
    <RowDefinition Height="Auto" />
    <RowDefinition Height="Auto" />
</Grid.RowDefinitions>

<TextBlock VerticalAlignment="Center" Text="Name:" />
<TextBox Grid.Column="1"
        Text="{Binding Path=Name}" />

<TextBlock VerticalAlignment="Center" Grid.Row="1" Text="Age:" />
<TextBox Grid.Column="1" Grid.Row="1"
        Text="{Binding Path=Age}" />
</Grid>
```

Just as template bindings refer to properties on the target control, so these data binding expressions refer to properties on some source object. Data sources don't need to be anything special—Example 20-26 shows an extremely simple class that will work just fine as the data source for Example 20-25.

Example 20-26. A very simple data source

```
public class Person
{
    public string Name { get; set; }
    public double Age { get; set; }
}
```

The code behind can create an instance of this type, and then make it available to the binding expressions in our user interface by putting it in the `DataContext` property as Example 20-27 shows.

Example 20-27. Setting up a data source

```
public partial class MainPage : UserControl
{
    private Person source = new Person { Name = "Ian", Age = 36 };

    public MainPage()
    {
        InitializeComponent();

        this.DataContext = source;
    }
}
```

As you can see from Figure 20-15, the UI displays the two properties from the source object thanks to data binding. This may not seem any more convenient than just writing code to set the `Text` properties of the two `TextBox` elements directly, but data binding can do a little more than that. When the user types new values into the text boxes, the source `Person` object's properties get updated with those new values. If we were to modify the `Person` class to implement the `INotifyPropertyChanged` interface—a common way to provide notification events anytime a property changes—data binding would detect changes in the data source and update the UI automatically.

Arguably the most important benefit of this kind of data binding is that it provides an opportunity to separate your application logic from your UI code. Notice that our `Person` class doesn't need to know anything about the user interface, and yet the data it holds is connected to the UI. It's much easier to write unit tests for classes that don't require a user interface simply to run.

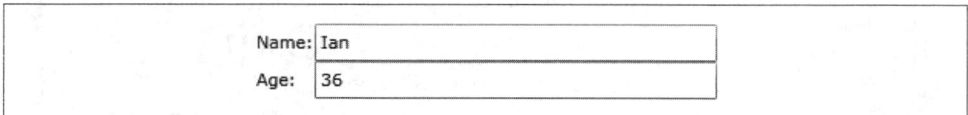

Figure 20-15. Data-bound text boxes

A classic rookie mistake with WPF and Silverlight is to write code that relies too much on UI elements—an example would be to use `TextBox` elements as the place you store your data. That might seem like a simplifying step—why add a class to remember the `Name` and `Age` when the UI can remember them for us? But that would mean any code that needed to access that data would have to read it out of the UI elements. This causes two problems: first, it makes it hard to change anything in the user interface without breaking the whole program, and second, it makes it impossible to test any individual part of the program in isolation. So while the separation illustrated with this example may seem excessive, for any nontrivial application it turns out to be very useful to keep the UI code completely separate from the rest of the code, hooking things together only via data binding. This tends to lead to code that is much easier to maintain than programs where a lot of the code deals directly with user interface elements.

Example 20-25 uses just a couple of ad hoc binding expressions in a user interface, but there's a slightly more structured and very powerful data binding feature you can use with item controls: data templates.

Data Templates

Just as a control's appearance is defined by a control template, you can create a *data template* to define the appearance of a particular data type. Look at the user interface in Figure 20-16—it shows a pair of listboxes, in a typical master/details scenario.

The `ListBox` on the left looks fairly ordinary—it lists product categories, showing each one as simple text. You might think this works by fetching the list of categories and then iterating over them with a loop that creates a `ListBoxItem` for each one. In fact, it's much simpler than that. Example 20-28 shows the Xaml for the `ListBox` on the left.

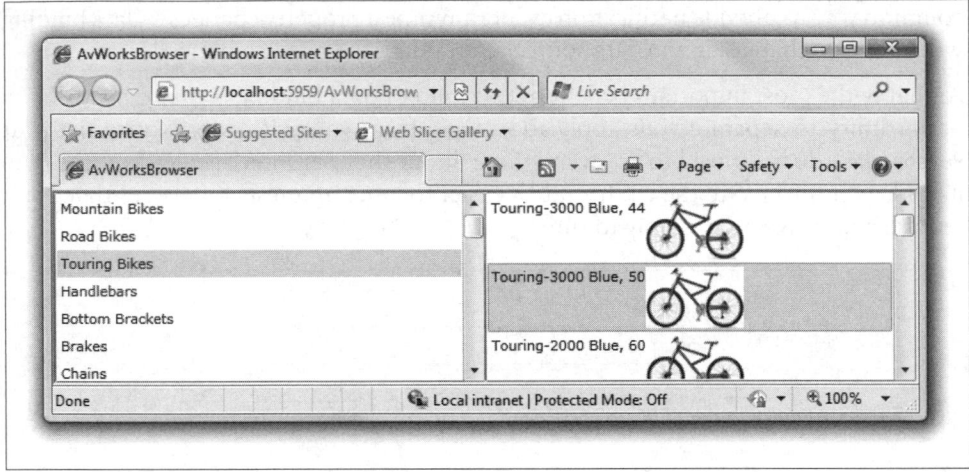

Figure 20-16. Lists with data templates

This application is using the Adventure Works sample database introduced in Chapter 14, which the hosting web application is making available to the Silverlight client with a combination of the WCF Data Services mechanism described in the same chapter, and some of the networking features described in Chapter 13. The precise details of the server code are not directly relevant to this chapter, but you can get the code by downloading the samples from this book's web page: *http://oreilly.com/catalog/9780596159832/*.

Example 20-28. ListBox displaying simple text

```
<ListBox x:Name="categoryList" DisplayMemberPath="DisplayName"
        SelectionChanged="categoryList_SelectionChanged">
```

Example 20-29 shows the code that puts the categories into it.

Example 20-29. Providing items for a listbox

```
categoryList.ItemsSource = categoryViewModels;
```

Obviously, we left out some code—that `categoryViewModels` variable, which contains a list of objects each representing a category, had to come from somewhere. But right now we're focusing on how the data gets hooked up to the UI, not where it came from, so to avoid distracting you with details irrelevant to this chapter's topic, we're just showing the code that deals with the UI aspects. And as you can see, it's really very simple. `ListBox` derives from `ItemsControl`, from which it inherits an `ItemsSource` property, and you can assign any collection into `ItemsSource`. The control will iterate through the collection for you, generating an item container (a `ListBoxItem` in this case) for every object.

The Xaml sets the `DisplayMemberPath` attribute to `DisplayName`—this determines which property on the source object the `ListBoxItem` reads to work out what text to display for the object. And that's why the lefthand list displays the category names. But clearly the list on the righthand side of Figure 20-16 is much more interesting. It shows all the products for the currently selected category, but it's not just displaying text—it's showing an image for each product. The product list is updated when we select a category, and Example 20-30 shows the code that handles the `SelectionChanged` event of the category `ListBox`, which was hooked up in Example 20-28.

Example 20-30. Loading the selected category's products

```
private void categoryList_SelectionChanged(object sender,
                      SelectionChangedEventArgs e)
{
    CategoryViewModel currentCategory =
        categoryList.SelectedItem as CategoryViewModel;
    if (currentCategory == null)
    {
        productList.ItemsSource = null;
    }
    else
    {
        productList.ItemsSource = currentCategory.Products;
    }
}
```

View Models and Details

While we don't want to distract you from the data binding details too much, there are a couple of points about the data sources in Example 20-30 that are worth being aware of. First, you'll have noticed the term *view model* cropping up in the names. This is a common name for a class that is not part of the view—it contains no UI code—but which is designed to be a data source for a particular view. We rarely data-bind directly to underlying domain model objects, because user interfaces usually introduce view-specific state and logic that does not belong in the domain model. We want to be able to test this logic easily, so we don't want to bake it into the view code. We therefore add a layer between the view and the model, sometimes called the *view model* layer. You'll also sometimes see this approach described as *separated presentation*.

Second, you might be wondering why the `ListBox` can't handle master/detail binding on its own, without us needing to add an event handler. Actually it can, but in this particular application, we don't necessarily have all the details up front—we might want to fetch a product list for a category on demand, rather than making the user wait until the whole lot has been fetched before showing anything. In these situations, testing is often easier if you add explicit event handlers so that you know exactly when child data is going to be fetched. In the experience of the authors, supposedly clever code that implicitly relies on obscure tricks to get data binding to do the work in these situations is usually more trouble than it's worth.

This has some code to deal with the fact that we sometimes get a `SelectionChanged` event to notify us that nothing at all is selected. But the interesting code here looks much the same as before—once again we're just setting the `ItemsSource` of a `ListBox` (the one on the right this time) to a collection of objects, the products in the selected category.

Example 20-30 sets the `ItemsSource` in much the same way as Example 20-29, but the two listboxes—on the left and right of Figure 20-16—look very different. That's because the Xaml for the second listbox is different:

```
<ListBox
    x:Name="productList"
    Grid.Column="1">
    <ListBox.ItemTemplate>
        <DataTemplate>
            <Grid>
                <Grid.ColumnDefinitions>
                    <ColumnDefinition />
                    <ColumnDefinition />

                </Grid.ColumnDefinitions>

                <TextBlock Text="{Binding Path=DisplayName}" />
                <Image Grid.Column="1" Source="{Binding Path=Thumbnail}" />
            </Grid>
        </DataTemplate>
    </ListBox.ItemTemplate>
</ListBox>
```

Instead of using `DisplayMemberPath` to specify what text to display, this sets the `ItemTemplate`, which does for an items control's data items roughly what a control's `Template` property does for the whole control—it defines the appearance. For each item in the `ItemsSource`, an instance of that `DataTemplate` will be created, with its `DataContext` set to the source item in question. So those two `Binding` expressions will pick up the `Text` property for the `TextBlock` and the `Thumbnail` property for the `Image` from the data source object for the product.

 The fact that our source object provides a `Thumbnail` property is a good example of why we need a *view model* class that's distinct from the *model*. The underlying model may well offer the bitmap—indeed, in this example, there is a model object (not shown, but available for download) with a property containing the raw binary data for the bitmap. And while WPF can automatically convert a byte array to the `Image` `Source` type the `Image` element requires, Silverlight cannot, and it becomes the job of the view model to transform the data into a suitable data type. So although the view model has no dependencies on the view code itself, it provides data tailored specifically for the view, even to the point of offering properties with types specific to WPF or Silverlight.

There is a connection between data templates and content controls: any content control is able to load a data template. (In fact, the heart of the mechanism is the `ContentPresenter` type that appears in any content control's template, as you saw in Example 20-20. This is the element that knows how to load a data template.) The reason items controls are able to instantiate a data template for each item is that the item containers (`ListBoxItem`, `TreeViewItem`, etc.) are content controls. So you can use data templates in all sorts of places—for the content of buttons, the headers and contents of tab controls, the labels on tree views, and so on. Just as items controls offer an `ItemTemplate` property, you'll find similar `ContentTemplate` and `HeaderTemplate` properties that also accept data templates.

Summary

In this chapter, we discussed how you can build the structure of a user interface with Xaml, and how the associated code behind file can handle events and provide the UI elements with the information they need to perform their work. You saw some of the more important control types, and in particular, you looked at the content controls that can contain anything you like as content. You also saw how to connect your application's data to the screen with data binding.

CHAPTER 21

Programming ASP.NET Applications

Developers are writing more and more of their applications to run over the Web and to be seen in a browser. As we saw in Chapter 20, Silverlight lets you write C# code to run on the client side in the web browser. As for the server side of a web application, the .NET Framework offers ASP.NET.

The focus of this chapter is to illustrate where ASP.NET and C# programming intersect when using Web Forms. ASP.NET is a huge topic, and for intensive coverage of ASP.NET, please see either *Programming ASP.NET 3.5*, Fourth Edition (*http://oreilly.com/catalog/9780596529567/*) by Jesse Liberty, Dan Maharry, and Dan Hurwitz, or *Learning ASP.NET 3.5*, Second Edition (*http://oreilly.com/catalog/9780596518462/*) by Jesse Liberty, Dan Hurwitz, and Brian MacDonald (both published by O'Reilly).

Web Forms Fundamentals

Web Forms brings Rapid Application Development (RAD) to the creation of web applications. From within Visual Studio or Visual Web Developer, you drag-and-drop controls onto a form and write the supporting code in *code-behind* pages. The application is deployed to a web server (typically IIS, which is shipped with most versions of Windows, and Cassini, which is built into Visual Studio for testing your application), and users interact with the application through a standard browser.

> ASP.NET supports other models besides Web Forms. You can work directly at the HTTP level, for example. And .NET 4 introduces a new model called *MVC* (which stands for Model View Controller). MVC is more complex, but is ultimately more powerful and flexible, making it a good choice for more complex web applications. Since this is not an ASP.NET-specific book, we will look only at the simpler, RAD-based Web Forms model.

Web Forms offers a programming model in which web pages are dynamically generated on a web server for delivery to a browser over the Internet. With Web Forms, you can create an ASPX page consisting of HTML and web controls, and you write C# code to respond to user actions and add additional dynamic content. The C# code *runs on the server*, and the data your code produces is integrated with the controls on your page to create an HTML page that is sent to the browser.

You should pick up the following three critical points from the preceding paragraph and keep them in mind for this entire chapter:

- Web pages can have both HTML and web controls (described later).
- ASP.NET processing happens on the server in managed code. (You can, of course, use ASP.NET in conjunction with AJAX or Silverlight if you want client-side code.)
- ASP.NET controls produce standard HTML for the browser.

A web form divides the user interface into two parts: the visual part or user interface (UI), and the logic that lies behind it. This is called *code separation*; and it is a good thing.

The UI for an ASP.NET page is stored in a file with the extension *.aspx*. When you run the form, the server generates HTML that it sends to the client browser. This code uses the rich Web Forms types found in the `System.Web` and `System.Web.UI` namespaces of the .NET FCL.

With Visual Studio, Web Forms programming couldn't be simpler: open a form, drag some controls onto it, and write the code to handle events. Presto! You've written a web application.

On the other hand, even with Visual Studio, writing a robust and complete web application can be a daunting task. Web forms offer a very rich UI; the number and complexity of web controls have greatly multiplied in recent years, and user expectations about the look and feel of web applications have risen accordingly.

In addition, web applications are inherently distributed. Typically, the client will not be in the same building as the server. For most web applications, you must take network latency, bandwidth, and network server performance into account when creating the UI; a round trip from client to host might take a few seconds.

 To simplify this discussion, and to keep the focus on C#, we'll ignore client-side processing for the rest of this chapter, and focus on server-side ASP.NET controls.

Web Forms Events

Web forms are event-driven. An *event* represents the idea that "something happened" (see Chapter 5 for a full discussion of events).

An event is raised when the user clicks a button, or selects from a listbox, or otherwise interacts with the UI. Of course, in web applications these user interactions happen on the client's machine in the web browser, but ASP.NET events are handled on the server.

For this to work, user interactions require a round trip—the browser needs to send a message to the server, and the server needs to respond to handle the event completely. This can take a while, so our hands are somewhat tied compared to classic Windows application event handling—it's just not practical for ASP.NET to offer server-side event handlers for things like mouse move events. So ASP.NET offers only a limited set of events, such as button clicks and text changes. These are events that the user might expect to cause a significant change, and for which it's reasonable to perform a round trip to the server.

Postback versus nonpostback events

Postback events are those that cause the form to be posted back to the server immediately. These include click-type events, such as the button `Click` event. In contrast, many events are considered *nonpostback*, meaning that the form isn't posted back to the server immediately.

 You can force controls with nonpostback events to behave in a postback manner by setting their `AutoPostBack` property to `true`.

Nonpostback events are raised at the point at which ASP.NET discovers it needs to raise them, which may be some considerable time after the user performed the actions to which the events relate. For example, the `TextBox` web control has a `TextChanged` event. You wouldn't expect a web page to submit a form automatically the moment you typed into a text box, and so this is a nonpostback event. If the user fills in several text fields in a form, the server knows nothing about that—this change in state happens on the client side, and it's only when the user clicks a button to submit the form that ASP.NET discovers the changes. So this is when it will raise `TextChanged` events for all the text boxes that changed. Consequently, you can expect to see multiple events during the handling of a single submission.

View state

Users tend to expect controls in user interfaces to remember their state—it's disconcerting when text boxes lose their content, or listboxes forget which item was selected. Sadly, the Web is inherently a "stateless" environment.[*] This means that every post to the server loses the state from previous posts, unless the developer takes great pains to preserve this session knowledge. The Web is rife with sites where you fill in a form, only for it to lose all of your data if anything goes wrong. Developers have to do a lot of extra work to prevent this. ASP.NET, however, provides support for maintaining some of the state automatically.

---

[*] There are good architectural reasons for this, but it's bad for usability.

Whenever a web form is posted to the server, the server re-creates it from scratch before it is returned to the browser. ASP.NET provides a mechanism that automatically maintains state for server controls (ViewState). Thus, if you provide a list and the user has made a selection, that selection is preserved after the page is posted back to the server and redrawn on the client.

Web Forms Life Cycle

Every request for a page made to a web server causes a chain of events at the server. These events, from beginning to end, constitute the *life cycle* of the page and all its components. The life cycle begins with a request for the page, which causes the server to load it. When the request is complete, the page is unloaded. From one end of the life cycle to the other, the goal is to render appropriate HTML output back to the requesting browser.

 Since ASP.NET is a server-side technology, its view of the lifetime of the page is quite different from the user's view. By the time the user sees the page, the server has already finished with it. Once the HTML has reached the browser, you can switch off and unplug the web server and the user will be none the wiser for as long as she's looking at that page.

The life cycle of a page is marked by the following events. ASP.NET performs specific processing at each stage, but you can attach handlers to any of these events to perform additional work:

Initialize
> Initialize is the first phase in the life cycle for any page or control. It is here that any settings needed for the duration of the incoming request are initialized.

Load ViewState
> The ViewState property is populated. The ViewState lives in a hidden input tag in the HTML—when ASP.NET first renders a page, it generates this field, and uses it to persist the state across round trips to the server. The input string from this hidden variable is parsed by the page framework, and the ViewState property is set. This allows ASP.NET to manage the state of your control across page loads so that each control isn't reset to its default state each time the page is posted.

Process Postback Data
> During this phase, the data sent to the server in the posting is processed.

Load
> CreateChildControls() is called, which creates and initializes server controls in the control tree. State is restored, and the form controls contain client-side data.

Send Postback Change Modifications
> If there are any state changes between the current state and the previous state, change events are raised via the RaisePostDataChangedEvent() method.

Handle Postback Events
> The client-side event that caused the postback is handled.

PreRender
> This is your last chance to modify control properties prior to rendering. (In web forms, "rendering" means generating the HTML that will eventually be sent to the browser.)

Save State
> Near the beginning of the life cycle, the persisted view state was loaded from the hidden variable. Now it is saved back to the hidden variable, persisting as a string object that will complete the round trip to the client.

Render
> This is where the output to be sent back to the client browser is generated.

Dispose
> This is the last phase of the life cycle. It gives you an opportunity to do any final cleanup and release references to any expensive resources, such as database connections.

Creating a Web Application

Visual Studio offers two ways to build ASP.NET applications. This isn't just a case of two different menu items for the same feature—the two options work quite differently in ways Visual Studio doesn't make especially obvious at the point where you make the decision. You can use the New Project dialog, which offers various ASP.NET project templates under the Visual C#→Web section, which produce various kinds of *web application projects*. Alternatively, you can choose File→New→Web Site from the main menu, and this lets you create various kinds of *website projects*. Web application projects are fully fledged Visual Studio projects that are built in much the same way as other kinds of projects such as libraries, console applications, or WPF applications. Website projects are somewhat more lightweight—there's no *.csproj* file to represent the project, nor do you need to build the project; your project consists of nothing but source files and you end up copying these to the web server. For this chapter, we'll use a web application project because it's the most similar to all the other project types we've looked at in this book.

To create the simple web form that we will use in the next example, start up Visual Studio .NET and select File→New→Project. In the New Project dialog, select the Visual C#→Web templates and choose ASP.NET Empty Web Application from the templates.

As the template name suggests, Visual Studio creates a web application with no pages. It contains a *Web.config* file to hold website configuration settings, but nothing else. To add a web form, select Project→Add New Item and choose Visual C#→Web from the templates list on the left. Select the Web Form template, and call it *Hello-Web.aspx*. Visual Studio creates a *HelloWeb.aspx.cs* code-behind file as part of the web form, which you can see by expanding the *HelloWeb.aspx* file in the Solution Explorer. (You'll also see a *HelloWeb.aspx.designer.cs* file which is where Visual Studio puts any code it needs to generate automatically. Don't put any of your own code in there, because Visual Studio deletes and rebuilds that file anytime it needs to change the generated code.)

Code-Behind Files

Let's take a closer look at the *.aspx* and code-behind files that Visual Studio created. Look at the HTML view of *HelloWeb.aspx*. (When you edit an *.aspx* file, Visual Studio can show three different views. The default view is the "Source" view, which shows the raw HTML. There are three buttons at the bottom left of the editor that let you switch between a "Design" view, which shows the content with the layout and design it will have in the browser, the "Source" view, which shows the raw HTML, or a "Split" view which shows both.) You can see that a form has been specified in the body of the page using the standard HTML form tag:

```
<form id="form1" runat="server">
```

ASP.NET web forms require you to have at least one form element to manage the user interaction, so Visual Studio creates one when you add a new *.aspx* page. The attribute `runat="server"` is the key to the server-side magic. Any tag that includes this attribute is considered a server-side control to be executed by the ASP.NET Framework on the server.

 Although the form tag is standard HTML, the runat attribute is not. But ASP.NET removes that attribute from the page before sending it to the browser. The attribute only has any meaning on the server side.

Within the form, Visual Studio provides an opening and closing pair of div tags to give you somewhere to put your controls and text.

Having created an empty web form, the first thing you might want to do is add some text to the page. By switching to the Source view, you can add script and HTML directly to the file. For example, we can add content to the div element in the body segment of the *.aspx* page, as the highlighted line in Example 21-1 shows.

Example 21-1. Adding HTML content

```
<%@ Page Language="C#" AutoEventWireup="true"  CodeFile="HelloWeb.aspx.cs"
Inherits="ProgrammingCSharpWeb.HelloWeb" %>

<!DOCTYPE html PUBLIC "-//W3C//DTD XHTML 1.0 Transitional//EN"
"http://www.w3.org/TR/xhtml1/DTD/xhtml1-transitional.dtd">

<html xmlns="http://www.w3.org/1999/xhtml">
<head runat="server">
```

```
    <title></title>
</head>
<body>
    <form id="form1" runat="server">
    <div>
      Hello World! It is now <%= DateTime.Now.ToString() %>
    </div>
    </form>
</body>
</html>
```

This will cause it to display a greeting and the current local time:

```
Hello World! It is now 4/4/2010 5:24:16 PM
```

The `<%` and `%>` marks work just as they did in classic ASP, indicating that code falls between them (in this case, C#). The = sign immediately following the opening tag causes ASP.NET to evaluate the expression inside the tags and display the value. Run the page by pressing F5.

Adding Controls

You can add server-side controls to a web form in three ways: by writing markup in the *.aspx* page, by dragging controls from the toolbox (to either the Source or Design view), or by writing code that adds them at runtime. For example, suppose you want to use radio buttons to let the user choose one of three shipping companies when placing an order. You can write the following HTML into the `<form>` element in the HTML window:

```
<asp:RadioButton GroupName="Shipper" id="Speedy"
    text="Speedy Express" Checked="True" runat="server">
</asp:RadioButton>
<asp:RadioButton GroupName="Shipper" id="United"
    text="United Package" runat="server">
</asp:RadioButton>
<asp:RadioButton GroupName="Shipper" id="Federal"
    text="Federal Shipping" runat="server">
</asp:RadioButton>
```

The asp tags declare server-side ASP.NET controls that are replaced with normal HTML when the server processes the page. When you run the application, the browser displays three radio buttons in a button group; selecting one deselects the others.

You can create the same effect more easily by dragging three buttons from the Visual Studio toolbox onto the form, or to make life even easier, you can drag a radio button list onto the form, which will manage a set of radio buttons as a group. When you select a radio button list control in the Design view, a smart tag appears, prompting you to choose a data source (which allows you to bind to a collection; perhaps one you've obtained from a database) or to edit items. Clicking Edit Items opens the ListItem Collection Editor, where you can add three radio buttons.

Each radio button is given the default name ListItem, but you may edit its text and value in the ListItem properties, where you can also decide which of the radio buttons is selected, as shown in Figure 21-1.

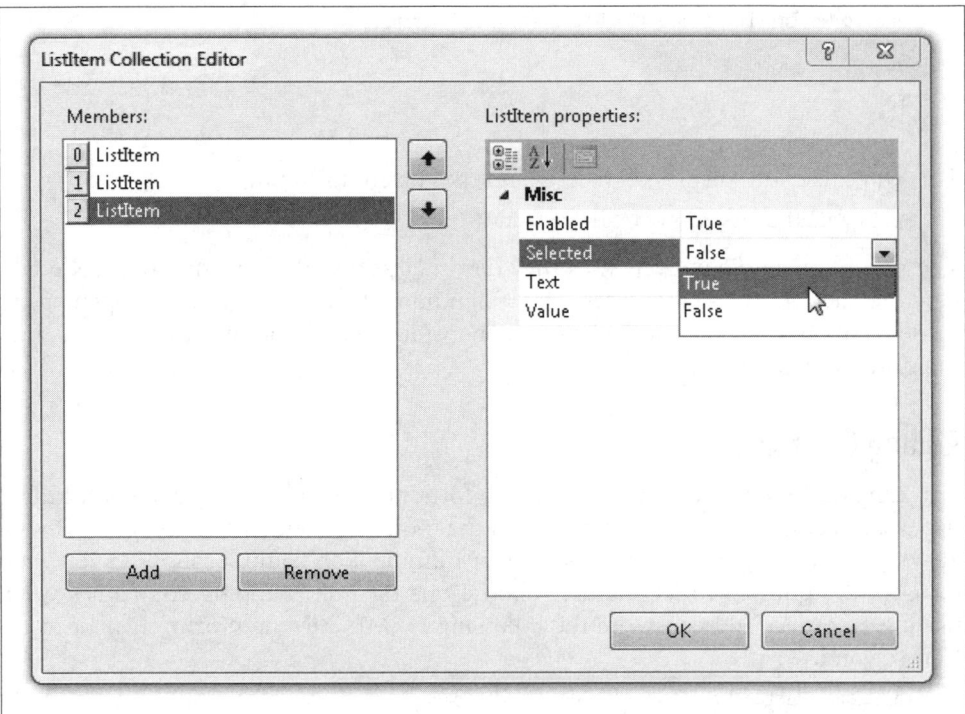

Figure 21-1. List item collection

You can improve the look of your radio button list by changing properties in the Properties window, including the font, colors, number of columns, repeat direction (vertical is the default), and so forth, as well as by utilizing Visual Studio's extensive support for CSS styling, as shown in Figure 21-2.

In Figure 21-2, you can just see that in the lower-righthand corner you can switch between the Properties window and the Styles window. Here, we've used the Properties window to set the tool tip, and the Styles window to create and apply the ListBox style, which creates the border around our listbox and sets the font and font color. We're also using the split screen option to look at Design and Source at the same time.

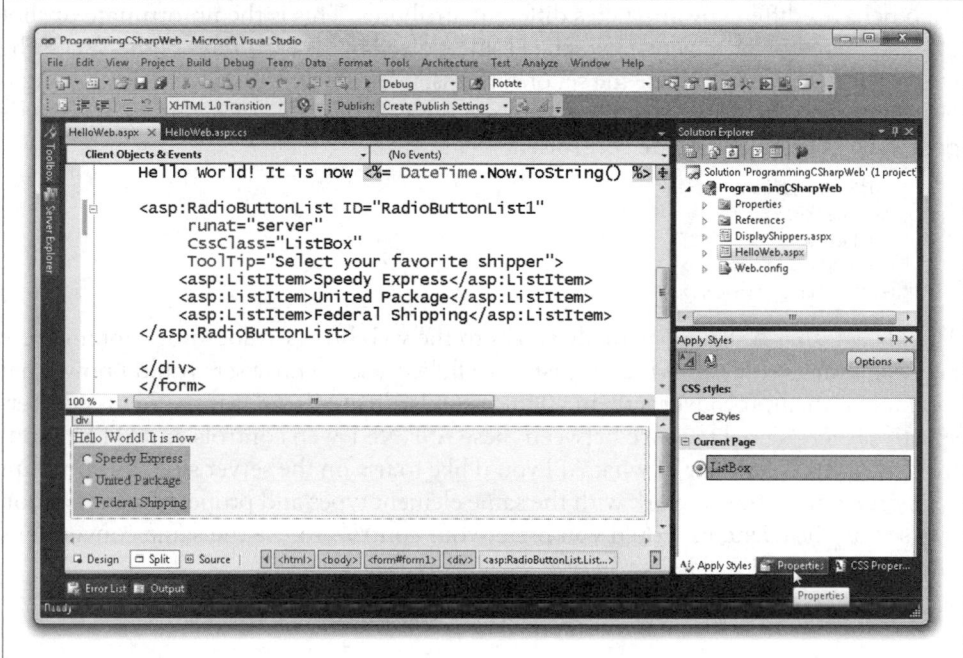

Figure 21-2. Using properties and styles

The tag indications (provided automatically at the bottom of the window) show us our location in the document; specifically, inside a ListItem, within the ListBox which is inside a div which itself is inside form1. Very nice.

Server Controls

Web Forms offers two types of server-side controls. The first is server-side HTML controls. These look like normal HTML controls, but with the extra attribute `runat="server"`.

The alternative to marking HTML controls as server-side controls is to use ASP.NET Server Controls, also called web controls. Web controls have been designed to provide a more convenient server-side API for working with standard HTML controls. Web controls provide a more consistent object model and more consistently named attributes. For example, with HTML controls, there are myriad ways to handle input:

```
<input type="radio">
<input type="checkbox">
<input type="button">
<input type="text">
<textarea>
```

Each behaves differently and takes different attributes. This is the unfortunate upshot of the rather haphazard way in which HTML evolved in the early days of the Web. The web controls try to normalize the set of controls, using attributes consistently throughout the web control object model. Here are the web controls that correspond to the preceding HTML server-side controls:

```
<asp:RadioButton>
<asp:CheckBox>
<asp:Button>
<asp:TextBox rows="1">
<asp:TextBox rows="5">
```

The HTML that ASP.NET actually serves to the web browser does not contain these tags beginning with `asp:` which is just as well, because no browser would know what to make of them. It converts them all into standard HTML, so from a client-side perspective, there's no difference between these ASP.NET web controls and HTML controls. It's purely a matter of what API you'd like to use on the server side: do you want your server-side code to work with the same element types and property names as you will see on the client, or would you prefer your controls to use the same conventions as all the other .NET classes you use?

The remainder of this chapter focuses on web controls.

Data Binding

While some of the content in a web application may be fixed, any interesting website will change over time. So it's highly likely that you'll want some of the controls on your web page to display data that can change from time to time, and which is probably stored in a database. Many ASP.NET controls can be data-bound, which simplifies display and modification of data.

In the preceding section we hardcoded radio buttons onto a form—one for each of three shippers. That can't be the best way to do it—relationships with suppliers change, and there's a good chance that we may want to work with different shippers in the future. We don't really want to have to go back and rewire the controls each time that kind of business relationship changes. It makes more sense to store the list of shippers in a database, and have the UI reflect that. (In fact, if you're familiar with Microsoft's sample databases, you may recognize the three shippers in the earlier examples as the ones provided in the "Northwind" sample database.) This section shows you how you can create these controls dynamically and then bind them to data in the database, by using the `RadioButtonList` control's data binding support.

Add a new web form called *DisplayShippers.aspx* to your project. Put the editor into Split mode. From the toolbox, drag a `RadioButtonList` onto the new form, either onto the design pane or within the `<div>` in the Source view.

 If you don't see the radio buttons on the left of your work space, try clicking on View→Toolbox to open the toolbox, and then expanding the Standard tab of the toolbox. Right-click on any control in the toolbox, and choose Sort Items Alphabetically.

In the Design pane, click on the new control's smart tag—the little arrow that appears at the top right of the control. Then, select Choose Data Source and the Data Source Configuration dialog opens, as shown in Figure 21-3.

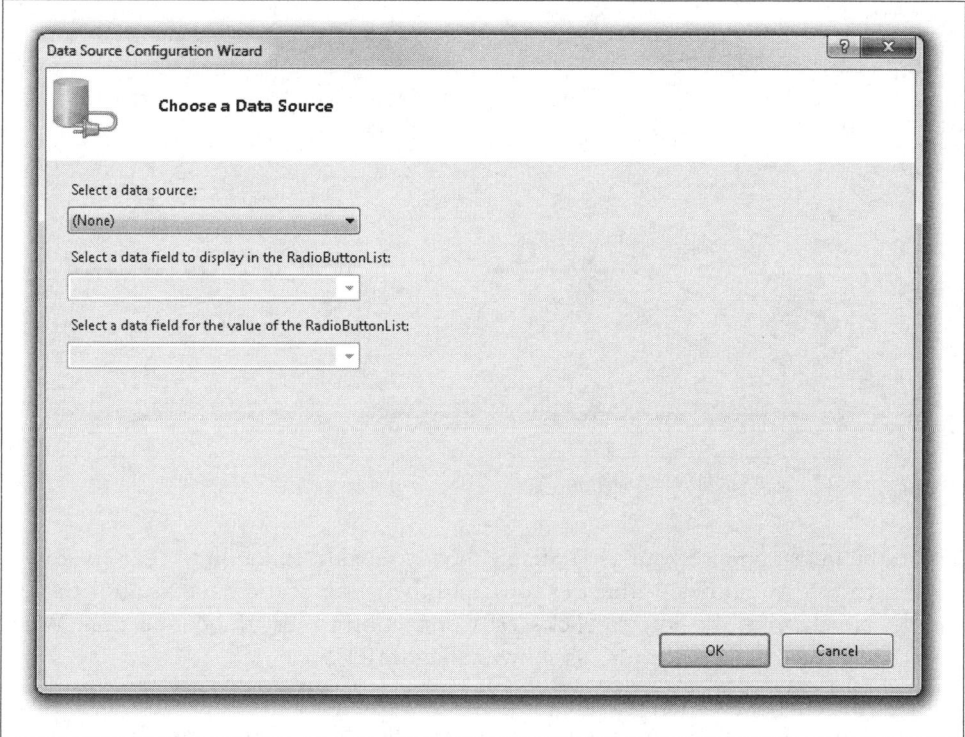

Figure 21-3. Data Source Configuration dialog

Drop down the "Select a data source" menu and choose <New Data Source>. You are then prompted to choose a data source from the datatypes on your machine. Select Database, assign it an ID, and click OK. The Configure Data Source dialog box opens, as shown in Figure 21-4.

You can either choose an existing connection, or in this case, choose New Connection to configure a new data source, and the Add Connection dialog opens.

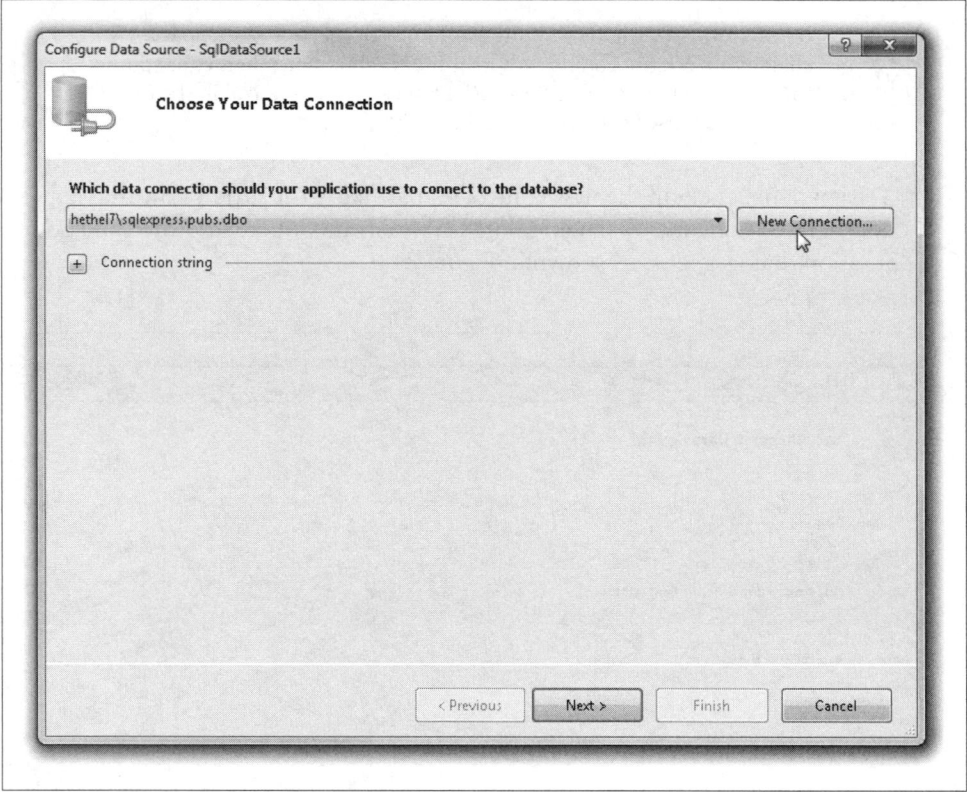

Figure 21-4. Choosing a data connection

Fill in the fields: choose your server name, how you want to log in to the server (if in doubt, choose Windows Authentication), and the name of the database (for this example, Northwind). Be sure to click Test Connection to test the connection. When everything is working, click OK, as shown in Figure 21-5.

After you click OK, the connection properties will be filled in for the Configure Data Source dialog. Review them, and if they are OK, click Next. On the next wizard page, name your connection (e.g., `NorthWindConnectionString`) if you want to save it to your *web.config* file.

When you click Next, you'll have the opportunity to specify the tables and columns you want to retrieve, or to specify a custom SQL statement or stored procedure for retrieving the data.

Open the Table list, and scroll down to Shippers. Select the ShipperID and Company-Name fields, as shown in Figure 21-6.

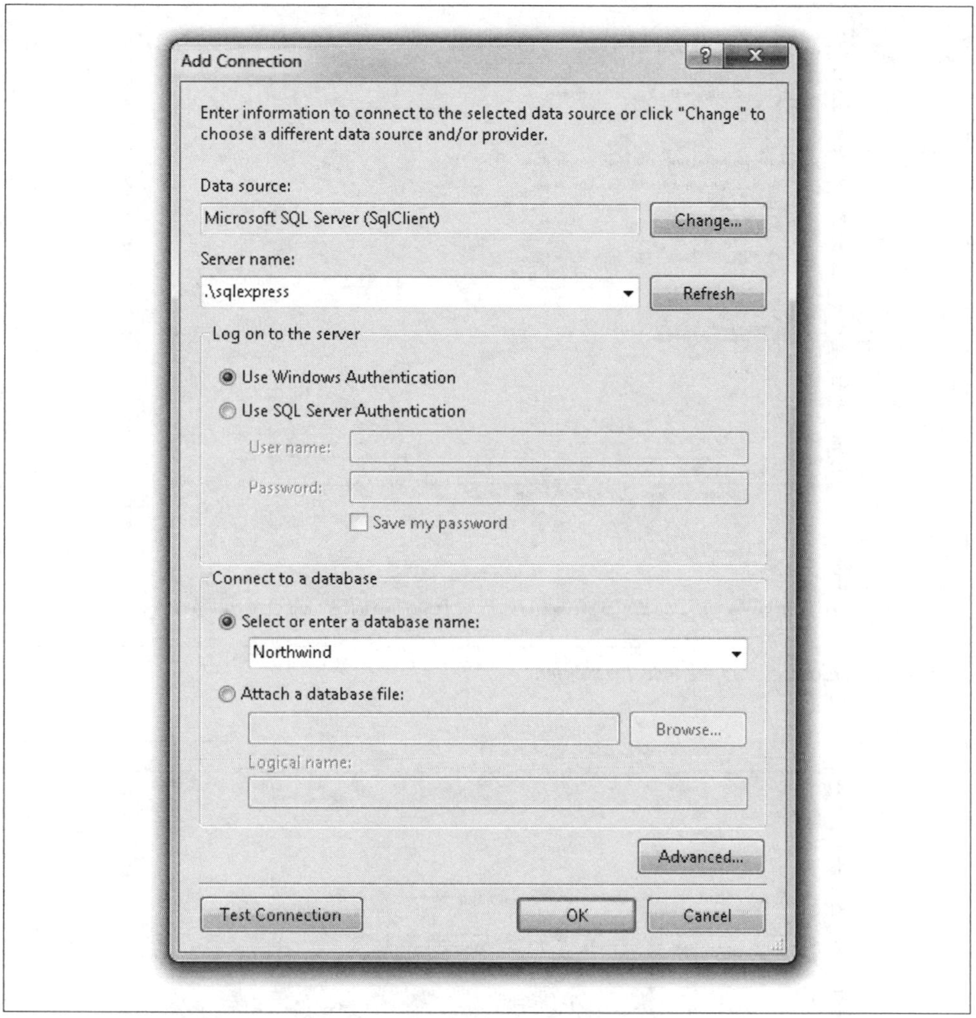

Figure 21-5. The Add Connection dialog

Click Next, and test your query to see that you are getting back the values you expected, as shown in Figure 21-7.

It is now time to attach the data source you've just built to the `RadioButtonList`. A `RadioButtonList` (like most lists) distinguishes between the value to display (e.g., the name of the delivery service) and the value of that selection (e.g., the delivery service ID). Set these fields in the wizard, using the drop down, as shown in Figure 21-8.

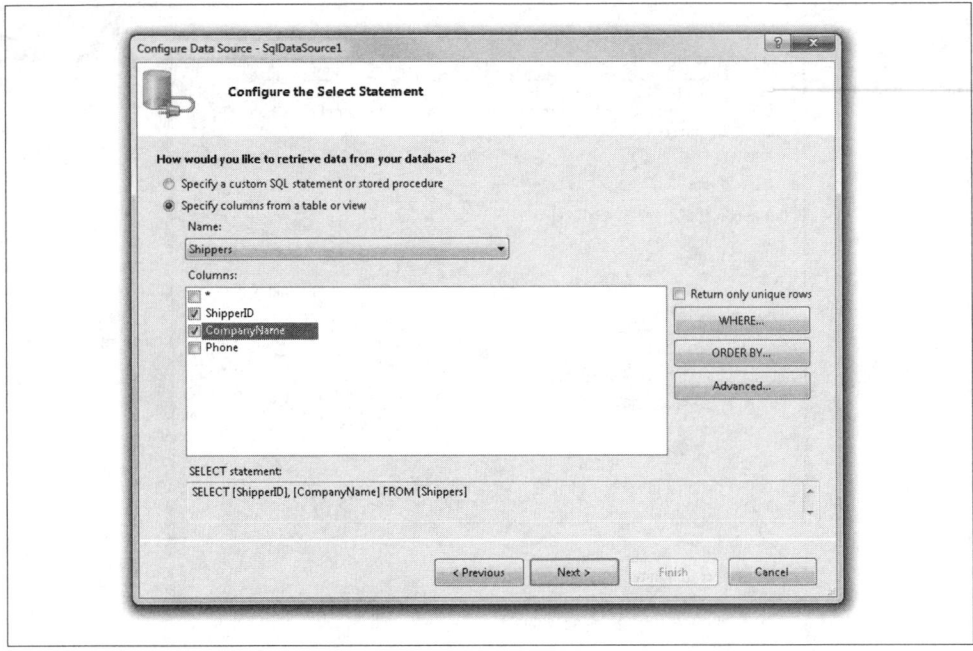

Figure 21-6. Configuring the Select statement

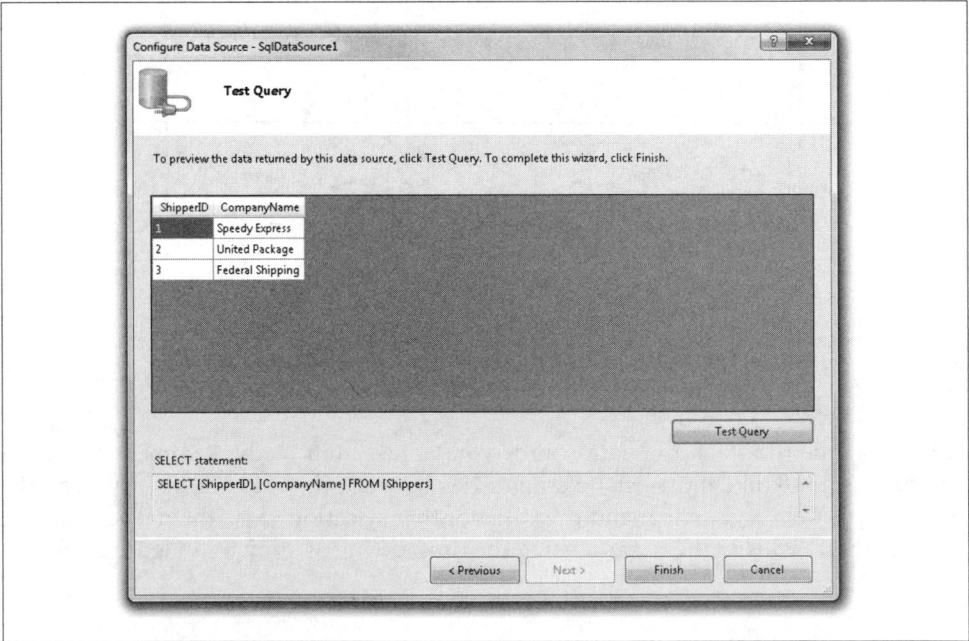

Figure 21-7. Testing the query

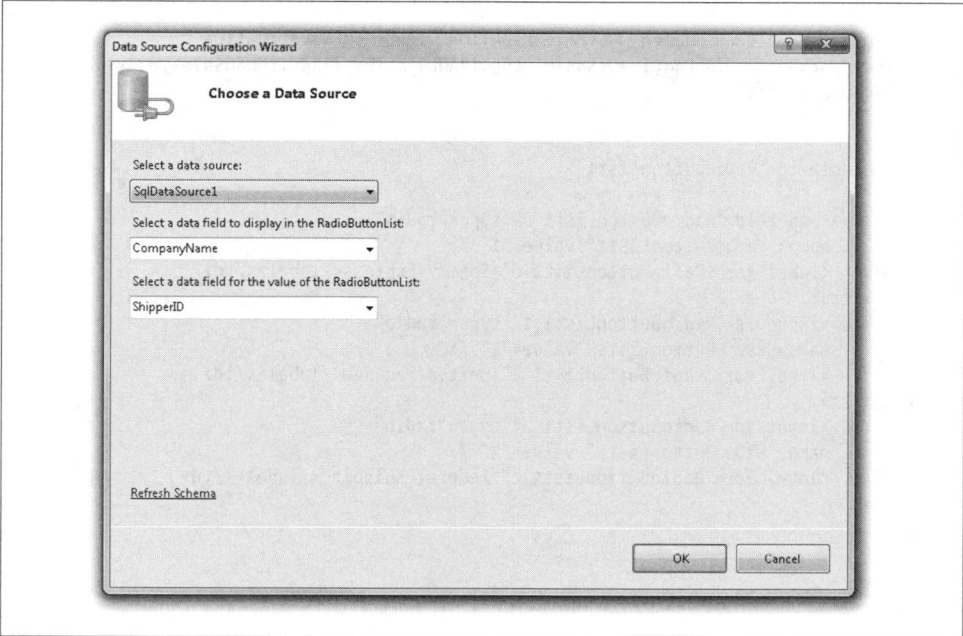

Figure 21-8. Binding radio buttons to the data source

Examining the Code

Before moving on, there are a few things to notice. When you press F5 to run this application, it appears in a web browser, and the radio buttons come up as expected. Choose View→Source, and you'll see that what is being sent to the browser is simple HTML, as shown in Example 21-2.

Example 21-2. HTML Source view

```
<!DOCTYPE html PUBLIC "-//W3C//DTD XHTML 1.0 Transitional//EN" "http://www.w3.org/TR/
xhtml1/DTD/xhtml1-transitional.dtd">

<html xmlns="http://www.w3.org/1999/xhtml">
<head><title>

</title></head>
<body>
    <form method="post" action="DisplayShippers.aspx" id="form1">
<div class="aspNetHidden">
<input type="hidden" name="__VIEWSTATE" id="__VIEWSTATE"
value="/wEPDwUJMjMzNjY1MzU4D2QWAgIDD2QWAgIBDxAPFgIeC18hRGF0YUJvdW5kZ2QQFQMOU3BlZWR5
IEV4cHJlc3MOVW5pdGVkIFBhY2thZ2UQRmVkZXJhbCBTaGlwcGluZxUDATEBMgEzFCsDA2dnZ2RkZCOksd8
IILjpH4OAdNkxGqjSaORYAA3N2F8zJz4lyxsv" />
</div>

<div class="aspNetHidden">
```

```
    <input type="hidden" name="__EVENTVALIDATION" id="__EVENTVALIDATION"
    value="/wEWBQKO2+CfAgL444i9AQL544i9AQL644i9AQL3jKLTDWylFXks1YMe8G5o7AkyHjJysQkO
    Cliwu8U/2yTrYA/Y" />
</div>
    <div>
        <table id="RadioButtonList1">
        <tr>
            <td><input id="RadioButtonList1_0" type="radio"
                name="RadioButtonList1" value="1" />
                <label for="RadioButtonList1_0">Speedy Express</label></td>
        </tr><tr>
            <td><input id="RadioButtonList1_1" type="radio"
                name="RadioButtonList1" value="2" />
                <label for="RadioButtonList1_1">United Package</label></td>
        </tr><tr>
            <td><input id="RadioButtonList1_2" type="radio"
                name="RadioButtonList1" value="3" />
                <label for="RadioButtonList1_2">Federal Shipping</label></td>
        </tr>
    </table>

    </div>
    </form>
</body>
</html>
```

Notice that the HTML has no `RadioButtonList`; it has a table, with cells, within which are standard HTML input objects and labels. ASP.NET has translated the developer controls to HTML understandable by any browser.

 A malicious user may create a message that looks like a valid post from your form, but in which he has set a value for a field you never provided in your form. This may enable him to choose an option not properly available (e.g., a Premier-customer option), or even to launch a SQL injection attack. You want to be especially careful about exposing important data such as primary keys in your HTML, and take care that what you receive from the user may not be restricted to what you provide in your form. For more information on secure coding in .NET, see *http://msdn.microsoft.com/security/*.

Adding Controls and Events

By adding just a few more controls, you can create a complete form with which users can interact. You will do this by adding a more appropriate greeting ("Welcome to NorthWind"), a text box to accept the name of the user, two new buttons (Order and Cancel), and text that provides feedback to the user. Figure 21-9 shows the finished form.

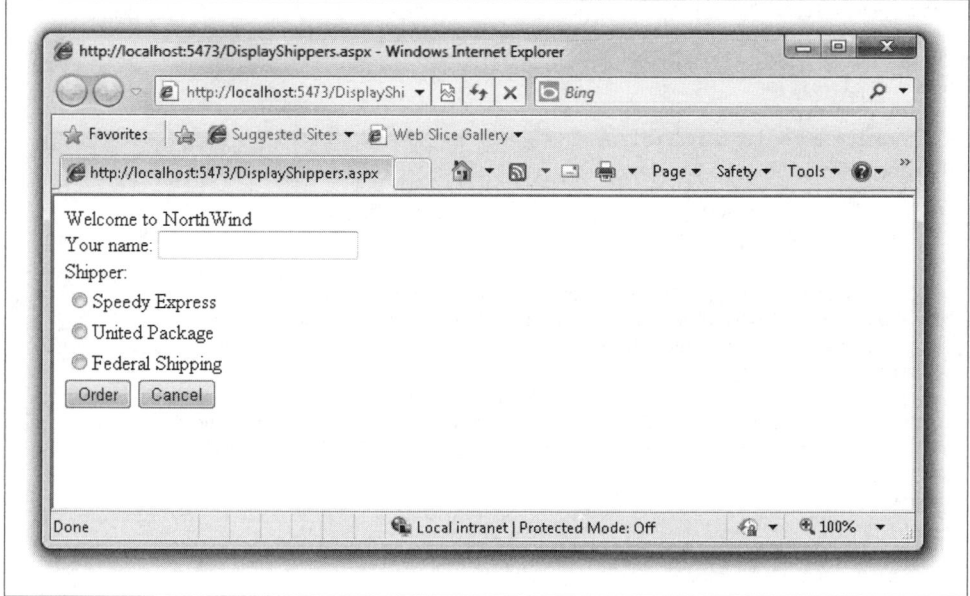

Figure 21-9. The completed shipper form

This form won't win any awards for design, but its use will illustrate a number of key points about Web Forms.

I've never known a developer who didn't think he could design a perfectly fine UI. At the same time, I never knew one who actually could. UI design is one of those skills (such as teaching) that we all think we possess, but only a few very talented folks are good at it. As developers, we know our limitations: we write the code, and someone else lays it out on the page and ensures that usability issues are reviewed. For more on this, I highly recommend every programmer read *Don't Make Me Think: A Common Sense Approach to Web Usability* by Steve Krug (New Riders Press) and *Why Software Sucks...and What You Can Do About It* by David Platt (Addison-Wesley).

Example 21-3 is the complete *.aspx* file.

Example 21-3. The .aspx file

```
<%@ Page Language="C#" AutoEventWireup="true"
 CodeBehind="DisplayShippers.aspx.cs"
 Inherits="ProgrammingCSharpWeb.DisplayShippers" %>

<!DOCTYPE html PUBLIC "-//W3C//DTD XHTML 1.0 Transitional//EN"
 "http://www.w3.org/TR/xhtml1/DTD/xhtml1-transitional.dtd">

<html xmlns="http://www.w3.org/1999/xhtml">
```

```
<head runat="server">
  <title></title>
</head>
<body>
  <form id="form1" runat="server">
  <div>Welcome to NorthWind</div>
  <div>
    Your name:
    <asp:TextBox ID="txtName" runat="server"></asp:TextBox></div>
    <div>Shipper:</div>
  <div>
    <asp:RadioButtonList ID="rblShippers" runat="server"
        DataSourceID="SqlDataSource1" DataTextField="CompanyName"
        DataValueField="ShipperID">
    </asp:RadioButtonList>
    <asp:SqlDataSource ID="SqlDataSource1" runat="server"
        ConnectionString="<%$ ConnectionStrings:NorthwindConnectionString %>"
        SelectCommand="SELECT [ShipperID], [CompanyName] FROM [Shippers]">
    </asp:SqlDataSource>
  </div>
  <div>
    <asp:Button ID="btnOrder" runat="server" Text="Order" />
    <asp:Button ID="Button2" runat="server" Text="Cancel" />
  </div>
  <div>
    <asp:Label id="lblMsg" runat=server></asp:Label>
  </div>
  </form>
</body>
</html>
```

When the user clicks the Order button, you'll read the value that the user has typed in the Name text box, and you'll also provide feedback on which shipper was chosen. Remember, at design time, you can't know the name of the shipper, because this is obtained from the database at runtime, but we can ask the `RadioButtonList` for the chosen name or ID.

To accomplish all of this, switch to Design mode, and double-click the Order button. Visual Studio will put you in the code-behind page, and will create an event handler for the button's `Click` event.

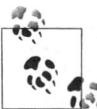 To simplify this code, we will not validate that the user has entered a name in the text box. For more on the controls that make such validation simple, please see *Programming ASP.NET*.

You add the event-handling code, setting the text of the label to pick up the text from the text box, and the text and value from the `RadioButtonList`:

```
protected void btnOrder_Click(object sender, EventArgs e)
{
    lblMsg.Text = "Thank you " + txtName.Text.Trim() +
```

```
                    ". You chose " + rblShippers.SelectedItem.Text +
                    " whose ID is " + rblShippers.SelectedValue;
    }
```

When you run this program, you'll notice that none of the radio buttons are selected. Binding the list did not specify which one is the default. There are a number of ways to do this, but the easiest is to add a single line in the Page_Load method that Visual Studio created:

```
    protected void Page_Load(object sender, EventArgs e)
    {
        rblShippers.SelectedIndex = 0;
    }
```

This sets the RadioButtonList's first radio button to Selected. The problem with this solution is subtle. If you run the application, you'll see that the first button is selected, but if you choose the second (or third) button and click OK, you'll find that the first button is reset. You can't seem to choose any but the first selection. This is because each time the page is loaded, the OnLoad event is run, and in that event handler you are (re)setting the selected index.

The fact is that you only want to set this button the first time the page is selected, not when it is posted back to the browser as a result of the OK button being clicked.

To solve this, wrap the setting in an if statement that tests whether the page has been posted back:

```
    protected void Page_Load(object sender, EventArgs e)
    {
        if (!IsPostBack)
        {
            rblShippers.SelectedIndex = 0;
        }
    }
```

When you run the page, the IsPostBack property is checked. The first time the page is posted, this value is false, and the radio button is set. If you click a radio button and then click OK, the page is sent to the server for processing (where the btnOrder_Click handler is run), and then the page is posted back to the user. This time, the IsPostBack property is true, and thus the code within the if statement isn't run, and the user's choice is preserved, as shown in Figure 21-10.

Example 21-4 shows the complete code-behind form.

Example 21-4. Code-behind form for DisplayShippers aspx.cs

```
using System;

namespace ProgrammingCSharpWeb
{
    public partial class DisplayShippers : System.Web.UI.Page
    {
        protected void Page_Load(object sender, EventArgs e)
```

```
    {
        if (!IsPostBack)
        {
            rblShippers.SelectedIndex = 0;
        }
    }

    protected void btnOrder_Click(object sender, EventArgs e)
    {
        lblMsg.Text = "Thank you " + txtName.Text.Trim() +
            ". You chose " + rblShippers.SelectedItem.Text +
            " whose ID is " + rblShippers.SelectedValue;
    }
  }
}
```

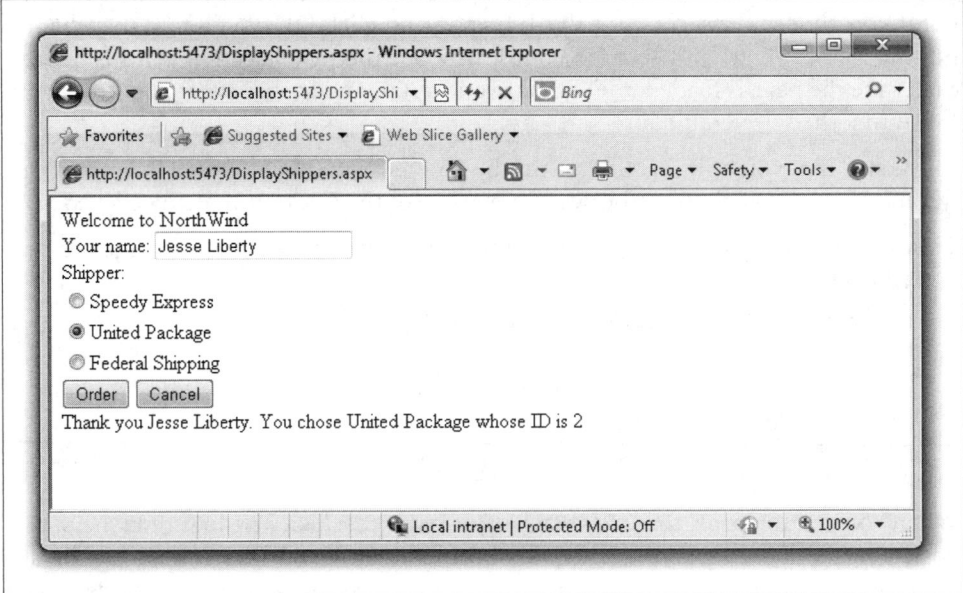

Figure 21-10. The user's choices preserved on postback

Summary

In this chapter, we saw how to create a simple ASP.NET web application using Web Forms. We bound a list of radio buttons to a database table, and added server-side event handlers that respond to a user's interaction with a web page.

CHAPTER 22

Windows Forms

Windows Forms offers a way to build Windows desktop applications using the .NET Framework. This may sound rather familiar if you're reading the chapters in order—surely WPF does that? The two technologies do overlap, but they work very differently. Windows Forms is essentially a wrapper around the classic Win32-based UI: when you create a Windows Forms text box, you get an ordinary Windows text box with a .NET wrapper. That's not true in WPF—in order to escape the limitations of the Win32 UI its controls are all rebuilt from scratch. So while they go to great lengths to look and behave like their Win32 counterparts, they're not based on them. (And Silverlight can run on Mac OS X, so it's clearly not dependent on any of the Windows common controls either.)

Since WPF rebuilds so much of the UI infrastructure from the ground up, it took awhile to emerge—it only appeared in .NET version 3.0, almost half a decade after .NET 1.0 shipped. Windows Forms was available from day one, presumably due in part to its less ambitious scope—since Windows provided the underpinnings it has less to do than WPF.

While this history explains how we ended up with two different technologies for building Windows desktop applications in C#, it leaves the question: why might you care about Windows Forms today? WPF was invented to get away from some limitations of the underlying Win32 UI system, so it's more powerful than Windows Forms, but Windows Forms offers a couple of advantages.

First, because Windows Forms was around long before WPF, it's very well supported, both by Microsoft's tools and by third parties. In Visual Studio, the Windows Forms designer is more mature than the WPF one—in Windows Forms, you can get a higher proportion of things done in the designer than in WPF, where you can end up needing to do more things by hand in C# or Xaml. And if you're looking to reuse existing controls, you might be able to find Windows Forms controls that offer more of the features you would like than the nearest WPF equivalent. (You can mix WPF and Windows Forms in a single application, so you might end up using a Windows Forms control in a WPF application, although using two different UI frameworks can complicate your program.)

The second advantage of Windows Forms is that it tends to be somewhat more frugal. WPF applications often have a larger memory footprint than an equivalent application would in Windows Forms. Of course, it's not always possible to build an equivalent application in Windows Forms, but if you're not exploiting any of the potential benefits of WPF, you may be paying for things you don't need. If your application needs to run on older machines with low specifications, this may be the deciding factor.

If neither of these benefits is useful to you, WPF is likely to be a better choice. Windows Forms lacks WPF's powerful composition-based model, exemplified by the content model and powerful template system. Windows Forms is less strong graphically, and has no animation support. It doesn't have styling features, has a much more basic data binding system, and has no equivalent of Xaml, which seems to have had the result that very few tools outside of Visual Studio offer any kind of Windows Forms support, whereas tools that can export to Xaml are rather more widespread. (And while it's technically possible to create Windows Forms user interfaces in Xaml, Visual Studio doesn't support this, and it's rather cumbersome because Windows Forms was not designed with Xaml in mind.) Moreover, Microsoft has indicated that Windows Forms is unlikely to see much significant new development—it will be fully supported for years to come, but it will not grow many new features.

Since you've continued reading, presumably the benefits are of interest to you, so in this chapter, we'll walk through the creation of a simple Windows Forms application to show you the Visual Studio designer support and the main aspects of the programming model.

Creating the Application

We'll build a simple application for showing and editing a to-do list. To create a new Windows Forms application, open the New Project dialog (Ctrl-Shift-N) and in the Installed Templates on the left, select Visual C#→Windows. In the templates in the middle, select Windows Forms Application. We'll call our project ToDoList. Visual Studio will create a new project with a single *form* called Form1—a class derived from the Form base class. A Form is just a window—the name reflects the fact that one of the tasks Windows Forms is particularly well suited to is making line-of-business applications that involve filling in forms.

Visual Studio will be showing the empty form in a design view that you can drag controls onto. However, before we start adding the UI, we're going to define a class to represent the to-do items in our application. So we'll add a new class called ToDoEntry to the project, shown in Example 22-1.

Example 22-1. Class representing to-do list entries

```
public class ToDoEntry
{
    public string Title { get; set; }
    public string Description { get; set; }
    public DateTime DueDate { get; set; }
}
```

 If you're following this in Visual Studio, make sure you build your project after adding this class. We're going to be using some design-time features of Visual Studio that will need to know about your class, and you need to have built the project for these to work.

Next, we need to make sure Windows Forms knows we're using this class as a data source, which we'll do by creating a *binding source*.

Adding a Binding Source

The BindingSource class keeps track of how a Windows Forms UI is using a particular data source. When you have a collection of items, such as the entries in our to-do list, the BindingSource tracks which item is currently selected and can coordinate additions, deletions, and changes. Using a BindingSource can also make life easier in the UI designer, because it provides Visual Studio with information about the data you're working with so that it can help connect that data to your controls.

We add a BindingSource by going back to the design view of Form1, making sure Visual Studio's Toolbox is open (which you can do from the View menu if it's not already visible), and then expanding the Data section of the Toolbox. This section contains a BindingSource item, which we drag onto the form.

 Utility components that aren't visible at runtime, such as timers or data sources, don't appear on the form itself at design time. A panel at the bottom of the design view, outside the form, contains all such nonvisual components.

Visual Studio picks a nondescript name—bindingSource1. We can change this by selecting the item and then going to the Properties panel—we'll set its (Name) property to entriesSource. Next we need to tell it what we're using as a data source. The Properties panel will show a DataSource property for the BindingSource, and if you expand its drop down, a pop up showing available data sources in the project will appear, as Figure 22-1 shows. There are none right now, so we need to click on the Add Project Data Source link at the bottom.

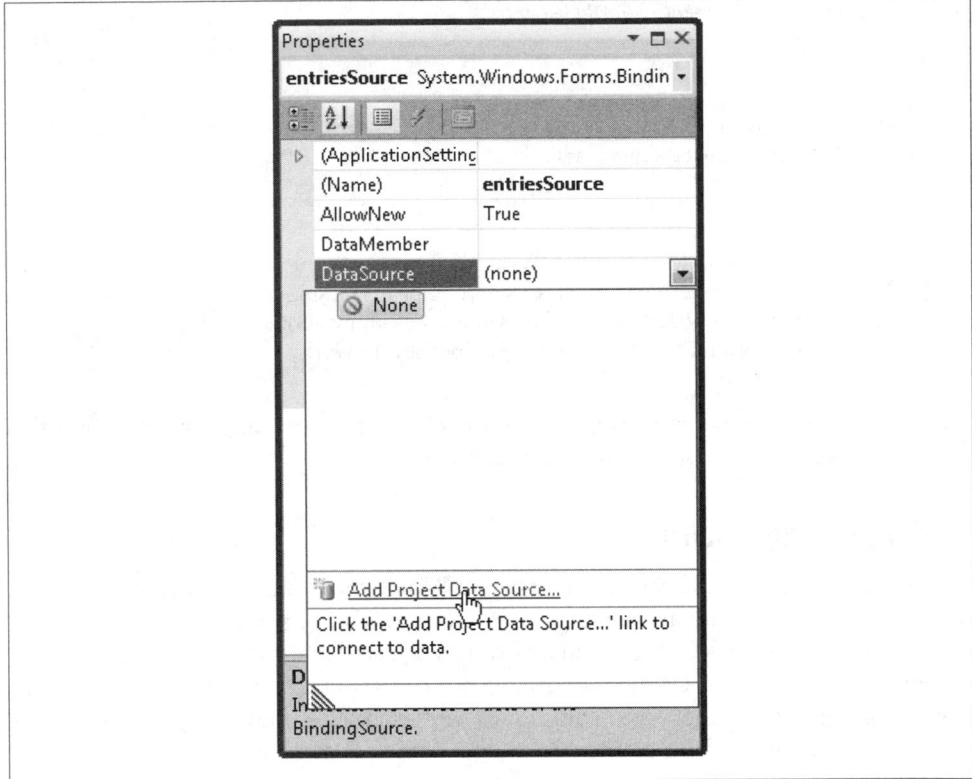

Figure 22-1. Configuring a binding source

Clicking this link opens the Data Source Configuration Wizard window. This supports a few different kinds of sources. It may vary depending on exactly which edition of Visual Studio you have installed, but you may see Database, Service, Object, and SharePoint offered. We're binding to objects—that's why we added the `ToDoEntry` class—so we'll select Object and click Next. The next page, shown in Figure 22-2, lets us choose the object types we plan to bind to—the `ToDoEntry` class in this case.

When we click Finish, the `BindingSource` now knows what kind of object it will be working with. The final step is to supply it with the specific objects. If we had connected to a database, Visual Studio could arrange to fetch the data automatically, but since we're binding to objects, it's our job to provide those objects. We do this in the code behind. By default, Visual Studio shows you the design view for a form, but if you right-click, you'll see a View Code option (or you can just press F7) to see the code behind. As with WPF, Silverlight, and ASP.NET, the code behind is a partial class in which you add code to handle events and work with the UI—Visual Studio generates the other part of this partial class based on what you do in the designer. We'll modify the code behind by making the additions highlighted in Example 22-2.

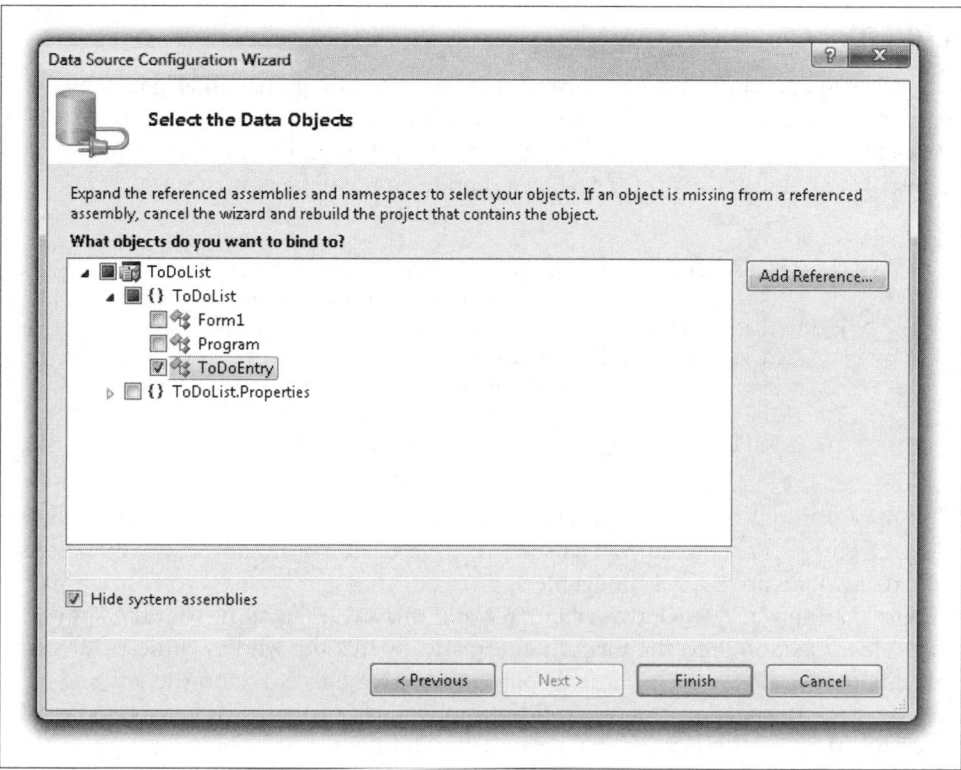

Figure 22-2. Selecting a source object type

Example 22-2. Supplying objects to a binding source

```
public partial class Form1 : Form
{
    private BindingList<ToDoEntry> entries = new BindingList<ToDoEntry>();

    public Form1()
    {
        InitializeComponent();

        entriesSource.DataSource = entries;
    }
...
```

The BindingList<T> class raises events when its contents change, enabling the Windows Forms data binding system to remain up-to-date if we add or remove data items. So the binding source now has the objects, and because we've configured the source appropriately, Visual Studio will know exactly what properties are available and will be able to connect those to any controls we add to our user interface. So next, we're going to need to add some controls.

Controls

The `Control` class in Windows Forms is the base class of almost all visual elements. A handful of exceptions—most notably menus and tool tips—work differently in Windows Forms because they also work differently in Win32, but the vast majority of UI elements you'll use in a Windows Forms application will be controls.

 This is a significant difference between Windows Forms and WPF. WPF's `Control` class (the one in `System.Windows.Controls`, as opposed to the Windows Forms one in `System.Windows.Forms`) is more specialized, as you saw in Chapter 20. In Windows Forms, not only do interactive elements such as `Button` derive from `Control`, so do layout elements. The nearest equivalent to the Windows Forms `Control` class in WPF and Silverlight is actually `FrameworkElement`.

Our application is going to have a list of entries at the top, and some fields to edit the selected entry at the bottom. We'll use a `SplitContainer` to arrange these two sections— `SplitContainer` provides a draggable splitter bar that can be used to resize a pair of panels sharing some space on-screen. We add this by dragging it from the Toolbox's Containers section onto the form. It automatically fills the whole window. However, it splits the window with a vertical splitter—the two halves are on the left and right, but we wanted them on the top and bottom. This is easily fixed, because like many controls, the `SplitContainer` offers a pop-up window for performing common tasks. At the top-righthand corner of the control, a little arrow in a box appears, and if we click on this, the pop up appears, as Figure 22-3 shows. Clicking "Horizontal splitter orientation" gives use the orientation we require.

In the top half of the UI, we want a list showing each to-do entry. We're likely to want to show at least a couple of pieces of information—the entry title and its due date, for example. The simple `ListBox` control is not sufficient here. Unlike the WPF `ListBox`, Windows Forms cannot easily add multiple columns, because it's based on the Win32 `ListBox`. It wouldn't be completely impossible as you can write code that customizes how each item is rendered, but that seems like an unnecessarily complex solution when the `ListView` provides multicolumn list support.

While `ListView` is the right control for presenting the information to the user, we just caused ourselves a problem. Support for data binding in Windows Forms is somewhat uneven, and while you can data-bind a `ListBox`, you can't do that with `ListView`. This puts us in a tricky situation: either we use a `ListBox`, compromising the UI to make life easier for us, the developers, or we have to do more work by hand to use the `ListView`, in order to do right by the end user. Or we could use a data grid, but for such a simple application, it seems like overkill—the `ListView` is something all Windows users will be familiar with, and it fits the bill. And because it means doing a few things by hand, it also gives us an opportunity to explore a few details of the data binding system that we might otherwise not have seen, so we'll go with that.

The `ListView` control is in the Common Controls section of the Toolbox. When we drag it onto the top panel in the `SplitContainer`, we need to fix a few things with the Tasks pop up. First, we want the list view to fill the whole of the top panel—there's a `Dock in parent container` task just for that. We also have to change its `View`—the default is `LargeIcon`, but we need to change that to `Details` for the multicolumn view we want. And finally, we need to tell it about the columns, by clicking the `Edit Columns` task.

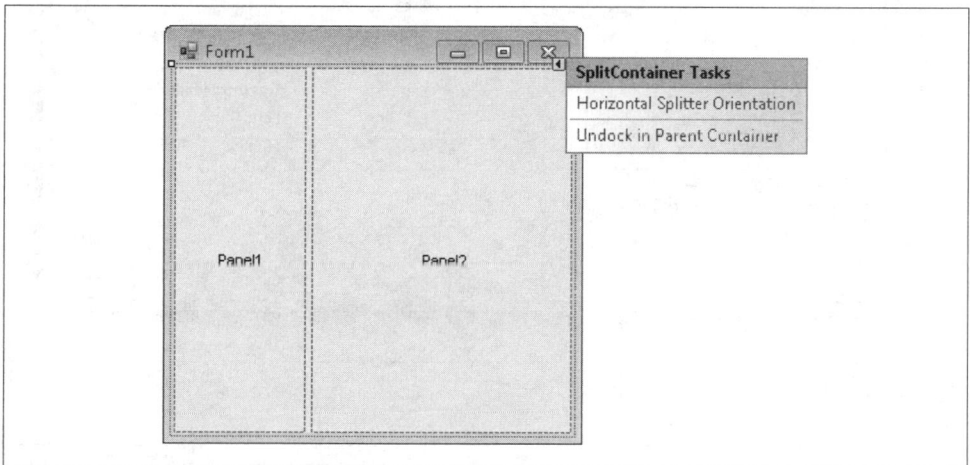

Figure 22-3. Pop up showing common tasks

The ColumnHeader Collection Editor opens. Clicking Add a couple of times adds two columns. As Figure 22-4 shows, Visual Studio has been characteristically unadventurous with the names—`columnHeader1` and `columnHeader2` don't say much. These are the names it will give to the fields that make these objects accessible to us in the code behind. It's usually a good idea to provide more informative names each time you add anything in the Windows Forms designer—whether it's a control, a nonvisual component, or a column like this. Otherwise, your program rapidly acquires a long list of incomprehensible identifiers. So we'll set the (`Name`) on the right to `titleColumn` for the first column, and `dueDateColumn` for the second.

Of course, we also want the displayed text in the column headers to be a bit more useful than the default, `ColumnHeader`, so we'll change the `Text` property of the two columns to `Title` and `Due Date`, respectively. Finally, to ensure that the two columns make reasonably good use of the space initially available, we'll set their `Width` properties to 200 and 70. Figure 22-5 shows how the form looks once this is done. We haven't given the `ListView` itself a good name yet, so we'll call it `entriesListView`.

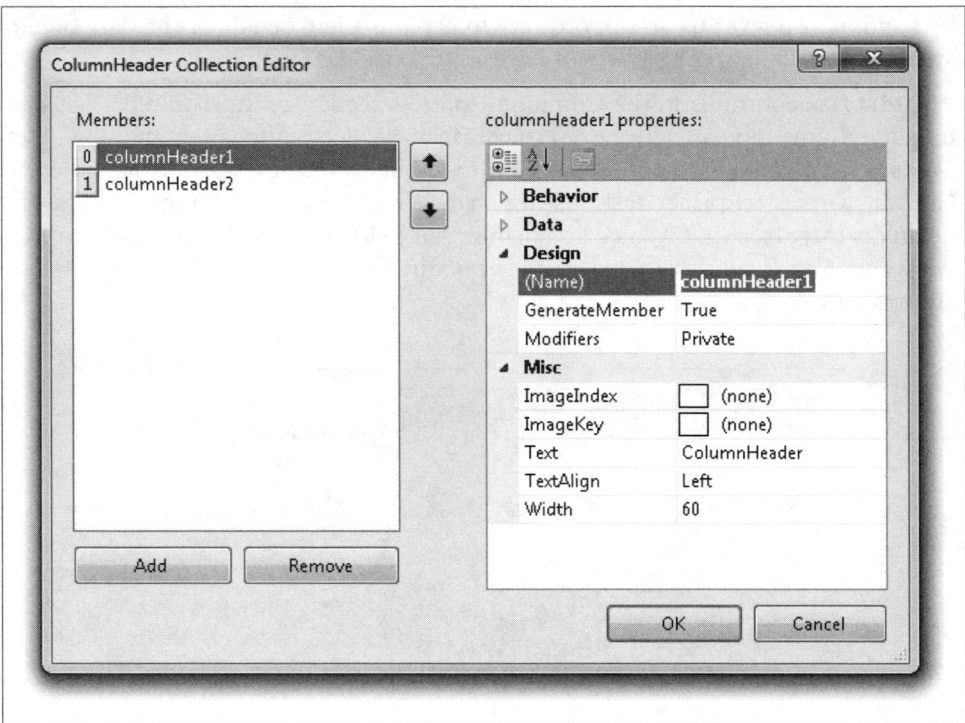

Figure 22-4. Editing ListView columns

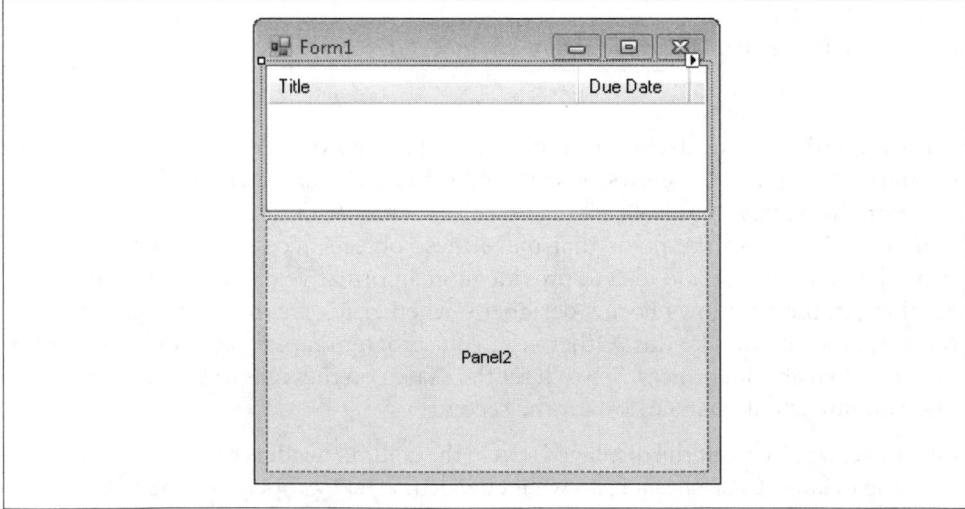

Figure 22-5. ListView with columns

Some developers have a stylistic objection to field or variable names that include information about the type, and would argue that entriesList View is unnecessarily verbose. However, it's quite common in UI applications to have several different objects all representing the same thing at different layers—we've put the underlying model in a field called entries, we have the binding source representing that model to the data binding system, which we've called entriesSource, and we have a control displaying the information, called entriesListView. Clearly these objects can't all be called entries. We could call the control entries View, but that sounds less like an individual control and more like a description of the whole form we're building right now. So entriesList View feels right because it seems to be a minimally descriptive and unique name.

We would not recommend just slapping the type name on the end of your control names out of habit, of course. Choosing identifier names requires thought (and that goes for all identifiers, not just those in Windows Forms apps). You should aim for the shortest possible name that will make it easy to understand the code when you return to it six months after you wrote it. If that happens to be a name that includes the type name, that's fine, as long as you thought about it first.

Finally, ListView supports multiple-item selection, but we want to have only one item selected at a time. Since multiple selection is the default, we need to set the MultiSelect property to false.

Next, we'll add a TextBox so that the user can edit entry titles and a corresponding Label so that the user can see what the TextBox is for. These controls are found in the Common Controls section of the toolbar. We'll set the Text property of the Label to &Title:—the ampersand denotes an access key so that the user can press Alt-T to put the focus into the text box. Access keys make user interfaces much easier to use from the keyboard.

When you give a Label an access key, it puts the focus into whichever control is next in the tab order. By default, the tab order will be the order in which you added the controls to the form. But you can change this by selecting the View menu's Tab Order item (which is present only when a Windows Forms design view has the focus). When you enable Tab Order mode, you can click on the controls one after another, and the order in which you click will define the tab order.

Therefore, your life will be marginally easier if you add each Label control just before you add the associated TextBox control because you won't then need to go back and redo the tab order.

We'll also add a label with the text &Due Date: followed by a `DateTimePicker` control, and finally another text box with a label of `Descri&ption:`. (Note that we've been careful to avoid ambiguous access keys; Alt-D is for the due date, so we had to pick a different letter for the description—Alt-P.) For the description, we'd like the user to be able to write multiple lines of text, so we need to do two things. We need to set the `AcceptsRe turn` property to `true`—this prevents the Return key from having the usual effect of clicking the form's default button, and lets the text box handle returns instead. We also need to set the `Multiline` property to `true`. These two properties may seem redundant, but sometimes it's useful to support multiple lines with word wrapping but still have the Return key click the default button, which is why these two aspects are separated out. In this application we need to set both.

Finally, we need a couple of buttons—one to add new items and one to delete items. We'll set the `Text` properties to `&New` and `&Delete`, once more taking care to keep access keys unique. Again, we want all our controls to have sensible names, so we'll go with `titleText`, `dueDatePicker`, `descriptionText`, `newButton`, and `deleteButton` for the various controls we've just added. (The names of the `Label` controls are not so significant, as we won't be using them from the code behind, but out of a slightly obsessive sense of neatness we'll called those `titleLabel`, `dueDateLabel`, and `descriptionLabel`.) Figure 22-6 shows the work in progress.

Figure 22-6. The basic layout

In fact, we're not quite done here because there's a problem when the user resizes the form. As Figure 22-7 shows, the `ListView` fills all the width, but the remaining controls have somewhat disappointing behavior. Fortunately, we can fix this.

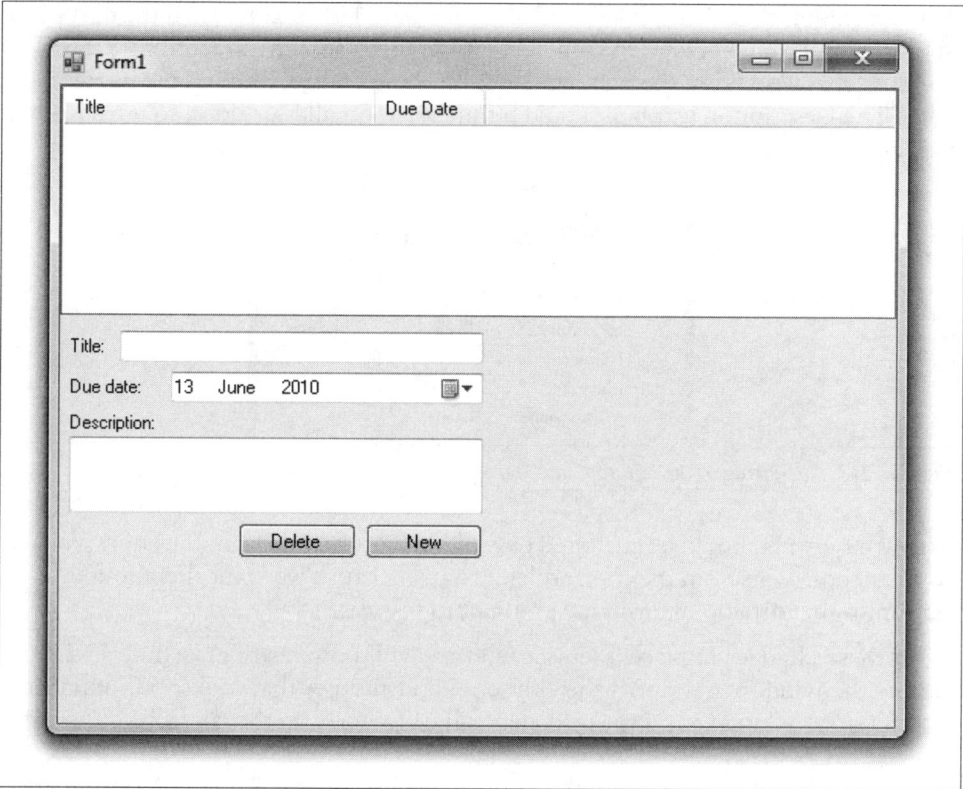

Figure 22-7. Poor resize behavior

Docking and Anchoring

Windows Forms controls support a couple of kinds of automatic resizing behavior. They can be *docked*—we already have two docked controls, in fact. The `SplitContainer` is docked to fill the entire form, and the `ListView` is docked to fill the top half of the `SplitContainer`. If you edit the `Dock` property with the Properties window (instead of the Task pop up we used earlier) you can also dock controls to a particular edge of their container, rather than having to fill the whole thing—this is useful for menus and toolbars that need to appear along the top edge of a window.

The other form of automatic resizing is *anchoring*. An anchored control doesn't have to fill the whole width and/or height of its container, but instead can resize or move as its container resizes. You can anchor the top, left, bottom, or right of any control to the corresponding edge of its container. In fact, by default, controls are anchored to the top and left sides of their container—this means that when the container (e.g., the window) moves, the contained controls go with it, but if the user resizes the window by moving either the right or bottom edge, the controls remain as they are.

We can exploit this to make our controls resize. The Title text box and the date picker should both be anchored to the top, left, and right, as shown in Figure 22-8. So as the window changes width, the righthand edge of these controls will follow its righthand edge. The Description text box should be anchored on all four sides, so it resizes both vertically and horizontally.

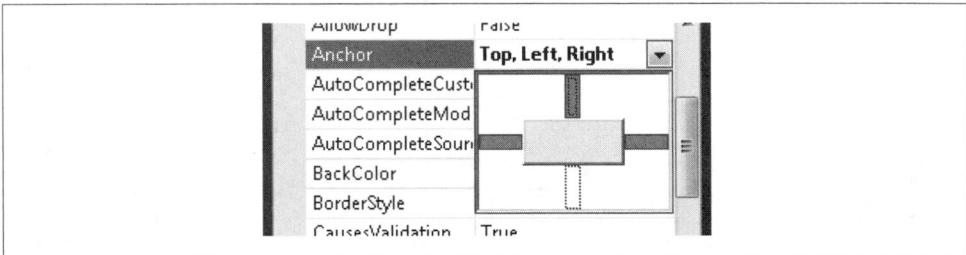

Figure 22-8. Anchoring to the left, top, and right

The two buttons should be anchored only on the bottom and right, meaning you need to unanchor them from the top and left. That's because we want them to follow the bottom-right corner of the window, but not to resize.

With these changes in place, the user interface will now resize gracefully as the user resizes the window or adjusts the splitter. Good though that looks, our application doesn't do anything yet. So the next step will be to hook up the controls to the data.

Data Binding

Earlier, we configured a data source and then we added some controls to represent our data. Now it's time to connect the two. If we select the text box for the title, and then in the Properties panel scroll to the top of the list, there's an expandable (`DataBindings`) item, inside which is a list of properties you're likely to want to bind. (You can bind other properties, but most controls have only a handful of properties that it's likely to be useful to data-bind to.) If you show the drop down for the `Text` property, the reason for adding a binding source earlier becomes apparent. As Figure 22-9 shows, Visual Studio offers a list of available data sources (just the one here —our form's `entriesSource`), which you can expand to select the property you require.

We'll bind the two text boxes and date picker (binding the `Value` property in that case) on our form to the three properties. To check that this is working, we'll need some data—the list we created earlier is currently empty. We'll add a helper function to create a new item; we'll need this for when the user clicks the New button, as well as for creating an initial item for when the application starts:

```
private void CreateNewItem()
{
    ToDoEntry newEntry = (ToDoEntry) entriesSource.AddNew();
    newEntry.Title = "New entry";
```

```
        newEntry.DueDate = DateTime.Now;
        entriesSource.ResetCurrentItem();
    }
```

Notice that we're using the AddNew method offered by the binding source—this means the binding system is aware that a new item is being created, and if other controls end up being bound to the same source, they will be aware of the change. We then modify two of the properties.

 Since we're using a BindingList, the data binding system would also be aware of a new item if we just added it directly to the entries collection. However, there's a subtle difference with AddNew—rather than just appearing on the end of the list view, this new item will become the selected item. And in fact, it'll be in a tentative state until we move to a different item or add another new one—this program happens not to exploit this, but we could cancel the addition of a new item if the user presses the Escape key.

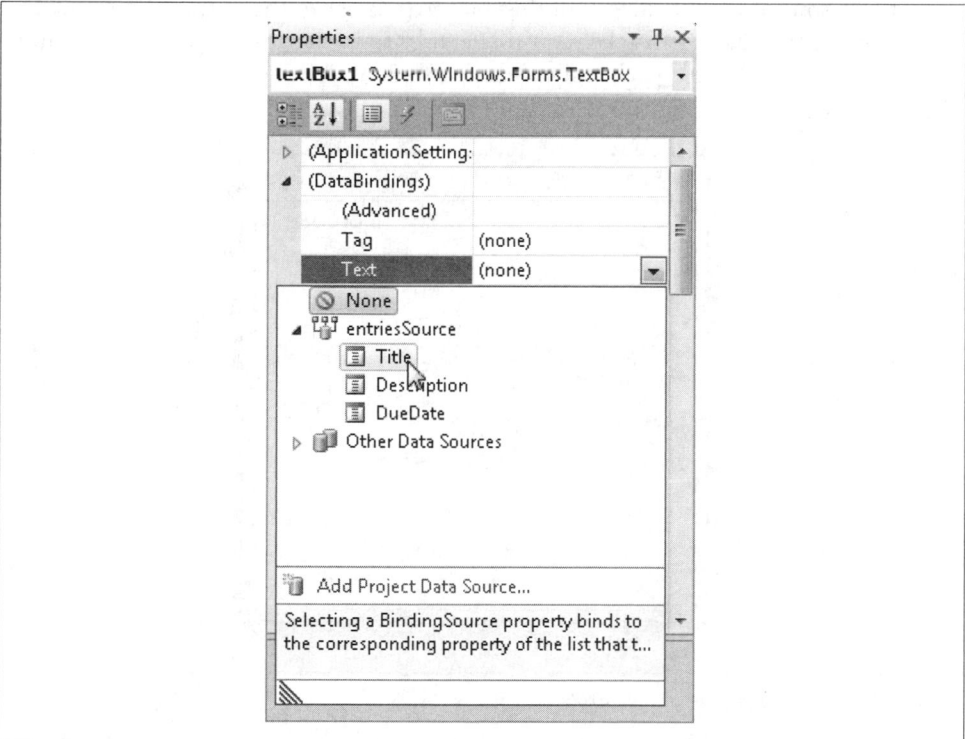

Figure 22-9. Binding a property

Our `ToDoEntry` class doesn't offer change notification events, so we had to tell the binding source that it needs to refresh any controls bound to the current item by calling `ResetCurrentItem`. If we implemented `INotifyPropertyChanged` on `ToDoEntry` so that it raised an event anytime a property changed, this last line would be unnecessary.

We need to add a call to this new method in our constructor so that we have one entry to start with:

```
public Form1()
{
    InitializeComponent();

    entriesSource.DataSource = entries;

    CreateNewItem();
}
```

With this in place, we'll see the `New entry` title set by the `CreateNewItem` method appearing in the Title text box as Figure 22-10 shows. The description is empty for now, so there's nothing to see, and although the due date is now bound to the `DueDate` property, there's no obvious evidence of this—`DueDate` is set to the current time and date, which is what the `DateTimePicker` control defaults to in the absence of any other information, so we can't see any change resulting from data binding for that control yet.

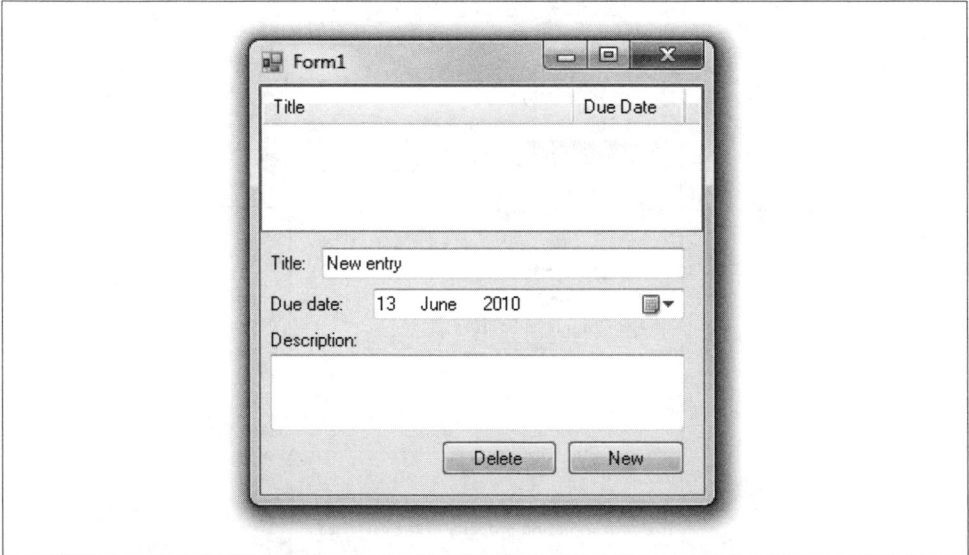

Figure 22-10. Form with bound controls

There's one glaring omission: the ListView isn't showing any data. And that's because, as mentioned previously, it doesn't have built-in support for data binding. We're going to need to write some code. Fortunately, it's relatively straightforward—the binding source raises events to let us know whenever something has changed. If you select the entriesSource item in the form's design view and then go to the Properties panel and select the lightning bolt symbol to show the available events, there's a ListChanged event. We can add a handler by double-clicking that event. We expect three kinds of changes in the application—addition of new items, updates to existing items, and deletion of existing items—so we'll be writing three methods to handle that. The change event argument tells us which kind of change we're getting, so we just pick the relevant method based on the change type, as Example 22-3 shows.

Example 22-3. Handling changes

```
private void entriesSource_ListChanged(object sender, ListChangedEventArgs e)
{
    switch (e.ListChangedType)
    {
        case ListChangedType.ItemAdded:
            MakeListViewItemForNewEntry(e.NewIndex);
            break;

        case ListChangedType.ItemDeleted:
            RemoveListViewItem(e.NewIndex);
            break;

        case ListChangedType.ItemChanged:
            UpdateListViewItem(e.NewIndex);
            break;
    }
}
```

You might be wondering why we are asking the binding source to tell us when items have been added and changed, when we're writing the code that adds and changes items in the first place. The main reason is that there are certain tricky cases, such as what happens if you have an event handler for a text box's TextChanged event that runs as a result of a data-binding-related change, but which in turn causes further data binding changes; it's easy to tie yourself in knots, or end up with code that's rather fragile because it depends on things happening in a specific order. But if we just perform updates when the data binding system tells us to (via the events that BindingSource raises) things tend to run more smoothly.

Let's start with the code that handles the addition of a new entry. We need to create a new ListViewItem for the list and ensure that it contains two columns. Since a new ListViewItem already has one column by default, we need to add a second one, as Example 22-4 shows. And then we just insert it into whatever position the binding source said it was added to—in this application we always expect that to be the end, but since we're given a specific index, we may as well use it.

Example 22-4. Adding new list items when new to-do entries appear

```
private void MakeListViewItemForNewEntry(int newItemIndex)
{
    ListViewItem item = new ListViewItem();
    item.SubItems.Add("");
    entriesListView.Items.Insert(newItemIndex, item);
}
```

This code doesn't bother to provide values for the newly created item, because the binding source immediately follows a new item notification with an item change notification. So by putting code to update the list view item in the change notification handler, shown in Example 22-5, we cover two cases: new items and changes to existing items.

Example 22-5. Making list view items reflect changes

```
private void UpdateListViewItem(int itemIndex)
{
    ListViewItem item = entriesListView.Items[itemIndex];
    ToDoEntry entry = entries[itemIndex];
    item.SubItems[0].Text = entry.Title;
    item.SubItems[1].Text = entry.DueDate.ToShortDateString();
}
```

Finally, Example 22-6 shows the code for handling deleted items. We've not added the code to perform deletions yet, but we need this method in place for Example 22-3 to compile.

Example 22-6. Removing list view items for deleted entries

```
private void RemoveListViewItem(int deletedItemIndex)
{
    entriesListView.Items.RemoveAt(deletedItemIndex);
}
```

Running the application will now show the title and due date for a newly created entry in the list view immediately. And updating the title or date will also cause the list view to update. There's still one small problem. By default, data bindings don't perform an update until the focus moves away from the control in question. This is only mildly annoying for the text box, but it looks quite odd with the date picker—selecting the date involves clicking on a day, at which point the pop-up calendar disappears. This is a sufficiently positive action that it feels weird to have to move the focus somewhere else for the action to take effect. We can fix this by setting up the bindings manually, because that gives us the opportunity to specify exactly when data is transferred.

To do this, we must first remove the bindings we set up with Visual Studio—if we're creating them manually we don't have any need for the ones the designer created. We do this by going back to the (DataBindings) section in the Properties panel, right-clicking on the relevant bound property, and selecting Reset. (If you switched to the event list with the lightning bolt earlier, remember to switch the Properties panel back to property mode.) You need to do this for only the due date and the title—the description isn't shown anywhere other than in its text box, which means the default updates are good enough, so we can leave that as is. Then, we can add the highlighted code shown here in the form's constructor directly after the call to InitializeComponent:

```
public Form1()
{
    InitializeComponent();

    titleText.DataBindings.Add("Text", entriesSource, "Title", true,
        DataSourceUpdateMode.OnPropertyChanged);
    dueDatePicker.DataBindings.Add("Value", entriesSource, "DueDate", true,
        DataSourceUpdateMode.OnPropertyChanged);

    entriesSource.DataSource = entries;

    CreateNewItem();
}
```

The first three arguments of each of these specify the control property, the data source, and the source property—this defines what information the binding connects. The true argument that follows says it's OK for binding to format the data if necessary. These arguments just do the same thing Visual Studio did for us previously. The final argument is the interesting one. We're saying we want the binding to refresh anytime the property changes, rather than the default setting of waiting until either the focus moves or something else means we can't wait any longer (e.g., different data is about to be loaded).

With this in place, changes to either the title or the due date will show up immediately in the list view.

So we now have some controls that present the data, and in the case of the text boxes and date picker, which will also modify the data. The next job is to make those buttons do something.

Event Handling

To respond to user input in Windows Forms applications, we can just use ordinary C# event handling—user interface elements are all represented as objects, and they raise events in the usual way whenever anything interesting happens. As you already saw with the binding source change notifications, Visual Studio can generate the event-handling code for us.

Controls define a default event, usually the event you are most likely to want to handle for the control in question. So we can handle the Click events of the two buttons by double-clicking on them in the designer. Visual Studio will add event handler methods with suitable names and signatures, and will add the code to handle the event in the generated part of the partial class. We simply need to provide the code. The New button handler is pretty straightforward, because we already wrote the code to add a new item:

```
private void newButton_Click(object sender, EventArgs e)
{
    CreateNewItem();
}
```

Deletion is slightly more involved:

```
private void deleteButton_Click(object sender, EventArgs e)
{
    if (entriesListView.SelectedIndices.Count != 0)
    {
        int entryIndex = entriesListView.SelectedIndices[0];
        entriesSource.RemoveAt(entryIndex);
    }
}
```

The ListView control is able to support multiple selection. We've disabled this, but we still have to negotiate an API designed to support it—it offers a SelectedIndices collection, providing all the selected items. We just make sure it's not empty, and then use the first index. We remove the object via the binding source so that the data binding system knows what's going on, just as we did when adding a new item. (In fact, it would work if we didn't do this because this example uses a BindingList to hold the model, and that raises change notifications. Unlike AddNew, there's no particular advantage to going via the binding source here, but since we're treating the binding source as the central point through which all changes are handled, it's good to be consistent.)

We can now add multiple entries. This reveals a missing piece—we have done nothing yet to ensure that when the user selects an item in the list view, the corresponding entry's properties appear in the rest of the form. So we need to add a handler to the list view's SelectedIndexChanged event. That's its default event, so you can just double-click the list view in the form designer. Then all we need to do is set the binding source's Position property:

```
private void entriesListView_SelectedIndexChanged(object sender, EventArgs e)
{
    if (entriesListView.SelectedIndices.Count != 0)
    {
        int entryIndex = entriesListView.SelectedIndices[0];
        entriesSource.Position = entryIndex;
    }
}
```

We've had to jump through the same hoop to get the selected item index. There's really just one line of interest here—the one that sets the Position.

 We have to do this only because the `ListView` doesn't do data binding automatically. The `ListBox` and most data grid controls will automatically synchronize the current data binding position with the selected item.

One little bug remains. When we delete all the items, the text boxes and date picker are bound to nothing. This doesn't crash the program; it just means the user can type in details that go nowhere. There are a couple of ways we could fix this. In the list change notification handler, we could look at the number of entries, and disable everything except the New button to make it clear that there's nothing to edit right now. Or we could handle change notifications in the text boxes—text box controls raise a `TextChanged` event, and we could handle that (as well as changes to the date picker or description) and create a new entry if the user types into an empty list. Since neither of these would illustrate anything you haven't already seen we'll leave this part up to you.

Summary

Windows Forms provides a .NET wrapper around the Win32 user interface model. Visible elements are represented as objects that derive from the `Control` base class. Control features are configured with normal .NET properties, and we can use ordinary C# event handlers to respond to user input. Data binding automates some aspects of connecting data to the screen, although the support in Windows Forms is not as comprehensive as in WPF, and we needed to do some extra work to get the effect we required on the control we wanted to use. Windows Forms may be less powerful than WPF, but it has a smaller memory footprint and may be more suitable on low-end hardware, or if you need to use controls that are available only for Windows Forms.

Index

Symbols

!= not equal to operator, 43
& address-of operator, 720
&& Boolean combination operator (if both true), 43
* dereference operator, 720
* multiplication operator, 35
+ addition operator, 35
++ increment operator, 38
+= adding value operator, 38, 630
- subtraction operator, 35
-- decrement operator, 38
-> member access operator, 720
. delineation operator, 19
/ division operator, 35
/* */ multi-line comment, 25
// single-line comment, 25
/// XML Documentation Comments, 26
32-bit processes, 5, 30, 236, 713–716
3D graphics, 755
64-bit processes, 5, 30, 236, 713–716
: calling one constructor from another, 86
: part of ternary operator, 44
; end statement, 24
< less than operator, 43
<= less than or equal to operator, 43
= field initializer operator, 74
== equal to operator, 43
=> lambda expression, 163
> greater than operator, 43
>= greater than or equal to operator, 43
? part of ternary operator, 44
@" " string literal, 321
[ ] array index, 222

\ (backslash) escape character, 319–322
\n line feed, 346
\r carriage return, 346
{} braces, C# containment, 17, 24
|| Boolean combination operator (if either true), 43

A

∀ universal quantifier, 292
abstract base classes, 121–127, 139
abstracting ideas, 59–63
accepting incoming connections, 533
accessibility modifiers, 67, 114–116
ACL (access control list), 490
Action<T>, 156–160
ActiveX Controls, 707–710
Add method, 245, 257, 308, 576
Add Reference menu item, 23
AddAnything method, 691, 697
AddBefore/AddAfter methods, 312
adding value (+=) operator, 38, 630
addition (+) operator, 35
AddNew method, 807
AddNumbers method, 254, 258, 259
AddProcess method, 159
AddRange method, 246, 279
AddTo methods, 574
administrative privileges, 490
ADO.NET, 540–544, 571
Adobe PDF Reader control, 708–710
affine transformations, 747
aggregation, 105, 292
air traffic control example
    constructors, overloading, 88–92
    declaring an enum, 79–82

We'd like to hear your suggestions for improving our indexes. Send email to *index@oreilly.com*.

defining classes, 64–66
defining methods, 95–98
defining variables/types, 82–87
initializing with a constructor, 68–72
object initializers, 92–95
setting protection levels, 66–68
setting up fields and properties, 72–79
specs for, 62
static fields and properties, 99–102
aliases, 30
All operator, 291
ampersand (&), address-of operator, 720
anchoring, 805
animation, 753
anonymous methods, 162
anonymous type, 283
Any operator, 291
APM (Asynchronous Programming Model),
    652–655, 663
appdomains, 605
AppendLine method, 350
application isolation, 434
args variable, 39
argument exceptions, 216
arrays, 39
    construction and initialization of, 222–225
    custom indexers in, 247–253
    custom types in, 225–230
    jagged, 236–238, 241
    List<T> as resizable, 243–254
    members/elements of, 230–236
    multidimensional, 238
    params keyword, 225
    rectangular, 238–243
    size of, 236–243
as keyword, 141
ASCII, 361
ASP.NET (see Web Forms and ASP.NET)
.aspx extension, 776
assemblies
    loading, 601–605
    naming, 598–601
    overview, 589
    protecting, 595–598
    referencing, 590–592
    writing libraries, 593–595
AssemblyInfo.cs, 21
assignment statements, 38
associations, 104, 108, 556–558

asterisk (*) dereference operator, 720
asynchronous file operations, 425–428, 517
asynchronous programming, 651–656, 663
Atom, 514
attached properties, 741
attributes, 456–459, 671–677
authentication, 518
Authenticode signature, 434
auto properties, 73

B

backlog, 533
backslash (\), escape character, 319–322
base classes, 106, 116–118, 121
Base64 encoding, 444–446
basic authentication, 519
basic profile, 474
Begin methods, 652, 663
BeginTransaction/EnlistTransaction methods,
    579
behaviors, 754
Berners-Lee, Tim, 512
BigInteger, 31
binary, 20, 33, 444–446, 589
bindings, 508, 763, 767–769, 784–787, 806–
    811
bit fields, 81
bitmaps, 751
bitness, 713
blocking APIs, 651
BlockingCollection, 650
BOM (Byte Order Mark), 363
bool type, 42
boxing, 127
braces {}, C# containment, 17, 24
brackets [ ], array index, 222
break keyword, 46, 53
breakpoints, 50, 200, 438
buffering, 423
bugs, defined, 185
Bustamante, Michele Leroux, 486
button element, 732–735, 740–748, 755–765,
    777, 784–793
Byte Order Mark, 363

C

C#
    compared to Java, 6

creating a new program in, 11
improvements in version 2.0, 258
improvements in version 3.0, 92, 265, 284
improvements in version 4.0, 7–9, 725–727
Internet resources for, 9
language style, 3–7
and managed code, 5
overview, 1–9
C++
    memory management issues in, 5
    and .NET Framework, 3
caching, 302–305, 520
calculated properties, 71
call stack, 57, 200
callback interface, 501
calling base class methods, 116–118
calling client from server, 505–508
camel casing, 65, 154
CancelAsync method, 656
cancellation, 663
cancelling events, 177–180
Canvas panel, 742
carriage return (\r), 346
cascading deletes, 576
cast operator, 33
catch blocks, 207–215
chaining enumerations, 262
char types, 317, 360
characters, 341, 343–344
charmap, 365
child elements, 450
Church, Alonzo, 163
cipher text, 440
classes
    defined, 62
    how to decide on, 63
    how to define, 17, 64
    in .NET, 3
    nested, 159
    sealing, 119
CleanupTestDirectories method, 394
CLI (Common Language Infrastructure), 87
ClickOnce Publication Wizard, 434
Close method, 9
closures, 169
CLR (Common Language Runtime), 3
code pages, 361
code points, 362

code separation, 776
code-behind files, 733, 775, 780, 793
codespace, 362
collection classes
    defined, 56
    dictionaries, 299–307
    HashSet and SortedSet, 310
    IDictionary<TKey>, <TValue>, 308–310
    lazy, 261–264
    linked lists, 312
    and polymorphisms, 254–258
    queues, 311
    stacks, 313
    when working in C++, 3
colon (:), calling one constructor from another, 86
COM automation, 7, 689, 693
Combine methods, 387
command-line inputs, 39
comments, use of, 25–27
Common Language Infrastructure (CLI), 87
Common Language Runtime (CLR), 3
comparable types, 234
CompareBytes method, 417
CompareFiles method, 410
CompareTo method, 233
comparison operators, 42, 355
Comparison<T>, 233
compilation, 20, 91, 250, 271, 285
Compile method, 567
composability with delegates (see extensibility with delegates)
composing strings, 344–348
composite formatting, 337
composition, 105, 273
Concat method, 345, 691
concatenation, 279, 345, 387
conceptual models, 549
Concurrent Programming on Windows (Joe Duffy), 632
Configure method, 154
Connect method, 504, 531
connection handling, database, 571–573
Console Application template, 12
const modifier, 75
constrained layout, 744
constructors, 68, 87–88, 423–425
Contains method, 310
contended resource, defined, 186

content controls, 755–761
contention, 611
context switches, 620
contextual keywords, 71
continuations, 661
ContinueWith method, 661, 666
control characters, 361, 362
controls
    ActiveX, 707–710
    Adobe PDF Reader, 708–710
    Silverlight/WPF, 755–761
    web form, 783, 790–793
    Windows Forms, 800–804
    Xaml libraries, 759
conversions, 37, 296
cookies, 521
copying array elements, 234
CopyTo method, 235, 421
Count method/property, 246, 293
countdown, 650
coupling, 144
CreateDirectory methods, 387
CreateEncryptor method, 443
CreateFile method, 399, 720
CreateInstance/CreateComInstanceFrom/
        CreateComInstanceFrom methods,
        684
CreateNewItem method, 808
CreateText method, 397
CRUD (Create, Read, Update, and Delete)
        operations, 574–576
CryptoStream, 443
.cs extension, 12
culture sensitivity, 338–340
currency values, 323
current working directory, 376
Curry, Haskell, 163
custom attributes, 673–677
custom dynamic objects, 702
custom event storage, 181–182
custom exceptions, 218–220
custom indexers, 247–253
custom interfaces (COM), 694
custom numeric format strings, 329–332

D
Dahl, Ole-Johan, 62
data access with LINQ, 4
data binding, 767–769, 784–787, 806–811

data parallelism, 666–670
database LINQ providers, 544
databases
    changing the mapping of, 554
    connection handling, 571–573
    context and entity lifetime, 583
    creating, updating, deleting data, 574–576
    Entity data model, 548–550
    and ESQL, 568–571
    functions delegates versus expressions, 567
    generated code from .edmx, 551–554
    and object context, 571–573, 583
    optimistic concurrency, 581–583
    queries, 563–571
    relationships between tables, 555–562
    and SQL Server 2008 Express, 547
    transactions, 576–581
    WCF Data Services, 546, 584–588
DataSet class, 543
date and time strings, 332–335
daytime service, 527, 534
deadlocks, 632
deadly embraces, 632
debugger (Visual Studio), 50, 205, 379, 438
decimal floating point, 34
decimal format, 324
declarative pinning, 722
decoding, 363, 365
decrement (--) operator, 38
decryption, 445
default constructors, 87
default named parameters, 89–92
deferred execution, 263, 274, 544, 563
degenerate query, 282
degrees, in relationships, 560
delegates, 150–156, 165–167, 271
Delete method, 381, 400
DeleteObject method, 576
deleting files, 381
Dequeue method, 311
derived classes, 106–109
Descendants method, 466
Deserialize method, 469
design by contract philosophy, 202
dictionaries, 299–307
digest authentication, 519
digital signing, 599
Dijkstra, Edsger, 54
directories

creating and securing, 388–394
deleting, 394–396
inspecting, 371–375
disambiguation, 15
Disconnect method, 504, 507
disconnected operation, 543
DisplayMatches function, 409
DisplayResults method, 411
Distinct operator, 295
divide-by-zero problems, 190
division (/) operator, 35
division, integer versus floating-point, 36
DLL, 19, 589, 602, 716, 759
.dll extension, 19, 589
do while Statements, 53
docking, 805
DockPanel, 743
document processing example (see extensibility
     with delegates)
Domain Name Service (DNS), 524
Don't Make Me Think (Krug), 791
dot (.) delineation operator, 19
double keyword, 28
double type, 31–34, 191
Download methods, 512, 513, 651, 655
downloading from URL, 512
dry (don't repeat yourself) principle, 72
dual-mode sockets, 532
Duffy, Joe, 632
duplex clients, 509–511
duplex contracts, 501
dynamic keyword, 9, 693, 695, 700, 703
dynamic object types, 693–703
dynamic programming, 7, 687–693
dynamic properties, 305
dynamic type, 690
DynamicWhere method, 704

E

∃ existential quantifier, 292
EDM (Entity Data Model), 549
.edmx extension, 551
EF (Entity Framework), 548–550
    and ADO.NET, 571
    connection handling in, 571–573
    and CRUD operations, 574–576
    and EDM, 548–550
    and ESQL, 568–571
    first release, 544

inheritance, 562
and Link to Entities, 563–571
and mapping, 555
multiplicity, 560
and navigation properties, 556–558
queries in, 563, 567
versus LINQ to SQL, 545
and WCF, 546, 584
elements
    array, 230–234
    graphical, 748–755
    method, 465
    UI, 738–748
    XML, 450, 455
embarrassingly parallel tasks, 626
empty strings, 355–357
encapsulation, 60, 71, 150
encoding characters, 360–370
encryption, 439–446
EncryptString method, 442
End methods, 652, 654, 663
EndGetHostEntry method, 654
endpoints, 490
English, cultural variants in, 338
Enqueue method, 311
Entity Data Model (EDM), 549
Entity Framework (EF) (see EF (Entity
     Framework))
entity lifetime, 583
Entity SQL (ESQL), 568–571
entry point, 589
enum keyword, 79–82, 197
EnumerateFiles method, 266
enumerations
    FileMode, FileAccess, FileShare, 422
    filenames, 266
    lazy, 261–264
    and variance, 257
equals (=), field initializer operator, 74
Equals methods, 300
errors
    custom exceptions, 218–220
    debugging with return values, 200
    deciding what to catch, 215–218
    exceptions, 201–214
    overview, 185–191
    setting return values, 194–201
    task handling, 665
    try, catch, finally blocks, 207–215, 260

when and how to fail, 191–194
escape characters, 319–322
ESQL (Entity SQL), 568–571
evaluation order, 37
event keyword, 171
event overlaps, 291
event storage management, 181–182
EventHandler<T>, 176
events handling, 171–182, 649, 776, 790–793, 811
exception types, 215
exceptions, 201–214, 260
    custom, 218–220
    for files, 400–409
.exe extension, 19, 589
existential quantifier, 292
ExpandoObject class, 701
explicit
    element types, 224
    interface implementation, 136–139
    loading, 604
    member access, 97
    TreeViewItem containers, 757
exponential form, 325
Expression Blend, Microsoft, 736
expression trees, 164
Expression<T> type, 567
expressions, 35–38
extensibility and polymorphism
    all types derived from Object, 127–132
    association through composition and aggregation, 104
    calling base class methods, 116–118
    checking types at runtime, 141
    deriving interfaces from other interfaces, 135–140
    inheritance and polymorphism, 106–108
    inheritance and protection, 114–116
    marking a class sealed, 118–121
    multiple inheritance, 132–135
    replacing methods in derived classes, 109–114
    requiring overrides with abstract, 121–127
    XML, 452
extensibility with delegates
    creating delegates with lambda expressions, 163–165
    delegates in properties, 165–167

functional composition with delegate, 150–156
generic action with Action<T>, 156–160
generic delegates for functions, 167–171
generic predicates with Predicate<T>, 160–162
notifying clients with events, 171–182
setup, 143–150
using anonymous methods, 162
extension methods, 268–270, 344, 698
external client, 480
external party web service, 479

F

F#, 4
factory methods, 92
fall-through in case statements, 46
fetching, 512
fibers, 613
field initializer, 74
fields, 72–79
File.Exists method, 401
FileInfo object, 377, 406
FileOptions enumeration, 425
files and streams
    asynchronous file operations, 425–428
    concatenating path elements safely, 387
    creating and securing directory hierarchies, 388–394
    creating temporary files, 381
    CryptoStream, 443
    dealing with exceptions, 400–409
    deleting a directory, 394–396
    deleting files, 381
    examining directories, 374
    FileStream constructors, 423–425
    finding and modifying permissions, 404–409
    inspecting directories and files, 371–375
    isolated storage, 428–439
    managing user storage with quotas, 436–439
    manipulating file paths, 375–377
    MemoryStream, 444
    reading files into memory, 409–413
    reading, writing, and locking files, 422–423
    streams, 413–421
    streams that aren't files, 439–446
    well-known folders, 383–387

writing text files, 396–400
filtering, 275
finalization, 666
finally blocks, 207
FindAll method, 231, 237, 254
finding and replacing content, 353
fine-grained concurrency, 659
firefighter training and simulation example (see
    extensibility and polymorphism)
firewalls, 502, 535
fixed keyword, 721, 724
Fixed-point format, 326
[Flags] enum, 81
flags-style enumeration, 425
floating point types, 31–34
flow control, 39–54
flushing data, 423
fonts, 316
for statements, 50
ForEach methods, 628, 667–670
foreach statements, 48, 254, 258–260
format characters, 362
format items, 337
formatting data for output, 322–329
friendly feed rendering, 586
FromAsync method, 663
Func<> types, 167
functional coding/style, 18, 143, 273, 279
functional decomposition, 61
functions, 60, 167–171
futures, 661

G

GAC (global assembly cache), 603
garbage collection, 5
general format, 326
GenerateIV/GenerateKey methods, 441
generic classes
    List<T>, 243–254
generic delegates
    Action<T>, 156–160
    EventHandler<T>, 176
    Predicate<T>, 160–162
generic types, 244
get accessor, 64–71, 130
GetAccessControl method, 405
GetAllFilesInDirectory method, 266
GetCipherText method, 445
GetEnumerator method, 255

GetFiles method, 374
GetFolderPath method, 383, 387
GetHashCode method, 300
GetLength method, 243
GetMachineStoreForApplication/Domain/
    Assembly methods, 436
GetMembers method, 682, 683
GetMethods, 683
GetRandomFileName method, 382
GetResourceStream method, 604
GetStream method, 517
GetString method, 367, 723
GetTempFileName method, 381
GetType method, 468, 680
GetUserStoreForAssembly/
    GetUserStoreForDomain methods,
    432
GetWeb methods, 515
global assembly cache (GAC), 603
global namespace, 16
Go method, 614, 621, 630
GoNow method, 642
governing type, 80
graphic characters, 362
Grid panel, 739–742
groupby clause, 286
grouping, 280–282
guard clauses, 202

H

hardware threads, 612
hashes, 300
HashSet, 310
heap, on the, 84
heap-allocated objects, 5
Hejlsberg, Anders, 65
"Hello, world", 2, 12, 18, 21, 24
hexadecimal format, 324
hiding methods, 109–111
hierarchies, directory, 388–394
high surrogates, 362
HighlightTrademarks method, 155
HorizontalAlignment, 744
Hurwitz, Dan, 775
hyperthreading, 612

I

IANA (Internet Assigned Numbers Authority), 527
ICollection<T>, 293
IDataReader, 540–544
IDictionary<TKey>, <TValue>, 308–310
IEnumerable<T> and IEnumerator<T>, 255, 269, 273
if statements, 40–45
if...else statements, 44–45
IL (Intermediate Language), 5, 20
images, 751
immutability
    of sources, 273
    of strings, 341
    of value types, 84, 251
implementation, switching of, 71
implicit transactions, 579
Implicit type conversions, 37
in keyword, 257
Include method, 559
IncreaseQuotaTo method, 436
increment operator (++), 38
indexed properties, 725
indexers, 247–253
indexes, array, 222
IndexOf method, 353
infinite series, 263
inheritance, 106–108, 562
initialization vector, 440
initialization, field, 74
initializer list, 223
InitializeService method, 585
inline array initializer, 224
inlined methods, 162
inner exceptions, 212
inscrutable identifiers, 302
InspectDirectories method, 373, 406
integers (int), 29–31, 80
IntelliSense, 165, 339, 696, 734
interface keyword, 133
interfaces, 132–140, 255
Intermediate Language, 5, 20
internal protection level, 66, 596–598
Internet Assigned Numbers Authority (IANA), 527
Internet Protocol, 523–528
interop assemblies, 711–713
interop scenarios, 423

interop syntax enhancements, 725–727
interoperability, 7, 707
into keyword, 281
intrinsic ordering, 233
Invoke function, 152, 684
IP/IPv6, 523–528
is keyword, 141
is-a association, 106
IsAssignableFrom method, 682
ISet<T>, 311
IsHighSurrogate/IsLowSurrogate methods, 362
IsNumber/IsLetter methods, 362
isolated storage, 371, 428–439
IsWhitespace method, 360
iteration statements, 47–54
iteration variables, 51

J

jagged arrays, 236–238, 241
Java, compared to C#, 6
JavaScript, 694, 737
Join method, 617, 641
joining of sources, 295
JSON (JavaScript Object Notation), 474

K

key pairs, 600
key type, 300
keys, 342, 586
Kleene, S. C., 163
Krug, Steve, 791

L

lambda expressions, 163–165, 271, 700
late binding, 683–685
layout panels, 739–748
layout properties, 743–748
layout slot, 743
lazy enumeration, 261–264, 274
lazy loading, 558
Learning ASP.NET 3.5 (Liberty, Hurwitz, MacDonald), 775
Learning WCF (Bustamante), 486
least-significant byte (LSB), 369
let clauses, 271
Liberty, Jesse, 775
libraries, 22, 593–595

life cycle, 778
LIFO (last in, first out) queues, 660
ligatures, 362
lightweight value types, 85
line feed, 346
linked lists, 312
LINQ (Language Integrated Query)
    aggregation, 292
    concatenation, 279
    concepts and techniques, 271–275
    conversions, 296
    data access with, 4
    and databases, 544
    filtering, 275
    grouping, 280–282
    joining, 295
    namespace, 15
    ordering, 276–279
    projections, 282–288
    query expressions, 265–268
    searching in XML with, 461–464
    set operations, 294
    zipping, 288
LINQ to Entities, 563–571
LINQ to SQL, 544
LINQ to XML, 452–455
Linux, 7, 730
Liskov Substitution Principle (LSP), 107
Liskov, Barbara, 107
List<T> class, 129, 148, 243–254
listening, 533–534
literal expressions, 35
literal strings/chars, 318
little-endian form, 369
livelocks, 632
Load method, 455, 558, 604, 680
LoadFile method, 416, 604
LoadFiles function, 410
loading assemblies, 601–605
localhost, 525, 532
lock keyword, 641
locking, 637–649
logical processors, 611
loops, breaking out of, 53
low surrogates, 362
lowercase letters, 347
Lowy, Juval, 486
LSP (Liskov Substitution Principle), 107

M

Mac OS X, 7
MacDonald, Brian, 775
machine isolation, 435
machine language, 20
machine translation (see extensibility with
    delegates)
Maharry, Dan, 775
Main method, 18, 39, 97
MakeTestDirectories method, 386, 404
Managed Extensibility Framework (MEF),
    604
many-to-many relationships, 562
mapping, database, 548, 554
media, 753
MEF (Managed Extensibility Framework),
    604
member access (->) operator, 720
members of a type, 682
memory, reading files into, 409–413
MemoryStream, 444
Message property, 203
metadata, 496, 589, 677
methods
    abstracting ideas with, 59–63
    anonymous, 162
    calling base class, 116–118
    declaring, 95–99
    defined, 17
    hiding, 109–111
    and LINQ queries, 267
    needs of users and developers, 60
    overloaded, 89–92
    overview, 55–57
    replacing, 112–114
    static, 98
    versus functions, 60
    virtual, 112–114, 120
MIME features, 536
ML programming language, 4
monitors
    BlockingCollection, 650
    events, 649
    locking, 637–649
    notification, 641–645
    overview, 634–640
Moonlight project, 7
MoveFile method, 716
moving/copying array elements, 234

MSB (most-significant byte), 369
multidimensional arrays, 238
multiple inheritance, 132–135
multiple sort criteria, 277
multiple sources, 286
multiplexing, 608
multiplication (*) operator, 35
multiplicity, relationship, 560
multithreaded coding, 629–633
mutable strings, 349–353
mutexes, 648

N

namespaces (.NET), 14–19, 22
NaN (not a number), 191
navigation properties, EF, 556, 575
nested classes, 159
.NET client/server, 477–480
.NET Framework
    and array size, 236
    and assemblies, 589
    and C#, 2–4
    and C++, 3
    class library, 2
    and collections, 254
    continuity with Windows ecosystem, 6
    and cookies, 521
    and data access, 539–544
    and default constructors, 91
    memory management in, 84
    and multiple inheritance, 132–135
    multiple language support in, 3
    order of static initialization, 101
    security model of, 6
    types derived from Object, 127
    version 4, 7–9
networking, 473
    (see also WCF (Windows Communication
    Foundation))
    bidirectional communication with duplex
        contracts, 501–511
    choosing technology, 473
    client-side code, 474–477
    external party web service, 479
    HTTP, 511–519
    Internet Protocol, 523–528
    .NET client/server, 477–480
    sockets, 522, 528–536
new keyword, 109, 226, 283

NHibernate, 546
NIST (National Institute of Standards and
        Technology), 528
no-PIA, 9, 712
nodes, 465
noninterop scenarios (dynamic), 703–706
nonpostback events, 777
not equal to (!=) operator, 43
NotePosted method, 507
null character, 320, 356
null keyword, 83
numbering from zero, 40
numbering items, 288
numeric format, 327
Nygaard, Kristen, 62

O

object context, 553, 571, 583
object-oriented programming, 62
objects
    defined, 62
    initializers, 92–95
    and Xaml, 735–737
Office, Microsoft, 7–9, 687, 689, 712
one-to-many relationships, 560
one-to-one relationships, 561
OnGetHostEntryComplete method, 654
OnProcessing/OnProcessed methods, 172
Open method, 9, 693
OpenRead/OpenWrite methods, 422, 515
optimistic concurrency, 581–583
order of evaluation, 37
OrderBy method, 278
ordering, 276–279
Organize Usings item, 16
orthotopes, 239
out keyword, 257
output
    formatting, 322–329
    to console, 2
overexpression of concurrency, 659
overloading, 88–92, 141
overriding, 112, 121–127

P

P/Invoke, 716–720
Page_Load method, 793
Parallel class, 667–670

parallel execution, 607
Parallel LINQ, 669
parameter list, 18
parameters, avoiding SQL attacks with, 542
params keyword, 225
parent-child relationships, 659
parental element, 450
partial keyword, 554
partial-trust scenarios, 720
Pascal casing, 65, 154
Path class/methods, 375, 387
patterns, 92
peer-to-peer networking, 536
percent format, 327
permissions, 389–394, 391–409, 424
PIAs (primary interop assemblies), 9, 712
pinging, 536
pinning, 721
"pit of success," designing for the, 75
Platt, David, 791
PLINQ (Parallel LINQ), 669
POCO (Plain Old CLR Object), 553
pointers, 720–725
polymorphism, 107, 254–258
    (see also extensibility and polymorphism)
popping, 57
port numbers, 527
post conditions, 202
Post method, 623
postback events, 777
PostNote method, 497
precedence, 37
preconditions, 202
predicate, defined, 159
Predicate<T>, 160–162
primary interop assemblies (PIAs), 9, 712
printable characters, 361
private protection level, 66–69
procedural coding, 18
Process method, 178
Program.cs, 12
Programming ASP.NET 3.5 (Liberty, Maharry, and Hurwitz), 775
Programming WCF Services (Lowy), 486
programming, basic techniques
    comments, regions, and readability, 24–27
    expressions and statements, 35–39
    flow control with selection statements, 39–54

getting started, 11–14
methods, 55–57
namespaces and types, 14–19
projects and solutions, 19–24
variables, 28–35
project
    creating in Visual Studio, 27
    defined, 12, 19
projections, 282–288
properties, 64–71, 165–167
Properties panel (Solution Explorer), 47
property elements, 739
protected internal modifier, 114–116
protected modifier, 114–116
protection levels, 66–68, 595–598
Proust, Marcel, 723
proxies, 497–501, 520
public protection level, 66
Pulse/PulseAll methods, 641
pushing, 57

Q

quantifiers, 292
quantum, 613
query expressions, 265–268
queues, 311
QueueUserWorkItem method, 621
quotas, 436

R

race conditions, 629–631
RAD (Rapid Application Development), 775
radio buttons, 781, 784–793
RaisePostDataChangedEvent method, 778
raising events, 172
random numbers, 382, 441
range checking, 192
range variables, 266
Rapid Application Development, 775
Read method, 415, 421, 721
read-only fields and properties, 76–79, 101
ReadAll methods, 48, 409, 624
reader/writer locks, 647
ReadLines method, 409, 687
ReadNumbersFromFile method, 55
ReadToEnd method, 529
rectangular arrays, 238–243
ref object, 726

refactoring, 57
reference types, 83, 226, 230
reference versus value, 83
References item, 23
references, assembly, 590–592
reflection, 677–685
Refresh method, 583
regions and readability, 24–27
Register method, 664
Remove Unused Usings item, 16
Remove/RemoveAt method, 245
RemoveAt method, 636
repaginating (see extensibility with delegates)
Replace methods, 354, 688
replacing methods, 112–114
responsiveness, 608
REST (Representational State Transfer), 477
RESTful Web Services (Ruby and Richardson),
        477
rethrowing an exception, 211
return keyword, 56
return values, 194–201
Richardson, Leonard, 477
Right method, 343
root element, 450
round-trip format, 328
Ruby, Sam, 477
runnable threads, 612
runtime, 141

S

Sandcastle, Microsoft, 27
SaveChanges method, 574
schedulers, 612, 662
Schneier, Bruce, 440
sealing classes, 119
search axes, 466
Secrets and Lies: Digital Security in a
        Networked World (Schneier), 440
security issues
    access control lists, 490
    accessibility modifiers, 67, 115
    authentication, 519
    directory hierarchies, 388–394
    dynamic queries, 568
    encryption, 439–446
    exceptions, 400–409
    fields initialization, 75
    firewalls, 502

.NET security model, 6, 429, 439, 790
    Silverlight, 720
    stack traces, 491
    WCF contracts, 483
    WCF data services, 546, 584
Seek method, 419
select clause, 267
Select method, 268, 282
selection statements, flow control with, 39–54
SelectKeyAndIV method, 441
SelectMany method, 287
semicolon (;) end statement, 24
separated presentation, 771
serialization, 220, 467–471
server configuration, 508
server-side controls, 778, 781, 783
service contract, 482
session-based communication, 503
set accessor, 64, 130
set-based operations, 294
SetAccessControl method, 405
shapes, 748–751
sharing contracts, 496
side effects, 163
signed assemblies, 432
signed integer types, 29
Silverlight, Microsoft, 729
    (see also WPF (Windows Presentation
    Foundation) and Silverlight)
    and assembly references, 592
    and cookies, 521
    and Data Access, 546
    and graphical elements, 748–755
    loading from, 603
    and partial trust, 720
    script objects, 694
    and WCF, 474–477, 489, 514, 584, 731–
        737
Simula 67, 62
Skip operator, 289
SMT (simultaneous multithreading), 612
SMTP relays, 536
sockets, 522, 528–536
Solution Explorer, 21
solutions, 19
SortedSet<T>, 310
sorting arrays, 232, 253
source code, 20
sparse arrays, 306

special folders, 383–385
special permissions, 389
speculation, 608
spellchecking (see extensibility with delegates)
SpinLock, 646
Split method, 347
splitting strings, 346
SQL injection attacks, 542, 568
SQL Profiler, 564
SQL Server 2008 Express, 547
stacks, 57, 84, 200, 313, 613–620
standard numeric format strings, 323–329
Start method, 614, 645
StartNew method, 658, 661
state sharing, 614–619
state, view, 777
statement-form lambda, 164, 170
statements, 36
static fields/properties, 17, 98–102, 598, 687
static keyword, 97
static versus dynamic, 687–693
Step Into item, 50
storage management for events, 181–182
store schemas, 549
stores, 429
Stream buffering, 423
streams, 413–421, 439–446, 514
StreamWriter/Reader, 397–400, 430
StringBuilder, 349–353
strings
    accessing characters by index, 341
    checking character types, 360
    comparing, 42, 355
    composing, 344–348
    composite formatting with String.Format,
        337
    converting to other types, 336
    culture sensitivity, 338–340
    custom numeric format, 329–332
    dates and times, 332–335
    empty, 355–357
    encoding, 360–370
    exploring formatting rules, 340
    finding and replacing content, 353
    formatting data for output, 322
    getting a range of characters, 343–344
    immutability of, 341
    literal strings and chars, 318–322
    manipulating text with, 348–353

overview, 315–317
    standard numeric format, 323–329
    string and char types, 317
    trimming whitespace, 357–360
strongly named assemblies, 600
strongly typed DataSet, 543
struct keyword, 86
styles, 764–765
subscribing to events, 171, 173
Substring method, 343
subtraction (-) operator, 35
Sum method, 699
surface area, minimizing, 67
Swann's Way (Proust), 723
switch and case statements, 45
symmetric algorithm, 440
synchronization primitives
    monitors, 634–640
    notification, 641–645
    overview, 634–640
System namespace types, 14
System.Double type, 191

T

Take method, 650
Take operator, 289
target, attribute, 671
Task Parallel Library, 656–663
tasks, 656–663
TCP (Transmission Control Protocol), 526–
    534
templates, 761–773
temporary files, 381
ternary operator, 44
ternary relationships, 560
test command-line switch, 379
test directories, 386
Test method, 704
text
    and culture sensitivity, 338–340
    encoding/decoding, 360–370
    encryption, 439–446
    fonts, 316
    manipulating, 348
    reading and writing, 430
    strings, 316
    and text boxes, 623, 768, 803, 806–813
    and TextBlock, 734
    whitespace in, 356–360

writing files, 396–400
TextWriter, 398
this keyword, 86, 97, 247, 269
thread pools, 620
threads, 634, 651
   (see also asynchronous programming)
   (see also synchronization primitives)
   affinity and context, 622
   multithreaded coding, 629–633
   myths regarding, 623–629
   and OS Scheduler, 611–613
   overview, 609–611
   safety and, 636
   and stack, 613–620
throw keyword, 212
Thumbnail property, 772
tightly controlled deployment, 478
ToArray method, 56, 254, 445
ToBuffer method, 445
ToLowerInvariant/ToUpperInvariant, 348
ToString method, 322, 333
TPL (Task Parallel Library), 656–663
transactions, database, 576–581
transforms, 747
Transmission Control Protocol, 526–534
triggers, 754
trimming whitespace, 357–360
try blocks, 207–215
TryGetValue method, 305, 308
TryParse methods, 336
turtle robotics example
   custom exceptions, 218–220
   debugging with return values, 200
   deciding what errors to catch, 215–218
   exceptions, 201–214
   setting return values, 194–201
   setup, 186–191
   try, catch, finally blocks, 207–215
   when and how to fail, 191–194
types
   bool, 42
   and discovery, 679–681
   and equivalence, 712
   implicit conversion of, 37
   namespace, 14–19
   numeric, 28
   and parameters, 244
   variable, 28–57

U

UI (user interface), 776, 791
UML 2.0, 105
unboxing, 128
"unexpected" errors, 185
unhandled exceptions, 205
Unicode, 362, 365
Unified Modeling Language (UML) 2.0, 105
Uniform Resource Identifiers (URIs), 512
Uniform Resource Locators (see URLs)
universal quantifier, 292
universal sortable form, 334
unsafe keyword, 720, 722
unsigned integer types, 29
UpdatePosition method, 97
UpdateUi method, 662
uploading methods, 514
uppercase letters, 347
Uri class, 512
URIs (Uniform Resource Identifiers), 512
URLs (Uniform Resource Locators)
   appdomains, 605
   Daytime Protocol, 527
   defined, 512
   Dijkstra letter on go-to statements, 54
   Exception class, 203
   MEF, 604
   misleading MSDN documentation on
      structs, 84
   MSDN on culture-sensitive string
      operations, 348
   MSDN on long paths, 402
   naming/capitalization conventions, 65
   .NET Framework class library namespaces,
      15
   NHibernate, 546
   precedence in expression evaluation, 37
   Project Gutenberg, 723
   Sandcastle documentation tool, 27
   secure coding in .NET, 790
   Silverlight Toolkit, 743
   Spec#, 202
   strong names, 601
   Visual Studio Express (free edition), 11
   Visual Studio logging privileges, 491
   Wireshark, 486
UseItem method, 637, 641
user controls, 760
user interface (UI), 776

user state, 427
user storage, 436
UseStream method, 430
using directives, 14
UTF-8, UTF-16, 362–370, 399, 444
utility features, .NET Framework, 2

V

VALUE keyword, 569
value types, 83, 127, 228
value versus reference, 83
var keyword, 266, 285, 301, 692
variables, 28–35
variance, 257
VB.NET, 3
VBA (Visual Basic for Applications), 689
Vertical Stack panel, 741–743
view models, 771
virtual methods, 112–114, 120
visibility and accessibility modifiers, 67
visual state manager, 766
Visual Studio, Microsoft
    2010, 3, 7–9
    free Express version, 11
    generated code in, 554
    handling of libraries, 23, 593–595
    New Project dialog box, 11
    and references, 591
    running client and server copies, 535
    and Xaml, 732
void keyword, 18

W

Wait method, 641, 658
WaitAll method, 658
WaitUntilReady method, 642
WCF (Windows Communication Foundation),
    3, 305
    contracts, 482–483
    creating a project, 481
    Data Services, 546, 584–588
    and Entity Framework, 546
    hosting a service, 486–493
    Test Client and Host, 483–486
    writing a client program, 493–501
    and XML, 481
weakly controlled deployment, 479
web application projects, 779

Web Forms and ASP.NET
    adding controls and events, 790–793
    adding controls to, 781–784
    code-behind files, 780
    creating a web application, 779
    data binding, 784–787
    events, 776
    examining the code, 789–790
    life cycle, 778
    overview, 775
WebClient, 512–515
WebRequest and WebResponse, 516–522
website projects, 779
well-known folders, 383–387
where clauses, 271, 466
Where method, 268, 704
while and do statements, 52–53
whitespace
    in C# code, 24, 65
    in text output, 356–360
Why Software Sucks (Platt), 791
Windows Communication Foundation (see
        WCF)
Windows Forms
    and ActiveX, 708–710
    adding a binding source, 797–799
    controls, 800–804
    creating the application, 796
    data binding, 806–813
    docking and anchoring, 805–806
    event handling, 811
    versus WPF, 795
Windows, .NET and, 6
word wrapping, 743
WPF (Windows Presentation Foundation) and
        Silverlight, 3
    control templates, 761–765
    controls, 738, 755–761
    data binding, 767–769
    data templates, 769–773
    elements, 738
    layout panels, 739–748
    overview, 729–731
    transforms, 747
    versus Windows Forms, 795
    visual state manager, 766
    and Xaml, 731–737
WrapPanel, 743
wrappers, .NET Framework, 2

Write method, 421, 723
"write-only code", 24
WriteAllText methods, 397, 399
WriteLine method, 18, 36, 430, 534
writing data with streams, 421

X

Xaml, 731–737
Xaml Browser Application (XBAP), 474
.xap extension, 592, 603
XBAP (Xaml Browser Application), 474
XHTML, 451
XML 1.0
    attributes, 456–459
    creating documents, 452–455
    elements, 450, 455
    extensibility, 452
    and LINQ, 459–464
    overview, 449
    search axes, 466
    serialization, 467–471, 671
    single node search, 465
    and where clauses, 466
    XHTML, 451
XML Documentation Comments, 26
XML documents, 363
XML literals, 5

Y

yield return, 259–264
yielding, 647

Z

zero, dividing by, 190
zero, numbering from, 40
zero-day attack, 502
zipping, 288

About the Authors

Ian Griffiths is an independent WPF consultant, developer, speaker and Pluralsight instructor and a widely recognized expert on the subject. He lives in London but can often be found on various developer mailing lists and newsgroups, where a popular sport is to see who can get him to write the longest email in reply to the shortest possible question. Ian maintains a popular blog (*http://www.interact-sw.co.uk/iangblog/*) and is co-author of O'Reilly Media's *.NET Windows Forms in a Nutshell* (*http://oreilly.com/catalog/9780596003388/*) and of *Mastering Visual Studio .NET* (*http://oreilly.com/catalog/9780596003609/*).

Matthew Adams is the Director of Development at Digital Healthcare Ltd. The last three years have kept him fully occupied in the development of a C#/.NET-based distributed imaging platform for healthcare applications. Before that, he studied Natural Sciences at Cambridge University, worked on banking and imaging applications in North America, became a fully-paid-up C++ junkie, and was the lead architect on software solutions for drug-discovery for a large US corporation. He thinks that .NET is a major philosophical stride forward for the computer industry: so much so that he almost doesn't miss his first love—generics—in C#. He has written articles and given papers on the subject to both technical and non-technical audiences, and looks forward to the day when he doesn't have to answer the question "So, what is .NET?" any more!

Jesse Liberty, "Silverlight Geek," is a senior program manager for Microsoft Silverlight in the Silverlight Development Division where he is responsible for the creation of tutorials, videos, and other content to facilitate the learning and use of Silverlight.

Even before joining Microsoft, Jesse was well known in the industry in part because of his many bestselling books, including O'Reilly Media's *Programming .NET 3.5* (*http://oreilly.com/catalog/9780596527563/*), *Programming C# 3.0* (*http://oreilly.com/catalog/9780596527433*), *Learning ASP.NET with AJAX* (*http://oreilly.com/catalog/9780596513979/*), and the soon to be published *Programming Silverlight*. He has over two decades of experience writing software, consulting, and training, with stints at AT&T as a Distinguished Software Engineer and at Citibank as a Vice President in the Information Division.

Colophon

The animal on the cover of *Programming C# 4.0*, Sixth Edition, is an African crowned crane. This tall, skinny bird wanders the marshes and grasslands of West and East Africa (the Western and Eastern African crowned cranes are known as *Balearica pavonia pavonia* and *Balearica regulorum gibbericeps*, respectively).

Adult birds stand about three feet tall and weigh six to nine pounds. Inside their long necks is a five-foot long windpipe—part of which is coiled inside their breastbone—giving voice to loud calls that can carry for miles. They live for about 22 years, spending most of their waking hours looking for the various plants, small animals, and insects they like to eat. (One crowned crane food-finding technique, perfected during the 38 to 54 million years these birds have existed, is to stamp their feet as they walk, flushing out tasty bugs.) They are the only type of crane to perch in trees, which they do at night when sleeping.

Social and talkative, African crowned cranes group together in pairs or families, and the smaller groups band together in flocks of more than 100 birds. Their elaborate mating dance has served as a model for some of the dances of local people.

The cover image is an original engraving from the 19th century. The cover font is Adobe ITC Garamond. The text font is Linotype Birka; the heading font is Adobe Myriad Condensed; and the code font is LucasFont's TheSansMonoCondensed.

Related Titles from O'Reilly

.NET and C#

ADO.NET 3.5 Cookbook, *2nd Edition*

Building a Web 2.0 Portal with ASP.NET 3.5

C# 3.0 Design Patterns

C# 3.0 in a Nutshell, *3rd Edition*

C# 3.0 Pocket Reference, *2nd Edition*

C# Cookbook, *3rd Edition*

C# in a Nutshell, *3rd Edition*

Data-Driven Services with Silverlight 2

Head First C#

Learning ASP.NET 2.0 with AJAX

Learning ASP.NET 3.5, *4th Edition*

Learning C# 3.0

Learning WCF

LINQ Pocket Reference

MCSE Core Elective Exams in a Nutshell

.NET & XML

.NET Gotchas

Programming Atlas

Programming ASP.NET 3.5, *4th Edition*

Programming ASP.NET AJAX

Programming C# 3.0, *5th Edition*

Programming Entity Framework

Programming MapPoint in .NET

Programming .NET 3.5

Programming .NET Components, *2nd Edition*

Programming .NET Security

Programming .NET Web Services

Programming Visual Basic 2008

Programming WCF Services, *2nd Edition*

Programming WPF, *2nd Edition*

Programming Windows Presentation Foundation

Restful .NET

Visual Studio Hacks

Windows Developer Power Tools

XAML in a Nutshell

Our books are available at most retail and online bookstores.

To order direct: 1-800-998-9938 • *order@oreilly.com* • *www.oreilly.com*

Online editions of most O'Reilly titles are available by subscription at *safari.oreilly.com*

Buy this book and get access to the online edition for 45 days—for free!

Programming C# 4.0, 6th Edition
By Ian Griffiths, Matthew Adams & Jesse Liberty
August 2010, $54.99
ISBN 9780596159832

With Safari Books Online, you can:

Access the contents of thousands of technology and business books

- Quickly search over 7000 books and certification guides
- Download whole books or chapters in PDF format, at no extra cost, to print or read on the go
- Copy and paste code
- Save up to 35% on O'Reilly print books
- **New!** Access mobile-friendly books directly from cell phones and mobile devices

Stay up-to-date on emerging topics before the books are published

- Get on-demand access to evolving manuscripts.
- Interact directly with authors of upcoming books

Explore thousands of hours of video on technology and design topics

- Learn from expert video tutorials
- Watch and replay recorded conference sessions

To try out Safari and the online edition of this book FREE for 45 days, go to *www.oreilly.com/go/safarienabled* and enter the coupon code DHVTPVH. To see the complete Safari Library, visit safari.oreilly.com.

Spreading the knowledge of innovators   safari.oreilly.com

©2009 O'Reilly Media, Inc. O'Reilly logo is a registered trademark of O'Reilly Media, Inc. 00000

Get even more for your money.

Join the O'Reilly Community, and register the O'Reilly books you own.It's free, and you'll get:

- 40% upgrade offer on O'Reilly books
- Membership discounts on books and events
- Free lifetime updates to electronic formats of books
- Multiple ebook formats, DRM FREE
- Participation in the O'Reilly community
- Newsletters
- Account management
- 100% Satisfaction Guarantee

Signing up is easy:

1. **Go to: oreilly.com/go/register**
2. **Create an O'Reilly login.**
3. **Provide your address.**
4. **Register your books.**

Note: English-language books only

To order books online:

oreilly.com/order_new

For questions about products or an order:

orders@oreilly.com

To sign up to get topic-specific email announcements and/or news about upcoming books, conferences, special offers, and new technologies:

elists@oreilly.com

For technical questions about book content:

booktech@oreilly.com

To submit new book proposals to our editors:

proposals@oreilly.com

Many O'Reilly books are available in PDF and several ebook formats. For more information:

oreilly.com/ebooks

O'REILLY®

Spreading the knowledge of innovators   www.oreilly.com

©2009 O'Reilly Media, Inc. O'Reilly logo is a registered trademark of O'Reilly Media, Inc. 00000